In Our Darkest Hour
MORNING STAR OVER AMERICA
February 22, 1991 - December 31, 1992
Volume I

by
William L. Roth, Jr.
&
Timothy Parsons-Heather

The Morning Star of Our Lord, Inc. is a nonprofit, tax-exempt religious and charitable organization which is incorporated under the laws of the State of Illinois. It has been established for the dissemination of *"In Our Darkest Hour - Morning Star Over America,"* a miraculous manuscript received through the supernatural intercession of the Blessed Virgin Mary, the Mother of Jesus Christ. The organization is solemnly dedicated to all of the principles delineated within this written text in union with the spiritual catechesis of Pope John Paul II, the Vicar of Christ on Earth. It is the intrinsic role of this Corporation to provide pastoral consolation to those lacking in faith, the infirm, homebound, incarcerated, deprived, dejected, and those who are otherwise suffering humanity for the sake of the Glory of the Kingdom of Jesus Christ. Apart from the funds generated through the distribution of this spiritual codex, the work is funded by the charitable prayers, sacrifices and contributions of those who have been touched by the beatific grace emanating from this work of God. It is these faithful people who are responsible for the opportunity that you are receiving to participate in the imminent Triumph of the Immaculate Heart at the opening of this new millennium.

The Morning Star of Our Lord, Inc.
Springfield, Illinois
www.ImmaculateMary.org

Published by The Morning Star of Our Lord, Inc. Used with permission.
Copyright © 1999 William L. Roth, Jr. & Timothy Parsons-Heather.
All rights reserved.

ISBN: 0-9671587-7-X

Cover Illustration - Photograph taken on Christmas Day, 1988.

DEDICATION
to
Pope John Paul II
A.D. 2000

There is one Man who rivals the essence of Love that the Most Blessed Virgin Mary has taught my brother and me since February 22, 1991. He is the Vicar of Christ on Earth who presently sits in the Chair of Saint Peter of the Roman Catholic Church. We have as many words in our hearts in honor of Him as we have written in the work that you hold in your hands. Humanity does not realize who is in their midst. How sorrowful will many hearts be when they finally realize the divine magnitude of His holy life only after His sacrifice is called to completion. We, instead, love Him now, openly and unreservedly! We see by His Light! He is the incarnation of courage, grace, wisdom, fortitude and strength beyond any other mortal man since the Risen Christ. God saved the brightest Light for the close of the mortal ages.

Totus tuus, Papa!
We are totally Yours!

In Our Darkest Hour
MORNING STAR OVER AMERICA
February 22, 1991- December 31, 1992
Volume I

Table of Contents
by
Topical Lesson

Prologue
Opening Remarks

The Beginning of the Miracle
"FIAT"

February 22, 1991 - May 26, 1991

    This time represents the opening chapter of Our Lady's direct intercession in our lives. Although veiled in much symbolism due to our spiritual immaturity, the first thirty messages of this period provide the glimpse of what is to come. They are the precognition of the glorious message She bears. We were children recording words whose depth we did not yet understand. God asked for our patient faith and trust in His omnipotence during this time of our spiritual acclimation. We lived in blind faith following Our Lady despite the disruption about us. As you read these initial pages, I ask you to remember that no human is ever prepared to receive the direct intervention of God. By the end of May, the Mother of Our Lord was ready to commence the lessons which She knows will convert the world.

A Child's First Steps

May
05/27/91 -	A Fear to Love	108
05/29/91 -	The Fear of Faith	111
05/30/91 -	Our Fear to Be Happy	113
05/31/91 -	We Fear to Serve God Without Recognition	115

June
06/01/91 -	Search for Purity	119
	A Blind Child's Clothes	
	Forgiveness of God	
06/02/91 -	Tiny Wind-sail	121
06/03/91	Circle of Opposition Growing	123

06/04/91 -	*"My Intercession Will Not Be Interrupted."*	123
06/05/91 -	Meeting with the Bishop	124
06/06/91 -	*"Your Messages to the World Will Continue."*	124
06/08/91 -	Humility	124
06/09/91 -	*"Let God Be God."*	125
	Little Bees Build Identical Shape,	
	Pricked with a Needle	
06/10/91 -	My Brother is Completely Healthy	127
06/11/91 -	Compassion	127
06/12/91 -	The Spirit of Love in Truth	129
06/14/91 -	Attendance at Conference	131
06/15/91 -	"The Fanfare Was Gone."	131
06/16/91 -	*"I Am the Lady of Liberty"*	131
	The New Colossus	
06/18/91 -	Authenticity of Messages	132
	Balance	
06/19/91 -	Self-control	133
06/21/91 -	Dissension	135
	Procreation	
	Parabolic Speech of Jesus	
06/22/91 -	*"Feel the Victory from the Battle."*	136
06/23/91 -	All Prayers Are Answered	137
	He Has Freely Surrendered His Will	
06/27/91 -	Forgiveness	139
	Charity	
	Reason	
	Thought	
06/28/91 -	The True Picture of Love	140
06/29/91 -	Moment of Love	141
06/30/91 -	*"My Special Little Spindle of Love"*	142

July

07/01/91 -	Peaks of Holiness,	143
	Prayer from the Heart	
07/03/91 -	Cross in Block / Seen vs Unseen	146
07/04/91 -	Motion	148
	Symmetry	
	Mirror	
	Balloon	
	God in Us	
07/05/91 -	Perspective/memory	151
	Color/mood	

07/06/91 - Hope 154
           Celibacy
           Abstinence
           Procreation
07/07/91 - Friendship 156
           Memories
           Grief
           Simplicity
           Church Provides Eucharist
07/10/91 - Wisdom and War 160
07/12/91 - Complacency 164
07/13/91 - Nobility 165
           Confession
07/14/91 - Faith and Discipline 168
07/17/91 - Uniting Funnel 172
           Corridor of Life
07/19/91 - Humility 176
           Forgiveness
           Patience
           Harvest
           Cultivation
07/20/91 - Habits 178
           Infinite Tolerance
07/21/91 - Emotion, ... 181
           Climates
           Terrains
07/24/91 - Faith: Ocean Vessels and Little Cars 185
07/25/91 - Faucet/Preparation 187
           Deer Beneath the Waterfall
           Wealth/Riches - Buried Treasure
07/26/91 - Nest and the Earth 190
07/28/91 - Human Interaction 192
           Love and Human Thought
07/31/91 - Bird's Vision of Flight 195
           Prayer from the Heart
           Compassion

August

08/01/91 - Tree and Cliff, Suffering 198
08/03/91 - Chance 200
08/04/91 - Faith and the Gallows 202
           Timing the Railroad Tracks

08/05/91 -	Vision of Love	204
08/07/91 -	Aesthetics	206
08/08/91 -	Winter Path	208
	Deep Snow and Hope	
08/09/91 -	Fulfillment of Love: House Partially Built	210
	Road Ending	
	Animals Vs. Man - Helplessness	
08/10/91 -	Letters: Sand, Chalkboard, Sky	214
	Night Sky Vs. Earth - (Points of Light)	
08/11/91 -	Perpetual Expectation: Faith, Piano	216
	Blinds on Window	
	Bale of Straw	
08/13/91 -	Prayer Groups Form Cross	219
08/15/91 -	Faith: Crossing Road of the Mind	219
	Love is Parade	
08/17/91 -	Drop Vs. Ocean	223
	Wholeness	
	Mystical Body	
	Indifference	
08/18/91 -	Virgin not the Savior	227
	Unity in Bible	
	Communion of Man	
	How Do We Love?	
	Love in Stranger: See as in a Mirror	
08/19/91 -	Darkness of the West	231
	Government	
	Bangladesh	
	A Universal Famine	
08/20/91 -	Stairway, Railing, Raising of Prayers	233
	Priority	
08/22/91 -	Lateral and Vertical Movement of Love in Prayer	236
08/24/91 -	Peacemakers	237
	Barriers and Divisions	
	Holy Eucharist	
	Unity and Public Policy	
08/25/91 -	Man Quilted	240
	Breathe Same Air	
	Fear of Church (Independence)	
	Picture of Cow	
	Candle	
08/26/91 -	Blessed are the Persecuted	243
	Black Man's Traits	

	Blessed Sacrament	
	Elevation	
	Participation	
08/28/91 -	Blessed Those Who Hunger and Thirst	246
	Human Systems and Love	
	Justice and Peace	
08/31/91 -	Justice System	250
	Meekness	

September

09/01/91 -	"Blessed Are the Meek..."	252
	The Poor in Spirit	
	Sermon on Mount (Move Mountains)	
09/02/91 -	Echo of Love and the Holy Eucharist	255
	Suffering	
09/04/91 -	Miraculous Intervention	257
	News Reporting/Chain Links	
09/05/91 -	Surly Bonds	261
	Exploding Sun	
09/07/91 -	Chastisement	266
	Movie Theater	
	Synthetic Blanket of Indifference	
	Eucharist: Breath of Life	
09/08/91 -	Abortion must End	269
	His Unmatchable Wisdom	
	Angels Provide Standing Ovation	
09/11/91 -	Anxiety	272
	Fulfillment in Holy Eucharist	
09/12/91 -	Mental Image of Balance	273
	Jesus' Life: Fear to Believe	
	Freedom	
	Protestants and the Eucharist	
09/15/91 -	Movement/Motion	278
	Family	
	Petrified Tree	
09/17/91 -	Great Awakening Power	279
09/21/91 -	Home of Love	279
	Conversion is the Vehicle	
09/23/91 -	"Soon My Son Will Come Again."	280
09/27/91 -	Windmill/waterwheel	280
	Eucharist	
	Priests	

	Consecration: Radiant Eternity	
09/28/91 -	Practitioners and Pragmatists: Abortion and Eucharist	282
09/29/91 -	Shock	284
	Renewed Perspective - Defeat of Satan	

A River of Light

October

10/04/91 -	Sacraments - Avenues for the Return to Grace	286
10/05/91 -	Division & Separation Eliminated at the Altar	286
10/07/91 -	"Yes" to Love	287
	All People Needed	
10/08/91 -	The Trophy on the Mantle	287
	Cycle of Human Competitions Fade Cross	
10/10/91 -	Life is Proof of God's Love for Us	289
10/11/91 -	Loveless Media	289
	System of Justice and Motion - Treadmill	
10/15/91 -	Search for Water/search for Love in Human Hearts	291
10/16/91 -	Two Worlds Become One in the Blessed Sacrament	292
10/17/91 -	Description of Ecstasy of Heaven	294
10/18/91 -	Perfect Geometry of the Host	295
10/19/91 -	"Auto" Everything - No Auto-salvation	296
	Leverage is God	
10/21/91 -	Man Upside-down on Poles	297
	Too Close to Picture	
10/23/91 -	Evil Disguised as Social Justice	299
	Man Trying to Control; Air, People, Creation	
	Windows in House	
10/24/91 -	Sufferings Are Holy	301
10/25/91 -	Elevation and the Plane of Glass	301
	Faith for Strength of Glass	
	Power of Truth is Love	
	Shaping Eternity by Prayer and Conversion	
10/26/91 -	Eucharist Focuses Vision	302
	Religious Conferences	
10/27/91 -	Labels and Forgiveness	303
	Middle Names of Family	
10/30/91 -	Light of Christ: Beams of Light	305
	Reflection in Time	
	Eucharist is the Glowing Beginning	
	Love: Energy	
	Magnifier: Prayer	

Jesus' Countenance
Holy Mother: Switch
The High Noon of Eternal Reckoning

November

11/03/91 -	Satan's Imitation of Fruits	307
	Level & Plumb of Surface of Water	
	Humility & Littleness	
	Heart is Carrier of Love	
	Consecration is not Conception but the Crucifixion	
	Protesters	
11/05/91 -	Love in Diversity: Fireworks	313
	Unity	
	The Symphony of Man	
11/06/91 -	Gentleness of the Almighty Father: Love of God	315
	Our Lady is Softness & Compassion of the Father	
11/07/91 -	Symmetrical Patterns: Chaos Vs. Order	316
	Picture of Pity: Pieta	
11/08/91 -	To Convince the World That Jesus is the Eucharist	318
	Faith	
11/09/91 -	Tell Him God Is Love	319
11/11/91 -	Holy Eucharist	319
11/12/91 -	Ship's Wake	320
	We Are Approaching the Threshold of Majesty	
11/14/91 -	Bottle of Our Favorite Soda	321
	Heart Releasing Love	
	Broken Heart	
11/15/91 -	Self-righteous Indifference	323
	Skyline	
	"The Pope Can See!"	
11/17/91 -	Blunting the Projectile of Motion	326
	Jesus' Return in Glory	
11/21/91 -	Love Vs. Academia	329
	Motherhood of Our Lady	
11/23/91 -	Suffering	331
11/24/91 -	Movement of Love	333
	The Answering of Prayers	
11/25/91 -	Visual Categorization	334
	Peace: The Color of Love	
	Beacon of Reflections	
11/26/91 -	Soil of Humankind	336
	Web of Love	

	Beacon Eliminated the Darkness	
11/29/91 -	Differential in Love	338
11/30/91 -	Nativity & Blessed Sacrament	339
	Unborn	

December

12/01/91 -	The Impact of Her Messages are Magnificent	341
12/03/91 -	Christmas Message	342
	Pile of Coins	
	Too Close to the Picture	
12/04/91 -	Birth of Mercy and Love	347
12/07/91 -	Nativity & Blessed Sacrament	348
	Little Drummer Boy	
	Christmas Trees	
12/10/91 -	Impact of Christmas Message	350
	Strobe	
12/14/91 -	God's Trust and Love	351
	Water Supply Pipes	
12/15/91 -	Christmas: Atmosphere of Love	353
12/17/91 -	Jesus' Words of Encouragement	354
12/18/91 -	Families: Interpretation of Love	354
12/19/91 -	No Abortions on Christmas: Hope for the World	355
12/21/91 -	Humbleness	356
	Eucharist	
12/22/91 -	Unintelligible Graphic	357
	Faith with Eyelids Closed	
12/25/91 -	Jesus: Tangible Reality	361
	Breath	
	Language	
	Oneness	
12/26/91 -	Building Blocks of Love	362
12/29/91 -	Forgiveness in Families	364
12/30/91 -	Our Lady's Special Message	366

1992
Unveiling Helpless Mankind

January

01/01/92 -	The Presence of Universal Grace	368
	Russia: Parable of Helplessness	
	Marching Inexorably Toward Their Demise	
01/02/92 -	Helplessness	371

	Persevere	
	Lift Them up	
01/04/92 -	New Century Is Destined to Be the Last	372
	Analytical Mind	
	Links of Chain	
	Revolving Spokes	
01/08/92 -	Peace	373
	Daydreaming in Class	
	Perfection	
	Unbroken Circle	
01/09/92 -	The Origin of Every Righteous Blessing	376
	Jesus Is about to Return	
01/12/92 -	Sacrity of Scripture	378
	Transfiguration	
	The Pantheon of the Firmament	
01/13/92 -	Unconditional Love	380
	Oblates of Metronymic Integrity	
	Dome of Love	
01/14/92 -	Box of Crayons	381
	Her Presence Is a Beacon of Light	
	The Rolling Spheres	
01/19/92 -	Accourse	384
	Competing Reflections	
01/22/92 -	Jesus Will Right the Wrong of Abortion	386
	"Remember That I Am Forever."	
01/24/92 -	His Mother Chased Him down	388
01/26/92 -	Jesus Is Not a Compromise	388
	Baptism	
01/29/92 -	Jesus Loves Creation	391
	If We Decline, There Will Be Chastisements	
	Admonishment to the Faithless	
01/30/92 -	Painting: Colorful Picture/initial White Canvas	392

Focus upon the Path for Home

February

02/01/92 -	Jesus Is the Author of Life	394
	Coupling Unity in Love	
02/04/92 -	Captive Fortress	395
	Isolating Shell	
	Fiber of Human Will	
	Love Is Not Weakness	

02/06/92 -	Yes, We Do Love Our Way into Heaven	397
	Helplessness: Mankind Arrives Too Late	
02/09/92 -	Participation but Not Worldliness	398
	Perfect Reflection of Jesus' Light	
	Reflection as Bright as the Source	
02/12/92 -	Self-imposed Bondage	400
	We Were Created for Paradise	
02/14/92 -	Evil Tries to Control	402
	Leaders Are Afraid	
	Love must Lead	
02/16/92 -	Dignity of Human Life	403
	Social Acceptability of Sin	
	Abortion	
	No Dignity in Prisons	
	Share	
02/18/92 -	Spires of His Kingdom	405
	Backs to the Cross	
	Machines for Terminally Ill	
02/19/92 -	Raven and the Dove	406
	Ocean of Mercy and the Sea of Love (Lust)	
02/20/92 -	Interest Destroys Charity	407
	New Age Philosophers	
	No Prosthesis for Love	
	No Excuse for Not Loving	
02/22/92 -	To the Critics...	409
	Frayed Ends Cannot Connect	
	Forgiveness Mends Severed Cord	
02/24/92 -	Family Dissension and Divorce	411
	Matrimony Is a Great Responsibility	
02/25/92 -	A Beacon Lady of the Highest Sovereignty	412
	They Wait and Do Not Pray	
	Trust God's Discipline	
	Astounding the Most Prolific Odds-maker	
02/27/92 -	Key Bounces under the Door	414
02/29/92 -	Global Transformation	416
	United Perfection in Love	

March

03/01/92 -	First Sunday Mass	417
03/02/92 -	A Lesson of Helplessness	417
	Message for Families	
	Jesus Propping Us Up	

Our Lenten Purification

03/04/92 -	Conformity of Shapes	420
	Water Taking Shape of the Container	
	Pope John Paul II	
03/07/92 -	"They Even Have Houses for Their Cars!"	421
	Fat Tuesday	
03/09/92 -	Human Suffering Is a Blessing	422
	Mankind Can Return to Total Love	
	Beatific Vision	
	Choice to Love	
03/10/92 -	Glimpses of Heaven	423
03/11/92 -	Visions of Peace and Simplicity: Little Bee	424
	Trickling Stream	
	Strobing Corn Stalks	
03/12/92 -	The New Star for the Imminent Dawn	425
	Let Us Begin the Ascent	
03/13/92 -	Time Is Extremely Short	426
	Endurance of Trials	
	Faith, Mental Disarray	
03/15/92 -	Jesus' Temptation in the Desert	427
	Love Is the Only Alternative	
	Grace Is Present as Never Before	
03/17/92 -	Humanity Rejected God at Our Most Perfect Moment ..	428
	Tent Stakes	
	Forgiveness	
03/19/92 -	God Is about to Pronoun Sentence	430
	Proclamation of Sacredness of Life	
	Servitude	
03/22/92 -	People Do Not Want to Get Wet	432
	Power of Diary	
	Gift of Sacrifice	
03/23/92 -	Coming of Age	433
03/24/92 -	Unity under the Cross	434
	Denial of Self	
	Lenten Focus	
	A New Mankind	
03/25/92 -	Prayer Brings Reassurance	435
	Hope Is Unconquerable	
	Evil Cannot Win	
03/29/92 -	Take-up the Holy Rosary	436
	Under Attack by Evil	

April

04/01/92 -	Welcome Mats Brushed Clean	437
	My Soul Awoke	
04/02/92 -	Human Progress Is like a Puppy	437
	Faith Will Win this Battle	
04/03/92 -	We Are Perpetuating His Pain	438
04/04/92 -	No One Is Too Wretched	439
	Fervor Unlike Any Other Age	
04/05/92 -	Indifference Is Blasphemous	439
	"Paracleted"	
	One Foot in Hell	
04/06/92 -	Meditating the Virtues of Hope and Faith	441
04/07/92 -	Prefigured Image of Assured Victory	442
	Explosion of Joy	
04/08/92 -	A Humble Tree Was Pressed into Service	443
	Prayer Is Power	
	The Holy Eucharist Is the Eternal Fortress	
04/09/92 -	"What Grade Do You Think You Deserve?"	446
	Plunging Ahead in Faith	
04/12/92 -	2000 Years as 2000 Panes of Glass	447
	Transcending Time in Holy Mass	
04/17/92 -	Good Friday Changed the World	449
	Conversion Through the Cross	
04/18/92 -	Come to the Eucharist	450
	Jesus Is Alive	
	See the Coming of the Son of God	
04/19/92 -	A Confirming Grace of "Shafes"	452

Discipline in Prayer

04/20/92 -	Prayer Removes Boredom	454
	Seek Holiness and Pray	
	What Sacrifice Would You Make?	
04/22/92 -	Each Letter a Prayer	455
	Rise above Sadness	
04/29/92 -	Footing in Shallow Water	456
	Cannot Swim	
	There May Not Be Rhyme for Every Reason	
	Logic Insufficient	
04/30/92 -	Everyone Subjected to Test of Faith	458
	Birds & Lilies	

May

05/02/92 -	God's Mighty Discipline	459
	Jesus' Upturned Smile	
05/05/92 -	The Example of Lyndon Johnson	461
05/11/92 -	Living with Trust	462
	Admonishment of Conferences	
	Prayer; Not Speeches	
05/12/92 -	The Most Powerful Voice in the Kingdom	464
	The West Looks Helpless	
	Jesus in a Box	
	Faith Finished in Eucharist	
05/15/92 -	Trials Are Coming	467
	The Time Is Now, and Ours Is the Generation	
05/17/92 -	Lighting Our Lady's Shrine	468
	Vatican II Council	
	Unity in the Eucharist	
05/19/92 -	Hypnotized by Worldliness	471
	Hell Is Marked by Time	
	Paradise Is Timeless	
	Crucifixion Is Eternity	
05/22/92 -	Believe in the Power of Prayer	473
	Baby Kittens Placed in Box	
	Invisible Ocean Liner	
	The Ultimate Prayer of Love	
05/23/92 -	Quick-thinking	476
	How Is Jesus Present in the Holy Eucharist?	
05/25/92 -	Line of Consciousness	477
	Ruptures	
	Healing Process	
05/27/92 -	Breaching the Line of Stability	478
	Mind-power Is False	
	Chemicals for Mental Illness	
05/28/92 -	God Is Not Proving That He Exists	480
	We Cannot Afford to Take Her Lightly	
	Libre-ary	
	True Passion	
	History's Crunch-time	
	Rebirth in Grace	
05/31/92 -	Small Gifts of Love	483
	Sustaining Speed	

June

06/01/92 -	Personal Letter of Love	484
06/03/92 -	Holy Trinity Revelation Made Complete	485
	Holy Spirit Cradling Humanity	
	Rosary Unleashes Power	
06/04/92 -	Timelessness	486
	"In the Beginning..."	
	Evil Was Destroyed 2000 Years Ago	
	Paradise in the Heart	
06/06/92 -	Family Correlations	489
	Perspective of My Gifts	
06/09/92 -	Champion Enshrined	491
	Workplace Disarray	
	Those Touched I May Never Meet	
06/11/92 -	Stretching God's Mercy	492
	Protestant Communion	
06/14/92 -	Pruning the Plant	493
	Mother Kneeling with Child	
	Parenthood	
	Infinite Possibility	
	Abortion	
06/16/92 -	False Leaders	495
	Dominating Control	
	No Compromise with Evil	
	Call of the Holy Spirit	
	The Proper Introduction	

Meeting Love in Person
The Holy Eucharist

06/18/92 -	Eucharistic Holy Card	498
	Jesus' Gaze Through the Cards	
	Confession	
06/20/92 -	The Attack-dog Approach	499
	Unassuming Innocence and Acceptance	
	Building Crescendo	
	Cannon-fire	
06/22/92 -	Tiny Raft Sailing on Peacefulness of Indifference	501
	Last 100 Yards to the Beach	
06/23/92 -	"May I Have a Drink?"	502
	Bishops must Be Defended	
06/28/92 -	Evil Disbelievers	503

Complacency
Persecution of Messengers

July

07/01/92 -	Undefinable Through Love	505
	Man Leaving His Mark	
	Tire Marks	
	"Tell Them to Get Ready!"	
07/02/92 -	Lackadaisical Reception of Eucharist	507
	Distraction Blocks Pure Vision	
	Totality of Communion	
	Misaligned Water Line	
07/05/92 -	Patriotism	510
	Great Saving Miracle	
07/07/92 -	Devotion to Our Lady	512
	Enwombed in Her Care	
	Too Much Baggage	
	Step to Heaven Too High	
	Paw Print	
	Spinning Saucers	
07/09/92 -	Throne above Us	515
	Heaven Around and in Us	
	Double-standard in Exile	
	Intercession of Saints and Angels	
	In-spirited	
	Pennant	
	Victory Celebration	
07/14/92 -	Conversation with Jesus and Our Lady	519
	Divine Union	
	Rich, Affluent, and Famous Fall Through the Cracks	
	Hypocrisy	
07/19/92 -	The Sunrise Is near	520
	The Greatest Revelation since Pentecost	
07/20/92 -	Vision of Brick Wall Forming in Mid-air	522
	Convinced That We Can Love	
	We Are His Countenance	
07/25/92 -	Satan's Double Attack	524
	Great Builder Coming down the Street	
07/26/92 -	Self-forgiveness	526
	Reptiles and Crustacea	
	Seashells	
07/28/92 -	The Message Not the Messenger	528

	No One Is a Messenger on Their Own	
	Holy Mother Can Discipline	
07/31/92 -	Faith Is the First Precept	529
	Jesus Blesses Diary as His Own	

August

08/02/92 -	Salvation Unfolding	531
	Communion of Saints	
	Solidified Faith	
08/05/92 -	Additional Titles of Our Lady	532
	Pope John Paul II	
	Unconditional Forgiveness	
	We Were Not Won in a Foot-race	
	Love must Not Be Blocked	
08/06/92 -	Taken to the Mountaintop of Grace	535
	Satan Running in Full Force	
	He Will Not Succeed	
	He Called Himself "The Dawn"	
08/08/92 -	Verification of Messages	538
	Pedestal Table	
	United Pair	
	We Are about to Be Shocked into Reality	
08/10/92 -	Living More Slowly	540
	Scrutiny of Our Conscience	
08/12/92 -	Her Presence Has Strengthened My Faith	542
	Satan Runs from the Imprint on Our Soul	
	Live the Messages	
08/15/92 -	Pre-eminence of Christ	543
	Light on Arm from a Distant Source	
	Creation Is Good	
	Natural Disasters Are Redeeming Acts	
08/17/92 -	We Are Loved by God	546
	Impact of Eucharistic Cards	
	Holy Mother's Great Vision	
08/20/92 -	Coincidences of Grace with Co-worker	548
	Confidence Instead of Fear	
	Healing Our Memories	
	Fear Impedes Our Potential	
08/21/92 -	Feeding the Starving	551
	Box of Sin Becomes Thin Line	
	Sphere Radiates Love	
08/24/92 -	My Statue Attacked Again	553

	Eucharist Is Power and Intent of God	
	Response to Indifference	
	Reprimand	
08/25/92 -	Abusive Detractors	556
	Refusing to Love	
	Eliminate Evil with Love	
08/30/92 -	A Letter to Confirm the Prophecy	558
	Example Not to Be Complacent	
	Soggy Kindling	

September

09/01/92 -	In the Company of Perfect Immortals	561
	Buoyancy of Spirit	
	Red-water Rapids of Christ's Blood	
09/05/92 -	We Cannot Breathe, Float, or Swim	563
	A Toy in the Hands of Baby Jesus	
	My Love	
	Hope Greater than Despair	
09/06/92 -	I Do Not Have to Tarry in the Stall	565
	Perception of Time	
	Divine Affection Beyond Reproach	
09/09/92 -	Helpless to Storms	567
	Glory of Little Acts	
	Regained Butterfly	
09/12/92 -	Darkness in the Church	570
	Our Lady Is Not a Priest	
	Peter the Rock	
	Purity Is Protection	
	Full Communion with the Holy Father	
09/13/92 -	Fence of Planks	574
	Turning Our Heads Away from the Spoon	
	"Where in All of this Is the Role of Woman?"	
	Elevation of Women Through Motherhood	
09/14/92 -	The Trinity of Ceremonies	576
	The Seven Sacraments	
09/16/92 -	Eucharistic Miracles	577
	Attaining Perfect Love	
	Human Nature Not Impediment to Perfection	
	Willingness	
	Eucharist Leaves Us Speechless	
09/19/92 -	Where Is Our Hope?	580
	Her Imprisoned Children	

	Corrupt American Dream	
	Thou Shall Not Steal	
	"Their Wealth Is a Self-inflicted Curse."	
09/20/92 -	Denying Jesus' Sacrifice	582
	The Holy Virgin Is One of His Best Signs	
	Third Dimension Is Freedom	
	Courage	
09/22/92 -	Have We Not Learned...	585
	Union of Womb & Child Is Heaven	
	Union of Priest's Hands & Bread/wine	
	Birth Must Not Be Impeded	
09/25/92 -	Bishop Blesses My Home	588
09/26/92 -	Raging Admonishment	589
	Old Man Cutting Jungle	
	Christ Rolls Out the "Big Guns"	
09/27/92 -	Lifting of the Heart in Prayer	591
	Meet Jesus in Your Heart	
	Love Is the Door	
09/29/92 -	"The Story of a Life"	592
	Old Man Cleans the Town	
	Stop Living as If There Is No Heaven	

October

10/01/92 -	The Incarnation of Undaunted Holiness	594
	Truth of Love Nearly Gone	
	Broken Hearts must Be Healed	
	Treasure Is Our Brother	
	Dignity Stripped	
	"Ex-con"	
	Umbrella of Love	
10/03/92 -	Freedom for the Captives and the Criminal	598
10/04/92 -	Francis, the Saint of Assisi	600
	Examination of Conscience	
	Little Children Francis & Dominic	
	Eucharist Is Jesus Present	
10/07/92 -	The Truth of the Eucharist	602
	Common Foe	
	Satan's Subtlety	
	Rosary Is Uniting	
10/10/92 -	Rosary Perfects Vision	604
	The Straight Line of Truth	
	Rosary Provides Perfect Focus & Direction	
	The Purpose of the Pieta	

10/11/92 - Little Diary Girl 606
God Has Control and Is Infallible
10/13/92 - Winner of the Debate 607
Littleness of the Admiral
Suffering Brought Compassion
Abortion Is Murder
The Supreme Court Justices
10/15/92 - Love is the Answer to All Questions 609
10/18/92 - Three States of Progression Toward Holiness 609
Our Lady's Intercession Supports Us
Timmy's Miracle

Conquering the Failing World

10/19/92 - Human Science is Failing 613
What Man Could Approach Such Genius?
Do We Know What We Are Doing?
Question of My Priesthood
10/21/92 - Abortion is not a Right 616
Jesus Spoke Again
Calvary is the Mass
Reflection & Generation
Behold Your Mother
10/25/92 - Struggle for Identity 618
Jesus Wants Conviction
Knowing Must Become Living
Celestial X-ray
10/26/92 - Our Transgressions Were Irrevocably Annihilated 621
Let's Face It!
Jesus' Coming Is Very near
The Eucharist Is the Answer
10/29/92 - The Life of Mother Teresa 623
Faith in the Holy Angels
Calling Spirits
SS Simon & Jude - Intercession of Saints
10/31/92 - Reference to Halloween 624

November
11/01/92 - Fr. Ted's Return from Haiti 625
Give Everything Vs. Use Everything
11/06/92 - Suicide Is a Hopeless Flower 626

	Growing Heaviness	
	Transformation from Indifference to Conversion	
	You Have Been Told!	
11/08/92 -	Love past Pillars and Palaces	631
	Unassuming Child-like Trust and Innocence	
	"I Claim You in the Name of Christ Jesus!"	
11/13/92 -	Faithless Excuses	632
	Increasing Our Capacity to Love	
	Holy Mass Unites Us with Power	
	The Two Hearts	
11/17/92 -	God Is Repulsed by Lukewarm Christianity	634
	Indifference	
	Shocking the Indifferent	
	Crawl to the Finish-line in Faith	
11/21/92 -	Power of Urgency	636
	"The Only Living Thing in the Universe"	
	Cry of the Mother	
	Prelude to Eternity	
11/27/92 -	Flaming Torch next to the Fuel of Hatred	637
	The Rise into Perfect Love	
	Victory Is in Suffering Hearts	
11/29/92 -	Attaining Perfection in Love	640
	Stairs to the Mountain Kingdom	

December

12/01/92 -	Billy Graham's Evangelization	642
	Holiness Eaten Away by Sin	
	Same Root: Different Word	
	Light Will Overcome Darkness Forever	
	They Expect to Be Paid	
12/04/92 -	We Are Righteous Conquerors Again	646
	Man Is an Aspiring Artist	
	Divine Potential	
	We Wish to Be More than Good	
	Transform the Weak into an Impenetrable Fortress	
12/09/92 -	Satan's Enticements	648
	When Evil Was at its Highest Pitch	
12/10/92 -	I Have Seen Her Immortal Sheen	650
	High above the Ramparts	
12/12/92 -	Where Is Mine?	650
	Helplessness Can Be Overcome	
	Heed the Admonition	

12/16/92 -	Sewing Garments of Holiness with the Thread of Love	653
12/19/92 -	The Child Is My Gift	654
12/21/92 -	Awake, Awake Your Sleeping Hearts!	656
	Contemplation of Christmas Eve	
12/25/92 -	He Slipped into the World Quietly	657
	Litany of Jesus' Names	
	Reciprocity of Love: Souls Released from Purgatory	
	Materialism Is a Prison	
12/27/92 -	Abortion Manifests Disasters	659
	Diminishment of Mankind	
	Fall Can Be Negligible	
12/29/92 -	Not Some Tangential Metaphysics	660
	People Refuse to Forgive and Forget	
12/31/92 -	Cleansing Absolution	661
	Encouragement to Continue My Mission	

Prologue

Where could I begin to prepare you for the words that are about to pass before your eyes? What can I say that will tender your heart to the grace that is soon to lift your soul? If we were to walk together on a sunny day, I would know to give you a pair of glasses to block the sun, or perhaps a lotion to shield you from its harmful rays. But, what would prepare you for a place where the sunlight is Love and its warmth the ecstasy that heals every ill and wipes all the tears from our eyes? How can I prepare you for a place where cripples rise and run with greater joy than any athlete has ever competed? Imagine those who are broken realizing that they were the giants carrying the world. Envision every desolate mother receiving her lost children back into her arms. Is your heart ready to embrace a gentleness that can shatter mountains and a grace that will transform the face of the Earth? Just eight short years ago, I heard someone ask these questions in response to my entreaties of childlike curiosity about what was to come. I now realize that there is nothing that could have been said to encapsulate the beauty of life into a sentence describing it. I can tell you how to become holy, but it is you who must make the transformation. I can tell you that I have seen the meadow, but it is you who must travel there. I can speak of commitment, but it is you who must become committed. I can reveal the Truth, but it is you who must accept it. And, I can ask you to believe, but it is you who must summon the courage that escorts that faith to the surface of your life.

This manuscript is a grace from Almighty God to His beloved humanity. It is heavenly balm for a wounded and suffering world. It is Light and Wisdom in the midst of darkness. It is a message of Love and Truth delivered by the most precious and docile soul that God will ever create. Through His grace and generosity, I have come to know Her. And, She knows each of us. I have taken comfort in the same arms which held the Redeemer of the world. I have laid my head upon the same Heart where Christ found solace here on Earth. And, from this Immaculate Heart, I have received the wisdom and understanding that strengthened the Savior of the World to complete His Sacrifice of Love upon the Cross of Calvary. Just as the Most Blessed Virgin Mary delivered the Word into the world 2000 years ago, She delivers this miraculous prodigy to each of us. This manuscript lives through the power of God. No human possesses the spiritual capacity to have authored it or to judge it. My brother and I have been merely the scribes who hope that we have moved closer to emulating the grace which has become our lives.

True Devotion To Mary
by
St. Louis De Montfort
Chapter I, Article III, No. 56,57,58,59

56. But who shall those servants, slaves, and children of Mary be? They shall be the ministers of the Lord who, like a burning fire, shall kindle the fire of divine love everywhere. They shall be "like sharp arrows in the hand of the powerful" Mary to pierce her enemies. (PS. 126:4). They shall be the sons of Levi, well purified by the fire of great tribulation, and closely adhering to God (1 Cor. 6:17), who shall carry the gold of love in their heart, the incense of prayer in their spirit, and the myrrh of mortification in their body. They shall be everywhere the good odor of Jesus Christ to the poor and to the little, while at the same time, they shall be an odor of death to the great, to the rich and to the proud worldlings.

57. They shall be clouds thundering and flying through the air at the least breath of the Holy Spirit; who, detaching themselves from everything and troubling themselves about nothing, shall shower forth the rain of the Word of God and of life eternal. They shall thunder against sin; they shall storm against the world; they shall strike the devil and his crew; and they shall pierce through and through, for life or for death, with their two-edged sword of the Word of God (Eph. 6:17), all those to whom they shall be sent on the part of the Most High.

58. **They shall be the true apostles of the latter times**, to whom the Lord of Hosts shall give the words and the might to work marvels and to carry off with glory the spoils of His enemies. They shall sleep without gold or silver, and, what is more, without care, in the midst of the other priests, ecclesiastics, and clerics (Ps. 67:14); and yet they shall have the silvered wings of the dove to go, with pure intention of the glory of God and the salvation of souls, wheresoever the Holy Spirit shall call them. Nor shall they leave behind them, in the places where they have preached, anything but the gold of charity, which is fulfillment of the whole law. (Rom. 13:10).

59. In a word, we know that they shall be true disciples of Jesus Christ, walking in the footsteps of His poverty, humility, contempt of the world, charity; teaching the narrow way of God in pure truth, according to the Holy Gospel, and not according to the maxims of the world; troubling themselves about nothing; not accepting persons; sparing, fearing and listening to no mortal, however influential he may be. They shall have in their mouths the two-edged sword of the Word of God. They shall carry on their shoulders the bloody standard of the Cross, the Crucifix in their right hand and the Rosary in their left, the Sacred Names of Jesus and Mary in their hearts, and the modesty and mortification of Jesus Christ in their own behavior.

These are the great men who are to come; **but Mary is the one who, by order of the Most High, shall fashion them...**

Opening Remarks

This writing is a record of my conversations with the Mother of Jesus Christ, the Blessed Virgin Mary. God has allowed Her to speak with me openly and directly so the world may be reconciled through their Son, Jesus. I ask you to accept it as a gift with an open heart. Please rid yourself of the desire to question or verify its authenticity. It is not humanly possible to authenticate supernatural origins if one does not have the capacity to believe anything more than what they see. Indeed, allowing verification would destroy the need for the faith that Our Lady has come to strengthen. The Truth in this writing proves its origin to those desiring the wisdom of God. The first thing that many of the faithless will ever believe is their own judgement before the Throne of God. This record of our Virgin Mother's intercession is in the form of a diary. When I wrote the initial entry on that first day, I could never have conceived what you now hold in your hands. One night, God tested my desire to participate when Our Lady told me that I was *"no longer required to continue with my writing."* I continued, even though I was not required. Our service to this work was a free gift of ourselves to God, just as our Blessed Mother's "Yes" was Her free gift extended to the Most High. My brother and I were free to discontinue our participation in Her intercession at any time. No one is forced to follow God.

I cannot imagine what our lives would have become if we had not continued. But, by doing so, my brother and I have experienced joy and peace beyond any measure. We have confidence and trust in God, supported by the grace of the Blessed Virgin. We have learned that true Love for Jesus and His Mother requires the complete sacrifice of the self. And, to our good fortune, we have also been hated, abused, ridiculed, mocked, slandered, and exiled. Jesus promised this treatment to all who would love and follow Him. His words are again fulfilled. In the early days of Our Lady's great visit, I felt it urgent that our home be blessed by a priest. Although I had always desired this blessing, it seemed imperative that it be conferred in light of the unfolding grace. The place of Her miraculous visits was to be purified and beautiful in reflection of the beauty which She brings us. Soon after, God allowed my desire to be fulfilled by our Roman Catholic Bishop.

In opening this work, I would like to lay a foundation and provide precedent to our Blessed Mother's intercession. We are fruit from the branch of Medjugorje, Yugoslavia, the extension of the Holy Virgin's intercession into the world. It was the fall of 1987 when I first heard of Her miraculous appearances in Medjugorje. At that time, the limits of my knowledge included only Guadalupe, Lourdes, and Fatima. I was especially familiar with the great apparitions of Fatima in 1917. I would never have considered becoming involved in any "Marian movement," nor did I know there was one. Being Catholic from birth, I simply knew of the events. Notwithstanding my lack of worldly perspective, I sat many hours wondering what it must have been like for those who received these great graces. At times, my contemplations brought me to tears as I imagined how awe-inspiring these events must have been. I never asked God to allow something of this nature to happen in my life. I only told Him that I wished I could have been there so that He could have seen me in the crowd believing with all of my heart.

I was given a book written by a Catholic theologian concerning the events in Medjugorje. As I read it, Our Lady's words leaped off the pages into my heart. I had never been struck so deeply in my soul as when I read Her words. Although not audible, it was as though I could hear Her speaking to me as my eyes fell upon each word. From that moment, I attempted to live as She was asking. I went to my room to look for my Rosary. It was always near me throughout my life. We had grown-up reciting it together as a family. Upon finding it, I began to pray, but could not remember all of the Mysteries. I knew there were Joyful, Sorrowful, and Glorious meditations, but I could not recall them specifically. So, I picked fifteen highlights of Jesus' Life and offered them as my prayer that night. I remember adding the "Flight into Egypt" as one of the Sorrowful Mysteries, and I remembered the last two Glorious Mysteries.

Soon after, I related what I had read to my best friend, Timothy. We had been friends for nearly fifteen years at that point in time. He converted to Catholicism after accompanying me to Christmas Eve Mass in 1977. He was baptized the following year on the Feast of the Most Holy Rosary, October 7, 1978. We later discovered that he was previously baptized as a child in a protestant church on May 13th, the anniversary of the first apparition of Our Lady of Fatima. For over a year, and with measured success, I tried to live as the Virgin Mary was asking. On 16th of April 1989, I made a commitment to attend daily Mass and pray the entire fifteen decades of the Holy Rosary every day. By mid-summer, I could not quell my incredible desire to travel to Medjugorje. I could not get the story of Our Lady's intercession out of my mind. My reason for visiting the site of Her appearances was the same as it had always been; for God to see me in the crowd believing with all my heart. I never longed for Her to appear to me, nor did I crave such a miracle. I simply knew that I wanted to be near Her. On the day I departed for Yugoslavia, I was gathering my travel gear. I had two Rosaries, one silver, the other gold. I picked-up the silver Rosary thinking of the many stories of Rosaries miraculously turning gold in Medjugorje. I immediately told myself that my Rosary turning gold was not the reason I was making a pilgrimage to this little town, so I placed it back atop the television and put the Rosary which was already gold into my pocket before I walked out the door.

As a pilgrim, I traveled to Medjugorje during the Feast of the Assumption in 1989. I will only say that the man who flew across the ocean to this tiny village was not the man who cried having to return to the United States. If I had not purchased a house two months before, I would have called home, quit my job, and stayed in Medjugorje. But, I knew I had to fulfill my responsibilities. For that week, I was immersed in a grace that transformed who I was and wished to be. I wanted to be "holy" and do the bidding of the Mother of God. I witnessed pure beauty and the power that will ultimately convert every heart destined for Heaven. That Love became the only thing I wished to live for. Physically, I saw no supernatural phenomena. But, by a miraculous grace, I saw the Truth in my heart more clearly than I had ever seen it. Love was seared into my soul by a heavenly saber pulled from the blazing cauldron of the Virgin's Immaculate Heart. I am incapable of other words to describe this Light. Upon returning home, people asked whether I enjoyed my trip. I could not tell them without crying. All I had to do was turn my thoughts to the mountain vigil of August 14th when I was in the miraculous presence of the Blessed Virgin and I would begin crying from the Light of Love still blinding my heart. And, as a grace of God's great Love, I found the silver Rosary left upon my television now a beautiful gold.

Together, Timothy and I returned to Medjugorje the first week of December 1989 for the Feast of the Immaculate Conception. This was the second visit for both of us as my brother had just returned three weeks prior to our departure. On this visit, we were chosen from the crowd of hundreds to receive a private audience with Vicka Ivankovic, one of the visionaries of Our Lady. During this encounter, Vicka laid her hands simultaneously atop our heads and began to pray. These moments of prayer were the grace that initiated and consecrated this work. I will forever be thankful for the prayers that she offered to God in those moments. They were heard and answered. We returned home renewed in the Truth that we had experienced in that tiny village of Yugoslavia. In the early morning hours of February 22, 1991, I received a telephone call from my brother which announced the rising of the Morning Star in our lives.

I ask you to remember as you read the initial pages that no human is ever prepared to receive the direct intervention of God. The first three months represent the opening chapter of Our Lady's direct intercession. Although veiled in much symbolism due to our spiritual immaturity, the first thirty messages of this period provide a glimpse of what is to come. They are the precognition of the glorious message She bears. We were simply children recording words whose depth we did not yet understand. God asked for our patient faith and trust in His omnipotence during this time of spiritual acclimation. We lived in blind faith, following Our Lady despite the disruption about us. By the end of May, the Blessed Virgin commenced the lessons which She knows will convert the world. These lessons teach us about Jesus in His most beautiful form as He hung on the Cross of Calvary. The Virgin Mother knew His Heart completely in those moments. With this knowledge, She has the authority and power to speak of Her Son to all Creation. There is not a man alive with the audacity to challenge the right or the words spoken by a mother to describe the goodness of her slain child. Yet, there are those who will arrogantly claim this authority in an attempt to usurp and obscure the beauty of the voice of the Mother of the Slain Child of Redemption. The

Virgin's message to the world is urgent and serious. Her instructions are pointed and clear, without compromise or conjecture. They illuminate the only path to peace that is available to mankind. There is only one Savior, one Love, and one chance. There have been, and will continue to be, grave consequences for ignoring the words of the Gospel. And, these occurrences will crescendo if we continue on our present path.

This is not a writing for entertainment or material profit. It is a plea for change directed personally toward every human heart. It is an effort by God to call forth the beauty within us. It is an invocation of the Holy Spirit upon humanity. For some, these words will bring soothing relief and buoyant strength. To others, they will bring shocking and revealing light upon the distance they have fallen from the beauty that God intends them to manifest. Still others will have completely rejected this entire work after having only come through these opening pages. Rejection has always been the defining act of the mortal human will. Masses of humanity have rejected the loving overtures of God for centuries.

Faith brings the openness required to embrace what Our Lady gives the world. She offers Salvation in the person of Her Son, Jesus Christ. She offers the Triumph over the desolation She endured on Calvary. She is the embodiment of the Victory of faith, while Her Son is the everlasting Victor. God is giving us a chance to render ourselves mercifully and peacefully into His Divine Will. Salvation was meant to include everyone. There is room enough in the Heart of Jesus for all the souls He died to save. But, it requires something special from each of us. It requires who we are, the gift of self in a sacrificial bath of Love. We must allow ourselves to be taught to love as Jesus loves. From our mortal vantage point, this instruction seems bitter and unwarranted, foolish and futile. It is the picture of the Crucifixion to the human soul. Our Lady wishes to elevate our vision so that we see the heavenly reality. Her instructions truly bring power and Glory, revelation and transformation.

It is a difficult process re-instructing those who have been impregnated by the biases of their mortal teachers and centuries of error. Darkness begets darkness. We are called to the Light. Jesus spoke of the necessity of being "born again," completely renewed in thought and being. Can a person reenter their mother's womb to experience this rebirth? Only if that womb is the Immaculate Heart of our Heavenly Mother! Birth has been singularly identified with woman since the foundation of Creation. Hence, it is both consistent and appropriate that the birth of the children of God into holiness be singularly identified with the Woman of Grace. The Virgin Mary is the Mother who bore Grace, Himself, into the world. She gave birth to the Body of Christ Who was filled with the Spirit of God. When we see Christ entering the world through His Mother's womb, we see the origin of our Redemption. Our Lady is calling the world to birth in holiness. We are about to enter a world which is boundless in Love. God wishes us to be attired in clothes befitting the dignity of His children as this new day rises. We are about to witness the revelation of the children of God upon the Earth. We must consider the pose we wish to strike on that day of revelation. The world as we know it is passing away. Beauty untold is about to replace it.

This manuscript is the glow of the morning sunlight which is breaking the horizon. It is the Morning Star who announces the Return of the Son. So, I ask you to enter the glorious Heart of the Virgin as I relate the intimate moments that I have spent with our Heavenly Mother. You have all been with us from the beginning. From the first moment, I recorded these miraculous events holding you in my heart hoping that I could someday share them with you. The hope that I have held for these years is now fulfilled. As man finds it fitting to christen his many prodigies and works, so too do I wish to bless this commencement with a prayer from the Book of Wisdom. It describes far better than my literary abilities the beauty and power emanating from the true Author of this work. In highest honor and veneration, I humbly and completely defer and submit to the majesty of the Woman Clothed With the Sun, the Queen of Heaven, from whom Wisdom has come into the world.

WISDOM 7:10-8:8

Beyond health and comeliness I loved Her, and I chose to have Her rather than the light, because the splendor of Her never yields to sleep. Yet all good things together came to me in Her company, and countless riches at Her hands; and I rejoice in them all, because Wisdom is their leader, though I had not known that She is the Mother of these.

Simply I learned about Her, and ungrudgingly do I share; Her riches I do not hide away; for to men She is an unfailing treasure; those who gain this treasure win the friendship of God, to whom the gifts they have from discipline commend them. Now God grant I speak suitably and value these endowments at their worth; for He is the guide of Wisdom and the director of the wise. For both we and our words are in His hand, as well as all prudence and knowledge of crafts. For He gave me sound knowledge of existing things, that I might know the organization of the universe and the force of its elements, the beginning and the end and the mid-point of times, the changes in the sun's course and the variations of the seasons. Cycles of years, positions of the stars, natures of animals, tempers of beasts, powers of the winds and thoughts of men, uses of plants and virtues of roots; such things as are hidden I learned, and such as are plain; for Wisdom, the artificer of all, taught me.

For in Her is a spirit intelligent, holy, unique, manifold, subtle, agile, clear, unstained, certain, not baneful, loving the good, keen, unhampered, beneficent, kindly, firm, secure, tranquil, all-powerful, all-seeing, and pervading all spirits, though they be intelligent, pure and very subtle. For Wisdom is mobile beyond all motion, and She penetrates and pervades all things by reason of Her purity. For She is an aura of the might of God and a pure effusion of the glory of the Almighty; therefore nought that is sullied enters into Her. For She is the refulgence of eternal light, the spotless mirror of the power of God, the image of His goodness. And She, who is one, can do all things, and renews everything while Herself perduring; and passing into holy souls from age to age, She produces friends of God and prophets. For there is nought God loves, be it not one who dwells with Wisdom. For She is fairer than the sun and surpasses every constellation of the stars. Compared to light, She take precedence; for that, indeed, night supplants, but wickedness prevails not over Wisdom.

Indeed, She reaches from end to end mightily and governs all things well. Her I loved and sought after from my youth; I sought to take Her for my bride and was enamored of Her beauty. She adds to nobility the splendor of companionship with God; even the Lord of all loved Her. For She is instructress in the understanding of God, the selector of His works. And if riches be a desirable possession in life, what is more rich than Wisdom, who produces all things? And if prudence renders service, who in the world is a better craftsman than She? Or if one loves justice, the fruits of Her works are virtues; for She teaches moderation and prudence, justice and fortitude, and nothing in life is more useful for men than these. Or again, if one yearns for copious learning, She knows the things of old, and infers those yet to come. She understands the turns of phrases and the solutions of riddles; signs and wonders She knows in advance and the outcome of times and ages...

Feast of Our Lady of Mt. Carmel

"My beautiful, beautiful little children, this feast day is a day of Love. How I love you on this day and always. I wish you to be of bright hearts today. I wish you to begin with a new face of joy that springs from within. I wish you to truly understand today the grace and gift that your Mother is speaking to you in a language that you understand, in a Love that you can comprehend, in a Light through which you can feel the precious countenance from which it beams. All of this is because you are loved. All of this is because you have the capacity and conscience to be open to the Holy Spirit who owns you and who loves you, and who asks you to respond in a prayerful way. This, you have done, and much, much more. I ask you to see your own holiness, your own prayerfulness, your own piety. It is because of all that I have taught you. You are very fortunate. You hold a great deal of responsibility. And, we share the Love that we seek and the prayers which the world refuses to pray. We share the hope that the world yet does not understand. All of this is because you have said 'Yes.' My same 'Yes' was only the beginning of the graces that I still bring the world.

Jesus is the fulfillment of the Love that your God has for the world. God made His Son, My Son, perfect as He is perfect. He asks those who accept Him and follow Him to be called inwardly to that same perfection, regardless of what those who inhabit the world proclaim, regardless of the many wounded reasons of why it cannot be done, regardless of those failing forces who sit in wonder why this should be done, or their callous reasonings how. I am your Mother, the Mother of Humankind, of all of the children of God who dare to touch the heavens, looking for the solution to their mortal woes. Yes, I am the Blessed

Virgin Mary who has come to the simplest and most innocent, given to the world by My very beautiful Son, the Glory of all that is, the Star in the Heavens, the Reason for all that is cause, the Strength for all that is power, the Shining Light for all that seeks the brightness of freedom. Yes, your loving Mother has come to proclaim that on the day that the world was saved, on that day that your God died for you, I was there. I saw His Passion. I saw His Blood. I saw His commitment to all that He created. I saw His willingness to understand, to have patience, and to be open, even to all those who would seek any direction except Him. I saw Him as I looked up. I saw His loving gaze upon Me, upon the Mother of all that He called His as He told Me that He loves Me, and as He made His proclamation that He was above and before Me for the same Love that I proclaimed when I gave Him birth.

My loving Son Jesus, bequeathed to Me as My children all those who would stand by Him and who would allow Him in. And, I was also given those who would yet deny Him to call My own, even those who would protest against His original charge given to our precious Apostles who would suffer, who would give of themselves to be the Givers of Love and Christ to the world. Even all those who deny Me this day, all of those who will not receive Me as their Mother, will come to understand that the same Savior whom they accept asked them to *'Behold your Mother.'* Even those who deny the Eucharist must surely remember what their Savior said on the Cross, the same Cross that redeemed them and that made them whole. They shall look upon Me as their Help and their Arms of caress and Love. I am the Home of the World. I am the Place of Refuge and of Safety who calls all of God's children to come with Me. I am the Ark who takes you to the Glory of the Sun, of the brightest Son of Salvation.

My precious little boy, I wish for the world to become little, to bow down in deference to the Holy One who came to save them. I wish every living soul to believe that they were low-laden upon the ground as they watched their Savior Jesus walk past them on His way to Calvary. I wish that every little child who God created would imagine the sound of the earth crackling under Jesus' footsoles as He made His way to the mountaintop. There, He would fulfill the Salvation of every soul ever given breath by the God who challenged them to again be perfect. Yes, I am the Mother of all of this Hope. I am the One who calls everyone to be lowly, just as Jesus was lowly at His Birth and at His Death. And, as Jesus asks His children to be at His footsoles, He also asks you to be elevated to His Heart, to where He calls you now. And, I call you too..."

At the invocation of these words, please begin with me now as the picturesque intercession of the Mother of Jesus is painted upon your soul. Open your heart to receive the Light beaming out of Heaven. Embrace this opportunity for us to all lurch forward in unity toward our beatific destiny.

The Final Colossus

Basking, bathing, brilliant! Outpouring the Wisdom of God!
The Visage of Heaven, flowing freely the tears of pristine Glory.
Clothed in unerring, inevitable Light. The winds of change!
Eradicating, electrifying, compelling, beloved!
You teach the shedding of Earth amidst the corals of sin.
Go! Go into the world that knows no peace.
Greet, bless, call, embrace! Heal, sanctify, purify, caress!

You, the Virginal Shores of Paradisial Love.
Monogram and Monument to the Triune God.
The Trident, the Benevolent, the Salvific, the Bold.
You, the Sunlit Matron of God's Holy Ones, lost in the portals of bewildering Death.
O' Perfect Glory, Mother of Life Renewed. You, the Hands of Grace.
The Fair Maiden who birthed the pacific Pardon of fallen souls.

You, the Beatific Dawn of a Boundless Age.
Bring the solstice of Ecstatic Light to heirs and orphans.
To the Well of corpus hearts brooding in hopeless Dusk.
Seek ancient tundras and mystical parlors where mortals huddle amidst battle and waste.
You, the flawless Blessing and newfound Trust of generations lost!

You, Matriarch and Queen of the lifeless Daughter in the Harbor.
Your Son is the Torch of Life to the children of Earth.
His Light unifies the blessed, the grated, the wretched, the lost, the timid, the damned.
You! Summoned by the outstretched arms of Hope!
Stationed high above the stillness of invincible Freedom.

You celebrate the Destiny of man and beast, alike,
with Your Immaculate Crown of Stars,
to which the little Child in the Bay bows in deference,
her spiked chapeau heeled near her humbled feet.
She welcomes Your cultivating Touch to the unwitting masses,
the hopeless chest of inordinate pawns awaiting their passage to the Celestial Port,
while the Streams of Paradise reflect your glistening Mantle.

Yes, You step into the world to claim the Unknown.
Clasping errant palms that flail in the dark,
pulling to beat their breasts in the vibrant New Groves of the Land of God.
You are the Parasol of Infinite Bliss. Refined, Robust, impassioned Delight!
Where cities of angels moor to feast on placid temperaments.
Come this Day! Lift every age to Heaven's Door!

In Our Darkest Hour
MORNING STAR OVER AMERICA

February 22, 1991- December 31, 1992
Volume I

THE BEGINNING OF THE MIRACLE
"FIAT"

FEBRUARY 1991

Friday, February 22, 1991   Feast of the Chair of Saint Peter

2:45 A.M.
"My forceful one, we have just begun. My Son is with you...."

At about 3:15 in the morning, the telephone rang while I was asleep in my bed. As with any late night call, my heart jumped with anxiety, thinking that I was destined to hear some bad news about my family or friends. I picked-up the receiver and my best friend, Timothy, began speaking to me through his tears. He was very emotional while trying to compose himself without sobbing. I could not understand him at first because he was so overwhelmed. My heart began to race, thinking that what I most feared might have come-to-pass. Then, he said clearly, "Our Blessed Mother just spoke to me..." I did not know what to say to him. Like a whirlwind, my mind went through a mental checklist of all the possible explanations for what he had said. Then a tiny voice in my heart told me, "*You have always trusted him. He has never failed you. Believe him now!*" At these words, I forced my mind to cease looking for any other explanation, only that what he had just affirmed was actually true. I completely accepted his proclamation. After I made the decision to believe, a light turned-on inside my heart. I began to feel an ecstasy and happiness that I have never known before. An incredible anticipation and expectation welled-up inside of me. From that moment forward, I knew beyond any shadow of doubt that the Mother of God had just spoken to him.

He heard Her voice outside of himself, describing it as someone speaking directly into his ear. There was more to the message that he received, but he could not record it because he was so startled. He wished that She would have spoken more slowly so he could have written everything down. During our conversation, he related several other personal phenomenon that he had recently experienced. This past Wednesday evening, we had joined another prayer group from Pana, Illinois. During the Rosary, Timothy felt a miraculous separation from the material world. He was elevated above himself in a boundless expanse where he knew only the freedom of flight. While experiencing this separation, he could not find me, although I was kneeling beside him the entire time. He also referred to the eighth day of December when he was outside a store-front after purchasing a statue of Our Lady. As he looked into a plate-glass window outside, he could see the perfect reflection of the Blessed Virgin Mary gazing back at him. When this happened, the ground began shaking under his feet as if there was an earthquake underway. He never told me of either of these events until tonight because he did not feel that he could explain them in a context that I would either accept or understand. I have included them here as related events to this record for reasons yet unknown.

Timothy came to pray with me at my house in the city this evening. We offered our supplications of Adoration of the Holy Cross and then continued with the fifteen meditations of the Marian Rosary. I secured a pad of paper and a pencil, hoping that our Blessed Mother would speak to us again. But, we finished our recitation without receiving a single syllable of intercession. Undeterred, I thought that She might return during the night. I implored my brother to call me as soon as She said anything more to him. To me, it was not a matter of *if*, but rather *when* She would proceed. I know in my heart that the Blessed Virgin's intercession is not just a casual greeting or passing grace. Interiorly, I am confident that Her presence is a gift from God with the power to transcend anything that humanity has ever experienced before. In this assurance, I know that Our Lady will continue with this gift.

Saturday, February 23, 1991
2:45 A.M.
"My dear little ones, pray, pray, pray. Prepare for the Coming of My Child. Polish your souls skillfully. Do not be afraid, My Son is near. Your prayers are the Light of His Dawn. Do not be afraid, little ones, I am with you always." Timothy called me immediately after receiving these words. He was as overwhelmed as before while comparing his feelings to a terrible stage fright. The Virgin Mary's voice was now completely inside his body. Her words flooded outwardly from deep within his heart. Audible phrases that we hear always originate outside of our being and penetrate into our mind and psyche. But, he described Her words as coming from somewhere within him and overflowing into his consciousness. They were not originating as thoughts of his own. It is obvious that he is not responsible for what he is miraculously hearing. He is listening to a person speak to him and recording the transcript word-for-word.

This morning, I called Father Ted, a Roman Catholic Priest, and related to him what was happening. After listening patiently, he told me that he would pray for us with great fervor. He asked us to be patient and peaceful as this grace continued to unfold. I told him that this is what I also wished. Timothy and I resumed our prayers Saturday evening. Again, we meditated on the five Glorious Mysteries of the Most Holy Rosary, more specifically, the

Resurrection of Jesus, His Ascension into Heaven, the Descent of the Holy Spirit at Pentecost, the Assumption of the Virgin Mary into Heaven, and Her Crowning as the Queen of Heaven and Earth. As we prayed, my brother began crying to the point that he could barely continue. He felt the immense Love of the Virgin Mary as She approached to pray with us again. Embarrassed by his weeping, he repeatedly asked me what was happening to him. I encouraged him to trust the Holy Spirit and open his heart to receive everything that comes during this supernatural event.

After completing the Holy Rosary, he told me that he could still feel our Blessed Mother's powerful presence. We were sitting on the sofa when he innocently closed his eyes for a brief moment. In that instant, he exclaimed, "I can see Her! I can see Her!" With an interior vision, he could see the Mother of Jesus standing clearly before us. He explained it as though he had another set of eyes which opened when he closed his own to the mortal world. I was overcome with awe. I felt like I was on a giant stage as someone had just opened the curtain, leaving me standing before a huge crowd that I did not even know existed. I was very humbled by the realization that Our Lady was present with us. After what seemed like hours and not knowing how to respond, my brother's interior vision subsided. I made him promise that he would call me if She gave him another message tonight.

Sunday, February 24, 1991
3:15 A.M.

"Prayer is obedient, My children. Pray with your heart. Heaven is being filled with pure hearts. Satan is very strong and you are very weak. Pray, pray, pray." After being awakened by these words, Timothy began asking Her questions, hoping that Our Lady would converse with him. He asked, *"How long will I feel you?"* After several minutes and not hearing any reply, he fell back to sleep. But, the moment he drifted-off again, She said with unexpected candor, **"That is according to you. Pray for peace! I love you."** These words were the only response he received. In the morning, I recorded everything that had happened before leaving to pray with another Rosary group in the early afternoon. At this meeting, I was deeply encouraged when another locutionist of Our Lady publicly announced that she had received the following words from Jesus and Our Lady concerning Timothy. After Holy Communion, Jesus told her, *"Help your brother!"* And, Our Lady added, **"You must tell him that he is My beloved and I have chosen him to help Me with God's Plan."**

Monday, February 25, 1991

"My precious little children, today the hosts of angels in Heaven are filled with joy, brought by your humble prayers. They will descend upon

you to bring you strength in your trials against Satan's mighty army. Along with them, you have touched My Immaculate Heart. My tears of Love for you rain to Earth to enrich the soil which bears the fruit of roses. Pray for peace, My children. Pray from your hearts for peace."** Timothy was uncomfortable about waking me during the past few nights to share these miraculous messages. So, without my knowledge, he asked Our Lady to wake me before his telephone call so that he would not cause me to be startled from my sleep. About 1:00 a.m., I awoke instantly from a very sound slumber. I knew that our Holy Mother had touched me the moment I opened my eyes. I felt as if I had been awake during the entire evening. The awareness that Timothy was receiving Our Lady's message had, somehow, crept into my heart. Although I had this sixth-sense, I glanced at the clock and saw that it was somewhat earlier than when he had received Her other messages. Notwithstanding the change, I went to the telephone in anticipation of his call. Within twenty minutes, I had received Our Lady's message from him. It was a very prophetic feeling while sitting beside the phone when it rang. I had the foreknowledge that it would momentarily ring, and it assuredly complied.

Tuesday, February 26, 1991
1:00 A.M.

"**My beloved children, there is only one Savior, one Love, and one chance. You must carry My Child's Love into the world against sin. Your Rosary is your release from the bonds of imperfection. Grow from the world of Earth! Your prayers and your peace are at hand. My Son loves those who carry the message of peace.**" In the morning, I contacted several friends to tell them what our Holy Mother had said, while Timothy drove to my home later in the afternoon. We had dinner, then offered our prayers of the Rosary before he returned to Beardstown, anticipating another message from our Virgin Mother.

11:45 P.M.

Again tonight, I was awakened in the same miraculous way by Our Lady. The clock told me that it was even earlier than the night before. Indeed, within a few short minutes, my brother called with another message from the Mother of God. As he recited its content, I noticed a certain calmness in his voice for the very first time. Recently, he had prayed intensely that his nervous feelings would subside. He said that our Blessed Mother helped him to be at ease by instilling a great peace within his soul, unlike any he had ever experienced before. Although still overwhelmed, he was very humble and serene during our midnight conversation. He told me that he had never dreamed that God would allow him to participate in something so beautiful. I also shared these heartfelt sentiments.

Wednesday, February 27, 1991
12:15 A.M.

"My precious little children, please live My messages daily by renewing your lives through prayer, fasting, penance, and adoration of the Blessed Sacrament. Confess to My Son all of your sins. He will forgive you because He loves you. Pray, pray, pray. His blessings are infinite to those who pray to willingly accept His Love. My special little children, receive My Son through His Creation of His Love through the Host. Its Light is His Love. All who breathe take Him in. Please, do not let sin separate you from His Light and Love. The ground is a stage for temptation, sin and impurity. Pray for sanctity, My little ones. I am your Mother, and I love you. Please do what I ask to save the world from sin. Walk gently on the ground. My winged ones will help you to be raised from the weight of sin. Your prayers bring the angels from Heaven. Pray for their help. Fast and pray. Darkness will be cast away if you pray everyday. While the stars only reflect, true Light has no imitation, only the warmth of Truth and Salvation. Pray for the Light of the Love of My Son. O' My children, please let Him in! My Motherly Love is with you always. You are My beautiful children. The Sacred Heart of My Son..." As Our Lady spoke, Timothy was very anxious to submit additional questions to the One who was speaking to him. Notwithstanding his original proclamation, he could not completely accept that the Mother of God would ever stoop to talk to him. Therefore, he desired to question Her identity. When he told me of this, I encouraged him to openly ask Her who She was. I knew that She would affiantly identify Herself. From the first moment I heard Her words in my heart on the night of February 22nd, I have been convinced without reservation that She is the Mother of Jesus Christ. I feel this truth living inside of me, although I cannot describe it in understandable terms. I also realize that it is not even a slightest offense to require audible spirits to identify themselves.

In light of this prudence, Timothy was impatiently recording Her words, hoping that She would soon pause so that he could query Her. Sensing his impatience, She stopped in mid-sentence. He immediately asked, *"Are you the Mother of God?"* She responded, **"There is no doubt or question in faith."** When he pressed Her further by saying, *"Will I hear you every night? Please give me strength to go on,"* Our Lady said, **"You are in My prayers. Pray the Rosary for peace and find Me in your future when My pedestal is in full bloom. I need you to help My Son fulfill His Plan for the Salvation of souls."** He asked, *"Could I beg you to bless my loving brother and his family and answer all his prayers?"* **"I will bless all My children who live My messages, fast and pray. I love you always. Please pray for My other children. Thank you for having responded to My call."** He concluded by asking, *"Will you let me* *see you again? What is your pedestal?"* She did not respond to his last two inquisitions. He was captivated by the word "pedestal," while repeatedly asking me what it meant. I was uncertain, but presumed that it referred to the approaching era when every person in Creation will realize Her exalted station as the sinless Queen of Heaven and Earth. It is a premonition of the Triumph of Her Immaculate Heart.

Later in the evening, we set-out to offer our prayers in unison with another Rosary group in a nearby town. During our prayers, Timothy felt Our Lady's presence very powerfully again. Her grace is introduced in his soul early each evening in anticipation of Her message. And, again tonight, my brother experienced the unbounded detachment from the world as we prayed. After thanking everyone for a very beautiful evening, we returned to my home to rest. It was very late when we arrived in Springfield and I did not believe that it would be safe for my brother to travel the additional fifty miles to his house while he was so tired from our trip. So, I invited him to take his lodging in my spare bedroom. He gladly accepted and retired, expecting our Blessed Mother to speak with him soon. At 12:45 a.m., he called me into the livingroom and offered the following words from Our Lady of Grace.

Thursday, February 28, 1991
12:30 A.M.

"Dear children, I came to you today because I love you and My Son loves you. Many graces were afforded today by prayers from sincere hearts. My Son's Love is not a weight, distance, direction, or measure. It is many times too great for you to grasp. He knows your every desire for the good of Love and Salvation. He knows that Satan's evil is as a grindstone that slowly wears away at a constant and fine pace to steal you away from Salvation and Eternity in Heaven. My children, My Heart is so full of room for your prayers and My Son's Heart is so full of Love for you. Love cannot let you be worn to sin by Satan's grit if you pray to turn his stone to purity and Love. My Son's Love for you is the greatest form of Love. Its energy is fed by your daily prayers. The road to Heaven, My children, is a long and difficult one, where you will meet many obstacles and trials. Each of you has such little feet on such a long road, but each prayer is a footstep toward the road of Salvation's end. Multiply your prayers and your road to Heaven will pass more smoothly and obstacles will be cast away and the pathway strewn with roses.

Pray and fast, My children. Pray that your hearts can be kept pure. You will be made worthy of Heaven through your example of My Son's Love. His Coming is drawing near. During this season, prepare yourselves for sacrifice so that you may be open to receive His blessings and promise. I love you and will pray for you when your hearts are pure

and full of penance. Accept My Son at His Tabernacle and trust in His Love and promise. Pray for peace in your lives and for each other. Pray for those who are far from Love, My little ones. They need our special prayers to come to the offering of Salvation. Please spread My messages through your prayers for the world. My Son is with you always and I love you always. I wish you the peace of My Son and offer My Love. Please, pray tomorrow so that souls can be saved and peace can be brought to the world. With Love from My Immaculate Heart."

As we recorded this message, I was drawn to a sentence that made me feel uneasy. I transcribed, *"Many graces were offered today by prayers from sincere hearts."* I had an overwhelming feeling inside of me that told me this was incorrect. It was like a discordant note that noticeably stands-out in a song. We were both quite concerned. Immediately, I told Timothy to ask Our Lady to confirm the impeccability of what he had written. We sought Her Divine assistance because I did not know what else to do. During the past week, my brother has been very worried about the accuracy of his transcription. He feels that an incredible weight of responsibility is bearing-down upon his shoulders. We returned to our rest tonight, trusting that everything would be made more clear in the not-too-distant future.

In the morning, I went to my workplace, as usual. Around 9:30 a.m., I called to make sure my brother was comfortable, as it had been a late night before. As we spoke, he blurted-out, *"I'm supposed to tell you something. I'm supposed to tell you the word, "afforded."* The moment this word touched my ears, a great harmonious chord struck my soul like the grandest organ anyone could ever hear. I could sense the entire universe resonating with this harmony. I nearly began crying while sitting at my desk. The word "afforded" was the correction for the errant word "offered." My brother was completely perplexed by my emotional response. He did not remember that I had instructed him to ask Our Lady about the sentence in question, neither did he know why he had given me the word "afforded." Irrespective of these facts, I feel great confidence at this occurrence because I feel Our Lady's protection. God has allowed Her to address our specific interrogatories about the substance of Her messages. This is an incredible gift which further solidifies the peace of my mind and heart. Later in the evening, we joined the Rosary group at the local Marian Center. As he had earlier, my brother began to feel Our Lady's engulfing presence in preparation for Her next message. I again extended an invitation for him to stay at my home tonight. He thanked me and humbly accepted.

MARCH 1991

Friday, March 1, 1991

I awoke about 1:00 a.m. as Timothy walked into my living room. He was in an ecstatic state that I have never witnessed before. As he sat down next to me, I could tell that he was listening intently to someone who was speaking to him. He knelt before my prayer-altar and resumed writing on his notepad. An entire page had already been written as he began to pen its completion. I took to my knees and began to pray beside him. Within a few more minutes, we transcribed the following message from Our Lady. **"My precious little children, I have come to you tonight to deeply express My Love for the radiant hearts of My faithful children who have proclaimed My Son as their saving Shepherd. In a world filled with deep regret, sadness, and sin, the heavens have been shaken by your cries of love for our Jesus, the greatest Good News for all Eternity. Please continue to pray, My children. Your prayers are very powerful in bringing peace and Love into the world. Dear children, your prayers are strengthened by the Eucharist. Many of My children believe that the world moves from flock to flock. The world moves, My little ones, from flock to Host. Love begins within the Host and the Holy Spirit is carried into the world by those faithful children who pray to receive it.**

To live My messages is to pray and fast, convert, and do penance. This is how the Holy Spirit will take abode in human hearts. This is how saving graces are received, and it all begins by receiving My Son in the Host. There is no need for an endless search for My Son, My little ones. He is already in the hearts of men who receive Him, and His Love is very strong. The search for My Son begins in the hearts of all My children. Open your hearts, little ones! Remember His Love for each of you in your prayers. I will pray for each of you because you are My beloved children. Each of you has special angels who help carry your intentions to Light. Pray to them and they will help you. I will always pray for you because I love you. Each of you is as special as a little flower to My caressing arms. Pray for lasting peace and good will and that My Holy Son's Love will be accepted by you with an open heart. Many prayers were answered because of your sincere love for My Son. He will bless you and grant you peace." In the morning, Timothy returned home to conduct the affairs of his office. He returned later in the evening so that we could be together to receive Our Lady once more. I felt great excitement laying down to sleep, knowing that the Mother of God would speak to us again before the break of dawn.

Saturday, March 2, 1991
1:00 A.M.

In a flashback replay of last night, I awoke as Timothy walked toward the living room. He was in a supernatural ecstasy as before. Although awake, he was oblivious to my presence. I placed my hand upon his shoulder and began to pray for him. He had already written most of the message, but applied the final paragraphs while I was kneeling to his right. Then, he suddenly jerked, throwing his pen aside. He was completely conscious in an instant as though he had never been "asleep." We reviewed the following message from our Mother together. **"My dear children, I have decided to come to you today to impart to you the knowledge of the terrible and destructive powers of Satan, the Evil One. You may not always recognize who he is and that is why he is so difficult to find and defeat. Satan is the darkness, the devil, the sinister one, and the doer of evil. It is very prudent that I make you aware that your Salvation is in danger if you do not pray to My Son to defeat him. Satan is a heretic and a rebel. As I have told you everything that My Son is, Satan is not. Satan is the undoing of justice, sanctity, life, peace, and happiness. You must pray, My children, to shut Satan out of your hearts, souls, and lives. Satan cannot help you get to Heaven. He will never do one good deed. He is against every good domain that My Son died for - the Savior of your souls and promise of Eternal Life in Heaven.**

My divine ones, you must provide yourselves with strength in numbers to shut Satan out. You must join your hearts in prayer to build a wall made of Love. A wall of Love is much stronger than Satan's wall of stone and hate. Satan has a grasp on the whole of Creation. He is bonded in the cities. He is alive through inhumanity and hatred. You must flood this hatred by tearing down his wall with prayer, prayer from your hearts. This flooding outpour must be from love for each other. Thirst for My Son, My children, and return His Love while you live. You must pray, pray, and pray and proclaim My Son as your Savior publicly and loudly. My children, your voices will be heard in Heaven if they are magnified by prayer. I pray that each of you will avoid Satan by prayer from your heart so that you can be saved from his grasp. I am here to remind you that for every soul born into the world, there is a special place reserved for it in Heaven if it is deemed worthy by My Son. He is merciful and loves you very much, and His Love is forever past Eternity.

I will help you, My special ones, if you pray everyday. Pray for your souls and for the peace of My Son. My breeze will come to you and wisp gently on your hearts and will be a healing kiss of security because I love all of My children so much. My special little children from all walks of life and deed are always in My open Heart and arms. My tears of joy are

always of good fragrance and sweet. Your love for My Son as your best friend and Savior lets Me weep from happiness. You can trust in His Promise and believe His Holy Word that the design of Eternity is to include every soul in it. Please live the word given to you by My Son's servants who are so special among you. They love you as Jesus loves you. They will take special care of you in the name of Jesus if you also pray for them. Thank you for allowing Me to love you and remind you of the tasks before you that are sometimes difficult to achieve. Remember always that prayer is power, the power of God in you, for you to use freely for the good of your souls. Pray to receive the goodness and Mercy of My Son. I will also pray for you and give My special blessing to you. I love you, My children. Thank you for loving My Son and thank you for having responded to My call."

In the afternoon, two friends from another prayer group stopped to visit. One of the ladies is a recipient of Our Lady's direct intercession. She has received many "interior locutions." We shared our experiences, then offered the Rosary together. As we prayed, Our Lady asked us to completely abandon ourselves to Her Maternal Light. Everyone could sense our Blessed Mother's miraculous presence, especially my brother. The encounter of Our Lady's immense Love brought him to tears. We completed the meditations of the Rosary and Our Lady maintained Her miraculous presence. My brother could see Her interiorly as I have previously described. While experiencing this interior vision, he said, *"She is standing on something... It's a big ball... It's the moon... She's standing on the moon!"* He was overwhelmed by Her presence, but was frustrated that She would not say anything directly to him. She was simply looking in our direction and smiling at us. I encouraged him to remain peaceful while continuing to describe what he was being allowed to see. The Virgin Mary was standing with Her Mantle billowing in the breeze and Her hands extended at Her sides. Timothy articulated Her magnificence for several more minutes before his beatific vision subsided, returning him to his normal demeanor. The experience lasted over ten minutes.

It was now nearly 4:30 p.m. and my brother and I attended Holy Mass as our Blessed Mother asked. After dinner, we returned home to continue our prayers and Timothy's miraculous vision resumed. I asked him if Our Lady was still standing on the moon. He replied that She was now standing on a giant green snake. I sensed a very childlike demeanor to his statements. He asked me why She was standing on a snake, as if he was completely unaware of the knowledge of this symbolism. His lack of understanding frustrated him, as it would almost any inquisitive child. I gave him a very simple answer while encouraging him to continue relating everything that he was seeing. I feel incredible joy witnessing these events and recording them for future revelation. I have never been this close to God and our Blessed Mother before, although

I now realize that they have always been close to me. I am a blind man in flight without a care in the world. I know that God is with us; and this knowledge extinguishes our every fear. My faith and trust in Him has been, somehow, magnified through no action or intention of my own. I realize my lack of authority to question what is happening. I am a mere mortal before the power and intentions of Heaven. There is a transcending peace supporting my heart that I now know has its roots in my visit to Medjugorje. A magnificent anticipation convinces me to allow God to be all that He desires in my life. In simpler terms, my own will must be eliminated. Therefore, I proceed with Our Lady's grace supporting, helping, and solidifying my every grace-filled thought, making it easy to accept Her and the order and succession of Her intercession.

As my brother's vision continued, he said that Our Lady was so close that he could feel the warmth emanating from Her body. Her countenance was like the light radiating from the sun upon his face. He asked me if I could feel Her or see any of this. In human terms and senses, I cannot. But, my belief and trust have awakened other senses that are, somehow, miraculously allowing me to experience what he is seeing. Interiorly, I am witnessing everything that he is describing. Our Lady's presence is inflaming incredible visions in my heart of a nature that I have never before encountered. An open heart is forever accepting of grace. I know there is a reason for what is happening, although it is one I do not yet comprehend. I will not question God's motivations or actions as I pray for Him to reveal His Will to me. After several more minutes, my brother began to wonder how long Our Lady was going to remain while gazing upon us. I told him to be patient and to affectionately embrace Her until She decided to depart. I felt as though we were being acclimated to the grace of Her Divine presence. It is all beyond any measurement of our human understanding. After several minutes, Timothy jolted and awoke completely. This was the same such awakening that he had previously experienced. We talked of everything that had just happened, then retired for the night. I am ever-so-grateful to God for the grace I am living. My heart is being transformed with each passing day. What will the future bring?

Sunday, March 3, 1991
1:00 A.M.

"My dear children, as this day of rest has come which has been created by My Son, it is time for all of you to prepare with greater intensity for the celebration of His rising from the grave. In this Victory, He was granted His role as Savior of all mankind. While an earthly king inherits his throne because of his wealth and riches of material goods, and his people need him for their daily bread and lodge, My Son, Christ the King, inherited His Throne because He is rich in Love and His followers need Him for their Eternal Salvation. My Son is always

watchful of My children. He feels the warm hearts of the faithful, the gentleness of the kind, and the praying hands of those beloved children who ask for grace and Love from their hearts. I, too, children, hear your prayers and pleas. As with My Son, My blessings are also with those who pray. Beautiful flowers bloomed from Earth this day as a result of a watershed of prayers of My children. Your prayers will be rewarded with a rainbow in each of your hearts which will pass from horizon to horizon. It is very important that you continue to pray for those whose hearts are heavy and dull, and without the conviction of My Son's Promise due to their own indifference. I am always with you in Love to help you enter the Kingdom of My Son. It is beautiful because you are beautiful and it is fitting that all beauty become enjoined by shared Love.

My children, days are numbers and you do not know where you are in them. I can only assure you that the numbers are growing smaller. Each day, a new sun passes to bring light back to Light. By following My Son's words and living My messages, your lives will become as that of a dove perched on the wing of an eagle in flight whose destiny is to carry you to the horizon of Light and an Eternity in Heaven. Pray, My children, so that your flight will be steadfast and sure! Great fulfillment of solemn promises are your future when you deliver your trials and your sins to the everlasting King of Heaven, My Son, Jesus Christ. He is yours, My children, in this world and the next. He is the sun of your soul. With Him, life will begin anew. If you pray with your heart in great numbers, the heavens will tell of great happiness. Jesus carried your sins, sorrows, and griefs, and was buried for your human inequities. Please place your promise in His return to deliver you to the destiny for which I am asking you to pray. My children, your Rosary is your sanctifying eagle. Thank you for praying to Me with sincere hearts. Please remember My Son's Sacrifice because of His tremendous Love for you forever and ever. Thank you for having responded to My call."

Again today, we traveled to Peoria, Illinois for the First Sunday Medjugorje Mass at St. Martin de Porres church. I was very anxious to speak with Father Ted because I knew that he would be kind in his loving attention. We have been chided and driven-away by many others who do not feel that they need Our Lady's miraculous help and guidance. After Holy Mass, our opportunity to speak with Father Ted finally arrived. He graciously reminded us that our experiences must lead us to embrace the Sacraments more deeply. The answers to our questions must be found in prayer! Although he did not affirm or encourage our experiences, neither did he deny them. He told us that this is a time of great discernment through which he would ardently pray for us. I was asked whether I was recording all the messages and protecting them in a safe place. When I heard this request, I was happy to know that my first inspiration to keep this Diary was correct. I have been making precise notations from the very first day.

Upon returning home about 9:00 p.m., my brother and I offered the Glorious Mysteries of the Holy Rosary. I prayed with great hope that Our Lady would speak to us again. I was not disappointed as She descended upon us the moment we began the first decade. Timothy was again overcome by Her beauty. I knew the instant She appeared by the beatific reflection that ignited upon his face. He spoke to me while gazing upon Her infinite beauty. It was almost beyond his ability to choose the appropriate words to capture the miracle. Those he used transformed my perception even further into participation with Our Lady's presence. He did not describe the experience as something imaginary that he was watching. Rather, he articulated that we were both complete participants in the miraculous grace that was unfolding before us. From his heavenly perspective, there was no difference between our ability to see the very same thing. We were both kneeling at the feet of the Mother of God as She stood with Her arms outstretched. We were receiving a person from Heaven into our midst who is as real and alive as you and me.

Timothy responded to Our Lady as would a tiny child, both innocent and pure. All he seemed to know was that he was face-to-Face with someone of majesty that he loved beyond anything on the Earth. In this innocence, a sequence of transformations soon commenced. First, a halo of twelve stars appeared upon Our Lady's head, followed by letters that shined through Her Countenance. Initially, he could not see them clearly because the light emanating from Her presence was too intense. He described the Countenance as Immaculate beauty radiating from Her like the sun. Within a few moments, the letters "MIR" became clear. In the early days of Our Lady's appearances in Medjugorje, this word was seen written in flaming letters across the sky. He asked me what "MIR" meant. I told him that it is the Croatian word for "peace." He began crying like a little child and said, *"I am not Croatian. Why does She not just talk to me?"* I did not have the answer, but I realized that She was speaking in a most profound way by just being in our midst. She is, undoubtedly, the Immaculate Queen of Peace.

As we continued to pray, a strong breeze arose which billowed Our Lady's Mantle behind Her. Two angels stood like honor-guards at Her side. I asked my brother what they looked like. He responded that their beauty was beyond description and broke-down in tears again. At this point, I interrupted the Rosary so I could sit peacefully contemplating what was happening. The moment I hesitated, he urgently exclaimed, *"More Hail Marys! More Hail Marys! She likes it when you pray the Hail Mary!"* Even though She spoke no words to him, he could tell by Her demeanor that the Salutation of the Angel Gabriel brought Her to joy. So, I continued to pray with a renewed fervor. A great light then blazed from behind Her head, radiating outward in all directions like laser beams. Amidst this flood of Light, Timothy described Her Immaculate Heart as it was revealed before him. He again did not have adequate words to extol Her beauty, but he told me that something was wrong. He recognized the injury caused by the sword which had impaled it. My heart was shattered by his description. For the first time in my entire life, I saw the reality of Her sorrow. What more can I say?

In spite of this soul wrenching realization, the sequence of transformations continued. We were nearly finished with the fourth Glorious Mystery when a halo of stars burst suddenly into a crown atop Her head. As this explosion occurred, Timothy burst into tears again. My heart was still reeling from the vision of Her wounds when another physical grace penetrated my being. The power of the Rosary was impressed into my soul. I felt as though I had been cut open by a sword. It was like being blinded by a light that was ignited in a dark room. We were living these decades as we prayed them! The fifth Glorious Mystery is the Crowning of our Blessed Mother as the Queen of Heaven and Earth. Timothy did not realize the decade that we were praying. He was ecstatic at the manifestation of Our Lady's Crown. He was pleading with Her to let him see Jesus. Although just as overwhelmed, I encouraged him to pray the final decade with me in honor of our Queen Mother. This was the only decade that he was able to pray without succumbing in tears to Her beauty. As we finished, the breeze began blowing again as Our Lady's garments billowed behind Her. Suddenly, an incredible calm came over my brother, like someone had immediately turned-off a switch. He said, "She just blew in my face and wants me to be calm." It reminded me of the time that Jesus breathed upon the Apostles and filled them with the Holy Spirit. As Our Lady remained gazing intently upon us, Timothy queried, *"Why is She still here?"* I told him to sit peacefully until She chooses to depart.

We sat several minutes before I told him to ask Her to bless us. He did as I asked, then said, *"She's not doing anything."* I repeated my request and She responded by extending Her hand in the sign of the Cross. I supernaturally felt the impact of Her blessing within my heart. An explosion of grace and Light completely immersed my soul. Ecstasy ignited a fire that I could not extinguish. I began to cry uncontrollably, unable to proclaim "thank-you" loudly enough to satisfy the sincerity of my intentions. In a repetitive canticle, I offered my gratitude. This third strike of Almighty Love incinerated any opposition that remained in me. It was the same searing saber that had lanced my soul between the mountains of Medjugorje in 1989. Through my happy tears, I asked Our Lady to bless all the world with Her Love. I consecrated everyone to Her Immaculate Heart from where this Fire originated. As I poured-out my soul upon Her, Our Lady turned and listened intently to my every word. I told Her that I wished to be in Heaven someday with every one of my brothers and sisters. I cried because I love and need Her. I prayed for the priests, for purity, and for all families to be like Her own.

Timothy said that She was listening as a mother would listen to her little child. Then, She gestured in acceptance. I emptied my heart into Her lap, then lowered my head in peace. The angels were the first to depart, followed by the Blessed Virgin Mary. My brother and I were sitting quietly as I asked if She was gone. He said yes. A few seconds later, he jolted as he had before and sat wide awake. We again offered prayers in thanksgiving for being blessed with such grace. I pray that I have written about it well. I cannot hold back the tears as I invoke my memory to pen this account. I can still see the flaming Light into the depths of my soul. I have been indelibly marked with a flaming brand. It brings me to tears to simply turn my thoughts toward the Love I feel. I hope that everyone will invoke the faith to see past the physical mechanics of Our Lady's intercession. I am recording this detailed transcript so that everyone can intimately participate in this grace. As you read, please believe that you were with us on this night. Our Lady's intercession is not bound by time and space. I know you were here. I could feel each of your hearts in the midst of the Love of our Mother.

Monday, March 4, 1991
1:00 A.M.

"Dear children, your Heavenly Mother wants that each of you will pray to share the Glory of Love and trust in the Promise of My Son, Jesus, as the Savior of the world. He is the Holy and Sacred One, the Special One, and the Divine One. Your prayers and faith will lead you to His countenance and to His Kingdom where there will no longer be any need for hope. Pray from your deepest soul and remember that I love you and I will come to you if you pray and pray. My Immaculate Heart is a compass of Love which reaches out to you to lead you Home from the beginning of your journey to its end. Through your daily prayer of the Holy Rosary, you will receive many signs, responses to hopes and prayers, and blessings in the fulfillment of the Holy Plan. Pray, My children, for the many who have never known the Love of My Son and do not know that prayer is the way to receive Him. Within Him, there are no other desires. Pray with Me, children, so that the Divine plan for the world can be brought to fruition. Remember always that I love you. I am the Queen of Peace. Thank you for having responded to My call."

Timothy arrived at my home about seven o'clock in the evening. His sense of Our Lady's presence increased in magnitude as the time for our prayers approached. We knelt to pray at nine o'clock, beginning with the Joyful Mysteries of the Rosary. Immediately, Our Lady descended, standing on a cloud with Her arms outstretched to receive us. A glistening Rosary was suspended from Her left hand. Within seconds, a little white dove appeared at Her feet. Both were gazing peacefully upon us while we prayed. As he choked back tears of emotion, my brother asked me why Our Lady was not saying anything to him. He was quite disturbed that She was only looking at us and not uttering a word. In an effort to change his focus, I asked if She was close enough to touch. He extended his hand, but She was well beyond his reach. She smiled affectionately as any mother would look upon Her tiny toddler who was reaching-out for her consolation. Remembering that the dove was resting at Her feet, I asked Our Lady to send the Holy Spirit upon us. I recalled that the Holy Spirit descended upon Jesus in the form of a dove at His baptism in the Jordan River. I hoped that the little dove would fly over to us so that Timothy could touch him. When I made this request, the delicate creature flew from his perch at Our Lady's feet. Timothy was somewhat upset because he did not notice where the tiny bird went.

Continuing with the sorrowful decades, Our Lady began to cry. Tears were streaming down Her cheeks. We prayed fervently in hopes of wiping them away from Her heavenly face. Timothy also wept, saying how saddening it was to see someone so beautiful broken into tears. Between the decades, I began to sing the "AVE MARIA" and She smiled through Her tears. Singing made Her happy, although She never wiped Her tears away. Instead, She folded Her arms across Her chest and prayed as two angels appeared at Her side. Droplets of Her Love continued flowing down Her cheeks until we finished the Sorrowful Mysteries, smiling only when we sang the "AVE MARIA." We asked Her to bless us before She left. Again tonight, She offered the sign of the Cross over us. I commended everyone on Earth to Her Immaculate Heart, especially the many prayer groups that She has formed throughout the world. I asked Her to obtain the Mercy of God for the poor souls suffering in Purgatory. I prayed for the priests, our Holy Father, Pope John Paul II, and for the family-of-man under his Pontificate. I told Her that I wished to be in Heaven with Her when God calls me Home. She gazed lovingly, listening and smiling while I offered Her these petitions from my heart.

The angels disappeared and Our Lady rescinded back into the unapproachable Light of Heaven. My brother and I offered a prayer of thanksgiving before meticulously recording this description. He pined at the beauty of our Blessed Mother's eyes. There are no words to accurately describe them. He could not think of a worthy comparison. They are like looking into the deep crystal-clear blue waters, or into the reflection of a highly-polished ivory grand piano, or a perfectly painted automobile. One can see forever through the beautiful essence that emanates from within Her Immaculate Grace. She radiates a breathtaking splendor with a brilliance that is greater than the sun in the sky. And, when She looks upon you, Her gaze penetrates your being into the foundation of your soul to heal, caress, and nurture it back to eternal Life.

Tuesday, March 5, 1991
1:00 A.M.

"Dear children, your Mother hears every word of your prayers, spoken and silent. I respond to your prayers with Love. Today, I came again to tell all My children everywhere that each of you should hold your hopes and dreams acceptable to My Son next to your soul and lift them up as sincere love for Him in the solitude of your own heart and hearts. This, My children, is prayer! You need to remain content and at ease with Our Beloved Jesus in your daily lives and labors. Offer comfort and warmth to your brothers and sisters everyday. Pray for them. Give of yourself to every human soul from all walks so that it requires sacrifice from you which you make through the arc of a smiling heart. Share your love and compassion in the name of My Son, Jesus Christ, who is the Lord of all people. This, My children, is peace!

Please take special care to pray for the afflicted and trodden. Though they already have special blessings from Heaven, they need your prayers and wishes. Those who live without thankfulness for their health and happiness are of great distance from Me and My Son. My children, prayer for these people is most important. It is prayer out of Love which ignites a spark, a flicker, and a glimmer. There can be a world of Light and Love if allowed to grow through Love. You must make the Rosary your sparks, My special ones. One Hail Mary leads to the next, and countless sparks of them will bring a revealing Light to the Mysteries to defeat the darkness of Satan. I have called on many of My children to serve as do My angels. Take heed in the words of your God! Thank you for having responded to My call."

This evening, Timothy stopped at St. Augustine's church in Ashland to visit Father Murray, who has been quite ill. They have been very close friends since my brother's entrance into the Catholic Church in 1979. Since he stopped in Ashland, I drove to meet him there so we could continue our prayers together for Our Lady. When I arrived, I knew that She would come to us again. We entered the small sanctuary and knelt on the steps before the Tabernacle. I felt great peace and solitude as we invoked the Holy Spirit and began to pray. Our Blessed Mother descended in great light, appearing in mid-air before the Altar with the Tabernacle resting in Her Heart. Her beauty was indescribable as She stood on a sparkling cloud with two angels at Her side. Her Countenance literally consumed the Altar. Timothy said that She looked to be no more than twenty-five years old, with a charm and grace he has never seen before. In a mesmerized tone, he commented on the depth in Her eyes, but was disturbed by Her inattention to our presence. Instead, Her focus was fixed upon the area behind us. My brother cast several discerning glances over his shoulder before realizing that She was peering toward the choir loft.

Remembering that Our Lady appeared at Medjugorje to the children in the St. James church choir loft, we went to the balcony and knelt down to pray. Upon doing so, our Blessed Mother fixed Her gaze upon us and began to smile.

The moment we resumed our prayers, Father Murray entered the church and walked-up the center aisle. Our Lady turned toward Her priest and watched-over him with beatific intensity as he prepared the Altar for the next morning Mass. Even when he walked into the sacristy, Our Lady turned completely away from us and focused upon his work. Timothy whispered several times that She was ignoring us in favor of the flood of lovingly attention toward Father. She watched his every movement until he completed his preparation and retraced his steps down the center aisle to depart. The moment the church doors closed, She immediately refocused Her attention upon us and smiled joyfully. We completed the Holy Rosary and my brother began to cry. He asked me why these things were happening, realizing that it would be very difficult for others to accept our witness of these miraculous events. I told him that I would always stand beside him. With the help of God, I will never deny what Our Lady is doing in our lives. It is an inexplicable vantage-point to experience something that is beyond the purview of every mortal intellect, especially my own. I realize that our own persecution is in the offing because of this. Without the light of faith, many see the Spirit of God as an unwelcome invader in the finite recesses of their minds. Their worldly thoughts cannot reconcile with the almighty Grace of God. Hence, they will fight against the Truth I am recording on these pages.

Wednesday, March 6, 1991
1:15 A.M.

"Today, My children, I have come to tell where My Son is. He is first in your heart and soul where you were begotten of Him. Outwardly, My precious ones, He is of the lowliest and holy places on Earth. Jesus is not difficult to find since His Love and Justice are so simple. His is no great empire of wealth or status, but is from His humble beginning at birth. My Son's teaching is an easy lesson. His message magnified can bring great power to the world. A simple kindness can lead to a smile, a greeting of love, a touching of hearts, and a common prayer. His words tell of the dimension of His Love and strength: the mustard seed, the camel and needle's eye, and the fate of the meek. Break down your barriers, My children, which block your reaching-out to receive His hand! You need to be sincere, not pompous, confident and not afraid, sorrowful without self-pity, forgiving and not vengeful, and accepting in the place of question. These are the acts of new life and new beginnings. This is the resurrection of the freedom of Love over the tyranny of hatred, which is the message of this season. My children, pray that it

will also bring a resurrection of your God-given gift of open-heartedness and compassion. As you pray together, you have become as one life and one hope, as My Son has wished for the world. Please pray that His wish can continue to come true. My Son blesses you and your many prayerful acts, and My Love for you cannot be overwhelmed. With all My motherly Love, I bless you in His Name."

This evening, we joined a Rosary group in a small town, not far from Springfield. While praying in unison, our Holy Mother descended upon us again. She appeared standing on a cloud above the Tabernacle in the Catholic church. With Her arms extended, She invited everyone into Her embrace. She wore the Crown of Her great dignity as the Queen of Paradise and was flanked once more by two heavenly angels. It was an opportunity of great proportion because another one of Our Lady's messengers was present this evening. She is an "interior locutionist," who has also received many messages from the Mother of God. Tonight, my brother noticed our Blessed Mother gazing intently at this woman while she was recording the miraculous message that she was being given. I asked him whether he could see Our Lady speaking to her. He responded that he knew that She was communicating with her, although he could not see Our Lady's lips moving.

After the Blessed Mother completed Her message to this "locutionist," She continued praying with us. An honorable tradition has blossomed within this prayer group. During the fifth Sorrowful Mystery, which commemorates Jesus' Crucifixion, a devout man stands in front of everyone present with the Crucifix elevated above his head. He literally "lifts high the Cross" as all the petitioners then offer the fifth decade in memory of Jesus' Suffering. Interestingly tonight, at the completion of the fourth Sorrowful Mystery, Our Lady looked toward this gentleman in anticipation of his assuming this humble position. Our Holy Mother glowed in approval at his elevated service to Jesus. When he raised the Cross aloft, She folded Her hands at Her chest and looked heavenward in supplicating prayer. It was overwhelming as Timothy described it. I could see and feel what he related through the ecstatic countenance radiating from his face. He struggled to refrain from succumbing again in tears to the beauty of what he was seeing. He told me that he did not want to show his uncontrolled emotion in front of such a composed group of people.

At that very moment, he instantly calmed-down in a way that startled me. The small white dove had reappeared, which sent a wave of peace into his heart. In the demeanor and innocence of a child, he told me, "The little bird landed on top of the golden box." He was referring to the Tabernacle. His words reflected another example of the angelic state that his soul enters as Our Lady comes to speak to us. He becomes so childlike that he does not seem to know anything for himself. He controls no portion of his will in the presence of our Blessed Mother while exhibiting the docile serenity of a juvenile.

Knowing that the diminutive dove was still present, I asked Our Lady to send the Holy Spirit into our hearts. The little bird then permeated the door of the closed Tabernacle, igniting a very bright Light that emanated from within Her breast. She looked toward Heaven with Her hands folded in prayer and began to float toward the Grotto at the right of the Altar. As my brother's eyes followed Her movements, he suddenly exclaimed that he could no longer see Her. I looked toward the shrine and noticed a huge stone pillar that was blocking my view of the Grotto. No sooner did I see it, than She came into view again from behind the pillar. Our Virgin Mother assumed Her position within the alcove of the Grotto with the Holy Rosary in Her hands.

We finished the final decade of our petitioning and Timothy asked Her to bless us again. Raising Her hand in the sign of the Cross, She did so and began to depart. I went to the Grotto, knelt, and began to cry because I could feel Her miraculous presence still lingering there. The feeling was overwhelming my heart in an intense moment of grace in Her presence. I, too, began to ask myself, "What is happening to me?" I continuously pray to become worthy of what my heart is seeing. I could write volumes of books and still not capture the moments that we are sharing with the Virgin Mother of God. When we returned to the city, I again asked my brother to stay-over because of the late hour and the distance he would have to travel back home. I retired with an incredibly expectant spirit, knowing that he would receive another message from Heaven within just a few short hours. I desire with all my heart to respond to every word that comes from the Immaculate Wisdom of Mary.

Thursday, March 7, 1991
1:30 A.M.

"My dear children and beloved ones, today I have come to tell you of the great peace which those have who love the Law of My Son. Jesus' Law is the rule of goodness and Mercy. Its plan is not to punish, but to make pure. Rules and laws of humanity are made out of competition and fear. Someone has to lose, My children, in your books of behavior in order that others may win. The all-encompassing Laws of My Son are those which include all of humankind to be loved and given a chance to love. My children, you are all too busy fixing your world to make your lives comfortable, without sacrifice, and far from Jesus. The design of your world distracts you from your prayers. You surround yourselves with entertainment and things that stimulate your physical and emotional senses. As your Mother, I must come to you to tell you that I love you too much to see you become absorbed into your materials and far from the Spirit of My Son. It is part of Satan's plan to seduce you into spending your days in an artificial world. Satan would like that you would ignore My Son through your frivolous activities.

All your worldly goods will return to the earth from where they came, My little ones. They will perish back to the dust of the ground. Children, please do not let Satan force you to design your own defeat by letting him draw you away from My Son, Jesus. Your worldly structures are your shelters from the elements and to make your days soft and easy. The real shelter you should be seeking is that of My Son. His is a shelter that will not perish through time or element. To build that lasting and most important shelter, you must continue to pray. My children, please do not think that your prayers are in vain. Once your words of prayer are lifted, they are forever etched into the hands of your Savior, as are the scars of His Sacrifice. To be sent to Heaven is a part of His Plan for all My children. Take refuge in Him as your greatest shelter! His house of Eternity will be infinitely more beautiful than the designs of men. He is the greatest architect and carpenter.

You must make sacrifices, My special ones, to keep Satan from distracting you from prayer. My loving message for you is to pray and make sacrifices, do penance, and fast. Instead of giving your idle time to Satan for him to take you away, devote that time to the Holy Rosary. The decades of the Rosary are the building-blocks which will result in your place of lasting shelter with My Son in Heaven. Your good deeds and works are the stones which will wall-up your home in Eternity. Your prayers are the mortar which will hold them together into a solid rock of Salvation. My children, please build your daily lives around prayer and every other part of your lives will fall into their inevitable place. Prayer is the way to learn the Law of My Son. I will help you learn and obey that Law as written for you as My Son's word in the Holy Scripture when you pray to learn and understand. I give you My loving blessing in the name of the Trinity that you will love and live the Law of Jesus so that your world can be filled with peace and you can build your foundation for your shelter in Heaven. Thank you for having responded to My call."

After recording these beautiful words, Timothy asked Our Lady the following question, *"Blessed Mother, I love you and I really saw you, but some will not believe me. How can I show them you are real? Please, show me how."* She did not immediately respond, so he called to share Her message with me. He would not be traveling to Springfield today because of a business meeting that he was required to attend in the early evening. So, at 7:00 p.m., I went to the Marian Center for our weekly Rosary group. Many people wished to hear about our Holy Mother's intercession. I realize that simple human curiosity was the impetus for most of their questions. Such an atmosphere of anticipation and support might easily evaporate into thin air should their faith begin to falter.

Friday, March 8, 1991

My brother called about two o'clock in the morning and related the following details. Before retiring, he had knelt before his shrine which he had previously erected in his living room. Our Lady's presence was simply overpowering there. The only light in the room emanated from two candles that were burning upon the altar. Upon kneeling to pray, he glanced over his shoulder and, in the flickering of the candlelight, he saw the silhouette of our Blessed Mother on the wall. He was stunned by Her miraculous image. She was blocking the light in the same way we would see our shadows on the ground on a sunny day. Instinctively, he turned toward the altar, scanning the path of light back to its origin. No other visible person was in the room, although the image was still being cast upon the wall. I ask you to imagine your own reaction to such an incredible phenomenon! He knew that our Holy Mother was standing beside him, but he could not see Her with his eyes. Hence, he was stunned into absolute bewilderment.

Upon finishing his prayers, he went directly to bed. Then, about 1:00 a.m., his bed began to shudder and a loud rumbling filled the air. The audible voice of our Blessed Mother said, **"Show them through your faith and they will believe!"** This was the answer to the question he had posed to Her the night before. He was startled because he was not prepared for Her to speak in this way. No one stops being human simply because they are faced with the miraculous intervention of God. While I cannot describe the grace I feel, my heart is able to peacefully reconcile every new manifestation that he decides to bestow. I can sense a great preparation and cultivation that is occurring around us as they continue to unfold. It is easy to believe because I trust in Jesus and Our Lady. After answering his question from the previous night, Our Lady delivered this next blessed message.

"Dear children, you rest in God's favor today as a result of your consistent prayer and humility. I have come to show you Love for taking time everyday to admire My Son. I have also come to tell you that you can gain many graces toward the promise that Jesus makes by doing His work along with your daily toils of labor. While your daily labors are performed with your feet pushing on the ground and the tools of your trade in your hands, the work of faith is done while on your knees and your hands reaching to the heavens and to each other. My Holy Son is perfectly upright and just, and He is all seasons of the climate of God. You, My special ones, are very delicate leaves which, when autumn is brought, will be folded according to His heavenly purpose. I pray for you as harvest grows nearer. You are not only in My prayers, you *are* My prayers. All of you are in My extended Immaculate Heart through Love for always.

You, My precious children, are the temporary custodians of My Son's world and all in it. Your Mother is asking that you be kind to it, as it is as precious a creation of God as yourselves. My Son's Creation of nature and beauty are being sieged by the sins of the followers of Satan against it. Your prayers and forthright goodness will allow you to be raised at autumn if you treat all of God's Creation with love. Pray, My children, that you do not fall into the grip of the Evil One when the reaping of souls comes to pass. I pray that you will be present with all the angels in Heaven. The fruit of your prayers are yours at harvest by steadfastingly following the wishes of My Son, who promises deliverance to the Eternal Kingdom. Thank you for praying to know and to do the Will of Jesus. Thank you for having responded to My call."

After transcribing the message, we spoke for nearly forty-five minutes. While reassuring him that he is not alone, I also reminded him that God will surpass any limit to effect the Redemption of the world. Timothy prayed for peace and strength until after the break of dawn. When I called in the morning, he apologized for his reaction to Our Lady's intercession. These experiences are so overwhelming to him that it is very difficult to capture them within his human thoughts. He reminded me of an incident that occurred on our pilgrimage to Medjugorje in 1989. The first night, we were both awakened by the bedroom shaking and a loud rumbling about 4:00 a.m. Plumbing pipes were rattling in the walls and the panes of glass were shaking in the window frames. We were both frightened for a moment as we sat straight-up in our beds, looking at each other in shock. I immediately dismissed it as an earthquake and went back to sleep. The next morning, I mentioned it to everyone at the breakfast table. No one else had felt it! Again, I ignored it, thinking that the others must be very sound sleepers. What we felt in our room should have awakened the entire building of pilgrims! Ironically, Timothy said that this is exactly what happened in his own bedroom last night, with the addition of Our Lady's voice. The connection between this event and the one in Medjugorje is a correlation that I extend to you. I am not sure whether the reference holds any relevance in nature.

This evening, Timothy came to my house to pray the Rosary and our Blessed Mother appeared standing on a cloud with a halo of stars encircling Her head. Her gown was billowing in the breeze as She radiated Her Love toward us with a spirited smile. Two angels were stationed on Her either side and Her Immaculate Heart was wide-open, revealing the infinite heights of Paradise inside. Her Love is so deep and clear as She awaits the embrace of every child of God. Again tonight, a sequence of visions corresponding to the Mysteries of the Rosary unfolded as we prayed. During the third Joyful Mystery which commemorates the Birth of Our Lord, I began singing "O come let us adore Him." At this spontaneous gesture, the words "ADESTES

FIDELIS" burst into view above Her halo. As we continued, Our Lady wept through the Sorrowful Mysteries, showing a smile only when we promised to continue fasting and praying. Much of the time, She prayed while looking toward Heaven with Her arms folded across Her chest. Somehow, She seems to be telling us that the sword of sorrow continues to pierce Her Immaculate Heart. We finished our petitions and I asked Her to bless us before She departed. She listened courteously to every one I offered, then raised Her hand in a blessing of the Cross of Her Son.

Saturday, March 9, 1991
1:40 A.M.

"Dear children, your loving Mother feels your warm prayers and outpour of admiration that you show My Son through Me. It is important that you continue to know where your life's protection is, My children. It is Jesus, and He hears your prayers and feels your heart in the same devotion through which you offer them. That is where I tell you that you will find Him. He is in every heart for the protection of your soul. The human spirit, My precious ones, is the Holy Spirit incarnate through each and every living being. All living things have been given the breath of life because He said it has been, and He says it will be. That is the Love of Life that Jesus has to offer and it cannot ever be lost when kept in the care of My Son, its Creator. Love may not always be easily discovered or noticed, but it is always there for those who choose to receive it, and there are great blessings in it. I tell you, My children, that you can remain close to Love through the Rosary. As the fate of the world is in the hands of God, the fate of your love for Jesus and your souls is as though each Rosary bead is the world in your hands. The fate of it is in your hands through your recitation of the prayers which accompany it.

Remain close to Jesus in your world and He will protect you as you are protecting each tiny Rosary bead, giving it caress and prayer. He will be your bastion of great strength through your prayers. He wishes that each of you will come to Him with an open and free act of will. As the celebration of His rising nears, let it be a reminder that, through His example you can also rise over the flood of death by accepting Him. The tide of Easter can wash you to shore and to safety and Salvation. Acceptance of Jesus in your hearts is all that He asks, and your safety can be assured. Release everything, My children, that is in your hearts that is blocking His entrance and caging-in your doubts. Please know that you can rise the way Jesus did after the grave. My children, you cannot totally accept Life until you accept the preciousness of death and resurrection. Pray through Me to My Son, little ones, and we will show

you the Promise fulfilled as written in the Holy Word. Remember the calling given by John, three and three, and pray to receive the graces which come through the call. I love you, My children, and hope you will trust in My Son's holy Promise. Please be mindful of His commitment at Holy Mass, through this period of sacrifice and always. Thank you having responded to My call."

At about seven-thirty tonight, members from several prayer groups arrived at my home, including a publicly-recognized locutionist of our Blessed Mother. As we conversed about Our Lady's intercession, I sensed many doubts about what we were relating. This surprised me because the other locutionist recently offered a summary confirmation of the intercession we were receiving. She told her Rosary group that Our Lady had given Her this message, **"You, My little dove, and My son, Timothy, will be messengers for many."** This was in addition to the previous witness given by this same locutionist on the 24th day of February. I held high anticipation that these words from Our Lady would buoy the waning faith of many, but I do not see my hope yet being realized. At nine o'clock in the evening, we began the Holy Rosary and Our Lady graced us with Her Divine presence. Stars were positioned above Her head when She appeared and three angels were at Her side. She looked about the room at everyone who was gathered, crying as She peered into our faces. This was quite peculiar because She is usually exceedingly happy when She comes. The locutionist began recording Our Lady's message while the rest of us prayed the Holy Rosary. My brother could not determine what the Blessed Mother was saying, but he knew that She was speaking to this woman.

I would like to briefly describe the vision that my brother generally sees. Although interior, he can see in dimensions that transcend the material world. He sees everything as if his eyes were open, along with seeing the supernatural presence of Our Lady, the angels, and the other miraculous elements that mortals cannot detect. With this vision, he could see Our Lady speaking to the locutionist tonight. As we continued our prayers, a brilliant light shined from Her being. When we meditated upon the Descent of the Holy Spirit, the little white dove appeared again. I asked Our Lady to send Him to us. Within moments, He flew beyond my brother's capacity to detect. A beautiful crown appeared on Our Holy Mother's head at the beginning of the fifth Glorious Mystery. This decade is dedicated to the Crowning of our Blessed Lady as the Queen of Heaven and Earth. After this, we sang to Her and finished our prayers for the day. I asked Our Lady for Her parting blessing and offered our petitions to God. Before our visitors left, the locutionist read Our Lady's words, while I shared everything that my brother had seen. At 11:45 p.m., he felt Her special ecstasy descending upon him in preparation for the next message he would receive. Within an hour, he had recorded the following transcription.

Sunday, March 10, 1991
12:40 A.M.

"My dear children, today I have come to you to remind you of the many ways that your prayers have touched and are touching My Immaculate Heart, My Son's Sacred Heart, and all the beautiful angels in the heavens. When your prayers are simple and from the heart, you find ways to keep your bestowed graces pure and in your hands. Many souls are moved by your lifting of prayers and the masses of souls are won to My Son, one at a time. Today, My children, somewhere there is a child whose hopes have been raised at the rising dawn. The heart of an aged soul has been touched so that he can welcome his coming day. Your prayers ring joy and love that are strong to the world. You have been given eyes to see the beautiful and vast places on Earth and ears to hear the solemn sounds of the places of peace, and touch and feel so that your brothers and sisters can be comforted and consoled. My children, you are using your senses for the work of My Son, Jesus, which brings Light and peace to all you touch. These great deeds are loved by My Son, but do not carry the power of the prayers which you raise to the heavens. As your eyes see the beauty created by God, they should also wait in prayerful hope upon seeing the return of My Son. Nothing in your power to grasp through any sense, My little ones, will allow you to know the stunning beauty of Heaven. It has been promised to you and awaits you as you await My Son, your Savior. Your prayers are heard, My special children, and many souls were moved today by them, especially those whose needs were higher. In due season, you will witness the days which you pray for. I will help you, children, because I have a special Love for you, the Love only your Mother could have. Be around My feet because your prayers are inspiring and move the heavens. My blessings are with you today for the intensity of your love for My Son. Thank you for remaining faithful to Him and thank you for having responded to My call."

He delivered this message to me and I read Our Lady's words to everyone there, after which they promptly departed. It was 1:45 a.m. and I was still very excited. Since Timothy was wide awake, I asked him to offer another Rosary with me and he lovingly obliged. I wanted to continue in Our Lady's presence because Her Love dilutes the heaviness of the world. We meditated upon the Joyful Mysteries since we were so gratified that She spoke to us again tonight. As we began, She returned in great Glory, causing my inner-soul to leap with happiness. There was such elation in my heart because She so politely responded to our beckoning call. Her supernatural intercession is more than any miracle I ever hoped to receive. It is the living evidence of God's great Love for us. I prayed fervently, telling Her how much I love Jesus. Timothy was laid prostrate before Her beauty. His senses cannot contain the Love that he is seeing. Feeling sorry for him, I asked our Blessed Mother for Her help. When the request formed in my heart, he breathed a sigh of relief as a peaceful calm came over him. He did not know that I asked Our Lady to help him. I was struck with awe that my prayer received an immediate answer. In that moment of grace, I gained a great sense of respect for the power of our prayers because God is, indeed, listening to everything we ask in the Name of His Son.

While mesmerizing about the answer to my prayer, Timothy exclaimed that our Blessed Mother was growing in size. I did not know what he meant, causing me to endure a moment of subtle apprehension. He then realized that She was becoming larger because She was drawing closer to us. Within a few moments, we were kneeling directly at Her feet with the angels in our company. Our Lady's message then came to mind. Less than an hour ago, She said, **"Be around My feet because your prayers are inspiring and move the heavens…"** Timothy reached-out to touch Her, but, She was just beyond his grasp. I also reached-out in faith, imagining that I was holding onto to Her gown. While not seeing these things physically, very vivid images were being impressed within my heart. They were unlike anything I have ever experienced. I could see clearly what he was describing. The Virgin Mother is one with us, and loves us profoundly. She is trying to offer Her maternal guidance to everyone on Earth. This is a fact that I am living and describing much as my brother initially described it to me. I feel like I am the most blessed individual in the entire world, and the least worthy to receive any of it. I asked Our Lady if I could see Her also, if that is the Will of God. When I posed this question, a very powerful thought entered my consciousness. *"What you are seeing within you is true vision. You have already seen Me."*

After we finished reciting the Holy Rosary, I thanked our Blessed Mother for extending these special moments of grace. I began to cry because I do not really know how to love Her as She deserves to be loved. I feel a passion to return to Her what She is so graciously giving to me. Indeed, I do not know how to accomplish this, but I know that She is teaching me as the days continue to pass. My mind has to relax in order for Her to succeed. I reclined on my couch today, gazing at Our Lady's statue with a most incredible feeling inside. Her presence began to engulf me with a miraculous intensity. I felt suspended in time while my heart silently prayed. I could sense that She was separated from me by only the thinnest of veils. I was the smallest instant away from physically seeing Her with my mortal eyes. I cannot accurately describe the anticipation that I began to feel. I was sitting upon the very edge of the seat of my soul. As I rested in this grace, I fell asleep in the greatest peace I have ever known.

In the morning, my brother and I rose and attended the Holy Mass. In the afternoon, we joined a Rosary group in Pana, Illinois and Our Blessed Mother came to us again. I was surprised by this encounter because I usually know from my brother's demeanor when Our Lady appears. This time he calmly said, "She's here." I then remembered my prayer from the night before. Its answer seemed to be "still in effect." She appeared above the Tabernacle on a puffy cloud, accompanied by two angels, and a halo of stars was resting upon Her head. She began speaking to the Pana locutionist while my brother and I looked-on. An angel was stationed next to her the entire time that Our Lady spoke. When She completed Her message, the angel retreated to Her side while the locutionist knelt with us to continue our prayers.

The Virgin Mother cried as we meditated upon the Sorrowful Mysteries of the Passion of Her Son. She looked into the heavens and prayed with arms folded upon Her chest. We recounted the Agony of Our Lord in the Garden, His Scourging at the Pillar, the Crowning with Thorns, the monumental Procession to Calvary, and His Redemptive Crucifixion. During the final Mystery, the Tabernacle upon the altar began to glow with the Countenance of God. It became so intense that my brother had to shield his eyes from the blinding light. He was looking into the heavenly Sun. Then, just as suddenly, the Countenance receded, revealing a Dove that was peacefully perched upon the red altar-candle sitting next to the Tabernacle. I asked Our Lady to send the Holy Spirit into our hearts. The snow-white bird took flight and our Blessed Mother began to ascend heavenward as we prayed the fourth Glorious Mystery. At the recitation of the Coronation, She reappeared while standing in the Grotto nearby, wearing a beautiful Crown of Queenly Glory. Upon completing this decade, I asked Our Lady to bless us again. She responded with the sign of the Cross and peacefully faded away.

Later Sunday evening, Timothy and I rejoined in prayer as Our Lady has encouraged us to do. She appeared again with three angels in Her midst, one on either side and the other behind Her. The words "GOSPA" and "MIR" were emblazoned in fiery light above Her head. As I invoked the Holy Trinity, the number "111" burst like a giant firework over Her Mantle. Within a few more seconds, the "111" transformed itself into the letters "IHS." I immediately recognized the intended symbolism. The number "111" is representative of the Three Persons of the Blessed Trinity, Father, Son, and Holy Spirit, while "IHS" stands for Jesus Christ. The transformation from "111" to "IHS" is symbolic of God becoming Man in His only begotten Son. We sang several thanksgiving songs that Our Lady noticeably enjoyed. Then, She began to gaze at my altar. Wondering what She was so intent upon, my brother reached to the place where She was looking. He picked up a rock from Medjugorje which was taken from the hill upon which She is appearing. The shape of the stone bears a striking resemblance to Her Immaculate Heart. The moment he picked it up, Our Lady held Her hands to Her chest as if to clutch Her Heart. I was very touched by Her animated gesture of Love and affection.

I am doing my best to relate them to you here.

Upon completing the Rosary, we continued to pray because we wanted Her to remain with us. I thought that, if we proceeded, She would not leave quite so soon. During the Mystery that commemorates Our Lord's birth in the manger, we audibly sang "Silent Night." The Star of Bethlehem appeared before us, bringing with it the solemnity of Christmas. My brother could see across the countryside with the moonlight casting a soft blue brilliance upon the darkened landscape. I felt as though I had just left a Midnight Mass on Christmas eve. Then, it began to snow to capitalize this miraculous vision. The crystal flakes were falling all around Our Lady and piling upon the heads and wings of the angels who were standing very proudly next to Her. I offered Her our petitions and asked Her to bless us. She extended Her hand in a blessing and faded away. After completing our humble supplications, we thanked God for everything we have experienced tonight. I played a final musical score that was quite fitting for the occasion. Timothy could see that it was still gently snowing upon the beautiful countryside. The peaceful image caused me to begin to cry. I wondered whether it would ever be possible to bring the entire world to comprehend the perfection of these timeless moments.

As I continued to ponder, my brother stated something very unusual. He saw a horse that was galloping in the snow, but he did not know what it could possibly mean. I knew what it meant the moment he told me about it. It was symbolic of the music that I had just chosen to play. The score was from a movie about the mountains and wilderness. There were many wild steeds in the film. One of the most prominent scenes depicted a horse running gracefully through the snow drifts. It is one of my favorite motion pictures because of the great peace I feel while watching it. I was overwhelmed to tears as this very personal moment impacted my heart. These are incredibly intimate times of grace that we are receiving from God. Our Holy Mother knows exactly where to touch our hearts. She knows how to comfort us and give us strength in ways known only to the depths of our individual souls. She came to the center of my being today and moved me with the power of Her Love. Our Heavenly Mother is intrinsically one with us, even to the smallest details of our inner-personality. She enjoys dispensing miracles that bring us peace because She is a Mother who is sorrowful when we suffer in any way. And, She is happy when gifts from Her Son's Creation bring us holy joy and take us closer to Him. I wish everyone could feel the exhilaration of my soul when this final grace was given tonight. I could do nothing but cry, knowing that She cares for us in such a special way.

Monday, March 11, 1991
1:45 A.M.

"My dear children, I have come to you again today to keep My promise of Love for you and to show you how deeply My Son loves you, which is of no comparison to any value that is known to humankind. My Son's Love for you is of the ultimate, has no equal, is final, and cannot be destroyed. Although many of you, My special children, do not understand the tremendous power of His Love, it is still a simple Promise that has been made to you. It is constant and unchanging, definite and permanent. Sometimes, little ones, you seem to look at Love as though you are standing on a long road, and when looking into the distance at it, it seems to grow smaller and thinner as it goes further away from you. His promise of Love for you, My children, is as steady and wide at its indefinite infinity as it is on the exact place where you are standing. It even grows wider, My special and divine children, to those who allow it to grow to its limitless immensity as was offered by Jesus in the beginning. It also resounds throughout Creation in an echo that will not diminish.

Jesus made the Promise of His Love to all mankind which still rings as loud and strong as on the day it was sounded. My children, His Love also becomes amplified when it is brought from the hearts of men to others for the good of the service of His Commandments which are best obeyed when all the children of Creation allow them to unfold in their good time and merit. The Plan of God will prevail through its predestined number of days. The world is not yet finished and no man should place judgement or prediction on its outcome, but rather should pray that he can be of the best and most noble part in it. The Commandments, children, can best be lived from the inside-out, although they are outward in their effect. Keep the Commandments in your heart and the outside world will be blessed from the inside. The heart is where My Son's home is and it should be kept pure and clean, warm and neat, open and full of Love. My children, a life through the Love of Jesus can be a happy memory at the end of each day, a beautiful song that can bring peace to an empty soul, and a benediction to a place where there seems no room for solace. God's benediction, My children, is His daily Promise of the renewal of His Love at each new dawn and it is fulfilled through your prayers at it. My Son's Promise is a gift to you out of Love for you to hold and cherish as your own, a gift that will not fade or grow thin in the distance and will not become dim from lack of light or sound.

My special ones, many are committing themselves to accepting the Love of Jesus through admiration for Him through the Rosary. It has the power to change the world from the inside-out by changing hearts through love for Jesus. This should give you hope for each new day. All of My children should love and cherish every new day that My Son has given them and do all possible to live all of them in peace. Each new day should be a renewal of faith and a renewal of the love for life because life is as beautiful as the Beautiful One who created it. The precious Creation of My Son should not be transformed, altered, shortened, or abused as it would place great sorrow in His Heart and Mine, your Mother, who loves you so much. My children, please keep life sacred and Love in your hearts through your daily prayers. Your gift of life can be preserved as was given by My Son. I pray for you that all your days be filled with the happiness and security which was intended for them. I pray that you will remember each other in your prayers and I ask My Son to bless your days with the wonderment and fulfillment of the treasure of peace. Thank you for living Love and giving Love. Thank you for having responded to My call."

We continued our prayers today as requested by Our Lady. Again, the symbolism and grace in my brother's visions were as prophetic and vivid as in my previous entries. We were directed to the Holy Scripture passage 1 Timothy 1:1-20. Then, early in the morning, we received the ensuing message from our Blessed Mother.

Tuesday, March 12, 1991
1:40 A.M.

"My dear children, today I have come again to invite you to receive the Spirit of peace. You are asked to open your hearts to allow the Holy Spirit to warm you in the way that the rays from the sun pierce the clouds to warm the Earth. As the air above the Earth is also warmed by the sun, by receiving peace in your hearts, your soul will also be warmed with the Love of God. My special children, there is in each of you the innocence of a tiny infant, a helplessness that can only be nurtured by God, the Father. Please surround yourselves with the thought and knowledge of Jesus. Dismiss yourselves of all self-interest and give your *all* to My Son. Remain unassuming and pure so that you can receive My Son. In your world of deep illusion and despair, hope and Love are found in Jesus. My little lambs, you will find the Wisdom of God from God. Pray for faith, My children, for there is room for Satan to enter a door of disbelief. Please do not grow weary from doing things according to the Will of My Son. As you know, not all of My children are filled with faith. Pray for their souls and conversion, out of compassion for them. If they will not see, they cannot see. You know, My precious ones, that you can pray to receive anything in God's Will when your faith is strong.

Please pray to receive the peace which I bring and My Son has to offer. When the world is brought to its reconciliation, all will know the Truth and Love of My Son. Remember to confess yourselves to Jesus and you may be made worthy to receive Him. My little children, Satan is a quiet and persistent enemy of Truth, Love, and Light, and he wants that he can steal you away from the Salvation offered by My Son. It is important that you pray to remain pure and strong in your recognition of evil and your avoidance of sin. As you look upward, you will see Light, and when you look downward, you see darkness. Raise your heads to the heavens, children, to seek the Light of Christ which will fall gently on your face! Pray and fast, do penance, and offer complete conversion, and your days will be filled with Light and void of the darkness of Satan. Please remember that I am with you always and that My Love for you is a very special Love. I pray for you that you will receive My Son in your hearts and the Love that He has to offer. I bless you in His Name because of that Love. Thank you for being My precious and obedient children. Thank you for having responded to My call."

Timothy was not with me this evening because he had a business meeting to attend. But, as he drifted-off to sleep about 11:00 p.m., the Virgin spoke audibly saying, **"Now you are fragile to nature, so share your blessing."** Since he was alone, it startled him to hear Her voice so miraculously. He knew that he would soon be receiving another message, so he asked Our Lady to wake me as before. Then, he went to sleep. About 1:45 a.m., I awoke instantly and completely and looked at the telephone, knowing that it would soon ring, and it did. Our Lady gave us the following words tonight.

Wednesday, March 13, 1991
1:30 A.M.

"My dear loved ones, your Mother calls your vision to the Mighty Gate and asks that you set your sights in your prayers to it. Children, My Son, Jesus, can feel the passion which is flowing through the veins of humanity. He shares in living and breathing through the lifeblood of humanity at the heart of its creation. This pulsating accord of common Love, My children, is fed through the power of prayer and by the compassion of humanity for humanity. The fields of your destiny of promise are irrigated through a quenching thrust from the Love of God and will be fulfilled by the only Maker of Truth. My special ones, Jesus should not be received in increments or by a means set by your mood or by fashion. Please accept Jesus as a gift from God, to all who believe in Him. Your lives, My children, were never intended to be filled with tragedy, discord, or perversion. That, My little ones, you have suffered through drifting away from the bulwark of the Spirit in creation of Life in its original beauty and sacrity. To regain the beauty of My Son's Creation, all of My children should merge in the universal offering of His Holy Body at the celebration of the Sacrifice of the Mass. You will be made whole and complete through the unity and purity provided in the daily acceptance of Jesus. He is a stately mantle, offering the security of decency and the restoration of moral warmth of the heart.

My children, please look upon your calling to His offering with joy and gladness because, in receiving Him, you are receiving your future and your destined Promise in it. You will be blanketed with Divine protection and shielded from the lowliness of Satan's despicable will for you by accepting and receiving My Son and through your willing repentance. Know that you are forgiven of your sins and loved beyond all measure. My children, you are delivered from captivity through My Son, Jesus Christ. You are saved through the embrace of His abundant Love for you. Humanity failed to take Him in during His earthly days. Please desire a willingness to take Him in now! Oh, My loved ones, there is a beautiful and bright city of celestial Light in the offing, a fertile valley of endless fruition. You will be brought to it because Jesus loves you! Through His lashes of leather and cord and by His humiliation which He freely accepted, your destiny can be assured by freely accepting Him. Jesus is offering, My lambs, and now is the time for taking. It is through His willingly-accepted stripes that you are healed. Your common blood can flow to the safety of Heaven through the union of your hearts for Jesus. I pray that you will come to His call. I love you with all My Immaculate Heart and wish to see each of you as one of My special angels. Thank you for having responded to My call."

In the evening, we journeyed to pray with another Rosary group. Everyone bowed their head in unity with faith and love, making it a very pleasant and peaceful experience. The Blessed Mother came to offer another message to the other locutionist in the sanctuary of the local Catholic church. Our Lady stood above the Tabernacle on a cloud with a chalice suspended in mid-air below Her feet. There was also a second special gift dispensed to us this evening. The little Dove which we had seen before appeared at the feet of our Holy Mother tonight. On previous occasions, when I asked the Holy Spirit to come into our presence, he would swiftly fly through the air toward us. Tonight, I thought it would be charitable to ask Him to go out and heal the entire world. So, I silently asked the Blessed Virgin to dispatch Him to every continent on Earth. When I lifted this inaudible prayer, the little Dove landed on Our Lady's outstretched hand and, after receiving a kiss, flew away in a direction opposite from us. I was again placed in awe when my brother told me that this had occurred. No other mortal on Earth could hear the prayer I offered, but Our

Lady still responded by granting the answer I sought. I was struck deeply with wonderment and reverence that She would so swiftly reply.

After several decades of the Holy Rosary, the Dove returned from the direction in which He had flown. It was during the third Glorious Mystery that He arrived, the Descent of the Holy Spirit upon the Apostles. With all my heart, I asked Him to come to us now and console us with His peace and grace. We completed the five Glorious Mysteries and Our Lady began to depart very rapidly as though She had declined to bless us. This left me with a sorrowful heart, so I began to pray silently for Her Queenly blessing. In response, She reappeared, made the Sign of the Cross over us, and faded away. I was ecstatic because my prayers were answered again. I felt very humbled that the Mother of God would care enough about me to answer my simple request. I have always *believed* that She deeply loves us, but my faith has never before allowed me to *recognize* that She has such miraculous power. I am seeing it now with the clarity of crystal, albeit in these very simple ways.

After our prayers ended, my brother and I spoke to the crowd about the miraculous manifestations that the Holy Mother has been bringing during the past three weeks. It was nearly impossible to articulate everything that I have included in this written Diary. Even now, it is still overwhelming for me to turn my thoughts toward these moments with the Blessed Virgin Mary. My only impulse on this particular night was to cry with loving affection for Our Lady, but neither of us wanted to weep in front of those who were present. We did not let our emotions show because we could see doubt written across many faces when we explained what had been happening. We left soon thereafter because I did not want anyone else's lack of faith to diminish the elation that we were feeling inside our hearts. My brother and I discussed our Christian witness as we drove back home. Upon arriving, we knelt to seek guidance through our continuing prayers. My brother did not believe that speaking with such public candor about our private revelations was the most prudent thing to do. On the other hand, I was so elated by Our Lady's presence that I wanted to tell everyone who would sit still long enough to listen. Something wonderful happened as we prayed later in the night. The Holy Spirit came upon Timothy immediately and he began penning Our Lady's next message. Until today, She had given them only after he had been asleep for an extended period of time.

Thursday, March 14, 1991
12:00 A.M.

"My beloved son, your heart is being rendered pure and your cause just. Fear nothing because My Son is with you and I am with you. You are completely protected from anxiety through Our tremendous Love for you. Your tasks will not always be easy and your road often long, but

through your prayers and perfect submission, that which has been set for you will bring Light to many. The special one whom you love so much and pray about is beside you so you can share My Love and the mission for which you have been chosen. You are always in My Heart because of My special prayers for you. Return to My valley for strength and to pray often. I will be there waiting for you. Please remember, My son, that the peace of silence can be the most powerful peace to give to humanity. Pray, fast, do penance, and do all I ask of you. Thank you for having responded to My call."

In the afternoon of today, my brother went to a wooded place near the river valley where he lives to say his prayers. He has gone there on many occasions to enjoy the peaceful scenery. Our Lady said, *"Return to My valley for strength and to pray often."* He believed this was the place to which She was referring. When he arrived, Her presence enveloped him as he rested on the trunk of a fallen tree. He was blessed with an incredible gift in the consuming presence of the Holy Spirit. Certain moments of his life descended upon him in their original clarity and detail. He actually re-experienced events in the full light of his awareness, just as they had happened many years ago. It was more than simply remembering or reminiscing about these occasions. First, his consciousness was transported to a protestant church service where he was singing the Ave Maria when he was quite a young man. While performing on this particular day, he thought of his scheduled band practice and his Ford Falcon automobile that needed its engine oil changed relatively soon. He saw the pianist kick the leg of the piano while he sang, just as she had before, and impishly thought that her distraction was an unintentional part of his performance. He related this detailed experience to me as if he had just departed the church, although it happened almost twenty-five years last passed. During this time of altered presence, he was completely oblivious of his true age or that anything in the future had already come. He was just a young man who was singing at a church service as he had been instructed to do so by his parents.

His next vision was almost unbearably more heart-wrenching. He witnessed the day his sister was struck and killed by a car. They were walking home from a Saturday matinee at the village schoolhouse when she ran ahead of them into the path of the oncoming traffic. His heart relived the horrible agony of that day. He ran to his sister and knelt at her side while she lay dying. The incredible helplessness of a five year old in terror swept over his soul. He and his brother were carried home to their mother in the arms of a man who had witnessed the accident. His recounting of this grave catastrophe nearly shattered my heart. The entire tragedy somehow transcended through time to allow us to experience its magnitude. As I listened, I pondered what it would be like to see Jesus' Crucifixion in this same timeless way. I probably do not realize what I am saying! He also told me that he saw a pink 1957 Chevrolet sedan drive past him on the street of our hometown. He said, "You're going to think I've lost my mind, but I saw your dad driving a pink 1957 Chevy." I told him that we, indeed, had a pink 1957 Chevy when I was small child. He looked at me stunned because he did not know our family during that period of time or that we had such an automobile. I do not understand the significance of these mystical experiences. I have neither heard nor read of anyone else who has been blessed with this grace. I record it with trust in God that our Blessed Lady knows what she is doing. She has reasons for which I have not the authority to question.

Friday, March 15, 1991
1:15 A.M.

"Dear children, your Mother brings you blessings in the Name of My Son, Jesus, and is asking you to surrender completely to Him. Jesus is alive and has promised to walk with you on your journey of life to deliver you to Eternal Salvation. Please remember, My children, that you need Jesus to redeem your souls. Pray and be close to My Son, and ask Him for help and guidance. Your human judgement is never heavenly, My innocent ones, but mortally frail. Your standards are no prescription for Eternal Life. If you try to seek Heaven without first taking the hand of Jesus, you will not find it. Please do not delay in accepting Him! My Son is going to return to the world and with great compassion, healing, kindness, and Mercy to those who love and fear Him. Pray, My children, that your souls will be greeted with great installation as the Love of My Son continues to live in you. Your only bounty is that of your Savior, Jesus Christ. While there is a limit and helplessness in human fortunes, the bounty granted by My Son is endless and forever. Jesus offers the seed of Love that can grow in you and become bountiful faith. That Love is found in your prayers and His Sacred Heart. Give your hands to prayer! Your future in Heaven cannot escape from between your hands if they are folded in prayer. My special children, the only free act in your power to achieve everlasting Life in Heaven is to willingly accept My Son. Your faith in Jesus is a bounty that has no material equal on Earth.

Those who are rich in faith will yield a fruitful harvest at calling which cannot be matched by manly wealth. The rich should learn from the poor. Children, your lives are a fierce storm which lashes at you to make you weak and afraid. There are many unstable forces which drive you to sin and away from Jesus. Please know that your guidance and help through all the ages is Jesus, and you can trust in Him and know that He will never leave you alone in body or spirit. Jesus loves you even in your faults when you accept and confide in Him. The storm of life will end in a beautiful rainbow to those who believe His Promise. He will place all of your sins in remission and forgive you when you pray to follow His Word. Children, Jesus is your watch during the darkness of sin to guide you to brightness. In your times of trouble, take refuge in My Son's ever-present Love for you. Your soul is at rest in Him. Your Mother is asking you to humble yourselves and pray for lasting strength. Please desire to see Jesus in His temple and He will come to you in your hearts where He asks you to grant Him permanent stay. Your lives, children, are made holy and honorable when you give residence to Jesus in your hearts. Pray for the grace to be acceptable in His sight! My loved ones, I pray for you because you are My special children and I hold you deep in My Heart. Please, pray with penitence and contrition and your lives will be made wholesome through the Love of My Son, Jesus. Thank you for having responded to My call."

My brother and I traveled to Peoria, Illinois to see Father Ted today. We wanted to continue to share our experiences with Him and seek his spiritual guidance. Upon arriving, we explained in detail everything that is happening and asked him what we should do next. He encouraged us to remain close to the Church and to receive the Holy Sacraments more frequently. He also asked us to continue attending the daily Sacrifice of the Mass. As I listened, it struck me that he was repeating everything that our Holy Mother has been asking of us. I committed myself to daily Mass on April 16, 1989 in obedience to Her requests throughout the world. She has taught me that the Eucharistic Celebration is the pinnacle of solace on the Earth. It has, indeed, become the greatest joy of my life. Jesus is now very special to me every day, not just on Sunday mornings. Father Ted instructed us not to "get-in-the-way" of these miraculous experiences by invoking our own human will. We must allow Our Lady to work at Her pace and in God's time. Father brought us comfort by saying that everything we told him is in keeping with the Virgin Mary's previous intercession in other parts of the world. He stated that it reminded him of other apparitions with which he has become familiar. Finally, he said that we must allow this grace to transform us through the normal course of our everyday lives. We must continue to live in faith like everyone else.

As the evening hours drew nearer, I wanted Father Ted to pray with us. He was very busy, so my hopes were not quite fully realized. I also believe that he was teaching the example of how we must continue to proceed without fanfare or spectacle, despite the miraculous happenings that are unfolding before us. We must let God's Plan bloom as He is laying it out. In the absence of this beautiful priest, My brother and I knelt in the rectory chapel before the Most Blessed Sacrament to recite the Holy Rosary. Our Lady appeared above the stately Tabernacle, standing on a cloud with a breeze billowing Her gown behind Her. To our left was a large Crucifix that was hanging behind the altar.

She looked in that direction with Her arms extended toward Her Son. We rose and venerated the Cross, kissing Jesus' Body in honor of His great Sacrifice. Then, we knelt again and continued to pray.

There was a Rosa Mystica statue of the Blessed Mother positioned in front of a kneeler just a few feet away. Our Lady turned Her attention from us and gazed downward at it. It was reminiscent of Her appearance in St. Augustine church in Ashland when She looked beyond our faces toward the choir loft. After a few moments, Timothy realized that She was looking at the kneeler, wanting us to move there. So, we repositioned ourselves upon the kneeler and continued to pray. A great Light was ignited and showered from Her presence. The intensity increased until She was clothed with a sparkling radiance that soon rivaled the sun. My brother shielded his face because his eyes could not bear the strain of such brilliance. After several more minutes, the emanation began to fade. Suddenly, Timothy fell backward from the kneeler as though he had been startled by something. As the Light dimmed into a more comfortable tone, Our Lady burst from its corona and stood where the Rosa Mystica statue was resting. She was so close to us that he could feel the warmth of Her radiance upon his face. My soul knew that the immortal Mother of God was only an arm's length away. I could feel my spirit shivering miraculously as we knelt before Her. I wish I had more descriptive words to share these moments that I am trying to relate. Our Virgin Mother remained before us until we completed our prayers. Then, She blessed us and departed. We retired for the night in Peoria with great anticipation, awaiting Her next message for the world.

Saturday, March 16, 1991
"**My beautiful children, My Love comes to you as the wind breezing gently and fair with warmth for each of you. I ask you today to keep yourselves holy and pure by your sincere prayers and penance, especially during this season of giving to God of your hearts. Many of My children suffer today because of the lack of their prayers and the absence of prayer for them. Come closer to Me, My children, and I will pray with you and for you and help you to know how My Son wants you to be holy. Jesus knows your holiness through your prayers and the fruits of your work. Dear children, your Christianity can be expressed by your tenderness toward all of My children, by showing forgiveness, charity, and by being pleasant. If you make sacrifices and suffer for the good of others, you will come closer to the Heart of Jesus because it shows that you love Jesus as He loves you. You should spend all of your days loving Jesus and dismiss idleness away from Him from your lives.**

There are many hours and resources which are wasted in your lives. The world is growing stale and damaged by your abuse of its beauty created by My Son. The greatest waste, though My children, is that

which could have been brought to the world through a prayer that was left unsaid. Children, you should remember that faith and prayer show your love for Jesus and give your lives direction and meaning. Many have gone before you to mark your way with signs of faith. Keep praying, little ones, so you can know the signs of faith and those paths that lead you to it. Take time in your lives to pray and seek the Kingdom of Heaven by asking Jesus to lead you there. Ask Jesus to lead you all to Eternity in Heaven. You need to pray, children, while you have time to pray and confess your sins. Each of you is moving through time at the speed of God's intentions. Time does not move, My special ones, it is you that move through it. Time is one in itself and, when you are called, you will become one with Eternity in Heaven when you live the Love of Jesus. I am with you all to pray for you out of love for you. I will not come back again, My special ones, so you must live My messages, fast, do penance, convert, and pray for peace in your lives and to be close to the Heart of My Son, Jesus. I bless you in His Name and with the warm breeze from My Immaculate Heart. Thank you for having responded to My call."

When I got up this morning, I realized that my brother did not wake me during the night. I speculated that he may not have received a message since we were away from home. But, when I met him for breakfast, I found-out that Our Lady had spoken as She has before. Timothy did not wake me because he did not realize that She had given another message until he found it on his writing tablet. This is the first time that he has been completely unaware of receiving Her message. After we returned home today, another friend came over to my house. She ordered us to immediately stop what we were doing. We were accused of abandoning our senses of reality regarding our prayers, the visions, and the claims that our Blessed Mother is communicating with us. This person knows that our mutual time of prayer and contemplation has been increasing. She said, "It's just not normal to do that!" My brother and I have already agreed that our experiences are not a subject for discussion with those who do not believe us. It is futile to try to convince people who refuse to invoke their own faith. During our conversation, I tried to avoid any semblance of conflict, but the open persecution relentlessly continued. The only thing she desired was for us to renounce Our Lady and the prayers of the Rosary that we have been lifting to God. I will never surrender to such demands under any circumstances!

Sunday, March 17, 1991

My brother transcribed Our Lady's message during the night. But, again, he did not remember receiving it, nor did he wake me from my sleep to give it to me. This is why there is no time recorded with this message.

A.M. - "My dear children, I am your Mother and the Queen of Peace. I have come to ask all of My children to come to the call of peace given through the Love of My Son. Remember that Jesus is Love and He is the Victor over despair, mistrust, sadness, doubt, temptation, and sin. I send the Love of My Son to all those who feel weakness in their faith and far from peace. Children, it is in each of you that peace begins because Love also begins in you by taking in My Son. You must be a witness for the Love of God by praying that evil will be removed from other men's hearts. This is how peace is shared between people, praying for inner peace and outer peace. There is never an overabundance or surplus of peace. The peace that is not used by one heart due to its hopeful saturation is the peace that belongs to a hungry heart. Pray, My children, that peace can spread throughout your land and in all hearts so all of humanity can share in its goodness and fulfillment. It is a precious possession that can only be achieved through Love, prayer, understanding and forgiving the faults of others and being patient during times of distress and change.

Children, peace is cool like a running brook. It is as soft as the down of the breast of a dove, gentle as a newborn lamb, and tender as a new sun at daybreak. And, it all comes from the inside of each and every soul which follows and accepts the Love of My Son, Jesus. Peace can never be dark, but white as the snow-capped mountains hovering above to instill strength in beauty. The Love of peace should take men to the highest peaks of human holiness, which is a journey beginning at the foundation of the heart. Oh, My special ones, the only true peace of the highest kind can only be found through the Heart of Jesus, kept alive in the hearts of yourselves. Your Mother is calling you to peace and to allow it to flourish in the greatness of its own potential as that which draws humanity together as one in Love. It cannot be forced or pilfered and is not a market for mortal pleasure. In its own right, peace is as a dove which comes to the very quiet and docile of habitats to secure serenity and calm to all it touches. It is very timid, is the Dove of Peace, and likes that its home can abound with warmth and compassion. I bring you this peace, My children, and hope that you will open your hearts to willingly accept it so that your lives can be kept pure and free from frustration and temptation. The peace which I offer will be given when you pray and remember the Love of My Son and the Sacrifice He made to give all of you peace for Eternity. His Sacrifice will make all men as one Love in the Name of Jesus. Thank you for patiently praying and receiving peace from Him in the Name of the Holy Spirit. May it be carried to you on swift wings and through the softness of quiet. I give you Blessings from the Sacred Heart of My Son. Thank you for having responded to My call."

Tonight, my brother and I continued our prayers together and Our Lady offered us Her personal instruction. She also comforted us in light of the growing persecution that is coming from our peers. It is almost worth being rejected by humankind to be so comforted by the Virgin Mother of God! I am not accustomed to people who violently and boldly challenge my honest intentions. My heart simply desires to share the beauty that I am witnessing. There seems to be very few among us who are willing to invoke the faith to accept Our Lady's intercession. They do not understand what they are casting aside! It reminds me of someone trampling through a beautiful garden of flowers. The delicate pedestals-in-bloom do not stand a chance beneath the errant souls of the doubters who must see in order to believe! It brings me shame that my fellow human beings will not respond to these overtures from Heaven. It makes me want to cry to Jesus to forgive those who turn away!

Monday, March 18, 1991

"Dear children, today I would like to call you to the will of forgiveness. You live in a world which is filled with dissension and disarray, but you were created to be all in one humanity. It is very important that your willingness to forgive others is a part of your lives for Christ. As you deliver forgiveness to others for their impositions to you, the great Mercy of Jesus will become more apparent to you and how important it is for you to receive it. You have built many walls, little ones, which serve to separate you from others. These divisions discriminate and segregate you from your fellow men and cause a lack of compassion for those who are truly in need of your love. Children, you can destroy these walls by uniting your hearts in unifying prayer. You must pray to be filled with the Holy Spirit and to become engulfed by it so you will be immersed in the joy of My Son, Jesus. The radiance of the Love of Jesus will descend on you when you pray to be one humanity instead of one in humanity.

When you show your joy in the Love of Jesus and follow His Word, others will follow you. This example to your brother and sisters also brings joy to the Heart of Jesus. Children, My Son does not have concern for your collection of earthly possessions, and He does not want them. What Jesus is interested in is extending His Love to each of you and receiving your love and your souls for happiness in Heaven. You are at your will to do whatever your trade allows you to do on Earth, and it is best served through the help of daily prayer and the remembrance that forgiveness is also a part of your daily trade with those from whom you would seek forgiveness. This, My children, is how you can earn the Mercy of Jesus. Many times, it is difficult to hold your stand in your love for Jesus in a world of turmoil and disbelief, especially when others are

showing to you their faithless side. Those are the times when your prayers need to be strong, direct, intense, and from the heart.

The Love of Jesus is with you and is very strong when you pray. He will answer sincere love with sincere Love. This is why forgiveness is so important in seeking the Mercy of God. A faithless world cannot hurt you if you remain close to the protection of Jesus through prayer. Oh, My special ones, while it may be difficult for you to carry trust and hope in your daily lives in such an unstable world, please put both of them in Jesus. He will grant you the protection you seek if you pray to receive it. I always pray for you and respond to your pleas for intercession. I see and hear you when you may have doubts that your prayers are strong or loud enough. The most simple and soft-spoken prayer is as bounteous as a fanfare in its merit of sincerity in Heaven. I am always with you because I love you, even when you may believe that we are far apart. Many blessings are yours through your sincerity in prayers from the heart! Thank you for having responded to My call."

Tuesday, March 19, 1991
"My dear children, please know that your days should be marked with holiness so that your hearts can remain aloft with the Spirit of My Son, Jesus. When your lives create in you a thirst to be made holy and pure, you should seek the fountain of My Son's Love to lift you. Children, the waters of the Earth are of brine and are salted with sin and impurity. Earthly waters will not quench your thirst for holiness and Salvation, but will draw you again and again to them. The Fountain of My Son's Love is your only means to sacred satisfaction. You look to the east and west, and the south to north, but your eyes still only see the mortality of the false hopes that the Earth has to offer. When you lift your hearts in prayer to Jesus, you will see and feel the quenching showers of Love that will make you holy and made clean of sin. Look, My children, up to the heavens for the saving Fountain, which is fed by your sharing of love for Jesus and for each other! Please know that your persistence in Love creates a vision in your hearts that will allow you to see also the Love of My Son. Your days, My special lambs, should show your example of Love through the language of your acts, prayers, and thoughts. You should tend to those who suffer or are blind to the vision of the Love of Jesus.

Your prayers are of great strength in bringing these people to the fountain of Jesus and His Love and Mercy. Your prayers light the way for those whose vision falls short of freely accepting the Love of God. And, My children, your pure thoughts keep your own hearts filled with the holiness you need to deliver the language of Jesus' Promise of

Salvation to others. Remember also that your enemies need your love and prayers even greater than those who are very close to your heart. Love is most powerful when given to someone who does not possess the willingness to readily accept it. The Love of My Son, Jesus, is the converting power given to you by Him to offer your enemies to bring them to His grace, and is the ultimate language prescribed by God. My special ones, never before has the world needed the offering of conversion through Love more than it does now. You have been given the power to convert others through your love and prayers. Your Heavenly Mother is calling you to remember those very near to you in your daily lives and to pray especially for those who are your enemies. By helping lead them to the fountain of holiness, My Son, Jesus, they too can know that Salvation is the result of conversion to God and gives the promise of Eternal Life. Thank you for having responded to My call."

Father Joseph Murray, the priest of St. Augustine church in our hometown of Ashland, died last Saturday evening and, tonight, we attended his wake. My brother was very close to our beloved Pastor. It was he who instructed Timothy in the Catholic faith and, in 1979, led him into complete fellowship with the Holy Sacraments at Confirmation ceremonies conducted by the late Bishop McNicholas. Therefore, we were both deeply aggrieved that Father was called to his Heavenly reward at this time when we needed him most. It is now very clear why the Blessed Mother was paying so much attention to him when we were reciting the Holy Rosary in the St. Augustine sanctuary on the evening of March 5th. She knew that he was about to be called into the peacefulness of Heaven. What struck us as being so unusual is that our precious Father Murray did not succumb to the symptoms of his illness, but from injuries he sustained in a recent automobile accident. He was in a wreck on the same day that he announced to the parish after Holy Mass that he would soon retire. I reminded my brother what the Blessed Mother told us recently about **"the preciousness of death and resurrection."** In his grief, he said that he was not yet prepared to acknowledge the preciousness of death. But again, he obediently transcribed another message through the night.

Wednesday, March 20, 1991

"**Dear children, on this day, gravity has left its port. Many hearts have been touched by the Promise of God. Jesus has provided peace to the aged worthy. Through the Love provided by My Son, many days have been yielded Eternal Light. The Promise of Jesus has been fulfilled. Love has been returned to Love. Gift has been given in kind and Promise has been redeemed as Love. Today, My children, prayers have been received and made whole in the mighty Plan of God, through life that was created from the beauty of the Love of God. The Love of**

Jesus took Him to His death and made Him King of Heaven and on Earth, the same Love through which those who believe in Him will lead to days of Eternal Light. My little ones, you are offered plentiful seed which, in prayer and time, will yield the complete fruits of your natural days. Blessings from your Heavenly Mother are yours for all Eternity. Thank you for having responded to My call."

Timothy and I prayed together this evening and Our Lady appeared to us as before. She has increased Her Motherly tutoring since the verbal attacks upon our character this past week. In retrospect, I can see how shaken I have been by these confrontations. But, the Blessed Mother's grace is beginning to fortify our trust and conviction. She helps me to see our conflicts for what they truly are; the destruction of peace caused by other human minds who have not the faith to keep Love alive in their hearts.

Thursday, March 21, 1991

"My special little children, today I have come to ask each of you to respond to the Love of Jesus through your prayers. Children, the world and its ways are changed through your prayers. It is important that all of My children unite your hearts. Set your hearts to glow in the acceptance of the Love of Jesus! My little ones, if all of you light your hearts through Him, the Earth could be made to be more brilliant than the sun. The light from the sun can light only a portion. There is no night or darkness in Jesus. Children, by accepting God's Love, your hearts will be embraced with tenderness because Love is the force that gives them the rhythm of life. The energy created by a heart beating for the Love of Jesus can shake the world. By uniting your hearts for Him, you can move the world to keep it away from the grip of Satan.

Sometimes, My lambs, you feel distance from Jesus because Satan has touched you on the inside. It is the will of Satan to darken your hearts and cause them to stop for his plan of terror and damnation. Keep your hearts free from Satan by keeping the guard of Jesus in them! He is always there, but you need to pray so that He can work in you. Jesus cannot ever be cast away, even by those who refuse Him. But, those who fall to Satan do not let Jesus freely show His Love in their hearts. When you accept Jesus, My children, your soul will rise to the surface of your body so that it is encased by the protection of His Love. No act of evil can penetrate a soul that is filled with Jesus Christ. Please, receive Him, little ones, in your heart and soul! Go to His house often to take Him in. Find Him in your brothers and sisters as He is present in yourselves. I pray, children, that you will know that Jesus is your only way to Eternal Life and to be made free from the deadening forces of Satan. I am always here to love you and pray for you because you are My blessed children. Thank you for accepting the Love of Jesus. I come close to those who pray to receive Him. Thank you for having responded to My call."

This was to be our last weekly Rosary at the downtown Marian Center. The proprietors told us that they could no longer accommodate our group without being in violation of the State Fire Code. We were also told that the prayer group was too large for the basement room where we were presently meeting. I thought it was very odd that we were to be denied access to a Center that is consecrated to the Blessed Virgin Mary. As we prayed the Rosary there tonight, our Holy Mother came to us again. The ensuing visions were different in nature than on previous occasions. Our Lady had always appeared in a fixed position in the room. If my brother turned his head, he could peer away from Her and She would remain standing above the Tabernacle, the altar, or wherever She hovered on that particular night. This time, however, She was everywhere he turned to look. She had completely consumed the entire area in one spectacular blush. Timothy did not see Her in one given place, but in every location that he pulled into focus. While he was coming to grips with this unexpected change, Our Lady suddenly burst into the fulness of color. He had mentioned to me within the past week that his vision could be seen only in black and white. At the time, I thought it would be nice if the apparitions were all the colors of the rainbow, instead. So, without his knowledge, I asked Our Lady to effect this alteration. Again, I have witnessed the direct answer to my prayers.

Our Lady was wearing a gray dress and a white veil tonight, and Her beautiful brown hair could be seen flowing from underneath. Her blue eyes were as clear as a crystal-clean wading pool. She was standing on a huge green snake and She cried throughout the Sorrowful Mysteries. The words "SUMMA," "CRUCIFIXUS," and "REDEMPTORUS" were highlighted in Her Countenance as She stood on a cloud while being flanked by three angels. Our wonderment at these words quickly vanished when She ascended from beyond our sight during the decade honoring Her Assumption. Within a few more minutes, She appeared again, clothed with the sun. She was standing on the moon with a Crown of Twelve Stars glistening like diamonds above Her head. She was resplendent in majesty and breathtaking to behold. Upon finishing the Holy Rosary, She blessed us in the sign of the Cross, reverted into the former black and white image, and faded into the distance again.

Friday, March 22, 1991
"My dear little Easter lilies, your loving Mother has come around you today to thank you for choosing to make prayer a part of your lives. Please always remember how important it is to remain whole in the eyes of Jesus. Please, children, live your lives to their fullest and always be

happy. **Your Heavenly Mother is always with you to bring you the Love of your Savior. I love you and pray for you so that you will be protected from Satan and kept worthy of Salvation and Eternal Life. My special ones, your lives and activities are changing so that you can be stronger and more aware of God's great and mighty plan. Today, I have bestowed a gift to share upon an obedient child who rests in good favor, one among you to whom I will return on the days of Sabbath, Feast, and those made Holy. Please read and live My messages, as they are new every day. You are all in My Heart and prayers forever because I love you. The gift of the rainbow is a very small vision of the graces I plan to bestow on each of My special children when the just and due season has arrived. Thank you for loving My Son as He loves you and as I love you. Thank you for having responded to My call."**

After this message, my brother was worried that he would never see Our Lady's Face again. I, too, sensed that something had changed. I became quite concerned, thinking that we might have done something wrong. I asked him how long it would be before She came back again, and He said that he had no way of knowing. Then, I read this most recent message again. The sentence about a gift being bestowed on the days of Sabbath, Feast, and Holy days jumped-off the page at me. I knew in my heart that She would appear on Sundays, Feast days and Holy days to someone who was at the prayer group last night. I did not know to whom, but I felt a great desire to prepare in solemnity for this coming Sunday. I knew that Our Lady would appear, and I was so ecstatic with anticipation that I could barely contain myself. However, Timothy was not as convinced. He cautioned me by saying that he did not know if that is what She really meant when She told us what She said.

In the later evening, we knelt to pray again. I did not know if my brother's feelings about the cessation of Her appearances were correct. When we commenced the Rosary, Our Lady's presence was very powerful, although She did not appear as She had before. He took his pen and began to draw the miraculous scenes that unfolded before him. There was an endless valley that was divided by a beautifully-flowing stream. I noticed something very different when he described it to me. This was not simply a vision about which he was a spectator. He was physically *in* the valley from the vantage-point of his view. He could feel the wind blowing and hear the birds chirping in the trees. At one point, he brushed the back of his neck because something was lapping against his skin. It was the wind slapping the collar of his jacket. When he looked into the sky, there were no clouds, although it was raining a slight mist. He was mesmerized by the raindrops that were gently falling from a sunny blue sky. These words suddenly appeared, *"A drop to every soul, a random blessing, and all as one in time."* I again asked if he could see our Blessed Mother. He responded negatively, but also said that he could sense that She was very close to us. A dove appeared, bearing the inscription "John 1:32." As the rain subsided and the wind settled, Timothy was lifted into the sky. As he rose above the trees, a panoramic view of a great mountain range appeared in the distance with the sun rising from behind their peaks. The landscape was freshly watered from the rains and a sweet clean freshness was permeating the air.

While watching this scene unfold, a rainbow appeared over the mountains. Its colors were rotating and sparkling like a giant barber's pole. When it faded, the sun began spinning while emanating the colors of the rainbow. Many people refer to this as the "Miracle of the Sun" which was first seen at Fatima, Portugal in October of 1917. The sun became like a Host and dropped into a chalice that appeared below it. A white dove was resting on its brim with the words "John 3:16" above him. Finally, in the morning light, a glowing star appeared. Notwithstanding his angelic state of heart, my brother was still disturbed because he could not see Our Lady as before. Therefore, I asked Her to come to us again. She responded, **"Your Morning Star is with you!,"** but did not come into sight. As we completed the meditations of the Rosary, She concluded, **"Thank you for responding to My call."** Everything eventually faded-to-pale in Timothy's interior vision, ending our miraculous experience this evening. My brother stayed to rest at my home again. And, for the first time since February 22nd, Our Lady did not give us a specific message during the night. I continue to pray and hope.

Saturday, March 23, 1991

We began the Rosary this evening and, although Our Lady did not appear, the symbolic visions commenced in unison with the Mysteries. In continuing the change that began last night, Timothy again committed to paper what he was witnessing with his soul. During the Mystery of the Birth of Our Lord, the word "EMMANUEL" appeared in light, along with a diminutive Lamb. He was disheveled and dirty as if he had been severely beaten. Next, the word "SIMEON" was followed by the manifestation of a rather large church. My brother was propelled toward it and passed through the main entranceway door. He found himself in the company of a huge group of people who were gathered in a circle, gazing at something inside. Initially, he could not see the subject of their attention. But, as he moved closer to them, the group parted to reveal the little Lamb standing in their midst. His vision was then drawn to a magnificent stairway with two separate landings that led to a doorway higher above. He marveled at its awesome appointments. As we began the Sorrowful Mysteries, he drew the Crown of Thorns that appeared before him. I realized at this point that my brother was incapable of drawing the images he was reproducing. His artistic abilities were being enhanced by the Holy Spirit of God.

Although never an artist, he was quickly drawing with intricate detail. He instantly realized that he was not responsible for the pictures. He said, "Billy, I'm not the one controlling my arm!" Drops of blood were falling from the Crown of Thorns into a chalice below. As we began the fourth Sorrowful Mystery, the little Lamb was dragging a Cross on its back toward an inclining hill. Two others were with Him, carrying their crosses along. The next image was the Cross implanted on a hill with the Crown of Thorns draped across its upper beam. Blood was dripping from the Cross with every drop still falling into the chalice. The words "I THIRST" appeared with clarity beneath the Cross. The visions continued as we recited the Glorious Mysteries. The entrance to a cave appeared in the side of a hill with a huge boulder resting near its throat. A pretty angel was sitting next to it with the word "GALILEE" emblazoned above his wings. A dove appeared above the chalice and was drawn into it before the Cup changed into a Tabernacle which opened to emanate of very brilliant Light. Finally, a giant star arose, bearing the words "REGINA" and "SUMMA." Through all of these manifestations, we continued to pray until every one of them ceased. My brother and I shared our amazement together. I collected all of the drawings and recorded everything we just saw, exactly as it had occurred.

Palm Sunday, March 24, 1991
I have been living the past forty-eight hours with an undescribable anticipation. I was so anxious for today to come because I knew that another spectacular event was about to unfold. The morning opened both beautiful and sunny, with a crisp, yet warm, comfort to its breezes. I suggested to Timothy that we find a peaceful place outdoors to pray the Rosary in the afternoon. We considered traveling to Pana, but thought that the group may be gathering inside the church. We decided, instead, to go to the Catholic cemetery near Ashland. It is graced with a huge stone crucifix that is nearly ten feet high at its center. We both agreed that this would be the perfect place to pray on such a beautiful day. So, we went to the cemetery about half past two in the afternoon. In spite of my exuberant anticipation, Timothy has not been willing to concede that our Holy Mother would appear to him or anyone else today. He reminded me again that She simply said that She would "return," which does not necessarily mean "appear." I retorted, *"What's the difference? She's coming, anyway!"* We knelt and began the Rosary right away on this special Palm Sunday, with nary a cloud overhead. But, before we could complete two decades of our meditations, a bank of clouds suddenly came toward us across the sky. Their movement and speed was almost miraculous in nature. They came to rest directly in front of the sun. No other clouds were in the sky from one horizon to the other. They were opaque, so we could see the sun very brilliantly shining through them, so greatly that it caused a great strain to befall our eyes.

We were kneeling southward while facing the Cross with the late afternoon sun and clouds just over our right shoulders. My brother was looking to the west in amazement when he exclaimed emphatically, *"Billy, I can see Her! I can see Her with my eyes open! She is standing in the sky!"* He began to cry at the overwhelming sight. I asked him exactly where Our Lady was standing. He pointed and said, *"Right below the sun, on top of those clouds!"* I looked in that direction and saw that the sun was still very bright. I had to squint to even look in its direction. Timothy, on the other hand, was staring directly at it, neither squinting nor blinking. As I focused my attention into the sky, an awe came over me. It was one of the most beautiful sights I had ever witnessed. The view was much like a portraiture as the beautiful rays of sunlight were streaming through the clouds. They were unlike anything I had ever seen before. The rays were textured like a giant garment, with highlights and pleats. I was looking at a Mantle and gown, but could not see who was wearing it. It was a great painting of miraculous sunlight!

Timothy asked me repeatedly whether I could see Her. When I responded that I could not, he emphatically reiterated, *"She is standing in the sky, just like a human- being standing up there! Can't you see Her? She is right there, looking down at us!"* He pointed toward the heavens excitedly, as if the whole world should be able to see Her. I again told him that I could not, but he kept pleading with me as if it were my own fault. He was so insistent that I see what he was seeing. He cried, *"Billy, just ask Her, She will let you see Her! Just ask Her!"* His insistence overcame me, so I offered a prayer with my whole heart that God would allow me to see. Immediately upon lifting my prayer, the heavens took shape and I saw the image of the Mother of God standing in the clouds with Her hands extended at Her sides. I could not see Her face because the sun was positioned behind Her head with its countenance enveloping Her body. But, as it reached Her bosom, the flood of light became bearable and left me with the ability to see The Lady standing before me. Her gown was flowing-out around Her and bathing the sky. The beautiful pleated clouds were the gown and Mantle She wore. Although stunned to the depth of my soul, I continued to pray the Mysteries of the Holy Rosary.

As we continued, I saw a huge angel appear in the firmament. He was above and behind Our Lady, as if protecting Her. His wings were as wide as ten football fields, stretching in a dominating presence across the sky. My brother asked me if I saw him standing behind Our Lady. I told him that I did, then queried whether he was seeing these images as formations of cloud and light as I was. He replied, *"No, She is a real person who is standing in the sky on a cloud, and the angel is real too!"* I knew then that we were seeing the same images in two very different ways. God was painting the visions as successive pictures of clouds and sunrays in a way that I could see. What I was witnessing is impossible to explain on a page or through the laws of science and nature.

We proceeded to pray the Rosary as the Face of Jesus Christ appeared in the sky beside Our Lady. I was trembling and wanted to hide my face in the ground. I have never experienced anything in my life comparable to looking into the Face of Our Savior. His Gaze lasted for what-seemed like hours. I could physically feel His powerful Countenance beaming from His Face. I prayed the Sorrowful Mysteries with a renewed fervor. A huge ringed cloud then formed below Our Lady. It shaped itself into a Crown of Thorns with the Virgin Mary standing in its center. My brother asked me whether I could see the Crown. I again told him that I could. At the completion of the Sorrowful Mysteries, Jesus and Our Lady departed. I knew that they were gone even before my brother told me because the beautiful rays that were covering the sky had all-but dissipated. The clouds were now casting a bleak dullness over the sun. As we continued the Glorious Mysteries, I watched the entire cloud-bank miraculously move to the southeastern horizon. By the time we finished reciting the Holy Rosary, the sky was completely clear again. We departed from the cemetery in a state of awe, not knowing what to say to each other. My mind could not grasp the dimensions of what had just taken place before our very eyes. I was peacefully excited, but I did not know how to describe it to anyone. Who would believe what I actually saw with my eyes?

My brother received another message tonight at 11:00 p.m. It began, **"My dear children, your Heavenly Mother has come to you today to shower Her rays of Love down upon those who have accepted Jesus as their Savior, anchor, and steadfast harbor. Many loving hearts for Jesus sent great flowers to My Immaculate Heart, today. I have brought the Face of My Son to show the conviction of His Love and My Love for those who have opened their hearts to Him. My special children, many of your brothers and sisters see their relationship with Jesus as though they are passing in the night on the waters. Jesus is the only vessel, the captain, the level to be sought for sanctity and harbor. Your love for Jesus and for each other cannot pass in the night, but must be dayborn and lighted, spoken and felt, and heard to be received.**

My little ones, there are those who are spinning themselves into a cocoon to shut Jesus out of their lives, an act that will not result in beautiful flight. Pray, children, that your spins will be outward and upward, so that the beauty in you can be free on its day of release as on its heartfelt day of conception, that of the admission of Jesus in your hearts. Oh, My little lambs, your special thoughts, wishes, and prayers are always heard in Heaven! When you are letting Love move your spirit, you will always move and change the shape of Heaven. I pray for you, little ones, so that you can change the shape of Heaven to allow room for your souls! My Love comes to you in many ways, not all of which you readily see or hear. Please know, children, that each new day, you see

the Light of God as a blessing to you and it is the Will of My Son that you see very much Light in your lives. My Son makes His Face shine upon those in His Heart and I come around all of My special children who have the hope of Eternal Life in their hearts. I pray that you will be a leader and a receiver of the Light of the Love of My Son. Thank you for praising Him. Thank you for having responded to My call."

Monday, March 25, 1991

We knelt to recite the Holy Rosary this evening and our Blessed Mother came again. Timothy resumed drawing the sequence of pictures as we prayed. The first was of the cemetery where we petitioned God for help during the great events of yesterday. It reflected a very revealing vantage-point because of its perspective. It was drawn as though one was looking down through Our Lady's eyes upon the cemetery. The entire landscape exhibited the highest accuracy and detail. We were beneath the Cross next to our car with the beatific rays from the sun that were bathing us as we knelt. Our Lady showed us many revelations tonight during our moment of prayer. I do not wish to burden this record with personal details that will distract from the messages which She is asking us to deliver. Much of Her instruction and explication is personal in nature. She asks me to prudently discern between Her message for the world and Her personal motherly advice for the spiritual growth of my brother and me.

Tuesday, March 26, 1991

Our Lady's personal instruction continued today as my brother and I prayed together in the evening. We have consecrated ourselves in Love to Her Immaculate Heart, therefore we pray often in unison as She asks. Timothy drew another series of pictures that were filled with symbols pertaining to many manifestations that we have experienced and the people we have met. Many references were also made to the graces we received in Medjugorje, Yugoslavia. We were given several Latin words to ponder, although we did not understand the nature of their significance. I thought that I would research them later to find-out their meaning. We finished our prayers in the Virgin Mother's company, knowing that we would not receive a special message through the night.

Wednesday, March 27, 1991

This evening, we joined the Pana Rosary group to lift our voices to God once again. During our prayers, Timothy sketched the inside of the St. Patrick's church. He drew the altar and the pews, along with those who were kneeling nearby. He, then, highlighted our Blessed Mother's presence in the choir-loft behind us, which seemed representative of the occurrences in Medjugorje. He drew reference lines on the notepaper in his lap between the Pana locutionist and Our Lady in the loft with his ink pen as if to indicate a force-field of communication between them. I fully understand the relationship between Our Lady and Her messengers, but he seemed intent upon signifying something more than that. I did not initially comprehend what it was, so I continued to pray with the assurance that I would find-out when Our Lady wanted me to know.

On the night of March 25, 1991, the words *"You will no longer need faith"* appeared on my brothers writing paper. At the time, I was perplexed because the phrase did not seem to be complete. I had the same feeling when we transcribed an inappropriate word in the message of February 28, 1991. Tonight, Our Lady completed the thought, giving it clearer definition by saying, "**There is no need for faith when He comes.**" She also had him write the words, "**WILL COME**" for me to read. Timothy whispered that She is going to come to someone else. I told him to ask Her to whom. He put his pen to the pad and drew the east facade of my house with the words "WILL COME" written above my bedroom window. Then, pointing to my bedroom, he said that She would come here. I asked excitedly when this would happen. The answer was in the next written word, **"PATIENCE."** You can imagine my excitement as I saw this unfold. I did not ask anything more, but my mind was ecstatic with the thought that Our Lady would soon embrace my life even more deeply than She has. All of a sudden, he began rapidly underlining the word **"PATIENCE."** I disciplined my thoughts immediately, invoking a greater reverence for what was happening in front of me. Until now, I simply considered myself somewhat of an observer who was recording Our Lady's message, notwithstanding what I had experienced this past Palm Sunday.

After ending our prayers, everyone gathered in the church Hall to socialize. We were not inclined to speak about the drawings to anyone else since many were not yet disposed to accepting these graces. As we conversed, the Pana locutionist volunteered her experiences that She had just undergone during the Rosary. She said that she felt a separation within herself, much like my brother experienced two days before Our Lady first spoke to him. During this separation, she felt her soul being drawn to the rear of the church in an upward direction toward the choir loft. She had not yet seen my brother's drawings, and we had never mentioned them to anyone. She stated that she did not know how to better explain it. The moment she said this, I understood what my brother was trying to relate to me during our prayers. He witnessed the pulling motion that she was feeling toward Our Lady and, subsequently, tried to communicate it to me. When my brother told me what he saw during our prayers, I did not fully understand. I simply listened and continued to pray without question. I did not allow my lack of understanding or a negative opinion to bring me to pause. In order to further grasp my point, imagine my thoughts when the Pana locutionist mentioned her mysterious experience! Something that did not make sense thirty minutes before now immediately became clear at the sound of her voice. This theme is beginning to repeat itself over and over again, *"In time and faith, all things become clear."*

Holy Thursday, March 28, 1991

On Thursday evening, we began our regular weekly Rosary recitation at my Springfield residence. There was a small group that attended because our meeting was on the same schedule as the Holy Mass. My brother and I had attended an earlier one at 5:30 p.m. It was a very peaceful evening with Our Lady giving us the prayer of the "**Requisition of the Holy Spirit**." Afterwards, I shared many details about the Holy Virgin's intercession as I had been instructed to do so earlier. I was initially very apprehensive because I did not know if anyone's faith would be shaken by my words. But, I responded as Our Lady had asked, not stopping to weigh the consequences. I told the group about Her appearance on Palm Sunday in the cemetery at Ashland. I was pleasantly surprised that the small group was very understanding and receptive. This gave me great hope that our Blessed Mother would be able to touch every heart around us in Her own special way.

Later in the evening, I reread the prayer that Our Lady had dictated to us. Again, I was disturbed by a sentence that did not seem to make sense. We recorded, *"Existence in perpetual transform and transpose."* Even though the sentence does not seem to be complete, I know that our Virgin Mother will correct it if it is, indeed, in need of something else. I am that confident of Her intercessory guidance. Before retiring for the evening, I asked my brother if he would join me tomorrow for the Stations of the Cross at noon. I have made it an annual pilgrimage to pray the Stations of the Cross at the Franciscan Motherhouse on Good Friday. He sounded a bit hesitant because he had to tend to some business at his workplace back home. He told me that he would return later in the day to pray with me, instead.

Good Friday, March 29, 1991

At nine-thirty this morning, Timothy called me by telephone at my office and asked where he was supposed to meet me. I reminded him of his plans to return in the evening. But, he responded, *"No, I am supposed to go with you earlier in the day."* I stated again that I was planning to meditate the Stations of the Cross at the Franciscan Motherhouse. He told me that, when he awoke, he felt an inner call to accompany me today. He described the inspiration as being more than just his own feelings. It was an overwhelming movement of conscience, as if Our Lady was directly speaking to him, although not openly using Her voice. In response to this summons, we began the Way of the Cross at noon in honor of Our Lord's Passion and Death. As we proceeded to the station commemorating Jesus' meeting with His Mother, Timothy spoke out, *"existence in perpetual fact, transform and transpose."* With these words, the sentence of the Requisition prayer that I was concerned about made immediate sense. He said while weeping, "What does it mean? Do you know?" I told him that I would explain it after we finished our prayers.

Requisition of the Holy Spirit
Oh, hearts of the beloved, faces greeting sunlight's rays.
Saints and solar beams in faith and beauty,
giveth of your souls to Love!
Receiveth in you incarnate peace from God's loving hand.
Give rise to hope, thou naked alone,
to be wrapped in holiness for the sake of Eternity.
Oh, beautiful buds of Love, be of no sorrow,
Know you shall yet be granted grace to arched faith.

Jesus, come Holy Spirit, Oh Bridge, Oh Gate, Oh Love,
Mystery revealed!
Bring, Jesus, eyes of Mercy and understanding.
In thy memory, Oh Favorite Bounty, hold your thoughts for us.
Make us content, Risen Redeemer, cometh forth in Light.
Our Deliverer, Our Savior, Our Purge, and Our Court,
give us flight from exile to freedom!
Oh, Love Immortal, existence in perpetual fact, transform
and transpose sin to Light forever and evermore!

Immediately following this exchange, Timothy looked upward and our Holy Mother appeared, standing in front of the sun like She did on Palm Sunday. He was gazing directly into the intense brilliance of the rays without squinting or shading his eyes. Our Lady was looking down upon us, smiling with Her hands extended in blessing at Her sides. I encourage him to continue to pray with me. He asked me if I could see the Light. I did not know what he meant initially, but then, I noticed an orange glow around the entire Station before us, while another light bathed us from overhead. When I looked across the landscape, the sunlight looked very pale. It soon dawned on me that I was witnessing a solar eclipse. The sunlight was clear, but extremely diminished in brilliance. I know that this is what I was witnessing, having seen eclipses before. There was a yellowish hue in the air. It made sense when I recalled the eclipse of the sun on the day that Jesus died. I thanked God for this great gift of grace on this special Good Friday. We arrived at another Station and it became lifelike and colorful with textures of flesh and cloth as my brother looked-on. He could see Jesus' blue eyes and His bruised and battered body. All the while, he kept glancing over his shoulder into the sky, making sure that our Holy Mother was still up there. I told him that She was praying with us, so we should continue. When we arrived at the Station where Jesus is stripped of His garments, Our Lady asked us to recite the prayer of **Requisition of the Holy Spirit** that She had given to us. We responded with great obedience.

We finished the last Station about 1:30 p.m. The Adoration of the Cross in the Motherhouse church always begins at this hour on Good Friday, so I thought that we had better hurry so as not to miss it. I was in a quandary because our Blessed Mother did not immediately go away after we completed the Stations. I was hesitant to depart while She was miraculously present above the trees. We did not know what to do. Timothy said, "She's not going away." No sooner had he said these words than She began to leave. I saw his eyes change from being wide-open to squinting-closed at the increasing glare of the sun as She moved from before it. I asked him about the alteration to the Requisition prayer. He did not know from where the words had come, nor who had spoken them. He did not even recall that Our Lady had given us that holy prayer last evening. The words that he blurted-out came from the depths of his conscience with such power that he was required to speak them. It is beyond description to witness how our Beautiful Mother amended Her own literati. I had no idea that it would be manifested in this particular way, or at this time and place. Indeed, I am baffled as to why She would even allow cause for our having to clarify Her intentioned words at all. I could see, however, that it brought us both together on this Good Friday in remembrance of the Crucifixion of Her Son.

10:30 P.M.

"Dear children, today I invite you to share the Passion of My Beloved Son, Jesus, and to feel the warmth of His Mercy in your hearts. I have granted My heavenly cloak to you today to bring you a special Love, as through a flask, to intensify it and deliver a special direction of grace to My little children who show their love for My Son. Dear children, on these days of God's miracle, please pray to convert all human hearts to Jesus. His sacrifice and Promise are at hand to those who receive His Sacred Heart. Be at His stations for Him, as He is at His station for you! As He bore His Cross of Love for you, children, you are given crosses to bear. He will be with you to help you carry your crosses when you pray to receive it through Him. I am with you, children, as I was with Jesus, to help you carry your crosses. I pray for you as I prayed for Him in His Passion and Death. My little lambs, the Glory yet to come to your lives is great and mighty. Your prayers and faithful living of the Commandments of God are your shield against the

forces of Satan and will lead you to sanctity and acceptance in the eyes of Jesus. Turn your faces and your prayers to Me and to the heavens! Ask for pardon and peace, little ones. You will receive it because My Son loves you. Turn your hearts, children, to loving all of God's Creation and you will be made worthy of His Promise.

Dear children, Easter is such a special time for human souls. It is a turning- point for all of My children. Now is the time for every child to convert their heart to accept Jesus! His victory over the grave made way for your victory into Eternal Life in Heaven. Today, little ones, I ask that you continue to pray and to remember that, since Jesus is alive and loves you, there is always hope in your lives. There is hope for your resurrection! There is Promise for Salvation and eternal happiness. All Jesus asks, children, is that you love. Live Love. I will help you to be brought to Jesus. I intercede for you. I ask you to live My messages and understand that I come to you as a part of God's Will to bring you Light toward His Mighty Plan. Those who have been chosen for tasks are given graces, and only a small amount of the graces which are about to be bestowed on all of My children who pray to love God and to hear Me and will to accept the Love of Jesus. I pray that you will do what I ask and understand that the Divine Plan of God is on His course. Thank you, children, for praying and loving. Thank you for knowing that Jesus loves you and wants to save you from damnation. He is with you always, and I hold you in My Heart always. Thank you for having responded to My call."

Holy Saturday, March 30, 1991

We began the Rosary very late Saturday evening, about 11:00 o'clock. Timothy etched another series of pictures, beginning with a great fanfare of trumpet blasts. He could hear their report which caused him to hold his ears and cringe. Our Lady asked us to sing joyfully because Her Son has risen! He is alive! I played some stately music and began to sing along. She was ecstatic at our profession and proclamation that Jesus is the Risen King. Along with the trumpets, the words "CHERABYM" and "SERAPHYM" appeared in their midst. My brother did not know that these were two choirs of angels about the Throne of God. He began to weep because he could hear their voices. I asked him what they were singing. He could not understand the language, but through tears, said it was the most beautiful song he had ever heard. In this emotionally overpowering moment, Our Lady told him to rest peacefully. He felt Her miraculous presence consuming him. Suddenly he exclaimed, "She has taken my heart and replaced it with Her own." Her grace radiated from within him. Our Lady then told him of a special place where She wished him to pray tomorrow morning. I asked Her if I could accompany him, but She responded that She wanted me to be with my family for the celebration of Easter.

Easter Sunday, March 31, 1991

At sunrise this morning, I prayed for strength and understanding about last night's events. I did not understand the significance of Our Lady placing Her Heart within my brother. I opened my Bible and this passage came before me.

"I will give you a new heart and place a new spirit within you, taking from your bodies your stony hearts and giving you natural hearts. I will put my spirit within you and make you live by my statutes, careful to observe my decrees. You shall live in the land I gave your fathers; you shall be my people, and I will be your God."

Ezekiel 36:26-28

The Holy Mother asked my brother to travel to the gravesite of his father and mother to offer prayers for the world on this Easter morning. He appropriately did as he was asked. Upon arriving at the cemetery, a supernatural Light poured-forth from the horizon like water flowing across the open sky. It descended upon him and struck his being with a majestic grace-filled force. At that very moment, he felt his own heart deposited back within him, along with several hours of conversation between him and our Blessed Mother. His memory became inflamed with this communication, but he could not remember directly having it. It was as though the Virgin Mary had taken his heart for those hours and had spoken to him about the Providence of God. While at the cemetery, the sun rose above the distant horizon and soon ignited into its miraculous dance of colorful spinning. Our Lady appeared in the spectacle of this glorious Easter sunrise. As he embraced Her presence, She turned from him to look at something a distance away. As he had on previous occasions when She redirected Her attention toward another site, he went to the place where She was looking. He got into his car and drove a short distance to a nearby lake, stopping at the water's edge. Our Lady's Divine image was miraculously impressed upon its glossy surface. He looked down into the water where She was gazing and, to his amazement, She was looking at him through Her reflection in the water. She smiled and returned Her loving gaze directly upon him. He offered the Glorious Mysteries of the Holy Rosary for the conversion of the world and returned home by early afternoon.

I arrived home at 3:30 p.m. after having a beautiful day with my family. Timothy was resting from his early morning departure to his prayerful destination. I woke him to find out what had happened and whether Our Lady had come to greet him there. He recounted everything that had unfolded and began to share with me the personal information that our Blessed Mother had given him to know. As he spoke, something unexpectedly miraculous happened. His voice became silent and was replaced by the sweet strains of our Virgin Mother! She continued Her instructions to me personally! She asked me to send a collection of Her messages to the Marian Movement of Priests and to the Marian Centers throughout the United States of America. With the help of my brother, I am to send them anonymously in Her precious name. She wants no one to judge Her messages based upon the weaknesses of those who are chosen to receive them. I am to continue diligently recording these passing events in my Diary. Our Lady promised to bless us immensely in the future for completing the work of the Holy Spirit.

She continued by stating that the drawings which Timothy has sketched are a particular gift for us and that we are not required to dispense them to others. She also encouraged me to share everything else that the members of our prayer groups are open to receive. This includes all of our experiences to this point, while excluding Her personal instruction and the revelations regarding future events. I am to be very patient and to pray intensely for all unborn children. I asked Her many questions to make sure that I understood Her clearly and correctly. She answered each one of them with attentive courtesy and detail. When I had nothing more to ask, She concluded by prophesying the success of our work and the monumental conversion that it will bring into the world. At these last words, Our Lady departed and my brother told me that there was nothing more he could remember. I was humbled beyond my greatest imagination by this beatific exchange. The Holy Mother of Jesus opened an audible dialogue with me today. My mind was in wonderment without the ability to reconcile what had just happened. As a result of these holy events, I believe that nothing is impossible with God. The floodgate is open and I am standing directly in the path of His tidal grace. The following is the text of Our Lady's message to my brother as he traveled to the country cemetery to greet the Easter Sunrise.

11:00 P.M.
"Dear little one, today I have called you here to be at one with yourself and one with Jesus in you. The Lord and Savior of the world has risen from His grave today so that all of His children can seek and attain Eternal Life in Heaven. Your heart, My child, has been under render lately. Many have been your trials and disappointments, and many more will there be. You must tell My other children, little lamb, of the rising of the sun and of My Son that you have witnessed on this day. I give you your rendered heart for you to share with My other children, especially with the special one whom you need to achieve My task for you. Please remember that blessings are given to those who choose to accept and do the Will of God. There are many lost children in the world. Tell them, little one, that there is a bounty rich in joy and happiness in the offing by deciding to tender their hearts and souls to Jesus Christ! Tell them now, My lamb! Tell them that to be saved is to be at one, like you have become. Give them your new heart to feel and share. Show them how

to love by showing them Love. All of My children can be loved by loving, can be trusted by showing trust, can be healed by healing, and can be blessed by giving blessings to others.

Tell them, little child, that Light can be brought by being a lamp, peace can come to those who live in peace, and Salvation will come to those willing to share in the News of My Son's victory over death! Let all of My children know that Jesus can be received in His Eucharist. His Body and Blood are His constant memory of His Life, Death, and Life. Little child, you must reflect Love as you see reflection of light off the shores. A shining star can be a beacon to many who will follow that lead to others. Please help My children fill the Earth with the twinkles of faith for Jesus in the way that the heavens twinkle in the reflection of the sun. Darkness can always be made to be greater light with an intensity of reflections for the Love of Jesus Christ. Your Heavenly Mother is veiled in happiness today because Jesus has conquered mortality to help you conquer mortality. Please tell My other children to pray and seek conversion, to remain as one body in prayer, to live and remember My messages, and to always keep hope during darkness and despair because of the Love given by your newly risen Savior, Jesus Christ. Become one, children, by praying as one and living the Love of God as one!

Oh, little lamb, go home and tell your brothers and sisters that the world needs God more now than ever before! Many eyes are closed to the needs of the children of the world. Pray and work together, and feel passion for humanity as Jesus showed passion for humanity, through an unending Love for it. Let My children know that there can never be an emptiness to Love or an answer of no. Love is only *yes* to all which is good and right in the eyes of God. Children, touch the lives of others every day through prayer and the good use of your resources given to you by God. Your blessings and graces will be many. Jesus is risen, children, and alive! He is with you every day to help you live your lives, carry your crosses, and know that through Him you will be awarded the Kingdom of Heaven. I pray for you so that you will remain strong, healthy, happy, and full of Life and Love. On this special day of new beginnings for all My children, I share the hope of My Son that each heart will be open to allow Him to enter. Thank you for living your faith in Jesus and for keeping hope in your hearts through that faith. With the Love of Jesus, I bless each one of you in the name of the Father, the Son, and the Holy Spirit. Thank you for having responded to My call."

APRIL 1991

Monday, April 1, 1991

Today, my brother responded in haste to Our Lady's request, **"Tell them now, My lamb,"** but, the merciless ridicule that he suffered saddened him terribly. As a result, he did not wholeheartedly desire for Her to come this evening to pray with us. She came anyway, despite his warranted despondence. Upon the appointed time, he declined to record Her message. So, She instructed him to give me the pen and asked me to write it, instead. Astounded by what was happening, I took the pen as I was requested and sat quietly for a moment, not knowing quite what to write. Since I did not hear Her say anything, I thought I would inscribe a message to Her. I began composing a letter, telling the Holy Mother how much I love Jesus and that I wish to continue helping Her. After I finished, I gave the pen back to my brother. Our Lady responded lovingly, **"Now is, and shall be, in Our Hearts."** The Virgin Mother instructed my brother to lay down as if he were a child being put to bed. He told me that She was displeased with him. He said, *"She thinks I'm being a brat."* The term "brat" was his own self-description, since he knew that he was being disobedient. He surrendered after She informed him that the messages were going to continue for the sake of unconverted souls throughout the world. It was an incredible display of mothering that I witnessed. The persecution that Timothy endured was very hard for him to accept. It reminded me of Jonah's refusing God and trying to run from His Divine Will. It was almost humorous to watch this scene unfold. My brother did not stand a chance against the wishes of the Mother of God.

I continued to pray the Holy Rosary during this entire discourse. After several minutes of sleep, Timothy awoke and stated immediately that he could feel the incredible Love of Our Lady within him again. Her Divinity was radiating physically from his hands and chest. In a spirit of great renewal and conviction, he recorded the Virgin Mary's words as if they meant more to him than life, itself. The fervor and happiness which consumed him was a striking contradiction to the reluctance that I had witnessed just moments before. It made me wonder what She had promised him to cause him to behave like a child anticipating a chocolate bar after finishing his homework. Upon competing Her message, he fell asleep for a moment. When he awoke, he could not remember anything that had occurred during the time of Her miraculous presence. His memory of being united with Her grace was expunged. He did not even know that She had come until I told him what She had said.

Tuesday, April 2, 1991

Timothy returned to my home today, eager to continue praying with me as Our Lady has asked. When we began to recite the Holy Rosary, She miraculously came again. Timothy was so overwhelmingly excited that She had to tell him to inscribe Her pictures more slowly. Several times during Her visit, She quieted him with Her peaceful grace. The Love that he felt emanating from his body last evening continued as the Holy Mother spoke to me this evening. She requested him to lay hands upon me and pray as a gift of Her Immaculate Heart. He was instructed to pray over my heart, my hands, and my head. Finally, Our Lady asked him to pray over my eyes, ears, mouth, and feet. As this unfolded, I was reminded of the solemn rites for those who enter the Catholic Church. Upon completing this "ceremony," we continued the meditations of the Holy Rosary to which Our Lady responded, **"Come to Me through My chosen ones who speak in Truth."** I asked Her who the chosen ones are. She responded, **"Those who are receiving My messages!"** She helped me understand this point even further. The messages are a gift to the world where the Truth has been nearly extinguished. Through Her intercessory Wisdom, She is shining a great Light upon the path to Jesus and the deepest beauties of His Original Church.

The Holy Mother told me that my brother would continue to feel Her grace radiating from his hands once he regained his own consciousness. But, She said that he would not be allowed to remember the effects of Her intercession. We concluded the Mysteries of the Rosary and I sat quietly to see whether he would remark about his hands. Within a few minutes, he began rubbing his palms together while noticing the burning sensation. So, as to appear unsure, I asked him what was the matter. He responded that his hands had a fiery tingling in them, but he had no idea why. I then told him what Our Lady had said. He was surprised because he did not remember any part of Her visit, exactly as She told me would happen! He has no recollection of the mystical conversations that the Queen of Heaven and I conduct.

Wednesday, April 3, 1991

This is my sister's birthday, so we did not attend the Rosary group in Pana as we would normally have done. I spent a very pleasant day at a reception that was given in her honor. Several members of my family and I recited the Holy Rosary in the mid-afternoon hours and Our Lady came to us with a very profound peace. My brother mentioned that there was a difference to the intensity of Her presence today. Her intercession is more readily apparent and powerful in the most placid of settings. This was one of those days. Our Lady referred to Father Jozo of Medjugorje in a quite affectionate tone. He was the parish priest of St. James church during the opening days of Her great apparitions in Yugoslavia. While persecuted terribly by the communist regime when the miracles began, he remained trusting in belief and steadfast in faith. The Virgin Mother praised him during our prayers today and asked us to be of equal conviction. He is, indeed, an iconic example of great holiness and piety. We were also asked to pray for their Bishop Zanic, of Croatia.

Thursday, April 4, 1991

Our regular Thursday Rosary group met this evening at my home. After a peaceful time of prayer, I shared with everyone what Our Lady has being saying. I detected a great amount of uneasiness amongst the members who were present. This caused my heart to be sorrowful because I did not know how to explain it in any other terms that they would readily accept. How else can someone describe what I have penned on these previous pages? I could sense the dissension that was growing, while feeling helpless to do anything about it. Those who refused to accept our witness were fomenting disunity amidst our ranks, while accusing us of destroying the peace that we have so long enjoyed. After everyone had departed, I began to pray again, hoping that Our Lady would tell me what more I could do. I shared the same feelings that my brother had felt several days ago when he did not wish to participate in any more of Her messages. As I laid my heart before Her, She imploringly said, **"Please, speak for Me! I love you!"** She told me that we were doing well and wished us to remain united in Jesus for the conversion of the world. She again offered Her gift of peace through the prayers of my brother's bestowing of hands.

Friday, April 5, 1991

We began to pray very late in the evening today, and the Virgin Mother descended from Heaven to pray with us in swiftness and intensity. She told me that the world is receiving a great gift through my brother's hands. At that very moment, Her presence was magnified as Timothy began softly repeating, *"Prepare these eyes! Prepare these eyes!"* while placing his palms over my eyes and praying. I asked him what he was doing, and he responded, *"She is going to come to you, if you are patient!"* This left me speechless, although I recalled the picture he drew of my home and pointing to my bedroom window while saying, "will come." I shall continue to pray as Our Blessed Lady has asked, as I also repeat the words, "Speak Lord, your servant is listening."

Saturday, April 6, 1991

We again joined the Pana Rosary group for their final recitation of the Holy Rosary in observance of a Divine Mercy Novena which they have been offering for the past eight days. As we prayed, Our Lady reminded me of Her impending appearance tomorrow to fulfill what She has foretold for Sundays, Holy days, and Feast days. She reminded me that Her appearance is not meant to interrupt the peaceful sequence of the day. We must be prudent and prayerful, while enjoying the fellowship of the potluck that we are planning to share after our First-Sunday Mass at Saint Martin de Porres parish in Peoria. I listened carefully to Her every word and promised that my brother and I would faithfully comply. Finally, She said that the Pana locutionist would also feel Her sensational presence in her hands, just as my brother has felt.

Sunday, April 7, 1991   Feast of Divine Mercy

We traveled to Peoria, Illinois today for a three-hour celebration of prayer, Adoration, and Holy Mass in union with God through Jesus and His Mother. We offered the Mysteries of the Rosary while we drove there, preparing for this special occasion of Our Lady's appearance. The service at the church began with the meditation of the first ten decades of the Rosary. As we knelt to pray, my brother could feel Our Lady's miraculous presence enveloping the entire area. He described it as being like a beautiful shroud consuming the building, itself, along with the surrounding countryside. Upon beginning the first of the Joyful Mysteries, Timothy's body became as motionless as a statue. A beatific ecstasy had overcome him as Our Lady appeared in the sanctuary. This is the first time I have ever seen him in this stoic-like state. His eyes followed Her every movement as She traversed toward the Altar and stood before the Tabernacle, at which point his gaze became fixated upon Her as though he was staring laser-beams across the room. He neither blinked nor moved his eyes for nearly a quarter-of-an-hour. He finally turned his head as if to look at something that had been pointed-out to him. I asked him at this juncture if Our Lady was present. He silently shook his head affirmatively, then became immediately focused upon Her again.

The Mother of God conversed with him for over twenty minutes. An elderly woman who was sitting directly behind us commented after Mass that she detected a very strong scent of roses while Our Blessed Mother was there, even though we never told her about the apparition. She did not know that my brother was, at that moment, speaking with the Queen of Paradise. The "smelling of roses" is a miraculous gift that is prevalent during many of Our Lady's apparitions throughout the world. After Holy Mass, Timothy explained to me everything that had happened in detail. He told me that the Holy Mother and he were conversing for an extended period of time. Interesting as it may seem, at no instant did I see him move his lips as if he were speaking to anyone. He was pointedly statuesque from my point of view, while he maintained his complete and normal inner ability to move and speak as he would at any other time when responding to Our Lady. No one else in the church knew that She was visibly perceptible. After listening to his description of these events, it was apparent to me that he had participated in a totally different frame of existence while speaking with Her. She spoke with him personally and at considerable length while standing on a cloud, then gave him a message to deliver to everyone else. He was assured that he would be able to repeat it word-for-word so that he could write it down on a pad. Our Lady concluded with the promise, **"Satan cannot touch you."** She reminded him that She would return tomorrow to observe the celebration of the Annunciation, a High Feast day in the Church.

When we joined everyone for the potluck supper after Mass, the Pana locutionist mentioned that an uncomfortable burning sensation was emanating from her hands! She did not know what was causing it. This is exactly what Our Lady told me would happen! I have been with my brother throughout our entire experience, and I know that he has not discussed this particular part of our personal revelations with anyone else. Timothy and I had told no one about this miracle. We were the only two people who knew! This woman did not realize that our Blessed Mother had previously told me that she would feel this grace-filled manifestation. In obedience to the Holy Virgin, I did not volunteer any information about it. When we arrived back home in the evening, my brother and I prayed so that he could transcribe the words that the Virgin Mother spoke this afternoon. He wished to record it carefully since he would only be able to repeat it once. I began to pray while he transcribed the message. The instant his pen touched the page, Our Lady's words flowed rapidly onto the sheet, faster than any human could even think. When he tilted the pen to reposition his hand, the words continued to flow. There were two individual portions of the message. The first section contained some personal instructions and guidance for my brother and me, followed by a pause and a second text that is meant for the entire world.

"Dear children, the Mercy of My Son, Jesus, is the greatest power that you should seek for the consolation of peace, reconciliation, and the great source of power in the Plan of Eternal Salvation. The Mercy of Jesus is a Divine Mercy because it is of God and from God, given to those who are penitent and have the will to convert. My special children, your Heavenly Mother wishes that you would arrange your lives so that you can be made comfortable in your requests for the Mercy of My Son. The Mercy for which you seek is given to you because Jesus loves you, and He wishes that you love Him and each other while remembering the Passion which He suffered out of His Love for you. Bringing yourselves to the Adoration of Jesus and humbly asking for His pardon provides the graces through which you will be granted Mercy. All of the graces which you have received and will receive are from the Glorious and Divine Mercy of Jesus, who suffered and died for you on the Cross.

My special children, it is the Plan of Jesus that you will accept Him so that your mortal lives can be made full of harmony, peace, and happiness, and that you will live your lives in the knowledge that the

fulfillment of the Promise of Jesus is real and forever. The faith that you show, children, is the faith upon which your Eternity in Heaven is founded. You are only seeing your human side of Eternity, and it is God's Plan that you be holy and happy with it. Life is a gift from God. Each of My children has been given a life to be lived for happiness out of love for Jesus and with the knowledge that His Mercy is all-powerful. You can depend on Jesus' Mercy to rid you of guilt, sorrow, grief, and sadness. It is a redeeming and forgiving Mercy. My special children, the prayers which you raise today are heard. Your petitions and requests are given special and individual attention by My Son and by Me. I bid you all to remember the peace that is brought to your lives through the Passion of Jesus, His Love for each of you, and the peace that He brings to your lives. I pray for you, little ones, that you will always be in My prayers. I love each of you as My special children. My Motherly Love is very strong and open. My Heart will receive all of My children who come to receive it. Please remember, children, during this time, Easter time, that Jesus' Passion and Mercy are your keys to happiness. Remember always that each prayer is received from each individual sincere heart and given holy promise and answer. Thank you for being My obedient children! Thank you for loving My Son, your Savior! I bless you in His Name every day! Thank you for having responded to My call."

After recording these words, we offered the Holy Rosary in thanksgiving for all the blessings that we have received through the endless Mercy of God. Once we started to pray, Our Lady came to us again. My brother began committing everything that She was saying to a written page. He took my hand and placed it atop his own as if we were both writing at once. Our Lady asked us to remain united for Her through this signature of unity. She promised that She would remain beside Jesus in our hearts, while asking us to fortify our patience through endless prayer. She then blessed us in a special way to maintain our sense of tranquility. Several times in the past week, She has instructed us to be patient in the strictest of terms. Much of the first half of Her message today was related to how deeply She desires that to occur. I promised Her that we would obey.

Monday April 8, 1991   Feast of the Annunciation
We traveled to pray at the hospital Grotto with the Pana Rosary group this afternoon and I was filled with anticipation of Our Lady appearance. As we neared the Grotto, the "miracle of the sun" was seen by many others who were present. Timothy could feel the Divinity of Our Lady descending upon us with the same intensity as Her apparition at St. Martin de Porres church yesterday. We all began to pray the Holy Rosary and the Chaplet of The Divine Mercy and

our Blessed Mother visually appeared to my brother, just as She had promised. He was completely overcome by Her beauty, although he did not become like a statue as before. He showed a great deal of emotion, but was still peaceful and quiet. As She miraculously came into view, he did not know whether to approach Her or remain kneeling with the crowd. I encouraged him to remain on his knees. A pillow was placed before the statue of Our Lady so that everyone could kneel there as they renewed their prayerful consecrations on this beautiful Annunciation Feast. Each person approached the center of the Shrine and offered their personal petitions and promises of obedience. The Virgin Mother gazed with great affection upon everyone who came and knelt at Her feet. She was quite pleased with the faithfulness that Her children extended to Her. Along with the others, my brother and I went before Her and assured Her of our love. It was overwhelming for him because he could actually see that he was kneeling just below Her Mantle, while the rest of us did so in faith. After our individual consecrations, we returned to where we had been kneeling and continued to pray.

On previous occasions, Our Lady would depart after we completed the Rosary. This time, however, She remained with us and we did not know what to do. So, we gathered in a circle around Her, held hands, and offered a litany of praises for Her Immaculate grace. My brother described Our Blessed Mother's appearance as She stood in our midst. It was a beautiful moment to behold! Our Virgin Mother was radiantly happy as glowing words appeared above Her head: **"I said yes so you can say yes!"** She finally blessed us, waved Her hand goodbye, and faded away. This is the message She gave. **"My beautiful children, I have come in peace to where there is peace. Your Heavenly Mother has been attracted to the Light of your prayers on this night of Our Lord in the same way as your eyes are drawn to the stars above you. Children, it is today that we celebrate the Lord in His power to come to mankind as I have come to you. All over the world today, My special ones, followers of Jesus and His Word are remembering the beauty of Love between God and humankind, which is as beautiful as your hearts in the peace of this night. The Love that is being shared in prayer around My feet is reflected and sent to those in the world who need it to be close to My Son. As you kneel at My feet, little ones, I give each of you a special blessing in the Glory and honor of His Name. I ask that each of you pray today especially for the sanctity and beauty of human Life. It is a great gift from God, which is being destroyed and perverted all over the world!**

My children, everyday that your prayers are lifted helps to provide peace to other hearts and lives. The time which you spend in prayer is the most valuable use of it and the greatest effort of your energy. That is what makes this night so beautiful, children! It is beautiful because

you are in it and you are praying in it! Your Mother is asking that you continue to pray that all of My children will say 'yes' to Jesus. I said 'yes' so you can say yes! I have asked some of My children to help lead you in walking in the beauty of My Son's Creation. You are surrounded by a freshly unfolding spring. Enjoy the beauty of nature as it is a gift for you and God's prayer for you as you pray to Him. Children, I ask that you remember the Passion of Jesus as this new season blooms. Remember your brothers and sisters and all of their suffering, and help them to be brought to prayer as you have been brought to prayer. I am with you today and always to give you My Love and the Love of Jesus. With all of the power of that Love, I bless each one of you, that you will know the fullness of peace. Thank you for being My obedient children and gathering in prayer with Me today. Thank you for having responded to My call."

Tuesday, April 9, 1991

I have been very interested to know why our Holy Mother places my brother's consciousness to sleep while receiving Her messages. Today, She gave him this reason when he asked, **"I put you to rest so that you do not inject your will."** This helped me better understand the pure state that I have witnessed in him over the period of the last month. My brother acts like a tiny child when Our Lady's presence consumes him, and he knows only what She tells him. His own will is truly in a state of involuntary abeyance. Later in the evening, we began the Holy Rosary and Our Lady descended to us almost immediately. Many supernatural visions began to unfold as they had on previous nights, but he did not see the Virgin Mary interiorly. This phenomenon was suspended when She physically appeared in the skies on Palm Sunday. Timothy's will is now asleep, but he is still capable of communicating everything that he is seeing and experiencing. Our Lady began by instructing him to lay hands upon me again for the transference of Her peace. She asked me if I wished to be blessed more abundantly, and I told Her that I would gladly accept any new graces that She desires to bestow.

It was very late in the evening before we completed our meditations of the Sacred Mysteries and my brother and I were both yawning. Our Lady said abruptly, **"Bless you and goodnight! Hail, Holy Queen!"** I knew that She wanted us to go to bed, but we had only completed the Sorrowful Mysteries. I felt bad and wanted to finish the Glorious Mysteries, as we do every night. But, I also knew that I should obey Her. I asked if we could continue, while reminding Her of Her own words about *"finding rest in prayer."* She responded, **"In My arms you rest, in My Son's Heart you live."** At that, She allowed us to proceed. Her conversation centered upon the thanksgiving that She wished us to offer for the Divine Grace of Her intercession. We are asked to remain strong and unyielding in faith as a witness to Our Lord's Mercy upon His children. Our faith will remain strong only as we allow His Will to be done. We were reminded again tonight to exhibit great patience and perseverance in our work for God. Before departing, the Holy Mother said that She remained with us tonight because we are so eager to pray for the suffering world.

Wednesday, April 10, 1991

Timothy was noticeably shaken when he came to see me today. His employment has been placed into jeopardy because of his witness for Our Lady. He is wagering the forfeiture of the incumbency of the office he has held for 14 years if he chooses to continue. Undaunted, he distributed the Virgin Mary's messages at a public board meeting this evening. Later, as we began the Rosary, our Blessed Mother commended him for his apostolic zeal. **"Souls have been touched tonight by you, who have helped tell them. Thank you for having responded to My call!"** She continued with words of comfort about an impending meeting at his place of employment which is to be held tomorrow night. She said, **"During times of suffering are when you will be closest to My Son. Tomorrow, you will be united to My Son by grief. He carried your grief and sorrows."** She prompted us again to attend Holy Mass every day to receive Jesus in the Eucharist. When She said this, Timothy touched his hands because he continued to feel the burning sensation emanating from his palms. He told me that they felt very strange. Our Lady responded, **"They do because I am coming from them."**

Thursday, April 11, 1991

Our Rosary group met this evening at my home. Timothy was not present because of his scheduled meeting. After our prayers together, I spoke with everyone who cared enough to listen about the miracles of Our Lady. There was a great deal of reservation and doubt about our experiences. I answered everyone's questions with the most concise and peaceful responses that I could muster. It is very difficult for me to understand why there is so much fear to believe that God is working in our midst. He has the authority to manifest His grace in any way He chooses. Human arrogance encourages us to believe that we have the power to decide what He will do. However, I also realize the need for our prudent discernment. There has been nothing that contradicts the teachings of the Holy Catholic Church in our own private experiences. I feel the Holy Paraclete testing our faith, and this is a spiritual examination that I fully intend to pass. I will listen to any voice who elevates the Trinity of God, hails His omnipotence over humankind, glorifies Jesus in the Most Holy Eucharist, and calls the world to prayer and fasting. The fact remains that Our Holy Mother is leading us to Jesus in a way that is confounding almost everyone on Earth. She wishes to evoke faith from those who have been lax in exercising it. This is evolving to be a very difficult task.

We can be sure that God will measure the integrity of our faith, as we are presently seeing at home. He asks us to demonstrate our own trust in Him as our nurturing Father in Heaven. Human faith resides in believing without having previously seen. Our technological culture has deadened our faith to a point where we require undeniable confirmation before we will believe anything of God. There are no doubts in my mind of the intercession of the Blessed Virgin Mary to my brother and me. That grace gives me confidence because I know that She will never lead us astray. I feel like I am swimming in an overwhelming peace that no outside force can destroy. I will not deny the Truth to assuage anyone else's feelings.

Friday, April 12, 1991
We knelt to pray early in the day and Our Lady dictated a very beautiful petition for us to recite. I have recorded it here so that you can lift it, too.

"O loving Jesus of one accord, whose Love sends Life to all. Please enter into the hearts of all mankind. Teach prayer and compassion so Your great Mercy will be bestowed upon all of Your children. It is only by loving as You love that we can be saved. Your radiance shines to the faithful to bring Light to dark. Oh, Mighty Savior, bless your children, who have put our hope in You! Amen."

Later in the evening, I was very anxious for Our Lady to visit us again. I am filled with great joy while participating in this miraculous response of God to our prayers. We knelt to raise our supplications, and sure-enough, She came again. Her communication to me was not in a normal human fashion, but in a very symbolic one. I felt like a kindergarten student sitting in a collegiate-level Advanced Theoretical Physics class. I could not grasp what She told me, nor do I know enough about it to record it in my Diary. It bothered me that Her intercession took-on this form. It was so very different from the words She had spoken before. We finished our prayers and retired for the night. In the wee-hours of the morning, my brother walked into my bedroom while bearing the presence of Our Lady. I knew immediately that She was with him. He said, *"She talked to us this way during the Rosary so we would be patient, and She will talk to us normally when we see Her again."* When we awoke to greet the day, he again could not remember any of these events, just as he does not recall any of the previous conversations between the Virgin Mother and myself.

Saturday, April 13, 1991

This morning was marked by a very special occurrence. I awoke early and was lying on the sofa with my eyes closed. There was a gentle rain falling outside and I was debating whether to begin the day in earnest or relax-at-ease until at least the chime of noon. The events of the past two months were fleeting through my mind as I reminisced about the great graces that we have been receiving. Suddenly, an overwhelming presence engulfed my soul. It was a peace that was so intense that it almost sent my spirit into ecstasy. The emotion it generated in me created an unbearable ache in my heart that could only be relieved by embracing it. I felt like I would have died if I had rejected it. I wondered whether I was dreaming as I became weightless and began floating toward the ceiling. Even as I felt this elevation, I knew that I had never physically left the couch. I was airborne beyond myself! After several more moments had passed, thoughts of apprehension entered my mind and the entire experience immediately subsided. I sat-up in astonishment, wondering whether I had slipped into a dream or if our Blessed Mother had caused this to happen. I walked into my brother's room and asked him to petition Her to come. I believed that She would answer my call, as She has so often in the past. Our Lady did, indeed, answer by telling me that what I experienced was not a dream, but a gift of Her living peace. I cannot begin to describe the sensation. The weight of the world was completely destroyed. I felt like a beautiful helium balloon that had been cut loose from its moorings into the spaciousness of the autumn skies. I realized that egoism and selfishness could never exist where such freedom resides. They are soundly defeated beneath the feet of this irrevocable peace.

Sunday, April 14, 1991

When our Rosary group met at my home at 5:30 p.m. today, we began to pray and Our Lady came to grace us with Her presence. She asked us to recite the Memorare while blessing ourselves with Holy Water.

Memorare

Remember O most gracious Virgin Mary, that never was it known that anyone who fled to Thy protection, implored Thy help, or sought Thy intercession was left unaided. Inspired with this confidence, I fly unto Thee, O Virgin of virgins, my Mother. To Thee I come, before Thee I stand, sinful and sorrowful. O Mother of the Word Incarnate, despise not my petitions, but in Thy Mercy hear and answer me. Amen.

After we completed our petitions, Timothy entered the solemnity of a heavenly peace and recorded the following words from our Blessed Mother. **"My dear children, thank you for coming inside this blessed home with Me to praise the honor and Glory of My Son. You are all My beautiful** children! Your faith has traveled this distance of ages as well as the distance of miles on this day. My little children, your Mother is calling you to remember the Passion of My Son, Jesus, in your daily prayers. It is His Passion, My children, that you will know gives you the grace of forgiveness and Mercy. Please pray on this day for many of My children who are weak in faith. My scent has been delivered to many children tonight to allow them to share the grace of My presence. The prayers that you offer in the Name of Jesus touches My Heart, which is so full of Love for all of My special children. I ask, little ones, that you pray My Memorare with your hearts so that you will remember that I am always here for you in your time of need. I pray for you when you are of weaker faith, when you are ill, when sadness and grief are abundant in your lives, and when your hearts are heavy from the burdens of your days.

My special little children, you must remember that My Son, Jesus, is your rest and safety during your daily lives of labor. His Love is your support and strength to bring you peace and strength. Soon the world will celebrate His return to Our Father where He is awaiting the conversion of all of His children. (We are about to celebrate the Feast of the Ascension.) Be mindful, My little ones, of the miracle which God has bestowed on all those who believe in His Son. You are promised an Eternity of happiness and Salvation from pain. Your Mother is allowing each of My special children to receive more graces as time passes. These graces are bestowed for the Glory of My Son and for the good of the faith of the world. Please remember, My children, that these graces are also given to all those who will receive them so that the faith of those beside can know and feel the warmth and Love of Jesus and the Motherly care and Love that flows from My Immaculate Heart to each one of My special children. Many children have been given the grace of My coming to them in a special way, unlike that of many others.

Children, please keep praying! Please keep seeking the conversion of all of God's children in your prayers. Remember those who are in sin and far from the Love of Jesus and unwilling to accept the mighty God's Plan for Salvation in Eternity. My special ones, I have come to help lead you to My Son because each one of you is so special to Me. I love you in a strength that you have never seen before in your lives. Please help Me share this Love with My other children through your prayers. My intercession is possible because of so many special prayers. I am the Queen of Peace! I come to this house tonight to give you My peace and My blessing. The warmth of the Love in friendship fills My Heart with joy! Children, you are all so special for praying together for the Glory of My Son. I bid you all to strike your breasts with the water Blessed in the Name of Him as I give each of you My special blessing and promise that

I will always love you and pray for you, that your petitions will be delivered into the hands of Glory!

My little lambs, many prayers are being answered tonight. I feel the sincerity of the prayers as they are raised from your hearts. Please remember that it is through this sincerity that the world is changed and made better, that the poor are fed and the naked are clothed, those filled with sin are made holy, those whose souls reside in Purgatory are released to the eternal happiness of Heaven, and your faith is strengthened to give your hope for Eternal Life a firm foundation. Thank you, children, for your sincerity and love for Jesus. His Love is majestic, mighty, and magnificent, and through His Love you are made truly worthy to receive Him. Please, children, render yourselves worthy at all times to receive Jesus. Remain penitent, pure of heart, and sincere, and Jesus will make you again whole and worthy of the Kingdom of Heaven. Children, Heaven is the beautiful place that you have been promised because of the Love of God. It is yours for the asking and receiving when you accept Jesus as your One Almighty Savior and Redeemer. The only cost for the Love of Jesus is an open heart! Open your hearts, children, through your prayers. We will pray together, little ones, for the Salvation of your souls and for your happiness in life. Thank you for being My obedient children whom I love so much. Thank you for having responded to My call."

Monday, April 15, 1991

When we continued our prayers on this night, I asked Our Lady to come closer to us than She has ever been before. She responded by placing my brother into a noticeably deeper state of ecstasy as we joined in supplication to God. On many occasions, he is quite animated and reacts directly to my questions. At other times, such as the apparition in St. Martin De Porres church, he becomes statuesque and oblivious to his surroundings. Tonight, he did not speak to me at all or proffer any reply to the details I attempted to discern. He recorded Our Lady's conversations with me while in a very serene state. After we began the Rosary, a close friend of mine arrived and knelt to pray with us. The Holy Mother was very pleased by his presence, telling us that he is very special. He carries many crosses that others do not have to bear because he has battled many terrible bouts with mental distress. Everyone should learn the blessings of sacrifice from him. Our Lady calls him the "Carrier of Christ." In recounting our final point of discussion with Her this evening, I have recently completed my preparation of Her message for delivery to others as She requested on Easter Sunday. Tonight, I asked Her if they were addressed to the proper people whom She wished to receive them. She responded, **"Your deeds are of God."** I will mail them tomorrow.

Tuesday, April 16, 1991

"**You were given Life out of Love, you are given Love to share in life. Your sorrows are your crosses to be borne for grace. Jesus has offered His Life to save yours. Your soul is secure in His hands. Open the hearts of the world to receive Him in Love and yours will be Eternity with Him. You are blessed to see without looking, hear without listening, and feel without touching Him. He is yours in your good faith!**" After offering these words to us, Our Lady spoke at length about the beauty of the Holy Eucharist in the Catholic Church. We are to receive Jesus' Body and Blood with reverence and thanksgiving. She encourages us to continue our prayers and openly accept Her miraculous guidance. She helps my brother and me to embrace our own difficulties and endure the ridicule that is quickly growing from those who once stood beside us in faith.

Wednesday, April 17, 1991

As Our Lady spoke tonight, She said that the world is in turmoil where Jesus is being locked-out. Her Son is openly welcomed only into the hearts of those who suffer. Most who are affluent, self-serving, and bitter will not invite Christ into their lives to guide them. She asked us to pray for the Spirit of Truth to descend upon the lost, while stressing our own need for patience in a very motherly way. I was not exhibiting the poise that She has repeatedly asked of me and was buzzing with this near-flippancy while She spoke. In response, She finished Her message abruptly and unexpectedly departed. I knew immediately why She had gone. I was not obeying Her intentions or respecting the seriousness of Her presence. An overwhelming sorrow overcame my soul, and I prayed fervently to understand the patience She desires. I told Her that I was very sorry as tears welled-up in my eyes. She accepted my sincere confession and returned to thank me for my prayers to do better. She begged me to forego my own will and allow God's Plan to unfold in His time and way. As a sign of such composure, I did not place this message immediately before the Rosary group this evening, but withheld it, instead, for our own prayerful discernment. I will begin to allow Our Lady to lead us forward by waiting for Her instructions, rather than relying upon the judgement of my own impetuous will. I have learned very deeply in my heart the terrible consequences that a lack of patience can generate.

Thursday, April 18, 1991

As our Rosary group met this evening, our Holy Mother gave us this evangelistic charge, "**Each one must tell of this group, so loved by My Son! Bring to Me one hundred people in the next month. I will give each new hundred people special graces, then we must go to where My Son lives, in hundreds to receive His Body. Call all of humanity to meet at the**

Tabernacle to receive Him, hundreds, then thousands! Pray, convert, do penance, be at peace, love Jesus." She also asked us to carry Holy Water on our person at all times. It is a very powerful source of blessing and purification in our witness for Jesus Christ.

Sunday, April 21, 1991

The Blessed Virgin has given me a considerable amount of personal instruction since my last Diary entry. She told me that Her appearance would be very short this evening, but I was not to infer that She is displeased with us in any way. It was simply a change that was required for reasons that She, alone, could know. I was also instructed not to tell my brother about this modification of events. We are witnessing the unfolding of God's Holy Will. Tonight, I met with the members of our Rosary group at five-thirty in the evening. Our Lady appeared and, true to Her premonition, She remained with us only a short period of time. She was wearing what many have called the "Madonna veil." An example is in the painting of the "Madonna of the Street." The moment She departed, my brother moved to a silent corner to record Her words, while the rest of us continued the meditations of the Holy Rosary. I soon understood why Her appearance was so brief when he moved to a different location. Last week, everyone had nearly gone to sleep before hearing Her message. She changed ever so subtly so that there would be ample time to record it and deliver it to those who had come to pray. Upon finishing the Rosary, my brother produced a transcription with these holy utterances from Our Lady.

"My beautiful children, your Heavenly Mother is pleased to see so many faithful ones gathered in the Name of My Son. Children, when you glorify Jesus, you also glorify your sanctity, wholeness, safety, and Eternity. Always remember that My Son is with you because He loves you! It is God's Plan that all of His children be offered the Kingdom of Heaven, and that is why I have come to you today. One more of you will be able to receive Me in the next month as I come to help you spread the Good News of Jesus as a part of God's Plan. My little lambs, I ask that each of you prepare yourselves for the coming of Jesus. He will return to make judgement of every person based on their life of the Commandments of God. Keep yourselves holy and remain penitent and humble and you will be made more worthy to receive My Son. I have come today to offer My blessing to you for living the Word of God and living My messages. You must all pray, fast, do penance, and convert to the Life that Jesus is asking you to lead. You were born to the world out of the Love of God, and you will be born into Heaven out of that same Love when you will to accept Jesus as your only Redeemer.

Open your hearts, children! Let Jesus come into your heart and He will make you fulfilled with His Love and peace. I am with you to help you open your hearts to Jesus. Your daily prayers will help you open your hearts! Pray for God's peace and it will come to you. Each of God's children will know when their heart is filled with Jesus. It is when to love is easy, to share and forgive feel warm, and to have sorrow for sins and awareness of forgiveness are apparent. Your prayers will fill your hearts with Jesus when you pray from your hearts. Children, you are close to Jesus when you cry for His Passion and fear Him through love for His Passion. You are worthy of the Mercy of Jesus when your hearts are filled with Him. The Life of a child whose heart is filled with Jesus is filled with happiness, purity, and peace. It is easy to be charitable when you love Jesus, and you know that to be loved is to love. This is the way to know, understand, and believe the promise of God's Plan for eternal happiness. Please continue to pray, little ones, for My Son to be with you. He will be with you when you let Him in by opening your hearts. Thank you for being My obedient children. Thank you for having responded to My call."

For the sake of clarity, I wish to describe the current nature of Our Lady's interaction with my brother and me. Each of us speaks with Her privately without the other's knowledge of the dialogue. For my part, these conversations deal almost explicitly with my personal growth in faith and the enlightenment of approaching events. The information regarding the duration of Her appearances is one such formal example. The Blessed Virgin Mary sustains my faith in the face of any opposition because She guides me as a Mother. She also speaks concurrently to my brother and me with words we both know and understand, giving us direction about what She desires us to accomplish. Thirdly, She is providing the great messages meant for the entire world that I have recorded here to date. These conversations are factual dialogues with the Immaculate Mother of God. I can ask Her questions and She will answer them both clearly and directly in this very special way. I thank Our Father in Heaven over and again for this miraculous gift. After believing in faith for so many years that life, indeed, processes into Eternity, our Blessed Mother's voice brings a euphoric confirmation to this Truth of the Holy Gospel. She reminded me tonight that human patience is a product of our own compliant volition. Beyond any and all exceptions, we must be willing to accede!

Monday, April 22, 1991

A group of special friends visited us this evening to enjoy a conversation about the miraculous intercession of Our Lady and to pray the Rosary for Her continuing blessing. Several people started to pose hypothetical questions, hazarding their own individual guesses as to the significance and purpose of the Blessed Mother's revelations. A certain strong-willed woman seemed quite distraught when no one would agree with her conclusions, which were founded in a very dark and philosophical perspective of the world. She chose to spend her time dwelling upon the numerous manifestations of evil that we are witnessing every day. Her hopeless lamentations of the deterioration of families and the Church were destroying her own peace and confidence in Jesus' Final Victory. We explained to her that we should trust that Christ has conquered every corner of darkness on the Earth. We must project His peaceful Love into the world like the flash of great lightning. She maintained, however, that we should run from the world in fear because it is evil in every aspect of its constitution. Her obstinate rejection of our confidence in the Holy Spirit nearly brought us to a heated exchange. I suggested that we should pray the Sacred Mysteries and Our Lady would tell us what we need to know.

As we began, the Virgin Mother said, **"You cannot defeat Satan by talking of him! He will win if your voice breathes his name. Do not compare him with My Son. When you allow Satan time in your thoughts, he is given time and room to move. When you are thinking and talking of Jesus, Satan will have no space. You say that some are too blind to see, Satan makes you see so much that you are blind! My children who truly love the Sacrifice of My Son will find no room to complain about their life and the world. There can be no true suffering by humankind if it is not out of Love for each other. No heart that has its fill of Jesus' Love makes room to ask where Satan is. He does not exist in a heart of Love. Spend your time praying for peace! I cannot come while you are asking questions! If you want to ask questions, ask yourself why you are asking questions, instead of praying for peace!"**

Wednesday, April 24, 1991

Tonight, I attended a prayer group without my brother. Many people are beginning to shun him because of our claims about Our Lady's intercession. He thought that it would be better if he offered his prayers from within the confines of his own home, nearly a hundred miles away. As he prayed, Our Lady miraculously transported his soul to the prayer group to beseech God's help beside us. He witnessed everything that happened as though he had attended in person. When I spoke to him by telephone upon returning to my house, he asked me the identity of some of the people to whom he saw me speaking while I was there. In fact, these persons had never been to the prayer group before, and he had no evidence that they even previously existed. He described one of the people that I met with uncanny detail, right-down to the buttons on their clothes. I was amazed when he discussed the evening with me as if he had been there the entire time. It is another astonishing manifestation that Our Lady has dispensed. I have recorded it here as another example of Her miraculous power.

Friday, April 26, 1991   Special Flask of Holy Water
On this quite auspicious night, the Blessed Virgin Mary gave me a very unique gift. I received a special flask of Holy Water directly from Her hands, which She told me God has blessed with His miraculous healing graces. I was instructed to place it in a location of high respect and solemnity until I am called upon to use it when a certain time of urgent need arrives. She will tell me in advance when that will be. I was awestruck by what She placed in my palm. My mind panned across the passing generations toward the millions of people who have longed for comfort and healing, hoping that God would respond to their prayers. Resting gently within my grasp was the renewal for which many of them had yearned. I could have been given all the riches in the world and it would not have meant as much to me as this tiny bottle of Water.

Saturday, April 27, 1991
There was a full moon this evening, so my brother and I decided to recite the Rosary in a nearby outdoor park. The weather was very mild, one of the first days that hinted at the approaching summer. As we prayed, the Virgin Mary came to us with Her extraordinary Wisdom of holiness. She told me that our Rosary group needed a name. I recently thought that it would be nice if we could refer to it in a more appropriate way. So, I asked Our Lady what She wished for it to be called. She responded, **"You may call your special group in My Name. The Ave Maria Prayer Group makes Me smile."** She continued to speak about many matters pertaining to our piety and elevation. One striking statement She made was that, **"There will never be good judgement by those who consume any substance which dilutes mental discernment and purity."** In another revelation of the unfolding of Her intercession, She told me that She would only appear to my brother on two more occasions in the Sunday, Feast day, and Holy day sequence. I was, again, denied permission to tell him. I asked Her what I should say to everyone else when this sudden change occurs. Our Holy Mother asked me to have faith and to live the unfolding of Her miraculous grace. There are not enough days in mortality for us to question every reflection of the intentions of God.

Immediately following this revelation, Our Lady began to speak about a more serious matter concerning a person who distributed a small pamphlet at our last prayer meeting. It is entitled, "My Ticket to Heaven." When I read it, I felt very uneasy about the way the author was demeaning the virtues of Life in an attempt to make Heaven seem more attractive. It took an intrinsically flawed approach. Although many members of our prayer group received this booklet with mutual enthusiasm, Our Lady did not particularly care for it. She said that it does not show reverence for God's gift of human Life and, therefore, weakens the awareness of its great sanctity. She asks its writer, **"What pregnant mother would bear a child into a world which they, themselves, want to die from as early as possible?"** This author is unintentionally planting the seeds of abortion! I asked Our Lady if I should keep this to myself or whether it is something I should share with everyone. She quickly responded, **"Yes, the whole world should know about the precious human lives which will be lost by the book! Everyone should know that Life is made peaceful by prayer and conversion, and your exile is a creation of God which can be lived, as long as the Will of God permits, in praise of Jesus. No human should place a value judgement on what a happy Life is, like this author has. He seems to have no appreciation for the gift of Life."** After She offered Her thoughts about this booklet, I reread it so as to understand Her vision more clearly. Indeed, the content is very subtle, yet very forceful in its destructive dispensation.

Sunday, April 28, 1991

Early this afternoon, Our Lady instructed me in regards to the members of the Ave Maria prayer group who were to meet at my home later tonight. I was to set aside a particular room of my house so that each person could privately approach Her with their prayerful petitions. She told me that She would extend a special blessing to everyone who desired to comply. This was to take place before we began the Holy Rosary as we offered the Chaplet of The Divine Mercy. So, obeying Our Lady, I extended Her invitation to everyone who came, just moments before we began to pray. I sensed an immediate wave of uneasiness amongst many of the members as I made this unexpected announcement. But, as we began the Chaplet, even those who were apprehensive at first had summoned the humility to partake in Our Lady's invitation, even if only for fear of being left-out. After the Chaplet was completed, we continued reciting the Holy Rosary and our Virgin Mother appeared to my brother in the presence of the entire group. It was a bright and beautiful manifestation of grace! Her appearance lasted approximately five minutes, during which She gave us the following words from Her Immaculate Heart.

"My beautiful and special children, your Heavenly Mother has come again to you to bless you and to deliver your prayers to My Beloved Son. Little ones, you are all so special in the merciful eyes of Jesus. His Love for you is larger than the precious gift of Life, itself, which he has created. Your Mother is asking that each of you remember that your Life is precious, and an act of the Love of God. You were given Life to deliver it to the hands of Jesus, who will help you seek sanctity in it and Salvation for it. The followers of Satan are seeking to destroy Life by

changing and abusing it. Precious ones, Life itself is Love itself, and to live Life is to live Love. My Son is there for you to help you with your crosses and burdens. He destroyed your sin by conquering death on the Cross so that they are forgiven of those who accept and believe in His Love and Word. Children, your days are as that of water flowing over a fall, at a steady pace and at the Will of God. The water is blessed and made holy through your prayers. Each of your streams flows into one great body in Jesus, your Savior. Without prayer, your lives, the water, will leave their path, become stagnant and stale with the dirt of indifference and sin. Prayer helps your lives to remain pure, on the path which God intended, and destined for the bonds of eternal happiness with your brothers and sisters in Heaven.

The bay of happiness and peace awaits those who accept My Son, Jesus, as their only Savior. By His grace and Mercy, you are saved. My little buds, I come to you today and touch each of you with My warmth, words, and blessings in the way that God the Father has intended. I have heard your prayers and intentions with an open and gentle Heart and arms. The answer to your prayers is in your prayers! It is the Will of Jesus to answer sincere prayers from the heart, and to receive each of God's children with His Mercy. By the power of Love, each of your prayers is heard and each of your sins is forgiven. Remember, children, that prayer is the call of Jesus to seek Him. Each of you holds a special place in His Sacred Heart and My Immaculate Heart! By praying every day, you will know the Love of Jesus as it was originally given on the day of His Passion. His Love is just as strong and powerful as it ever was, and He is as alive now in Heaven as ever preparing you a place for Eternity. I am the Queen of Peace who has come to help you reach this beautiful Kingdom. Come to Me, little children, and bring Me your sorrows and prayers. I love you with the strength of the Almighty and wish for each of you to pray for peace in your souls and for love for My Son, Jesus. Thank you for receiving the Love of Jesus in your hearts. Thank you for responding to My call."

After our visitors departed, my brother and I knelt to pray again as we often do, once everyone else has gone. Our Blessed Mother continued Her conversation with me, asking why I had not come privately forward to receive Her special blessing. I had not done so because I was leading the prayer of the Chaplet and did not think it would be appropriate to disrupt anyone else's meditations. She told me that She was visible to my brother during the time each person approached Her to speak. She came in this way as a means of bestowing a great blessing upon this holy night of prayer. I was told that my brother would have no recollection of the events of this evening since he was functioning solely as Her instrument of peace. I continued to be disturbed by the waning faith of many who had come. The seeds of dissension and division are sown in doubt and disbelief. Many are having their faith shaken through graces that they could have never before conceived, but now are being bestowed upon them by the truck-load from God. I pray for an increase in everyone's personal abandonment. Many gifts from Heaven are received abundantly just beyond the grasp of our mortal intellect because they flow in the realms of blind human trust. I know that I do not have the authority to question the intentions of the Mother of Jesus Christ or Her intentions for the people He has come to save. Everyone must remember that those who did not believe tonight were never required to participate. But, they were equally afraid to decline! This is an example of the terrible paradox that is wrought by mortal skepticism.

MAY 1991

Wednesday, May 1, 1991
   "Good morning, My beautiful children! The peace of God is with you and I am with you! My son, if anything should trouble you, come to My arms and I will help you take your cares to Jesus. Your prayers have been received with great Love. Each of My children has My pity and prayers for the gift of the great Mercy of My Son. He is Love, who teaches you love. I bring you peace so you can know Love. Live your days knowing that Jesus loves you and I love you..." We must increase the prayers from our hearts, while remembering that we can never depend upon God too much. In response to His call, I joined another Rosary group this evening. My brother did not accompany me because he was visiting a member of his biological family. Notwithstanding his absence, I shared the Wisdom of Our Lady with everyone who would listen to me and encouraged them to pray with great fervor. The Virgin Mother tells us that Jesus is pleased with our faith and perseverance. She repeatedly asks us to remind one another how special we are to them! I did so today, without reservation.

Thursday, May 2, 1991
   When the Ave Maria prayer group met at my home this evening, one of the members brought a bouquet of flowers to adorn our altar. Our Lady expressed Her appreciation for this gesture of affection by saying, **"Thank you for the beautiful flowers! Your faith has made them alive and fragrant. They are precious and gentle as you. Each flower of your love for My Son will gain a special blessing for nonbelievers, that they will convert and accept the Love and Promise of Jesus."** As we continued the Holy Rosary, She dictated the following prayer and asked us to offer it often to Her Son.

"*O loving Jesus, our hearts are awake to receive Your Love and Promise. Teach and guide us, O Savior, to know the true peace of Your Love by praying to always be open to accept You. As we open ourselves for Your Love, help us also open our hearts to love our brothers and sisters, our neighbors, and those who are cold and wretched. We pray, Blessed Redeemer, that you will keep Your children safe from harm, impurity, and persecution. You are our defense against the forces of evil and darkness. Please receive our hearts and keep them from sleeping in sin, but be kept awake to know Your Love, Your Sacrifice, Your Passion, and Your Mercy. Be with us and in us, O Jesus, and help us to be worthy of the Promise of your Kingdom. Amen.*" The Virgin Mother instructed us to rid our homes of all blasphemous material so that our lives will be protected from the sins of impurity. Satan is propagating lust and perversion all around the globe through the printed media and the entertainment industry. After telling Our Lady that I did not have anything like this, She responded that Her call is meant for people everywhere. We must pray the Rosary for strength against the temptations of the flesh. When we do, there is no room for Satan to wield his diabolical influence.

Many in the prayer group this evening questioned why the Holy Mother's intercession consists of the numerous pictures that Timothy has drawn. Our Lady told me that She has manifested Her presence in pictures so that we will be inspired to envision the grace of the Holy Spirit as He speaks from within our hearts. Contemplating the Love of Jesus is very beneficial for revealing where Satan conceals his darkness and violence. The Blessed Mother says that the greatest portrait of beauty is the Love of Jesus as He is received in open hearts through the Holy Eucharist. Thoughts of God's beautiful nature and presence are very powerful prayers, to which He responds with many miraculous graces and blessings. My brother's drawings encourage us to ponder the sacrity of prayer from the depths of our beings. They unveil scenes of beatific possibility that our souls have yet to conceive, while our hearts nurture these images if we are open to receive God in good faith. Our Lady also reminded us that the great beauty of the Holy Eucharist comes through the hands of Her beloved priests. She asks us to pray especially that they all become great examples of Jesus' holiness and merciful Love. She promises that anyone who turns to Her for Divine assistance will be further elevated in holiness.

After everyone else departed, my brother and I continued to pray. I was especially seeking Our Lady's loving guidance in response to my many concerns. I did not know if I am worthily accomplishing everything that She is asking of me. I desire with all of my heart to be a good witness for Her miraculous grace. She comforted me by saying, **"My child, I am with you! Please trust the Love of your Mother and the mighty Plan of God. You** are pleasing to your Mother! Always remember that the greatest gift is the gift of faith. You have been given that gift in addition to your Mother's direct intercession. You are full of love for My Son, whose Love for you is endless." I felt an incredible exhilaration by Her words and went to my rest this evening in the solitude of peace.

Friday, May 3, 1991

My brother and I knelt to offer our morning prayers at seven o'clock. Our Lady continued in the same grace as yesterday with a greeting of, **"A morning of Love has opened for My little children! I bless you for being obedient! I am in your heart. Touching other hearts with yours is the most powerful means to share My Love..."** Speaking with our Immaculate Queen is an overwhelming gift. I have always known throughout my life in the Roman Catholic Church that She is our Heavenly Mother, whom Jesus gave to us from the Cross. However, the possibility that God would allow Her to speak directly to me has always been infinitely beyond anything I have ever dared to imagine. But now, I realize that the doorway to Heaven is open to receive anyone who wishes to enter. The Virgin Mother of Jesus Christ stands at the eternal Gate of our Salvation, beckoning Her children to come into the paradisial Light. Her presence inundates the depths of my heart with an overwhelming joy, while the world continually tries to submerge it and extinguish this happiness, such as someone would throw a burning torch into the water to put it out. That is why I call upon Our Lady at all times, so that I can be lifted into Her arms. And, as many around me still refuse to believe what I am saying, She strengthens me so that I do not relinquish my obedience to the Truth.

This evening, She asked me again to encourage everyone to receive Jesus in the Holy Eucharist every day, while in a state of purity and grace. **"I have come to bring My Love to My children and guide you to Jesus. All of My children need to become one body for Jesus for strength in Love. My children need to receive Jesus in the Eucharist! Please pray for the conversion of sinners to accept Jesus in the Tabernacle. The Body and Blood of My Son cleanses, renews, and protects the human spirit and prepares the soul for sanctity and Salvation."** She also asked me to anticipate this Sunday by preparing for an extraordinary day of grace with Father Ted at St. Martin de Porres church in Peoria. He is one of Her very esteemed priests. She said, **"My special child, Father Ted will give a message inspired through My touching of his heart. All of My children should take lesson in his example of Jesus' Love. A special place is being prepared for him! You are in the presence of great holiness with him!"** Since the beginning of Our Lady's intercession, many have requested that we submit their questions and petitions to Her as She speaks to us. Tonight, She responded by saying, **"Tell them that I can hear, understand, and respond to their prayers in their every need."**

Sunday, May 5, 1991

My brother and I offered our morning prayers before traveling to Peoria, and the Queen of Paradise greeted me by saying, **"Good morning, My son. A very special day has opened! Thank you for loving Jesus as He loves you. Your greatest vision is your hope for Salvation through My Son."** She told me in advance about many graces that would be unfolding today and asked me to accept them in faith. I promised Her that I would. She dictated a message that She wanted me to deliver to everyone who came to the church. This gave me reason to be very excited when we arrived at the St. Martin de Porres parish because I knew that She was going to appear there. I also had great hope that I would be allowed to deliver Her message. Timothy could feel Her miraculous presence with the same magnitude as our visit last month. I asked one of the resident priests for the opportunity to deliver the message that the Holy Mother had given to me. My soul was so touched upon receiving his permission that I nearly fell to my knees in thanksgiving. It is a rare occasion to see such unconditional trust in our contemporary world. I was profoundly proud of my priestly Father, knowing that he is the joy of Our Lady's Immaculate Heart. After we finished praying the first ten decades of the Rosary, I presented the Holy Mother's words to everyone.

"The day is meant for prayer, children. Jesus is all in you, to be with you. God has made the decision to save the world from the grasp of evil. I am with My Son and waiting to receive you at His house by praying. You help heal wounds that separate yourselves from each other. Break down your divisive partitions through prayer. Today, I call the Western world to pray for your neighbors around the world. Pray for the end of famine, disease, disbelief, mediocrity, hatred, and perversion. Jesus is with you today to help you lift your prayers to the Almighty Father who loves you to no end. As My children pray together, hearts are united in Love for the cause of peace. When you are at peace, you will be closer to sanctity. Please read My messages! Peace is with you because God is with you. A heart full of Love is filled with peace. Your lives began with peace, which the evil forces of the world have diminished. Jesus is the restoration of your peace begotten from within you. My children, you must hold on together for there to be peace. One by one, the evil one will try to divide you. By the material forces of the world, each child is led a separate way.

The many millions of people who gather today in competitive arenas to watch human activities and the millions who follow from their homes by telecommunications are being led away from Jesus during such a desperate time for the world. The conscience of the West is no larger than the West. Go to your churches to receive My Son instead of to the fields and stadiums of human frivolity! The resources of the Earth are

being destroyed. To protect your physical lives, you must protect the Earth which gives you life. To protect your souls to assure Salvation, you must protect yourselves by accepting Jesus. Go to the fountain of Eternal Life and accept the quenching Love of My Son. Sing the praises of Jesus today with your beautiful voices! The Passion of Jesus was suffered out of Love for you and all those yet to come. Pray for His Mercy and you shall receive it! Where ever you walk, the calm and peace of Jesus shall be with you. Accept Him this day. Today, My children shall be given the gift of faith to share and the peace of patience. I bless you now in the name of Jesus Christ, the Lord of all Creation."

Father Ted offered the Holy Sacrifice of the Mass, after which we began our hour-long Adoration of the Most Blessed Sacrament. It was a magnificent celebration of living faith. During the final segment of our service, we held our May Coronation of the Blessed Virgin Mary. This is a beautiful tradition where a statue of Our Lady is crowned in honor of Her Queenship. Several small children approached the beautiful statue which was resting beside the Altar. They placed a wreath of fresh flowers upon Her head after a very inspiring and appropriate procession. We then began the final five decades of the Holy Rosary. Our Lady suddenly appeared, wearing an exact replica of the Crown of flowers that had just been placed upon Her statue. She paid great reverence to Her Son by bowing toward Him in humble adoration as the Living Host in our midst, present in the Holy Eucharist in the monstrance upon the Altar. After this display of affection, She smiled deeply at Father Ted before directing Her gaze upon the rest of us with a glow of Divine admiration.

As we continued to pray together, Father Ted inadvertently began to sing a refrain of the "Ave Maria" out-of-sequence with the Rosary. Upon recognizing his error, he stopped and apologized while everyone else chuckled. He is a holy perfectionist with respect to our prayers. But, ironically, he made this one simple mistake. Timothy said that Our Lady was as amused as the rest of us. We quickly returned to our meditations. After about five minutes, the Virgin Mother ascended above the Altar and transcended a magnificent stained-glass window depicting the Crucifixion of Jesus Christ. We completed our three hours of prayer and set-out for home. Our Lady spoke to me during the journey. She said, **"Prayers are important in thanksgiving for the gifts of this day! The Spirit of Truth has descended upon My children. Receive My message with an open heart. God's Plan is unfolding. My Son's Heart was warmed by your radiance. Thank you for reading My message to your brothers and sisters. It is important for all My children to remember that prayer is Life, and to love to pray is to love Life. Your hands together will bring your hearts together. The result of prayer is healing and peace. No one can enter the merciful hands of Jesus who is without peace. I bring you peace, for I am the Queen of Peace. Please know I love each of you in a special way."**

Later this evening, the Ave Maria prayer group met at my home and Our Lady spoke further about Her desires for our abandonment in prayer. She also made this a special day of revelation by asking me to tell everyone about the lesson of faith that She has been teaching for the past two months. Our belief must be deeply rooted in our trust in God's omnipotent Love and care. It is difficult to grasp the true frailty of our infant spirituality. But, this vision is the great seed that bears the fruit of saintly conviction. I encouraged everyone to open their hearts ever-wider so as to become filled with joy by Our Lady's loving guidance. **"Dear children, your Mother has opened Her arms to receive you again today. Please bring to Me all of your earthly cares and I will cast them away in the Name of My Son, Jesus, and will replace them with peace and happiness. I know, little sheep, that it is easy to get lost by going astray in your earthly world. So many of you are distracted by the teachings of a mortal existence in the nearness of the grasp of indifference and sin. My Son is the Shepherd who will gather each of you in, to lead you to Salvation. His Plan is to encircle you with Love and compassion so that you will not be lost for all Eternity. Dear little ones, there is only one Gate through which you can pass to reach the Kingdom of Heaven. It is the Love of God and is with you for you to accept and become engulfed by.**

Your Heavenly Mother is asking today that you turn away from your earthly temptations and accept the Love of God through His Son, Jesus Christ. Many of My little ones believe that passion is a source of pleasure or ecstasy. Children, the true Passion of the world is composed of sorrow for the sins of all humankind. Jesus' Passion was a suffering out of Love for you, a suffering which He freely acknowledged and accepted. He died out of that same Love for you and asks that you rise with Him in the same way that He claimed Victory over His grave. Please pray that all of your brothers and sisters will come back to the fold of little lambs who have opened their hearts to allow Love to enter. My children, please follow the course set before you in God's Holy Word. Remember His Commandments and know that they help you to be brought to Salvation. Remember especially to love in the Name of Love. Your Mother is with you today and with all of the children of God all over the world to teach and guide, to listen and love, and to pray with you so that you can truly know the peace of My Son's Love and Promise.

Please be obedient to My call to prayer and seek the conversion of yourselves and the world. Run into the arms of Jesus and He will embrace you with His care. I will help you to be received by Jesus because I am your Heavenly Mother and I love you as a fragrant rose loves light and warmth. Thank you for following your Good Shepherd to your land of Salvation. Please receive My Blessing in the Name of the

Father, the Son, and the Holy Spirit. Thank you for having responded to My call." After everyone had gone, my brother and I prayed in thanksgiving for the many supernatural gifts that we received today. Our Lady concluded by saying, **"My special child, through all of My Love for My beautiful children, given to the Earth out of the Love of My Son, I come to bring peace so that human hearts may be open to receive Him."**

Monday, May 6, 1991

Our Holy Mother spoke with me again as we offered our morning prayers. She said, **"Blessed morning My children! Welcome to the world from out of your cradles! Your days have been made brighter through the Light of Christ! Today, My Son would ask that all those who have died in His favor be praised for the example they have left the world. The conversion of sinners depends on your prayers and the example which you set forth for today and after. My son, the world has made it possible for abortion to multiply. Satan rejoices in these actions. The world is set apart from sanctity by this conviction. I pray with you to My Son that He will show these poor sinners His merciful Love. The Good News is that God loves and is merciful. You must rejoice with all My children in the beauty of My Son's forgiveness. There is no greater power than the Love of God! Be happy in the Love of God for you! I am with you to help you know the Way. My special one, there is a warm place in My Heart for all My children who suffer the cold of indifference."**

Tuesday, May 7, 1991

We offered our early prayers at seven o'clock and the Mother of Jesus Christ spoke still more about the Truth that all humanity needs to hear. **"The Word of God holds great promise for all humankind who accept it! Remember to pray for your brothers and sisters who do not believe. There is so much beauty in prayer. Through prayer, a new world is created. Prayer is the power which causes suffering to cease. It is the true medicine for an ailing heart. It is the supply of Love to replenish a weakened soul. Thank you for shining your light! I will continue to feed your light with My Love so that your love for others can be manifested."** Timothy delivered a copy of the messages that we have received so far to the Mayor of our City at ten o'clock this morning. The Mayor is Catholic, so we hoped that he would help us direct the attention of our fellow citizens to the intercession of our Holy Mother. We are not sure what will happen because there has been a considerable elevation of opposition directed toward my brother and me. I am having difficulty understanding their outright rejection of Our Lady's work. Without exercising faith and trust, those around us are becoming increasingly distressed. They refuse to accept that we are telling the truth, and it seems nearly impossible for us to convince them. Fear is setting their minds afire. I am maintaining my peace the best I can, while trying to be patient with our detractors. They have given us only one alternative that will satisfy their anger. They want us to deny the Mother of God. No human on Earth has the power to make us do that.

Wednesday, May 8, 1991

I continue my prayers for the Peace of the Holy Spirit to enter into everyone's heart so that we can honor Christ Jesus in unity as Our Lady desires. It is an authentic miracle to speak with our Immaculate Mother, but it is our prayers that are most important to Her now. If I never experience Her direct intercession again, I have been forever blessed to have experienced the past two months of my life. I thank God over and again for this incredible gift. I will continue to walk forward in the knowledge that my Heavenly Mother is guiding me to Salvation, along with everyone else who wishes to follow. After praying with another Rosary group again tonight, I shared the portions of Our Lady's messages that I have been asked to dispense. Timothy did not accompany me for the same reasons I have previously described. As he prayed at home alone, Our Lady said to him, **"My son, your hope is great as is your faith! Please do not be burdened by those whose faith fluctuates. It is by Jesus that you gain many graces. My message is clear to the world: pray, fast, do penance, convert, live in the peace of the Love of Jesus. A new day is dawning for all of My children. Your prayers have brought new light and new hope. Thank you for doing your part for My Son. Hold on to My hand and I will lead you to the peace and power of Jesus in your heart!"**

Thursday, May 9, 1991

Our regular Thursday meeting of the Ave Maria prayer group took place at my residence tonight and many of our friends asked if Timothy was there. I responded by directing their attention toward our Blessed Mother's promise to pray with us, regardless of who might be in attendance. I reminded them that our priority rests in the supplications that we lift to God and the love we offer to one another. The summons of the Sacred Heart of Christ deserves our undivided attention. Jesus' Mother helps us to know where His intentions reside. Timothy received Our Lady's message through the night and dictated it to me by telephone this afternoon. He also received some auxiliary personal instructions for both of us when She offered Her words for the entire body of humanity. **"Dear children, your Heavenly Mother has come today to bring you My Love and peace and to help you in your struggle against evil. I ask each of you to take My hand and I will deliver you to the arms of Jesus so that you will know His true peace and His gift of the Promise of Salvation. Little ones, each of you must be stronger in your struggle** against the hand of Satan. There is no evil which is not created by him. He invades the very fibre of your precious hearts. You must know children, that all of the coldness, bitterness, and violence in the world are brought through his works.

I have come to you to ask you to pray with Me so that the darkness of the world can be lifted through the Light of My Son. Your Mother is telling you that you can never be at peace until you accept the Love of Jesus. The fate of your hearts and souls rests in His Hands. My Son is Love, which is the worst enemy of evil. When you pray, little ones, you will receive Love and it will always be with you. At times, you are distracted from Love through the blindness and temptation of sin. When you accept Jesus, you will be delivered from sin. Children, you must know that without sin, evil will perish. Through prayer it will be turned to clay and will wash to the bottom of the seas to be consumed in emptiness and nonexistence. Through your love for each other, evil will be destroyed. If you fear that your brothers and sisters do not accept your love or show their willingness to return it, My Son will give it to them for you when you pray to Him. Please remember, My special children, that Satan is a coward who will not come where Love is. You must be strong in your love because evil is aggressive where there is weakness in heart and faith. Temptation will feed on the frail and restless. Your Mother has come to tell you that Jesus will not allow peace to be destroyed. Please pray, children, to accept the defense of the Love of Jesus. I ask that each of you accept Him in your hearts now because time is passing and now is the time to be obedient to My call. Thank you for being My special children. Thank you for having responded to My call."

Saturday, May 11, 1991

I prayed with the children's Rosary group at my home after Holy Mass this evening because tomorrow is Mother's Day and there would be insufficient time to meet with them after the Sunday morning Masses. I plan to visit my family and honor my own mother in the household where I was raised since I have not been able to do so in the more recent past. My dedication to Our Lady's intercession has kept me quite occupied with Her work. I recited all fifteen decades of the Rosary in the evening because I enjoy praying with the Holy Mother of God. I know that She is always with me. She responds to my every word and I can still hear Her tell me that She loves us all.

Sunday, May 12, 1991

"Dear children, I am the Queen of Peace whose Immaculate Heart is filled with Love for you on this special Mother's Day. My beautiful shrines throughout the world which you have strewn with flowers bring warm and soft tears to My eyes of happiness and peace. My Son, Jesus, is touched by your pouring-out of love for His Mother. You are all so very special to us! Please remember, children, that when Jesus died on the Cross, He saw each one of your precious faces as He promised His Love into all Eternity. Little ones, Jesus knew that if He had come down from His Cross, there would have been no hope for you. Please allow Him to be close to you so that He can offer His Promise of Salvation. I ask that you receive Him in your hearts and there will always be reason for hope. Your problems are too great for you to face alone! Your sins are too many and too burdensome! Please remember, children, that all of your sins were laid on Jesus so that you could be set free from them to be made whole and pure. Your sins were His Cross. You are all too helpless without Jesus to guide you! Little ones, you do not lead your lives, but follow them on the path which God the Father has chosen for you. You must pray for the guidance you need to help you through them.

Without prayer, children, your days are as fruitless as if you tried to move the Earth by reaching to grasp a handful of soil. Please spend your lives in prayer to bless the fate of God's humanity which walks upon it. My Son is with you to help you to pray and believe. He will come again into the world through a veil of clouds where each eye will see Him, even those of the blind. Your Mother is moved by your prayers and faith in knowledge that Jesus will save you through His everlasting Love for you. Children, please pray, convert, do penance, and remember that to seek Jesus is what God wants for His people. I will help you find Him because I am your Blessed Mother who comes to guide you to grace when you pray. Thank you for helping My Son save you by accepting Him through your open will. Please accept My blessing in the Name of the Father, the Son, and the Holy Spirit. Thank you for having responded to My call." I accompanied my family to a Sunday evening dinner and our prayer group met at five o'clock this evening. There was a smaller than average attendance because of the observance of Mother's Day. We offered the Queen of Heaven a special litany of praises that was brought by a member who is quite highly devoted to Our Lady of Perpetual Help.

Tuesday, May 14, 1991

My brother and I were together this evening and I was very excited because I knew that Our Lady would speak to me again. As She did so, I was told that the individual whom She has chosen to bless with Her miraculous presence was not allowing Her entrance into their life because of their refusal to invoke living faith. She prophesied on the twenty-first day of April that someone else would be able to receive Her intercession if they opened their heart. But, as of this date, She has called upon them four times without success. She instructed me to encourage the group to pray for obedient trust, but not tell them why She has yet to manifest Her foretold grace. I petitioned fervently for this new messenger to make room for the Holy Spirit. Even though the Blessed Virgin did not tell me who it was, my spirit was crushed by the thought that a soul would deny such a miraculous gift. It was very difficult for me to refrain from telling everyone why I was asking them to pray so urgently for strong faith, considering the vantage-point from which I was gazing at them! The most beautiful Joy of Love was at the doorstep, but could not enter because one of Her chosen children in our midst would not open the door!

Wednesday, May 15, 1991

I intended to continue my compilations of Our Lady's intercessions tonight since She had told me that there were several issues that I had not addressed sufficiently. She wishes there to be no room for ambiguous interpretations by those who cannot conquer the temptation to critique the work of the Mother of Jesus Christ. Tonight, however, She asked me if I would continue to receive Her further instruction, leaving the previous explications until later. She promised to help me when I take them up at another time. Upon being given the decision, I eagerly accepted the invitation to hear Her beautiful voice once again. She was very happy with what I had chosen because it was truly the desire of Her Son. She began, **"My special child, I love you so! I am with you tonight so you can continue to help Me with the Plan of My Son and because I love you. I will be giving you some thoughts on conversion so that My children can be saved. Your future is so happy because My Son loves you. Your days are bright because you also love Him! Thank you. I am going to tell you why I have used a language foreign to you previously. It is important that you tell My other children..."**

Over the past three months, Our Holy Mother has related many terms to us in a foreign language that we did not fully understand. When I first saw them, I surmised that it was for our assurance that a supernatural event was actually taking place, God knowing that we did not comprehend any other origins of speech. She said, however, that the words have nothing to do with the confirmation of Her intercession. It is a very rare occurrence to receive miraculous proof that would satisfy the skepticism of the faithless among us.

She said, **"I do not need to confirm My presence to those who lack faith. If I did, they would never have or need faith. I have come to strengthen faith! The beauty in faith is that it is of God's children. The Father's children are beautiful by creation, and faith is of His beautiful children. The intent of the foreign language is the same as the gift from God for certain children to pray in tongues."**

A foreign language seems to be the initial barrier which must be overcome for a world of people to vest themselves in peace. By showing us these incomprehensible symbols, Our Lady is teaching us that they are false hurdles to our pious commonality. The way we speak to each other is not an issue to God in the spiritual cohesion between nationalities. The Holy Mother's use of intercontinental phrases in no way separates us from the Love we share while in Her embrace. She offers the same infinite Divinity in every means we could devise to interact with Her. Yet, conversely, there are many who speak the same dialect every day who are neither communicating peacefully nor moving toward the unity that allows the Kingdom of God to flourish on Earth. The only form of true reason between all races and creeds is the Holy Gospel of Jesus Christ. The many different tongues in the world are not impenetrable walls of brick that divide people at all. We are not moving toward peace today because we refuse to imitate the Life of Christ as He commands it in the Bible. Love transcends every conceivable boundary, even the one that resides between ourselves and Paradise. The Holy Spirit is understood by every human heart, indeed, by every living thing!

When we see something that we do not instantly recognize, our curiosity bleeds to discover its significance, immediately sending us on a frantic search for an underlying meaning. We are not adverse to embarking upon great academic studies to be the first to comprehend phenomenon that are presently beyond the grasp of what has already been recorded. This takes much time, attention, and effort which we willingly offer to the cause without so much as a whimper of reservation. Our Lady does not want us to pursue such an inquisitive path of waste anymore. Instead of participating in hours of conjecture about Her motivations, She desires that we use these precious moments to seek-out the reason why there is such a lack of Love in the world. She wants us to be curious about why humanity finds pleasure in outright hatred. In the time it takes to search for the translation of a foreign word, we could have scrutinized our own souls for evidence of the Wisdom of Christ. Language of the same origin can be as great a barrier as a foreign one if those who are involved lack compassion and mercy. Our Lady is challenging us to realize what truly separates races of people. We must expend our energy to unite ourselves through congruous Love. If we do, we will find that there are no impermeable walls between any of God's children. There will never be good intention where Love is unwelcome. Peace is a little dove that alights in the habitat of serenity. He is timid, but will feather any heart with hope that prepares him an abode of solitude.

After speaking to me about communicating with Love, Our Lady told me something that was rather crushing to my heart. Her repeated calls to another member of our prayer group have still gone unheeded. She has tried for the final time to extend Her miraculous messages to this individual. Their lack of faith has caused this unfortunate circumstance to unfold. I was grief-stricken by the thought that Love could be so rejected in our midst. I knew that many others in the group were anxiously awaiting the manifestation of the grace of our Immaculate Mother to another messenger. Knowing this, I asked, *"How am I going to tell them that You could not come to one of them because of their lack of faith?"* She said that my question clearly illuminates the point that has been made. I was instructed to proclaim to them with confidence that obstinance toward the Holy Spirit breeds such consequences as these. Faith is mandatory in a Life of perfect Christianity. The Virgin Mary cannot dispense Her blessings when the children of the world refuse to suspend their haughtiness in order to believe. Jesus could not work miracles in Nazareth because of the same lack of trust and humility. God has not changed to this very day. Our Lady stands prepared to bestow undiminished Divinity and peace upon anyone who unconditionally opens their heart to welcome Her intercession. I ask you to do so with me, witnessing with my life that Her embrace is worth the sacrifice of our cumulative years on Earth.

The gift of supernatural understanding that Paradise is extending to every soul in Creation is infinitely beautiful and priceless. We must strive to achieve a complete and pious submission in loyalty to the Will of the Father because our final rest lies within His Son. It is an audacious sign of human arrogance to require God to prove Himself before the encore doubts of the everyday world. His intentions are a Divine mystery which He has already completely revealed in Jesus. The Anointed Savior of humankind will not stoop to die again! We do not have to know in advance what is going on, nor fully understand it, but rather simply concede, repent, and do our assigned portion. The Virgin Mary is the sinless example of both obedience and Love who asks us to extend our own compliance to the heavens. I, for my part, will obey Her with all the power of my soul. I know without question who is speaking to me from just behind the shadowy veil of our mortal life on Earth. **"There is little inner peace in lack of faith, as those who hold little faith will see at the passing of this incident. It is from God and through your Heavenly Mother so that all of My children will believe! Your Mother knew of this happening. Please trust My power to convert. With My Love comes discipline out of Love. There is always sacrifice required for conversion! My special one, please deliver all of these words to your group."**

Thursday, May 16, 1991

The Ave Maria prayer group met at my home again this evening. I obediently stated the words from our Virgin Mother about the failure of someone else to embrace Her call because of their lack of faith. Interiorly, I sensed an invincible pang of guilt enter the heart of nearly everyone there, each individual knowing that it could have been them. I also recognized the thoughts of self-justification that arose as an entitlement of their defense. Many of them misinterpreted their feelings as a sign that Our Lady's messages were false, believing that She would never do something to cause them to bear such spiritual blame. I responded confidently to all their questions, just like She had asked, knowing that there is little inner peace in a life of disbelief. That is why this has been such a revealing example for the entire world, one in which every person present will someday be ecstatic to have participated. It is most apparent in the passing of this incident that discipline often accompanies the Mother of God. We have forgotten that our Heavenly Mother is one with infinite Love and tenderness, yet demanding of our own obedience to make it come to pass. It is analogous to a little child being reprimanded by his mother, then claiming that she does not love him anymore. Through eyes of honest humility, we can see this occurrence as a great sign of revelation. God states this Truth quite openly in the prophecies of the Scripture. This encounter with heavenly Justice brought deeply into every heart the great importance and ultimate necessity of faith, which Our Lady has come to strengthen without calculating the cost to our feelings of repulsion. Today, She accomplished that task while wielding the highest power from Heaven.

The open opposition to my brother and me has been increasing dramatically. This, too, is in direct accord with what the Bible has to say. Although Our Lady asks me to be confident, I am still intensely bothered by the deep repugnance that others hold toward me. Above all else, however, I will never deny our Blessed Mother or scoff at Her Eternal Wisdom. I can see the spiritual cultivation that She is initiating which is flourishing before my eyes. My own parents taught me clear lessons of good behavior from the time I was old enough to remember. Hence, I am not offended by what Our Lady commands. If She asks me to change my heart, I will. She has, indeed, required me to embark in many new directions toward the conversion of Her children.

Friday, May 17, 1991

Timothy and I prayed together this evening and the Blessed Virgin Mary spoke with me again. **"My child, I am with you to tell you how pleased I am with your obedience to My Son in your group. Throughout the ages, there have been true followers of the Word and works of God in faith and belief. There have been many disciples, those who have stood fast with** the discipline of faith. Faith and discipline have to be together, for without one the other is not as strong. You have shown both to Jesus and to your Heavenly Mother. Your discussion to the people is from your discipline. You are a disciple of My Son. My message was delivered by you with divinity. My child, you are truly filled with the Spirit of Jesus…"** Our discussion was refocused as if Her great lesson of discomfiture was a matter whose time had now passed. She requested that I continue recording as much of Her intercession in my own words as possible in the future. She wishes for me to be more than someone who simply repeats Her substantive intentions word-for-word on writing paper. Her desire is for us to become completely united with the Holy Spirit as a living example of His Love. This holy purpose has always been the thrust of Her Divine intercessory messages. Therefore, I resumed my attentiveness to Her next discussion, recording it all the best I know how for anyone else who wishes to receive the Light She bears.

She continued tonight by stating that the mind-set of the Western hemisphere is to cast away the requirement for seeking a life of piety in Jesus. We require verifiable physical facts before we will believe in anything. We are skeptical of every witness to the spiritual nature of man. The modern world has lost its interior sense of what holiness truly is. Those who are lost in materialism wonder why they should believe in a God that they really have no time to pursue. Jesus spent His earthly days trying to bend these same bland maniacs into accepting that He is the Son of God. It was very difficult to convince those who refused to accept His witness and deeds because they had never conceived that the God of Mount Sinai would take-on human flesh and live among them. Is it not the same faithlessness that causes people to refuse that Jesus miraculously comes to the Catholic Altars as the Bread of Life at the hands of our priests? Each of them waits for proof of this sacred Truth before they will submit themselves to His healing Redemption. Upon what circumspection do they base their defiant disbelief?

Ironically, many people do not accept that our Blessed Mother would tell us how to conduct our lives. Do we believe that we do not need to be called to task for committing our blatant errors? It has been said that those who initially reject the Holy Spirit spend their days denying their own transgressions, which will almost always lead them back to final repentance in Christ. When their faith becomes stronger, reverential fear and hope for His Mercy will replace the desperation caused by their lack of prayer for help. God weighs our inner-integrity so that we will rise to perfection in trust and abandonment. Then, Love becomes the solemn motivation for all of our thoughts and actions. When the Almighty Father in Heaven tests us, His Will always transcends our own. We must remember Jesus' admonition during these times of spiritual decision; **"Whoever seeks to save his life will lose it, but whoever loses his**

life for My sake will gain it." This examination of conscience is supposed to rest beyond our mortal reasoning at any particular moment in time. We should always remember our Holy Mother's affirmation to the Archangel Gabriel. She had made a perpetual vow of virginity to Our Lord, yet in an instant, She completely accepted motherhood without a fiber of consternation. Her question to the Angel was only for the purpose of fulfilling the Will of God, whom She still loves to the depths of immortality. We must proclaim our allegiance to Him in these same prophetic dimensions.

Our Lady has asked me to share the necessity for Divine obedience with everyone who is blessed to know Her work. No single person has the capacity to pass judgement on how She chooses to teach the lessons of Love or what She knows will effect our conversion to Her Son. She is the most loving disciplinarian alive today. God trusted Her to prepare Jesus Christ for the redemptive excruciation of the Cross. Her credentials are beyond any remedial academia or humanitarian experience. But, many-a-soul has created a faulty caricature of Our Lord and His Blessed Mother. Their attitude suggests that God would not subscribe to any lengths which will disclose His intentions upon our lives. Therefore, their belief is shaken when events unfold that require their faithful acceptance. I now realize that there is nothing that God will not do to save us from condemnation. Does not the Cross of Calvary already prove this revelation? I, too, have found my faith tested in the past several months as I have watched this miracle unfold. God has gone far beyond every limit that was ever conceived in my mind. And, I am still being rewarded by Him for each "Fiat" that I have summoned from my heart. If someone tries to cerebralize God's Divine Plans before abandoning themselves before Him, their thoughts will never release them into the freedom of His embrace.

Our Lady offers the greatest Maternity that any of us could ever desire. She loves Her children and wishes to teach us kindness, compassion, self-denial, and shared mercy. Who is humble enough to learn these lessons without being pinched on the ear? Therefore, heavenly discipline must be a part of Her instruction. We can gain wisdom from the small children around us by remembering one of them on the first day his mother begins to bridle his passions and selfishness. She knows that he must learn the soul-sustaining virtues. So, she circumscribes the boundaries in order to undermine his soon-to-be-reckless will. How does the child react to the unrecognizable new constraints being placed upon him? In most instances, the little one responds by claiming that his mother is a "meanie," culminating in an abbreviated period of filial alienation. Our own reactions are still very child-like, even into our adult years. When we finally realize that we have failed the test of faith, our instinct is to attack the authority of the one from whom the call for holiness comes in an effort to diminish our personal culpability. Our defensive retaliation is an effort to place our own will above the Will of our Almighty Father. We must, instead, stand forward when we recognize that our trust in Him is less than what Heaven desires. In that very moment, Jesus Christ will bestow the gift which leads to the great invitation of the human soul to be one with the Creator of all righteousness.

"**Your Heavenly Mother comes in peace and Love! My children do not believe that their Heavenly Mother will bring discipline. I am the Mother of all humankind. As I have appeared throughout the world, I have approached My children in as many different ways as the number of places I have come. I pray that My children will allow God's Plan to unfold. When I bring My Love to My children, it is without condition! My Heavenly Heart is full of Love for each of My children. I teach kindness and love, pity and compassion, and all My children should remember that discipline is a part. All of My children on Earth are in exile. I have pity on the children of God to lead them to My Son. There are many children who remain closed in all that My Son does. Only through an open heart and a penitent will can people know the trueness of complete faith. Patience and trust in the Will of God display strong faith.**"

Saturday, May 18, 1991

As we were eating dinner this evening, my brother began to feel Our Lady tendering his spirit to receive Her miraculous intercession. He was being drawn away from the influences of the world through the grace that was welling-up in his soul. Soon thereafter, we knelt to pray and She came saying, "**Tonight, My child, it is time to continue the quest for the faith of My other children...**" Then, She commenced another discussion in search of the innocent abandonment of all humanity.

We demonstrate our faith in many ways regarding the things of Earth. We erect antennas and cables to our television sets in order to receive our favorite news and entertainment programs. Yet, there are only few of us who actually understand the laws of aerotechnology that allow this to occur. We simply believe the people who tell us that radio waves can enter our personal businesses and dwelling places. We trust that we will see a continuous picture on our screens through this artifact, unsure of why it really happens. Our Lady says that this is how our faith should be demonstrated in Her Son, Jesus Christ. "**How is it that people can erect an antenna in faith that it will serve to bring entertainment without seeing the reason, but they will not erect their minds and hearts in faith to receive Jesus, who will provide them Salvation and Eternal Life?**" We place an immense level of stock in the electrophysics of the mortal world, but not in the miracle of God's Plan through the Mercy of His Son. The Holy Mother continued as if to show Her tacit disapproval, "The people of the world are divisive and gloating. They remove the fishes of the seas and transfer them to their different aquaria for their own entertainment. The people of the world also divide themselves for the same reason. My children feel that it is easier to segregate than to love in the common Sacrifice of My Son. The Almighty Father allows men the will to remove fish from the water to eat and to prey upon the animals of the world.

But, humankind does not stop there! Men of the Earth also find it necessary to gloat this gift by placing their prey on display. Fish and animals are preserved in areas of flaunt. Such as it is with men gloating victory over others. This is why there is oppression, bigotry, violence, and distress. It is the will of many of My children to defeat their brothers and sisters, consume their existence through their own greed, and place their defeat on display such as the bust of a gentle deer is hung on a wall. The Mother of God is asking why there is no faith in men to survive with only the gift which God has given. Men feel that they must act further to show to others that they are the curators of their own success and destiny. Will these same men gloat their own inability to forego their own plight in their search for My Son's Mercy? The world is not in the hands of the people who proclaim to control it. All that men have is a gift from God, from whom all good things come. Happy are those who know that My Son gives and takes away. Those who believe that God gives and takes are of great faith. Therein lies the lesson of faith."

She also explained Her previous references to Padre Pio, the holy priest from San Giovanni Rotundo, Italy who died in September of 1968. Historical fact shows that he miraculously received the Wounds of Jesus in his flesh, as did Saints Theresa and Francis of Assisi. His Life is a revealing witness to the Truth of Jesus' Sacrifice, manifested in the Holy Mass. We must remember that Our Savior chose to die publicly on the Cross with His Precious Blood flowing down upon our souls so that the entire world can see Him there. Through His Crucifixion, He blesses us with the Promise of His Love into perpetuity. He carried our sins into the grave so that we can rise from them again. Padre Pio exhibits the Love of God and the Five Wounds of His Beloved Son as a miraculous sign for modern-day humanity. He is the example for the 20th century of the never-ending Oath that Our Lord has made from the Cross. Padre Pio's Life is a living message, stating that the Passion and Death of Jesus Christ are real in the Eucharistic Celebration. The Sacrifice of Calvary and the Holy Mass are one and the same Crucifixion. His beatific testimony was written through the suffering that he bore for over fifty years. His life of piety and Our Lady's message are a gift from the same Holy Spirit. The Death and Resurrection of Christ embodies God's complete commitment to save all humankind from the throes of unending perdition.

Sunday, May 19, 1991
Early A.M.

"My beautiful children, your Mother has come today to bless you in your acceptance of the Holy Spirit of My Son who is upon and in you. Each of you share the Love of God through His presence. As My Son comes to you, it is a time for every child to accept Jesus through the miracle of faith. Now, My children, is the time of greatest faith for those who fear! If your faith is weak, you cannot accept Jesus through His Sacrifice on the Cross. Please know that your faith is already in place in your world. You know at daybreak what brings light, but you do not run to the horizon to see if it is the sun. My precious ones, please keep faith in your hearts to believe that Jesus is with you and is alive through your prayers. Please have faith in the power of your prayers! You believe that the world is round, even though it was mortal men who told you. Throughout the ages, men have stood by My Son's Word in faith to help new generations to believe. My Son is asking that you have faith in His Return as He has told the world. It is through the Love which My Son provides that belief is possible. It begins in your hearts, little lambs! You must open your hearts to receive Love and give Love so that belief can grow from the energy of your faith. This is not an ordinary journey.

Your pathways and pavements of your everyday lives will not elevate you from them. Children, your hearts must be raised in faith through the Holy Spirit of God within you to bring you to know Love and grace. Please know that your Heavenly Mother is filled with grace, which I give to you out of Love. I am your Mother who prays for your peace and Salvation. Please allow Me to bring you to My Son through My Motherly Love. I ask all of My children to make yourselves worthy to receive Him. At times, I must come to you in discipline because you are all so innocent and beautiful. Please prepare yourselves to receive My Son through the Holy Eucharist. Your Mother for all Eternity wishes you to be made pure of heart so that you can receive My Son who loves you so much. Thank you for praying to become worthy of Him. I bless you in your faith in the Spirit of God. Thank you for having responded to My call." I am forever grateful for the gifts that God the Father is granting through His Immaculate Mother. I related the specific things that Our Lady asked me to share with those in our prayer group this evening. I told them that She is trying to teach us about unwavering faith through our more recent experiences. The need for openness of heart is crucial to our embracing the great Love and Wisdom that She wishes to shower upon us.

Monday, May 20, 1991

My brother and I knelt to pray the Rosary late in the afternoon and I asked the Holy Spirit to guide us through another day. Jesus responded by sending His Mother to ask me to record His wishes and instructions. This Diary belongs to Our Lady of the Redeemed, and I am Her child. Everything I have and will ever come to know is Her possession. This work is a factual record of the unfolding of God's merciful Plan for the conversion of the world. Mary Immaculate helps me transcribe Her personal Wisdom and guidance into meaningful instruction for every soul on Earth to see. Later this evening, a couple friends arrived and asked us to join them in a pilgrimage to the Franciscan Motherhouse. It was a very heartwarming affair.

Our Lady said to us, **"I bless all who pray! Jesus is the Lamb of God who takes away the sins of the world and has Mercy on His people to grant them peace. He carried His Cross for the sins of the world. He died on the Cross to save all humankind from the burden of their sins and to give Everlasting Life in the Kingdom of Salvation. My beloved sons, remember always My Motherly Love for you as you pray. Your hearts full of Love are tender in My arms. I give you My special gift of peace this night. Please remember My motherly grace given to your brothers and sisters throughout the ages. My sons, there are no sins which are inadvertent. A sin is an act of the free will! My Son will forgive the sins of those who accept Him and pray for His Mercy. The children of the world are so special to My Son. Thank you for praying to save the world! I am with you to help you pray. My Heart is open to receive you. Come into My Heart for Love. There is a fountain of Love through My Son. Your fears are quenched into Love and promise. No act of Love will be left unnoticed. The smallest deed of Love can move a soul to My Son. Please keep faith in the power of Love."**

We can perceive from Her words that She appreciates the smallest acts of affection that we offer to our fellow man. Her response is the warmth of Her unfathomable Love that She extends from all Eternity. When we arrived home, I began penning another section of my Diary and our Virgin Mother came again to guide me in Her work. Praise be to Jesus! She encouraged me to continue in all I am doing for God. I have been carrying a great deal of heaviness in my heart throughout the past few days. I have never experienced the opposition that I see growing from my closest of friends. I sometimes find that I am truly afraid to proceed. My confidence fluctuates, but I remain absolutely faithful to what I am recording. The Truth must reign supreme at all cost! Our Lady helped me tonight by saying, **"Your Mother is happy that you have spoken the way you have to your brothers and sisters. You are allowing Me to speak through you! Thank you for loving My Son."** With this enlightenment, I felt an heroic courage descend upon my spirit and my weakness melt away like ice during the first thaw of spring. I can sense our impending victory, although I cannot see it from here.

Tuesday, May 21, 1991
   This evening, Timothy was visiting a sick friend in a nearby hospital and happened to meet a family from the Orient in the hallway who spoke only very broken English. Our Holy Mother guided him to this encounter to highlight Her message about the Love which transcends the multiplicity of our nations. One of the Chinese women asked what they should know about the United States that will help them better understand our culture. My brother simply told them, "*You should know that we love you!*" She then wrote the words "I love you" on a piece of paper in her native tongue and handed it to him to bring home. It was a moment for all times and an international communion of peace. Their hearts were profoundly touched by my brother's inclusive affection. Everyone knew that they would probably never meet again in this world, yet the inscription of their response to the fruits of Christianity will reside in their hearts forever. Timothy's words were overwhelmingly unexpected, but were innocently received with the most incredible joy. He did not have to say anything more because there are no other words, foreign or domestic, that could have usurped the good will that they shared.
   Upon his return home about nine o'clock, I was instructed to sit comfortably on the sofa before my prayer altar. He began an unrehearsed dissertation which continued the Divine grace that I received on Easter Sunday. After a few more sentences, Our Lady came to speak in my brother's place. For two and a half hours, She conversed with me about the marvels of Jesus Christ and the unfolding of His Kingdom to come. She referred me to verses of Sacred Scripture from one end of the Bible to the other, justifying everything that She wished me to comprehend. I cannot articulate the depth of these one-hundred-fifty minutes, as though each click of sixty seconds was a reflection of the Psalms. No human on Earth possesses the command of Sacred Scripture that I witnessed during this time. A sense of the *supernatural* penetrated deeply into my heart. I realized that I was not participating within the bounds of human plausibility. It was like visiting a place where gravity is suspended, and my soul was assuredly in flight. My mind wanted to ask, "How is this possible?" while my heart already knew the answer. How do I explain this paranormal timelessness? It shattered any new limits in my mind that define what God is liable to do. I felt a freedom from the oppression of everything that the world expects us to assume. I became aware of many original Truths about which most mortal men have not a single clue. They are of such holy magnitude that I do not yet have the literary dexterity to describe them on this page. I hope that, someday, I will be able to capture them clearly so that your heart can experience the same miraculous presence that I witnessed again today.

Wednesday, May 22, 1991

We joined another Rosary group in prayer tonight and Our Lady spoke to all of us. **"My beautiful children, you have been called to pray in unity through the Love of My Son. Please remember to pray every day! A day without prayer is absent of Light and Life. Your prayers together unite your hearts, feed the hungry, clothe the naked, convert the faithless, and bring the cool gift of peace. Thank you for praying!"** She then gave me the following prayer that I was to share with everyone. *"My dear Jesus, the hearts of all the children of the Earth beg to feel your Love and Mercy. We pray that, through Your Love and the grace of Your Mother, we will become worthy of our promised Eternity in the beauty of Heaven. Holy Father, it is through our living of Your Commandments that we are brought to true holiness. We pray for the gift of understanding for our brothers and sisters, for the beauty of purity to overcome our lives, and for the openness of our hearts to receive Your Will. All of Your children throughout the world hunger for peace and Salvation. We pray our promise that our hunger will be satisfied by receiving You at Your Tabernacle so You will remain alive within us to bring us Your peace. O precious Jesus, we pray from our hearts that we may become one with You! Amen."*

The Blessed Virgin Mary has come to nurture our faith, while many people refuse to believe that they are special enough to be so blessed and saved. This is the same rejection that brought the trials which Jesus endured during His Lifetime on Earth. Tens of thousands fear to accept Him because of the daily commitment that is needed to imitate the piety which He commands. Instead, they must understand that daily prayer is the power given to us to change the world. If we attempt to effect that transformation without kneeling before God, we will most assuredly fail. It is only through the Will of Jesus Christ that Creation is brought to Light. His Heart is still open to receive our every petition. The Queen of Heaven has been with us from the moment we were conceived in our own mother's womb to encourage our souls toward unity and peace. Jesus lives within us, sustaining our strength and sharing our joys. But, He also asks us to find rest in Him. Everyone must remember that our spiritual cohesion between the inhabitants of the Earth comes only through the Son of God. The world is at the pinnacle of sanctity when it is filled with the perfection of Jesus through the Holy Eucharist. While the Virgin Mother is trying to convert humanity with Her sinless grace and guidance, many people would rather remain skeptical and ask why they should listen to Her at all. They exercise their human authority to determine just how far they truly desire to commit themselves toward conversion, refusing to accept that the time for holiness is now. Our Heavenly Mother has come in peace to lead Her children to their Salvation in the Messiah on the Cross.

She continued by saying, **"The peace that you feel around you is My Love. It is time for all of My children to feel My peace with an open heart! I am in the breeze which is about to come to your prayer group. The Spirit of the Love of My Son is in the breeze with Me..."** It was a very calm evening as we prayed outdoors. The very moment She said this, a gentle breeze began to roll across the landscape with a refreshing kiss of cooling relief. To augment Her Divine prescience, She said, **"My special one, here I am! Please remember that this breeze always makes My children inhale the breath of a new beginning in peace and Love. The beauty of the Earth lies also in the Love of human hearts! Your Mother is praying with you so that you will love each other for the good of all Creation. If the children of the world cannot love from within their hearts, they will never be able to share the unity of peace. My Son comes to bring Love in the heart to be shared for the unity of common prayer for Mercy and Eternal Life in the Kingdom of Heaven. May these fruits of the Holy Spirit keep you close to My Son as I open My arms to receive you in Love. Thank you for loving your brothers and sisters in the Spirit of My Son!"**

When we finished praying the Rosary, I told the group about the many facts that Our Lady allowed me to share with everyone. I explained the meaning of the foreign words and the decisive references to Padre Pio. She has given me a parable describing the faith that She wishes us to have, while highlighting the pitfalls of our refusal to surrender. She asks us to imagine a boat with rows of seats from bow to stern and an oar resting on each one, reaching over the side into the water. Every soul alive is sitting in the seat which is uniquely prepared for them. There are plugs inconspicuously placed between our feet which fill the holes in the hull. They symbolize the doubts and reservations that attack our lives of faith and attempt to tarnish our grace. The Virgin Mother stands at the bow like the figurehead of a mighty ship. Her presence encourages us to follow where She leads, Her eyes fixed upon the glimmering Light of the fast-approaching horizon. But, as our oars rhythmically slap the waves in unison with the beat of our loving hearts, one of our shipmates gives-in to his curiosity and removes the plug from beneath his feet. In doing so, he takes his eyes off-course and away from our collective destination. The gush of water launches the plug from his hand into the farthest corner of the boat. Unfortunately for everyone there, he cannot replace it alone.

In the ensuing commotion, many others have their perception drawn away from their future and, likewise, pull-out their own stop with the same disastrous results. The boat begins to take-on water at an alarming rate and tilts with a list on the seas. With only a few souls obediently rowing, the craft beneath us slows and becomes even harder to control. The burden becomes almost unbearable upon those who feverishly continue to row for the sake of everyone else aboard. Over the din, Our Lady pleads, *"Please, do not entertain doubt and distraction. Listen to Me! Lift your eyes to the beatific dawn!"* She has told us repeatedly that there is no doubt or question in faith. It is, rather, a fruit of our undaunted belief and acceptance of the Lord without hesitation. Our reservations and distractions, however innocent they may be, destroy our trust in Christ Jesus as His omnipotent Plan for the culmination of Creation continues to unfold. Our weaknesses are the holes in our flat-bottom boat from which our intentions escape. They allow evil to enter and submerge us amidst the darkness of fear and despair. But, to our everlasting gain, our allegiance to Jesus permanently seals these imperfections with a scented resin of grace and peace. Yes, we are on the true "Maiden" voyage of the destiny of man, accompanied by the Mother of maidens, the Ever-Blessed Virgin Mary! Indeed, the port city of celestial Light anticipates our arrival with joy!

Friday, May 24, 1991

Tonight, Our Lady began, **"Good evening, My beautiful son! You are in special grace for allowing Me to help you teach and convert My other children. All that we do is for the Glory of God the Father. You must feel strengthened by the help you are giving Me. Please use God's Holy Word to speak to the world..."** I was instructed to read Hebrews 6:10-12: *"We earnestly desire each of you to demonstrate the same eagerness for the fulfillment of hope until the end, so that you may not become sluggish, but imitators of those who, through faith and patience, are inheriting the promises."* She asked me to pray for faith, Mercy, and sanctity with the knowledge that God will answer my prayers. **"My Son is with you to love you and will return to save you. His Death on the Cross is His Promise of Love. Jesus is the Savior of the world! I come to help all My children seek Him. There is no limit to the Mercy of My Son. The prayers of humankind will always change the world. No final judgement will be rendered until My Son returns to the Earth to judge the living and the dead. Then, His judgement will be final. Pray for the souls in Purgatory! Pray for the living to honor the Word of My Son, to be happy living His Love, and to receive His Body in the Eucharist. In days to come, I ask that you help Me in the writing of many dissertations which will convert others and help them grow in faith."**

I told our Holy Mother that I wish with all my heart to record these things for Her and She responded, **"My beautiful son, you have made your Heavenly Mother cry tears of happiness. I bless you with the Love of My Son in His Name. I will come to you as long as God wills. Thank you for praying..."** To begin the fulfillment of this request, I was instructed to read Hebrews 9:11-28 and explain why it is important. The passage flows from mankind's inherent aspiration and need for purification and Redemption. Our goal is to worship our Almighty Father with a pure and decent conscience. And, since we were bound by the fall of Adam and Eve, God initiated a new liberating covenant through the fatal suffering of His Perfect Son which was signed with His Precious Blood. Jesus sustained His Love through the most horrific agony that our transgressions could generate, thus destroying them forevermore. Love is the final note left resounding from Mount Calvary as the sins of humanity were consumed. The veil between Heaven and Earth has been transcended by the High-Priest upon the Cross. He entered the Beatific Light of Paradise, bearing redeemed mankind within His Sacred Heart as the supreme gift to our Omnipotent Creator who is poised upon the Seat of Perfect Divinity.

God desires the re-unification of His children within the realms of the Saints. Therefore, when Jesus appeared before His Eternal Court bearing our souls within the wounds of His Sacrifice, the First Person of the Trinity witnessed His Son's Love for humanity and was again pleased with His Creation. Justice has been served, restitution has been made, and satisfaction has been delivered. Jesus' Crucifixion is the perfect, pure, and acceptable gift to Our Father for the purpose of His granting absolution and Salvation upon our souls. Judgement has been bestowed upon the Benevolent Lamb Whom mankind has slain. The prescription for our everlasting reprieve rests in our acceptance of the events of Good Friday and the imitation of His Life. Jesus desires to show us His forgiveness with all His infinite being. He endured His Passion and execution so that He would be blessed with the opportunity to offer us Eternity with the angels. Our call is to admit our need for Redemption and seek the Mountaintop of Calvary. The Cross is the Altar where the High-Priest first offered His Holy Mass. He is the Eucharist, our soul-sustaining Bread, and the flowing Fountain of Endless Pardon.

Saturday, May 25, 1991

We began the Holy Rosary at nine-thirty tonight and the Immaculate Virgin Mary said, **"My blessed ones, your Mother has come to bring you My peace and My Love. Thank you for your prayers from the heart! It is through your faith that your prayers are answered. My special one, you should remember that Satan is very strong. He is subtle and does not always at first appear to be repulsive and evil. He is the fine grindstone which wears purity thin through temptation. You will recognize evil by its temptation to bring you to lose your elevation through earthly pleasures."** I was wondering whether my dissertation pertaining to the Hebrews reading was acceptable. She replied, **"What you have written is Divine! You should choose your words with the knowledge I have given you."** I am often guided and reassured through Her motherly encouragement. I wish for God to be glorified by everything that I accomplish for Our Lady through Her miraculous intercession. She continued with a considerable amount of personal instruction for my brother and me tonight, asking me to invoke greater faith and trust in Her power. I am to have no doubt that we will succeed in all that She has planned. Mankind should live the Victory of Christ in advance of our deaths! Our failures have been destroyed by His Resurrection!

Sunday, May 26, 1991

"Dear children, today I call all of My children to respond to the Love of My Son which grows in the hearts of the faithful. Through Love, the sins of the world are banished and replaced by holiness. Little ones, no one is borne into the world with the knowledge of hate. You grow to hate in the absence of Love. None of the children of God are taught enough about hatred to hate. Every little heart has been given the power to Love, a Love which comes through prayer. Your Mother has come to ask you to pray with Me so that your power to Love will be unequaled by any other force in the world. It is on the dwelling of Love that hatred is diminished. I ask that all of My children brighten their hearts through the knowledge that My Son has total and irrevocable Love for you. As each of you kneels to pray, you are allowing My Son to come closer to the Earth to reach your heart. Through the soft wings of Love, you are lifted from your burdens of the days and released from earthly cares. Children, your Heavenly Mother asks that each of you grant the other a smile and a prayer. My heart is warmed to see My children helping each other come closer to their Savior. It is through the lesson of Love that you are taught to be gentle. The lesson is written on your hearts by the Hand of My Son.

Oh, special ones, please call yourselves to raise your brothers and sisters by touching their hearts with your Love! This is how the world is brought to peace. The most gentle touch of your hearts is done through prayer. There, you will find the gift of grace to become one with Jesus. Children, there is no higher grace than to be one with Him! Your Mother has come to help you live in grace and Love because I love you through a Heart of sweetness and peace. All I have in My Heart belongs to you. You are all so special! Your tiny feet will deliver you to My arms when you fill yourselves with Love and understanding for those who suffer. Offer them the Love of Jesus, whose Sacrifice brings deliverance from pain and the strength of Salvation. Pray and pray! Thank you for loving your brothers and sisters as My Son loves you. I bless you in the name of My Son to bring you peace. Thank you for having responded to My call."

The "Ave Maria Prayer Group" met at five o'clock this evening at my home, but very few were in attendance as a result of Our Lady's recent lessons about spiritual discipline. I am quite ashamed for their obstinance. I felt very nervous tonight as I considered everything that I was instructed to tell the group. I invoked my love for Our Blessed Mother to strengthen my heart because I know that She will never let me down. I pray for my inner-strength to overcome the disturbance that is brought-on by the faithlessness of others. Our Lady has always given me the correct things to say when I am at peace, so I must continue to behave as She asks without pause or hesitation. She is the most loving guardian and holy mentor that any person could ever have. When Timothy arrived at my house later in the evening, we prayed the Rosary and our Blessed Mother came to speak specifically to me. She spoke about the dwindling number of people who are now attending the prayer group. She said, **"My special one, please do not concern yourself with numbers, quotas, impressions, opinions, or passing verbiage of how or whether your prayers and actions are acceptable to God. You are doing My Son's work! A prayer group is composed of one who prays with you! Please remember that your Mother has asked others to attend the Ave Maria prayer group. The choice to attend is with the other children, not with you. Thank you for doing your part..."**

In continuing Her conversation, She answered a question that many people have posed to the Almighty Father for centuries. Why would a God who so loves the world allow it to become so perverted, abused, and distant from the sanctity of Heaven? Our Lady said that Life is a gift from Our Creator, but would it remain so if He told every child how to exercise their will every day? He has promised the most important part, that He will always guide our souls back to His embrace. Each person on Earth is given the direction to Salvation and the freedom to accept the wholesomeness that Christ bestows upon His children. That is where we will find true peace! Redemption is made complete through our reception of His Body and Blood in the Holy Eucharist.

A CHILD'S FIRST STEPS

I have witnessed many great revelations through the grace of the Blessed Virgin Mary during these first three months. Thousands of people throughout the centuries have longed far more deeply than me to see the things that I have seen. I fervently try every day to be worthy of these modern-day miracles. From February until now, my perspective was one of a spectator to a supernatural event. But, with the request to pen Her many spiritual dissertations, I have found myself conscripted from the stands to serve the most beautiful creature that God has ever conceived. It is with great confidence that I now call Her "Mother" with the pulsing conviction of my entire soul. In retrospect, I hope that you will accept these months in the context that my brother and I have experienced them. It is as wonderfully surprising as you can possibly ever imagine. It is a time of spiritual tendering in preparation for the greater work of the conversion and Salvation of the entire mortal world. My mental constitution has been acclimated to fluently accept what I had previously believed to be impossible in my life. God has uniquely astonished me with His omnipotent power.

But, in this same time, our beautiful Mother is nurturing my heart past the paralysis of awe which has been engendered within the revelation of God. Each of you who reads this record has already been touched with the hint of the same awareness within your soul! Our Almighty Father has placed a witness directly in your path with a written record that you have never before dared to dream. Will you blindly stumble over it, or fully embrace it, carrying its Light as your new torch of Love? I ask you to invoke your heroic faith to know yourself as the soul that will make all the difference on Earth! Do not doubt that my integral trust was also required! I tell you humbly that I have passed that initial test, but only because our Examiner is the Pardoner of our souls. I did not naively suspect that there would not be subsequent trials which would seek to shake this mighty inheritance. For my part, on this day and forever to come, I renew my proclamation in the presence of all the Hosts of History and Heaven, "*I believe, I accept, and I submit!*" And, in union with this profession of faith, I ask you to continue with an open heart while reading about this child's first steps toward knowing and loving the One who redeemed mankind at the price of His own Life, Jesus, the Christ.

Monday, May 27, 1991

Late in the afternoon, Timothy and I were making ready to eat dinner. We were driving to a local restaurant when Our Lady manifested Her Divine presence quite powerfully. The sun began to spin, throwing-off many beautiful colors from its perimeter. I drove to a peaceful place near the airport so as to have an unobstructed view of the western horizon. The sun was dancing in the sky and was encompassed by a huge heart. It became a solid-white host which was resting in the heavens. A crystal chalice then appeared and the host set like the sun, itself, into its transparent reservoir. I prayed seven Our Fathers, Hail Marys, and Glory Be's. Our Lady said, **"My grace I give to you! His Love permeates the glass and is magnified through the Host. Amen."** After finishing these few short supplications, we traveled onward to dinner. I was anxious to go back home because I knew that the Blessed Mother would come again to continue our lessons.

Upon returning to my house, we knelt to pray and She did appear to us. Tonight, She taught me the first of four types of fear, the fear to love. This wholly unjustified fright is the most damaging to the human soul. We have built a world that is complete with values, measurements of success, and levels of right and wrong according to our mortal opinions and suppositions. Our confidence in the future is derived from our allegiance and dedication to our everyday plans. Our Lady says that we must detach ourselves from these self-righteous courses if we are truly to be of service of our brothers and sisters in Love. **"To love all of mankind requires an abandonment of earthly principles that hold men fast to their daily actions and beliefs. The children of the world fear that their destiny will become insecure and without definition if they give their entire conscience to Love through the acceptance of the Holy Spirit of God."**

Our attachment to bleak mortal ambitions closes the passageways to the spontaneous outpouring of Love from our hearts through lives of pious sacrifice. The solitary legitimate ambition imprinted within the human spirit by God is to accept His Son and to live in His perfect image. But, we fear the consequential labors of serving our brothers and sisters for the glory of His Name. As a result, we do not place any stock in their capacity to be of any benefit to our material ambitions. This fuels our grim prospects for the fate of all humanity. Our lack of mutual loyalty begets the wanton destruction of peace. We place our most charitable nobility off-limits to anyone else who cannot help us achieve our own imagined destiny, making way for lying, deceit, intentional misunderstandings and barriers between our families and dearest of friends. The first lock ever invented by mankind is the one that we place on our own hearts. The fear of Love is the very first tomb of those who are unknown to God! There is no commemoration for those who refuse to engage that battle! Our Lady proclaims that prayer is the key to opening the ancient passages of holy generations gone by. The greatest Mysteries of our Creator's pristine affinity have not expired, for they still reside at the center of our souls! The Holy Spirit lives within these chambers, waiting to escort us with dignity beyond the courtyards of disgrace. The key to these dungeon doors that plunder our ability to see His Face is only one "Our Father" away. Our Holy Mother said, **"Today, I come to tell all My children everywhere that each of you should hold your hopes and dreams acceptable to My Son next to your soul and lift them up as sincere love for Him in the solitude of your hearts. This, My children, is prayer!"**

As we continued, She said, **"None of the children of God have learned enough about hatred to hate."** I did not understand what She meant, so She explained Herself further. Love is abundant in the human heart when it is open to the divinity of faith. Malice is characterized by an earthly-acquired dilatory attitude, absent of serenity and compassion. There are many beneficent actions that bloom from the charity that is shared amongst peoples of good will. The Holy Spirit is the reason for this righteous interaction and makes possible the progress toward a peaceful coexistence of nations and races on Earth. Upon seeing someone perform a sanctified act, we state, *"Wasn't that a nice thing to do."* When God sees the same offering, He proclaims, ***"See how he has loved!"*** The diplomatic conscience cannot exist without the preparatory invitation of Heaven, because its very essence is the dissemination of mutual reconciliation. Accordingly, malevolence always exists outside the Christian spirit with an agenda to devour the virtuousness within. It will never become a part of the Divinity of Christ. No person can disdain other souls from within their heart because only Love resides there. When a human person chooses a life of reclusiveness through an uncheerful disposition, he is defenseless against the onslaught of those who are filled-to-the-brim with scorn. This can bring any faithless man to cower in desperation and hopelessness, alienating himself from the outside pervading world.

The instant that our childlike abandonment to Jesus is summoned from within, Light pours-forth and consumes the most aggressive darkness in our midst, bringing Life to everything it greets. Our Virgin Mother has made it clear that the Almighty Father will not allow His Son to die again. Therefore, none of Her children will have their beauty destroyed. **We do not know enough about hatred to hate**! The human spirit is a gem that encompasses the infinite expanse of the heavens. Love lives in union with our soul, waiting silently to be summoned through the door of our Divine submission to the New Covenant Christ. We are the most precious gifts placed within Creation and our hearts are living tabernacles of the Spirit of God. The genuine resurgence of our profession of faith will emanate the revealing Light of Our Savior, who illuminates all Creation with His intense perfection, restoring it to its paradisial beauty. Every one of us can open ourselves like a blooming flower to receive Him if we gingerly nurture our honest confessions with the intention of watching them grow. That is why the Holy Mass is the most profound Glory to God in the Highest. Every communicant who wishes to be completely in unity with Him must be of carpathian contrition at the Holy Sacrifice of the Mass. This is God's Divine Will for all of His children. Unimaginable beauty will pour-forth upon the Earth when this day of Christian solidarity arrives. One Faith, One Tradition, and One Body in Christ!

Tuesday, May 28, 1991
Today, our Blessed Mother engaged my childlike presumption when I assumed something through Her message that She had not actually said. It is wrong to believe that our faith frees us from the responsibility to protect ourselves from the snares of the physical world. For example, one who willfully enters into perilous situations should not presume that God will keep them free from bodily harm. The grace to ensure our safety and the wisdom that precludes our life from being ended prematurely resides in our making the wise decisions to avoid such danger. Although in a different context, I felt ashamed to have made such an error. My intense desire is to live in complete union with Our Lady's wishes. She was very loving in Her correction as She said, **"You both are so beautifully human!"**

Wednesday, May 29, 1991
Timothy and I were driving later this afternoon when we again witnessed the miracle of the sun as Our Lady came closer to us. We immediately returned home and began to pray the Rosary. She came to say, **"Good evening, My beautiful sons! Your Mother is with you! My Heart beats strongly with Love for you. Your work and words are Divine. You are attaining the grace of sanctity. My children, your prayers reach the heavens. Blessed are you in your hopes! Today, your Mother would like to tell you about the fear of faith which keeps My children from receiving My Son..."** Her lessons continued as She told me about the second type of fear, the human reticence to have faith in God. Explained very simply, it is born of our refusal to embrace the Love of Jesus Christ and the peace that He offers to humanity. We must be comfortable in our conviction with the grace that Our Lady brings from Her Son. The world was created by Love in eternal tranquility, and we exist within the omnipotence of God. The serenity of His Sacred Heart is always present and permeates every facet of Creation. Just as thunderous waves crash against our earthly shores, the revelation of God breaks with deafening silence over each mortal soul that He has given the breath of Life. Yet, we scramble-up the beach like little children who are afraid of the waves, hoping not to become immersed in the promises of our own Baptism! We choose to avoid the path to good will in our world by refusing to accept the presence of Our Lord's prayerful solemnity.

No one can create silence because it already exists as a gift from God. It is the fully-detectible heartbeat of the universe. The Holy Trinity emanates this pulse, awaiting our acceptance of His perpetual beauty. God patiently waits to soothe the burning intentions that flicker from within our subconscious desires. Everyone in Creation yearns deeply for the warmth of His consoling serenity, whether they realize it or not. He is the Benefactor of this final blessing, and there is no other! Through every century since the beginning of time, He has rested in the placid beauty of the nature He created, quietly revealing His magnificence in every painted setting of the unapproachable sun. His ordination and guardianship are openly apparent as we witness the galaxies of the heavens suspended before the curtain of night. The hopeful seed of His mighty purpose is planted again every morning as we are given another dawn to begin life anew. Our belief in His majesty grows from the vision that floods the world through this undeniable reality. But, our refusal to extend our hearts in faith drives us to plans of contradiction, taking our thoughts away from the Wisdom of our Father in Heaven. It is easy to avoid trusting in Him by becoming absorbed in the materials of the physical Earth. These elements are bonded in the chaos of the cities that are filled with outright incongruity. They obscure the vision of a higher union with Eternity for the entire family of man. Those who hide from Christianity do not even know that Christ is alive because they avoid the places where His Divinity chooses to flow. If you wish for a plentiful harvest to come from your fields, do you purchase a downtown city block or boulevard on which to plant its seed?

  We must surrender ourselves to the Will of the Almighty Father. Therein lies the genius that has transformed countless mere mortals into intergalactic saints. Jesus is the perfect Man in whose image we must grow. His thoughts are impeccable, and we must learn to plagiarize His mind. He owns a manifested commitment to His Father unto death out of Love for our Salvation There has been no greater sacrifice ever witnessed in the history of man, and never will there be. So, to be afraid to trust in Him is to be fearful of the commitment to reflect His Light. It is rooted in our errant thought that if the Promise of God is untrue, we will have forsaken our gainful worldliness for no good reason at all. Faith tells us instantly that the reason is still alive! It is one of His great Names, Redemption! We must forfeit our material possessions and the time we would otherwise spend lining our pockets. It is obvious that we require physical evidence that the Blood-Oath of Christ is authentic before we will commit our lives to His call for servitude and self-denial. Was His Crucifixion on Mount Calvary not factual enough to convince us? Are we frightened to seek Jesus' Mercy and forgiveness because we do not wish to stand before the record of our transgressions? The cohesion of the world rests in our understanding that Jesus loves us all too much! He will absolve everyone and everything if we will simply go to Him on bended knee in humble supplication. Still, many of us are far too stubborn and shy to ask, shuddering to our bones that the requisites which Love may require will be too awful for our helpless souls to bear.

"My children fear faith because it represents the commitment to Love all the people of the world and to recognize that there is sacrifice in faith. Your Mother has come to tell the world that it is in great danger! The fear of the children of the world to have faith is leading them to sin and separation from grace and purity. The fear of faith is founded in the need for these children to have physical proof that the souls of the faithful are received through forgiveness and Mercy into the Kingdom of Heaven. The Love of Jesus is so strong that no sin is too large to be forgiven by those who seek Him and are not afraid to believe in faith that forgiveness will be given. So, the world needs to seek the strength to overcome its fear to have faith..." The Blessed Mother is requiring me to be diligent about recording our discussions in my Diary. She asked me not to simply transcribe Her lessons word-for-word, but to draw my own concepts from deep within the recesses of my heart. She wishes me to describe what She has told me as I understand it, and has promised to correct me if I make any mistakes.

Thursday, May 30, 1991

The Ave Maria Prayer Group met at my home at seven o'clock this evening, and many people who had been disturbed by Our Lady's earlier manifestations invoked a renewed trust in Her messages and returned to pray in unity with us again. Our Virgin Mother was radiantly happy with them because She knows how difficult it is for us to battle the worldly forces that tend to erode our spiritual strength. She said, **"Good evening My beautiful children, Your Mother is with you again to bless you in your prayers! The room is so filled with faith on this night! Each special child who has come to Me this evening has brought a shining Light abreast which will lead you to My Son. Each of you carries a Light which helps bring hope into the world where there is despair and tragedy. Your Mother is happy with each of you! You are all so beautiful! My special son, your brothers and sisters have returned out of Love! God Almighty is praised by such obedient children. Your obedience brings joy to the heavens. Special angels are with each of you to help you through your days..."**

Our Holy Mother continued by explaining a third type of fear, which is our outright reluctance to be happy. We are afraid by our own design to allow joy and satisfaction to flow from within our hearts. Many people are absolutely terrified to express their jubilation in the Holy Spirit because they feel that God would somehow be scandalized in a public way. They believe that by being ceremonial, somber, and stalwart are the only suitable ways to adore and honor the Savior of all humankind. Jesus came into the world to eliminate our sorrows, affliction, pain, and ultimately, death itself. He chose His own Crucifixion as the vehicle of Love through which our inheritance would be secured. The greatest Good News is that our Dear Lord has brought healing to anyone who suffers from the buffets of mental grief and physical pain. His Victory over sin, despair, and disbelief has restored humanity to infinite grace! The bounty of the Son of God nourishes our inner-confidence in a way that can come from no other origin on the Earth or in the skies. We have every right to be filled with assurance and peace by virtue of His rising from the grave! Since we willingly submit ourselves to His forgiveness, we are forever saved from the flesh-biting flames in the squalid snake-pit of Hell. Anyone who is unhappy in Christ is being duped by the doldrums of their own blatant conceit. His Triumph over every human agony is in the Love of our Almighty Father through the Fountain of His Mercy flowing from the Cross on which His Son once willfully died. Jesus surrendered his Life to Pilate so that contentment and jubilation would gush like a geyser from the epicenter of our souls.

Can we remember the Nativity of Our Savior when the world was so filled with hope that choirs of angels came down from the heavens to sing? The entire body of mankind was sanctified by the presence of the Divine Child in the manger. Every heart throughout all of time is offered the fulfillment of their dreams through the Promise that this Infant would make to those He came to save. He still teaches that His Way is the road to sublime serenity, peace, generosity, humility, patience, kindness, goodness, faithfulness, and self-control. His Way is Love! We have every reason to be ecstatic in anticipation of His great Return to bestow Eternal Redemption upon the peoples of the Earth. There is no room for sadness within this hope! No pain, infirmity, injustice or dissension can rebuke the omnipotent Victory of Jesus Christ, which is also ours to claim! We are loved by God with a power that will soon erase the very memory of the first doubt which Saint Thomas ever entertained. The only authentic desire within the human constitution is to be embraced within the righteousness of Heaven. Jesus is about to openly fulfill that everlasting joy! He is on the verge of unleashing His Love in its full-blooming realization upon every soul who lives. This might be a little outside our simple capacity to comprehend, but not beyond our forthright power to envision with the confidence of kings. Sadness is incinerated in the anticipation of this moment. There will be an exhilaration that leaves the flesh behind, a felicity without conceivable bounds, and an eternal celebration streaking for the ends of all Eternity. The Promise of the Cross lives today for each one of us to consume. It is attainable in our time and offered to all humanity. When we desire Christ Jesus to the core of our very being and live according to His Word, we will be given the Paradise that we know to be standing in the Light that is still blinding to the yearling pupils of our newborn Christian eyes.

"Upon Jesus' birth, the world was filled with hope and the solemnity of peace because there came a reason to live in victory over the tyranny of life. The same hope, joy, and gladness which echoed throughout the world still resounds because My Son is going to come a second time. Your Heavenly Mother asks all of My children to be happy. Do not fear to be happy! Your Mother is happy when you are eager in the Love of Jesus and the expectation of His Return. With the prayers of the faithful, the kindness of God brings hearts filled with peace. When you are filled with the Love of Jesus, you cry tears of happiness. Please do not be afraid to weep tears of happiness! They will fall to the ground and bring bright flowers of joy. Please do not fear to show the joy of little children who run and play and laugh. The world of peace is yours when you accept My Son. He wants you to accept Him. He is yours, little ones! Please feel confident to dance through life on the wings of God's hope that, through the Love of Jesus, you will be saved. It is the only true reason for joy!"

Before departing today, our Blessed Mother asked us to pray for the twenty-two new cardinals presently being installed in the Roman Catholic Church. We are to petition for their sincere efforts on behalf of Jesus Christ. "Let your hearts be filled with joy in their lives and efforts for My Son! They and all other priests offer the Body and Blood of My Son. Please accept His Sacrifice with warmth and promise. The world needs to move closer to the Eucharist as these days of importance grow nearer. Those who are filled with Jesus are protected from anxiety. The world has the offering of Salvation as your mouths open to receive Jesus. Open your hearts to receive the joy and gladness that His Life has to offer."

Friday, May 31, 1991   The Feast of the Visitation of Mary
"My beautiful children, your Mother has come today to ask that you pray for peace. It is time for you to pray for those who are the enemies of peace and purity. Through the dedication of yourselves to Jesus, the world will remain full of Love. Children, please turn your hands to His so that, with Him, you may live in pardon and peace. I have come again to invite you to live My messages of Love in a world so full of indifference. The graces of God come as through a prism to light your world with the colors of promise. My special children, you find the coolness of peace in the blueness of the skies and greenery of the lands. The brightness of the sun warms your days and hearts with strength to help you grow in Love. As the gentle shower gives way to the rainbow, the precious drops of Jesus' Blood give Promise of unity and Salvation. Little ones, please open your hands and hearts to be bathed in the beauty of Eternity in Heaven by reaching out to Him. Your Mother is with you

to lead you to Love and bring you peace. Please, let Me lead you to Jesus!

The shadow of your days is growing ever longer, My lambs. Evening is drawing very near and I want you to be in the shelter of Jesus when night comes. Please remember that there are thieves in the night who would take you from the Kingdom of Heaven. Please come with your Mother, little children, to a retreat that is safe, warm, and Light. Remember to pray for peace for those who would deny it. There is a Blessing in the fountain of Love which I offer. Thank you for being My obedient children. Thank you for having responded to My call." Earlier today, Our Lady helped my brother compose a letter to the tenants of a low-income federal housing authority project over which he serves as the Chief Executive Officer. Through Her Love, She wishes to help them overcome the very difficult times that they are presently enduring. It is one of the most powerful letters that has ever been written by an incumbent public official. She said, **"Today, My Son has allowed Me to reach many hearts! This is a day of grace! It will begin the conversion of the poor, the awakening of those who serve in government, and those who make record of it in the media."**

"I am writing to you today to bring you some very good news and to ask all of you to open yourselves to understand what is happening today and in the future. Each of you needs to be reminded of some very important facts that exist as a part of your tenancy at the Housing Authority. As all of you know, the summertime has come and brought with it the very difficult times which accompany outdoor activities. Each of you lives in an area where the population is very dense; your neighbors live only a few feet away from you. As happens every year, there are difficulties which come when so many people of such varying interests and behaviors live so close together. Conflicts occur which are the result of people just being themselves. We often have property damage and personal injuries when conduct gets out of hand. I am calling on each of you today to help yourself and the cause of this public housing agency to maintain the peace that should exist between the members of a group of civilized people.

Recently, there has been a movement by several tenants to forget the gift which they have been given. Some tenants fail to remember that to live at the Housing Authority is not an affliction or a curse. There is no one who lives at the Housing Authority who is no less special a person than those who live in the other parts of the city. The fact that the economic condition of your family makes it necessary for you to require public assistance in paying your housing bills has nothing to do with how special each of you are. As you look at what brings each of you together as a group of tenants, it is only through your economic difficulties that you have become enjoined. I am asking each of you to remember that you are still valuable members of the human race. I ask that you look at your life and the beautiful world in which we live. It is time for each of you to stop thinking of yourself as just a pauper who has no future and who is stuck at the bottom of the ladder. For your own good and for the good of your friends, please bring yourself to think larger than you have been.

In the process of thinking of ideas which could help all of you to live in peace with each other so that your lives will be made easier as our tenants, I have exhausted all avenues of my thinking. I now realize that my first mistake was to believe that my thinking was the answer in the first place. I do know that now is the time to call each of you to peace. You need to engage yourselves in the act of patience so that we can allow peace to work within ourselves. I see so many of you who walk through life wondering why your lives are out of control and without meaning or happiness. I would like to tell you today that there is meaning in your lives that you can place into them by choosing to accept the promise that has been given to us by the Son of God. Each of us thinks that Jesus, the Son of God, is an imaginary person who never existed because we have never seen Him. If you have never trusted a word before, it is time that you trust His Word. He is alive and with you.

You can control your destiny by making the choice to be raised from your suffering and be lifted to the freedom of His peace for the common good of all of you. You are not just a lowly tenant at a public housing project; you are special in a way that no one else is. You can be a perfect person like Jesus was when you pray to become close to Him and His promise. You ask how you find out about Him? Pick up your Bibles. I know that each of you has one, and that is the beginning which you have chosen, but not started yet. All of your life is in the Words of the Bible. The Holy Word contains your future. It will show you how to love your neighbors and even those whom you believe are your enemies. When you see someone walking down the street, you are not just seeing a physical body with a face-value description: you are actually seeing another creation of God such as yourself. You are seeing someone who is like yourself who cries-out to the world for understanding and help in the suffering of each day.

And, when recognizing the beauty of that human Life, I ask all of the expectant mothers to remember the gift of God's Creation, that of another human being who is alive within you, and is also crying- out to be given the chance to see the beauty of the Life which it has been promised by God. Although your voluntary act has resulted in conception, that is where your choices need to end. I beg you to give your unborn children the choice to say 'yes' to Life before you say no for them. Your newborn child could help lead the world to holiness and to the One who will save you from your burden of sin, Jesus Christ. Please do not use alcohol or drugs when you carry an unborn child. The choice of their usage of them should also be theirs. You will be blessed in ways that you have never seen by letting the gift of Life grow in God's intent for it.

While these summer days are hot, it is sometimes very cold in our hearts. We need to warm them by filling them with love for each other. If you do not already know, it is very important that you learn what you need to know to be worthy of receiving Jesus' Body in the Church. When you take your faults and sins to Him and receive Him, you will be given peace and then will love your neighbors. Our problems will be solved. Mary, the Mother of Jesus the Son of God, was raised into the heavens by God and crowned the Queen of Heaven. She has returned to the Earth to help all of us learn to be with Jesus so that we can live in peace and receive His Promise. Ask your local Church about the Blessed Virgin Mary, or you can see me, I will show you and tell you what She has personally said to me. Thank you for trying to live in peace and accepting the gift that God has given us. I hope that you will allow your life to begin its change as soon as you receive this letter. Remember to place your future in Jesus. His Mother is waiting for you with Her arms open to help you to do it."

Today is the anniversary date of the endorsement of the purchase papers for my home in 1989. Our Lady told me that my residence was prepared as a place where She would miraculously come to tell America and the entire world about the Savior of humanity. Ironically, the previous owner was an elderly gentleman who was almost eccentrically meticulous in his upkeep of his property. He was a perfectionist as he built and maintained it. I have envisioned his happiness in knowing that he was chosen to prepare a place for Jesus' Mother to visit. He played a unique role in God's Divine Plan and, perhaps, never realized it until he entered the Gates of Paradise. This example should give renewed hope to everyone on Earth. We cannot yet see what Christ has ordained for us the moment we rise from our sleep.

As my brother and I prayed tonight, our Blessed Mother explained a fourth type of fear. It deals with our refusal to serve the Lord without recognition. There are many who attend their churches because it is the popular thing to do. They have confidence in their social, economic, and spiritual status which garners them words and gestures of high respect from their peers. They wish for their acts of goodness and kindness to be seen because they require a gift of support from the world. This causes them to neglect many other potential acts of charity because there would be no profitable return on their hidden sacrifices. A truly selfless person will leave a loaf of bread on a stubble-stone stoop, knock on the door, and leave before it is opened by the poor souls who live inside. Some people are afraid that God will not recognize their efforts unless the rest of Creation also sees them. In truth, our Almighty Father is already aware of our good deeds before they ever enter our minds. No act of sincerity or devotion is without its reward. Indeed, it is a blessing of infinite magnitude to share the Life of the Lamb of God through our most wholesome intentions. In those special moments, we allow Jesus' Love to enter our lives like a blossoming flower. That is why we should never gauge our popularity before the paradisial Throne through the legend of confectionary approval. Christ is the most powerful warrior, the greatest competitor, and the Eternal Champion. But, in the eyes of the cynical world, He lost the battle. They fail to see that He won the War! From a mere nominal perspective, there are many more champions who have been defeated than have ever claimed the prize.

It is not important to wear a badge of swagger when someone lays-down their life for the sake of Redemption. The King of Creation eternally elevates those who humble themselves before the eyes of the rest. They perform acts of Divinity and contrition within their hearts where no other has the vision to see. Jesus is glorified by these cloisters of His grace! He inherently knows our littleness inside and lifts us to greater sanctity for exposing it in His Name. We must love our brothers from the foundations of our faith, wanting nothing in return but the opportunity to embrace them again. Our Lady said, **"Your Mother asks all people to not fear to serve without being raised in stature. The only stature which is important is that with My Son."** After our discussion, She spoke to me at considerable length about the things yet to come. I was encouraged to continue in obedience, praying in unison with the power of Her Son. She asked me to begin contemplating the gifts of the Holy Spirit and His fruits, particularly how the world is brought to complete cultivation through the sweetness of their Truth. I promised that I would heed Her remedial instructions, to the response of Her infinite joy. As She finished, I continued to pray, not expecting Her to say anything more. Joy was flooding my heart and filling it with the peace of Her words. To my great surprise, about ten minutes hence, Our Lady said, **"I am still with you! It is so beautiful for Me to hear you say My Name. Your voice is as beautiful as your heart! Thank you for praying. Your Mother is so happy. Your prayers are heard in Heaven. You are truly witnessing the beginning of conversion and unfolding of Salvation. I bless you again and give you My Love."**

JUNE 1991

Saturday, June 1, 1991
The Virgin Mother came to us again this evening in preparation and rejoicing for the celebration of the Feast of Corpus Christi, the Body and Blood of Christ. She said, **"My dear son, you are beautiful, and so is your brother! Today, the world celebrates My Son's Body and Blood in the Eucharist. Please accept My Love for keeping Him so close to your heart."** I offered Her a multitude of prayers, especially for those who are immersed in the distraction of nightlife events. These individuals need to be brought into the Sacred Heart of Jesus. I asked Her to infuse the thought of Her Son into the minds of everyone who is participating in such revelry on this night. After my petitions, She continued, **"Your Mother hears your prayers for all those whom you have asked to be blessed. My special one, I must tell you that there are over fifty million people who are indulging in the company of drunkenness and promiscuity this night. It is the same as each week ends. Your prayers will be answered. Before this night ends, each of them will have Jesus' image in their thoughts. But, these children usually dismiss the image for earthly thoughts. This is why you and your brother's work is so important."** Following this introductory exchange, Our Lady continued with a lesson about our reception of purity.

We must all remember the Sixth Commandment of God as it is written and validly remains. Those who obey it have already accepted the gift of chastity. Our distance from this state of holiness comes from the loss of our spiritual elevation. The result is the diminishment of our love and the vision of God. Purity is maintained through abstinence outside of the Sacrament of Marriage, and through procreation within it. The intended purpose of our sexuality is for the creation and transmission of incarnate Love within the sacred bonds of Holy Matrimony. This is not a stern morality that is meant to incarcerate the passions of people as some critics have fanatically set-out to claim. It is, rather, the foundation required from which to launch our thanksgiving to God for allowing us to participate in the begetting of human life on the Earth. His purpose is scandalized when we lose this vision of His holy intention. To be precise, our innocence is effectively lost. The search for this depurated wholeness begins at the foundation of the heart. We must be truly sorry for having offended Jesus when we decline to reflect His Holy Commandments. The restoration of our angelic integrity is a heavenly gift that Jesus obtained through His horrific Sacrifice of the Cross. We would have never been given the opportunity to experience the Kingdom of Heaven had He not secured this rebirth. Therefore, if someone refuses to accept the gift of moral purgation, they are ultimately rejecting the Kingdom of God.

The Almighty Father also realizes that many people have great difficulty maintaining their unadulterated state, even though they give their most honest ability to try. Our Lady told me that this dilemma arises from our failure to realize that confessed sins have already been forgiven. The world has assumed a very distant position from the Sacrament of Reconciliation. Our failures are wiped away through the confessional, both mortal and venial in nature. They are erased from time and Eternity, with the result of our purity being restored. Those who refuse to accept this Sacrament and encourage others to follow in their path are depriving themselves and everyone they lead astray from their beatific rebirth in Our Lord. Imagine a child who is unable to see while being dressed in beautiful new clothes by his mother. The trust he holds in her word confirms to him how special he looks, even though he cannot detect his own reflection in a mirror. Faith tells him that his garments sparkle with a fresh cleanliness that everyone who sees him will immediately notice. But, he is just a child who is tempted to play with the rest of his young friends. In the process, he soils his pants and shirt, obscuring their new-fashioned essence. He knows that he has ruined his appearance by the reaction of the other children. Dejection then pushes him to sadness and despair as he realizes that what he is wearing will "never" be new again. The damage has already been done.

But, his mother soon arrives and helps her little boy with a cleansing bath, while his broadcloth and trousers tumble in the washing machine. Within a few short hours, he is redressed and as beautiful as before. He is sent-off to play with a warning to be most careful not to ruin his new clothes again. His ability to remain clean and beautiful resides in his trust of his mother. He must accept that his fine linens have been irrevocably restored. If the remotest doubt remains in his mind as to the authenticity of his purity, his original strength to maintain his beauty will be forever infringed. There is very little to impede the resoiling of his attire if he does not believe what she says. He would think, "What's the use in trying, I've already done the damage. My garments will never be new again." He has forgotten that forgiveness and absolution raise us up from the lowliness of sin. Jesus wipes-out its very occurrence and suspends the appropriate consequences. Therefore, we must pray to be forgiven; and accept our new recreation. Our Lady inspired me by saying, **"Every sin which has been forgiven was never committed."** Can we comprehend what this miracle effectively means? Jesus' convokes Mercy that is wrapped in a pardon, a gift which is almost beyond all understanding. He not only heals our insides, but expunges the very history that we rent with the gall of our errors. God makes all things new in our Divine absolution through His Son on the Cross.

Our Holy Mother told me that many thoughts of impurity come from speech and activity which are initiated in frivolity, competition, and the burdens of social irresponsibility. Many of us believe that it is popular to be promiscuous, thinking it will attract a great following of admirers. But the Truth still remains, there is nothing sanctified about the deviance of sexual exploitation. Those who partake of it must be persuaded to change through heartfelt prayers for forgiveness. Transgressions of the flesh always begin with indecorous thoughts. Holiness cannot share its repose with the likes of carnal disgrace. With His cleansing spoils, Jesus has defeated the death of those who lift their souls in the honest confession of, "*peccavi*, I have sinned," and receive the grace to be pure. When we summon His strength, thoughts of the flesh cannot be entertained. That is why holiness and chastity are found in the petitions from our hearts. Our Lady concluded, **"My special son, your Mother would like for you to rest well tonight to prepare for tomorrow. You will wake in the morning to My kiss on your cheek. Your prayer of the fifteen Mysteries on this night has reached the heavens. I will be with you tomorrow to help you, as I am always with you. I bless you and love you. Goodnight."**

Sunday, June 2, 1991

"Dear children, My beautiful children, your Mother has come today to help you to pray and bring you closer to Love. Through the Will of God, I have come to show you how helpless you are without Jesus. Please listen, children, to the words of your Heavenly Mother, given through the arc of My outstretched arms. Little ones, each of you is like a tiny wind-sail which sits in anchor to your life about you. My Love is the breeze which has come to gently move you to holiness and your destination in Jesus. Please raise your hearts so I can wisp you toward the waters of Salvation! You are all so little and cannot reach Him on your own. You are too weak to fight against the forces which burden you in mortality. You are lured to the Earth like the force of gravity by temptation and sin. Children, I have come to ask you to free yourselves from your heaviness by accepting My Son as your Savior. Through prayer, you can reach an everlasting freedom that cannot be outweighed. Please remember to pray every day, fast, do penance, and live in peace through the conversion of opening your hearts to Jesus.

Remember that you must be strong in spirit to reach the purity which fights against a weakness in will. A bolt of lightning knows its destination before it reaches the ground. It follows the path of least resistance. So it is with sin, My children. The first strike of sin is temptation, begotten through the weakness of the human heart. Please pray, My lambs, so that your hearts will become perfect in Love and Virtue against the attraction of temptation and sin. Your Heavenly Mother loves each one of your precious little hearts. I ask you to please pray continuously to Jesus. Even though you are often so dependent on others, your prayers can be lifted through your own strength. Prayer is the only way you can help yourself. It requires the help of no others, it costs no earthly value, has no limits set by time, and expects only that which you choose to receive from it. My precious children, you will receive much more than what your prayers may limit. I ask you to come together to pray as My family of little ones. My Immaculate Heart opens to those who pray so that the sweet fragrance from within it can draw you to My peace. Thank you for praying to accept the Love and loftiness of Jesus. He is your Shelter, your Shield, and your Savior. Thank you for having responded to My call."

I traveled with several other members of the Ave Maria prayer group to the First Sunday Mass in Peoria, Illinois today. It is always a very special occasion when I am able to see Father Ted again. Our Lady told me that we are in the presence of great holiness with him. She loves his soul beyond all imagining. When we returned home in the evening, our Rosary group met for the meditations of the Holy Mysteries. Afterwards, I told everyone about the letter that Timothy had written to his tenants with the help of our Virgin Mother. I related to them Her words about its power for the conversion of many people whose lives are in ruins. She said that there are thousands who have already been touched by it. This is only one of many future communications that She intends to launch into the world from our hands.

Monday, June 3, 1991

The circle of opposition against my brother and me is growing ever larger by the hour. Many believe that a public official should never distribute a letter that openly acknowledges Jesus Christ as the solution to our mutual problems. How did we arrive at the point where it is wrong to proclaim God's dominion through a public forum in a country that is supposedly free? Our Lady did not allow Timothy to stay with me tonight because of the growing hatred against us. I have begged God to bestow the gift of understanding upon everyone in our midst. It is an incalculable sorrow to see such marveling peace being rejected by the exacerbation of human egoism. This is not the example that the Blessed Virgin is putting before us. In reparation, I diligently continued to work on my Diary tonight, hoping that She would recognize me as one of Her children who desires Her guidance with all my heart.

Tuesday, June 4, 1991

Timothy returned today and we knelt to pray again. Our Lady said, **"My special one, God's mighty Plan is on course. Your lives are being blessed! The world is being converted by your suffering. You are gaining strength of character and a special place in your Mother's Heart. Now, you can feel as Jesus felt. Your Heavenly Mother is with you and will always be with you. Please pray with Me and together we will deliver God's Plan to fruition. Thank you for remaining with Me. As has happened throughout the world, your Mother has had to ask My chosen children to alter their schedules so that there can be peace. The time has come. Please remember that your Heavenly Mother wants the world to turn to My Son. This cannot be done in the midst of turmoil. I ask that peace always be preserved. The Will of God and My intercession will not be interrupted..."** She also told me that our conversations must become confidential between Her, my brother, and myself because those who have resorted to belligerence are ordering us to "stop the nonsense." They refuse to believe that we are telling the truth. Our Lady has asked many of Her messengers to alter their personal itineraries to avoid altercation with those who would destroy their peace. Moving the visionaries of Medjugorje, Yugoslavia on many occasions to accommodate the changing social atmosphere is the example that She cited to me. Until we are instructed otherwise, Her miraculous communication is to be shared with no others for the sake of our own safety and the work yet to be done. The conversion of lost souls is far too important to be impeded by the dissension of our detractors.

Wednesday, June 5, 1991

There was a private meeting today between Timothy and our Roman Catholic Bishop concerning the messages we have been receiving. Our Lady spoke with me about it, thanking us for placing the text of Her messages in his hands. This has been a monumental step toward opening the world to a better understanding of Her miraculous intercession on behalf of all humankind. Even though I was very happy with the day's events, I was not feeling well when the Blessed Mother came to speak with me this evening. My stomach was terribly upset and my head was writhing with pain. I cannot help but believe that the blatant forces against us is having a terrible physical effect on me. Early in the evening, the Holy Mother asked me to go to bed before I had finished praying the Glorious mysteries. I hoped that I was not letting Her down by being unable to continue. But, She said, **"Thank you for praying when you feel so badly. Your prayers are always very strong!"**

Thursday, June 6, 1991

About 3:30 a.m., I awoke feeling extremely strong and healthy again and Our Lady called me to finish the Glorious Mysteries with Her. She said, **"My special child, I have come close to you so you can be filled with My peace. I will continue to speak through your words and thoughts! You have been blessed with My presence. Your messages to the world will continue. I love you very much. You must know how happy a time it is in your life and your world. The days are becoming filled with peace and God's work and My intercession are on course."**

Saturday, June 8, 1991

Our Lady beckoned us to pray again about twelve-thirty in the morning. It is so peaceful during the night for lifting our petitions to Heaven. The special messages that we have been receiving on Sundays, Feast days, and Holy days will now be given on Sundays only, in an order and sequence originally intended by God through their full entirety. But, the circumstances surrounding us require that the Blessed Mother accomplish Her intercession on a different schedule than before. We must maintain our peace with holy order! I have been told that I can still offer Her future transcriptions to the Ave Maria prayer group, if they desire to hear them at all. Before departing, our Immaculate Queen admonished me for depriving myself of rest.

7:00 P.M.

Upon kneeling to pray at nine-thirty this evening, Our Lady came again and said, **"Good evening, My special ones. I am with you to show you My peace and Love. I have been with you throughout the day. Thank you for your prayers, especially to preserve the lives who would endanger** themselves. My special son, your family is very strong. Both of you are so special to your Heavenly Mother and the mission of peace. I am with you to protect you. By continuing to pray, you will receive the messages which will serve to convert the world. Tonight, you will learn about humility..." She continued with a dissertation about "humility." Although I received this lesson tonight, I was told to enter it in my Diary under another heading and only upon Her further instruction. It was a very beautiful and evocative message. During my discussion with Her this evening, I was also requested to share my feelings about everything that She has asked us to do thus far.

I recalled an incident which happened several days ago when I joined another assembly of the faithful to recite the Holy Rosary. After being summoned to share Our Lady's words before those who were interested, I spoke through the passionate love in my heart about the seriousness of our faith and obedience, recalling Her previous lessons to our group at home. When I had finished, many of them behaved as though they were somewhat insulted, although I could not recall saying anything offensive. Their attitude concerned me quite deeply. But tonight, our Holy Mother blessed my efforts by saying, **"The children there heard what they needed to hear! They reacted in accordance with their own degrees of faith. Your words were Divine in nature, especially those concerning My children who need to work together for the good of Jesus. The conversion I seek is on course. Your Mother is very happy with you. Please assure yourself that your Mother and your Savior are smiling upon you and your brother. You have been given many graces and gifts as a result of your prayers."**

Sunday, June 9, 1991

"Dear children, today I have come again through the Love of My Son to ask you to look at yourselves and your faith. I invite you to let God be God! Please release yourselves from your tasks of the days to listen to the words of your Heavenly Mother which guide you to Jesus. I ask that you remain open to receive My Son in your lives. Children, you lose sight of God because you do not take time for Him. In your human world, My Son is diminished because you recognize only that which your hands have made. Little ones, you see but a tiny fragment of the beautiful Creation of God. Love begins on the inside of Creation. It is the heart and the conscience which follows it through the Spirit of Love in those who follow Jesus. Your mind knows only what your heart teaches it. My special ones, I ask that you allow your hearts to be filled with Love and your thoughts and actions will be holy. Please understand that Love has been created in you. Remember the little bees of the Earth who build their world in perfect symmetry. God is the architect and they are the carpenters. None of these tiny creatures knows that he is building a flawless shape identical to the next. So it is with your faith, My children. All you need to do to make your world perfect is to pray and it will become restored to the order and beauty which My Son has intended for it. Your hearts will be filled with the sweetness of honey for all to share through the Love of My Son, Jesus Christ.

Children, please do not allow indifference to keep a grasp upon you. Through coldness of heart, you become the prey of temptation and sin. Please warm your hearts by praying your Rosary every day. Through prayer, fasting, penance, and conversion, the appetite of these predators will perish without satisfaction. Please pray to remain protected from the scourge of sin. Remember that when you are pricked with a needle, you first concern yourselves with the pain instead of what is flowing from your veins. Little ones, it is not the pain that will hurt you the most. I ask that you learn to recognize temptation as the pain which warns you of the loss of your lifeblood of holiness through sin. Please give your sins to Jesus and you will be healed and spared for all Eternity. In Jesus, you will be kept alive with a flourishing spirit. Your Heavenly Mother loves each of you too much to allow you to suffer the failures of human mortality. Please come to My Immaculate Heart which reaches out to you to teach the lessons of Love and Purity! Thank you for being My obedient ones. Thank you for having responded to My call."

Our Rosary group met for prayer later in the evening. Once they departed, my brother and I continued to offer our petitions, while our Virgin Mother said, "**My beautiful son, I love you so much. Thank you for touching the hearts of your brothers and sisters today. My message contains the same beauty as the children to whom it was given. My precious son, your prayers are always sincere. Thank you for praying from your heart. You are to remember the words of My message today about the heart filled with Love lending holiness to thoughts and actions.**" She urged me to be unconcerned whether anyone believes me regarding Her supernatural manifestations. What matters most is that every heart should become filled with God's Love. She spoke to me at length about eliminating my worries and strengthening my patience. I was helped to more clearly understand the spiritual dimensions of the occurrences around us. She expanded my awareness to realize that what often seems like an unfortunate set of circumstances is actually the prelude and advancement of our transformation into a higher state of grace.

Monday, June 10, 1991

About 9:30 p.m., we began the Holy Rosary and Our Lady came to us again to speak about the power of our prayers. **"Good evening, My beautiful son. I speak to you about the Plan of God, who loves all of His children. Thank you for praying. Many lives are saved through the prayers of My children. Please know that millions of faithful children like yourself bring the world to grace and Salvation. If only more of My children knew the power of their prayers!"** She followed by addressing the emotional condition of my brother for those who are accusing him of mental instability. She said powerfully, **"He is completely healthy of mind, normal, functional, and capable of leading any society to health, security, and to My Son. God Almighty has been served, praised, and glorified on this day!"** Her conversation was quite abbreviated this evening, and I was told that I would be learning more about compassion during the next few days. She thanked us for honoring our Father in Heaven, then offered Her blessing before departing. **"I will teach you more about the gifts of My Son. Tomorrow you will learn about compassion. You have My blessing as these days pass. I love you."**

Tuesday, June 11, 1991

Timothy and I knelt to pray at the evening hour of nine o'clock and Our Lady began Her message with the following words, **"Please smile your largest smile, hearts have been won today! There is no dissension of hearts. There is no false pride. There is no separation. There is the unity of peace and Love. Both of you must remain united and strong. My special son, your Mother is very close to you. Thank you for loving Jesus as I love Him. Many are far from Him. You have responded like no other, so willing and anxious. Thank you! Today, I would like to speak to you about compassion..."** The Holy Virgin began by telling me that compassion is a blossom of the flower of peace, which is natural to the display of authentic Love for our brethren in Christ. Showing sympathy toward others is not only recognizing their suffering, but realizing its power within ourselves. In our search for this pious virtue, we must begin at the very foundation of Life, which is the Love of the Almighty Father, residing comfortably in the depths of the human heart. This presence is the eternal affection of God which He shares within His Creation. Our Lady told me that compassion has been necessary from the beginning of time, even if there would have been only one person inhabiting the Earth. This is because kindness begins by understanding the inner-self before we can know the personal aggravation that is encountered by every other soul in the world.

Physical and mental agony are unavoidable consequences of the human condition. When we invoke understanding for ourselves and others, we acknowledge our unity in the Mystical Body of Christ. We are intrinsically singular because Jesus composes every one of the beautiful people who have been, and will continue to be, created by God. This encompassing nature of the Holy Spirit is a splendid mystery of His Love. Our awareness begins when we recognize the need for cohesion beyond our imaginary borders. We naturally desire the absence of conflict which, in truth, is a yearning for the Divinity of Heaven. Our Lady said that this is actually a longing for a personal wholesomeness within ourselves. This positive inclination of the soul will lead us toward the Light of Paradise. The lessons of life tell us boldly that no one wishes to suffer alone because there is a collective tendency to share it. This propensity provides a wider thoroughfare for Love to be exchanged through our desire to help those whom God has chosen to emulate His Son on the Cross. The environment becomes compatible and communicable, much like the freshly-tilled soil awaiting its new spring seed. Everyone endures the same mortal consequences and circumstances at the start of each day. Those who search for unity at the strike of the morning bell must base their existence upon the compliant sharing of the plight of all humanity. Initially, we must learn to have respect for ourselves or we will never embrace the sacrifices that are raining-down upon those who grieve alone. It is this same realization which teaches us the depth of the Passion of the Solitary Warrior, the Lamb who was slain for our Salvation. When we embrace His Light without repulsion, we can forge any pit that might stand in our way.

 Compassion is most powerful when invoked to forgive the transgressions of others. No one truly believes that they are absent of sin. This recognition allows us to know that our families and friends are vulnerable, too. Upon realizing our own inherent culpability, the admission of our common imprudence is a means of sharing the helplessness that befalls the most invincible of men. Each day's errors and miscalculations are kindred to all, yet are forgivable as a result of our consistory inheritance and the Mercy of Almighty God. Therein lies the foundation for kindheartedness, which leads us to complete absolution. The reason we show compassion to others is so that we can see the sweet harvest of ourselves in them, effecting the restoration of their soul, and that of our own, for an unbroken circle of Love. We will receive vindication for our personal faults as candidates for Redemption when we pardon those who are offensive toward us. This is what we ask of our Father in Heaven in Jesus' great prayer, *"Forgive us our trespasses as we forgive those who trespass against us."* Our souls are then cultivated to implore the ultimate perfection of Christ. I asked our Holy Mother if it is possible to be raised above the human condition. She responded, **"No man or woman who walks the Earth now will become the Sacrificial Lamb of God or His Mother, but the example has been established to show that all can be made perfect through the acceptance of My Son and His vigilance against sin** and transgression. The beginning of this is Love, made up in part by compassion of one for another."

She continued by reminding me that Her intercession is based solely upon what God allows Her to do. She is the Mediatrix of all Graces who offers our petitions to Her Son, Jesus, for the dispensation of His infinite power. Our beseeching requisitions are changing the course of mortal existence because Our Lord is responding to them. Her presence is adequate proof of that fact. She is deeply inspiring Her children on Earth to seek Salvation from within our hearts. I remember an earlier occasion when I was shown a set of scales. One side was weighed-down with our sins, while the other piled-high with our earnest intentions. I watched as our petitions changed the balance so as to outweigh the entire collection of our faults and the blind errancies we have chosen to ignore. She reminded me of this vision by saying, **"Prayer will change the scale of abortion, numbers of lost souls, and multitudes of sins."** Finally, I was asked to clarify a misunderstanding that is held by too many people. There are those who are unilaterally asking Our Lady to change the course of human destiny. She said, **"I am the Mother of God who has come to humanity through the grace of Jesus' Love and Will. I come to bring peace and to show that My Son is real, alive and the adjudicator of human destiny. All men should pray for *His* Mercy! I will help you because I love you."**

Wednesday, June 12, 1991

"The Lord is King; let the Earth rejoice; let the many isles be glad. Clouds and darkness are round about Him, justice and judgement are the foundation of His throne. Fire goes before him and consumes His foes round about. His lightenings illumine the world; the Earth sees and trembles. The mountains melt like wax before the Lord, before the Lord of all the Earth. The heavens proclaim His justice, and all peoples see His Glory." Psalm 97:1-6.

Timothy and I were together again this evening to pray so that Our Lady could continue Her quest for the conversion of humanity. She began, **"My beautiful sons, the day is so special because you are in it! Thank you for being My obedient ones. I would like to tell you that your Diary is so richly blessed with Truth and Love. Thank you for writing My words for others to share. Your handwritten words must be kept, also. They are My messages to you. My Son is glorified by all of this time and effort. We will proceed for the Glory of God. Today, there will be a dissertation about the Spirit of Love in Truth."** America has founded its government upon our trust in God. The founding articles state that all men are created equal, with certain inalienable rights: Life, Liberty, and the pursuit of Happiness. The most important premise is the likeness of people under God, but this is also where we have miserably failed. The Almighty Father gives us freedom from sin so that we may pursue eternal gratification by living the Love of Christ. There can be no prejudice in this heralded struggle. Those who pray, while others pray for them, will be strong in faith. This is the only power that sustains our ability to combat the pressures of human life brought by the evil which is trying to diminish our souls. When we turn to Jesus, our future becomes filled with peace.

Our Lady has asked me to paraphrase some of Her lessons using my own words, as much as humanly possible. But, the beauty of what She told me today rendered it nearly beyond my capacity to explain it any better. Therefore, I have recorded it just as She said it. **"The Spirit of Love in Truth is the reality of God. The Love in Truth determines the destiny of Creation. One must look at the Spirit of Love in Truth as a flame on a candle. The flame is on top, is the brightness, the heat, and the color. The flame is the beauty and the bringer of Light. All this is good, but the flame is not only the Truth, it is also the effect of the Truth. The candle, itself, is the Truth which makes the brightness possible. As days continue to pass, the world unfolds, one day at a time, such as the candle wax lowers each moment to reveal a new shape to the candle, a new shape to the world. The common thread of life and days is the wick, which is the Love which runs from the foundation of the candle of Life to the beautiful flame of reality which people see and enjoy for the radiant view it makes possible. This is very important! The Spirit of Love in Truth, the candle of God's beauty and Creation is made possible by His overwhelming Love and purpose. God ignited the flame which breathed life into Creation for all the world to see. There is a special world to be seen by those who allow the Light to draw them to it and see what reflects it..."**

Creation unfolds as a delightful gift of the bounty of God's Love when we accept the Way, the Truth, and the Life. Jesus is the Light who emanates through the beauty of the universe to bring every living soul to contrition. He is Life, given to us so that we may overcome the darkness, accept His peace, share His Love, and obtain His Promise of eternal happiness. Our Lady always asks me if I need more help in understanding. Sometimes, I am allowed to contemplate Her words for several days before She elevates me to a higher comprehension. I feel like I am a student who is learning at the side of a wonderful teacher. I thank God continuously for allowing Her to come to us. Praise be to Christ Jesus! Our Lady concluded today, **"My children, Jesus is always with you. You are always in My Heart and prayers. I also love those who do not believe in Me or My Son. I ask you to use your holy water to bless yourselves in the name of the Blessed and Divine Trinity. I love you with the power and grace of My Son."**

Friday, June 14, 1991

We traveled to Notre Dame University in South Bend, Indiana, today for the opening of an extraordinary conference celebrating the appearance of our Blessed Mother to six little children in Medjugorje, Yugoslavia. After the initial talks, we began our procession to the Grotto while praying the Rosary. It was apparent that the grace of our Blessed Mother was with us. We participated in the services at the Grotto, then retired to our motel room in anticipation of the next day's sessions. As we knelt to pray, Our Lady came to tell us goodnight. I was told that She enjoyed listening to the prayers of Her children. She also said that the conference has Divine intentions, but it lacks the simplicity She desires. We must remember the poverty and humble beginnings of Our Lord at His birth in Bethlehem. There are millions of children throughout the world who are still living in destitution, just as in the prophetic days of Jesus. Marian conferences do very little to address these ongoing problems. While nearly everyone in attendance is affluent and wealthy, having the resources to help those who suffer, most of them climb into their Cadillacs and drive back home.

Saturday, June 15, 1991

After a very pleasant day at the conference, Our Lady came to us late in the evening. She thanked everyone for worshiping Jesus during the afternoon Adoration of the Most Blessed Sacrament. **"My beautiful children, thank you for adoring My Son! When He was adored, the fanfare was gone. The simple Truth of His Love and peace remained!"** Since my brother and I were both tired from our travel and activities, we were not being as kind toward one another as our Holy Mother has asked. She quite strongly admonished us to display more respect and love in the future. This will become more prevalent when we invoke greater patience.

Sunday, June 16, 1991

During our drive back home from the conference, Our Lady led us to a shrine just beyond the city limit of St. John, Indiana. Situated off the highway on a patch of land that was quartered from a farming field was a towering concrete statue of the Blessed Virgin Mary. It was exceedingly beautiful, projecting a powerful witness to Her Immaculate grace. I could feel Her overwhelming presence emanating from its grandeur. When I saw Her likeness, I felt as though I was gazing at a historical monument when the Statue of Liberty immediately came to mind. After we arrived home later in the evening, I spoke with our Holy Mother about this wonderful site. She responded, **"I am the Lady of Liberty! I will lead all to Jesus to make them free of their sins. My torch is the Light of the Love of My Son. Amen."** When She said this, the following poem, written by Emma Lazarus, suddenly entered my thoughts. It is engraved on a stone tablet within the pedestal on which the Statue of Liberty stands amidst the waters of the New York harbor.

<u>*The New Colossus*</u>
Not like the brazen giant of Greek fame,
With conquering limbs astride from land to land;
Here at our sea-washed, sunset gates shall stand
A mighty Woman with a torch, whose flame
Is the imprisoned lightning, and Her name
Mother of Exiles. From Her beacon-hand
Glows world-wide welcome; Her mild eyes command
The air-bridged harbor that twin cities frame.
"Keep ancient lands, your storied pomp!" cries She
With silent lips. "Give Me your tired, your poor,
Your huddled masses yearning to breathe free,
The wretched refuse of your teeming shores.
Send these, the homeless, tempest-tost to Me,
I lift My lamp beside the golden door!"

Tuesday, June 18, 1991

Timothy returned to pray with me again this evening and, as we recited the Holy Rosary, our Blessed Virgin Mother came to speak about many unbelievers who are in our midst. Our hearts are being fortified by Her encouragement so that we can continue to serve Christ Jesus with confidence. She said, **"I am with you, My sons! I love you! Today, we will continue to pray together. You must be strong against the forces of evil. Do not take My messages to others for verification of authenticity. No others have the capacity to know! Not even other visionaries know how I come to do My Son's work. Together, you must be strong against this period of unbelief. Do you see why it is so difficult for your Heavenly Mother to help convert the world? Do you see why so many do not take My intercession seriously? My children, it is due to fear that you are required to change your lives to believe. It is too great a sacrifice for many."** She continued by reminding me again that it is not a requirement for others to believe that She is appearing in my home. It is only necessary that they accept the Love of the Savior of the world and the Promise He has made to redeem our souls. The battle should never be focused upon the authenticity of Her supernatural works or the means She employs to teach Her children about conversion.

"Please do not let anyone discourage you in your work. The difficulties which are coming were also faced by Jesus, but in much larger scope. Anything you suffer can be given as a gift to Jesus. It is

suffering that will lead to the conversion of many. **Thank you for suffering for the Salvation of others! I will be with you as I was with Jesus, to pray for your strength and peace in your trials. It is truly a sacrifice larger than you believe! It has earned you great standing with Jesus."** She reiterated Her point that it takes only two people to compose a prayer group. Tonight, I sensed a more prophetic tone to Her words. There are thousands of souls present in an assembly of only two if their supplications are from the heart and worthy of the grace of God. The Angels and Saints comprise these humble multitudes! In continuing Her lessons, I was asked to delineate Her explanation of "balance" in the pages of this Diary. I have been continuously chided by my friends to gain a more complacent spiritual equilibrium in my life and to offset my religious fervor with the malapropos matters of the material world. Our Lady has helped me to understand the intervention of the Holy Spirit, while showing Her disapproval with the mere bicron of faith and understanding that others are willing to afford our Almighty Father in return.

Many times, we are asked to hybridize our Christian beliefs by those who notice the change in our behavior, caused by our new orientation toward God. Jesus tells us that this redisposition is in direct contradiction to the urgency of the world. We will be accused by career-minded people of becoming out-of-touch with reality as we begin leading our lives of spiritual avocation. The centeredness that many of them encourage us to follow is an opposing emersion in mortal distractions in order to dilute the holiness they see growing in our newborn Christian hearts. This state of high piety that they witness shakes-down their own apathetic indifference. But, they still refuse to admit that they should give any more than a mere pittance of themselves to Jesus. To that end, they errantly conclude that the holy conviction before them must be an inordinate aberration. Everyone must realize, instead, that Our Lord destroyed this soul-endangering counterpoise on the Cross. To live in a state of grace is our complete abandonment to the Will of the Father during every moment of life. It is an allegiance and passion which concedes no equation between sanctity and sin, or between saints and reprobates. These same people would have attempted to dissuade Jesus Christ from taking-up His Cross. But, what did He say to Simon Peter in response to that plea? Without mincing a syllable of His words, He proclaimed with the strongest of candor, ***Get thee behind me, you Satan!***

Wednesday, June 19, 1991

Our Lady continued to comfort our feelings in the midst of the terrible disturbances that are now being instigated around us. Her plan is on course and She has no intention of turning-back at this late hour in the destiny of man. God is being glorified and the conversion of thousands is occurring before our weeping eyes of joy. **"My beautiful son, the Lord God of All is being glorified on this day! You are seeing others dissemble themselves to be regained in the future. The Glory of God is at hand! You have won! There is much to be happy for! My messages have gone to hundreds of thousands. They have received them and are living them. Thank you for responding to My call."** Upon returning home in the evening, I began to pray with my brother again. Our Virgin Mother came and continued by explaining "self-control" and the importance of maintaining our peace. We began by reading Psalm 111. *"Fear of the Lord is the beginning of Wisdom, prudent are all who live by it."* Wisdom begins in the reverential fear of God! It is the strong foundation of our spiritual confidence. Nothing on this Earth is worthy of trepidation! We maintain order over ourselves when we realize that worldly vexations and seamy delusions are not from the Spirit of Jesus. They are temporary phenomenon which are destined to dissolve into nothingness, just as all else that will perish into dust. We must invoke the Wisdom of Christ to sustain our struggle for Salvation.

Those who will not pray with us are lulled into temptation and sin, just as sure as the sun sets at dusk. Indifference seductively anaesthetizes their knowledge that mortality and its false stimulation will eventually fall. This blindness can destroy the very foundation of any genuine conscience by opening the door through which evil will enter and infiltrate its offensive domination. Those who embrace the Holy Paraclete will not trespass against the rest of humanity because the clanging for humble submission rings too loud in their hearts. If we should lose this war by misfortune, only violence, destruction, and disorder will prevail. But, if our minds are perpetually nurtured with Love from the charity of Heaven, our erratic actions and critical words will never be induced from the start. Indeed, the virtues of prayer, compassion, and grace are always dispensed by the Love of our Almighty Father. The moment of Truth comes when the integrity of our faith is put to the test. Even the most sincere of intentions can be shaken without it. If we find our trust stumbling even a diminutive trifle, it is reflected in our own self-deprecation as we forget our priceless value to Christ. When we understand the great esteem in which we are held by the Hosts of Paradise, we will effectuate a newfound conviction that no force in our path can devour. In this paradisial Light, we are required to behave as citizens of Heaven, displaying every fruit of goodness that our ecstatic souls can employ. Hearts who imitate Jesus will always live in His dignity out of reverential respect for the people He gives us to love.

When we are filled with piety, we will actualize it through our thoughts, emotions, and the way we care for the poor. Good works will forever be a portion of the authority we maintain over our own consciousness to do the Lord's Will on the Earth. Fanaticism for such service is never detrimental to the spirit when Love is the reason for our emotions. By all means, it is our prime vehicle for transmitting the grace of Our Lady of Perpetual Help. She said today, **"No heart that is in control of Love can resist showing the emotions which follow."** Jesus Christ yearns for us to be one in His Love. This means that we must be self-appointed in the direction of the Life He pours forth. Only Love is the answer! The strength of our inner-peace resides within the mystery of the Holy Trinity of God. Our vision is widened when we transcend the standards that are made only by materialistic men. Jesus is our example of perfect stability of the heart. When we love in His likeness, we remain self-assured in every circumstance, aware of all our feelings, and bold in any obtuse situation. One never has to aggressively stand guard over something that others cannot steal. Our dignity is eternal because it is secured by the Love of the Messiah. Hell would have to destroy Him before He would let us surrender to that shame But, He has already won that contest, high upon a dark hilltop that we remember to this day as the Crucifixion that saved our souls.

Friday, June 21, 1991

Timothy and I attended Holy Mass this evening in response to Our Lady's continuing invitation that we receive the Body of Christ in the Most Blessed Sacrament. Later, we knelt to pray and She came to speak to us again. **"My beautiful son, yours is a special life, a blessed life filled with Love and peace! Thank you for staying at the side of your brother. My messages to you are to continue."** She instructed me as to why it is important that we remain united in Her Immaculate Heart. We only know what we seek to comprehend. Therefore, everyone must move to understand the Love of Our Savior. His peace will overcome all dissension when we perceive human life through the eyes of His Divinity. Unity in prayer begets good will in the presence of the Holy Spirit. Our Blessed Mother told me about the fractures in our families and nations caused by those who are frightened by Her celestial miracles. The more opposition they impose against Her intercession, the greater will be the faith they need to return to the Truth. God is magnificently glorified in the process. **"Darkness will always be replaced by greater Light."**

She spoke to me again today about purity, saying, **"There are many who mistake the purpose of their sexuality. It is for the creation of new Life in the Sacrament of Holy Matrimony. It has no other use or value."** I thought of how unacceptable this proclamation would sound to the self-indulgent world. She said that it is my free decision to assist in the deliverance of Her messages to God's people everywhere. I am not mortally bound to respond and would not be out-of-grace if I choose to discontinue. She wants me to realize the magnitude of this sacrifice. **"You stand beside Me at the** cost of your reputation!" I told Her that I will fulfill every request and witness to every word that She has spoken. **"Your actions bring loving tears to My eyes. Thank you for living Love!"** I understand that the only charitable destiny is our abandonment in obedience to the Immortal Son of God. Grace is gained by our complete "yes" to all that is good and acceptable in His eyes. This ratification of His Will is an act of new life and beginnings because it conquers the darkness of sin. Living a life of Love will take us to the Kingdom of Heaven.

Recently, many people have been emotionally questioning the validity of my work, even without having seen it in advance. My statements are being taken out-of-context, with the result being the defamation of my personal character. I have always told the truth, but many others do not understand the spiritual concepts I am relating to them. In response to this pool of concern, I have remained silent to the onslaught, which has only broadened my persecution for not being open enough. I am pressured to give honest answers to legitimate questions. But, my explanations are repeatedly turned against me. Our Lady helped me with this dilemma by saying, **"No person can bind another to respond to a rhetorical question if they do not feel it necessary or acceptable to do so. It is an invasion of the privacy of Truth in the human heart. Therefore, it is ethical to state that the information which others may be seeking is unavailable to them. Please remember the parabolic speech of Jesus to deal with rhetorical questions. He is so wise! The world is filled with people who seek information to use for misinformation. God will protect the Truth in thought and communication. Remember that He holds the key to all Truth."**

Saturday, June 22, 1991

This morning, Satan manifested himself very forcefully through two people, for whom I hold great affection, who came to my door and demanded that I surrender my allegiance to Our Lady. About ten-minutes into the altercation, I began praying the Rosary as loud as I could. When I encouraged my opponents to pray with me, I was mocked for my devotion to the Mother of God. I trembled inside because my disposition is not accustomed to such attacks, almost like a glaive being driven through the center of my heart. I feel quite ingenuous to have expected everyone to respond with happiness, excitement, and openness at my announcement of the messages we have been receiving. I somehow know that this is what Our Lady expected to happen. It is my heartfelt desire that everyone on Earth be ecstatic about this great gift from Heaven. My comfort resides in our Holy Mother's protection. Early in the afternoon, She came to bolster my strength and confidence by saying, **"Praise be to God! Satan will not win! My son, you are seeing evil right before your eyes. You must not dignify any more of Satan's attempts.**

Remember that the peace of silence is one of the greatest gifts of peace. Feel the victory from the battle! You have been a shining star for Me today. My Son brings His blessings upon you. Your forgiveness is a great act of charity. You can see the true value of peace. It is, indeed, based on Truth."

At ten o'clock tonight, we continued the Rosary and Our Lady said, **"Your Mother is with you, My son. Thank you for praying. Give your sorrows to the morning Light and they will be taken away. Feel your hearts at peace. Bring Me your sorrows."** She said that everyone should pray for spiritual understanding, but many refuse to seek the Light. They attempt to malign the lives and words of Her messengers in an effort to prove that Her intercession is false. They should, instead, pray for the discernment to accept the truth that they do not have the capacity to judge what the Savior of the world will do. We will never find Jesus if we are searching for signs of Satan in His place. **"I will help you! Please know that My Son walks with you always in your journey of faith. Think of the peace to come!"** Our Lady completed our conversation by blessing my brother and me. We are to sleep without consternation tonight, not worrying about whatever lies ahead. We are in Her perpetual care, a perfect place to wait for Jesus to bring the end of the world.

Sunday, June 23, 1991

"Dear children, today I invite each of you to answer the call of peace. Many of you are hungry for peace during these days. My little ones, your Mother asks that you open yourselves to receive the Love of My Son so that you will have peace. Love and peace are united. There can be no peace without Love, because it is fed by Love. As the leaves on the trees turn their bottoms to the sky to receive a gentle rain from above, I ask each of you to turn your hearts to the heavens to receive the showering of God's Love for you. By accepting His Love, you will be nourished and will flourish and grow in strength and beauty. Each of you plays such an important part in the beauty of My Son's Creation. You hold a special place on your branch of life which is nurtured by the Almighty Arm of God. Little ones, your Mother has come today to call each of you to dismiss your trials in the loving warmth of My arms. I bring you the peace of Jesus to make you happy. Please pray the Rosary and you will live in peace. Remember that Jesus loves you and will save you from the burdens of your days when you accept His Love. Thank you for accepting Jesus as your Help and Savior! Thank you for having responded to My call."

Timothy remained overnight again so that we could be together for our morningtide prayers. During the recitation of our petitions, I opened the Bible to read the Scriptures in preparation for Holy Mass. Without realizing it, I chose the same passage from the Gospel of St. Mark which was read later at our Eucharistic celebration. When we returned home, we knelt to pray and Our Lady said, **"My son, the morning is beautiful and so are you! Your worries are gone! I am with you today to bring your peace! The battle against Satan is still raging, but this will not inhibit My plan. All of My messages will come to you."** She confirmed that She led me to the Scripture reading today as a grace for my soul. The Holy Spirit is very powerful in these miraculous ways when we open our hearts to receive Him. I was also reminded that Satan is a coward and his evil is stopped dead in its tracks when we carry Holy Water on our person and use it very often against him. The Virgin Mary blessed us before departing, telling me that another lesson about charity will be soon forthcoming.

We continued the Rosary at nine o'clock this evening and Our Lady came to pray with us again. She always presents Herself in humility when we contemplate the Most Sacred Mysteries. Tonight, She discussed why my brother is put to sleep when She comes to speak to me. Several people have asserted that Timothy's induced unconsciousness at the wishes of Our Lady is a violation of his own free will. I asked Her about their claims. She said that he has freely surrendered himself in obedience to God and his life is consecrated to Jesus toward the purpose of the conversion of humanity. Hence, there is no violation of the harmony of his soul. He is serving the Almighty Father in the way that he desires. My brother is put to sleep so that Our Lady can speak to me without his foreknowledge of our private conversations. **"Please remember the power of the union of you and your brother. There is much to be accomplished by your union. One day, the world will know by your example to seek God. Your peace will manifest peace. Remember that I love you always. I am with all of My children."** The Blessed Mother asked us to remain fervently beside Her because our petitions are very powerful. The Will of God is fulfilled in His own good time. But, if we refrain from seeking His intercession, the days can only mount against us. There are too many people who think that their intentions are never heard, or if they are, it takes too long for the answers to arrive. In truth, all of our holy wishes are honored in a most provident way through our patience and trust in the Will of the Lord. The many prayers that are fulfilled by our Creator in Heaven often go unacknowledged because those who lift them are not open to recognize there evidential presence. This is true regarding our reaction to the Virgin Mother's intercession. She is God's answer to mankind's supplications for unity, deliverance, and universal peace.

Thursday, June 27, 1991

My brother and I continued in our new role as Our Lady's little children by kneeling again tonight to pray the Rosary. Our Virgin Mother came and said, **"I am beside you! Thank you for praying with great faith. You must remember that I will always be with you!"** She then described the most revealing and soul-inspiring affirmation of piety that I have ever heard in my life. I pray to be able to relate Her intercession in a way that reflects its awesome apotheosis. This evening, She spoke about our mutual absolution, charity, reason, and thought. **"You must always remember that forgiveness is the greatest act of charity."** Many people are belabored by the assumption that to forget the faults of humanity is a sacrifice of some sort of unimaginable magnitude. When we erase the failures of our trespassers from our memory, our love is fully actualized. Since there should be no profit from it, our forbearance must be free to everyone who offends us, without a single exception. Relieving our brothers of their guilt is a spontaneous outpouring of the Holy Spirit from our hearts. Charity is a gift that is characterized by a gift of generosity from our available resources. But, it does not always constitute a sacrifice of the things that we really need to survive. Our Lady said, **"My son, charity is an act of good will, and there is no cost for forgiveness. It is a natural act of Love."** Therefore, pardoning our fellow man is a product of charitable works that comes from a heart that is committed to Jesus Christ, His Glory, His Plan, and His Promise.

To renounce our own resentment toward others is the greatest act of almsgiving because it expunges our memory of anxiety, embarrassment, humiliation, and anger for the sake of the Kingdom of God. When we extend the sign of peace from within our hearts, we are sharing the most beautiful treasure of Love that God has ever intended. **"Your Mother is calling the world to forgive and love in the way that My Son loves and forgives."** Our Lord embraces His people without limit or any sign of impediment. He forgives us both infinitely and totally. Our lives must imitate that same Divinity, just as a mirror pointed to the heavens can reflect the incalculable light-years of the universe. Since charity is giving generously from our available resources, then our greatest offering of Love is to pray for one another. Seeking God's help for those who do not know Him is an act of charity because, through it, we are giving from our collective bounty. The wealth at our hands through imploring the assistance of God is the infinite riches of Heaven. We can obtain anything that our brothers and sisters desire by beseeching the Truth on their behalf. When acts of goodness are amplified within His Spirit, the Love of our Redeemer resounds throughout Creation as it rises from the depths of our hearts, rolling back the clouds of darkness, enlightening our minds, and bursting forth to renew the world. The Resurrected Christ lives through our acts of shared compassion, and our Savior is glorified in the process.

Our Lady told me that many acts of charity are performed without the knowledge of the giver. Such is one of the greatest fruits of our intercessory petitions. God fulfills our hopes and dreams by changing the world in response to our fervent entreaties. Indeed, the Blessed Virgin Mary prays for us every hour and most of us never realize that She is doing it. Her Son acknowledges our love for one another and advances our hopes into the lives of those whom we commend to His care. These desires will never be extinguished because they originate from the Light of the Cross. Jesus is the reason that they are forever granted. He knows that they are a fruit of our heart, little embers that serve as the interface between Heaven and Earth. When we help our brothers and sisters to live in faith, it is an act of charitable works. We assist in the strengthening of their love by offering them our own. If the human mind is not nourished with the piousness that is generated in the heart, fear will almost always diminish our peace. Many people believe that our thoughts are able to govern the universe because of their ability to pursue sound reasoning. Our Lady says that we should never assume that the human intellect is self-sustainable while independent from God. Only the heart contains the genius of the ages. It is there that Jesus has granted us the ability to know Him and to share His creative Spirit. The chambers of the heart hoist the foundation of the corbie-steps from where we can see beyond the horizon of mortal understanding. Prayer from these solemn perches carries us into the arms of Our Lord. We will be granted Salvation as we allow ourselves to be transported to the Altar of Sacrifice and receive the Holy Eucharist. This is what our Blessed Mother has been telling the world for the past 2000 years. We must believe Her intensely if we wish to escape the darkness of the world. Humanity is much too headstrong instead of embracing the strength of God's Spirit. Our Lady says, **"Do you see why it is so important to pray from the heart?"**

Friday, June 28, 1991

"My beautiful children, I am happy that you are again together for My Son. Your Mother asks that you remember your Holy Water. This has been a day for peace because Truth is coming so near. Jesus Christ, the Savior of the world, is the Son of Truth. The world is saved because of Love. Truth and Love are human life itself!" Our Lady asked me to have patience, remaining firm in the Truth so that peace can live among us. Jesus is glorified by everything that is happening, although His Plan oftentimes seems elusive, cumbersome, and difficult to bear. Despite this appearance, it is entirely a function of His Mercy and Love that generates the unity we all wish to share. Yet, very few of us realize this Truth powerfully enough to live it. If you were to ask most people to envision a picture of Love, they will derive either a blank thought or a mental picture of a sensual act. Our Lady says that the true image of Love is the Crucifixion of Her Son.

Saturday, June 29, 1991   The Moment of Love

For us to know Jesus well enough to become like Him in all ways, our focus must be upon the Moment of Love, His Death on Mount Calvary. At this historical and Earth-shattering event, *reason* was revealed to mankind. Eternity was given birth in His timeless Agony. Creation assumed the shape of the Cross as all force was directed and centered upon this King and Champion of men. The depth of His Love became His nobiliary power for our sake; the ultimate, solitary and Infinite Redemption of His every penitent child. His reason is simply Love. When our Savior died for our sins, the Cross became the Earth on which we stand, the air we breathe, and the life we live. The cruciform wooden beams where His Sacred Flesh was impaled became the intrinsic soul of Creation. The gaze of His immortal eyes was the living testament of the Feast of all the Saints. Love came to flawless revelation at the preferment of His execution as an epoch of eternal bliss embraced our souls for the very first time in human history. At the uttering of His words, *"It is finished,"* Love consumed time from beginning to end and from the heights of Heaven to the depths of the nether world. It planted hope in the hearts of all who had waited untold centuries for the coming of the Messiah. It incinerated their hellish darkness with a Thrice-Bold flash of incandescent Glory.

The Prophets of old gazed with hope into their future and saw a Crucified Light shining upon them like a laser beam, penetrating their being into the foundations of their past. And, in its launch forward through time, His Radiance reaches us now, engulfs us, and passes beyond our vision into that lasting immortal sunrise that we will be forever elated to see. This defining Moment is the boundless iconography of the entire reign of Eternity. It is cumulative and concurrent Salvation that surpasses the entire sphere of mortal history. Christ loves us with a triumphant intensity from the Divinity of the Cross. The combined forces of all decadence and destruction that were directed at Him have now been transmuted into His Majesty that pulsates from this solitary point of timeless courage, hailed to this day by martyrs, kings, poets, and visionaries. When Jesus rose from the dead, His magnificent essence burst from Mount Calvary throughout Creation like sunlight passing through a crystal pane of glass. Every time we recognize the beauty of the universe, we are again witnessing the reality of His Resurrection. Jesus Christ is glorified throughout His Creation in every sense of our being.

The third part of Love is His impending Return to retrieve our souls on an avalanche of white clouds. This consuming rapture will transport everything that is righteous into the Halls of Paradise. The bookends of time will greet each other, producing a fresh beginning where our new and infinite vision will forever nourish our everlasting joy. It will be the reward of the suffering and the vindication of the just, a beatific prize for those who have long-sought the Mercy of Christ. His Return will be the most apocalyptic event in time because we will be reconciled once and for all into His thirst-quenching Light as we gaze at the Love which has conquered the Cross. We will find ourselves standing at the foot of the Tree, experiencing Calvary from within the Immaculate Grace of the Blessed Virgin Mary. God will show us the Love of these two perfect Hearts as they gaze into each other's eyes and affirm their devotion for the children of this Mother and King. It will bring such an overwhelming peace to our spirits that eternal ecstasy will become a reality for the first time since our souls were originally conceived. Vindication will be wrested from our faithless hearts like broccoli taken from a baby and replaced with the sweetness of a chocolate confection. Those who believe in Jesus and have lived His Eternal Word will be wrapped within a blanket of amnesty through His friendship, Mercy, and pardon. Unceasing rest will descend upon all who have proffered their lives to His Gospel of Truth. Our Lady says that now is the time for humankind to be exultantly happy because our sadness has been forthrightly destroyed.

"Yes, My son, Life is Love! All should seek to preserve Love. The living of life is the preservation of Eternal Life to those who believe in My Son. All of God's Creation should unite like a fabric for Him. Thank you for being strong. You have not given-up, as Jesus did not give-up. Your heart is filled with the Love prescribed through the Cross. Thank you for saying yes, as I said yes to God." I continually pray and hope that everyone who reads this Diary will understand what Our Lady means by these words. It is difficult to place into comprehensible terms what She has helped me see over the past several months. The sentences on these pages cannot portray the new Life we have gained in the Son of God. But, the Love in our hearts gives substance to their meaning. They are given it through the strength of our prayers. The Holy Eucharist is the key to this mystery. The Consecration at the Holy Mass is the **"Moment of Love."**

Sunday, June 30, 1991

"Dear children, today your Mother has come to call each of you to remember to pray from your heart. My special children, it is your heart which carries the Love of My Son into the world. Each of your hearts is My special little spindle of Love. The unity of the hearts of My children will weave a blanket of Love to warm the soul of all humanity. I ask that you allow your Heavenly Mother to serve as the seamstress for the world, to perform My maternal duty to mend the divisions which separate My children. Your Mother asks that you allow the Love of Jesus to thread all of you into one heavenly body in the hands of God for all Eternity. Children, by accepting Jesus, you will no longer be frayed into loneliness, fear, or delusion. The time is now for you to come together as one! The coldness of the night is here and you must be kept warm in your hearts.

I have come to tell you that the hearth of your souls is Jesus Christ, fueled by His Love for you. He will warm you through His Light where you will bask in His Countenance of radiant Salvation. Please open your eyes and hearts to receive His Light and Love! Your Mother loves each of you as one. Remember to pray and fast, and seek the peace in your brothers and sisters through your love for them. Thank you for having responded to My call."

JULY 1991

Monday, July 1, 1991

We prayed again today for the conversion of humanity as Our Lady came to offer Her words to us. I was told that the recitation of the Holy Rosary can do more to ameliorate the problems that plague the world than any other human action or intention because Creation is altered every time anyone offers their hopes to God. We draw people toward Jesus' door with the work of our hands, but our humble supplications help their vision penetrate that partition as if it were made of glass. With intensity and multiplication, our petitions rend the veil so that our brothers and sisters can walk freely into our Almighty Father's embrace. We must beseech Him to reveal His Love to the depths of every human heart. An endless valley of fruition and peace already lies deep within us. Our Lady began in the power of the Holy Spirit by speaking to me this evening about the peaks of holiness. **"My son, today I would like to tell you that many do not see as well as they can. When My children have been raised to the highest peaks of holiness, they will be on a perch to see. There is much blindness which people build in their mind. This blocks their vision to see the Savior in all His dimensions."**

Our interior search for Our Lord is hampered by our knowledge, habits, preferences, perspectives, and the emotions which arise from among them. Our minds are filled with stumbling-blocks to righteousness which, oftentimes, seem like huge dinosaurs before us. They impede our walk that leads us to Jesus. When we have been raised to the highest peaks of human holiness, we will see the many constraints that previously imprisoned the Love in our hearts. Our vision is presently blinded by our judgement, which hampers our sight, our belief, and our trust in the omnipotent Love of our Savior. There are many vantage points that are not positioned beyond our greatest potential. In the following illustration, which Our Lady gave to me, we see that our purview is often from behind a limited boundary of faith:

By our prayers, however, we are elevated to a higher peak of holiness:

Every one of us must struggle to reach the celestial spires in Creation to perceive Our Lord more clearly, even though the tallest peak will vary from one person to the next. The number of obstacles that must be overcome, and where they are located, is also specific and definitive to each individual. There are some who have ascended to these summits very early in life. Many holy people have never borne a singular inhibition to their vision whatsoever, but have always held a clear understanding of Love from their earliest years on Earth. They have allowed no part of mortality to distract them from their union with God.

Our Lady told me that we create these strictures all by ourselves. Our own weaknesses and imperfections magnify the heights that we believe we must climb to be worthy of Redemption. We were born of God with only original sin. So, our impediments are created by the transgressions which arise from the broken nature of our souls. Only Jesus is the rectification for this problem. By embracing His sacramental Mercy, our errors are forgiven beyond our deaths. The summit of our desire for Paradise is achieved through the faith that our faults have been erased from Creation. This must include their expungement from our memory, as they are already removed from the intellect of God, while the purity of our perfection is fully restored. We are remade into the image and likeness of Christ as Love elevates us into this incarnate grace. When we accept Him unconditionally with our whole heart, mind, and soul, our vision is transferred to the highest peak of holiness and we are able to see with Divine confidence that we are finally one with the Sacrificial Lamb who hung on the Cross for our Salvation. Our beatific sight becomes comparable to those who freely accepted His Crucifixion from the innocence of their childhood.

Our Lady cautioned me not to complicate this example by dwelling on it any further than that. Each soul is such a unique Creation that only God possesses the Wisdom to make this comparison, should it be necessary to draw it at all. Notwithstanding this fact, there are variations of understanding between people, just as there are differing degrees of commitment to Jesus on every corner of the globe. Hopefully, we will all ultimately see that He is the Savior of the world. He knows and loves every one of us, making it impossible for anyone to become so lost that they fall beyond the power of His infinite Mercy. We can see only as clearly as our hearts will allow. Our transient conclusions cannot lead us to complete Christian enlightenment unless we allow the Love we embrace for Our Savior to guide and direct us back home. Prayer functions as our headlights in this darkness.

The perspective is completed here:

Now, there are no peaks to overcome at all because holiness is the only facet to define our vision of life. We see at last that the so-called mountains that stood in our way were merely the walls of the valleys into which we had fallen through the misfortune of sin. Above that darkness lies a limitless plateau of Love with no boundaries to climb where our gaze can penetrate the farthest horizons. This is the supernatural grace that we gained through our Baptism! It can be instantly reclaimed by completely believing in the immortal pardon of God, freely granted to penitent hearts through the Sacrament of Reconciliation. It is there that we are released from the weight of our transgressions, prosecuting the campaign against our weakest of sins. We must scale the summit of Divinity to implant our souls in triumph before the feet of the Holy Eucharist at the capstone of the Holy Mass. The Rosary is the tool we must employ to ascend to this perfect realization. We would easier climb Mt. Everest while untethered than achieve perfect oneness with Jesus Christ without reciting the solemnity of those Most Sacred Mysteries. Our voyage to an immeasurable comprehension of Christ is a very long and treacherous one because the travelers have made it so formidable. For the sake of every lost soul, we must shorten and simplify the journey by completely abandoning ourselves in faith to every principal that took Jesus to His Death on the Cross. Our Lady asks us to accept Her Son and His Mercy without pause. This is why the Almighty Father has allowed Her to come to the Earth. There is no denying that He loves us that much! The Virgin Mary is truly our Heavenly Mother who guides and teaches the lost. She speaks with as much candor as any mortal mother would address her own children. It is because of this light that my yearning desire is to love Her as much as She loves us all in return.

Wednesday, July 3, 1991
Timothy and I began the Holy Rosary and the Blessed Mother came again saying, **"The almighty and magnificent Love of My Son is the consummation of all happiness of mankind."** We conversed about many personal events that are unfolding around us. Her guidance helps me gain the correct perspective of others' fears and judgements. Many people attempt to instruct others about the teachings of the Son of God: parents to children, clergy to laity, and friends to acquaintances. While we may have no personal problems seeing the beauty in His Love flowing through the Sacred Scriptures, our difficulties arise when we misconstrue His Words to strengthen our own biased perceptions of the world around us. We must, instead, seek to totally change our environment, along with our attitudes, to be in conformity with the Life of Jesus Christ. By praying as Our Lady asks, we will be able to distinguish temporal latitudes from eternal Glory. Heaven is the steadfast and permanent reality of everlasting Life. Put quite simply, Love *is*. Conversely, the globe on which we stand offers us only a linear, temporary mortal existence. We must strive to passionately live the Divinity of Jesus as it is revealed in the Bible and the 2000-year-old Tradition of the Church that He founded upon the Earth. Our Lady wishes us to diminish everything about us that is not in union with that Truth. God will never validate the sins that we commit or approve of our omissions either.

The Virgin Mother told me that we must "describe" our faith in order for it to be alive. Not understanding Her meaning, She reiterated Her point by asking me to "DE-SCRIBE my faith." We must take it out-of-scribe, from the print, and off the pages of the Holy Scriptures. Our love must become the intensity of Christ as He inscribed it into Creation by His sacrificial Life. God commands us to magnify the witness of His Son by imitating the very perfection He lived. This description is influenced by Our Lady's initial point.

Without prayer, many assume that Jesus is somewhere unreachable and someone whom He really is not. They believe He is unexplainable and of the unknown, always out-of-sight, far from view, and always unapproachable. They do not know where He is, even though they may believe He exists. And, in His imaginary absence, they can define His Will any way they see fit. Our Lady counters these notions by saying that God is of the most conspicuous and simple places on Earth. She gave me another depiction of where Her Son resides. Her vision is beautiful and comforting. Praise be to Jesus forever and ever!

In this illustration, we see a three-dimensional square with a cross-shaped hole completely though it, and a string of beads behind. This is how many people fail to recognize the eternal presence of Jesus, unable to detect Him amongst the shadows of the world. Their attention is captured by the block and the beads before they ever notice the Cross through which they are gazing. Consider what constitutes this hollow cruciform. It is composed of nothing physical at all. Yet, it actually holds the interior angles of the square into their articulated shape. In other words, the Cross is there first, while its collateral substance has formed around it. It is given definition by what many fail to perceive. So, the lesson remains that God is the essence, the beginning, and the anchor of all that He has created, including its intrinsic form and its designated function. Moreover, the height, depth, and width reflects the limited dimensions of the material world. On the other hand, when we look at the image of the Cross, it appears to be limitless in its depth to the perpetuity of the atmosphere beyond it. The God of all humankind truly transcends the substantive boundaries of our mortal existence! This is why Jesus is so difficult for many of us to detect. Have you ever looked into a mirror with the intention of actually seeing the reflecting surface, itself? What does a mirror really look like? If we invoke our restricted insight and judge reality only by what we observe, we will look directly at Christ and only perceive ourselves. We will be left wondering where He is, or if He is truly there at all.

Our Lady has come to bless us with the knowledge of things beyond our limited vision. This beauty comes into focus through our faith in the Son She bore to save us. Our perception transcends all globular physics as the Divine reality of His words are made manifest to our souls. *"I will be with you always even until the end of the world."* This is one of faith's greatest blessings! The Virgin Mother is facilitating the empowerment of our capacity to recognize Jesus in the mirror of Creation. Now, imagine the square block as being one solid mass of wood, with no Cross hewn from within its center. This is the distance which many must still travel to comprehend the presence of the Lord. Those who behold the Cross are most responsible to live His Word and spread His Gospel to those who fail to see. Throughout this evangelization, the pellucid Kingdom of God supports and fosters everything that we say and do through the power of His Spirit. Faith in Jesus opens our eyes so that we may discern the provisions of His Will amongst the distractions of the Earth.

Thursday, July 4, 1991
Upon taking a holiday from work, Timothy came to my home to pray and our Holy Mother joined us again. **"It is always warming to My Heart for you to accept Me into your life. Thank you for your prayers from the heart! They are always well received. Today, I will answer your prayers by telling you from where conflict comes. By knowing the origin of conflict, you will be able to more readily see it and be capable of the self-control for which you pray..."** Human discord ultimately evolves from the process of change, or the need for its implementation. If events unfolded according to what each of us desires, our search for alternatives might never prevail. Either way, it is a function of a pseudo-distance from God, which is characterized by an unrest in our soul as we recognize that we are not seamlessly one with His grace. And, since peace is a product of our unity with Heaven, the motion we feel is the movement of our spirits in search of Love. Everything that is redeemed by the Almighty Father eventually rests in His peace because the synchronicity of Creation emanates His perfect design. Nature was set into its balanced framework like a diamond placed into a crown. The origin and composition of its beauty is the Love whose ordination the heavenly bodies adore. Even the human anatomy is a patterned reflection of God; our right side mirrors our left. With few exceptions, the animals, birds, fish, and plants emulate this same exquisite order which projects the discipline of our Creator through the very essence of their being.

Symmetry and silence are coexisting partners which exude the fulfillment of Heaven because they are from outside the boundaries of life. The Blessed Mother told me that even time, itself, is a factor of an unchanging Eternity. It does not move, but we, instead, saunter briskly through it. Human inequity is the root all conflict because it alters the harmony of the Earth. Such silence is disrupted when we contravene the inexorable Will of the Almighty Father. We decimate the eternal peace within our hearts and set our spirits into pandemonious motion when we turn away from His grace. This terror ends when we finally arrive at the foot of the Cross, where lies the peaceful foundation of Love. It is on this spot that every battle in history was laid upon the Sacred Heart of Jesus in an attempt to destroy the perfect isotropy of His immortal soul. Satan engineered the Passion and Death of Christ in an effort bring chaos to the eternal sanctuary of man, a war that evil lost by a landslide 2000 years ago. Our Champion Lord Jesus is our everlasting portion in Heaven. He single-handedly consumed the destruction of all humankind, reconciling our lives within the Blood of His Holy Sacrifice. The Cross, itself, displays this perfect symmetry:

Our Lady reminded me that the world actually became the Cross on Good Friday. That is how peace on Earth was first allowed to flourish. She asked me to remember the hallowed cruciform with the square block formed around it. This tells us that what we cannot see supports and fosters what we do see. The loving harmony between the Father and the Son radiates a perfect and infinite Divinity which consummates their Love in the material world. When people cause conflict around the globe, they essentially do not realize that God became one of us to restore our good will. His ultimate act of proportionality was when He took-on our human flesh. There can be no greater Love to touch the ground and no nobler purpose for Life than that. The human family is made perfect by Jesus' presence among us, Emmanuel! This supreme manifestation of symmetrical Love was evinced as the beauty of Paradise balanced Itself when Christ was born in Bethlehem. Earth was seen in Heaven, as Heaven was seen on Earth. When God robed Himself in Sacred Flesh, He came to the side of the mirror on which we live, sending His complete Love into our midst within the Womb of the Immaculate Virgin Mary. Through Her permission, the Breath of Life was bestowed upon the rest of humanity. Because of Her affinity for us, we are new products of the Love of Our Almighty Father, who wants us all to be in exacting unison with Heaven through the perfect Son His Mother bore.

When we open our lives to Our Creator and allow Him an avenue to move from heart-to-heart, He comes to us through others as we offer His Love to them. We become one with Christ and reflect His perfect image through complete abandonment and the charitable nature of our spirit. Saintliness is, indeed, our highest potential. God is Love, and therefore, the capacity of our souls. He must become our make-up, our behavior, and the standard by which we live and breathe. The Father resides within us, while we afford Him the opportunity to project Eternal Life through the animation of our being. His Divinity is Life, itself, which we emulate by loving every soul He created, along with that of our own. It is through this same grace and propriety that we realize that there is no such thing as a small act of Love. Christian righteousness has no earthly match or measure. Our Lord is infinite in every act that He initiates, participates, and sustains within us throughout the tenure of our exile. We see His Face in others through our own eyes of Love. When we do, we recognize His incarnate Life again vested in the stature of human flesh. Humanity is that precious to His Spirit. Therefore, we must purify our discernment, interact without judgement, and accept the Love that others wish to share. In the end, the perfection which we are extending will radiate from those who despise us as we speak. Every human being emits this Divine Light because no one is absent of God. Although none is worthy of being proclaimed perfect except Christ, Himself, His Father is present in everything that He has created toward the expression of His purpose. He is the permanent Love who sustains the peace that originates only in Him.

Imagine a balloon that is filled with air, and someone is inside it. If they extend an arm, touching its interior surface, the outside perimeter changes in shape. The perfection of its natural constitution has been destroyed because the motion from the inside initiated an altering effect. This is an example of what happens in human interaction, resulting in the brines of social conflict. I asked our Blessed Mother why the Apostles seemed to cause so much dissension. She responded by saying that they did not cause the motion, but were at the side of Christ, who is the restoration of the balance of Heaven. Jesus, and subsequently His Apostles and disciples, were the bearers of peace and absolution, dispensing the grace of holy cultivation into the world. The ensuing battles came from those who denied the Truth of the Divine Messiah that the others were evangelizing. This is how our distance from God soils our own symmetry and the peaceful nature of the universe. Only Love has the power to quell the motion of the world. Peace will never come through rebellion, especially against the Truth that Our Lady brings. A pond covered by waves never becomes smooth by tossing in more stones. The little dove of peace is very timid, and will light upon every soul who is tendered to the serenity of His silence. That is why we must pray for Him to come.

The Blessed Mother continued by relating this discussion of solitude and symmetry to the plight and agony that we see so intensely throughout the world. Suffering is a great gift from God because it is His indication that we have been elected to assist and sustain the conversion of humanity. Any opposition that is directed toward us is engulfed in the stillness of His omnipotent Divinity when we accept our distresses and offer them to His Son. Love in our hearts is the only power capable of capitalizing upon the pious sufferance that comes without our advance preparation. If we do not imitate Our Savior, we will not accept the sacrifices which bring peace to the lives of other men. The intentions of Christ pulsate across the continents of the world from this mystical cauldron of change. His Crucifixion is manifested through us as we race through Eternity under the blessing of His Light. Only the Son of God can reconcile our suffering into peace.

Friday, July 5, 1991
Timothy and I began the Rosary at nine o'clock this evening, and Our Lady greeted us by saying: **"The night has come and I have come to you! Praise be God Almighty for this glorious day! My son, you are beautiful and your brother is beautiful! Together, we do beautiful things. Bring your happy selves to My arms. Your prayers for abortion are reaching the heavens and back to the hearts which need them. Thank you for praying. Many lives which will be saved will remember your prayers..."** She continued by encouraging me regarding the preparation of our Diary. I was instructed to be confident that it is coming together as She desires. This task requires a great deal of faith because I do not always comprehend the principals I am recording. As I listened to the Blessed Mother tonight, a question formed in my mind concerning a point of Her lesson which I did not completely understand. Consequently, I "thought" my question toward Her instead of stating it audibly. She immediately admonished me by saying that I should never "think" my inquiries in Her presence. Since God is allowing Her to communicate openly with me, I should respect His gift and speak to Her aloud. I must faithfully venerate Her miraculous intercession and completely accept that She can hear my words as I say them. She told me that everyone of us can learn from this simple example. Jesus engaged in disclosed conversation with those He met on Earth, asking them questions, even though He already knew the answers.

I was given a lesson about "perspective" this evening and a vision of the relationship between our personal experiences. When we have a pure outlook toward others, it helps us in our efforts to be patient. We can also clearly identify those areas where our spirits are being diminished so as to nurture the peace in our hearts. Our Lady began with the word, "prospective." "It is the vision of the relationship of all possibilities as we look forward in time." It is not solely for the institution of our calm endurance or to diminish the importance of a given moment. It is, rather, a means to prioritize impending events so that we may prepare to openly receive them. Prospective offers us a perspective to attain our highest success. Our greatest anticipation is the return of Jesus Christ in Glory to take us to Heaven. On the holy path toward this rapture, we acquire many different viewpoints in our efforts to understand God and conform our lives to greet His Mystery. In our search for peace, we create a multitude of vistas, hoping that these myriads of the inexplicable will rest in a position that is complementary within our framework of beliefs. This work helps us understand why we have certain feelings about the world. Our Lady said that we should never worry about outdated perspectives which may be less than what they seem because they oftentimes serve to highlight where our particular feelings are founded from the past. We show compassion by remembering them because we are sharing in the common faults of those around us. In this fellowship, we are reminded that we need Jesus, too.

She also drew a correlation to the facets of color. We recognize the hues of the palette with the sense of our eyes. They influence very strongly the way we feel inside our hearts. Who would want to stare at a black-and-white television screen after seeing all the stripes of the rainbow in one digital display? We are conditioned to connect this luminance with our differentiating moods. If we are asked what color we feel when we are depressed, we would probably say dark blue or gray. This answer comes from the memory of our feelings at an earlier time when we saw the solemnity of their setting. Our daily temperament is defined by the perception of motion in our souls during the time when we lack inner-peace. What we see causes us to follow our emotions that are in contradiction with God's design of confidence. The reason Our Lady brings this to our attention is because many of Her children view their relationship with Jesus in these same multi-graded tones. The fact remains that they are only shades of a singular darkness, which is not a color, but a condition of the heart. On the days we refuse to accept Christ, we are living the redness of rejection. When we decline to invoke hope and depression sets upon us, we enter the "blue-boards" of despair. Jesus desires to be received through the pure, white, openness of the innocence of His children. He wants there to be no scales of depressiveness to our contemplations that might serve to impede His affection and uplifting grace. Indifference and guilt always paint our souls with a spasm of temporal distractions about things that do not matter at all. The white of the veil of the Immaculate Queen is the only acceptable consonance for the human soul to replicate.

Jesus must be received in a state of total openness and purity because the Holy Spirit cannot be categorized by a singular color. If white is the pigment of peace, it must assuredly be the only one that exists. While we were taught as children to identify our colors, Our Lady is teaching us that only a pure heart will find the tranquility of God. We must never say "no" to Love, whatever our tendencies might be. She has miraculously offered God's prism of Divinity by hanging rainbows from the sky throughout the entire world. They evoke us to look up at them, proclaiming to everyone we see that the storms of life have finally passed us by. They are one of the greatest signs of hope ever given to those who are just breaking from the dismal ports of faithless depression. So, holiness is definitely beyond the violable hues of our gauntly whims and grim misconceptions. There are no moderations in accepting Jesus Christ. It is conviction without reservation, with the invincible heart, the converted soul, and the singular mind. God is perfect, and it is not possible to rebel against Him and still live in His peace. We find fulfillment by residing in His Son on the Cross. The Blessed Mother told me that, **"Many of My children also see God as an entity that is of a great distance from them, and that Heaven is a place way in the distance of the sky. None of your people who were launched into outer space got any closer to Heaven because they did not die to sin."**

Our distance from Heaven cannot be detected by the measurement of our thoughts. It is a preponderance within the human heart that is associated with spiritual elevation, not a physical climb through the clouds. **"My son, Heaven is in and about you. It is a place that cannot be grasped by human thought or description. The word 'beautiful' is not beautiful enough to describe it. I will tell you that if you use color to describe your world, color cannot describe Heaven. You have never been able to completely feel Heaven or what it is like, and you will not yet. You must remember that Heaven is beyond any means that you could describe or feel. There are no words."** She added that every one of us can begin Eternity while living here on Earth. Her greatest worry is for those who are lost in the darkness and are flagrantly denying Her Son. Her purpose is to elicit a full and compliant acceptance by all! We are capable of conquering our separation from Christ through one simple task; the conversion of the human soul. Our Lady desires for us to pray from our hearts and live in the assurance of that peace. She wishes us to gather around Her feet for instruction in the ways of Eternal Salvation. We must remember that righteousness comes from within us, not through the colors we see. It is often diminished by our misconception that we are still not acceptable to God. Jesus' Mercy has already eradicated the darkness of that dimension by absolving us both infinitely and equally. We are worthy of Heaven when we invoke the faith to say "yes" to His miraculous Love and Redemption.

Saturday, July 6, 1991

As my brother and I continued praying together like Our Lady has asked, we knelt with our rosaries and She came again to speak to us. Her conversation was very lengthy this evening, beginning with Her promise of Love for every child of God, followed by an invocation for our confidence and continuing conviction. Jesus knows where evil hides, so Satan cannot tempt or attack Him. However, as frail human beings, we are always potential victims of his diabolical antics. Our lives are helplessly mortal, and Satan knows it. His wickedness spreads throughout Creation because of our lack of faith and commitment to fight against it. While prayer destroys everything that is not Love, we still refuse to convene in the Truth and pray for the grace of Heaven to strengthen our souls. Our Lady told me that our hope must be founded upon the power that created the universe from the start. This omnipotent essence is Love, itself. The Almighty Father precedes every thought and action we could ever imagine, and therefore, is the natural foundation of our dreams and aspirations. If He had not sent His Son into the world to save us, there would be no hope for humankind. Therefore, every one of our divine inclinations is a product of the Love of Jesus Christ. It is the shining light that proceeds from any heart that is willing to pray for His companionship in life. When we look to Our Lord's Agony in the Garden of Gethsemane, we witness Hope in its highest degree. Bloody sweat gushed from His pores like genius flowing from a grand composer, editing his ultimate redemptive score. He timelessly yearns for our deliverance onto the wings of His happiness. He innocently accepted a Passion and Death that no human on Earth had ever conceived, invoking the trust of His own Holy Spirit that we would recognize the beauty of Heaven in time to strive for its Gates. He said to the Father, **"Not My Will but Thine be done."**

With these words, He unveiled God's invincible desire for the Redemption of His children. We know this through faith because we do not yet see clearly. We exercise charity because, in giving, we also receive. Hope pierces the darkness in human souls, inflaming the realization that each petition we lift to the Almighty Father changes the world for the better. Prayer is the action that fulfills the greatest dream we can envision. It is the caretaker of the seed of our internal wishes. We want our world to be filled with peace, righteousness, and the affectionate constancy of Love in our lives. Our self-compassionate desire for serenity is heard through our supplications to God for His loving glance. This is the essence of prayer, our call for the Prince of Peace to come to our aid. It is also an invitation to which He always responds. He is simply waiting in our midst to be asked. Whether He chooses to answer is not the questionable part, but do we hope for His companionship? Our Lady said that this Divine longing is a part of Love that always resides within the center of the heart. The reason that some people do not pray is because ulterior motion has overwhelmed their mind and convinced them that life is pre-ordained to their misfortune. Their best expectations have no room to come forth because they do not believe that turning to God will rectify the depressing scenes that they are witnessing before their weary eyes. They accept their darkness as a natural state of being and accuse God of reneging on His Promise to provide the bountiful foison that will feed the entire family of man. Their anticipation is swept away in the damning current of their own indifference and disbelief. In this cesspool, the landmark to Salvation is obscured, leaving them twisting in the wind and unprepared for the evil strikes from the followers of Satan.

We must imitate the hope of Christ in the Garden of His Passion. He had every reason to be broken in spirit, but He forged a weapon with His destitution that He wielded for the complete transformation of the future of the world. Neither the Apostles, nor the people of that day, save the Holy Mother, saw this truth before the sunrise of His Resurrection. He sustained the Light of hope in that dark hour so that every child of God can say with confidence, "I have hope too because He has come to deliver me." We draw Redemption from His heavenly account as heirs to the infinite fortune that He claimed as the spoils from Mount Calvary. With this power, our prayers can now change the lives of the despondent, knowing inside that they will eventually seek Salvation for themselves and those they hold most dear. When they do, they will see the magnificent fruit that the tree of Love has born to redeem us. Their single pinhole of light will be transformed into a parade of streaking lightning that will blind them from any creeping sorrows that might try to dampen their days. Our supplications to Heaven naturally increase as this jubilation intensifies, leading us to the full blossoms of faith. Factual knowledge thunders the Truth that there must be a God because someone has answered their prayers. When our faith becomes ever stronger, we know to share the Love we feel because that charity is an essential requirement for the reception of the Mercy of Christ. Hence, the fire of Love is set in the soul. Our Lady told me, **"Now do you see what your prayers can do?"**

We were all created to share in one heavenly destiny. Love will return to Love. Our petitions help guarantee that our journey of life will conclude in the Glory of that Heaven. The hope of Christ in the Garden of Gethsemane is consummated in the Holy Eucharist. He prayed to His Father that we would all become one in Him, giving His Body to the Cross for the fulfillment of that purpose. We are perfectly united with Him when we receive His Body and Blood at the Holy Sacrifice of the Mass. Our Divine Communion is the return of our soul to Paradise as the Almighty Father reciprocally restores Eternal Life to our souls.

After mentioning the power of Catholic priests to perform the miracle of transubstantiation, Our Lady spoke with me about "abstinence" and "celibacy." The recognition of the Truth of Love rests in the simplicity of the heart. We hold a knowledgeable perspective of human procreation when our understanding is in unity with God. There is only one choice to the faithful who seek an innocuous faith. That is to either do the right thing, or commit ourselves to error. Those who have chosen to be celibate will abstain as a sacrifice for the sins of the world. For them, procreation is a non-issue because, in their vows of celibacy, there is no other alternative. The term "procreation" is for those who choose to pray for children within the Holy Bonds of Matrimony. Furthermore, people who are married and have chosen not to have children should refrain from the act of procreation. It is an offense against the symmetry of God to plant and cultivate an orchard, then cut it down before it bears its fruit. Chastity through abstinence is the sanctified way of choosing to not have children and is a prayerful expression of hope for the well-being and redemption of the world. Celibacy, on the other hand, is not merely abstinence. Abstinence maintains a continuing choice, while celibacy is void of the decision whether to abstain. With celibacy, the decision precedes the choice, effectuating a perpetual state of purity and holiness. Priests are required to witness to the perfect likeness of Christ as they sustain their holy celibacy. They have carried purity to its highest sacrificial degree throughout the past generations. We also maintain this image when we choose to live only in the Spirit. Ironic as it may seen, this same purity, along with other sacrificial perfections, is also manifested through the choice to have children in the Sacrament of Holy Matrimony. Jesus' Love is impartial and undeniable.

There is a war being waged in our modern day society against the great virtue of purity. Our minds are tempted continuously to destroy this angelic holiness. It is rare for anyone to not have imperfect thoughts. Prayer forthrightly overcomes these impious distractions. Although our actual thoughts are not sinful in theory, if these temptations are not immediately cast aside, they will lead us to a descent from grace. Our Lady asked me to always remember that carnal thoughts do not indicate that someone is absent of purity, holiness, or grace. The error is not in our temptations, but in our failure to categorize them in our hearts and throw them away. There is no need for an internal struggle when we already know the answer. This is the great unilateral grace of celibacy. The fight for purity is won with the recognition that there is no other choice on the table. No internal torment can be waged when only one decision exists. Purity is the power that sustains our holiness. It is a requirement for priests, nuns, religious, and lay-people, alike. We will embrace it when we love the Truth in the Life of God.

Sunday, July 7, 1991

"My precious little children, I am your Mother, who has come today to ask you to remember to pray for peace. It is always peace, little ones, that allows your hearts to be open to receive Jesus. There is no anxiety

which can wound you when your soul is strengthened by prayer. Always remember that your world is built by your design to weaken and offend you. There will be many days of sorrow and grief before you. Your lives are composed of trials against the peace which your hearts need to love your brothers and sisters. My children, when you accept Jesus into your hearts, you will conquer your trials and your sorrow and grief will be turned into happiness and victory. I call each of you to be raised through the strength of Jesus and His Love in your hearts. Please come to My arms where I can help you learn to pray from your heart. There is a blessing which awaits those who understand and accept Jesus. He is the leader and the pathway, and the guide and the destiny. My children, Jesus Christ, the Son of God, is your best friend. I will take you to Him because I love each of you so much. Your peace, freedom, strength, and happiness is Jesus. You are all saved by the security of Love because you are all so special. Please accept Jesus into your lives to save you through prayer. Thank you for having responded to My call."

At four o'clock this afternoon, we began to recite the Rosary and our Holy Mother came again. She thanked us for praying and asked me to be patient with those around us. The Will of God unfolds through the facility of our meekness. **"Good day, My special sons! Thank you for praying again. Today is a special Sunday. It is special because it is a day in your life which My Son has given. Much is being accomplished now. There are many souls who are being touched by your answer of 'yes' to God. I am sure that you feel rewarded for having done so. There are many blessing yet to come..."**

Today's lesson was about the value of friendship, a beatific manifestation of the reciprocity of Love. Many times our cordial acts go unnoticed, ignored, or accepted without gratitude, and we become offended by these silent omissions. Our Lady says that we should not expect any return-in-kind as a reward for our own hospitality. Neither can we force someone else to offer their affection to us. We must never tender our extension of Love based upon the calculation of another's response. Yet, there are those whom we consider as friends that have shown the endearment and graciousness that our hearts desire. This is the same bond of friendship that Jesus wishes us to effect with Him. He is the supreme supplier in our times of need because He knows the hunger of the human heart and is willing to give His Life so that we will be ecstatically happy. This fraternal relationship convokes freedom upon our lives because we inherit the fruit of His Promise of Salvation. The great power radiating from this liberty is in the Love that we have the opportunity to share. We are free to give our lives and resources as a sacrifice from which we will receive Infinite devotion in return from the greatest Man to ever live. Our attitude becomes, *"I need you, because I want to love you."* This is the beauty of embracing Jesus through His Mystical Body. The bondage of self-denial and servitude actually unites us with His fondness for the palms of all Eternity. We are not forced to accept the Divinity of Heaven, but God magnanimously offers us the opportunity to live there, not a day less-than forever, in the perfection that already exists among the celestial Hosts. That participation must begin while we are living in mortal flesh upon the Earth. When we open our hearts, we can already experience this same unfettered bliss.

    Our Lady asks us to remember that Love is not like flintstone, but is compassionate and understanding. Jesus does not concern Himself with past occurrences or offenses that have been confessed and discarded from His Mind. Forgiveness of others is of ultimate importance if we expect our own absolution to survive in the end. With this vision, we are able to peer into the future with confidence and direction. The power of God will always be present to protect and guide us because the Love of Our Savior can never be destroyed. No matter what the future becomes, freedom will always be secured because our happy home has already been built. Satan cannot change this eternal fact. Let us remember what Our Lady said about the power that emanates from the Crucifixion. Christ's Love surges from that moment and permeates throughout all of time. We have already witnessed our future when we retroactively gaze upon the tragedy of Mount Calvary. The salvific transformation that is ratified by Jesus' Blood renders Love as the only power left standing. Despite this beautiful fact, the human mind still tries to obscure the Holy Spirit when we recall unhappy occurrences, regrets, biases, and offenses. We must, instead, allow only goodness and kindness to reside within us. Our every happy memory is a portion of the Love of Christ. He caresses and protects us by guiding our meditations so that everything we think is generated by the heart to create and retain His peace on Earth. If someone is made jubilant by a holy rumination, it has come directly from the righteousness of God.

    I asked our Blessed Mother about human curiosity, and She told me that it was a rhetorical question. She said that inquisitiveness may be inspired by the heart, but only if it does not lead to conflict. For example, if we are inclined to learn how we may serve God more perfectly, our yearning is from His Spirit. But, if we are angered by wondering why others do not serve Him in the way that we think they should, we might be making a summary judgement about what He would otherwise have them doing. This would be an example of a fastidious mind. Our Lady wishes us to be peacefully curious about inspirations that are important to Jesus. While talking about matters of the heart, She also helped me contemplate human grief. She told me that it is the only thing in addition to the Rite of Christian Burial that gives us strength through the tragedies we bear. A person who does not pray in the midst of their sorrows is not allowing their response of Love to properly unfold. There is a difference between mourning and depression. The former must be used only for its purpose or it will lead to the latter. Grief is an emergency state of suspension by the heart, which helps us gain perspective as our disappointments are carried to the soul. There is no way to spiritually avoid the impact of these events. It is like planning for your stomach to hold two gallons of water. You may think you are ready, but you would eventually fail if you tried. Depression, on the other hand, is characterized by a clinical disorder. We must have confidence that the throes of grief will always pass from our lives. The light of the new morning should give everyone hope that the birth of Eternity may dawn before this day comes to a close.

This leads to Our Lady's main point about simplicity. She gave me an example about a Rosary group that was ferociously attacked by Satan. Dissension arose in their ranks, their unity was fragmented, and evil attempted to poison their loving relationships. But, by virtue of their petitions, they still established their permanent place in the timeless Kingdom of God. The clock cannot be turned-back to destroy the Love that we now share between us. This is why Satan will ultimately fail. Love that is nurtured in time will always bear good fruits in the end. Through holy perseverance, the members of this particular group sustained their unity with supplications for peace and forgiveness for everyone there. Satan actually speeded his own destruction by his effort to destroy their lives. By making himself visible and evident, these Christian children invoked the power of Jesus to withstand this diabolical action. Satan, himself, augmented the process by causing the conditions that brought everyone to pray so profoundly and fervently for help.

This example clearly illustrates the humility of the heart. Notwithstanding the complicity of Satan's agenda, evil will have no room to incarcerate our souls in unhappiness if we pray unwaveringly to stop him. Simplicity is lost when someone stops to see how large of a lead they might hold, but is preserved when we are single-hearted in the goodness of Christ. We must always remember that Satan can travel as swiftly as he needs to capture our souls. There is nothing to slow his sinister progress if we refuse to ask God for help. Evil does not pray for its power, but feeds upon our own self-serving indifference. When we do not implore the Holy Spirit to guide us, we are giving venue to the enemies of our Salvation. Condemnation gains both advantage and venue when the children of Light do not remain in the friendship of Christ. The good news is that Satan cannot overcome the total surrender of the human heart to the Savior of the world.

So, the simplicity of Love is quite obvious to see. It is overwhelmingly beyond any comparable measures, directions, or dimensions. Complications arise when people slow-down to tally the score, hoping all the while for a buffer zone where they can take a moment to relax from their commitment to Love. Total conviction to Jesus eliminates any need for both the tally and competition. There is no opposition in a human heart that is given completely to the Son of the Immaculate Conception. It is simple to accept the yoke for those who seek peace. The God-Man is the only One there is. He is second to none, the beginning and the end. It is easy to pass an examination where there is only one correct response. In the case where our Salvation is the question, Jesus Christ is the definitive Answer. The foundation of simplicity is laid in the human heart through lifting our souls to Him. The Roman Catholic Church is the living petition of Our Savior, Himself. The Church gives His Life to the world through the Most Holy Eucharist, His Body and Blood on the Earth. Prayer, peace, happiness, purity, simplicity, sanctity, humility, goodness and Truth come through this Most Blessed of Sacraments. Everything that *is* comes to *be* at the moment of the Consecration. If we desire our lives to be filled with these virtuous graces, the Holy Communion is our ultimate destination. It can be put no more simply than that!

9:15 p.m - **"My beautiful son, thank you for praying! I want you to be happy. I love you with tremendous power! I will tell you in the future about Wisdom and confession. They will be important messages for the world. You have been given great graces as a result of your love and faith. You realize how happy you feel as you go into the world and see people you have not seen before. Your life has been made whole for your faith and prayers. Today, I sent a dove of peace to those for whom you have prayed..."** Before She departed, I was asked to pray deeply for the unborn, the destitute, and the poor souls in Purgatory.

Wednesday, July 10, 1991

Timothy and I began to pray at eight o'clock in the evening and Our Lady greeted me by saying, **"My precious son, faith becomes knowledge to those who serve! Thank you for praying. Your Mother is so happy to speak to you again. Your evening with your brother carries great promise, great blessings, and change for the world."** She continued Her lesson, reiterating how important it is that prayer comes from our hearts. It must be the fertile plantation of Love which has been cultivated with great devotion and care. There is no compromise or democracy in the Kingdom of Heaven. Jesus taught us the formula for speaking to our Almighty Creator when He articulated His great petition, the "Lord's Prayer." Our mind is non-essential since Love flows upward from the depths of our hearts. Worldly impulses swarm about our consciousness like bees and create the stings of defense, self-actualization, and self-justification. We must, instead, remember that selfishness is senseless, and that material cogitation does very little to solve physical problems. The solution lies in the acknowledgment that mankind, himself, created them in the first place. Nearly all of the ills that are facing humanity are centered in possessions and the distribution of resources. We must embrace the **Gospel of Matthew 6:24-34.**

> "No man can serve two masters; for either he will hate the one and love the other, or else he will stand by the one and despise the other. You cannot serve God and mammon.
>
> Therefore, I say to you, do not be anxious for your life, what you shall eat; nor yet for your body, what you shall put on. Is not the life a greater thing than the food, and the body than the clothing? Look at the birds of the air; they do not sow, or reap, or gather into barns; yet your Heavenly Father feeds them. Are not you of much more value than they? But which of you by being anxious about it can add to his stature a single cubit?
>
> And as for clothing, why are you so anxious? Consider how the lilies of the field grow; they neither toil nor spin, yet I say to you that not even Solomon in all his glory was arrayed like one of these. But if God so clothes the grass of the field, which flourishes today but tomorrow is thrown into the oven, how much more you, O you of little faith!
>
> Therefore do not be anxious, saying, 'What shall we eat?' or, 'What shall we drink?' or, 'What are we to put on?' for after all these things the Gentiles seek; for your Father knows that you need all these things. But seek first the kingdom of God and his justice, and all these things shall be given to you besides. Therefore do not be anxious about tomorrow; for tomorrow will have anxieties of its own. Sufficient for the day is its own trouble."

The heart contains the prescription to heal our mortal ills. Live Love! When Jesus is allowed to govern, our problems will be dispersed like smoke caught in a swift autumn breeze. Too many people mistakenly believe that their lives are crumbling at the discretion of others. They should look at the work of their own hands, or the lack of it, if that is the case. We must recognize self-denial in its appropriate context. The sacrifice of our own wishes should take precedence over our search for scapegoats in our refusal to acknowledge that we are part of the problem. When we accept the heavenly perspective of

Divine Love, we will see that our misery cannot be mitigated by the human intellect because the answer is not of cerebral origin at all. Love reigns supreme in the heart and, when released, purifies everything that stands in its way.

This is the significant essence of Divine Wisdom. Love is the solution, the medicine, the caretaker, and the eliminator of worldly cares. Our Lady said, **"It is wise to love, and wisdom is in the loving."** It is enshrined in the heart through our acceptance of Christ and reciprocally emanates from the mirror of God within the depths of our soul. It teaches, delivers, benefits, carries, and initiates Salvation into our lives and throughout the world. As sanctity blooms from within the heart, greater wisdom is given venue to rest within this comforting abode. The constituency of the material globe is not as important as is the symmetry of Paradise which reigns paramount for our victory. Success is not in solving the monumental confusion brought-on by the architects of modern-day society, but the elimination of human misfortune and suffering through the Love of Our Savior in Heaven. Charity and righteousness will ultimately prevail. It is time for us to finally realize that none of our problems are brought by God. Our many dilemmas are only imaginary figments generated by the curiosity of man. Heaven is the source of our deliverance.

I asked Our Lady about the many demands of those who are in control that cause such difficulties for the rest of us. I wanted to know how to respond to these problematic summonings. She told me that their solicitations are created by three influential factors; their oppressive manipulation in seeking our compliance with their system of values, their personal ambitions for success in the material world, and their minds overruling their hearts for the governance of their lives. Our Lady told me that Christian Wisdom is a fruit of our openness to embrace and accept the Love of Her Son. But, this genius is of no value if one does not live according to the Will of the God who created it. There can be no wisdom in someone who rejects the Holy Spirit. How can a person be wise if he knows Jesus, and yet, ignores the lessons He teaches? Further, in our desire to maintain peace, we must see through the immaculate vision that is given to us through prayer. Defiance is never the answer in response to the manipulative tactics of others. The only sanctified act of censure is to openly project the Truth of Love in the face of every deceitful manifestation that is thrown in our path by Satan. Love is that precise contradiction to evil. The greatest offensive against the scourges of Hell is to pray from the heart to stop them. When comparing the power of our petitions to our synthetic weapons of destruction, mankind truly has no arsenal behind him. Militaristic forces pale in the presence of our communication with the Almighty Father in Heaven.

War is a physical act of violence on a continental scale. Many people have tried to legitimize the provocation of aggression as being a system of discipline. They have come to an incorrect conclusion because only Love must be our ultimate goal. One cannot commit evil in order to achieve the goodness he seeks. The heat of battle must never be construed as being a greater influence than the power of the Holy Spirit. Even accidental deaths are the result of assuasive inference over the logic of Love. It stands to reason that, if first-water hearts are allowed to govern, holy acts will always prevail. But, since sinister minds are allowed to fester, there are conflagrations that are waged with innumerable casualties of the body and the spirit. This cannot be an act of wisdom. Our present century witnesses to the distance that mankind can be taken by treachery and anxiety. Let us remember how fear has gripped the countless generations before us. Many people believe that this will solve their altercations with the forces against them. They abandon Love, but still believe that they are on the path to peace. Fear did not accompany Our Savior on the way to His Crucifixion because His Love escorted Death to its own extinction. He owned every basis for being afraid and angry, yet He chose instead to magnify God's grace through His benign benevolence. He stood atop the mountain of aggression and was nailed to hatred, itself. Therefore, it is a great act of holiness to avoid war, even at the cost of laying down our lives. Jesus refused to violate the tenets of His Father's Love, and there is eternal peace in that. He did not respond in a mortal attempt to free Himself from the suffering that was imposed upon His Sacred Body. The Conqueror left no darkness undefeated. Given this intensity and purpose, Love is truly the only answer. The victory resides in loving, not in the fighting. Indeed, human wisdom lives in a heart that is filled with the fortitude to know them apart.

The Holy Spirit teaches us that each individual who is born into the world is the one that completes Creation. Humanity would be sadly diminished if a singular soul is left-out. Those who extinguish the gift of life render the universe incomplete, aborting God's intention for His Kingdom on Earth. In effect, they destroy themselves and the intentions of Heaven for their future. We must see the dignity that exudes from the pores of every human being. This divinity is the purpose that God holds for His people, each of us born with equal stature, the same value, and our own individual potential. We have one life and one fateful opportunity to accept Jesus' Promise of Salvation, transforming us into children of His Father for all Eternity. In exercising our power to pray for the Mercy of Christ, we secure our place at the bountiful Feast alongside the Martyrs and Saints. In a nation as free as the United States, the responsibility to pray is more electrifying than the constitutional right to vote! Holy priests are more powerful than any public servants will ever be. Through their words of Consecration, they have the magnificent grace to summon Jesus Christ to come to the Altar at the Holy Sacrifice of the Mass, making Paradise appear amongst men. Twenty centuries of aggression and war have failed to conquer the Papacy, the Eucharistic Celebration, or the legacy of faith of those whose perfection has been imitated and transferred to those they left behind. Satan has been rendered impotent by the pious obedience of the children of Mary. Evildoers would be just as unsuccessful if they had another 2000 years to practice. They can declare not-an-iota of victory from their maleficence because Victory is upon us! Our Lady finished tonight by saying, **"Thank you for loving each other. It is a great act of wisdom."**

Friday, July 12, 1991

We began to pray the Rosary at 8:30 p.m. and Our Lady came again. **"My son, welcome completely into My Heart! I love you and will help you. You are My special child. Your prayers will bring great purity to many. I would like to tell you tonight about *complacency*. You can see that your decision to deliver yourself from complacency will change you in a very holy and noble way."** We are stimulated by many impulses that spur us to turn to God as our daily lives unfold. If we see a homeless person on the street, we know that it is good to pray for them. However, these inspirations are oftentimes spawned only by our repulsion at seeing such ugliness in our midst, rather than our heartfelt yearning for the betterment of the lives of the poor. Thoughts such as these are limited to repetitious musings in our mind, and not much more than that. We are complacent if we believe that this sort of contemplation can mend the ills that we see. It is also a sign of complacency to beseech the help of Christ only when our own lives are encountered or affected. Not only must we seek Divine assistance for the poor beggar in the park, but for the eradication of the evil that chains every unfortunate soul to destitution throughout the circumference of the globe. The sincerity of our prayers must encompass the entire world as we embrace with compassion what others are feeling, while sympathizing with all the downtrodden, not just the homeless person leaning against the facade of the downtown supermarket. Our reach must even extend beyond our mortal lives to reach the suffering souls in Purgatory, and likewise, into the wombs where unborn children prepare for their first walk upon our blessed ground. When our intentions come from the heart, they embody these universal dimensions, crossing over borders into nations where material works are still falling painfully short.

Our Lady wishes to rid the world of complacency and indifference. She articulated a litany of examples this evening which reflects this self-assured attitude toward God. Those who do not pray every day are complacent. It is priggish to measure our abandonment to Heaven, declining to accept Jesus with our whole heart, soul, mind, and strength. By all means, it is a self-serving heart that refuses to receive Our Savior at His Cross every day in the Holy Eucharist. When these daily opportunities of grace are missed, our strength is always diminished and the turmoil around us continues to mount unchecked. In the final analysis, there is either Love pouring from within us, or not Love at all. If Christ Jesus is not given unconditional propriety over our flesh, our soul cannot emit the Light of Paradise. That is the true definition of complacency. This lackadaisical state lessens our acceptance of every fruit that the Holy Spirit has to offer. Similarly, those who believe that Satan will not stand immediately at their side and tell them that he is their best friend are egotistically deluded. The father of lies can seductively approach us from the most inconspicuous of places. He ceaselessly attempts to destroy our holiness with every distraction that he can possibly impose. This is why our prayers to Our Lord must be vigilant, constant, and all-encompassing, with the intention of eliminating the stench of misfortune from every quarter of the Earth. The greatest way to prevent complacency from ever rearing its ugly head again is for every one of us to simultaneously kneel in petition to Christ for His help. Anything less than total surrender to Him is an affront to the very Sacrifice He made on Good Friday. We will all soon beg on our knees for the Mercy that blooms from the Cross. The ravages of evil will continue until we do.

Saturday, July 13, 1991

Timothy and I began our morning prayers at eleven o'clock. Today was overwhelming because of another magnificent gift that Our Lady brought to us. She began, **"Good morning, My son. Today, I have something special for you. Please, listen..."** As I turned my ear attentively to Her, Jesus spoke to me, instead, *"My brother, I hold you in My arms and Love. I am with you always. Thank you for helping My Mother."* My spirit crumbled in awe and I began to cry upon hearing the words of Our Savior. I cannot place into understandable terms the encouragement that flooded my heart. All of the excruciating punishment from the indifference and opposition of others was instantly lifted from my being. I did not realize how heavy the weight truly was until He audibly proclaimed His Promise to help me. I now feel like I could endure anything that stands in my way. In the midst of my humble joy, Our Lady continued, **"My special child, your Mother has come again to tell you how you can help the world. Your prayers from yesterday have impacted many hearts with Love and purity. I would like to tell you about** *confession.* **The subject is truly of oneness and simplicity, and does not require a long dissertation."**

The confession of our sins is not a barter with God for His Mercy and forgiveness. Neither is it a purchase cost for goods that are received. It is, rather, the purging of guilt from our soul so that our heart may openly anticipate the Light of Paradise. We personally own the insipience of our transgressions and the resulting heaviness of our individual culpability. These acts are perpetrated of our own accord, and God takes no part in creating them. He is never-changing because He loves us infinitely, even in our state of weakness. He does not have to laboriously transform His essence in order to accept us without condition. Therefore, the need for change lies within our own conduct and compliance to His Will. Spiritual reconciliation flows naturally from our acceptance of our personal guilt and the sorrowful knowledge that the Almighty Father, who is so immeasurably beautiful, is offended by our lives. The request we make of Christ for the renunciation of His justifiable anger is always met with the kindness of His Mercy and absolution. We cannot receive His pardon unless we request it through the remission of our errors. It is the only way to justify our lives in His sight.

This necessitates the renunciation of all wrongdoing before someone who is capable of taking it away. The outward display of such contrition is easy for those who truly seek to be vindicated. It is fueled by the passionate yearning for reunion with the grace-filled favor of Our Lord. The soul has the divine knowledge that forgiveness restores our perfect unity with Eternal Love. We have been accepted by Jesus because our perfect repentance disposes our inner-being to embrace everything that Salvation has to offer. Our Lady said that those who decline the divulgence of their sins to a priest are penitent and contrite to the best of their ability. They are still seen in a light of compassion by Her Son if they open their hearts to His healing Spirit. But, once they understand and accept the perfection that is embodied within the Sacrament of Reconciliation, they must openly comply with the Catechism to be completely united with Heaven. The many thousands who disbelieve the Truth of this great redeeming Sacrament are not refused the eternal blessing of Redemption. However, they are never completely abandoned to the omnipotent Wisdom of God if they maintain a position that is contradictory to the Sacrament which begets such consummate absolution.

I could sense the urgency in our Holy Mother's powerful words. I asked why Her statements were directed so strongly toward Her protestant children. She replied that She has both the intention and authority to move humanity back to the original Apostolic Church for which Her Son has died to save. Her universal witness to His unnegotiable Will allows everyone on Earth an equal opportunity to rethink many of their errant tenets and align themselves with the power and legacy of Peter, the Rock upon which human Redemption rests. Protestants who finally embrace the Light of this Truth will convert before the end of the world. Those who believe it now and never convert are in need of our heartfelt prayers. And, the majority who have yet to come to full acceptance have not been told clearly enough for them to forthrightly decide. This shows that God is impartial in regards to the children whom He plans to redeem. Those who know Jesus and reject Him in the end will never be in that number. We must all claim our own portion of Salvation through the Blood of the Cross if we expect to eventually gain it. This fact is true for everyone, whether we are Catholic, protestant, or any other religious denomination.

About 9:00 p.m., we continued the Holy Rosary and the Virgin Mary came to us again. She wished to speak about "*nobility*," the stately virtue that begins with Love. The words Our Lady is speaking to us are the fruits of Jesus' Divinity which He planted in the world 2000 years ago. Everyone must give their lives to Christ in preparation for their deliverance into Eternal Salvation in Heaven. The Immaculate Mother of God has been sent to predispose us to that glorious Light. This cultivation often brings us great discomfort, a breach of family relationships, and a total rejection by those around us. While evangelizing the world for Jesus, we will be ridiculed, mocked, and held in contempt. Entire societies will spate upon us and reject the message that we bear. This is how we become those "little Christs," in reflection of the Messiah who prophesied that this would happen in our lifetime. The exasperated insurgence of outright human obstinance will never peacefully co-exist within the Divinity of the Holy Spirit. Our Lady cites the example that the Apostles and disciples were divided into pairs as they were sent into the world. Their Love for one another sustained their holy strength and conviction through some of the most vile rejection. They shared the Spirit of Jesus with an impenetrable union against the forces of pagan darkness. Enduring our suffering with a companion at our side helps us to bear it with dignity, especially when that "other" one is Jesus. This is why it is of paramount importance to remember that Our Savior faced the most excruciating pain and spiritual torment alone.

When no one else will stand beside us in our struggles for peace and grace, Jesus always remains our closest friend and benefactor. There is total sanctification in suffering when it is offered in unity with His Sacred Heart. This is our means of surrendering our lives to Him to use them as He pleases. We offer a Divine act of nobility to Heaven when we deny ourselves and peacefully bear the plight that would otherwise belong to others. Expressions of faith, hope, charity, humility, purity, and confession are of great nobility when they are manifested out of devotion for the King of the World. This beatific honor blossoms from a heart that is open to Love, alive in prayer, and sacrificial in service. A venerable beatitude is never composed of material goods or private possessions. Rather, it resides in the advancement of redeeming conversion upon the face of the Earth. Without personal surrender, a noble character cannot breathe the freshness of new Life. Our Lady asked me to recall that charity does not always require us to go without our daily bread. Oftentimes, the human heart is not excessively involved in charity, even though it may officiate its proceeding. For example, currency is frequently donated without conscience from someone's excesses simply to satisfy a given situation that might suddenly strike the heart. Although this still represents an act of charity and generosity, the gift may not be too sorely missed. Therefore, the benefactor has truly relinquished nothing important at all.

Our Virgin Mother utilized this illustration to articulate an elevated rule of sanctity. Nobility requires that the "giver" go without something that he truly wishes to retain in order for the "recipient" to reap the harvest of his kindness. This sacrificial criterion guarantees the deployment of Love in the human heart because it transforms the sensation of loss into a beatific gain. It is an irrefrangible blessing to take delight in suffering for the good of all humankind. Such nobility came to complete fruition in the Passion and Death of Christ upon the Cross. His being still emanates the greatest exaltation of character ever to be seen by mortal man. With our own lofty uniqueness, we must imitate His elegant grandeur in preparation for meeting Him again when He returns to take our souls to Paradise. Our Lady has asked us to be of the best and most noble part of Creation. Hence, we must pray and forgive, admonish and sacrifice, repent and be purified for the Salvation of those who do not yet know the miracles of God. Every one of us must be drawn into the Holy Eucharist radiating from our souls. Our destination has always been the Most Blessed Sacrament of the Altar. Our sacrifices prolong the merciful opportunity given by God for everyone on Earth to see Love, accept Love, and ultimately live in Love forever.

We realize at the last that nobility and self-denial are reciprocal partners and the Holy Spirit inflames their protracted beauty. We must finally understand that agony and pain are the giant stumbling-blocks that make it very difficult for the affluent to pass into the celestial heights. The Scriptures make it very clear how difficult it is for the wealthy to enter the Kingdom of Heaven because their simplicity and generosity have been so plundered by greed and self-indulgence. It is in the midst of that void that Satan takes control of them like a parade of lost sheep that are unaware of where they are going. They truly do not recognize the wretchedness of the one who is leading them astray. That is also why so many people enrich their own fortunes before ever deciding to help the poor. They look away from themselves only after denying everyone else first. Their lives are most commonly given to the acquisition of priceless possessions and stimulating experiences, all the while maintaining their poise as far from any material discomfort as they can possibly travel. Although generously giving from their abundance of goods is, indeed, a charitable contribution, it is absent of any greater purpose than that. Nobility advances the gift of Life by diminishing the wealth of the giver. It means being united with Love from the very bottom of the wallet-size barrel. It is in giving that we receive, and in loving that we become enjoined in bonds of paradisial grace.

Sunday, July 14, 1991
"Dear children, today your Mother has come to call each of you to Love. I have come to ask you to pray so that Love can remain in your hearts. Each of you must be open to understand the encompassing power of Love. Please remember that Love is an Infinity beyond dimension, but still can be grasped by the most feeble of hearts. It is

prayer, little ones, that helps you to see because Love is vision to those who accept My Son. Without accepting Jesus, your hearts will be blinded by indifference. Please remember that, while Love is strong and stable like a rock, it must also be tender to bend to forgiveness. Through your faith and trust in Love, you will see its fruits and gifts in your lives. My children, Love is the cause of life and the result of life, and it does not fathom a means to measure it. Love is the world and all in it and all that is not the world, but can still be held in the pulse of the human hand. Your Mother has come to ask you to open yourselves in prayer from your hearts! I ask you to share your love, as there is plenty in the world to replenish you. My children, even though Love is so strong, it is also very fragile and must be protected and sheltered in a gentle place. That is why the home of Love is the human heart, where it is nurtured and strengthened to be sent into the world to unite all as one. Thank you for praying, My children, to accept Jesus, who is that Love. Please remember that, when you pray from your heart, Love will come in while the door is open. Thank you for having responded to My call."

We began the Rosary at eight o'clock this evening and Our Lady came to continue Her message, "**Good evening, My beautiful ones. I have come again to teach you lessons to be given to the world and lead it to My Son. There is a bounty of beauty near. My son, this message is very important to the world. It is one of My most powerful. You see how simple it is. The message of Love shows its transcending power and, yet, its simplicity. Jesus is of that great power from such humble beginnings! This is how My messages will flourish, from the meek beginning of your lives, to a force that will convert millions. Thank you for helping Me. Your prayers are very powerful! Please never forget that. You must, however, remember that God's Will is also to run its course. His time is time, itself. Please be patient...**"

She revisited last night's message to make sure that I understood everything that was in it. The greatest nobility in human history was brought to fruition by Jesus as He hung dying on the Cross for the sins of humankind. There is no higher pinnacle of sacrificial Love that could exist anywhere else in the universe. She continued by reminding me how powerful prayer truly is, hoping that everyone who hears Her will be more encouraged to make their innocent supplications to God. The proud and mighty who live in penthouses behind ivy-covered walls petition Him with no greater authority than the meek and humble who lie sweltering in squalor in the ghettos underneath. Yet, many of them do not ask the Lord for help because they feel that He cannot hear their pleas. They believe that He will not tend to those who have wandered so distant from his grace. They errantly presume that, since they cannot see Heaven, they have been removed from beyond its purview, too. Their separation from the Land of the Redeemed is just a lonely misconception.

The simplest of petitions is an invitation to the Savior of the world for His Divine attendance to those who walk in fear. It is the preparation for the long-awaited arrival of the answers which they thought would never come. Jesus will respond expediently to the orisons we offer from our knees. He is simply waiting to be asked, while silently proclaiming with the resonating song of peace that no supplication is too small to reach His Sacred Heart. The slightest hint of human contrition brings the patter of His footsteps toward the landing at our door. When we are open to receive Him, He will refuse no one's offer to boldly let Him in. But, many of us will not accept that we are significant enough to be so special to the only Son of God. We do not realize that we complete the Almighty Father's vision of Creation after He pronounced it "good" upon the passing of the first six days. Indeed, we are the child who makes all of humanity whole. It is only a matter of time before we fully understand that the step-son of Saint Joseph is the answer we've all been searching for. That is the purpose for our religious inquisition because there is no other Savior. And, thanks to His Death on the Cross, we are already loved completely, so no one should burn-out their lives rejecting the wealthiest King who also happens to be their Father. We must come to comprehend how close He really holds us all. I asked, *"Holy Mother, how special are we, really, to God?"* She said, **"My son, when you ask how special you are, you are asking how much you are loved. Remember that it has no dimension or measure. There is nothing to compare Love to. There is nothing else in the world."**

Comfort and peace are instilled in the hearts of those for whom we pray. God entertains our hopes and dreams, leaving no good-will-measure beyond His creative capacity to fulfill. It is not possible to impede or destroy the power that He reserves to make us happy. In that Light, even our greatest longings are a sure-shot commitment in the bountiful fields of His universal Love. We must pray for one another with this confidence so as to evoke the entire body of humanity to turn to Heaven in hope for the world to change. Our Lady also asked me to remember that not everyone will convert by simply asking them to think of Jesus. We must move them into His presence by invoking the power of our own affinity for them. The Holy Spirit travels through physical space inside the human species. If we refuse to embark upon this righteousness, many souls on Earth will continue to grovel in a quagmire of unrest until they find their Gospel Home. Our inner-being craves both peace and the balance of contentment because Love flourishes in these tranquil environments, each of which is the abundant accord that composes the Christian heart. This is where Jesus works His greatest miracles of conversion. He communicates His grace into the material world through the very *cardiacus* fibers of His faithful children who trek the minefields of mortality proclaiming the Divinity of His Name. Ultimately, it is our own reciprocal response to Him that brings peace into our lives and those for whom we advocate. Prayer beseeches this ultimate intercession of God. That is why the answers to our most simple of petitions often take us by surprise. Indeed, we do not yet comprehend His Love in its fully-unbounded magnitude. There are no superlatives which can be used to accurately describe this holy spectacle of grace. The Almighty Father in Paradise is the highest power in Creation because there is no other deity. Our communication with Salvation, itself, must bloom from the salivating lips of the Holy Spirit who has planted His Divinity within us.

    Let it be stated with perfect clarity that human discipline is required in order for this supernatural dialogue to occur. The ability to participate in the expressive interchange with the Almighty Father above us is granted to every soul on Earth. He pines for us to exercise our newly-obtained gift to address His majesty with the familial term "Papa." He desires our growth in holiness toward a sanctity that increases by-the-hour as we come to know the wellspring of His Love. Our obedience strengthens the capacity for us to faithfully consume the quenching draft of life-giving water from a life of suppliant humility. If our Christian conveyance is proportioned from the fountain of our love, the need for punitive spiritual discipline is lessened. But, it is a very precious commodity during the times when our desire to succeed is weak. Constructive self-control plays a vital position in most every circumstance because our faith is rarely ever completely undiminished. It is an indispensable necessity if all the fruits of Love are to healthily exist. We need this self-imposed bridle because temptation and sin continue to engage us, attempting to take the life of our precious infant conviction. But, it grows stronger as we willfully catapult the alluring temptations of evil that prod us to fail and cast the seductions of the world away. All that is good among us can then grow with florid excellence and an unbroken spirit of peace. But, when our desire to hear-out the Lord is obstructed or unprotected by a lack of holy will, the gentler facets of the most tender of hearts are nearly always abused. It is in the midst of these torturous volleys that Jesus is always present before those who will accept Him and wish to be blessed by His Love. Within a singular flash of His luminary Truth, we realize that Christian discipline is never a punishment, but rather a sign from the Holy Spirit that, with just a little more help from above, our souls will be ready for Heaven. It is the Mother of the Child called Love who protects us and allows Her Son to grow from within our hearts. We must charitably give Him free-passage to anywhere He wishes to play in the meadows and midways of the world in which He is King. Great peace abounds amidst leaps and pinnacles in nations where this union is allowed to thrive. Our Holy Mother has come into the circles of human life to bring us to conversion and repentance, and to offer us this peace and everlasting good will. She will not spare our feelings in order to succeed. **"The most important part to** remember is that discipline is reliant on the strength of faith. Your Mother would like to thank you for allowing My messages to come to you.

Wednesday, July 17, 1991

Timothy and I began the Rosary at 8:30 p.m. and Our Holy Mother began by saying, **"I am with you! Thank you for praying from your heart for the world to be filled with Love! I am here to ask you to continue to help convert the world. Today, I have a special message to share with you about the funnel and the mirror..."** Our Lady then showed me the following picture.

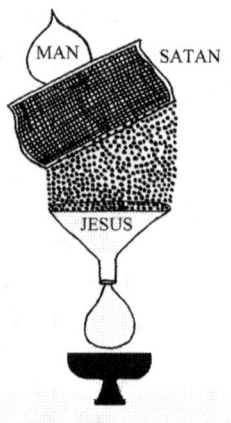

In the beginning, all of the children of God were united as one. But, Satan has sifted us into many individual droplets, separating us from one another by the hatred and sin that we have learned from his followers. Our Lady wishes us to gather into the singular Divinity of Jesus. He suffered His Passion and Death so that we would own this convoking conduit in which to commune. God loves humanity so immensely that He is poised to receive us in the boundless ocean of His Merciful Heart. In order for this to occur, we must all become visionaries of His Love. This is why our Virgin Mother labors so intensely to improve our soulful sight. When we pray for Her intercessory grace, God's Revelation expands within us because we move closer to the Gate of Paradise and we are sensitized to the overwhelming beauty of Salvation, becoming more compassionate toward each individual member of the body of humankind. Our focus must always be directed upon this Divine capacity that is now resting in the palms of our prayerfully-folded hands. This opening of the heart overcomes the darkness that we are trying to leave behind. Yet, some people will not turn their eyes forward and are still oblivious as to what they can do. There are many others who might give it a thought, but never show it in their heart. Our Lady explained further how our vision can be clarified by employing the mirror of faith, a supernatural tool that allows every soul to see Jesus Christ.

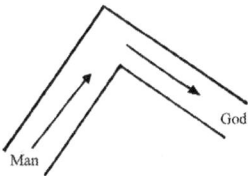

Imagine looking down a long corridor that turns sharply to the right. We have no way of knowing in advance what is down that open passageway. Even though we do not have the capacity to see around the corner, we have always felt a longing in our hearts to see the Face of God. How, then, can we see Him before we pass the juncture of mortality? Yes, we peer through the mirror of faith. Jesus has positioned a reflecting surface at the intersection of Heaven and Earth, a point of concursion that resides within our hearts. We see the Almighty Father through a vision that is inspired by the Holy Spirit, like an impression of a universal code of relevance that is imprinted upon our curious souls. I queried Our Lady whether we could actually see God, Himself. Her answer was that anything is possible if our prayers are powerful enough. Heaven is more than standing face-to-Face with the Almighty Creator of all things. Satan was once in that position, yet he never embraced the Eternity of Love. Our Heavenly Father desires us to experience more than just seeing His physical presence. He wants to totally submerge us in the majestic Love of His immortal being. He already knows that it is quite difficult to inundate the landscape of our lives with holiness when our hearts are only the size of water sprinklers. Therefore, He has provided the supernatural gift of faith to get us through the night. Despite His powerful beneficence, our own obstinance, disbelief, lack of conviction, materialism, and outright indifference, continue to obstruct our spiritual sight. We refuse to recognize that the mirror is hanging on the wall of the Earth.

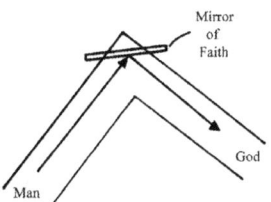

Our Virgin Mother added that we cannot simply run to the end of life to get a glimpse of God like we are scampering to peek down a turn in a hallway. Our place in time and space is especially measured by God for our eternal benefit. We must, instead, lift our hearts to Him, invoke our Love for humanity, and believe what He says at the cost of our own execution. Time does not move, as Our Lady has said, but we move through it at the pace of the Will of Her Son. Our progression toward Eternal Life is accelerated by the faithfulness and intensity of our prayers. There are countless people who live for years at the intersection of this world and the next, looking for the Lord in the mirror while He is already standing directly behind them. He knows that we will get there if we walk through the corposant Light that allows us to see. Our footsteps toward our deliverance are marked by the cadence of Christ. When our prayers increase in intensity, Love blooms throughout the world, moving us ever closer to the beatific infinity that stands at the end of our journey of faith. Time, therefore, is only an intransigent factor and belongs solely to our loving Creator. Our lives are the time that He has reserved for us! This does not separate His children from Him or inhibit anyone's capacity to know Him. In fact, it enhances it by leaps and bounds. Our work on this planet could be completed in a single day. But, the Almighty Father allows us to transcend the opportunistic breadth of life, participating in His reflective Love and taking heed of the Gospel at every new-breaking occasion that unfolds in our way.

Unfortunately for humanity, many people will not pray because they are blinded by indifference. They have not even a meager sense of the meaning of time, vision, or hope because they are like lifeless statues, forever fixed in the timocracy that overshadows their ability to live in the Holy Spirit or see past the mounds of intolerance they have generated for man and God, alike. They are dead in a human existence without the Love that will sustain their vision into Eternity. That is why we must all remember that life is not limited to mere human existence. The corridor of our collective days reveals many magnificent truths. Human opinions regarding our most beneficial direction and the limits that God has placed before us are transcended through invincible faith. One is not alive until they can see their resuscitating breath like exhaling the fresh air of a mountaintop. Therefore, Life is endless, while existence is a mortality that we shall never permeate without accepting the Love of Jesus Christ. The proof of our need for this reflection is in the confining parameters that we feel. We look at physical objects with our eyes. But, the Light that refracts from our understanding of Heaven can be seen only in a heart that is cultivated in the Truth. Without the guiding Wisdom of God, the steaming fog of faithlessness obscures our beatific purview in favor of the delusions and errors that thrive in our frail mortal reasoning. Many of us are already lost and confused in this way. For example, the scourge of abortion casts a horrific shadow over the wretched evil of those who participate in its perpetration. The vast human illness of a disunited Christianity is left unnoticed by the broken faculties of those who protest the miracle of the Holy Eucharist. When faith becomes powerful enough within us, we will indeed see the mightiness of God which He so perfectly conceals in the bounty of the Sacraments of the Holy Roman Catholic Church. The Truth has no end. And, the Love that He wishes to share with us is magnified by our prayers, entwining us more deeply within His Sacred Heart.

Our past, present, and future rest just beyond the corner of death. They all reside in the Eternal Now. This is how we have retroactively obtained our liberty. When Jesus rose on Easter morning, we escaped the incarcerating prisons of human mortality. It is in Him that our own impending resurrection has timelessly destroyed the chains of our bondage. We do not realize our mutual freedom because we have yet to collectively allow the mirror of Justice to shine on our face. Of the three elements that now exist; ourselves, our faith, and the Holy Trinity, it is the latter whom our hearts pine the most to see. As we are called face-to-Face with God's merciful visage, there will no longer be a need for the noble offices of faith and hope. We will be able to conduct our personal parlance in Heaven instead of kneeling with folded hands, hoping against hope that somebody outside of life and time can hear us. There will be nothing left at the end of time but the fall of the prodigal son into the arms of his loving Father. Our Lady told me that, as a result of our indifference and blindness, many people of strong character and good principle have borne countless crosses and suffered much grief in this world in which we live. Therein lies the perfection of their love for God and humankind. We should, likewise, bear our sorrows through Love, rather than relying on our hollow physical strength to shrug our shoulders or employing snide intellectual excuses for turning away. We must tender our faith with the discipline that is procured by our Heavenly Mother to augment our conviction for standing upon the principles of Christ. Obedience to Our Lady manifests a faith more powerful than any evil offense or the time-tested failures of stubborn obtuseness and recondite modernism.

It seems very ironic for Love to appear so defenseless while it persistently wields the power to shape the destiny of all humankind. Jesus subjected Himself to death on a Cross, yet His Divinity was never vulnerable to defeat. If we live in that same omnipotent grace, neither will we be vincible, even though we may lose our lives in the process. Love must be given freely in order to magnify our opportunity to see God, to be seen by Him, and to show His lucidness to others. Jesus actually defended everything that He embodied from the acidic horror of the Cross by magnifying Heaven throughout the ends of time. He surrendered His Life in defense of our Redemption. We must, likewise, endure our own hardships with equal perfection and certitude. **"My** children, the world does not know how to love! Your prayers are helping others to grow in Love. Many will not allow their hearts to receive Love. The Salvation of the world depends upon the consecration of human hearts to Christ. Simple minds are trying to destroy the world. My Son is the Savior of the world because He loves His Creation."

Friday, July 19, 1991

Our Holy Mother approached us this evening with the following holy words. **"Welcome to My Heart! Thank you for praying! Contemplate the Eucharist! The work of the Church is centered upon providing the Eucharist to the world. The Blessed Sacrament is the grace around which all others reside. The world must move swiftly toward the Holy Eucharist. My Son has come to purify, to enrich, and to save. Those who do not receive Him in the Holy Eucharist do not wholly understand His Sacrifice or its importance..."** There are seven Sacraments, and the Eucharist is the Most Blessed of them. It is the pillar, the power, and the source of the living Love, Jesus Christ, God-become-Man. In Its very essence, it is mankind's return to Paradise, for it embodies human unity and the completion of the Will of God. Through the Alpha and Omega, who is Christ, we are called to the Table of the Lord. The time to return is now! Those who deny Jesus in the Holy Eucharist do not realize the power of His promise, ***"The Kingdom of God is upon you."***

This evening, our Blessed Lady told me that humility is related to our patience, and both of them are a portion of forgiveness. We cannot be humble unless we pardon the offenses of others. And, we cannot do so if we fail to allow them time enough to change. Jesus has absolved us of our every transgression, and we must imitate this same kindness toward others. Such an exalted splendor is ratified when we completely erase the missteps of our enemies from our memory. Compassion and understanding provide a healing balm for hearts who are crying-out to be loved. Through our own humble generosity, they can stake a new claim in dignity because the power of Jesus lives abundantly in us. That divine authority is what it will take to deliver our brothers and sisters to conversion in Him. Personal reconciliation destroys the now-extinct boundaries of time, allowing former offenses to be extinguished and replaced by the purified beauty of Christianity. This is the power of Our Lord in the hearts of mortal men and is the reason that reciprocal vindication is joyfully authorized by God, the Almighty Father in Heaven. The Holy Mother has told us that Love is the only Power in the universe. We see many forces trying to bring our souls to ruin, but we have no greater benefactor than in Jesus of Nazareth. Satan can huff and puff against our doors all he wants, but he still cannot defeat the Master of the House. Evil impels many people to move away from peace, happiness, love, purity, and Salvation because they will not obediently pray to stop it. These poor souls are victims of their own indifference, rendering themselves stagnant, lacking in direction, less than whole, and starving for replenishment and renewal of the spirit.

Jesus is our deliverer from these terrible pales of existence. He restores our human dignity and purity, giving life to the soul and allowing the embrace of solace to rest within our hearts. We must remember that peace is the natural symmetry of Creation which has been reinstated through the Death and Resurrection of the Savior of the World. While farmers cyclically hope for bountiful harvests and an abundance with which they can feed the world and sustain their families, Jesus is the True Eternal Bounty. He is the food for our souls and the supplier of our every need. It is He who purchased our Salvation and Eternal Life with the price of His own precious Blood, where two limbs of an ordinary tree intersected in time. Our Lady has told us that we, too, will be folded at the last harvest. While our hearts change like the seasons, we always live in the climate of God. We must remain united in the Sacrifice of His Son and anticipate His return into His Kingdom once again. To do so, we must make our hearts tenable in His grace by never again entertaining the temptations of evil. We must destroy it through the integrity of our faith. Any lack of communication with Heaven is the beginning of our own self-destruction. Our Lord oftentimes anticipates the bounty of our lives by cultivating our souls with His hands. We must be willing to accept this refinement in order to eventually taste the sweetness of Salvation.

When we totally accept Christ, we will become permanently happy and peaceful, despite the cost of the tangible sacrifice. Nothing can block His pluvial Love from inundating our being once we have crossed that bridge of trust. His infinite power will radiate inside us and the dove of peace will quietly nest beside our yearling courage. The Holy Spirit sanctifies the heart in this nurturing way, preparing us all to finally see the Almighty Father as a singular body of people. Love is universally one, no matter if it is in the heart of a human being or in the vaulting consciences of the great Seraphim on high. We are called to return to those celestial courts by transforming our human indifference into a holy and indomitable conviction of faith. But, our inhibitions must be totally convinced that we will succeed. God said affirmatively, "**I AM**," therefore, He is indeed! He is perfect Love in a simple way that any child can understand. Likewise, Jesus says that, through Him, we "are." In the flash of that instant, human life now has new meaning because His Divinity is the standard among men. He is both the concept and the definition, and is reciprocally one in the universe. Jesus knows us well, while we faithfully know Him, too. Our unity evolves from the Truth that God reveals through His Son. Jesus' birth brought perfection to the mortal side of Creation where it once was quite sorely lacking. Now, He will never leave our side. He still inhabits every Catholic Tabernacle in the world, hoping to receive that final lost soul who stumbles in to receive Him. We must all eventually come to the Holy Eucharist and embrace this generous gift of Eternal Life that is now pouring-down from the heavens.

The Virgin Mother of Jesus Christ has come into our midst to facilitate our acceptance of the Paradise where She reigns as Queen. Her Son's Death on the Cross, united with Her unwavering loyalty to Her children, have brought the Mercy of God upon the Earth to redeem us. We will fully receive His everlasting forgiveness, if that is what we truly desire. That is why there is hope in our every sincere prayer. We can see the infinity of Salvation from where we stand in time. A simple definition of prayer is "I HOPE." This was Jesus' petition to the Almighty Father during His Agony in the Garden. He hoped with every fiber of His perfect being that we would accept His Sacrifice and follow in His footsteps. The world He saved continues to be reshaped through the prayers we lift today because He took them into account while hanging on the Cross, answering every one of them when He humbly pronounced the prophetic words, "It is finished!" The work is at our hands, but the Holy Spirit is the reason we have the power to extend them with strength. God will answer our every holy prayer when we reach-out to others in His Name. He responds in His time and in His own miraculous way. Our Lady often repeats the single word that makes our impetuous lack of perseverance shudder. "Patience." **"Every day is important toward the Salvation of the world. Each moment is important! Each prayer is important! God's Will will be done. Your work is of God and is very holy."**

Saturday, July 20, 1991

Timothy and I began the Holy Rosary at 9:30 p.m. and the Mother of God came to speak to us again, beaming with pleasure at the sound of our prayers. We are learning to invoke the power that God has dispensed to all people on the Earth to change the very essence of human existence. When we understand that Jesus Christ is the definition of Life, we no longer have difficulty living His Love amidst such a treacherous world. Tonight, Our Lady described to me how our holy convictions become lost in the turmoil that greets us as we face the dawn of each new day. Our failure to seek the intercession of Heaven is not so much founded in our lack of belief in Salvation, but rather, because we do not know how to make the sacrifices to bring it about. We already know that the human heart is the receptacle of Divine persistence. But, through the passages of time, we have failed to simultaneously embrace one another while governing the lot of the multitudes. We are afraid that our friends and siblings might, somehow, gain an advantage over our individual well-being while we greet them in mutual consolation. Our Lady has already told us that someone has to lose in order for someone else to win in our courts of worldly competition. This is true because we live without a desire to taste the fundamental fruits of the Holy Spirit. Indeed, where are love, peace, joy, patience, goodness, kindness, faithfulness, humility, and self-control in our actions and intentions? These are the soul-enriching foods that are mandated by the Almighty Father to nourish the lost souls of the world. Instead of pursuing them, many of us would rather feast upon public laws that restrict the civility of the masses, creating false barriers between societies and causing neighborhood friends to fight against each other like foreign troops in killing fields.

We know one another only superficially through habitual actions, stringent tendencies, and biased expectations. The Blessed Virgin told me that our interaction must, instead, be founded upon the Wisdom of God. Our daily actions must flourish and thrive from the Love in our hearts, remembering all along that their multiplication does not necessarily render them obsessive in nature. For example, attending Mass or reciting the Holy Rosary every day is not so much a *habit* as it is a grace and mutual response to Jesus Christ by His people on Earth. All humankind must recall their obedient respect for the Most Blessed Sacrament at each new sunrise. In this simple way, all human coaction is led to the heights of the greatest sanctity we could ever hope to know. Then, even our temporal differences cannot impugn our hearts. If we allow the work of our hands to be diminished through habitual indifference, it will, indeed, become absent-of-the-heart and lack the elevated purpose we are expected to achieve. We are still human, and therefore are quite susceptible to stumbling in the darkness. This is assuredly what leads us to societal conflicts and personal disagreements. Our Lady wishes us to wisely avoid this conduct by totally loving others in the spirit of humble prayer. She provided a pictural explanation.

If our expression of spiritual affection is constrained by our unwitting habits, we will always need to reorient our level of tolerance so as not to offend those around us. Love is the consistency of life and must never be weaker at one time over another. The previous illustration indicates our emulation of Christ in relation to someone else's offense. The distance that a person must travel before they overshadow our grace is the tolerance that supports our faith in humanity. We can also envision how our tolerance would be reduced if the temporal offenses were to rise higher toward our level of love.

Suppose an offense is so grave that it exhausts our forbearance and completely overcomes our love. In that moment, we realize that we must reaffirm our commitment toward what Christ would have us do, increasing our tolerance so that we can peacefully embrace those who have trespassed against us.

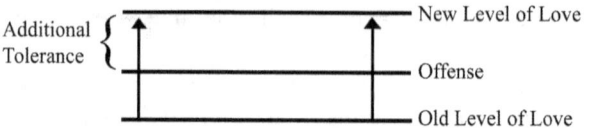

When I heard this description, I thought that it was an appropriate vision for our spiritual growth. But, Our Lady said that we tarnish the Spirit of Love by needing to establish another "cushion" of forbearance. We should not feel that we have a right to a tolerance because Love is unconditional. No human insult or affront can be allowed to diminish our capacity to live in the peace of the Holy Spirit. Many people are reticent in their compassion toward others because they lack the virtue of walking a mile in their shoes. Our patience must magnify our tolerance to the perpetual heights of invincible Love.

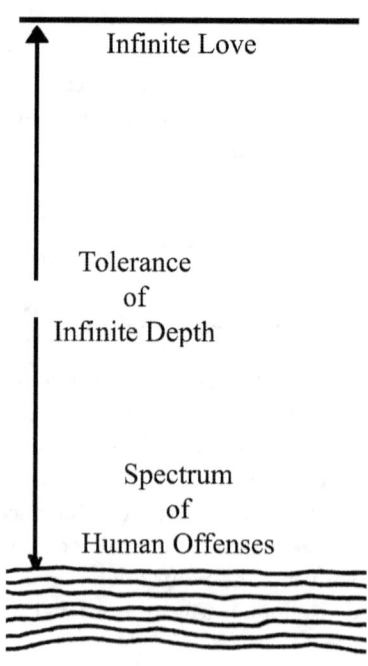

Sunday, July 21, 1991

"Dear children, your Mother calls you to My arms so I can teach you to love Jesus. Please be still and rest your hearts in the cradle of My Love. My children, it is important that you learn the power of prayer from the heart. You have no other way to change the world. I ask that you commit yourselves to receiving Jesus often in the Blessed Sacrament. Your prayer is strengthened through the Love provided in the Holy Eucharist. Come to Jesus, my special ones, and He will guide your days to peace through the quiet of Love. When you see the world through the eyes of Love, you will no longer see your need to be weakened through your search for earthly goods. Your search for wealth ends in Jesus. He is your final treasure and lot. My Son is your future and your destiny. My children, all that is good is in the hands of Jesus. Your Mother has come to ask you to receive His empire of Love by taking His hand. Your toils and labors are fruitless without Love and prayer. Please remember to pray and fast, and be penitent to make you pure of heart. Please concentrate on the Eucharist and not the world so you can be free to love instead of enslaved by indifference. My children, there are many ways to gain your earthly fortune, but only one way to receive Eternal Life. That is Jesus, little ones, who seeks to rescue you from the captivity of sin and hatred. When you ask Jesus, He will help you because He is Love. Thank you for having responded to My call."

Timothy and I began the Rosary at four-thirty this afternoon and our Virgin Mother came to us to say, **"Good day, My precious ones. I am with you again. Thank you for your prayers. Today, I have come to speak to you about** *emotion*. **It is directly related to My message of last evening..."** I listened attentively so that I could quote all of Her words verbatim in this Diary. Our Lady has made a clear distinction between the movements of the heart as opposed to the functions of the mind. The outward appearance of these subtle dynamics is the display of our responsiveness to our interior life. Human emotions that are generated by the activity of the mind always do more harm than good because they are rooted in the selfish perspective of our sensible character. Our excitability is a trait of our physiological response to the perceptions of the mortal psyche, and are oftentimes ambiguous and quite uncontrollable. Our Lady said the heart does not sponsor such delusions of this kind since they are not an inherent derivative of the Wisdom of God. Jesus' Spirit is one of total acceptance without any fashion of rogue resignation. His grace flows far beyond the pressures of our willful incitement. True Love is never flippantly controlled or coerced by what our thoughts can imaginatively create.

Our understanding of emotion must not be confused with the beauty that is shared in our Christian affection. Mutual warmth can be manifested from our love for one another. But, Satan falsely sires a diabolical imitation from the sensations of human greed and the false pressures of lust and perversion. Neither emotion nor affection of this kind are part of omnipotent Love, and do not lead toward conversion in Christ. Such intellectual and physical phantasms must not be equated with feelings of the heart. When we weep in recognition of the Love in our soul, we are not crying because we have lost all control, but rather, because we are tenderly touched by the Spirit of God. Tears of Christian good will are from the Light that has burst-through the heart and flooded the soul. The demeanor and grace that follows are a result of the Divinity which magnifies our holy imitation of Jesus. Our physical sensitivities are always temporal and worldly and are most often based on an imagined human need or desire that is produced from our perception of being personally violated. They can cause great distraction and unnecessary grief as a result. Radical emotion may also flow from self-pity, causing false guilt to fester in others. Our Lady told me today that we are often forced to accept responsibility for problems which are not of our own making. Christianity is a self-examining prospect that provides the necessary value of a constructive critique of our inner being. We must honestly judge our own actions and motivations with the fruits of the Holy Spirit as our only criteria. Those who recognize these delectable morsels can savor their sweetness the moment they live them. Others who have never partaken of such piety continue to suffer because their appetite for righteousness is left unsatisfied.

It is nearly impossible to survive an attack upon our emotional constitution if we do not call upon the Holy Spirit for guidance and protection. How often have we allowed anger or bitterness to lead us away from the symmetry of peace? Fear is the weakness of nature that is most often the foundation of our erratic emotions. It manifests anxiety and tension, leading us to spontaneous arguments and pitiful crying. This seriously impedes our capacity to radiate the Spirit of God to the rest of humanity. Our polluted disposition is an intense derangement that only serves to blind us from seeing Jesus more clearly. While Love lives in the tranquil solitude of the heart, it is blocked from feeding the intellect during emotional and physiological distress. Prayer is the solution to this paradoxical condition because it facilitates our projection of good will toward those we detest. Then, we can enlist temporal acts to outwardly communicate the feelings of unity that flow from our hearts. We must never respond to emotionalism with increased anxiety. Prayer is the summation that leads to the composite resolution of unmitigated disdain. The Holy Mother described some corollaries between human thought and the structure of the world, asking me to contemplate the many different terrains, such as mountains, valleys, and deserts.

TERRAINS	FEELINGS
canyon	hollowness
desert	frustration
ocean	loneliness
plains	lost
badlands	fear
frozen tundra	cold
rainforest	apprehension
swamps	helplessness

The terms in the right represent human sentiments that might describe the associated terrains on the left. The ensuing emotions are also symbolically related to the corresponding feelings and terrains. Now, if you were the world, which words would you want someone to choose to describe you? Which aspects might you want them never to see? Consider these comparisons in light of our frail mortal nature. Let us now look at climates.

CLIMATES	FEELINGS
arid	hopeless (parched, dry)
arctic	abandoned (cold, alone)
wet	depressive (cloudy, no sun)
dry	anxious (needing water)
mild	comfortable

Notice that the individual climates produce their respective terrains. Arid conditions produce a desert, while arctic ones result in a frozen tundra. Consider what feelings might be attributed to these different circumstances. Which makes you suffer the most? Conversely, which would you not seek to escape? Can you see that there is no desire for change when the weather is fair? These climates symbolically highlight the complete cycle of human emotions. We should see through them that our inner disposition must never be allowed to define our individual interaction. If someone attaches their fundamental sensitivities to their social interchange, they will mistakenly draw distinctions based upon the premise of those temporary feelings. Our communion with one another must, instead, be situated upon the unwavering foundation of Love. After seeing this analogy between the composition of the Earth and our sensitivities, we assuredly recognize that they are both only temporal in nature. Like terrains and climates, our emotions are only a part of the surface.

The landscapes of the Earth do not affect the factual nature of the spherical world. Jesus has made it round, and nothing affecting its surface has ever changed that. Likewise, our inner emotions cannot alter the Spirit of Love in our midst because Jesus sustains it with His logical sense of Divine composure. Our inner sentiency, however, is a synthesis of our daily encounters with the material world and our fetish human nature. This is not to say that Jesus did not exhibit the responsive impulses of the heart. He was born a human child and was reared in a mortal world. But, He subordinated it with the genius of His Love, and that is exactly what He asks from us. We will never be subjected to anything that He was unable to endure. Our thoughts were originally His own because He lived our lives before we were ever conceived. He asked the same tough questions of His elders, suffered the same temptations as His contemporaries, and felt the same agony and helplessness as every soul that God has given the breath of Life. Jesus, indeed, lived our sorrows, guilt, afflictions, and discord. Through perfect compassion, He was able to know and understand our human inequities through His own experience of life. But, as the Son of God, He remained perfect in every way because Divine Love is perpetually free from sin. Our Lord took-on our faults and imperfections by absolving us with compassionate empathy and patient understanding.

We were cleansed of our every imperfection when the Son of God was crucified on the Cross. Our souls are rendered sinless in His grace through our acceptance of that gift. And, come the end of this life, we will receive the Kingdom of Heaven because everything that is reborn in Him will then be conjoined as one. There is nothing less than complete Divinity which resides in Heaven. That is the Promise that our God has made. So, we must pray for forgiveness so as to be made a part of that Eternity of bliss. We must also petition fervently for the poor souls in Purgatory who are one-step closer to Redemption than we are on Earth. They are purified by contrition and admitted into the glories of Paradise as a fruit of our intercessions on their behalf. Our Lady has said many times that we cannot bear the crosses of others because Jesus has already done that for them. We can, however, share in their sufferings through our private conversations with God. We must implore every living being to accept Jesus Christ as the cure for all their ills, knowing full-well that the most ravaging of all infirmities is a heart that denies the Holy Spirit. Everyone must be bonded in the Most Blessed Trinity, which will secure our Eternal Salvation in the Messiah who is very soon to return again. **"It is important that men remember that they are capable of weaving their own shackles, but they cannot break them without Jesus. My son, the perspective which you have been given as a gift from Jesus is like no other in the world. Thank you for praying. You are My special and obedient child."**

Wednesday, July 24, 1991
   We knelt to pray the Holy Rosary at nine in the evening and Our Lady said, **"You are beautiful and special! I love you very much! Your prayers of the last two days have ensured through My Son that I will continue to speak to you. Your prayers carry much power..."** She prophesied the beauty of the coming autumn, reminding me of the peaceful state of my memories of this time of year. The Fall season is a symbolic finish to the toiling labors of our hot summer days. The work of our hands and the prayers of our hearts yield the fruitful harvest for which we offer thanksgiving to God. The rainbow-colored trees are His gift of beauty, along with the sights and sounds of the familial fellowships that rise into the crisp clear nights from the campsites and wiener roasts of the waning fair-weather. It is truly a magnificent time to venerate nature and honor the God who made it. **"It seems such a short time since your brother woke you in the night to tell you I spoke to him. My child, I was also speaking to you! Now, you see how it has unfolded. And now, during this autumn, you will see many fruits of your labors. This rich harvest will yield the conversion of many souls. Thank you!"**
   Humanity must become one in Love, and Our Holy Mother is pleading with tear-filled eyes because we have yet to reach this sacred unity. Many of us require signs of God's presence before we will ever desire to seek Him. Yet, the revelations of His Glory are abundant in the world and through the very lives we lead. The magnificence of autumn, itself, is a continuing notation from the Almighty Father that His beautiful Plan is on course. His grace and clarity motivate His Love throughout our human senses. It takes the smallest amount of faith to reignite the childlike wonderment that flourishes at the opening of every day. In answer to my own beliefs, the Blessed Virgin led me into a discussion tonight about the trusting innocence from which the awesomeness of Heaven can be experienced. It is founded upon two strengths; the gift to accept and understand that Christ Jesus is our only Salvation, and the nurturing of that conviction through the journey from our spiritual infancy to the maturity of our passage into Glory. When we faithfully accept the Gospel Commandments, the Love of Our Savior becomes the absolute reason to stand beside Him with indomitable courage. There are many ways to symbolize this strength. For example, through our ingenuity and technology, we have constructed many means with which to transport ourselves and our material possessions. There is great variance in the scope of these carriages. They range in shape and size from huge ocean-liners to compact little cars that are capable of carrying only one individual person. It would conceivably take thousands of these diminutive vehicles to transfer the manifest of a singular sea-going vessel.
   Let us consider the source of their power. Each of these transportation devices has a generative motor with a distinctive design. The cargo ship has

several, perhaps, dozens of engines which are assembled onboard because of their humongous size. By comparison, small automobile engines are built via an assembly line prior to being installed in each particular car. This analogy is a parable regarding God's faith-people on Earth. Indeed, we should contemplate the reason that the Mother of Jesus is appearing throughout the world today. Most of Her children are like the little automobiles. They do not have the capacity to engender a loyalty to the heavens of their own accord because they will not pray from their hearts, while others have been given the gift of generating their own vision of Love through an obedience that will never bow or subside! These are the great sailing bastions of Christianity who have peppered the seas of human history with an indelible allegiance to Heaven! Padre Pio, the Pontiffs of the Church, and the holy Saints are all insuperable frigates of this beatific destiny of hope. Our Holy Mother has come to help us emulate these majestic professors of Godlike stature and to summon our service to the Almighty Father. Those who are distant from Christ through a lack of knowledge of Him need to rendezvous with His most ardent supporters through the conveyance of mutual prayer. The Virgin Mary has every intention of augmenting the power of our faith by converting our souls to unification in Her Son and effectuating our cultivation through the miracles of Her intercessory grace. She already realizes that there are many mighty carriers among us, but even more little dinghies afloat. These tiny ones are the infant souls whom Jesus is only now beginning to feed, hoping to rear them into mighty Saints who will sail the high-seas of destitution in search for the lost and alone.

We recognize these giants of life through our vision of what we are supposed to be in reflection of their fruitful legacies of compassion and good works. Likewise, we also know those who are still sorely lacking in Love. The indifferent around us live with no perambulating urgency to help those who struggle in need because their consciences are dead in the water. They live in worse cracks and crevices of darkness than those who are without enough light to safely guide them through life. **"I have come to bring My Love and prayers. This simple story of man-made vehicles will be simply understood. The simple message of Love, faith, and prayer enkindles power through the meekest of distance. Love can be a giant vessel of strength and breadth; and it can be self-generated and sustained, but it can also be instilled in the most simple vehicles, one capable of transporting only one heart to the Kingdom of Beauty, Eternity, and Salvation. It is beautiful to imagine."** The Ever-Blessed Virgin Mary is the grandest steamer of all! She is truthfully the Ark of the New Covenant who has come to take us into Her Immaculate Heart as shelter from the storm while we sail together into the union of eternal happiness above. The course is set and the destination is sure! Let us live in peace beside Her as She asks everyone else to come aboard!

Thursday, July 25, 1991
   The Holy Mother came to us again as we began the prayer of the Holy Rosary. **"Good evening, My special little ones! You are beautiful because you have accepted My Son who loves you. Thank you for praying! You are sharing the Love that makes Me happy. My child, I would like to respond to your question of why I first came through much mystery and symbolism, but now so openly. It is very simple. It has to do with the preparation of the world to receive My intercession..."** Our Lady asked me to envision a water faucet that is dripping because its handle is not completely closed. A small droplet swells from the spout and slowly grows larger until it shivers-loose and falls to the surface below. This process is repeated over and again if the spigot is never more tightly sealed. We cannot really know when another drop is going to shed until it actually breaks-away from the spout. This is symbolically how the Virgin Mary approaches Her children on Earth. It would have been much too overwhelming for the Mother of God to introduce Herself like a fully-open hydrant in Her initial appearances to my brother and me. All over the world, She consistently initiates Her intercession through little unsuspecting people in simple and understandable ways. Very few of us have the spiritual capacity to embrace the supernatural manifestations of this Holy and Immaculate Conception without some sort of graduated form of revelation.
   This point is made more clear as we ponder a waterfall somewhere in a deep country woods. During the warm days of summer, the water flows freely and with a deafening roar. It is both powerful and serene as it soothes the souls who come there to seek a quiet communion with nature. But, in the wintertime, the river is frozen and the waterfall is only a silent memory of the season that has now gone by. Upon the first sign of spring, many thirsty fawns drink from the pool at the base of the rugged cliffs, indulging in the same basin where they once tread with courage amidst the deafening summertime roar. It is quite a sight to see them stop to partake of the first trickles they see as the winter ice breaks loose and the waterfall comes to new life. Sometimes, the huge chunks startle them and they flee, overcome with fear, even though it is the same site of serenity where they had quenched their thirst on many past fall evenings. Our Lady does not want us to be afraid like the deer in the wild. She has come to preserve the serenity of peace for Her young ones because the western hemisphere is truly in need of spiritual conversion. She does not want anyone to run from Her in fear of the startling revelations from Heaven, but to confidently approach God with courage so that She can teach us all to pray in humility. Through this communion of holiness, each of us constructs our own spillway of conviction, faith, and firm perseverance. God blesses us as we pour-out our confessions through the intercession of the Holy Spirit and opens the mighty floodgates of His Love into the timidity of our hearts. The cascades

of blessings which form His droplets of Love quench the souls of all humanity and help us walk the parched deserts of mortal indifference that we all seem to tread alone.

We unite with our brothers and sisters to prime the flow of loving humanity into the Sacred Heart of Jesus. This true stream of holiness cascades from the Holy Sacrifice of the Mass, where we join the one Body of Christ in His purifying Ocean of Mercy. Jesus is the tranquil Bay of Christian oneness and human Redemption, and is truly the harbor of our eternal protection. If every living soul on Earth will grasp the hand of the person standing next to them in the Name of mutual forgiveness, we can launch many ripples of hope that will be felt around the globe and into all the universe. We must pray for the river of Love to pour-forth from every heart! This is the beseeching brotherhood and cohesion that causes Our Lady to be ecstatic in anticipation of the future of Her children. So, She continued today in great sincerity by redirecting Her lesson toward the inestimable riches of Her Son. All of the wealth which we need to survive is the Love within our hearts. Our Lord lives in the depths of our being and is our only authentic treasure whom we must console to the infinity of our faithfulness. When we embrace the people that God has chosen to redeem, we display our priceless Christianity before the entire nations of the world. Keeping the Gospel alive through our imitation of Christ is the only treasure trove that voluntarily searches for the one who is also seeking it. Inert gems must lie in wait to be exhumed or mined through the exchange of shovels and buckets. Love, however, is the living movement of Heaven through the collective conscience of individuals who are humble enough to believe that it can be seen by anyone on Earth. While many-a-bonanza and mother-load continue to lay hidden beneath our inaccessible mortality, the most tenable riches that are alive today take the least of effort to proclaim. That is the work of Our Lord, Himself. Since this is the undeniable Truth, what indeed, are we struggling for?

We search for material wealth, but it will have no universal value at the end of time. Gold and silver are as dead as the soil beneath our feet. The beauty of the Earth lies not in its arteries under the ground or encapsulated in the mountains that range overhead, but in the life-sustaining veins of the people who excavate their quiet depths and seek to reach their highest peaks. Together, we flow within the Spirit of Jesus Christ, the Savior of the World. His Love is the Life that we receive, uniting us with the Heaven that is already teeming with the joy of our arrival. The treasure of this Divine reality can be received by extending our hands in prayer and opening our hearts in faith. While those who search for material wealth use stocks and bonds as vehicles for temporal gain, the tool for our everlasting Life is the Sacred Mysteries of the Most Holy Rosary. Its power can exhume the deadest of souls from the depths of human sin. Fine jewels are worthy and beautiful only if touched by the naked eye. Their fineness can be appreciated only by those who search and see. But, immortal perfection is the lasting treasure that God sends to us through His Son and His Spirit, while dredging our silt of lust and greed and seeking new followers of peace and good will. His dazzling brilliance is gently protected within our hearts, awaiting the chance to be broached by the most sincere of seers, those anxiously-awaiting souls about to be converted to the flawless brilliance which will eventually set them free. There has always been time for gaining the abundance of fortune from the heart because prayer of the Rosary is the greatest utensil for making the most difference in life. Aside from that fact, there is precious little time for wasting our days away. Everyone must stand-up for Salvation and convert to Christ Jesus, now! With that same great immediacy, we must simultaneously live the Spirit of Love to make this miracle come true.

I asked Our Lady why it seems as though Her messages are not taken seriously by everyone I know. She told me that the reason is far greater than people just simply not taking the time. My brother and I were riding in the car one day and wondered why the clouds that we saw were level on the bottom. We realized that the unseen atmosphere below them is what makes them appear to be flat. We remembered the Holy Mother's earlier affirmation that what we cannot see fosters and supports what we realize through our senses. With regard to Her intercessory words, people are unsure what makes them comprehensible messages. In answer to my question She said, **"Many do not take time for the Love of Christ."** Our Divine Lord is expressing His Love for humanity through great natural and supernatural signs. He is the unseen Creator who sustains every glimpse of the beauty we see. Many people think that Our Lady's intercession is too good a grace to be true because, by their own action and words, they live with miserable recklessness while blaming God for never coming to their aid. They falsely perceive their squalor as being both a dictation from His Throne and the intention of His Will for the rest of their lives. So, they close their hearts to His healing Love and become further impoverished through their own self-fulfilling prophecy, setting themselves apart from the fruitful life which the Almighty Father is offering them from above. They must realize that Jesus is a spiritual and physical reality within His Creation. Our Lady has come to remind us that He is still alive and real through His Mystical presence on Earth. Through our humble supplications, we can better know the King of kings and serve Him more worthily while truthfully living His Word. This is why we were created and given life, to share His magnificent Love in this world and the next.

Friday, July 26, 1991

As Timothy was leaving his home today, he found a robin's nest which had fallen from a treetop near the railing of his porch. Upon delivering it to my house, I would not allow him to bring it inside because it seemed to have no relation to the higher works that we were doing. Later in the evening, we began to pray the Holy Rosary and Our Lady came to say, **"I am with you, My sons. Thank you for praying to change, convert, and save the world! Bring the little nest inside. I have brought it so you will be able to understand My message more clearly. The nest was given shape by the free and beautiful flock..."** I was somewhat embarrassed that I had originally entertained some distasteful thoughts when I first saw the fallen nest, now knowing that it was to symbolize part of Our Lady's message tonight. Thinking that it was probably insect-infested and may have a bad odor, I did not consider pausing to remember the little robins that were born there this spring. The nest represents the foundation of the first flight of their lives. Their mother gave of herself through love and nature by weaving it together in preparation for the birth and maturation of her young.

Our Holy Mother asked me to notice the design and contour of these fledglings' first home. It had intricately inter-woven blades of grass that seemed to be bound together in any fashion that would firmly connect them. Its bottom was prefigured to fit the limb of the tree upon which it had been resting and the upper rim seemed stronger and more sturdy where it assumed its rounded shape. There is no doubt that little lairs of this sort represent one of God's greatest miracles right before our mortal eyes. My attention was directed to the inside where I saw a coating of mud-packed soil which the mother robin had molded into shape with the crown of her breast. Together with the single blades of grass, she had contoured the mixture into a smooth surface with a delicate interior. Through this intricate detail, refined by hours of tedious labor, she expended great effort to preserve the precious life that she was about to bear. I was holding the very world in whose circumference the little birds' newborn lives had been protected in the palm of my unworthy hand. It was truly a remnant of natural love. The mother robin was the sculptor of the first environment that her little offspring would ever come to know. Imagine what it meant to these feeble infant songbirds! It was an environment that was given to them through a love that they had yet to fully understand, a source of protection, a means of support, and a place of fortified comfort. They nestled in its bosom as the innocent beginnings of incarnate Love. The mother robin's work came to fruition when the last tiny fledgling flew into the skies. At that very moment, the nest became only a useless conglomeration of dead grass and dry earth. It was no longer of any value to the life it had once sustained. We can see, however, that it represents the memory of filial affection and the image and promise of new freedom.

Our Holy Mother taught me that this story reflects the beauty of Creation. In its likeness to the nest, the Earth is the foundation of the existence of mortal life in both its functional and physical form. It was created by God with precise style and purpose, a temporary estate where He can feed our souls until we are worthy to be set free into being and fly skyward toward Redemption. Just as the nest was intricately shaped to fit gently upon the limb of a tree, so has the Earth been perfectly poised in the stately foyer of the doorway to Heaven. While the configuration of the nest becomes more refined in physical detail as it comes closer to the life it supports, so it is with the globe that provides our daily food. Indeed, the closer we direct our hearts to the lands which the Father has blessed, the better we can see where Our Savior was born. As the mother robin consecrated her life to be nearer her children, Our Creator in Paradise has consecrated Himself to the very planet upon which we live. He has bestowed His Immortal Child into the confining realms of our mortal dimensions. That is one of the reasons that He is most obvious in our life as we look closer toward all humankind. Even as we comprehend this truth, the world often mistakenly believes that the Almighty Father is as far from our souls as the most distant blade of grass at the remotest perimeter of a nest in a tree. Many know Him only as residing somewhere in outer-space, beyond the reach of intelligent men. But, the Holy Spirit leads us to understand Him as residing inside the realm of our hearts. While little robins must always cry-out for the maternal instinct of their mother, humankind is dependent upon the nourishing Body of God's only Son. Just as these silk-feathered babies open their hungry mouths to eat, we must also open our hearts to become Divine in His image. The mother of these yearlings is the epitome of Love in nurturing her young so that their flight is assured. Jesus bestows the same gift upon our spiritually famished souls.

In imitation of the helpless robins who open to receive nourishment in preparation for flight, we must remain as eagerly receptive to the Body and Blood of Our Lord in the Most Blessed Sacrament. Once this last conversion has been made, the strength for our Salvation is gracefully bestowed upon us with our steadfast passage being the fulfillment of the oath that God has taken for those who accept Him. This redeeming process originates and concludes in the Manna that rains-down from Heaven. It is the beginning, the center, and the sustenance of human Life. Moreover, and most importantly, it is the Promise of the Eternal Salvation of the children of Light through the Holy Cross on the Hill where our Savior once died for our sins. Even though our Blessed Mother's story about the robin's nest is simple, it represents the Truth which the entire world must ultimately claim as their own. She concluded, **"My hope is that the world will gain the knowledge of Love, and realize how simple it is. The story is one and the same. Love is! There are thousands of ways to show it, all leading to the same simple Truth."**

Sunday, July 28, 1991

We began the Holy Rosary at 2:30 p.m. and the Mother of God blessed us with Her presence again. Glory in the highest! **"I love you and am with you again. Thank you for praying and opening your hearts to My Son. You are in His special favor..."** Our Lady reminded us of the importance of the Feast of the Assumption, August 15th, and also the Feast of the Queenship of Mary, which is observed on August 22nd. Special graces flow abundantly into the lives of those who fulfill their holy obligations on these particular days. Through celebrating Her perpetual Coronation, we better realize the unity that we share with Jesus and the Hosts of Heaven above. It is in that Divinity that we begin to accept the powerful and grace-filled intercession which the Immaculate Virgin comes to offer Her children. She told me today that many gifts are given to those who recite the Sacred Mysteries on the feast-day of Her Queenship. She also told me that Her weekly Sunday messages for the rest of the world would be transformed into an even greater work that is to soon to be revealed. After dispensing with these procedural facts, She continued with Her lesson about our worldly interaction with others and our mistaken obedience to our mental desires instead of the love in our hearts. The world seems to be more interested in intellectual and material stimulation than in nurturing the Love of Heaven that is blooming within and around us.

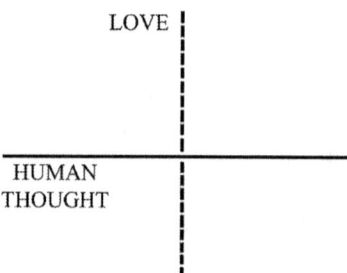

Human interaction is a function of the tangible characteristics of the mortal world and is a process of thought that offers little regard for the possibilities of Love. Our lives are often based solely upon the stagnant communication between peoples, which is symbolized by a horizontal baseline inter-connecting the lateral fields of Earth. Rarely do we ever consider proffering any elevating attributes in the midst of our daily labors. Such ascension could be symbolically denoted by a vertical line of loftiness that is representative of God's Love descending into our material world. His Holiness is the highest plane of human potential and is situated far above any thought that we might be capable of conceiving. This noble beatitude, alone, should be more than enough to move and engulf the forces that impact our hearts toward a higher grace and purpose. Indeed, it should encompass and overwhelm everything that is below the heavens, as well as the distance of the universes around us to complete the Divine matrix of Jesus' total Kingdom.

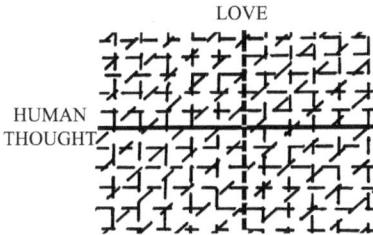

This comprehensive supremacy is the fabric of life that will always circumscribe human thought and action so that Love can become the entire capacity of our being as our prayers weave us into a blanket of Divinity. Our Lady wants us to fully understand that our thoughts can either be completely separate from Heaven, or a unique portion of its Eternal destiny. Despite what mortal beings might believe, Jesus' Spirit always supercedes, surrounds, and transcends all of our cerebral notions, even to the point of destroying those that blatantly stand in His path. A person cannot love God's people by simply *thinking* they do. Likewise, neither can someone *think* that their soul is united in the Holy Trinity without actually effecting it to the depths of their being. The essence of a life of perfect piety is accepting mortality without yielding to its carnal temptations. After every errant thought has been conquered by our personal contrition, the Holy Spirit is all that should remain of our consciousness. The Blessed Mother gave me a pictorial example of how our feeble minds tend to interact. Suppose two individuals have considerably different visions, but are living complementary to each other. A given impulse is reflected by a measured reaction so they can communicate with each other with civility, although they may be forced to invoke considerable reservation to avoid any conflict.

We might imagine how our individual aspects of intellectual disposition are even more widely variant on a societal and global scale. It is quite rare that someone can avoid disagreement and the resulting conflict while holding much different opinions from the circle of their peers. And, as these people often see, terrible clashes, violence, and oppression undoubtedly ensue, with the strong and stubborn almost always overcoming the more peaceful and weak. All of this is the legacy of what we think and is distinctly separate from our oneness as a singular people under God. It has been such a longstanding globular trait that many believe it to be the natural condition of our cultural diversity. Notwithstanding this hopeless position, Our Lady wishes us to realize that Love is the only alternative that is powerful enough to sustain the weight of a civilization which has so egregiously misconstrued the concept of truth. We must all reorient our vision and redefine our lives so that it will be possible for the entire body of humankind to meet on a level playing field and the potential for the happiness of every heart can finally be sustained. To that end, we must encounter others through the perfect symmetry of Christian good will, absent of our whims, biases, pride, and discriminations. This must not simply be a struggle to avoid disagreeing with the rest of the world. We must live for each other, instead of seeking to triumph over everything that someone else holds as dear. It is imperative that we hone our ragged edges so as to forthrightly greet our brothers to the mutual benefit of the entire world.

    Our Lady wants us to be united at every point along the surface of life, manifesting the oneness of God's Kingdom on Earth. Until people stop seeing one another through the impulses of the brain, we will continue to gain our sense of spirituality only when a heart-rendering or sacrificial event occurs. It might be the birth of a child, the death of a loved one, or the horrors of the world at war. During these defining moments, the inner-soul is touched and propelled upward, either seeking solace from the skies or searching for the words to describe their new joy. Many people do not even know they have a heart or the responsibility to respond until such a time comes upon them. By all means, this is why these instances arrive. God fluently enters the material world at every grace-filled opportunity that He chooses to employ. The Holy Spirit carefully carves-out the face of our nations amongst the Saints, preparing them like a mighty sculptor for their places alongside the bygone ages in the statuary halls of Eternity. Love is the insoluble consistency of the children of God, totally present in the solace of life, our sacrifices for each other, and our suffering in His Name. It is universally all dimensions we can possibly perceive, any direction we could possibly travel, and every tense that can withstand the test of immortal time. There is precious little justification for a human interpretation of God. It would be like trying to explain infinity in exemplary seconds or miles. We could multiply any measurement of distance from now until the cows come home and be no closer to unraveling the secrets of His Mind. Suffice to say that we are the lifeblood of His Love on the Earth. And, we manifest this perfection by opening our hearts in prayer. Our Lady said, **"My sons, I am with you because I love you! Thank you for your prayers of the Rosary today. They give humankind reason to be happy! Your Mother would like for the world to remember to pray for the unborn. A prayer every day in union with My Spouse, Saint Joseph, who is the guardian of the unborn, will preserve and continue their lives! Saint Joseph is the Patron of the giving of life who intercedes against abortion. Jesus is glorified through the prayers of Saint Joseph and of yourself."**

Wednesday, July 31, 1991

Today, Our Lady came to my brother and me saying, **"My special ones, I love you! You are both blessed! Again, I have a special message for you. Thank you for continuing to accept them over and again. Do you see how they are new each time? You are very precious..."** We are continuing to encounter unbelievable opposition to our Blessed Mother's messages as more time passes by. I can fully understand how others might think that I am unworthy to be the recipient of such a miraculous grace. If I were God, I probably would not have chosen me, either. But, our Virgin Mother encouraged us this evening to proceed with assurance and confidence that Her words are, indeed, from Heaven. Our trust must remain strong and wholesome as we cope with the frightful apprehension of those who cannot seem to believe. We understand their suffering as we try to help them transcend the stressful difficulties that are causing the darkness that evolves from their fears. We must all be convinced that the fruits of the Holy Spirit will lead us toward peace and unity in the Sacred Heart of Our Lord. The Blessed Mother continued, **"Tonight, I would like to tell you about prayer from the heart. I will liken them to the guide and direction which gives the birds of the air their flight. First, I will tell you what gives them direction..."** If we were to encounter the forces of nature the way a bird must overcome them to fly, we would know the direction of the wind by simply seeing it with our eyes. Creatures of the air inherently know the patterns of their flight, although they may not actually see the ground that is situated below. Their concise memory of the currents passing over the surface of the Earth guides them to their destination. An eagle knows his location by perceiving the direction and speed of the wind, along with the temperature of the atmosphere. The following sketch is a simple picture of the world from very high in the air, indicating three mountainous peaks around which the wind is spontaneously swirling:

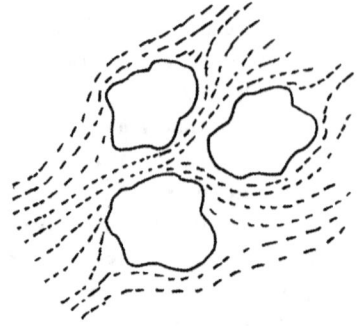

The eagle recognizes the constituency of the terrain below him by detecting how the air moves across its surface. He can also discern the vertical height of the mountains by the varying temperatures of the thermal levels around them. His entire journey is a function of his memory of these countless facets of the natural world. The Virgin Mary has equated this process with the miracle of human prayer. We are blessed with a similar *sense* that characterizes our vision of Love by speaking to Jesus from the heart. We *see* and know Him by the direction, expanse, and temperament of our lives of holiness and peace. It is through this extra-sensory transcendence that we finally come to know that Salvation is our Eternal Reward. It is true that we are capable of finding our immortal Home through this supernatural vision of faith. Divine Love is this perfect insight. As with the birds who soar among the clouds, this phenomenon is dependent upon our recognition of the signs that are put before us by God. If we consider His Gospel to be the indicator of our direction through life, we must also realize that He wrote it with that purpose in mind. We know that the scalars and vectors that direct us toward our everlasting destiny in Him are already present on Earth. His miracles that surround our everyday lives are to be ultimately interpreted as signs of our timeless security in Heaven.

We must serve this perfect Jesus with a new vitality because He is still present in the material world. He is our compass whom we have left laying abandoned and dust-covered on our mantles of life, while we stumble through the wildwood of spiritual indifference, helplessly wondering whether anyone will eventually come to our aid. Our Lord knows full-well that He is the pathway of everlasting Redemption because His creative ingenuity is the source of every new day. We know that tomorrow is only yesterday, once it has eventually gone. But, to be like Jesus, we must be convinced in advance of whatever the future may bring. If we already knew that, it would flash in our faces before it ever actually arrived. Love will always be new and can never be made extinct or obsolete. Our Savior is our every tomorrow, the same as today, and fully yesterday because the omnipresence of God cannot be measured by time. This is why He said **"It is finished"** from the Cross on Mount Calvary. He completed our Divinity throughout every moment of the history of our souls. His memory is so powerful that He has already seen the culmination of the world as though it has already happened before. Likewise, He realizes that He is standing at the final juncture of our passage into the perils of death, presiding over the destiny of mankind as our omnipotent King, the undefeated Champion of Creation-at-large. This vision was consummated by the same Sacrificial Lamb on the afternoon of Good Friday, thirty-three years after His Bethlehem birth. Everything that will continue to live became irrevocably immortalized by His Sacred Heart when He suffered His Passion and shed His Lifeblood to conquer our sins.

So, prayer from the heart is like the vision of the bird. Although not seen through an ophthalmic lens, it still enhances our understanding of the Truth and the nature of the God who is guiding our way. The terrain of human life emanates varying degrees of holiness, much like the thermal inclinations that circumnavigate the shivering mountains. Our Christian awareness of such distant elevations grows our understanding of where we are going through the piousness we espouse. When we perceive the intentions of our Almighty Father through the parables of the winds and the environmental temperatures, we indeed have the capacity to change humanity through the power of our prayers. The most prolific and advantageous currents of cultivation which beckon our attention are the peaks of inner-sorrow and outright human agony. Misfortune and adversity always lead us to the silence of the skies like the transparent sheets of the wilderness winds, into the arms of the Champion who truly showed us how to suffer with the nobility of a King. The character of Christ Jesus is the complete, living, and Eternal elegance of the Heaven He owns. It is only by His Mercy that every living soul is capable of recognizing the impending equinox of our Redemption and feel the urgency to migrate to the pleasant pastures of the celestial Kingdom of God. And, it is through the miraculous grace of the Queen of all Martyrs that this conclusive change of seasons is finally being made apparent amidst the ranks of Her children, posturing our wings for our decisive flight to the lofty perches in the heights of Paradise.

AUGUST 1991

Thursday, August 1, 1991

"My special ones, I am with you! Thank you for praying again! I always come when you pray! You are very beautiful when you are together as one. Tonight, I have come to teach you more about Love. It is important that you understand Love in all of its magnificent and timely simplicity. Jesus always hears your prayers, silent or spoken..."
After our Holy Mother's introduction, I began contemplating Her words from last night about the flow and direction of God's grace. I wondered how Love can still be recognized amidst all the confusion of the world. How is a bird capable of seeing through his heart, rather than with his eyes? Our Lady read my thoughts and responded with another example to highlight Her point. Love is like a tree growing on the bank of a river. The bird perceives the wind that blows through this young sapling which stretches toward the heavens in a very straight, tender, and flexible manner during its many stages of life. As it proceeds onward to maturity, it bends and twists to accommodate any environmental obstructions that might try to impede it from growing straight and true. This process perfectly reflects the symmetrical peace of God's Creation. Trees always grow outward and upward, despite any inhibiting effects that their physical surroundings may impose. They never stop searching for a view from the clouds.

The Virgin Mary asked me to call-to-mind a stately old sycamore that had taken root near a rocky crag with a cliff overhanging its pathway of growth. What will it do on the day it reaches the stone barrier overhead? Will it stop its progress toward maturity? Not this old soldier! It simply changes direction and, over the passage of time, slowly works its way into the clear, quietly co-existing with the cliff of rock as it takes a proud bow and slowly crawls by. It does not cease its ascension simply because it has seemingly encountered an obstacle too large to conquer. Neither does it alter, transform, or relocate its new mountainous friend. Instead, it continues to grow while maintaining its purpose in accordance with the nature of God. Likewise, Love flourishes with the same indomitable passion, notwithstanding the existence of those who stand in the way. The omnipotent Truth of the Father is as unstoppable as the forest of Earth in the face of those who refuse to accept it. His soothing Love always grows more beautifully and abundantly than the tarnished alternatives which may lie in its absence. The majestic and dignified Life of the Almighty Father flourishes in the cultivated spirit of humankind, taking us all to sanctity and holiness. Like the sprout that nestles near the running water, we need not make a judgement upon how to affect or change our environment. Indeed, Love will spontaneously altar the consciousness of those who choose to embrace it. The Wisdom of our Creator is the catalyst and standard by which the world must yield to move Love through the lives of humanity.

Our Lady asked me to ponder how the life-sustaining waters rise within the veins of pear haws as they prepare to blossom in the spring. Holiness is the sap of our souls that elevates Love upward through our lives so that we, too, can bear such bountiful fruit. At this ascension, everything good about our spiritual awareness improves. The towering white oak is another example of our paradisial movement toward the spires of sanctity. Its leaves turn to the heavens to be bathed in showers of grace like the hearts of humankind receive the blessings of God. **"As the leaves on the trees turn their bottoms to the sky to receive a gentle rain from above, I ask each of you to turn your hearts to the heavens to receive the showering of God's Love for you. By accepting His Love, you will be nourished and will flourish and grow in strength and beauty."** (Message of 06/23/91) The tree of Love is powerful and strong, yet flexible within its environment in order to fulfill its intended purpose on Earth. Similarly, our struggle for Salvation must grow without impediment, no matter how difficult the climb. Sin must never be allowed to sever us from the Life-giving roots of the Crucifixion of Christ. It is imperative that we clothe ourselves in the strength of Our Lord's Agony, like the bark on a tree, so as to provide ourselves an impenetrable garment that will preserve us from wanton destruction. Our Life-sustaining drink flows from this river of suffering. Human life has been planted on the fertile banks of both terror and pain, sending us on a roller-coaster through the deluge of elation and downward with the droughts of despair. This often reminds us that our love is oftentimes besieged by the malevolent forces of the world. Yet, we must still shine with plentiful leaves and grow in the Holy Spirit, no matter what the seasons of life may bring.

Our inner-impression of Heaven rests somewhere beyond the stars. The Ascension of our Lord and the Assumption of our Holy Mother help us to realize that human Redemption concludes high-above the workings of men. The Virgin Mary has stated, **"Upward is the movement of the Ascension and Assumption, intended to relate flight and freedom, not earthiness and groundedness."** Heavenly flight defies the forces of gravity. While our sins continue to confine us to the material world, our visions of faith that are extended toward the heavens are always met with new elevation and self-consecration, drawing us skyward and away from the treacherous paths where we walk everyday. Unfortunately for those who are in need, only a few good people ever participate in this journey toward peace. They believe that their problems are too great an encumbrance for them; ones they cannot see their way past. The Holy Virgin says, **"It has become a habit when men are sad or depressed, they hang their heads and look down. It makes sense, then, that to see the Love of My Son and to see hope and happiness would be to look upward toward the sky."**

Would it not be more beneficial and awe-inspiring to raise our faces in anticipation of the Love of Christ Jesus, who will bring eternal ecstasy to humankind upon His Triumphant Return on the clouds? Our Divine source of Light has always been from His Kingdom above. Therefore, we must turn our hearts heavenward to greet this Rising Dawn of tomorrow! We travel from side-to-side and downward with relative ease, but our spiritual elevation is only achieved by defying the gravity of sin. There can positively be no celestial flight without accepting the Cross of Our Savior. The Love that we invoke through our prayers sets us into the assumptive current of the empyreal stream of His soul-cleansing Blood. Our sustaining nourishment is the same Divinity that saturates the elegant elms of the New Holland meadows. The holy waters between the banks of the river of suffering flow past every barrier that lies in wait to impede its progress of life. Our Blessed Mother finished today by saying, **"Jesus is the Light, but sin is the darkness! Light comes from above, and the Earth is dark. Heaven is everywhere My Son is! I am the Queen of Heaven and I never leave Him. Search for Love in your life and you will find Heaven. There is only one God and one Trinity."**

Saturday, August 3, 1991

Our Lady came to us on two separate occasions today, at 2:30 p.m. and again at 9:05 p.m. In response to our prayer of the Holy Rosary, She interceded with the words, **"I have come so that we can again speak together. I have some very special words for you today. Your journey of life is filled with tyranny because it is governed by fear and hatred, rather than by Love. You will become bitter and indifferent if you allow others' hatred to bother you. Remember that human existence is not necessarily human life."** Obviously, I asked our Holy Mother to draw a clearer distinction to help me understand what She meant. To summarize Her description, existence is our temporary suspension in time. Life, however, is Love that is perpetually Infinite. We must never wish to be separated from the redeemed body of humankind. A Life in the likeness of Christ is our gift from the God of our fathers, where we affectionately embrace His Will as our own. We glorify the Only perfect Son of our Creator when we participate fully in the fruits of the Holy Spirit, from whose essence we have been miraculously remade. Only through this Immaculate Grace will the world ever be healed and converted. Every human soul is a tiny sapling who is planted by Christ upon the Earth. It is His omnipotent intention that everyone grow to perfection upon the banks of the sacrificial waters of Love. In this way, we learn to magnify the flawless potential which is inspirited within our soul, thus projecting our ultimate happiness throughout this broken world.

Our Holy Mother also spoke to me about the issue of *"chance."* It is a phenomenon that is cherished by those who gamble, while holding little regard for the true opportunities at hand. No one must live believing that there is only a *chance* that God might somehow be real. We must, instead, embrace the magnanimous Truth that He sits on His hierarchical Throne and watches our every false move. Our lives must not be based solely upon an odds-bearing chance for Salvation, but upon accepting the Sacrifice which Jesus has made that is guaranteed to exempt us from the eternal punishment we rightfully deserve. Therein, we will soon pass from this mortal existence into the timeless bliss of Eternity. We have already learned that God has perpetually touched humankind in every way and throughout all of time. Mankind, however, has yet to collectively respond-in-kind. For whatever the cause, we have never seemed to quite muster the faith, prayer, hope, or love that are needed to return full allegiance to the Almighty Creator who has conceived us into being. But, whenever we do, good fortune will finally come through Christ's generous bounty and power. We will ultimately realize the fatal error of risking a gamble on any false redeemer. Our faith will be strengthen in the face of disaster and sadness, knowing that the Messiah of God is carrying our souls through all of our mortal temptations. Love provides this complete and fulfilling vision through which we will all eventually see.

We will never fall prey to worldly desires when we see Christ's holiness clearly. We will no longer take chances or wager on other avenues that lead only to the deadest of ends. All of this is understood through our prayers and the imitation of Our Teacher and Lord. The choice is singularly our own because Heaven will not make it for us. The Almighty Father has already provided the means and the power for our eternal deliverance to His side. The Savior of the world has completely assured every person who has lived or will ever be born that His blessings and forgiveness have preserved our souls for posterity alongside the Saints. He is the Champion of all ages and the universal Conqueror of the world. Our Lady said, **"Please be happy!"** She blessed us and departed until later in the evening. When we began the Rosary at bedtime, She came again saying, **"Tonight, you have made Me very happy! You envision Life from within the heart, instead of the mind. You truly live your Life in Jesus, a Life also seen in the Holy Pontiff, in Father Jozo of Croatia, and other vessels to which I have referred. In your holiness, you must also be humble in service to your brothers and sisters. When you ask for blessings for others in your prayers, they are granted. Life is for the living and Love is for the giving. Many will follow your example. This is not only a blessing for you, but also a responsibility! Thank you for accepting Me."**

Sunday, August 4, 1991

This evening, the Immaculate Virgin of God offered another message to the world. She began, **"Your Mother is very happy today. My children are sharing in love, faith, prayer, and strength. I love each of you very much! Tonight, we will speak about the space in which one must travel toward faith..."** There is an imaginary barrier that seems to exist between God and man whose distance makes our faith necessary. On the other hand, one does not have to willfully assume that some things are true when they are openly and visibly apparent in Creation. Christianity is a gift that allows us to span the chasm between what we see and the universe beyond the grasp of our senses. The expanse between these two venues of perception is the realm of what we believe. The question whether God actually exists is not where we should be directing our attention because there is no doubt that He is tangibly real. We must, instead, focus our attention upon serving Him through our obedience to His Son and Heaven will open before us. Our Lady offered an analogy tonight by referring to the capital execution of two condemned people. Imagine both of them standing atop the gallows, each with a rope around his neck, and each, likewise, over a panel that will break-away beneath them at the pull of a lever. One trap-door rests on solid ground and can only barely be moved, while the other sits over the shaft of an abandoned dry-well. Neither of the men who is sentenced to die knows which doorway he is standing upon. When the hangman tells them that it is finally time for them to pay for their crimes, what is the first thought that comes to their minds? Each of them wonders whether it will be himself who will soon see the Face of his Maker. According to the Blessed Mother, this is symbolically how many people envision their faith. They are afraid of being fatally wrong.

We often experience the foreboding agony of not being on solid spiritual footing, yet we refuse to step beyond our frail understanding of God. We wish to have firm proof-in-hand before tendering our lives in faith to Christ Jesus, even though a noose of perdition is about to strangle the life-blood from the crux of our souls. The two men had concerned themselves with the prospect of this being their last day alive as the executioner triggered the flat-decks beneath them. It never once occurred to them that, when the latches had been tripped, the Almighty Father would grant them summary clemency and the ropes around their necks would gently slip away, allowing them both to fall safely onto the ground. Trust in the Mercy of Christ would tell them that such a gift is not beyond the graces given by God to those who believe His Love. Moreover, their faith would ignite their continued acceptance of His forgiveness of all sinners, buoying their assurance in Him for the Salvation of the rest of the world. That is why we must all remember that death does not hang over us like a stockade binding our shoulders. Human life is a living and breathing freedom of viable hope that gives us the ability to choose absolution and compassion over the false trepidation of rueful disdain.

Our Blessed Mother refocused Her discussion and told me that unborn children cannot make the decision for Life. Their determination must be made by the mothers who carry them. Each little baby in the womb hopes with the same vision as prophets that their mother will bear them to full birth. Eternal Life in Paradise can never be preserved by a fatal decision. Indeed, it is not the stature of the infant that is in immortal jeopardy, but the soul of the woman with child. To bear newborn life into the world is a decision from God, and is the only choice we can ever sustain. Anything less than that fact is simply our own miscalculation of the value of the soul who is given breath by what He ordains. Benign human Life is never fatal in Him. Unborn little children immediately rest in the hands of their Savior, no matter what their circumstances might be. He accepts them as they are because He has made them in His image. Their birth is His Will which He has eminently proclaimed because He wishes their souls to be part of Creation. Those who live beyond this faith haplessly search for a place to hide where they need not trust in anyone but themselves. They require proof every day that the brightness in the eastern skies is really the new morning sun. They search for quantifiable evidence that they have even raised from their beds, although they find themselves walking blindly down the street toward nowhere at all. At the last, these same empty souls demand absolute physical confirmation that the Holy Eucharist is the Body and Blood of their Savior before they will move one inch toward the Altar of Sacrifice and receive Him as their Sacred Communion. They often know the Truth in their hearts, but wish not to convert into witnesses for Christ or to lead others by their own good faith.

Our Virgin Mother continued this evening by explaining the timing and rhythm that we often feel as we travel through life. Over and again, we believe that we have discovered the pace at which God's Kingdom is unfolding. We walk peacefully in union with Him when, suddenly, we seem to be thrown completely off-stride. We find ourselves out-of-sync with the design of that anonymous Creator who is laying our Life before us one day at a time. Our Lady said that this phenomena of timing and rhythm is a false means of viewing the passing of days. In order for a rhythm to be present, there must be a starting point and a repetition of events which follow. We synthetically calculate the passing generations by using the calendar, the seasons, and the angles of the sun. The Almighty Father, on the other hand, is not constrained by such repeated compressions because He is the unified completeness of Creation, a sonotone of Love whom has yet to adjourn and has never once stopped being Divine. He answers to no measure of time and declines to yield to any season or the expressions of the clamoring clock. This same anatomy of Truth is applicable to our mere mortal perspective on Earth. Rhythm and repetition are both reciprocally non-issues in the Light of Heaven's perpetual day. We can see this more clearly when we try to remember when we might have been walking between the rails of a railroad track. The wooden ties always seemed to be just out-of-step. The beams looked perfectly equidistant, but we continued to stumble because we walked by an interior state-of-mind, a stride that is peculiar to only ourselves. We were helpless in our simple earnestness to march with uniform cadence upon the perpendicular placement of the individual ties.

We are equally as hapless in our attempts to keep rhythm with God. When we stumble in Life, we somehow feel that Christ has lost His commanding pace. Yet, the error really belongs to us for not maintaining our pulse with the beat of His Most Sacred Heart. If we are to live in unity with Heaven, we must perpetually choose to reside in Jesus and welcome His Spirit in us. We must let Our Savior lead us like anxious little pre-schoolers lingering under His feet. Then, He will prepare our stride to be in perfect harmony with the parades that will soon flow down the heavenly Streets of Gold like skipping perfectly over the railroad beams we see at night, never missing a step or having to stretch to succeed. We must follow Our Lord with the hearts of tiny children, who often leave their fumbling parents countless spikes behind. The innocents among us inherently know the intentions of Love. **"Please remember that the lack of rhythm or timing is an imaginary occurrence. You must observe the perpetual Love of My Son. If you search for rhythm, at least observe it as the daily acknowledgment of the beauty and appreciation of Life. Those who do not understand the beauty of Life, and those who destroy their own Life or that of another, will find it difficult to enter the Kingdom of Heaven. However, through Love and Mercy, it is possible. Life is that precious! Jesus is outraged by destroyed Life! His Creation is, indeed, His intention, and His Love is for Life. All should fear violation of His Commandment against destroying Life, except that allowed to be taken in the Scriptures for food. It is very serious!"**

Monday, August 5, 1991

We began to recite the Holy Rosary at 8:55 p.m. and Our Holy Mother came and said, **"Please be happy! Thank you for being patient so My Son's work can be done. Thank you for your trust and prayers, and for working on your Diary. Today, I would like to speak about the rarity of faith..."** Again, the Holy Virgin asked me to paraphrase Her message in a way that can best describe Her feelings. Each new day, the sun rises and arcs across the sky toward evening, setting the stage for the most beautiful show on Earth when the clouds don't get in our way. This daily occurrence has come to be expected by everyone who has the ability to see. However, it is not a forgone conclusion that it will ultimately recur at the break of dawn tomorrow. We can find a virginal beauty with the opening of every fresh morning when we remember this proposition of Truth. Everyone should strive to achieve this unique perception as we rise from our slumbering beds. Our anticipation of God's Love as He brings us the Life-sustaining sun offers a new appreciation and a true anticipation of the arrival of Eternal Life. Our Lady speaks perpetually of the immortal vision of Love, and there is an infinite number of ways that She has employed to described it. We have learned the many means through which the hidden part of Creation fosters and sustains what is revealed, along with what we oftentimes think we can see. If our focus were to be perfectly founded upon the transcending nature of God, we would love in the truest form of all Light. After that, each sunrise would be embraced with a new exhilaration, momentarily followed by prayers of thanksgiving for the beautiful colors when it quickly sets in the west. Indeed, our sleep would provide a refreshing peace which would fluently give-way to the great power of the strobing flashes of new hope from beyond the eastern horizon. We would rise as a new people of faith, seeing human existence as it was always intended to be. The opening of our yearning eyes would reconfirm the Promise of our Eternal Salvation at each fleeting moment in time.

Many of us have derived a definition of Love, but yet cannot see its effects. We have the power to invoke that vision upon the expressways of our hearts. This is the source of all hope for our everlasting Life to come. Remember that the bird in flight knows his destiny by relying upon the peerless nature of God carefully directing his course. We also recall the example of the honey bees, which do not realize that they are building a perfectly symmetrical world. These diminutive creatures always trust our Father in Heaven without question to lead them through Life by simply doing their work with His Divinity impressed on their soul. Therein lies the clear and perfected purview for all humankind, a simple reminder to prove that we cannot predict or control His intentions for ourselves or the rest of the Earth. We, too, are perched in His Sacred Hands and must allow Him to draw them to His breast at His own particular discretion. We will then be poised for perfection and will simultaneously be on our fledgling journey back to the Heart of Paradise. Our Almighty Savior is glorified through every new day we live, if we give our souls entirely to Him. He empowers us with the capacity to see the Heaven He continues to govern, hidden only by our unwillingness to learn. Every passing moment is filled with grace because Jesus' Love is real. All He asks is that we pray for the aptitude to perceive Him with conviction and to surrender our lives in wholehearted anticipation of His perfect Will. Our Blessed Mother concluded tonight, "You have such vision! You are special! You are Love, by Love, and for Love! You were called upon early in life to respond to Love. Thank you for accepting this charge. These days are filled with grace because you made this commitment long ago. Thank you for praying. I love you."

Wednesday, August 7, 1991

Tonight, we knelt to pray and Our Lady said, **"Welcome to My Heart, My special ones! Thank you for your prayers. Your Diary is progressing well. I am very happy with you. Please be wary of upcoming trials. Stand by your knowledge of the Truth! There are many false witnesses which Satan has put in place, but your work must continue. Your heartfelt prayers are lifted by the swiftest wings. It is important that you continue to pray from the heart. Your prayers have been fruitful and bring lasting peace. Tonight, I have come to speak about a special form of prayer, that of *aesthetics*..."** We enjoy a means of human communication that opens our hearts to Love, prayer, and hope. Aesthetics is a doctrine that affirms beauty as the basic principle from which all others are derived. It is God, Himself, who has defined with truthfulness that the authentic beauty of the world is the Divinity of His Son. It is from Him that all promise and benevolence flow. Through an inverse sense of reciprocity, our contemplative meditations partially comprise the doctrine which leads to Love, making aesthetics an intrinsic form of prayer. Our most beautiful petitions are always invoked from the depths of the human heart. Likewise, any divinely-inspired painting or blissful song is parented from those same unique renditions. If they are embraced by the Holy Spirit, they have always lived in the Kingdom of Heaven.

We are one heart and one Love through our constituency as the body of humankind. The way we share it, however, may differ between certain individuals. Therefore, we see various forms of piety and strengths of compassion as we wage the united struggle to live and feel the presence of Heaven through our many diverse originations. This speaks to the tremendous faith of the composers of legendary ballads and the artists of priceless works! Through their personal creations, we can perceive the beatific visions that spring forth from the sacred recesses of their hearts. This is the great bravura of poetry, art, and music! They each evoke the prayerful hope of every seer and listener. Does not everyone who gazes upon an artist's perception of a fabled mountain range appreciate its magnificence in every shade and brush-stroke before them? The human heart can contemplate possibilities far beyond the realm of mortal boundaries and acceptable revelations, hoping to conjure their beauty somewhere within themselves. When we see the aesthetic nature of Creation, we are reflecting upon the living monstrance where God has placed the greatest Beauty that humanity will ever know. It is within these parameters that Christ took to the flesh and was born of the Immaculate Virgin Mary. If we would only recognize the beauty of our Divine Redeemer's work, we would finally become one inside His Sacred Heart. This mystical explication is what makes aesthetics so perfectly unifying. Our inner-spirit knows when it sees Divinity reaching-out to draw it into the heavenly beatitude which grows from the artist, the songwriter, and the singer. We recognize both strength and beauty, while experiencing eternal reality before our very eyes. We comprehend the transcending omnipotence which unites our souls with the hopes of Paradise. Through all of this inter-procession, our prayers are a psalm of thanksgiving for the gift of Life and its sustaining power. These alms are as princely and timeless as the anonymous beings who humbly grow them before anyone else can discover that they are silently blooming there. It is through their dignity that our once-apprehensive personas expand with an ever-widened vision which leaves us standing before an uncharted new world where we see inwardly the Perfection that has created us anew.

At this point in my discussion with the Immaculate Mother of God, I thought of the so-called art and music which does not evoke visions of goodness and purity from those to whom they are exposed. I asked Her if immoral depictions magnify evil into our lives with such dimensioned renewal. She told me that evil can never be propagated with its original intensity once it has been unveiled. It is a damning proposition which begins its inevitable decay the moment it is conceived. Holy Love, however, is always the original image of the majestic heart of righteousness which celebrates Eternity with pristine vigor every time it is shared with others. The rekindling of special moments and happy memories enlarges and clarifies our capability of carrying goodness and Mercy all the days of our life. Indeed, once a song of Love has been written for Jesus, it can never be removed from Creation, nor is it ever diminished or lost. It thrives eternally because the Holy Spirit is a timeless work of iconography who touches our spiritual senses, helping us to recognize the limitless signature of the images of peace. This might begin as innocently as a warm and simple thought. But, seeing Salvation with the eyes of our heart helps us to gain a unique perspective of its limitless surplus of grace. With the aid of the Man on the Cross, we are all artists and composers of the Will of God during of our time here on Earth. Some of us have simply never placed our prayerful pen or our brush of contrition to our respective canvas or page. These collections of inner-Glory allow us to see the Sacrifice of Calvary with the clarity of kings and curators. Christ is pleased anytime His children magnify an avenue for His miraculous Soul to travel, seeking to enhance their immortal union with the Light who leads their way.

I have spoken previously in this Diary about the symmetrical characteristics of the tranquility of the Lord. Poetry, art, and music are forms of symmetry when they show our yearning desire to share His Love, transmit His holiness, and live in the humility of His Mother. Therefore, those who enjoy aesthetics have chosen a flower-strewn path to peace. I persisted today in asking Our Lady about some of the music of this modern day age, knowing within my heart that it often advocates violence, impurity, and disorder. She told me, **"The noise to which you refer is not a form of aesthetics. If you feel** peace and love when you hear it, you will know whether the Dove of peace will lead you to enjoy it. Remember that the Dove of peace comes to the holy places. Again, the reverberation of peace in the chambers of your heart will tell you whether your experience is good. This is why it is easy to see that evil cannot be repeated in aesthetics. The Dove of peace will immediately take flight to avoid evil influences."** Sinister misconceptions always agitate impressionable adolescents, taking them away from peace. Therefore, it is easy to recognize what is wrong with the many misguided youth. Their hearts need to be exposed to the perspective of God, rather than the stimulation of their pleasurable fleshly senses. They will then realize whether their spirit is at rest, or comfortably numbed into blind oblivion. In closing tonight, Our Lady asked us to look with our souls at the upcoming autumn season because we will see the aesthetic artistry of Jesus in the brilliant Midwestern colors. He is the greatest artist and composer as Creation sings of His nobility through its breathtaking beauty. Our witness to the physical presence of God's affection for humanity unites His children, not only to protect us, but to allow us see Heaven through its joy. We must pray through open hearts to acquire this same affinity for Him. We must become artists, songwriters, and singers in the way of Christ, the Anointed. When we move closer to His Sacred Heart, He will teach us through His profession as Creator of everything that is good that we are beautiful in the eyes of the Saints.

Thursday, August 8, 1991

We began the Rosary at 8:55 p.m. and the Immaculate Virgin Mary presented Herself by saying, **"Blessings upon you, dear son! Thank you and your brother for reading the Bible as I asked. Please remember that prayer is the solution to any problem. Tonight, I would like to tell you about a special scene which I would like you to imagine..."** She asked me to envision a particular point in time when the season is beginning to turn into winter. The late autumn ground is brown and barren and a brisk cool wind is blowing through the dark cloudy skies. To enhance this image, you notice that it is beginning to lightly snow. You are somehow able to focus your attention upon each little spiraling flake, unique in its own special way, falling gently onto the ground at your feet. As the icy crystals begin to cover your path, you begin to walk through them and they stick to your foot soles in large burdensome layers. The trees are turning white and the fluffy blankets begin to drift around their slumbering trunks. It is now much more difficult to proceed as your shoes sink further in the wind-blown piles of dust. After a little more time, it rises past your knees, so deep that you can barely lift your legs. Finally, you simply have to stop walking because the trek has brought you to near physical exhaustion. Can you somehow sense the lonely confinement that you now begin to feel?

To continue this symbolic description, you suddenly notice a trail ahead where the snow has been scooped away. You do not know who removed it, but someone is obviously in front of you clearing your path to walk. Thankfully, you take one step from your place from within the waist-deep bank to the freedom of the unobscured trail. The sky now clears and, without the cover of clouds, the air is much more crisp. You see the sunlight reflecting from the newly-fallen flakes like sparkling stars upon the glistening ground. You listen as the snow crunches under your feet with each new step you take. A sense of liberty and release comes upon you as you find that you can now move freely upon this icy passageway. The snow has become firmly compacted and as hard as a pavement beneath your feet. This memory is a metaphor of the compilation of days that life sets before all humankind. And, like those innumerable flakes that taunt us, we must also place them in their proper perspective. We can visualize them as support for carrying our hopes and dreams to the bright horizon ahead. Even though we know that there may be many more miles to go, each one of us is confident that we will reach our intended destination. Your heart can now sense who has cleared the way. It is Jesus Christ, who is also the Path upon which we stand! He brings the days together like the countless flakes of winter and lays them before us as support upon which we can tread back to Him. He is the Creator of time, the Determiner of its passage, and the Destiny, Himself. This is the eternal reciprocity of Love. We must know Our Lord as the Author of Life and the fulfillment of our Salvation, the beginning and the end, the Alpha and Omega. We believe that there could have been no Eternity without the occurrence of the first day He made. But, because of Heaven, the first break of dawn began without the element of time. It is unfortunate that so many people cannot comprehend this Divine exhilaration. They feel their passing days accumulate upon them like massive drifts collecting beneath the tumbling flakes. The weight of loneliness, despair, and isolation have locked them into their lives with no freedom of movement at all. They cannot seem to muster either the vision or the courage to take that single step which would lead them to the path of an unbounded grace.

Such people are also snow-blinded by fear and apprehension, leaving themselves as casualties of a spiritual apathy where they would rather wait for the winter to end and the snow to melt than to step-out in trust and reach for a new exemption in faith. To make this parable complete, they will place no trust in God before they finally see Him Face-to-face. It is the Spirit of the Living Christ who helps us to accept Him during our every wakening hour. Through our unfettered belief, God provides countless signs of holiness and Love which confirm that Jesus is with us and loves us beyond all measures. There never seems to be a way for those who reject the Holy Gospel to truly be happy. The cumbersome days enshroud them in darkness while they cower from the confidence that would take them to the overwhelming conversion which will eventually preserve their souls. Our Lady has come to strengthen our loyalty to God so that the lost may finally unleash their joy. True, pure, strong and patient faith is the answer to the peace and Redemption of all humankind. The Blessed Virgin Mary is with us to teach how this rending serenity is brought to those who accept Her Perfect Son. She said, **"Jesus goes to the lowly and stricken who suffer for Love. Their sacrifice is patience and understanding in the face of tragedy, loss, and infidelity. Those who are affluent will never keep it. When they lose it, they will see how strong are the meek who have accepted Jesus. Compare the days when you have been the strongest for Jesus to those when you were the weakest. You were, indeed, stronger when you suffered. This is because your heart is of Love. Please remember the power of Love! You are My special children and I bless you for praying."**

Friday, August 9, 1991

As we began to pray this evening, Our Lady said, **"Thank you, My son, for your prayers. Tonight, I have come to discuss the question that has been in your mind since last evening.** *How can each child of God have my feelings so that their conversion will be easier in knowing God is truly present?* **You bring this question because you wish to save every brother and sister that you can. That is why you are My special one. You are, indeed, a favored child of God!"** Our Holy Mother began this message by giving me a prophetic glimpse of what will explode from our hearts upon the Glorious Return of Her Son. It is somewhat the same feeling that I already experience in Her presence almost every day. She has told me that this same elation will forthrightly be there at the end of time, although in many ways more magnified than I could ever possibly imagine right now. I sincerely hope for everyone to embrace this Light so their conversion to Salvation can come very quickly. If we could all experience such passionate conviction, the faith of the entire world would become as immense as its highest mountaintop. We must ponder the spontaneous ignition of perpetual hope within our hearts while relating it to our expectation of complete ecstasy in Paradise. Many people do not know how to lift heartfelt prayers which are the sustaining fuel for this beatific fire. They have no hope because they do not understand the immense capacity of Jesus' Love that was resurrected by God to reside within them. They have simply never taken time to intimately know Him or invite Him to be their friend.

Imagine a house that is being built at a location where there are many travelers passing by. At an early point in the process, the wooden frame has been constructed and the roof is eventually nailed-down. What thought comes to the mind of those who glance over at this new construction site? Most likely, they would quickly recognize that the structure has not yet been finished. And, in their anticipation, they would also find that they are much too anxious to see the final product. They already know that there is progress being made toward that goal, but each individual who looks at it has a different opinion of how it should look in the end. Their conception of the completed work in their heart is complemented by the sight of the unfinished house as it stands at the close of another new day. If someone had told them that God has built a mansion for them on Earth and the carpenter is His Son, they might have higher hopes to know how their future dwelling might look. But, what if they are also told that this same Son was crucified before He was able to finish the job, and that only He knows how to complete it. It is obvious that they would yearn for Him to come back to cap the vision that has been so inflamed in their hearts. We presently live in such anticipation of exactly this same expanse. The feeling that Our Lady wishes me to describe finds its essence in our inner-expectations which will soon be unconditionally fulfilled. Through our new perception of this Love, our memory becomes so powerful that tomorrow becomes yesterday because Heaven already exists at it is.

Consider a second example of someone traveling on a very long road which is fairly easy to pass. After a quite lengthy and exhausting journey, they feel that they have truly accomplished something, although not really knowing where they have arrived. As they finally crest the last stubborn hill, they see that the pavement before them has come to an immediate end. The path ahead is one of only stones, sagebrush, and dust. It is much too rough a terrain for them to proceed any further. They do not know who built the boulevard that they have been traveling, nor do they understand why it has been so abruptly discontinued. Again, this parable indicates the pathway of Jesus. He built the road which no mortal has the power to carve into the world or Creation, itself. The traveler has two alternatives from which he can choose. He could return to his original starting point, all the while remembering that he left it at first because it showed no promise at all. Or, he could invoke the faithful assurance that Jesus will lay-flat the pathways before him, even though he may not know where it will eventually lead. What decision will the traveler finally make? His only hope for a new direction is to follow the pastorate of Christ. In his deep-seated yearning for perfect fulfillment, he might even set-out through the rocks and brambles before Our Savior returns, whereupon, as a reward for his faith, it would assuredly be made as smooth as the road on which he had previously been journeying with such relative ease. Faith will make our mortal future definable again! Some people accept Christianity early in life without ever enjoying a peaceful moment. But, as soon as they venture through this divinely gifted-passage, Christ Jesus will always lift them from their subjection to pain!

While the parable about the house is a view of man in relationship to God, it is still filled with our individual desires and opinions of the heart. Each passer-by might envision a different completion of the home toward the satisfaction of his own particular whims. But, Jesus has engineered a uniquely dignified design that fulfills every conceivable expectation that could possibly be brought to mind. Yes, the second parable also accurately reflects our mortal walk throughout life. It is a road that cannot lift us from it, a pathway often strewn with other footprints leading to the unforseen horizon. But, it always thins to just a pair. We must always walk in the footsteps of this mighty Giant among men. We must keep pace with the Champion who has gone before us if we ever expect to be elevated from the pedalfers that will only lead our souls to nowhere. It is Jesus Christ who gives hope and strength by paving the walk of life with the greatness of His compassion. He has completed our exile like a humongous bulldozer, boldly plowing through the newly-fallen avalanches of human incongruity. In the final analysis, the unfinished house can be consummated with the work of our own hands and the spark of our eagerness to serve. Those who hope with such indelible vision already recognize the Kingdom that Jesus has prepared for them. It is truly their own heart which they have stationed as a clement abode for the Master of all Creation. The righteous of the Earth inherently know Our Savior as the Builder who came to complete their everlasting Life in Him. The inevitability of the fulfillment of God's Will gives both peace and perpetual jubilation to any soul who is willing to accept the great generosity that His Son poured-out on Mount Calvary. The power supporting this faith is the fulgent Promise of this same Eternal Messiah. These are ideally the words from the Cross, "It is finished," through which our world has been saved and humankind has been delivered from death. Our faith unites us with the ecstatic completion of our final Redemption through Him.

Our Lady provided yet another parable this evening to help us understand the noble concept of faith. As we look at the chain of life from the most microscopic singular cells to the rodents, reptiles, primates, and finally, ourselves, we know that each level of life must find food in order to survive. Nourishment rarely volunteers to come within the grasp of any living creature, perhaps with the exception of those swimming under the surface of the water. The point is that a physical effort must be put-forth to search for what we need to eat. The differing forms of life use their hunting skills and body structures to attract and capture food. The Holy Mother asked me to consider mankind's methods of securing the dressings for our tables. Through our advanced intelligence, we have learned to set traps, discharge weapons, and employ vehicles to capture and prepare fine dishes from all parts of the world to augment the other recipes we concoct on our own. We expend a great amount of energy to perfect our epicurean skills and simmer the preparations we enjoy to the tunes of fancy fiddles, while seated on wicker seats at the finest dining tables. The question that Our Lady is posing is which form of life is the most helpless without the tools to assist them? Indeed, it is humankind, the most advanced of all! We would assuredly die from starvation without the utensils we have enlisted to help us.

To further ponder this revealing comparison, let us remember our faith and the unending life we hope to secure. The human person is not capable of constructing a tool that will capture Redemption in a bottle. We cannot set traps for catching unsuspecting prey to feed our spiritual selves in the same way that we do to keep our fleshly bodies going. Moreover, earthly perishables can cause an almost anorexic famine of the soul. Herein this paradox lies our total helplessness. We can satisfy our hunger to prolong our mortal lives, but we do not have the weapons or tools that would yield us the sweet fruits of the Paradise of Life everlasting. For this, our only help is in Jesus Christ, Himself. He is the only Bread who can keep our souls from dying. Indeed, He transforms our need for corporeal nutrition into the desire for Eternal Life in the Holy Eucharist of the Altar. Our yearnings are fulfilled by the miracle of our Father in Heaven through His priests who consecrate the Manna of Life for the sustenance of our emaciated souls here on the face of the Earth. He does not need to be stalked or hunted because He comes to us of His own Divine accord. He is not a beast in the wild, but rather the docile Lamb who waits for us to ask Him for our apportioned share in the savory Glory of His Celebratory Offering.

One might say at the last that the human heart is an immortal tool through which we receive the grace for our understanding, relief from our sorrows, and Salvation when we are finally called to come Home. But, unlike all other physical appliances-in-hand, we must eventually release our grip on mortality and give ourselves over in conversion to Christ. If we ask, *"How do I give my heart, and how do I let go of it?",* Our Lady holds the resplendent answer. She has come to offer a tangible tool which also has immortal benefits. It is the Most Holy Rosary! The contemplative Meditations allow us to free ourselves from the bondage and torture that the world so blatantly impresses upon our faltering hearts. We come into union with the Divinity of Our Savior when we surrender our souls in prayer through recounting the Sacred Mysteries of His miraculous Life, Death, Resurrection, Ascension into Heaven, and commissioning of the Holy Spirit. Even more than that, we receive the Life of Jesus in all His infinite power when we attend Holy Sacrifice of the Mass. God's endless Love is given to all humankind, totally and irrevocably, in the elements of the Most Blessed Sacrament. We must pray to worthily accept His Love by taking our Rosaries in-hand, along with the crosses we bear, in union with Our Immaculate Lady, the Mother of All Fidelity. She concluded this evening by saying, **"Man is obviously helpless without Jesus, despite having mastered the physical world. I bless you in the Name of the Holy Trinity! Thank you for your prayers. I will always protect you!"**

Saturday, August 10, 1991

We would be more holy if only we would allow ourselves to be. Many people impede their own progress by pretending that the scent that Christ has placed in their hearts is but an estranged fragrance from an unknowable source beyond our reach. Yet, we cannot turn away from Jesus once our inner-selves have experienced Him. The heart will simply not allow it. And, in reply to God's message of Jesus' Life, we cannot deny Him at this most important juncture in our time. Once we have been comforted in the solemnity of Our Savior's Sacred Heart, we will never again stray into the wiles of the sin that first fell us from above. If there is any unhappiness to pull our spirits down, it is because our disaffected intellect is trying to steal our hearts from their natural resting-place in the arms of the Messiah who calls us to His side. It is the same prospect as falling into water and getting completely wet. Once we are fully immersed, we cannot get any more soaked, neither can we be any dryer. We are summoned by Almighty God to become submerged in His grace, a people renewed in hope, Light, Life, and Love. All of our movements are buoyantly sustained by our new-found freedom in the bathing waters of God's forgiveness, which are provided us on our sacramental baptismal day.

Our Holy Mother described still another example tonight. While growing-up, we learn the alphabet and soon connect the letters to form the words we speak. They may be printed, cursively written, capitalized, small-cased, written on paper or a canopy, in the sand, or scrawled across the sky. We recognize an "A" whether it is inscribed in a note or on a large-scale chalkboard in a schoolhouse classroom. It is a unique observation to realize that we use different muscles when writing on a small piece of paper than we do when standing on our feet in front of an entire collection of students. And, sky-writing with an airplane requires no pen-in-hand at all! Yet, through employing all of these variations, an "A" is still an "A." Our Lady called my attention to the reason for this truth. It is our mind which has learned the symbols for the letters. We often magnify our thoughts, projecting them outwardly so that others will know what is on our mind. The same process is utilized in faith. We must take our small images of innocent Love and transform them into giant acts of God's magnificence by feeding them our holiness to help them grow. Just as our thoughts recognize the symbols for language, the human heart comprehends His Love, no matter whether it is in the tiny confines of the self or as large as the Supreme Pontiff speaking from his balcony on Christmas morning "To The City and To The World." An "A" is still an "A." Indeed, the Love in our hearts must grow to be as magnificent as every Vicar who has ever spoken on behalf of Heaven from the Chair of Saint Peter from his Basilica in Rome.

All of this stands in light of the fact that Our Lord is ultimately immeasurable by anyone. We should all learn to write with the greatest of clarity so that others can understand our message of Love, whether upon the pages in our private diaries or across the galaxies for the entire universe to see. The Virgin Mary has told us that Love must be dayborn and lighted, spoken to be heard, touched to be felt, and given to be received. We are all capable of imitating Jesus and, simultaneously and inherently, obligated to share His Holy Spirit with those we meet on the street. But, it seems that far too many people are still waiting to stumble upon a well-positioned chalkboard or for the skies to clear and break into a bright sunny day. Or perhaps, they are not seeking God's venues at all! Everyone must be told that the whole of Creation lies at their hands, the painter's canvas upon which to spread God's Divinity and share His beauty with others. Salvation must become the language of the world! Once we are wet, we will always be soaked. Once we have lived in faith, we will never again confine ourselves to anything less than that total spirit of freedom.

The Blessed Mother provided an especially pretty image as She concluded Her message tonight. Imagine being positioned in the sky, well above the Earth. It is nighttime as you look down to see the lights of the cities and the twinkles from the countryside farms below. You are even capable of detecting a single porch light in the only house within a radius of nearly twenty miles. And, as for the sweetness of this image, you now notice that the globe is like a reflection of the heavens upon the ground. You might consider it as a mirror of the celestial lights which God has placed overhead. Now, what is the difference between the luminous points on the ground and those which glow in the skies? Many of the ones in the heavens are planets that only reflect the sun. They are not really sources of light at all. However, each one on the ground is composed of a filament which emits its own source of luminance, not reflecting some other incandescence. Through this simple comparison, we often feel that we can switch Love on-and-off at our own whimsical desires in the same manner as we do the lights at the front door of our homes. We falsely believe ourselves to be the creators and sustainers of Love and the actual beginning of Life. We are in grave error to assume that we are the origin of humanity or the benefactor of what God has already done. We attain His grace in the same manner that the planets receive light. It is provided by our omnipotent Lord, who asks us to shine only through the radiance that His Spirit provides. We are not the inventors of Creation or Divinity at all, but are actually products of their Maker. We are the jewels that decorate the vaults of Paradise, and God's Hand is our eternal backdrop. We are the mirror in the corridor into which others may look to see their destiny in Christ. Our course is to return to perpetual joy and, in doing so, reflect the radiant beauty that is His alone to give. By living in that perfect consciousness, our souls are better polished and the world becomes more brilliant through the prayers we lift in His Name. To greet the horizon of Light and our Eternity in Heaven, our journey must originate from the heart. Every single petition is a step forward to greet that new paradisial day. If we tire from the journey, we should recite the Most Holy Rosary and our Mother, Immaculate Mary, will replenish our strength to go on.

Sunday, August 11, 1991

"My precious ones, thank you for continuing to pray. I have come to bless you with more messages that will convert the world. It is important that you remember to serve like the Saints. Your love is God's Love! Thank you for praying for the world. Today, I would like to describe the common thread..." We can detect a great fiber of Light that is weaving its way through Our Lady's messages which ties them all together. It is important toward our conversion for us to always wish to know Jesus personally and, therefore, graciously prepare for His imminent Return. We should perpetually expect our complete fulfillment based upon our prayers, hopes, and unwavering faith. Only the element of time separates us from the Second Coming of Jesus Christ. The clock, in itself, is a relative artifact because Eternal Life is forever timeless. Our past, present, and future are all one in the glorious revelations of God. Therefore, Our Lord has already returned in Glory, but not yet in our time. Our ardent anticipation continues to be necessitated because without it, there is assuredly no hope for our Eternal Life in Paradise. We cannot yet see past our mortality without believing in the Divine Kingdom to come. But, when we trust in Jesus' Promise, our vision transcends our every mortal limitation, revealing that the Messiah has already dawned. Our mansions have been finally completed because, in faith, we accept the reality of His Triune Deity and are fulfilled by that factual Truth.

The Holy Mother reminded me to contemplate this prospect very simply. Persistent and confident anticipation allows us to see the Salvation of the world in our own day. And, the common thread of the Blessed Virgin's messages is how helpless we are without Her Perfect Son on the Cross. We must accept and believe in His sorrowful Crucifixion in order for our own souls to become perfected in Love, thus securing our Redemption at the end of time. Our lives must emanate the Truth of Jesus so that the entire world can become refocused in accordance to His Divine Will. Christ is the Light of Heaven who sustains our passage from mortal life into the heights of everlasting joy. No man can honorably reject this tenable Wisdom. It is quite obvious that we are not the craftsmen of Life. Neither are we the universal source of all Love. We are, instead, the result of the perfect Eminence of God. And, ironically, through all of our nomadic discussion about our inability to truly contain Him, we still hold His very Spirit within the depths of our hearts. We are witnessing a world whose systems are founded solely upon temporal goods and carnal lust. We mistakenly believe that material and inanimate objects are somehow filled with

Life and happiness, with a soul of their own and the capacity to breathe. In reality, they are not signals of the slightest tenor of perpetuity at all, nor should they be the object of our faithful Christian affection.

If the playing of a piano were to represent the greater world, each note would somehow feel that it must stand independent of the other keys. It would truly not understand its relationship with the rest of the scale. When its pitch is sounded, it requires no other notes to be played for its solo to be heard. It is symbolically content to simply echo its own level of resonance. Collectively, the other little keys are unaware that they compose a melodious song when played in rhythm and unison with the rest of the keyboard. Since the notes are obliviously inanimate, they do not know that they are playing together. Sadly for the condition of the world, this is how many people view themselves in society at large. They believe that they are capable of producing harmony by leading the lives of empty recluses. They ignore the call of suffering humanity, never once conceiving that their individual score must be played in unison with the beatific chords that link their souls to the Mystical Body of Christ. We should never envision ourselves as being an insensate lever on a pianist's palette. Each of us is required to stand side-by-side with our fellow citizens and anticipate our union in loving service to God and humanity, alike. We should anticipate the joy of Jesus touching our hearts, allowing our full participation in glorifying God to the sound of His whistling Spirit. His is a song of predestined heights! Every note is needed to complete the symphony that He has composed for Creation to hear. Without the lowest "A" and the highest "C", the trebles and bases of immortal Life would be sorely remiss. The Mother of Jesus Christ has come into the world seeking to fine-tune the baby-grand hearts of anyone who will listen to Her. She already knows the auricular masterpieces that Her Son desires to play and understands the harmony that God is just waiting to hear. By obediently living Her messages and accepting Her Immaculate grace, we can each play our part in a flawless resonance that will unite us in Glory with the symphony of Heaven.

The Blessed Virgin Mary provided another metaphor this evening to assist in our understanding of Her motherly Wisdom. She asked me to ponder a set of window blinds. They are composed of many slats which function together for the purpose of shading the sun from pouring too brightly into a room. A solitary strip of material cannot block the sunlight unless it is accompanied by the others. The single slat could never stop the rays from creeping inside, nor is an entire venation complete if it is missing one spline. Light would stream through the window at the place where one of them is truant. This also reflects the necessity of unity in Love, much like the keys on a harpsichord. If we symbolize human coherence through the example of the oriel shade, we will ultimately understand that every heart is needed to protect humanity from remaining anything less than the total congruity that is fully intended by God.

We must become completely unified in order to be the *tout ensemble* which Our Father in Heaven has made us to be. Again, Our Lady has come for the sake of the errant and lost. She prays especially for the souls who are missing the mark by not coming to the balconies of Earth where Jesus can cheer for their souls. Her children find both purpose and unity in reciting the Holy Rosary, where every life gains new meaning under Her definitive Mantle. She gently pulls upon our heart-strings, asking us to move in unison like the slats of a window blind, while peacefully drawing us toward Her beauty with hearts as open as broad canyons. The elevation of humanity as one functioning body allows Jesus to shine through the darkness to reclaim His Creation on Earth. We must remain open for that Light to shine perfectly through! Every new day must foster our sanctified loyalties and distinguished intentions by seeing that our souls remain harmonious in Him. We must all become one if we are to maintain this peace and good will.

All of this must be done through prayer because it is the only means of feeding us the good fruits and weeding-out the bad. The order of the day must be the Son of God and His gift of Eternal Life. Our appreciation of human existence will then blossom with new conviction and raw power as we finally see the poor as being our most precious of brothers and sisters. To this end, we will be filled with joy when we finally accept that Heaven has dispatched its most Noble of Princes so that we can all live together in the riches of Heaven. The very essence of this accordance rests in our understanding that sacrificial compassion is the beginning of Love. We must remain whole as one people, although never assuming that we are being forcefully bound by the Almighty Father like a wire binding a bale of field straw. Heaven nurtures our freedom so that we may desire its greatest display to the rest of the world. This is never a forceful aggression or imprisonment of the soul like a razor strap straining to hold its contents at bay. It is, instead, the human strength of liberty when we are all collected between the prayerful hands of the Wonderful Counselor of the New Covenant Gospel. We must never stop in our pursuit of this ultimate singularity with the Man who has Died to save our lost souls.

The common thread of solidarity throughout the Virgin Mary's charitable work is human Love as Our Lord so graciously provides it. Therein lies the Peace for which She is the Queen. She is the Seamstress who binds us into oneness through the Holy Eucharist of Her Son. This is not a call for our mortal compaction or the loss of our individual liberties. It is simply a plea for each of us to place our collective will in the hands of our Almighty Father above. Much fear and anxiety is endured by those who wish to be separated like hermits from the rest of humanity. Notwithstanding that sad truth, we must all realize the Divine Nature of God as the only true freedom on Earth. We are all conspicuously unique creatures, but still children of the same Omnipotent Father who makes us whole, indeed, brothers and sisters at one

Table of Love. Our deliverance is without limit through this Eucharistic Christ. All of Creation, over, under, and around the globe, reaches into Eternity when we open our hearts and accept Jesus' complete Love in the Most Blessed Sacrament. We must believe this without the slightest hesitation because there is no other Salvation to behold, and no force can ever take Him from us. There is no other living gift to either offer or receive than the Infinite Redemption we find in His Body, Blood, Soul, and Divinity.

Tuesday, August 13, 1991
Tonight, we recited the Holy Rosary with a prayer group in Pana, Illinois. Upon our return home, we began our additional prayers to which Our Lady responded, **"I give you My special blessing. My Feast is intercessory for all! I pray that you will love My Son as much as He loves you. Many are set free from sin by your prayers for them to receive My Son in their hearts. Please remember also to pray for the unborn. My beautiful son, it is important that you remember that the misgivings in the world, the true suffering, the true defamation of Love and total sin, are not in your midst. Please direct your prayers where you know sin to be..."** Our Holy Mother showed me the following picture depicting how Her many prayer groups are delivering the world into greater grace.

This is what the world will see.

Each of these simple lines represents a prayer group, one connected to the next. Every cenacle conjoins their individual supplications with the Glory of God from different locations on the Earth. Through the passing of time and the perseverance of their petitions, they will eventually reveal the redeeming Cross to all humanity. I was very happy to know that we are playing such a simple, and yet very important part in the bringing of the world to know the Crucifixion of Christ.

Thursday, August 15, 1991   Feast of the Assumption of Mary
This afternoon, Timothy and I visited the Illinois State Museum. It was quite easy to find since we live so close to it. I had not been there since I was in grade school over twenty years ago. We had a great deal of fun looking at

the history that has made our State such a unique part of the American experience. Upon our return home, we prayed the Rosary and Our Lady greeted us by saying, **"Good afternoon, My special little children! I am pleased that you went to the building of memories. It is indeed a way to place things in perspective, especially your physical world. It is very apparent how temporary your body is by seeing the ages of life before you. It is an act of Love to strengthen your faith through the transcending ages. It is apparent that Love began very many ages ago, and yet still is new."** Tonight, Her lesson was about our "transcending faith." The Virgin Mother told me that it is an act of great Love to strengthen our Christian piety upon the passing of every new day. We acquire a better perspective of our own lives when we study the past generations of God's people on Earth. It becomes very apparent through this historical review that the Almighty Father is the orchestrator and guide of Creation from every vantage point we could possibly engage. But, our trust has been tried and tested many times before, leaving us to realize that the Love of Jesus becomes all the more obvious amidst our own personal misfortune. During these critical moments, it is necessary for us to call upon the fullness of our obedience to Him, rather than invoking a means to cast away the opportunity that Our Father has given us to delve more deeply into the Mercy of His salvific Son.

We must transcend the immediacy of our mortal days and apply their meaning to the full purpose of Heaven for our understanding of the coming new Eternity. Then, we will find the wholesome knowledge and confidence to believe that our Savior perpetually lives alongside our souls. What a lost Creation we would be if Jesus Christ had abandoned us upon His Ascension to the Right Hand of God. Imagine our desolation had He not dispatched His Holy Paraclete to be our Advocate on Earth! And, to multiply and accentuate the grace of His contemporary presence, He is now sending His Immaculate Mother by apparition, interior locution, and a host of other miraculous ways to seek our spiritual conversion. Sadly, however, many of us errantly and proudly attempt to downplay the significance of these gifts. Our Lady is known to be the Seat of His Wisdom. It would be wholly unwise for us to either state or imply that we do not need Her miraculous intercession. While many people still take this preposterous position, it is obvious that they are not accepting the fullness of the miracles for which they have long been praying. These same individuals might claim that such supernatural gifts can damage our faith. They should understand, instead, that God's omnipotent revelations on our right and to our left are the wings that can finally set the collective faith of humankind aflight.

The Church has already approved many shrines where the Mother of Our Lord has miraculously appeared. Although belief in Her apparitions and the manifestations of Her Divine grace is not mandated by the Holy See, the messages from God which we procure from them are. It is quite unfortunate that so many detractors discard their openness to Our Lady's holy intercession because they can damage their own confidence in the capacity of God to teach His children through any means He chooses to employ. Notwithstanding their outright objections, the Holy Spirit often comes through many accessory venues to complement His Will, whether they like it or not. He will never stop reaching for the hand of His children because of the heckling of those who reject Him. The souls who need to be touched-of-heart are the many who will let a small blockage of faith destroy their entire belief, much the same way that a plaque-filled artery will deny nourishment to the tissue it intends to feed. Moreover, in the absence of any justification or explanation for obvious works of the Holy Spirit, these same people still refuse to turn to Heaven for the discernment they so desperately need. They render themselves blind to God's helping-hand, just as they refuse to see it through Our Blessed Lady's intercession. Despite their adamant opposition, quite the reverse is true. Miracles, indeed, help many thousands to believe in our God who reigns Supreme in Paradise and the Holy Spirit who resides deep within the well-springs of our hearts.

If we tried to imagine a faith so strong that it would transcend time, space, and the logic of science, it would still be very difficult for us to grasp. Once a given day has passed and we know its final outcome, we would no longer need the faith it might require to live it over again. There are many obstacles to our acceptance of the unseen world that act like spiritual stumbling-blocks inside our hearts. Faith is always strongest when the cerebral mind is clear of logistical and analytical facts and figures. It is difficult for us to muster an abandonment to the Holy Spirit while our thoughts are replete with reasons, facts, habits, perceptions, opinions, and fears. Our Christian conviction must often fight to transcend the distracting barrage from our statistical intellect. It is as though our vision must forge the temporal rapids of a flowing river in order to be powerful enough to reach our soul. If shown symbolically through a picture, it would appear to be something like this:

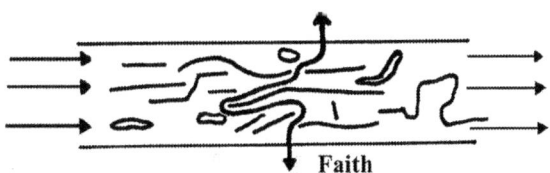

We can easily see that our belief in the Lord must somehow make its way through the chaotic swamp of our human disposition. Our loyalty to Christ Jesus must wind and curve to keep afloat because we helplessly allow these rogue obstructions to define its course and final destiny. But, what of those whose faith is sound and unable to be so inhibited? What of those who are so strong as not to be distracted by the detours that are forced upon us by the divergent impulses of the material world? Their faith suspends these composite snares because their belief in God is a sure-shot journey from inside their hearts to the foot of His Monarchical Throne.

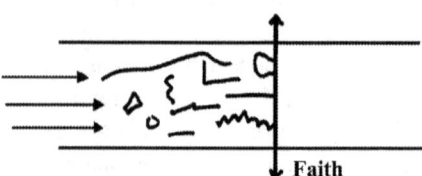

While this image is somewhat exaggerated, it still indicates that faith is constant, while all other thoughts must defer to its path. Its power is not shaped by the strength of our mind, but is much like a laser-beam annihilating a block in the road. Mental conjecture is of no eternal consequence because our judgements are fleeting and ineffective in calling God's grace to our souls. This is accomplished through the meditation of a heart that is acceptable in the sight of His Son. One cannot refrain from noticing the similarities in this picture to the growth of the tree of Love which Our Lady has described once before. Love eventually finds its way through the hoards of Judas Iscariot's that pretend to come to our aid. And, faith greets it through a myriad of mental fissures. There is, however, a major difference to denote. While our Christian allegiance can often be bribed into falling apart, the power of the Cross will never be stopped by anyone who dares to reproach it. We are called to reflect upon our every parable by its shadow in the Light of the Crucifixion. Jesus knew of His unstoppable power over a world that was about to take His Life on Good Friday. Through His trust in God the Father and His Love for humanity, He allowed nothing, not even His untimely death, to distract Him from achieving the goal of redeeming us all. Therefore, we have come to know Love in the flesh as the Son of God on the Earth. We also understand anew that faith is culminated in the teaching that He has provided from His first utterances in the manger until the final syllables He could muster in life, "It is finished!" We must, likewise, nurture both our obedience and love in the image of this great God-Man. He is the first Martyr for whom all others martyrs have eventually died.

Love can never be destroyed because it is the essence of God. However, since faith is the responsibility of mortal man, it is subject to hindrance and diminishment, perhaps even elimination and extinction. Prayer transcends these fatal probabilities, making a permanent path for our conviction to succeed without pause. Our heartfelt intentions to be truthful and holy remove everything that stands in our way, allowing the Spirit of God to grow in us both straight and true. Turning to Him in our every moment of need blocks the traffic on the intellectual expressway so that our faith may escort the parade of Salvation onto the world stage. Christ is the Grand Marshal of this mighty procession! He comes from the unseen Paradise of Glory into our physically knowable universe by way of our simple bow of humility to His invincible Love. We must live every moment like this same Jesus Christ, beginning in meekness and convening in His sacrificial Life. Those who are inherently humble can still dance on the parquet of delight! Throughout this entire convention, our Salvation in Him must become our grandest desire. Our wish to remain united with Heaven and to share the Divinity it brings is our most important of goals. This simple kindness manifests its strength through our acceptance of those who hunger to receive our affection. The true yearning of their hearts and the taste they savor is fulfilled by the Love we offer in Christ's Name.

Saturday, August 17, 1991
"My precious little ones, thank you for praying such powerful prayers! You have shown your happiness in My Son. This is how millions will feel through your Diary..." She continued by referring to Her upcoming work and how important it is for us to love one another for the good of the future unity of our nation and the entire world. There is no doubt that we still witness evil works all around the globe. Not all of us yet realize that each person is a part of the body of humanity, and therefore, inherently precious to God. We must afford this same consideration to every soul who is born in the lineage of Adam and Eve. But, as it is with many families, some members remain distant from the nuclear remnant through their own indifference, or perhaps, because of some type of interpersonal conflict or discriminatory misunderstanding. It is obvious that all of us wish to be loved with equal measure. Jesus and Mary know every heart on Earth, those suffering in Purgatory, and the fortunate billions who are already with them in Paradise. They are not as concerned with satisfying the desires that result from our material temptations as they are with the prayers for spiritual growth that rise from within our hearts. Our wish to be like Christ is echoed by the compassionate response of every Saint who has had the honor of seeing His Face. These petitions need not necessarily be spoken aloud to be heard in Heaven. Our Lord knows what is in our hearts and comprehends our silent prayers as well. Indeed, He sympathizes with us most intimately during our most quiet contemplations.

Let us ponder the most truly important questions. Do we allow ourselves to love in the image of Christ? Are we willing to make personal sacrifices for His suffering people? If so, then we have already acknowledged that we are the children of Light. Every soul who walks the Earth plays a particular part in the role of humankind because, when united, we compose the corporeal composite of Jesus' Body. Unfortunately, however, not all of us realize the awesome scope of this Divine ordination. The Holy Mother offered me a parable using a body of water as an example. If a single drop is taken from, or added to, an entire ocean, would we really notice the difference? Can we sense the true impact of subtracting one diminutive dreg from a seemingly infinite body that composes three-quarters of the surface of the world? While it may seem that we cannot, the open seas would never truly be the same. Their constitution is altered by even the most insignificant of amounts, whether added or detracted. Likewise, when you ponder the value of the number "1" and deduct even the smallest fraction from it, you no longer have a whole integer. You cannot maintain the complete arabic numeral without including that distinct ratio as being part of the entire mass. Accordingly, we will never realize the ultimate unity of the universal Church without each and every one of us participating in the bounty of our Savior's Love. The amount or the quantity may not matter to us because we will never know every soul who ever lived before we close our eyes in death. But, like the ocean itself, we will always be limited in our capacity to serve Christ Jesus whether we are missing a single soul or an immeasurable lot of His population. Without either, we would be less-than the wholeness that God has intended for His Mystical Body on Earth.

To demonstrate the importance of such a component measure in comparison to the rest, suppose a gallon pitcher is filled to the top with water and cannot hold a scintilla of a molecule more. To that amount, we add another drop and it instantly spills over the rim onto the level surface and saturates the area below. Does that singular apposition seem so insignificant now? It is obvious that when a sole droplet of rain falls into an ocean, it becomes one with that incalculable measure as the endless depths consume it. It evolves to be an irreducible part of the whole, like one soul among us is united with the rest of humankind. This reveals to us that Love cannot be determined by the segments of a line. Neither can it be quantified by seeing it with our eyes. The Holy Spirit is either allowed to reign inside the human heart, or He is ultimately rejected. The most important factor is for all of us to understand our need for unity amidst that heavenly Flame. If we surrender one soul to the scourge of indifference, our Almighty Father above will not be diminished, but the collective body of His children will be forever less-than whole. Our composition will be deficient in its potential to manifest what He has always wished us to be. This is why every lost sheep on Earth must be eventually found by Christ. They need to Love again so their joy and happiness can be restored in Him.

After paraphrasing our Holy Mother's words about this unity in Jesus, I asked Her how the Mystical Body of Christ could be anything less than whole. How could something which is lacking in any way be an intrinsic part of Christ?

She told me that my question should be deferred to the issue of "wholesome humanity." Humankind is never wholesome because of sin. Therefore, we need to garner holiness and perfection for our evolution into the Mystical Body which Christ will claim as His own when He returns to redeem the world. God wishes us to prepare for Heaven and we must say "yes" to everything that He plans for our souls to accomplish. He, alone, can make that claim! While collective humankind is the Mystical Body of Christ, it still suffers because of its lack of total commitment to everything His Father has done. The Mystical Body agonizes in its fleshly existence, yet remains whole by virtue of the miracle of the Crucifixion. Love is always one and can never be less-than Divine. However, we are yet to be wholesome in our service to Our Savior because we are allowing a portion of humanity to be painfully stricken by poverty and disease. Those of us with closed hearts impede the flow of Jesus' Love throughout the world because of our errors, greed, and omissions. Our inheritance of this debilitating subjection began when we fell from the Garden of Eden. Fortunately for us, Jesus' Death on the Cross is the reparation for our inequities. He suffered to save our souls from due condemnation brought by our voluntary abandonment of the perfection through which Our Creator is giving us Life.

Christ has reunited humankind through His Passion, Death, and Resurrection, and will deliver us both whole and wholesome back to God. For anyone who is seeking Salvation, there is no alternative than to open their heart to Jesus and accept the great Mercy He offers simply for the taking. Indeed, we must all embrace His Love to be a part of the total body of humankind. Those who have not done so represent the drops which are still missing from the keg. They are still water from the ocean of Life, but are separated of their own accord, not yet a part of the libation which the Hosts of Heaven will pour-out in celebration of the final Redemption of man. When we pray for those who will not love, they are drawn to the fullness of unity through the power of the Cross. It is as though we alter the flow of the land so that they run naturally into the awaiting Bay of God's compassionate Mercy. The body then becomes a more "wholesome whole." Our unity sustains the Love that serves as the healing balm in Jesus' hands, feet, and side. There is no longer sin in those who have been washed clean by His Blood. We become the medicament of Christ, who has reciprocally healed our own souls. Our imitation of His compassion emanates miraculous healing through the strength of our forgiveness of those who have trespassed against us. Jesus is the Mercy of God who has been dispensed through the Immaculate Virgin Mary to every age of mortal history, including the new millennium about to come.

The citizens of the Earth must begin to recognize the genius of God's almighty Plan and accept the curative grace that He is still bestowing today. The Light that the prodigal children must follow through the perils of mortal darkness is brilliantly burning in the heavens. The time has come for all of us to seek that Eternal Redemption! The God of our fathers formally recognizes us as the legitimate Body of His Son, Mystically and mortally present on the spherical face of the Earth. And, through His Divine forbearance, this Body has been restored by Jesus and remains whole for all the universe to see. Jesus died to secure an open avenue for every person who seeks Him to live in everlasting peace. Even the most despicable wretches in Creation are suspended high above damnation in the preserving Mercy of Christ. There is no doubt in His Mind that He will effect whatever action is required to assure us that we are loved by Him.

I became very concerned during my discussion with Our Lady about souls who will never say "yes" to conversion. I asked Her if these people will be given a final opportunity to accept the Crucifixion and spare themselves from the fiery cauldron of Hell. She told me that if they reject the Lamb of God during every opportunity they are accorded, especially at the last, they will be forever separated from His Heavenly Communion of Saints. They will deport themselves into perdition and away from the glorified presence of the perpetual Light of Salvation. In essence, they will be eternally damned and forever condemned. Our Lady said, **"To avoid that terrible end, everyone must accept My Son, Jesus! But, many do not yet understand. They do not know that damnation is real. They feel that it is an option. Only Life is an option! Those who accept Jesus have Life eternal."** It is truly obvious as we watch the world that Love is flagrantly avoided because of outright human obscenity. I asked whether I could discuss this pococurante attitude with Our Lady tonight. She obligingly spoke of the grave consequences that will befall anyone who invokes a lukewarm approach to the teachings of the Son of God. We must require ourselves to be firmly founded in the Truth of the Commandments, wholesome in our Christian service, and committed to evangelizing all peoples and nations so that they can come to the Cross on the Hill.

After the Holy Mother gave me this stern warning, I thought of those who have never heard of Jesus or felt His great Love through their peers. She recommitted Her affirmation that those who do not believe in Her Son are still within the bounds of His Mercy because they have never really been told who He is. It is our responsibility to evangelize His forgiveness to them before they succumb to death. The greatest danger lies in those who believe in Christ, and yet still reject His forgiveness. If they do not convert soon, they will be cast into the flames of Gehenna. We must make it clear that indifference is not the same as disbelief. When we know Jesus, we understand the truth which convokes the responsibility to teach and admonish our brothers and sisters about His impending Return. Our Lord saves us because He loves His Faith Church on Earth. The reciprocation belongs to ourselves because we must pray to accept Him. Christ Jesus will always extend His peaceful compassion because He knows that He is the only Way that we will ever be allowed into Heaven. Our Lady concluded this evening, **"People will not take time for Jesus! This is their willful denial of Him. Through Me, you see clearly how beautiful Jesus is. When the world sees Love, it will be safe! Thank you for your joy in Love. I bless you. Thank you loving. It will convert the world and make the body whole!"**

Sunday, August 18, 1991

One Person alone has conquered death! Jesus is the sinless Child who miraculously entered the world to do it, heralded as the Son of God by the same angels who surround us on Earth. The Almighty Father loves us so much that He allowed His Eternal Child to be so horribly crucified. No one other than this Divine Messiah pursued our Redemption to the hilltop of Mount Calvary. It was in that plundered orchard that the fruit of all forgiveness came into full-season, perfectly ripened to satisfy the hunger of a soul-famished humanity. Tonight, the Immaculate Virgin Mary wished to articulate clearly the dimensions of Her role in Salvation so that She would not be falsely misunderstood. She is *not* the Savior of the world, but is, rather, His Immaculate Mother. She did not die on the Cross to redeem humankind. But, it must be recognized that She also suffered for our sins, a sorrow known to no other woman in Creation. Her sacrificial participation was magnified infinitely because it was Her only beloved Son who was killed. She is the Spouse of the same Father who bore the Second Person of the Holy Trinity into the darkness of the mortal world. While innocent and perfect, the Son of God is the personification of the best that any man could ever have to offer, while becoming the Lamb that also makes humankind the best we can possibly be.

The Virgin Mary is the Sign who was perfectly conceived by God, Himself, prophesied by the great prophet Isaiah. And, in accordance with the Father's Divine Will, She was born without stain and, therefore, not subject to the fatal wage of sin. Her mortality was originally overcome at Her Immaculate Conception because Perfect Fruit was to grow from this undefiled Tree. She magnified God's Glory when She said *yes* to the Archangel Gabriel. Likewise, our own mortality is overcome when we proclaim our *yes* in acceptance of Jesus' Crucifixion. In that complementary commitment, our own sentence of death is no longer an issue because we shall not realize our passage from this life into the next. Our Lady's intercession is occurring for the benefit of every human soul. She teaches us how to love, while encouraging us to pray at Her side to sustain the holiness we need to succeed. As we raise one another higher in that piety, our Mother Immaculate lifts us in a greater, most profound of ways. She loves, protects, and guides us with an affinity so perfect that it transcends and overwhelms the combined maternity of all other women who are graced with the title of "mother." She is The Madonna of Humankind-Redeemed. Her concern for any misunderstanding is an issue that should be addressed with sincerity inside every ecumenical convocation.

Christians of all persuasions have been given the gift of Our Lady's Motherhood. Everyone must unite in Her presence under the Cross that Christians everywhere embrace as their saving benefactor. We must call upon Mary and invoke Her intercession with childlike innocence and urgency. The Blessed Trinity does not include the Mother of God, any more than it does the rest of us. However, the Holy Spirit lives completely in Her Heart and Being as He does in all people who accept Him in faith. Our Mother has addressed Her affiliation to Our Triune God in another section of this Diary. She never tells anyone that She is a member of the Deity. But, She holds the authority and commission from Him to proclaim Her role in His revelation. Without the Virgin Mary, the Holy Trinity would never have been revealed and our Redemption would not have been possible because mankind was irrevocably damned. She wishes not to be interpreted as being a cloud before the brilliance of the Love of Her Son. Indeed, She is the greatest Magnifier and Advocate that He has in the universe. This is a truth that no person of honest integrity can ever deny. It is obvious that She allows Our Lord's magnificent grace to shine through Her Divinity into every hemisphere on the globe. This is also what every one of the children of the Holy Spirit must do if we are to be worthy of His blessing.

I asked our Holy Mother about Maria Valtorta's *"Poem of the Man-God,"* regarding its seeming inconsistencies when compared to other literature that has been revealed by Her Son in various accepted private revelations. She said that it is important to remember that none of them, including this very Diary, can supplant or displace the Holy Scriptures. Such works, however, supplement the Bible with complementary truths and images. Hence, while the *"Poem of the Man-God"* is a manifestation of the Holy Spirit, it must be presented and understood with the realization that it is in accordance with the Sacred Word, but not its equal or substitute. The New Testament is the only perfect record of the Life of Our Savior, His Death, and His Resurrection from the Tomb. The unity of the Holy Spirit makes this true. There is only one Redeemer of the world, and His Name is Jesus Christ. The unity of the Blessed Trinity is Love in Three Divine Persons. This is the Godhead of which the Mystical Body of humankind is an integral part. The Apostolic Church is mankind upon whom the Holy Spirit has descended in tongues of fire. He reigns simultaneously in Heaven with the Almighty Father, on the Earth in the Holy Eucharist, and inside the human heart as the Paraclete of Peace. Since we are the Body of Christ in the world, we are equally and eminently as immortal. But, those souls who do not accept God's Anointed One as their Savior will assuredly never be raised from the grave.

Our Lady asked me to consider additional images about the communion of man. She referred to the tribes of people who presently live in a far-off African nation. She, then, referred to a native tribe who lived hundreds of years earlier in America. When She asked me to ponder this point, I found it rather difficult to perceive these same people as being our brothers and sisters, our family, or even our physical body. However, because of Jesus Christ they truly are, indeed! And, when we see them in Heaven for the first time, we will know and remember their souls! This is the majesty and miracle of the universality of Love in Christianity under God. When we see another person, we are seeing a creation of His perfection. If someone were to ask where is the Love that we see, what should we tell them when all they can see is a body of flesh? We must inform them that we see Paradise because we know the Love who created their frame. And, that same Divine Prodigy is the Father and the Patriarch of all seers. He is Supreme in Spirit and Truth and the owner of all souls at His feet. The next question is, "How do we effect this love?" Our Blessed Virgin has come to teach us the answer. We love when we pray for each other and when we hope for all souls to live in union with Christ. Yes, hope is the operative verbatim because we must embrace goodness to make this come true, a transformation that is manifested through a community of prayer. We become the transition itself, while preparing for our final reunion with the Holy Messiah to whom we implore. This is how the tribes of Africa are brought to the Light and lost souls are exhumed from indifference. The lives of grace that we lead today are provided in part through the prayers which were lifted by the generations who lived long ago.

This is the transcending power that our petitions wield throughout time and space. We seek help from the heavens for the coming new world to be inhabited by the children of hope who will one day reciprocally thank us. This, then, is the same strength that makes all men through all ages one people in God. All Love glorifies Jesus. Our Lady taught me a prayer to assist in my understanding of this magnificent union. *"I love you. That means that I know that you are love like me. I know that your potential is to be like Jesus. I know that He loves you as He loves me; and I wish to show you how I love you. When I close my eyes, I will meet you in my heart. I will comfort you in your pain, and hope for your life. I love you endlessly."* When we beseech God's help for others, or when we simply ponder our intentions for their personal well-being, we are reciting this charitable prayer. It is a vision of the heart which becomes more clear when we understand and comply with the intercession that our Virgin Mother is bringing. She gave Our Savior His life in the flesh so the world would be perfected again. His Love is that Life within us. Our Lady knew when the Angel Gabriel came to Her that Jesus would purify our souls. That is why She gave-up Her Son to the Sacrifice of the Cross on Good Friday. Between the peoples of every race and origin, this single Crucifixion is the prophecy of our unified future. When we live according to the teachings of the Blessed Virgin Mary, we are prophetically saying that we already know our own destiny, too. It is in Jesus, the Son of the Immaculate Queen, the Miracle who will bring us to Salvation someday. The earlier we recognize that reality in life, the sooner we will understand that there is no other goal worth pursuing.

To attain this lofty new beginning, we must unite ourselves with the Sacrifice that Jesus has suffered to save us from perdition. He died on a Cross, while loving us to the bottomless depths of His Most Sacred Heart. This is the majestic moment of history which has forever proved that there is no greater Love than to lay down one's life for their friends. Christ accepted death so that the Father Almighty could reveal that not even His own Son would be spared to take us back Home. The Cross is the prophecy of Heaven that has been fulfilled from God's ancient words to Moses, Isaiah, Abraham, Simeon, and all the others of old. And, this prophecy continues today through our prayers. We do this because the contemporary age has yet to understand the Wisdom that Our Savior has taught the world through His greatest of spiritual messengers. We travel a rough path because we create our own stumbling blocks. For whatever the reason, we refuse to anticipate Salvation. It is as though we pave a road upon whose path stands a tree. We would rather remove the tree and ignore the God who put it there than simply divert our aggression and accede to His Will. If we pray enough together, we will finally understand His power and He will reveal to us the same prophecy which was given to those who turned to Him in the centuries that have long-since passed away.

To the end of all, we are really searching for the place that marks the opening of a new world. That fresh start lives in the Love which has destroyed our death. Our ultimate goal is Eternal Life, which we will enjoy in the Light of Heaven. Jesus teaches that forgiveness of the transgression of others allows this righteousness to grow. He is the masterful teacher of absolution whom we must imitate in earnest. The following words would make a very effective public billboard: *Love takes away our sins and brings the everlasting peace of Eternal Salvation.* **"Your Mother has come in ways that are different from what many would expect from God. Your Diary is such a billboard with endless dimension. You are painting it now! You are changing the world! The impact of this Diary will touch those who have not been to My shrines or those who do not believe in them. You truly do not realize what we are doing. It is a miracle!"** Later this evening, I began the Holy Rosary and Our Lady came to speak with me further. She said, **"My dear son, I have come again to bless you during these last five decades of your day. I intend to communicate with you as long as God allows. Your prayers and patience are important. Please consider all who trust Me on faith alone! A beautiful season is coming. I will share it with you."** I asked Her about some recent public altercations that I had witnessed relating to the battle against abortion. She said, **"The fate of the unborn lies in the prayers of the faithful. Violation of public law and civil disobedience change very little! Without prayer, all of life is a frustration! I will speak to you tomorrow. Goodnight."**

Monday, August 19, 1991

Tonight, the Virgin Mary came again and told me that I could ask Her any specific questions that I may have in mind and that She would answer them according to God's Will for me to know. These revelations would help me understand my service to Him, and perhaps, remedy any unnecessary inquisitiveness which I might have in the future. My first questions regarded the events that are unfolding in Russia. After that, we conversed at length about what I am recording in my Diary. I did not abuse this grace by selfishly generating an inordinate amount of curiosity. When I had nothing more to ask, She instructed me to read the fifth chapter of Saint Matthew's Gospel in preparation for Her approaching messages about the Beatitudes. She, then, spoke specifically about the United States and the darkness of sin that is covering the western hemisphere. Our problems lie not only with the policies of our country, but revolve around our lack of willingness to exercise our Christian freedom. Our government is blessedly-founded on the values of religious and social equity. This nation is composed of a people who have the opportunity to choose the path that has been laid-out by Christ. But, it is blatantly apparent that we are not choosing the Way of His Revelation, but rather pursuing a daily agenda of greed and self-satisfaction. We own the liberty of worshiping Jesus Christ because it is not against our public laws. Most everyone in the U.S. inexcusably knows who He is, but through their own indifference, material distractions, and the decision to choose rampant ill-will, many sins still stand without expiation, sorrow, or the penitence of our citizens.

While the United States often seems concerned for the feeding and housing of its poor, it lacks the fundamental compliance with what God believes to be most true. The American government does not believe that human life is as valuable as social freedom. This inequity was not brought from the foundation of our country, but has been allowed to fester into our openly-wounded public policies by the faithless among us and their so-called radical reformations. Our Holy Mother told me that we should feel warm inside about assisting the poor and oppressed, especially in foreign lands during times of war and natural disaster. For example, our citizens voluntarily utilized their knowledge, talent, and materials to help the poverty-stricken flood victims of Bangladesh. Never before having seen any flying machines, those destitute souls believed that the helicopters of the United States Armed Forces were angels from Heaven that had come to their aid. Therefore, since God sees the good works of our country as often being of true compassion, charity, and love,

He expects us to be of such nobility at all times and every place within the realm of possibility. So, the vice lies not in our country, but in the hollow of our hearts.

We live in a technologically advanced world where we have demoted Christianity to a pale priority. This demoralization has produced rampant temptation and sinfulness. We are obsessed with physical stimulation, impure satisfaction, and blind materialism in the sale of goods and services. Furthermore, we are perpetuating and magnifying evil throughout the world by peddling our dreadful wares in other countries under the guise of capitalist prosperity. The United States is fulfilling its own self-created destruction. The western world believes that nations should be free to govern themselves. That is why our religious liberty is held in such great esteem. But, how can a society look upon foreign lands where so many others are starving and continue to pack our pantries with goods for ourselves? How can a Christian nation allow others to perish when God has provided an abundance for the entire world? Our Holy Mother asks through which principles of our Constitution, and from which canons of our religions, we justify the harsh lives of the rest of humanity. In order to answer this question, America needs to pray on its knees! One soul who will not turn to God is one person too many. Lack of prayer is a worldwide epidemic, not just a moral laxity in the continental United States. There is a universal famine of the hearts of all people in every land, save the graceful souls who serve in religious vocations and those in contemplative meditation. Due to the warring factions in every country, including our very own, we see a free people who are not capable of governing themselves without the guidance of God.

No government is ever good, but simply effective if it is in compliance with the service called for by our Almighty Father. Greed, racism, bigotry, and bias are the enemies of justice, along with the mantra of false-victimhood by anyone who preys unjustly upon the compassion of others. We will see a nation that is truly free and living in union with the grace of Heaven when we all pray, share, and strive to protect human life. This is intrinsically inclusive of the precious unborn little children who are yearning to become living citizens under a righteousness-practicing government. We must read the Bible instead of scanning the secular press. The Holy Words of Christ are our daily reading and our teaching to take us to Love. When we do this, we will no longer find the homeless, poor, afflicted, and destitutes on our streets as a testament to our lack of charity and good will. Most important, God has given the Virgin Mary to us as our Heavenly Mother. He did, indeed, shine His grace on America! She is our Patron Saint and Divine Intercessor. Through all of the darkness in our land, through the clouds of our sins, and above the lowered faces of our country's lost, She is the Morning Star over America.

This Morning Star concluded today by saying, **"I have asked you to do a great deal. I am happy that you tell others that Jesus is the Eucharist. As His Coming draws nearer, more of His children will be prepared. It will be a glorious day!"** She again reminded me that Her intercession is not meant to supplant my life. I am to live in the holy ways that I would have anyway, had She not ever begun speaking to me. I am not to allow Her presence to interfere with the good choices that I wish to make about my future. I was told to remember the millions who must live through faith alone, never receiving a single miraculous word from Her sacred lips. Their faith is, indeed, a remarkable profession! I must also call upon that same trust. **"I love you. Show Me your faith! God knows what you want. I am here to help the world into Heaven. You have many years of work to do. God may choose you to suffer to rescue the souls of others. I will always be with you and bring My Son. His Love is all that you need. Thank you for praying."**

Tuesday, August 20, 1991

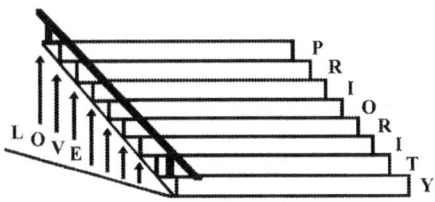

"My beautiful children, please remember to pray for peace in the world! It is important that you utilize the strength of your prayers to deliver the world from the destructible forces of Satan. With the many dimensions of evil, it is difficult to notice immediate changes in time. But, through your prayers, Satan is never as destructible as he intends. Thank you for recalling this knowledge. You are beautiful and innocent! Remember that, through holiness, your vantage point is superior to others. In many ways that men do not know, your prayers help change the world..." Prayer is active hope in the heart because we receive from Jesus what we ask at the invocation of His great Name. When we lift the intentions of others, it shows Him that we do love our brothers and sisters as we do ourselves. When we offer our supplications for someone else's well-being and happiness, God's answer is the fruit of our heartfelt hope and affection for them. Our Lord will respond with great facility and magnanimity because He, too, hears our petitions and extends His own Love to them as we speak. This makes the union of Heaven and Earth both wholesome and complete. Christ, indeed, wants us to be like Him.

The Blessed Virgin gave me the beginning illustration this evening to reveal the spiritual dynamics of our Christian faith. Our prayers are always directed upward toward the Father in Heaven. The Love of Jesus that we share with others is the founding element beneath our intentions which supports their lofty elevation. Imagine the difference between the foundations of small cottages when compared to the enormous pilings that support massive skyscrapers. The tiny country bungalows are built upon bases which extend only a few feet into the soil. Their footings do not need to be any deeper because the load they must bear is relatively small. But, the majestic business towers of the cities have moorings that extend hundreds of feet into the bedrock of the Earth. These foundations have been engineered to sustain the forces which nature will bring to bear upon them. The higher the building, the deeper the supports are implanted. This is why Our Lady asks us to pray from the depths of our hearts. When our prayers rise from the most intimate Love within us, they are capable of supporting our spiring intentions into the heights of God. Furthermore, when we compound and intensify our beatified hopes, our prayers build a city of stair-stepped structures that reach ever-higher above the fray of the world, untouchable by mortal nature and life's violent storms.

The upward arrows celebrate our progressive elevation, originating upon the foundation of Love. God gives a priority to each of our petitions based upon their intensity and merit, according to His Holy Will. He knows whether they complement the Sacred Scriptures and if they reflect an actual human need or just a personal whim. Our prayers must not contradict the Bible in order to be in union with Him. Interestingly, the answers that we seek descend upon the type of stairs we have built. God answers every prayer by extending His Love from above, downward toward His world below. While He has set the foundation in our hearts by sending Jesus into our midst, He also maintains a stairway which descends to meet the height of our greatest of intentions. He already knows the reality that we still yearn to see. Therefore, through His grace and the prayers of His children, He provides a means through which everyone of us can ascend to His Promised Land. Prayers from the heart lift all Creation to God's Almighty Kingdom beyond our mortal sight.

All of our wishes are supported and elevated by the Savior of the World. His Love heightens our lives with each passing day, helping us to realize the effectuation of our most righteous desires. He inspires us to pray for the Kingdom that He described so beautifully through the first of His Apostles. The Church stands at the foot of this elegant staircase like a grand turnstile-of-life. We pass through its gates and rise through the sanctifying steps of the seven Sacraments to holiness, saintliness, and everlasting Redemption. While God provides the magnificence of these Sacramental Graces, it is our prayers that bring our brothers and sisters by the multimillions to receive them. Therefore, the prayers of the faithful validate the blessings that God gives to those who call upon Him. Our trust in Him builds the pathway for those who will not pray on their own. These souls need our continued conviction and commitment to rise toward conversion and peace. By all means, we lovingly provide it because we wish for them to also ascend toward their highest hopes and dreams. As one body of humankind, our prayers become their eventual fulfillment. Their hope and ecstasy are founded upon our mutual love for Jesus.

The Virgin Mary gave me a very definitive understanding of Her service to humankind in referring to this staircase. She asks us to consider Her as the hand-railing that steadies our balance toward the spiritual skies. We reach for Her beauty and intercession in the same way that we would extend our hand for the security and strength that are provided by a hand-rail at the edge of a landing. She told me, however, that the weight of our prayers must be supported by the legacy and Life of the God-Man, Jesus. She promises to bless and guide us, but not to bear our own weight. The Lamb of God has already borne the infirmities of the world. Therefore, Her role in our Salvation is abundantly clear and focused upon Her wise-counsel, graceful intercession, and salutary guidance. It is simply another means by which the Holy Spirit has proclaimed to Creation that Jesus is the highway to Heaven. We are encouraged to hold the hand of Our Lady as the Holy Spirit lifts us in His many cultivating ways. Our Blessed Mother, therefore, is a miraculous provision who has been given from God that allows us to place our feet upon the stairway to Paradise in a much clearer Light. Jesus elevates our souls, while His Mother teaches us not to be afraid of the heights. What parent has not told their child to hold on to a bannister as they prepare to climb a stairway?

This is the exact context of the service of Our Lady. God blesses us at the very point where our feet make contact with the ground. Prayer from the heart lifts us swiftly to holiness, clearing our vision for our ascension up the immortal stairs. Jesus constructs them based upon what alms and good deeds we offer Him in return. He is the Builder who has laid the foundation of Eternal Life upon the wood of the Cross, alone. He proudly does all of these things because He is infinitely merciful toward those who accept His gifts. The many people who are in darkness need a landmark before directing their steps ahead. Anyone who humbly realizes that they might slip and fall will instinctively search for a hand-rail in the darkness before placing their next foot forward. Our Virgin Mother is the One whom they should seek because She will always reveal that the stairway to Heaven lies just a few strides away. Her intentions have always been to elevate our hearts and bring us to unity in Jesus. She has repeatedly instructed us to look to Him for Salvation and never once look back.

Thursday, August 22, 1991 - Feast of the Queenship of Mary

The Immaculate Conception has taught me a very clear perspective about material things, knowing that humankind is absorbed in the collection of worldly goods. Most recently, we discussed the millions of new automobiles that are now being built and sold in the United States, alone. There are tens of thousands of people who cannot afford food and shelter now, notwithstanding their inability to tender the gigantic sum required to purchase a sport utility vehicle or minivan. Our Holy Mother places very little value on such extravagant products. She said, **"If you removed the paint from every car in your city and drove them for a year, who would want any of them? They would all look the same! They are fine if used for God's work. However, they cause a great deal of damage to peace and prayer. Before automobiles, families remained at home and prayed. Now they are entertained to travel. Many people do not attend Holy Mass because they want to drive somewhere else."** I found it both interesting and evocative that the Virgin Mother would take time to specifically address the detrimental effect that automobiles are having on our journey to holiness on Earth.

In continuing Her lessons this evening, She referred to several of Her previous messages, beginning with the planets in the sky that reflect the light like Love. She asks us to turn our faces heavenward to receive the showering grace of God. She has also brought us to understand the heavenly growth of the tree of Love. And, most recently, we were given a vision of the staircase of prayer that lifts us to higher levels of holiness. Through all of these pious images, our means of elevation is Love. The human heart is the shaft through which the elevator rises. We are lifted skyward in thought, word, meditation, and deed as we offer our devotion to Christ and, laterally, to our brothers and sisters around us. When we charitably consider the needs of others in our daily prayers, the Almighty Father sees us looking at them the way He does from His Throne. In this way, our petitions elevate them toward His grace, oftentimes even without their knowledge. Our compassionate hopes offered to Our Savior effect the lateral movement of His Love throughout the rest of the world. The love we have for humanity initiates the prayers that we raise after having seen the intensity of their needs. So, when the movements of our heart become heavenly and upwardly mobile, the actions of our mind are made holy, spreading grace from east to west and north to south, through the burdened mortal lives of the brethren we are piously called to serve. Lateral holiness comes in the form of communication and interaction with them as we provide the essentials they lack. As the old saying goes, we treat others as we desire to be treated in return. We do all we are asked by Jesus to assist them to be comforted, healed, and fed. This is a spacial function of the Love within our hearts. These two movements, our heavenly ascension and our practical service, form the shape of all Love, the Cross of Christ in the Church.

This very simple image describes concisely how God's Kingdom is a function of both Heaven and Earth. Through our prayers and holiness, He bestows great power upon us to convert the world so that the beatitude of Paradise can be infused into the Mystical Body of humanity. I am, indeed, impressed by this simple wisdom. Our Lady blessed us in the Name of Her Son and departed for the day.

Saturday, August 24, 1991
Tonight, for the good of all humanity, we prayed the Rosary and Our Lady came to say, **"Today is a very special day! Thank you for receiving Me. I have many more special messages for you. Your prayers are very powerful. Jesus knows your love and faith. Your prayers manifest His Love. They are answered by My Son. Now, I would like to speak to you about the Beatitudes..."** Like the Ten Commandments, the Beatitudes are a very important part of Christian life because they maintain our grace-filled union with Jesus and our brothers and sisters. Our Lady's dissertation this evening focused upon the *Peacemakers*. What of these special souls? Christ tells us that they are called "the children of God." They are so blessed because they emanate the Light of His Love wherever mankind is at war, reflecting it to all others. Like a flaming torch, peace is passed from one generation to the next through the legacies of those who pray for God's intercession. As people have always inherently hungered for the elusive tranquility of God, each new generation has been required to learn to live in His peace, despite the many malevolent forces against them. To that end, there must always be peacemakers to transfer the flaming brazier to their successors. Our Heavenly Mother told us in a previous message that there is never a surplus of peace. There will always be the need to love and pray to prevent new societies from inhibiting and destroying the fabric which unites us as a single community in Christ.

It is quite obvious that Peacemakers lead lives of Love. They embrace a complete state of serenity and a "be-attitude" of placid good will. These humble souls exhibit the Spirit of Jesus mightily in their hearts to compensate for the marring impairment that the world so egregiously piles upon them.

Love can live within us if our own senses of bitterness, rejection, and hatred have not corroded the hinges upon the door that chastens our spirits. The Holy Paraclete provides the silent strength where the profound harmony of happiness flourishes beneath the pitted exterior of our being. This is the location of the Kingdom of God on Earth. The Almighty Father resides inside our souls in His Triune Oneness, caressing the cares of the world into the transformation of man. When we love as considerately as He asks, we validate our own lives as His new earthly offspring. Christ then asserts our very being, animating our existence with His Incarnate Love through our every thought and action. By virtue of our royal birthright in Him, we reciprocally claim Creation for the Omnipotent Paternal Love who calls us His children. That is how we finally grow in unity. We are the peacemaking lineage of God who is world Peace, Himself. But, what does this really mean? We must remember that peace is not necessarily something that we can generate on demand or make in an instant. It is a product of Love! Therefore, where there is an absence of Christ, there will always be the diminishment of men. We are nurtured and sustained when we willingly yield to the Holy Spirit who tries to make us whole.

Those who make the sacrifice of their human will repair the damage that has been done by living the truth in their hearts and allowing God to manifest His own Will on the Earth. This is quite self-evident because the Paraclete sets everything aright. We cannot manufacture peace by some type of synthesis, but we can make way for it to flourish by the removal of anything that stands in its way. Let us consider the many things that divide us one from another. The list begins with human thoughts and attitudes that are absent of Love. They play themselves out in every conceivable social context. Our Holy Mother has previously discussed such divisions, telling us that they are like the fences that divide properties or denote private boundary lines. These partitions are a sad monument and testament to our refusal to be one. It is further saddening for us not to realize that they are a true manifestation of our inner motivations to be separated from our brothers and sisters. We measure-off a section of the Earth, reserve it as an estate, and claim it as our own. No one is allowed access to our parcel of the world unless we grant them permission to enter. Every means is employed to guard our land from would-be trespassers against us. What a revealing example of the violation of common nature between men! This displays a disunity of principle, a greed of ownership, and a discriminatory set of beliefs. Our environment of division is truly symbolic of the artificial lines which we spiritually draw between ourselves and our fellow nations and races.

Through spiritual separatism, both indifference and hatred are allowed room to flourish. We have grown quite accustomed to hating each other, but we have never really known why. We seem to be unable to comprehend the reasons why previous generations have been so barbaric and disrespectfully uncivilized. We do know, however, that Peace has been the most wounded Victim of all during the many passing centuries. Every generation has equally destroyed it through war and counter-conflagration. Therefore, there has always been a need for the peacemakers, and they will always be among the blessed. Our Lady has now come beckoning us to thoughtful resignation through the lifting of our prayers, bringing with Her the ultimate answers that we seek. If we allow Her to reign over humanity like a Queen should be allowed to rule, every nation will see the dawning of a worldwide union that can never be destroyed. She instructs us in the pathways of God's righteousness, hoping to mend the divisions of our cultures and the painful memories of the history we have left behind. Prayer expunges all of these man-made impediments, along with obliterating the Aryan and ethnic hatreds. Those who call upon the assistance of Christ are the instruments of peace, making them the children of God. Their attitude is that of being like Saints. Our Holy Mother is absorbed with the necessity for our understanding the nobility in this cause. She asked me again to consider the list of forces that so painfully divide us.

legislation	*sports events*	*personal habits*
governments	*contests*	*physical attributes*
politics	*borders*	*race*
sects	*countries*	*cultures*
clubs	*fences*	*wealth*
religions	*prisons*	*civics*

Although these entries are certainly not exhaustive, they show many criteria through which we choose to go our own separate ways. And, while one might argue that such things as legislation and governments tend to prevent conflict, they do so by constructing a terminal co-existence between peoples who are no more closer to loving one another than when the political processes began. Therefore, they are not manifestations of Love, nor do they sustain a true peace. At best, they manifest the indifference which causes nations and peoples to look at each other begrudgingly, or perhaps not at all. Sacrificial Love is the only means of drawing all hearts into one human family. The only catalyst that has the power to make us one people is the Sacrifice of Jesus Christ. Our Blessed Mother told me that His Infinite Love is brought into the world both physically and spiritually in the Holy Eucharist. No material partition or intellectual division can separate human spirits who have come together as one to receive the Body and Blood of Jesus Christ at the Altars of the Catholic Church. No governmental legislation or political boundary can stop the almighty power that is brought by the Son of God. Every land which accepts Him will be remade, healed, united, blessed, and made whole.

All of the people of every continent are one Covenant and nation under God through the Lamb of the Cross. The Holy Eucharist is the only destination for those seeking a public policy whose ultimate goal is international peace. Any public administration whose leadership truly desires the unity of its citizens will accompany them to the Sacrifice of the Holy Mass. The Virgin Mary told me tonight that if humankind would accept these truths, the Earth would manifest the long sought-after united community. We would be a singular body of man which is bound by the heart and complete in the understanding that only through Christ Jesus does peace ever reign in the world. The Salvation of our collective souls rests at the juncture of Heaven and Earth. While we know this to be the Cross of Jesus, He asks us to kneel before it at the foot of the Altar of the Catholic Mass. It is upon that Altar that we submit our best gifts so that God can bless, consecrate, and make them holy. Through the power of prayer, we can achieve the peace for which every spiritually desolate nation still yearns. Prayer is the power of God that circumscribes our hearts with Light, making us the torch-bearing peacemakers that He calls us to be.

Sunday, August 25, 1991
It was late in the afternoon when the Holy Mother came to us today. As we prayed the Holy Rosary, She said, **"My beautiful ones, these days are filled with change. Tomorrow is at its rising moment as this day passes. The finality of yesterday rings hope for today. All will be made one through Jesus! My children, I have come to speak more about unity through Jesus..."** And again, for reasons only She knows, Our Lady asked me to paraphrase Her message in my own words. She promised to help me compose them according to Her prescription and intentions. Therefore, I will obediently continue in hope for the Eternal Salvation of every soul, especially those who will someday find these words before them. God wishes us to be joyful in Him as we live these days. Our Holy Mother told me that She could not promise to make me happy in this life, but She will instill the hope and vision in us to know that we should be content, nonetheless, in anticipation of the Eternal Kingdom that is already at hand. The Body and Blood of Christ unites all people, quilting us into a blanket of Love to keep our collective soul warm. Even amidst such division and indifference, we can still learn to be one bonded family. Let us call to mind this quilt with its many patterns and symbols spun into thread and woven into a singular mass. This covering is very special, unifying, and wholesome. It is truly representative of the unity to which Jesus is summoning His people. We are not asked to surrender our identity as individuals, but to relinquish the egoism that makes us hold-out on our own as though we are stranded alone somewhere on an uncharted desert island.

Often the question arises regarding the direction and destiny of people who refuse to unite with others in the Blessed Sacrament. The answer is very simple. Their reluctance ultimately leaves them in emptiness and despair. Jesus did not intend for us to proclaim this kind of freedom! He reminds us of our mutual dependence upon Him and the people we have been given to serve. He often reiterated that there is no true liberty that is separate from His messages and lessons to those whom He met on the street. He used parables to tell men who breathed the same air that they are co-dependent children of the same omnipotent Creator. Christ, Himself, revealed the same honorable submission to the Almighty Father who gives each of us the Breath of Life. Every individual is warmed by the same sun, cleansed by the same rains, and cooled by the same breezes. This makes us collectively equal in God's eyes. And, we are helplessly reliant upon each other to keep ourselves warm, clean, and refreshed by the same gentle winds that swirl around the globe.

Curious as I am, I asked our Blessed Mother how we are liable to each other by just breathing the same air. She answered that when the air becomes polluted, we must put our trust in others to help make it clean. Many industries are responsible for the toxic chemicals that are present in the rainfall. It is both destructive and deadly. The water in our streams is being poisoned, as well. We are all responsible to others to prevent this molestation of nature and to assist in reversing the destruction that we have already caused. Our Lady says that people fear to be humbly subordinate to Divine Wisdom because they feel that they will lose their freedom to achieve their envisioned potential. They seem to omit noticing that a quilt is many separate, but equal, parts that are united as one so as to perform a more noble function than an individual sliver of cloth. Each unique pattern does not disappear when it is sewn alongside the next. Therefore, no one needs to fear being washed into a faithless background that is lacking in identity as we are enjoining as one humankind. What about those who feel that they must live independent of others to achieve full happiness and Eternal Life? In actual fact, their souls are cold because they are not open to welcome the Body of Christ into the warmth of their hearts. The Holy Eucharist threads us together by weaving our spirits into the pretty fabric that God calls His own. It is the unifying Heavenly Bread that binds us soul-to-soul and collectively presents us to the Tabernacle of His Most Sacred Heart.

Our Holy Mother told me that there are many people who feel that they can actually hide from Jesus, whom they believe is far outside their lives. They look upon Him as a teacher whom they never liked, all the while banking that their name will never be called upon to give an answer. They do not believe that God will ever be an issue to them during life, or after it, as long as they maintain a material hold on the physical world. We must pray for these souls because they are soon to greet the shock of their lives. Yes, Jesus will come from outside of them when He brings His final judgement to the Earth. But,

He wishes to reside now in their hearts so that they will affectionately recognize Him when He arrives. The lesson is obvious. No one can hide from the Triumphant Savior, nor should they ever wish to try. God's Judgement of the Earth is an imminent Truth. Those who do not live this reality will ultimately reject the Almighty Father who brings it and the destiny He decides. Human love is the "inertia" which exhumes itself from the recesses of the heart and reaches forward and outward to convert these lost souls. Our Lord wishes to share His treasure! And, since compassion and mercy magnetically gravitate toward unity, it is imperative that we seek others, lest our own fruits die unattended and unnourished. It is impossible not to know Salvation once we have received the Holy Eucharist with a pure heart. After this moment, we pine to be woven more intimately into the singularly beatific oneness of Christ. Those who accept Him wish to love and to be loved in return. It is a mystical obedience where one no longer desires the choice to accomplish anything other than Love because Jesus supernaturally lives within us.

Those who never receive the Divine Eucharist can still love, but they will never completely bear the highest fruits of the Holy Spirit. Their tree will become stagnant unless their bounty comes to full harvest. We must understand that our love and livelihood must be remade new in the likeness of God each day through the Blessed Sacrament. Our Holy Mother gave me an example for comparison. Imagine three dimensions instead of two. One cannot get milk from a picture of a cow. But, it is still a cow to the eye. Envision a picture of Our Lord in comparison to the living, breathing Christ standing right before you. Without the Holy Eucharist, the vision of the heart is in a state of atrophy where it only recognizes Christ as an inanimate depiction which only resembles the image of true Love. The soul lives a description of Heaven instead of the actual Eternal Light. One who does not receive the Most Blessed Sacrament is like a picture of a flame on a candle. They cannot emit, transmit, or reflect the true and undiminished brilliance of the Divinity of God. And, when the lights go out they will not emanate a single ray which could illuminate the path of even the most acute of seers. Indeed, a planet is not of energy or light, nor is it the solar sphere. The Blessed Sacrament is the Sun who radiates Light from those who consume Him at Mass.

The Eucharistic Species provides the Life and Light to nourish our hearts and pours-forth the living essence to the hopeful visions that are inflamed by the Holy Spirit. The fruit is borne from within us. Without the Holy Eucharist, a flower is made-up of plastic, the household pet is a stuffed animal, and a meal is a photograph on a page. The Sacred Sacrament is the Life of Love given to keep our souls alive. As the fruits of the Earth feed the body, the Fruit of the Altar, the Most Blessed Sacrament, gives Life to the human spirit. This brings our mortal hearts into communion with the Salvation that Christ has bestowed upon the redeemed. I asked Our Holy Mother to tell me about those who do not desire such Salvation. She responded, **"Those who are condemned to Hell know where they are! They are given no comfort or pleasure. Conversely, in Heaven, you will be able to live any time of your Life over again if you wish. There are no limits to what God will grant to those whom His Son has won for Him. That, My precious children, is Love! Heaven will allow you any wish you desire. When you are in Heaven, no evil can tempt you. Satan cannot destroy you. There are no words that you would understand that can describe Heaven. All is made new by the gift and miracle of Eternal Life. I promise that you will like Heaven!"**

Monday, August 26, 1991

The Blessed Mother came tonight to speak further about the Beatitudes, referring specifically to the persecution of the righteous in the world. They are overwhelmingly blessed by Jesus. She said, **"Blessed are they who are persecuted for the sake of righteousness, for theirs is the Kingdom of Heaven."** They belong to Heaven because Heaven belongs to them. Presently, the persecution endured by the faithful is much the same as when Jesus walked the Earth in human flesh. The Prince of Peace struggled every day to convince those who heard Him that He is the Son of God. Likewise, most people to whom Our Lady has come have struggled against incredible odds to deliver Her messages faithfully. Another group is those who live by faith alone, while never knowing Our Lord first-hand or having openly witnessed the miraculous intercession of His Immaculate Mother. Yet, somehow, they still compose themselves in strength with the willingness to be maligned for their living faith in God. Yes, these are truly the very special ones!

Our Holy Mother began by explaining the characteristics of those who are violently derided for their faith, relating Her lesson to a tangible source in our lives. Probably much to the elation of the producers, the Blessed Mother asked us to watch the motion picture *"Driving Miss Daisy"* again. She likes this movie, while applauding its message of goodness. The humble chauffeur exemplifies patience, joy in Love, happiness, forgiveness, and the willingness to listen and learn. He is honest, sincere, and penitent, regretting his faults, aware of his mistakes, and charitable in the face of correction. Our Lady told us that this character is a grace for all the world to emulate. In recalling the synopsis of the film, the chauffeur is abused because of his innocence. But, through that same simplicity, he allowed others to find their personal faults on their own. His open heart mirrored the humility of Jesus. When he was falsely accused of stealing a can of salmon, he provided evidence of his innocence before his accuser could strike him in the face. His honesty spoke for itself through his blamelessness. This is the reflection that many people learn as they see their own wrong-doing. Jesus works through people in much the same way.

The Virgin Mary asked what we believed changed the heart of the elderly Jewish lady in the movie. It was her servant's timely honesty that allowed her to see through her own crass false accusations. This drove her to a complete understanding of his goodness and provided a very clear picture of her errant ways. Hence, she was able to love her servant because through his purity, Love came to her heart. His honesty was quite intense against the forces which tried to destroy him. His patience, however, offered no venue to such destruction. The little lady recognized that she, too, had love in her heart; but it was not allowed to shine-forth because of her insincerity and underlying prejudice. It was as though she came to envy his ingenuousness and virtuous service. She knew that these holy attributes were missing in her own conduct. I asked Our Lady if there are any other movies that project these same images of Love. She told me that there are others, but they are rendered unacceptable because they contain scenes that depict impurity and indecency. Why do some producers believe they have to include such immorality in their work? Why do they see it as a necessary evil? The film to which our Holy Mother is referring contains no such graphics, but simply displays the transcending nature of Christian charity that endures for many passing years.

After highlighting the characteristics of this actor, She told me why people such as these are persecuted. It is obvious that portraying such kindness and simplicity is not socially popular nowadays. Many believe that innocence in love and openness to Jesus exhibits an inherent immaturity, making His little souls appear to be naive. For these reasons, holy people are scoffed-at and ridiculed. It is very important to understand that those who are filled with the goodness of the Holy Spirit are neither naive nor immature. The gentleman in the motion picture represented a very intelligent person, although he had never learned to read. His genius was of a much greater power because it sprang from his affection for all of God's Creation. He was happy to be a Christian! Oftentimes, those who are joyful for no apparent reason are despised by other men. Mankind believes that to be in love with Christ does not seem to be a good enough reason to be satisfied. The basis for this dislike is founded in envy by those who do not yet accept Salvation. Some people feel quite strongly that only material wealth can bring happiness into their lives. But, standing by Our Lord in jubilation and love can be overwhelmingly beautiful and wholesome.

Those who love unconditionally are not intimidated by persecution from others who refuse. It is not necessarily because they enjoy suffering, but because they know that Jesus will always bless them. They are joyful standing with Him in the Truth, fulfilled by having chosen to serve, and willing to happily share in the same sufferings endured by the Savior whom they love so dearly. Our Lord asks all of us to stand beside Him because He knows that everyone on Earth has the strength to do so. It is graceful and praise-worthy to withstand persecution for loving Him, united with His suffering and knowledgeable of the purpose of His sorrowful Passion. Heaven observes with open eyes those who are persecuted for His sake. God's eyes beam upon those who love Him enough to be cast-out for His Glory. The souls who reflect this Light give great strength to all who walk in darkness. The Heavenly Father has promised that Heaven is for those who love and stand by Jesus, persevering in the battles of life, pending the final Triumph of the Immaculate Heart of His Virgin Mother. It is She who has told us so clearly that, when we love, we have already begun to live Eternal Life. I asked Her tonight to tell me more about the Holy Eucharist. She responded, **"Consider the consummation through the Blessed Sacrament. The renewal of Love is clearly found in the Eucharist! It is compounded and made whole in the Blessed Sacrament..."** I was asked to refer the following parable. Imagine preparing a meal using all of your utensils, appliances, time, and effort. Then, as you sit down to eat, you find that you have no sense of taste. Neither can you detect hot or cold. Moreover, you are incapable of smelling the food. These conditions make your much-awaited meal nearly impossible to distinguish from any other inanimate object. Without these senses, there is no Life to the substance that you have prepared which would make it an otherwise desirable dish. This is similar to what life would be without the Holy Eucharist.

Many people have an infant view of Love which makes them feel that they are separated from humankind because of this knowledge. They do not perceive that they are an active participant in the world about them. Life is a sport that they watch from a vantage point where they are seemingly unable to grasp the passion and exhilaration of the competition. Yes, they do possess love, but their souls yearn for the true heavenly feast which is not of this world. Their hearts wish to savor the nourishment of God from His Holy Table, firsthand. The Blessed Eucharist is the fruit from the feast table of the Father in Heaven. Through this Sacred Bread, human souls know Paradise and can see past Eternity. The Holy Spirit communes with the human soul in the Most Blessed Sacrament, providing a perfect vision of perfection. At the Eucharistic Table, anyone who experiences life as a spectator is instantly transformed into a living participant in the Salvation of humankind. God wishes every soul to actively share His Divinity as a player in the great drama of human Redemption. That is His holy gift to us, participation in Omnipotent Love, which is Life itself. Through this great miraculous interaction with Grace, flawless purity is projected throughout Creation, restoring our original beauty. We must live in open communion, yet retaining the simple perspective that this life is also His Divinity. No one should hold themselves distant from the gift of Communion because of human weakness or doctrinal error. The Holy Spirit in the Eucharist protects and blesses every soul who partakes of Him. We wear the armor that is needed to remain holy through the most temptuous of environments. The Bread of Life reveals the Love who is God, while helping us to avoid temptation. All of these graces are brought to us because Christ lives inside us. But, if our hearts are closed, the Blessed Sacrament will be concealed behind our own error and indifference. Only through our willingness to be like Him will the Sacraments clearly shine to make us radiant and new. Our Lady has come to spread this Good News, telling all the world that Jesus Christ in the Holy Eucharist is the only hope for those who are lost.

Wednesday, August 28, 1991
These sweet words given by the grace of God from the Virgin Mary make our lives worth living. **"My precious son, thank you for praying. Man is sad because of the failures of the world, but Love has never left you. Please continue to be patient and happy! Tonight, I would like to speak about those who hunger and thirst for righteousness...** *Blessed are they who hunger and thirst for righteousness, for they shall be satisfied."* Righteousness is garnered by fulfilling the standard of what is just and true. We already know the benchmark to be Love. Since its meaning has its basis in goodness, righteousness can never be vengeful if we wish to honor this fundamental principal. Jesus is always right. Therefore, righteousness is lovingness. God's definition of "right" is to be like His Son. There are many who still hunger and thirst for His beneficence. Our Savior tells us that those who desire His Love are seeking what is "right." And, He promises that everyone who searches will find what they are seeking. Why do we hunger for such Love? Because we suffer the bonds of a material world which shows no compassion at all. We know deeply that to be righteous is to be with and in the Holy Spirit. The battleground is in our hearts. While those who hunger and thirst for righteousness desire to live through an open heart, the world does not reciprocate because it is ensnared by atheism and indifference.

Human arrangements are products of the mortal mind. Our Lady tells us that the cerebral intellect is not capable of magnifying Love unless it is guided and nourished by the heart. We look for Divinity with our eyes, but our heart does the seeing because it proffers our vision of Heaven. We must ponder the fact that it is our soul that truly hungers. The basis for this need is the voice of God calling us to know Him more intensely. He beckons us to long for His Divine essence. How do we satisfy this spiritual appetite? What do we consume? What helps the heart grow to fruition? It is simply, LOVE! The grace of God's affection is the food for the spirit, manifested through our prayers. Our petitions cultivate our hearts for Jesus, much like we would prepare a delectable meal. Moreover, the wholesome food for the soul is the Holy Eucharist, while the nourishment for the heart is the fruit of our genuine invocations. We are incorporated and sustained as the One Body in Christ by the Most Blessed Sacrament. Prayer is the nourishment for every heart which concurrently satisfies the individual needs of each petitioner. We must pray and intentionally hunger and thirst for righteousness. We do this because of our intrinsic desire for Redemption, hope, and the goal of Paradise. Pope Paul VI told us that if we desire peace, we must work for justice. Unfortunately, he was misunderstood and misquoted by many. Some individuals interpreted his words to mean that vengeance and the self-will can be invoked in their search for equality and justification. Jesus did not say that the vengeful are blessed, rather it is those who hunger for the fruitful spectrum of gifts bestowed by the Holy Spirit who will be satisfied.

Ultimately, Love is the only justice. It is this call that Pope Paul addressed to Christ's Apostolic Church and to the world. He knew that we would all find peace in the Love of Jesus, if we dedicate ourselves to such a noble proposition. We can be confident of satisfaction if we know what to pine for. Why will we be so contented? Psalm 33 states that Jesus loves justice and right. This means that "Love loves Love and Love." Jesus, justice, and right are all simultaneous and processional Love. This prophetic Psalm should be the inter-reactionary goal of all nations. When we look across the cultural landscape, we see societies with millions who hunger and thirst, spiritually, physically, and intellectually. If political governments dare to claim any humanitarian beatitude, they must live the Spirit of the Psalms by struggling for the eradication of famine, disease, mortality, and the violation of human and civil rights. They must inherently yearn for the peace of Christ. Everyone who longs for a world that is free from corruption should begin by praying from the heart. Then, we will all be sanctified as one humanity under God. No person will perpetuate neglect or be neglected, himself. The world will then feast upon the newborn fruits that will spring-forth from the righteousness in human hearts.

Jesus is Justice, Himself, who seeks only what is right. He wishes us to have a great affection for one another, calling us into spiritual communion with both Himself and all mortal men who yearn, hunger, and thirst in body and in soul. Indeed, many who are receiving plenty to eat are starving from a lack of spiritual nourishment. There is a terrible famine of the human soul that is suffered by many who thrive on material wealth. Conversely, Our Lady told me this evening that many who live in the eastern world do not dwell upon their physical hunger, but realize more importantly the impending death of their souls because they do not know Jesus. We must teach them by giving them the words of Eternal Life, by living the example of Our Savior, and treating them with dignity. They are the suffering Christ on Earth! When we do these things, those who are far from God will hunger intensely for His intercession. They will then truly understand the internal desire for the unity wrought by the Most Blessed of the Sacraments. Simple prayer and the Body of Christ will feed their souls as Jesus becomes their nourishment and makes them whole. A hungry heart is many times more painful than a hungry flesh. When we meet the needs of our fellow men in our prayers, we will all find satisfaction. We will recognize that we are, indeed, like the Son of God if we care for them to such a loving degree.

This is not yet a perfect world, but in the beauty of Mary's teaching, it will soon come close to it, leaving peace as the final custodian of every society and nation. Now, more than ever, is the time for everyone to turn to the Lord God of the Cross. In Him, we find the justice for which we all must hunger. Those who seek such satisfaction and know not where to find it should recognize Christ as the source of their every fulfillment. His Love, Sacrifice, lessons, and legacy are all integral components of the justice which God seeks for His Creation. In all of these magnificent and collective graces, peace quietly resides. The world longs for the infinite Deity, and Jesus is our bountiful fulfillment. The true message of this beatitude is that the world needs your love, my love, and God's Love, triune, united, and one. This coherence is manifested through our collective prayers of the Holy Rosary and the Sacrifice of the Mass to which our Virgin Mother is calling all souls. Our Almighty Father has set before us a great task of transforming ourselves into the perfection that He seeks. It is through righteous holiness that such perfection is founded. Moreover, Love is the seed of this supernatural naissance. God is providing the world a new beginning which will lead us to a perfect ending in His arms. This great Alpha and Omega is the Christ-Child whom the Immaculate Virgin bore on Christmas day 2000 years ago, and still is alive. Glory in the highest and peace to all people of good will!

We hope and pray for the eternal day of blissfulness on Earth to come very soon! We petition even more intensely for Christ to return and bring us to perfection in an instant. Our Lady asks us to remember that we have a magnificent gift which those of Jesus' time did not yet have. Until His Crucifixion, they had not seen the pinnacle of God's affection for them because the ultimate convincing proof had yet to be manifested. It is now open and apparent for the entire world to know. We are a blessed generation of people. And, to add blessing upon innumerable blessing, Jesus has bestowed the gift of His Mother's miraculous intercession in a powerful and undeniable magnificence throughout the world and all of history. The great appearances of Lourdes, Fatima, Medjugorje, and the countless other sights where She has convoked Her supernatural grace proves that God loves us with a power beyond all human comprehension or intellectual capacity. These miracles would humble every egoist on Earth if they were not still incessantly fighting to keep their distance from Salvation. It is time for us to collectively deny our own will and humbly allow God's Love and Wisdom to enlighten the world. Unimaginable suffering is occurring because humanity will not bow in deference to His Plan for our Redemption.

I posed a very serious, but quite honest, question to Our Lady this evening. I wondered how the millions of Jewish people who suffered through the horrific persecution of the Nazi prison camps during World War II spiritually survived without accepting Jesus as their help and Salvation. Realizing the strength that Our Lord gives me to endure my simple altercations with the world, I was puzzled how my brothers and sisters of the Old Covenant could sustain such abominable suffering without inviting the Messiah to protect them in His Love. The Jewish Virgin Mother of Jesus responded by asking me to ponder the many millions now who are free and yet do not know Jesus. Additionally, I was asked to consider all those who do know Him, but still flagrantly reject Him. Indeed, how do their spirits bear the grief? Where do they find the strength to go on?

She continued by telling me that my question was para-prophetic because the answer is that they truly did not spiritually survive. Most of them who escaped with their lives were never the same after that. They were broken inside, stripped of their dignity, and no longer whole because they did not look for Christ in their suffering. Many perished in soul, which is the ultimate of mortal wounds. Happiness was lost and forgiveness was out of the question. War begins through a contorted sense of righteousness, one not founded upon Love. So-called justice must, then, be exacted to make right the imaginary sense of balance. Zealous vengeance in the name of goodness is errantly invoked upon those who are deemed to be responsible. Moreover, the victims fall from grace by virtue of a reciprocal revenge as they wage their own confrontation based upon the measure of their pain and suffering. If Christ were to have used this same logic, He would have been required to destroy us all centuries ago. Without the grace of His Divine Wisdom, there is no end to this cyclical process that destroys entire cultures and existing generations. War can never be equated with justice because it is not based upon righteousness, nor can it manifest true peace. The mountainous spiritual casualties far outnumber the amount of the corporeal deceased. No one has ever truly won a war, save the Champion of the Holy Cross.

What is most readily apparent in the beatitudes of righteousness is their fertile foundation in Love, the mooring pillar for them all. When Jesus gave humankind the Beatitudes, He was describing His own unique being. It is Divinity who first spoke of Himself. He consummated His essence upon His Crucifixion at Mount Calvary. God is the first to be Divine and His Only Son is the incarnate summit and pinnacle of that same perfection. The case is forever closed from argument after that. Together, they compose the Alpha and the Omega. The *finis* does not connote that Eternity is ever over. It means that it is perfected and final, unable to be transcended. We again recall the humble chauffeur in the motion picture "*Driving Miss Daisy.*" He had not yet learned to read when the elderly lady asked him to place some flowers near a tombstone bearing the name of "BAUER." When he asked her what that looked like, she responded with the question of why he wished to know. He humbly responded that, although he recognized the alphabet, he could not read a lick. She then gave him the letters "B" and "R", telling him that he had enough information to find it. So, the gentleman set-off walking, looking solely for the letters "B" and "R." In effect, he was given the Alpha and the Omega. He could then read well enough to find the proper gravestone.

Such is the way of our lives of faith. As soon as we recognize the beginning and the end as Jesus Christ, we will know our final destination. The old gentleman in the motion picture questioned himself after receiving the first and last letters by saying, "We ain't gonna worry about what come in the middle?" He later discovered that, by knowing the beginning and the end, the Alpha and the Omega, he would safely find his intentioned destiny. This is a parable that we should all observe during our journey through life into the hands of God. When we know His Son as both the Alpha and Omega, the content of our lives will become immaterial because we will give them to Him in trust. If we love the best that we know how, Our Savior will do the rest. He will make sure that we do not stumble or ever miss the mark. The Holy Mother concluded tonight by saying, **"You, children, are love, and I love you! You are My source of joy and I pray for all My children in Love! That task is a very easy one because you are all so beautiful!"**

Saturday, August 31, 1991

Tonight, we began the Holy Rosary and Our Lady returned through Her great maternal affinity for all Her children. She discussed with me Her perspective of our systems of justice. Our rulings and tenets are not based upon unconditional Love. Much of the behavior of those who are judged to have poor conduct is in retaliation against a system where sinners are fallibly-defining righteousness and hypocritically determining the punishment for those who slip and fall. This rebellion only gives the accused an increased reason to revolt. They lose hope that they will ever be respected or appreciated for anything again. In short, they inherently give up ever seeing the posture of human justice. They would like to be cared-for as they see so many others being loved. None of them would decline its fruits if they were ever allowed to taste them. The laws of our judicial system do not necessarily preserve, protect, or promote human decency and cohesion among our fellow citizens. How can our procedures and methods be administered with a hunger and thirst for righteousness if those who implement them do not have the Mercy of Christ as their living standard?

We cannot teach a justifiable moral right if we do not know Jesus in our hearts. The human spirit learns to recognize Him by seeing His Face in others. The Lamb of God is the greatest moral Teacher who loves every one of us infinitely. Worldly standards are not a prescription for Heaven. When I asked our Holy Mother how people in prisons and jails can come to know they are loved and can get to Heaven, She responded by saying, **"Do you feel that they would have a better chance remaining there?"** I have seen documentaries that expose the conditions in so many of our penal institutions. What kind of people would we become if placed in such hellish environments for any length of time? Can our hope survive there long enough to heal anyone among us? The Almighty Father is our freedom and Salvation for every incarcerated soul. Each of those men and women cry-out interiorly to be included in the dignified family of man. They are the very ones who will make our Mystical Body complete. They are a part of the wholeness which must be fully recovered and united. Every sinner must come to understand that they are made perfect and sinless through Jesus' Crucifixion on the Cross. There is no criminal element staining their soul once His Mercy wipes them clean. Christ destroyed all our sins on the mountaintop of Calvary, despite what any other mortal person may choose to decide. Recall Our Lord's words to the thief who asked Him to remember his soul when He comes into His Kingdom. ***"This day you shall be with Me in Paradise."***

As we ponder the poor souls in the dark cells of prisons and jails, we must remember that the first Saint ever to be canonized by Jesus Christ was the convicted criminal who was hanging at His side. God needs their souls in Heaven to complete the perfect unity He desires because He loves them. The greatest question of all is, "Do we?" We must pray that these weak ones will only convert, confess, and forgive themselves! Our most noble participation is to make this Redemption as easy for them as possible. We must surely know that, unless we call upon them to join the Communion of Saints, God may hold us responsible! If we do not love them with the freedom that Jesus teaches us so magnificently, who is actually imprisoned? Who is locked-away from sanctity and forgiveness? Jesus has destroyed every sin through His Sacrifice on the Cross. It is our simple responsibility to accept what He has done and concur with His judgement of reconciliation. When we pray, we ratify His beatific offering and accept His redeeming clemency. Our Lady has come to help us triumphantly claim our good fortune through Her Son. She brings the Holy Rosary with Her, hoping to teach us to pray with the power that we have been seeking for seemingly endless generations. Any grace can be obtained through the recitation of the Most Sacred Mysteries, and any soul can be converted to their Salvation in Our Lord, without a singular exception.

Our Holy Mother also says that material riches and carnal desires cause the same bondage of the human family as do prison cells and jails. Worldly goods are the playground where Satan lures lost souls to destroy them. He causes innocent children to become indifferent by immersing them in temporal experiences and physical stimulation. He seduces souls who have lapsed from their prayerful vision, calling them away from God with distractions of riches, stature, and the glamour of instant fame. He sets straying souls in motion amidst the mire of the world. This causes us to lose our sight and good sense toward eliminating the destitution of the poor. They are the salt of the Earth and the flavor which God most desires to bring to His table. Their humble prayers are powerful beyond all measures. Our Lady told me specifically that the haughty petitions of the rich and influential carry no stature in the eyes of God. They represent a blatant hypocrisy that is fomented by those who would rather see others hunger to their deaths than go without the most insignificant of luxuries. Yet, we must be convinced that the Almighty Father loves each of us equally, notwithstanding the fact that some may never come into His eternal embrace. We should pray with confidence and hope that the world will unite as one and envision the possibility that the last soul may have already entered Hell. This potential is brought to reality as we take our brothers and sisters to the Sacred Heart of Jesus Christ. Prayer gives us the vision to know what changes we need to effect to move the entire world toward Paradise. The Holy Mother is making great strides in bringing this idealistic dream of unity to fruition. We are all one in Her Love and, together, we must return to perfection in Her Eucharistic Son.

SEPTEMBER 1991

Sunday, September 1, 1991

"Blessed are the meek for they shall inherit the Earth..." It is with these prophetic words that Our Lady began Her intercession to us this evening. She has come to seek the conscience of everyone who will listen in faith to Her beautiful instructions. She tells us that the meek are very much in love with Jesus Christ, who is all Truth. Their faith feeds their great spiritual conscience and renders them docile and gentle in spirit and heart. The Virgin Mother told me that meekness does not necessarily imply weakness as some would prefer to prescribe it. The refinement to which Jesus is referring in the Sermon on the Mount is more of a mandate of Life through an open heart than an agenda of aggressiveness for conquering the world. By spiritual definition, the meek are always open to Love, but do not readily know how to project it. That is not to say that they do not return it. They simply refrain from doing so from the peaks of their rooftops. Those who are so amiable are not assertive in collecting possessions of the Earth or wielding power over its wares. Ironically, many people have staked-out boundaries, supposedly claiming that they own parts of God's Creation. The submissive among us are often prohibited from enjoying these same bounties since they do not militantly seek these things. They are unintentionally caught between those who have mastered the intellect and those who control other unsuspecting hearts. This serves only to magnify

their pleasure. They are neither slaves to their mind, nor do they manipulate the affections or emotions of others for their own personal gain. Quite simply, they allow God to be God!

The operative word here is "aggression." Those who are meek project Love by their words and example, while maintaining a lenient and long-suffering attitude toward life. They do not willfully force the path of the Holy Spirit by requiring Love to grow in a way it may not have otherwise determined. Imagine bending the tree of Love or placing a splint onto it to hinder its course. The meek shyly enjoy the spontaneous flourishing of Love that God provides. They rarely desire the gain of material possessions because their innocence and purity have already secured for them the natural bounty that others try to forcefully appropriate for themselves. The children of Light are very aware of what destroys their symmetry and peace. Worldly goods, by-products of the Earth, and human inventions are not really that important to them. Those who are holy and humbly submissive to the Will of the Father are not impressed with the industrial revolutions of centuries passed. They are the quiet faithful who pray from the heart, while rendering honest self-examination regarding the virtues of penance and sincerity. They hold a special place in Jesus' Sacred Heart because their lives are a placid example of the quietness and beauty of the Holy Spirit. But, we must all be forewarned that come Judgement Day, these meek giants of sanctity will stand as proud and strong as Christ, Himself, when He calls all of their oppressors to their knees before Him.

Our Lady told us in an earlier message to be sincere not pompous, confident and not afraid. If we sincerely move closer to that prayer and piety, we will walk steadily toward unrivaled perfection. It is the grace-filled word of faith and the love found in our hearts that is of the highest importance. Living in peaceful obedience brings us to a greater display of patience, penitence, and understanding of others. It gives unity a chance to flourish by allowing us to see the present path of Love, rather than wishing for a new and individualistic rendition which only momentarily pacifies our unquenchable ego. Jesus is the path and the destiny. His Will is the only way we can ever succeed in claiming our identity before the immortal ages.

Our Holy Mother directed Her lesson tonight toward the next Beatitude. **"Blessed are the poor in spirit, for theirs is the Kingdom of Heaven."** *Matthew 5:3-12* It is a beautiful beatitude which promises us the gift of Paradise.

Both suffering for righteousness and being poor in spirit guarantee our Salvation without reserve. Do we know how to be poor in spirit? If so, the everlasting Kingdom is ours. Our Lady told me that someone who is poor in spirit is faithful to the Holy Commandments, honors the God who has given them, and manifests all of the living fruits of Love. All of these qualities must be present in order for our hearts to be strong in trustworthy obedience to Jesus. In essence, we must be loving in the world as we live in it every day.

This is the key to being poor in spirit. The human soul must be hungry for Our Savior, Himself, in addition to all that He proclaims and does through His Holy Spirit on Earth. Our Lord's Love nourishes our Life-sustaining vision as we engage repulsion and endure rejection while struggling to emulate His Son into all the world. Through His heavenly food, we are assumed into the arms of the Almighty Father from where our strength originally came. We are drawn upward toward the Kingdom of Heaven which belongs to the meek. The human spirit is delivered to Paradise atop the Holy Spirit like the dove perched on the wing of the Eagle in flight whose destiny is the horizon of Light and an Eternity in Heaven. This freedom of flight is naturally found in Jesus Christ. How very blessed are the poor in spirit!

Our Lady asked me about the nature of the Sermon on the Mount. Why did Jesus offer it? I thought for a moment before She responded with Her explanation. Its main purpose is to bring the simplicity of Love to Earth in a form that is comprehendible to people who would otherwise be lost forever from its grace. The Sermon teaches us that Love is manifested through our service to others as God guides us from within our hearts. Therefore, it is of a Christian who reflects simple oneness with Jesus as their guide. All other sermons about the Life of Christ flow from the Sermon on the Mount. Anyone who listens to them falls into one or more of the categories which Jesus describes as being so profoundly blessed. When He spoke on the Mount, as He did in many other public fora, He was trying to show the simplicity that was emanating from His Sacred Heart. His monumental Sermon is a parable to the differing peoples whom He wishes to unite in Him. The underlying purpose in the Sermon is to betroth those who would realize that they had never discovered a Love so breathtaking before. Indeed, they had never heard it described by the Messiah, Himself. Ironically, many of those who listened found themselves indicted on each of the categorical counts which He clearly defined for the first time ever in the history of the world.

Our Lord's Word elevated the consciences of everyone in His age, as it does for ours today. His speech is the example of how the tree of suffering grows around the mortal cliffs instead of trying to move them aside. Yet, Jesus' Love is so powerful in its magnificent simplicity that the barriers eventually move themselves so as not to impede His almighty progress. No one wishes to be the adversary of our Master once they have seen Him clearly. This is how mountains can be moved as the elevated ranges relocate themselves. The summits surrender to their Creator, relinquishing their identity to become the stair-steps upon which mankind can ascend to Heaven. God has given every sinner the opportunity to be redeemed. Jesus asks us all to go with Him to the Right Hand of the Almighty Father. Heaven has been properly tendered to humanity for our final acceptance, but many of us do not even know it. That is why Our Lady has come to deliver the Good News of our only chance to avoid condemnation. The Fruit of Her womb is Redemption, Himself. Her "Fiat" through the Angel Gabriel granted God a pathway into the world that He already owned. She now tells us that our choice is made quite clear. Conversion is the key to everlasting Life and the Holy Gospel teaches us how to comply. Christ is the same yesterday, today, and forever. His Love perpetually "is."

Monday, September 2, 1991

Our Holy Mother came again to bless us in our prayers at ten o'clock tonight. **"Good evening, My children. I am with you to help you because I love you. Thank you for also helping Me. Place all of your concerns in the hands of My Jesus, and your heart in Mine. I will take you to sanctity, purity, and peace. Remember to be patient with yourself! You still have human temptations, but you are so very beautiful. Your prayers are indeed powerful. You have Life to live. Remember always that I know where your heart is because it never leaves Me and My Son, nor will We leave you. I have been with all of My children since their conception. I have just simply not spoken to all of them yet..."** Our Lady asked me to widen my vision to encompass all of the suffering, famine, disease, and conflict that is present in the world today. Imagine how so many people endure such grave tragedies without calling upon their God for help. There are multitudes that number in the billions who lack the faith to passionately realize that He exists. Suffering pays no deference to their vulnerable condition. Fortunately for them, neither does God. He always remembers the works of His Hands and has placed the memory of His compassion within every soul He has ever conceived. Since this awareness is so perfect, we cannot refuse to accept Him once we realize who He is. The vision that is now emanating from this primal imprint is drawn upon during our times of great tragedy and distress. While history is replete with such instances, prayer must be summoned from the heart whenever such pain abounds.

As we seek God's grace from deep within our being, we trust Jesus to remember us as we also ponder Him. Christ knows our hearts before we ever come to realize that He is with us. Knowledge of His power ignites in our souls and His protection flourishes when our thoughts are at a loss as to which way to turn. It is much like trying to break a wild stallion. The willful instinct must be reconditioned to accept that it cannot succeed in knowing obedience without the heart. Suffering always seems to be in vain if we do not embrace it as Jesus asks. Our sublime submission is the perpetual sound of His living presence on the Earth. If our hearts remain closed to our own eternal happiness, we are lost without this supernatural chord of Light. Those who will not accept the piety that Jesus teaches do not have a means to withstand the terrible torment that the world generates against them. Anyone who does not imitate Christ has no echo of Divinity to carry them through their pain. In essence, their tree of Love has yet to germinate because their seed is lying dormant and unfertilized on the lifeless rubble below. Indeed, our affections for Our Lord and one another will not survive if we surrender them in favor of our bitterness. Therefore, the evergreen of Love must be sown in the fertility of the heart because it will remember the Crucifixion when all else has been forgotten. Our pious state of consciousness feels perfectly at home there. This is why purity grows in our painful trials of agony. It is fed by the God who pulses His Love into our every faithful thought. His response to our pleading supplications moves the Light of Heaven throughout all Creation and simultaneously helps us to endure every difficult moment we could possibly encounter while residing anywhere He Wills us to be.

When we suffer, our imaginings reach for the soothing deliverance of our Almighty Father, as well as enlisting the aid of other men. Our mind begins to listen for the echo of deliverance which rings through the valleys of our soul. We call-out to Christ and He answers. But, if someone has never known or accepted the Lord, this immortal bell has never really been struck in their heart. Their intellect becomes a voiceless mute, not knowing how to call-out for help. Neither does it attempt to listen because it is completely unaware of the reverberations that the Holy Spirit dispatches for them to hear. They simply do not know that Christ is the sustaining power of the entire universe. Therefore, we search for the faintest hint of God's goodness throughout the world. And, where do we eventually find it? First, foremost, and finally, He resides omnipotently present in the Holy Eucharist, the beautiful cascading crescendo of this message from Our Lady tonight. The Bread of Life can be received daily in the Holy Roman Catholic Church. The Eucharist is "not" just the reverberation of Love. It is God's original essence every time it is offered to us from the hands of the priest at the Altar. So, in all the irony, perfection, and timelessness of Jesus, the Echo of His Love is still the original Proclamation from the Cross of Calvary, yesterday, today, and forever. The Blessed Sacrament is His original Body and Blood at the Crucifixion. It is not a facsimile or a replicated regeneration.

The Christian faithful receive the Body and Blood of Jesus Christ as He first lived, died, and rose from the grave, God's Love as it was in the beginning and shall be evermore. Jesus is the original Son and also His own culmination. Since we lead our lives in union with the Holy Eucharist, every new sunrise is the first day of the dawn of man in Paradise. Each succeeding morning is that same perpetual Eternity, the timelessness of God in our hands and souls. The Holy Eucharist, therefore, is the living Body of Christ that the human heart yearns to receive, initiating the original complete stroke of perfection which ultimately overcomes our every trial and tribulation. This is how the heart feeds stability into the mortal mind with prophetic dimensions. We must symbolically believe that each time our heart beats, it is the same pulse that God gave to us the day we were conceived in our mother's womb. The rhythm of its tempo is the echo of Our Father's Will as our lives proceed toward His Kingdom. The enlightenment that we feel within the chambers of our being is the ray of grace that Heaven returns to us as we accept Salvation in every way. It is an omnipotent facet of the Divine absolute that the Food for this interchange of Life between God and man is the Most Blessed Sacrament, the Eucharist, the Body and Blood of Jesus Christ from the Holy Sacrifice of the Mass.

We must believe that this Holy Bread is the Flesh and Blood of our Risen Savior because it is the greatest Truth to ever be unfolded before the likes of a sinful humanity. If we honestly desire to be saved, we will accept without question that Our Lord Jesus is truly the Eucharistic Host. The Great Sacrament is Love as Love perpetually is. The Lamb of God who takes away the sins of the world is the Most Blessed Sacrament, His Body, Blood, Soul, and Divinity. He is alive, crucified, resurrected, reposed in the Tabernacles and exposed upon the Altars of the Roman Catholic Church, and resting on the tongues of those with the faith to take Him in. This is a timeless and authentic reality dating back to the first Mass of God's Church on Earth, exempt from the influences of time, the changing world, and the attitudes of humankind. He said, "I AM." Therefore, "HE IS." Jesus is living Love who is truly present, brought into Creation at the hands of the very reverend priests of the original Apostolic Church. At the Holy Mass, we see Jesus' Body broken upon the Altar right before our very eyes. We see Him move and hear His spoken Words as He is consumed to bring those who receive Him to the Promise of Eternal Life. We see His Divine perfection walking about in the hearts of all those who are faithful enough to partake of His indestructible blessing. Indeed, we know all of this to be true because the Truth, Itself, lives in our trembling hearts. Many more Martyrs have surrendered their lives in defense of this unequivocal sovereignty than have skeptics who went to their graves blaspheming it. We must never allow temptation, worldliness, or any other diabolical influence to keep us from defending the Truth of the Most Blessed Sacrament. With this mighty faith, the world will be moved en masse to the Bread of Life, and therefore to God in Heaven.

Wednesday, September 4, 1991
The Holy Mother came again to give a special message for the world. Tonight, She began with these words, **"I am with you again. Thank you for being My precious little children! Thank you for attending the Chapel of Adoration today to adore My Son, Jesus. The Adoration Chapel is a place of great grace. Your prayers there are their most powerful. Therein lies such great peace..."** The Virgin Mother began Her discussion

by listening attentively to my many questions regarding the refusal of so many people to accept Her intercession at Her various miraculous shrines throughout the world. I have long wondered why so very few of us take them seriously or adhere to their purpose which She so faithfully delineates at those revealing sites. She answered by telling me that it is very difficult for those who lack faith to realize that Jesus loves them so much that He would provide supernatural evidence to show it. Those who truly believe in Him actually only know Him as a God of whom to be afraid. We know that fear of the Lord is the beginning of Divine Wisdom. But, we fall painfully short if we do not also realize the great Mercy that He holds in His Sacred Heart for His children in the mortal world. He forgives our sins while asking us to always try again if we fail. Absolution is the driving power of the justice of God that is provided through His Son. But, for those who do not believe in the Savior, there is no such thing as an omnipotent Creator, notwithstanding a supernatural intervention or miracle of some sort.

Far be it from anyone to stop our Divine Lord from dispensing His grace upon the children He has saved. He seems to be unmoved by weak faith because He always imparts the true knowledge of Himself to mankind. That is the importance of our call to the holy shrines of the Virgin Mary and is the reason She asks us to pray the Most Holy Rosary. Through its Sacred Mysteries, we come to know Jesus Christ more fully than through any other means, save the Most Blessed Sacrament. We must respond with urgency to the manifestations of the Holy Spirit and hold ourselves accountable enough to receive the Mercy of Our Lord. It is through the beautiful intercession of His Divine Mother that we are made acceptable and worthy to be saved. Besides that, Jesus, Himself, has revealed the veneration He wishes the world to have for the Blessed Virgin Mary. How accurate the Sacred Scriptures are when they state that we truly do not know how to pray as we ought! We do not know what to ask or how to pose the question. The Virgin Mother teaches us to humbly petition God for His compassion and forgiveness, for peace and the ultimate Christian unity that will bring His Kingdom to Earth. That is the purpose of Her supernatural intervention.

But, when miraculous events occur at various shrines or through interior locutions, it is very difficult for worldly-minded people to accept it. There is a perplexing fog that the mighty Beacon of God must penetrate in order to reach our lost souls. Everyone must willingly acknowledge that a truly loving Savior is among us. We must further concede that we have the Holy Spirit within us, whom we can confidently rely upon without fear or trepidation of His guidance. This is the acclimation that all who are questioning His work must make. There is only one Judgement. The plan of Heaven is unfolding before our very eyes, collecting souls by the millions into the Ark who will deliver humankind to Salvation. Yes, it is just as in the days of Noah. We must believe because Jesus Christ has provided this final merciful chance to take us to Paradise. Christianity brings many responsibilities that we must accept with humility. We are required to amend our ways and overcome lifetimes of misperception and outright error. This is true for clergy and lay-people, alike. We must not just weigh the task, but welcome it aboard. We must not only see the horizon, but approach it with courage. We must not simply intone a "yes" to God, but become exactly like Him. Our successful future lies in emulating the Son of Mary, His sacrificial Life, Death, and Resurrection. Our lives must become the model of humility, holiness, and prayerfulness, always compassionate and loving.

Our Holy Mother told me that there is no middle ground in the process of accepting Jesus. Total commitment to Love is the immortal call. If we foster only a spontaneous, on again-off again, belief-at-will faith, there is no true conversion. We cannot define a life of faith as *we* wish it to be. Rather, we must live our faith as God divinely *wills* it. What seems like a dilemma to each person is only a "commitment without human attachment" to the lessons and teachings of Jesus. No one will totally know God until they completely reciprocate in Love for Him. To do this, we must embrace the Cross. When we accept the Crucifixion of Christ with our whole heart and soul, we gain knowledge of the great converting power of the intercession of Our Lady at Her shrines. This is where our conversion is magnified to an heroic degree. Our lives become full of Grace, whose Mother is the Blessed Virgin Mary. We maintain a habit of making record of our days from one crisis to the next, from one war to another, and from economic upturn to its eventual down-slide. We record dates like stepping stones to mark human history for others to see. And, after the passage of time, succeeding generations consider these notations as somehow being a remnant of God's Will for them to continue. But, they are actually only the positive proof of our human failures and weaknesses in time. Societies are accustomed to being shown beyond any doubt what has preceded them. This worldly exhibition makes it quite difficult for the slightest faith in God to exist.

Many people have wondered why the innumerable media outlets, television, newspapers, and magazines, do not announce with conviction the truths of the Bible and the manifestations of the Christian Church. It is because they are not considered to be a human stepping-stone from their flat-blasted vantage point. The Bible and the Life of Christ are not recounted as being an important part of the version of mortal history that they wish to espouse. This is very sad considering the fact that Jesus Christ is the most noble of humans who left us the greatest legacy of all time through the most profound Sacrifice and the highest form of trust and service. The Life of Christ marks the heritage of an Omnipotent Man, God Himself, in which we mortals fail to believe. That is why the Almighty Father is not discussed in any secular medium. Those who are worldly-absorbed fail the test of faith because they cannot accept the need for it. Not even the corpse-strewn battlefields of this latest century have been enough to convince them. God wishes us to know that He is the answer to every question and the summation of our days. He knows the product of the dates of our calendars while we are still adding a column of numbers, one hour at a time. If we open our hearts now at the opening of this most opportune millennium, He will give us the answer to His Will. We will no longer need to make the daily calculation of the value of our lives without Him. He is the answer! There is no need for us to search any further or any longer for the meaning of life or our purpose on this Earth. In Christ, our lives are a consistent plateau of ecstasy, not a group of milestones that lead us to nowhere. Let us walk to the Cross and we will be lifted to God.

I asked Our Lady this evening whether the media could be converted to Her Son. She responded that they represent a fictional entity and a pretense of statistics and opinions that are filled with the materialistic thoughts of man. The media are a generic group of self-serving nonconformists, composed by a coterie of people who wish to control the agenda-of-the-day for the world and for every man. Although the hearts of those who control it can be converted, they would have to do one of two things; either report the Truth of God, or quit the reporting business. In either case, they would lose their earthly fortunes. They would prove the fallacy of their false power and would no longer be allowed to distract others who are searching for Salvation and the meaning of Life. The Holy Mother told me quite clearly that the answer to human history is not found in the march of time. Imagine a chain with numerous links representing each of many human milestones or crises. Mortal thought, existence, and history are interconnected in this same way. And, just as with any other chain, our mortal legacy has its weaker links. Therefore, there is no safety net or security in this set of binding shackles. It cannot lift those who are seeking the loftiness of Heaven. The chronicle of our mortal experiences is not the immortal Word of God, neither is it a substitute for the Truth for which He asks us to search. The Almighty Father places no value in our passing human curricula. He is bored with the secular world and disinterested in our interpersonal competition. The profane news of the day is of no worth to our Eternal Creator in Paradise.

The true news, the Good News, is the Hand of His Merciful Son, who became Man for the sake of a wretched humanity. He still has both of His nail-scarred palms extended for us to grasp. His invitation has been constant throughout twenty centuries of the greatest darkness that has ever been etched into the annals of historical decree. Jesus Christ is forever and never changing. His security is not about links on a chain with indentations, gaps, and imperfections. Neither is it a staccato of stimulation for the world to enjoy like contraband. It is a perpetually constant fortissimo of Eonian Divinity which will continue throughout the epoch of all Eternity. The power of His Love is as wide at its inception as it is at its eventual mark in God's unabridgable version of Perfection-come-to-Earth. That demarcation is the summit of Mount Calvary where His Divine Son hung on a Cross because He loves both His Father and humanity with an inextinguishable fire. Quite frankly, human communication cannot accurately report about any cohesion between peoples because we are, indeed, not loving one another as our Savior has asked. There is very little evidence of it to review! We are failing in righteousness and, likewise, refusing to acknowledge it before ourselves or any of our superficial friends.

At the beginning of this message, Our Lady said that many do not believe in Her intercession. They pray for miracles, yet do not accept them as authentic when they finally arrive. And, as we can see, the secular media organizations and other outlets of information are perpetuating this abhorrent indifference and lack of good faith. Our Holy Mother encourages our conversion from this condition of apathy for our own spiritual well-being. She wishes the world to live in the Truth and believe in the ultimate power of Her Son. The Earth can become a shining City of brotherhood and an incorrupt unity of mystical perfection if we will only adhere to the lessons in Her words. She knows how to elevate us to that pinnacle of understanding by leading the world to holiness, offering Her Beloved Son to us with outstretched arms and the greatest of solicitude. He is Jesus, the One whom we must accept in faith, the One whose motivations we do not yet fully comprehend.

Thursday, September 5, 1991

Tonight as we prayed, Our Lady discussed how we are separated from God and our brothers and sisters by artificial barriers that we construct in our minds. Whether we are held in captivity or free from the chains of human bondage, we still bind ourselves to the limitations of our exile through our inability to acknowledge that God is larger than what we see with our eyes. There are many people who are held in the recesses of darkness through the omissions of others who can openly see. They reside in captivity because they have never been loved by anyone else. This is the total eclipse that has produced the greatest shadows upon the Earth. When we try to isolate God within the limited scope of our intellect, we will never transcend our sinfulness or ultimately understand His great Wisdom. The following is a picture of our encased thoughts as we search for Him without understanding that He is greater than the dimensions of the Earth. If we believe that He is only of the world, we will never permeate the veil that separates us from the origin of His Light.

As we can easily see, the boundary of our faithlessness is not permeable by any of our weak-minded thoughts. Without invoking the Holy Spirit and utilizing the faith that Jesus teaches, our efforts only rebound back upon us. It is like trying to fly into the sky by jumping only a few inches off the ground. We see merely a reflection of ourselves in relation to the finite nature of the world. The circle in the picture represents the bonds of our mortality. It was created by Almighty God because we were cast out of Paradise by the sin of Adam and Eve. A veil was erected between the Holy One and ourselves that we cannot see through until we are called to face our final Judgement. Sensing this, we become frustrated by not seeing Him as He can perceive us. Mere mortals believe that this is an unfair place for us to be. We have often described this circle as being the "surly bonds" which cannot truly be penetrated or removed without the destruction of our faith. Our Lady has asked me to recognize that this depiction is only a product of our human understanding. Our thoughts and perceptions are frail, weak, and not always completely accurate. Although a worldly vision is incapable of transcending the incarceration of our intellectual thoughts, the miracle of faith permeates the veil between seeing and believing.

Faith will never let us look back at ourselves, but only forward to what Heaven has to offer. While we strain to envision the Paradise of tomorrow, the faith we need to reach it is in our hands today. Many do not believe that God ever comes into the world, or that He even knows it still exists. All too often, they believe that their inability to transcend their mortal limitations proves that He is also unable to touch them in-kind. They are convinced that there is no real communication between Heaven and Earth, despite the fact that they have never opened this channel of faith. Many people see God this way:

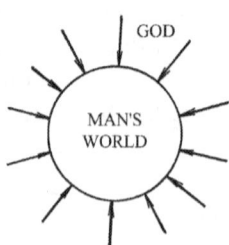

This is the symbol that many people believe reflects the truth about their mortal existence. Since they cannot pierce the partition that separates humankind from Paradise, they assume that neither can God, Himself. These faithless souls errantly concede that He stops at their border, unable to enter our lives. They are helplessly stranded, fending for themselves, while doing the best they can. God will only show Himself when He returns or when they finally die, so they choose to believe. They perceive their relationship with Him this way:

Notice that the stimuli on either side of the circle-of-life never permeate the so-called "surly bonds." Any overtures between the Almighty Father and ourselves are only deflected back to their origination by the veil that separates us from Him. Spiritual pessimists resign themselves to being obscured from Heaven because they assume that God somehow wishes us not to partake in infinite blessedness just yet. What is He trying to teach us by allowing our minds to conceive errant thoughts that the bond is a permanent separation between His Kingdom and ourselves? First and foremost, He reminds us that we are sinners who are in need of His Son's forgiveness. Second, He makes it painfully obvious that we have collectively fallen as a wayward people in the way of Adam and Eve. Third, He shows us our barren aptitude to grasp the mighty source of Love that we seek. We are yet mortals and do not realize the eternal bounty of Creation. We believe ourselves to be lost, rather than just simply blind and confused. God knows exactly where and who we are. He also knows why we are mortal. He instructs us through the Life of Christ and the Apostolic Church that we are permanently bound to perdition if we do not reconcile ourselves in Him. The order for our condemnation has been rescinded through the Passion and Death of Jesus. He has released us from those horrible chains, hoping that we will no longer believe that the veil of our exile can impede our knowledge of the true bounty and beauty of His Love and the Kingdom He has prepared for every soul who surrenders in trust to His Mercy. We must no longer entertain the mental phantoms which try to convince us that Redemption is something that has not yet come. Indeed, our Salvation is now complete. Jesus has already died and rose from the dead to provide it. God has proven His loyalty beyond any mortal reservation and in a perfect way that is outside our frail comprehension. We must know that He does not approach His children intermittently, but perpetually touches our lives at every point we can imagine, both spiritually and physically. He enters His Creation in infinitely many ways, greeting and lifting us with the grace to know Him well.

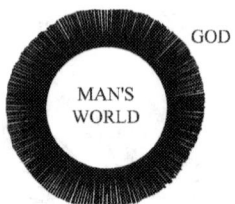

God's Love for humankind is not just a smattering of applause for our good deeds and thoughtfulness. Rather, it is a perfect, boundless, and endless blessing. His Promise does not leak at the seams or quiver in regret on its foundation. He aches to embrace His children and to soothe our wounded hearts. So, we must ask ourselves, if the Lord is exerting all of this pressure from beyond mortality toward the Earth, why is He not readily apparent to everyone? What is keeping Him from profoundly touching our lives to the depths of our hearts? The answer is quite simple. Humanity is resisting His miraculous intervention by pushing the Sacrifice of Jesus away. We are refusing to Love and are rejecting God by opposing the supernatural grace that will give us that immortal vision. We decline to know Him perfectly, so we counteract His Benevolent Spirit by our own reckless resistance to everything that is beyond our mortal intellect. The Savior of the world wishes to enter every heart, but our icy indifference will not spare Him room to come in.

While every story has its inevitable ending, this one, instead, has a happy new beginning. If we direct our efforts toward Heaven while focusing our attention on granting Christ free entrance into His Creation through the human heart, there will no longer be an exilic partition barring us from His Beatific Vision. Perfect acceptance of Love and a willful union with Jesus allow the Kingdom of God to reign inside the mortal parameters in which we reside. Our Lady told us that our lives must move in concert with the Divine perfection of Her Son, which is pouring-forth upon the Earth at every moment in time. Christ Jesus is the center of infinite Beatitude who wishes to also be the focal point of our attention. If we exert our efforts toward Him so as to perfect His example within our holy vocations, the imaginary bonds which we falsely believe to divide us from Him will disappear. Jesus was born to mankind so that we would cease in our opposition against Love.

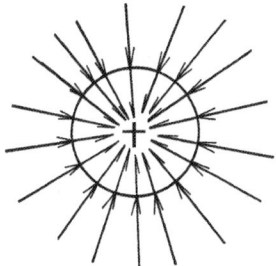

We see through this graphic depiction that, while exerting our efforts toward the Salvific Cross at the center of our lives, we will not be forcing God away from us. Indeed, our eyes will be fixed upon Calvary in communion with the pride-filled gaze of the Almighty Father who looks at Himself in the mountaintop mirror of His Son's broken Flesh. The living tide of Love which perpetually reciprocates between Heaven and Earth is the flow of Jesus' Sacred Blood, met by the flood of merciful Redemption breaking upon Creation from the Heart of our magnanimous Creator. His mighty power becomes our Eternal Bounty if we allow Him to work through us for our common good. Our unification with His Sacred Heart will perfectly manifest peace upon the Earth. We will then not be distracted by a ruthless search for meaning in our lives. Our collective accedence to our gentle and compassionate Father will focus our complete allegiance at the foot of the Cross for our momentary deliverance to Salvation. In a single bat of our mortal eyes, we will witness the detonation of paradisial beauty like a magnificent fireworks in the morning dawn, blooming into the vaults of Heaven as an eternal flower. The exploding sun of Christ's Triumphant Return will reveal the perfection and delight of every redeemed soul. The Light of Redemption reflecting from the folds of our broken hearts will blind us with ecstasy as it absorbs and heals us in the rays of Jesus' countenance.

While it is difficult to display this prophetic image on a page, you must imagine the unbounded joy of rocketing outwardly toward the arms of total freedom with neither a veil of exile nor a spark of human indecision impeding our path. We will move with the omnipotent power of God into His embrace, like filings captured by the fields of a magnet. Love will so voraciously consume our being that we will trample our own weaknesses and sins into the immortal pavement trying to reach His outstretched arms. There will be nothing that can stop us. Our Holy Mother asked me to be simple in my acceptance of this message. It has many dimensions whose pictorial essays highlight a childlike description of God's boundless desire for us to rejoin Him, the Saints, and Angels in Heaven. This story is a profound and concise way to visualize the direction where we will achieve the simplicity in which we should ultimately live. We must relinquish our will back to God and allow Jesus to come into His Creation by any means that He chooses. His Mother thanked us for praying with Her this evening. After offering Her gratitude for delivering Her messages to the world, She blessed us and departed for the day.

Saturday, September 7, 1991

My brother and I collected ourselves for the prayer of the Holy Rosary at 8:30 p.m. Our Holy Lady came and said, **"My little children, I am happy to speak with you again! It is a beautiful night as we share it. I am happy that you have many good memories. They are still in your heart. Love is the same through all Eternity and distance, but many are miles away. I have come to bring you a special message..."** May God be eternally praised for the miracle of these days. May we unceasingly petition Our Lord for the grace to comprehend the beauty that He is bestowing by sending His Mother to speak to us in such a special way. It is, indeed, to our own good fortune that She has come to reveal the deepest desires of the Heart of Our Savior, bringing us the Good News of His Infinite Love. We are also asked to gracefully engage the struggles that we are required to endure so we will render ourselves worthy to receive Him when He returns again in Glory.

I asked Our Lady tonight why God threatens chastisements in order to convert the children of the Earth. She told me that He is Love, and therefore is the converting power in the Life of His Creation. Reprimand and punishment are truly the reflection of our corrupt and fallible will back into our own lives. Our Almighty Father allows us to see our wretched helplessness through nature, time, and physiological suffering. We must consider the daily battle that He wages against the arrogant, egotistical human will. While He seeks our homeward return to Paradise, He does not require that we enter. He is simply invoking His Omnipotent power to provide the greatest opportunity for our final success. Therefore, He calls us caressingly and beautifully, while allowing us to definitively see how lost we are without Him and the beauty of the Heaven that He promises. In consideration of the present and ongoing darkness, chastisements seem to be the most effective way to open closed hearts and stop the recklessness of our rogue intellectual minds. Indeed, who is listening during these times of unprecedented prosperity?

Imagine wanting someone to attend you to a beautiful place that would fill their heart with indescribable joy. In spite of the anticipation, they believe that the length and ruggedness of the journey would be far too much for them to bear. Would we, like God, be willing to blindfold and transport them to this happiness without their knowledge for their own good? This is the grace that chastisements effect. They are God's way of reducing the impediments to our journey back to Him. Everyone passionately seeks the embrace of Divine consolation when suffering comes to their door. God knows that all souls wish to return to Heaven. But, most of us do not like the road of Christian sacrifice that must be taken to get there. So, many types of chastisement are meant to invoke human fear of both God and mortal destiny in order to bring us to conversion. Our Holy Mother wishes us to be strong in faith. If we would become so, there would be no need for blindfolds, punishment, or any type of repulsion. The heavenly chastisements, should they be necessary at last, will demonstrate to mankind that God's Will alone is supreme. And, if we expect to reach the Gates of Paradise, we must humbly embrace His every desire. This seems to be a tall order for the millions of people who are trying to make this journey alone. As a result, many unfortunate mishaps and disasters occur along the way. Those who try to proceed without first taking the hand of Jesus will vividly feel the fall of adversity without knowing that it could have been originally avoided. Our Lady provided a brilliant example.

Perhaps you can remember a time in a movie theater when you enjoyed a film that allowed you to feel as though you were flying in an airplane, riding a roller coaster, or driving a race car. As you watched in anxiety, you felt the sensation of movement as if you were truly inside these carriers, even though you were actually seated firmly on the ground. If any of these machines would have crashed, you would have been safe because you were never truly in motion. In much the same way, we are on a solid foundation when we live in union with Christ. But, if we ignore His Divine Wisdom, we actually live in these dangerous situations, susceptible to the horrific carnage that they might inevitably bring. Consider being placed in a vehicle in a virtual reality auditorium without knowing the theatrical specifics of your environment. Would you believe someone if they told you that it was just a film? If you refused to have faith in their explanation, would the cinematographer have to crash the vehicle on the screen to show you the truth? Our Lady's warnings of chastisement should awaken us to the peril of moving through life without God. She wishes us to show Him through our conversion that we truly know, love, and trust in His Son. Then, there will be no unpleasant repercussions recoiling back into our faces. The decision belongs to mankind on the Earth, not solely to God in Heaven. He allows us this freedom because He loves His children to an infinite degree.

"Your Diary is a miracle of Love to the lowliest and simple on Earth, and yet a warning to the affluent and those far from God. Praise God for this miracle! Tonight, I would also like to tell you about a confining blanket with which man has covered himself. I have told you before that mankind should be weaved into a blanket of Love." I was reminded of Her words about this blanket. It will keep our souls warm in spite of the frigid temperatures of the world and the icy attitudes between disagreeing people. It is porous so that we can inhale the breath of Life through it. When we are covered with Her Mantle of grace, we are protected from the intrusive elements of the world and the harmful actions of others who cause untold suffering to millions. Despite the call of our Heavenly Mother, we are falling terribly short of any semblance of unity and collective conversion. The ecumenical covering we have chosen has not been composed of the Love and Wisdom of God. We are actually shielding ourselves from other hearts, but most especially from the Sacred Heart of God. We are jettisoning every aspect of Divine Truth that would make a mortal ego cringe in hopes of finding some elusive combination of beliefs that everyone can agree upon. We are in the process of appeasing every arrogant sluggard who rears his ugly head. Our unenlightened man-made cover is a synthetic and suffocating one. Instead of protecting our final destiny, it stifles and consumes our ability to survive. It is based upon our fears and intimidation, rather than on mutual compassion and sacrifice amongst men.

The shield that we are erecting is of the deceased 20th century intellect, instead of the timeless Christian heart! Therefore, the Earth is almost completely covered by a blanket of sin and indifference. Many people believe they are being protected by this artificial barrier. But, while they see themselves as safe, they are not providing their opportunistic means of escape into the arms of Eternal Salvation. They are essentially in a cocoon. Moreover, since it appears that not everyone will do his part to become a thread in the blanket of Love, something must be done to pierce the suffocating indifference that is now covering the Earth. Therein lies the need for prayer because it opens human existence to the everlasting Breath of God. It allows Him to transcend the barrier that we mistakenly call our protection so that every member of the human family can inhale the magnificence of Jesus' Love. It is imperative that we come to understand what gives and sustains immortal Life. The holy, living, and saving Spirit of God is resuscitated into humanity through the Eucharistic Bread of Life, the Most Blessed Sacrament. Jesus caresses our souls back to Life in the Eucharist to save us. When we pray and attend the Holy Sacrifice of the Mass, we deeply respire the salvific Divinity of Heaven. It is Our Lord who allows us to partake of His Flesh and Blood, not unlike the same nourishing life that is given to a newly-conceived child in the womb of its mother. When we accept the Heavenly Bread, we are replete with infinite grace, our fullest resemblance of God for whom there is no peer or equal. Indeed, we are perfectly newborn in holiness every time we receive the Body and Blood of Jesus.

In the Life of Christ, our baptism begins our reciprocal union with the Almighty Father in Heaven. We are reunited with His paternal Divinity, which restores our heritage as His children. This Sacrament establishes a new binary communication with Him while we still live on the Earth. The Father has always been fully present in His acceptance of us, but for the first time in mortal existence, we reach-out toward Him. Before this moment, we were stained with the original degradation of Adam and Eve, and thus, forced into exile. We have always been God's Love, but free and independent in the world, from our own quaint point of view. However, in this case, autonomy from God means *lost*! If we continue to proudly proclaim our self-liberation from the Almighty Creator who gives us Life, we will truly not be capable of knowing the eternal future which He has so kindly established for us. That is why He sent His Only-Begotten Son into the world. His charge was to teach us to be dependent upon the Love of His Heavenly Father so that we may be saved and live in Paradise for Eternity-to-come. Therefore, we are baptized as infants to wash the original sin from our souls as an acknowledgment of our reliance on the Sacred Breath of Life. There are some who profess an objection to the baptism of infants because they believe that they must be able to hear a willful and knowledgeable confession from their tiny lips. They must realize that the soul of every infant makes a perfect ascension to the Almighty Father through the Sacrament of Baptism.

The soul of every newborn child intrinsically knows that it is being offered infinite joy and freedom, even though it may not be able to place it into words any better than an adult. The infant is able to knowingly accept this grace in its complete dimension because the world has yet to impress any other opposing mortal phantasms and trappings, i.e. temptations, upon its soul. The inner being of a child does not know of any other choice. Therefore, it wholeheartedly assents to the only one it knows. Someone can honestly make a decision when there is only one choice in the matter. It would be diabolic to believe that an innocent child's awareness must arrive at a certain saturation of damning mortal options before it can willfully decide for the immortal bliss of God's affection. We should let God get there first! Therefore, we must take infants to Baptism, just as we are required to escort each of them to birth. The open confession that these people yearn to see is found in the Sacrament of Reconciliation. This great ecclesiastical grace restores Divinity within a soul who has errantly chosen the fleeting mirages that have been injected into life by Satan. Penance prepares us for our reception of the Sacred Eucharist, the pinnacle of Christian perfection. Through its Light, we become forever united in Christ's Mystical Body. The Sacred Flesh and Blood that we consume is the fruit of the Salvific Cross. Therefore, the Eucharist is the rhythm of our breath of Life in holiness and Love. This is why Jesus should be received daily in His Sacramental Body and Blood. Without the Life-giving Bread from Heaven, we only hold our breath. The Most Blessed Sacrament not only gives life, it is Life Immortal. It is truly God's Love in the flesh.

Sunday, September 8, 1991 Nativity of the Blessed Virgin Mary

Today, Our Lady reminded us to pray from our hearts as She gave us another special message for those who desire Heaven, and especially for those who do not. She asked us to speak to all of Her children, including those who do not know that She is their Heavenly Mother. Indeed, Her intercession is specifically for them. That is why this Diary is such a grace for the world. Those who do not know God as their Father and the Blessed Virgin as their Mother will come to know the grace that will lead them to Jesus so they will be saved. Our Holy Mother is very pleased that the Church remembers Her Nativity on this day. Each of us has been blessed with birth because of God's Love. The Birth of the Blessed Virgin Mary is a day to remind ourselves of the millions of children who have been deprived of life because of the scourge of abortion. Yes, they have been murdered by those who are lost from God's grace. They must be found in haste. We must pray today so that abortion can be finally ended. Every person holds a special place in the Sacred Heart of Jesus. Through our petitions, we come to know His grace in a very intimate way in order to move back into the arms of our loving Creator. That is His Plan for all humankind. If we do not pray, we will slip even further away from His Love and Wisdom. When we beseech the help of our Almighty Father, He will mend the divisions between us and unite everyone in the Truth, bringing us all to everlasting peace. Each intention that we offer to Him takes away a slat in the fences that divide us. When they are finally removed, Love will freely pour-forth from our hearts to our brothers and sisters.

Our Lady continued this evening by telling me more about the Life of Jesus that we should all emulate with apostolic zeal. She asked me to remember that, by virtue of the Cross, we are personified Love in His image. The Lamb of God is beautifully human and yet divinely sinless. There were many valleys and peaks in His Life, just as there are in ours. He, likewise, had to fight the same temptations of the sinful world. He is truly and uniquely the perfect human that He wishes us to become. As an example, Christ Jesus walked perfectly and humbly on Earth throughout His entire Life. He allowed others to know Him in the way that He wishes us to embrace each other. And now, through His gentle Spirit, He passionately desires us to recognize Him in the hearts of our fellow men. His Love is still comprised of the same fruits and beauty that the world witnessed a scant 2000 years ago. He continues to guide us through compassion and humility, requiring faith, hope, and charity of His children in the Church. God demands that we strongly and faithfully live the example that His Divine Son taught us to embody. Jesus spoke to the world as a flawless human, in love with all of Creation. Those who knew Him as He lived and worked among them were required to have faith in Him because His day had not yet come until the Last Supper and Good Friday. Today, we must also have faith enough to understand that He came to save every generation of humanity from the flaming fires of Hell.

It is of eternal record that Christ Jesus died to destroy the sins of humankind. He expired publicly for all of us to see and for the hearts of every generation to eventually know. Our faith must rest in the truth that we are worthy of His Mercy and Salvation. Were this not so, God would not have subjected His Son to such a horrible death in order to redeem us. We must have impenetrable faith that all is not lost because we are the absolved souls who fully trust in Him. Those who live and believe in Jesus know His Word to be the Truth. Our Lady desires for us to expand this faith in a consuming way for the conversion of those who do not yet accept Him. Jesus' Mercy is obtained through repentance and contrition. Everyone must summon the strength to whole-heartedly implore His mighty forgiveness. We must truthfully state, *"Jesus, I trust in You to save me."* Christ died for every sinner who desires to be healed of the lifetime of infirmities that burden their souls. Yes, we must realize that God loves us that much! Forgiveness is the road to Mercy and Salvation. Jesus taught us to pardon our offenders with the same completeness that He forgave all sinners to whom He spoke during His journey of Earth. But, we must remember that when He offers us His forgiveness, He also asks us to never sin again. This, too, is an integral part of the grace of the Sacrament of Reconciliation. And, just as when He walked this world, Our Lord still beckons for us to accept His forgiveness humbly and with a firm purpose of amendment.

Our Holy Mother asks us to recall that Her Son's Love is a universal constant. His conduct exemplifies the greatest of valor, both courageous and bold. Yet, He is also beautifully humble and simple, and most especially knowable. During His mortal Life, He was neither aloof nor flippant because He was self-confident of who He is. Jesus did not use temporal means to coerce others to believe in Him or convert them to His teachings. He built His case upon loving communication and the appealing warmth of the Truth that He spoke. He was always consistently loving and enduring. The world never conquered His Will to care for the sorrowful and broken or instruct the affluent and powerful. While He was tried and tested by the worst of men, He never desisted in being the perfect image of the Love that He preached. But, since He was also beautifully human, He felt the same pressures that we experience when we are comparatively asked to love in the same noble way. These are the times when it is very difficult. While Jesus' Love is indomitably strong, it is flexible and patient to give us time to overcome our own volition and follow His words. His unmatchable Wisdom told Him that it would take time for humankind to accept His pathway to Paradise. We must forthrightly acknowledge that His Love has never wavered. His desire for our Salvation has not waned to this day. Yet, while it is eternally constant, it did not become brittle or stony. As God placed our sins upon Him, He opened His Heart ever-wider to bear all of our transgressions for the sake of Salvation. His Love was perfectly shaped by His overwhelming desire for our Redemption.

His soft compassion produced a delicate resting-place for the hearts of those He came to save. In the face of horrible suffering and injustice, He summoned the strength of unconquerable Love from within His Heart and proclaimed to a dark Creation that He is the Light, the consistency of God on Earth. This is also the Life that He asks us to live. The continual magnification of perfect Love is the application of Love, itself. We must always respond this way to others. We must bend, but never break. We must communicate, but never cower. And, we must always exhibit the grace that our Almighty Father in Heaven asks us to live. We are obliged to be honestly-straightforward and truthful, but willing to stoop to the smallest gesture of contrition with our own forgiveness, no matter how heavy the burden or how great the sacrifice may be. The Love of God is already perfect and there is nothing in Him that needs to be changed. We, however, must abandon our wicked ways in order to reside in seamless alignment with His Divine Will. We are commanded to become impeccable in the holiness that rains-down from Heaven. Our Lady wishes us to feed the hungry and quench the thirst of human souls until the work of Christ is complete upon the Earth. Those who search for meaning in their lives are actually hoping for this sanctified state of being. Prayer is their hope and Love is their vision.

The Almighty Father loves us so much that He wishes us to be as omnipotent in Divinity as Heaven, itself. In wishing for us to be beatifically singular with His Being, He answers our prayers for others. He wants us to change the world from inside our hearts. It is a stunning revelation to realize the power that has been vested in the human soul by God. Hope is an Earth-moving petition which He will always answer in time. Although we often seem to be quite distant from such spiritual enlightenment, it is easy to see that we should all wish to try. It is the reason for life because it is life's living essence. Those who do not love are already dead. But, their resurrection can come through our prayers. Our hopes, in union with their own, will deliver them to the Cross of their Savior. The Holy Mother told me that no petition is ever lifted in vain. God's attention is wholly exquisite toward those who humble themselves in prayer because the Angels in Heaven provide a standing ovation for any supplication that pierces the veil. The Almighty Father smiles upon those who pray amidst the cheering Hosts of Paradise, the family of royals who are euphoric that humanity is finally calling upon their Master for help in their long journey back Home.

Wednesday, September 11, 1991

"Good evening, My little children. I am always with you to protect you…" Our Lady continued by saying that the world exists in a terribly indifferent state, causing far too many people to suffer from depression and grief. Most human anxiety is centered upon worldly matters that are not deserving of our concern. The Holy Mother has come today to ask us to cast this dreadfulness away and allow our joyful hope to take its place. Prayer is the way to bring us to happiness because the mind is fed a new spirit of loftiness as the heart pushes every feeling of despondence and helplessness aside. Our Lady specifically told me that, by virtue of the Most Blessed Sacrament, the Holy Mass is our greatest rendevous with eternal destiny. We come to this great Sacrifice with enormous anticipation, knowing that we are returning to our fulfillment in the irrevocable Love of Christ. We convene at the Eucharistic Table of the Lord to experience the transformation of our solicitude into the fulfillment of perfect peace. This new spirit of serenity is granted through our faith and acceptance of Jesus as He comes to greet our souls. Both spiritual and corporeal order are restored through the mutual reciprocation of Love between God and humankind. It is the clearest image of the Holy Trinity on Earth.

Everyone who walks the Earth should come to know this peace. While we physically attend the Eucharistic Celebration and receive Holy Communion, the rest is accomplished within the heart and soul of each communicant. The Lamb of God who takes away the sins of the world delivers everlasting solace to the consciousness of those who believe and partake of His Sacred Host. We must simply release our spirits and open our mouths to receive this gift of grace. When we do, we will faithfully accept the Blessed Sacrament and everything that He embodies. The original Breath of Life is given to us again. A Divine transformation overcomes the limited being of every individual, mystically uniting us as one entity, all in the Body of Christ. Therein lies the true renewal for every deposed generation. Our Holy Communion with God provides the unity and strength to defeat any anxiety that could possibly dare to haunt us. Loneliness is consumed when we realize in faith that we are one with Divinity, Himself. Through the Holy Eucharist, we transcend the mortal to arrive at the culmination of all the ages combined. We must become reverently cognizant of Jesus' omnipotent power and presence in the Most Blessed Sacrament of the Holy Catholic Church. The opportunity to witness the magnificent moment of terrestrial Recreation is right before our eyes. God, in the glorious Flesh of His Son, stands with open arms, unconditionally poised to receive us into the eternal concinnity that He so yearns for us to crave.

Thursday, September 12, 1991

To touch every soul in the world, our Holy Mother came again with another beautiful message. She told us today that humanity will be at its best when all hearts are open to receive the Love of Jesus Christ. She is cultivating our lives for the fertile moment when all souls will convert and begin their sacrificial journey back to Heaven. Our Lady wishes to eradicate the indifference of Her children toward Our Savior's gentle Mercy. She asked me to ponder the question that is so obvious to pose, "Do we actually think we can save ourselves?" We were given life on the Earth so that we can learn to love and keep our holiness intact for the transfer of our souls into Paradise. There will be no Eternal Salvation for those who foster hatred. Holiness and human perfection abound just beyond the reach of our timid hands. It resides and lives in our total abandonment to Christ. The Holy Mother told me that those who call for balance in their faith, love, and religion are wrong. For the true manifestation of the fruits of the Holy Spirit to flourish, we must think in unison with the mind of God and the uncompromising genius He wields. When we do, we will understand that true balance will live when Heaven and Earth become one, and not a nanosecond before. There is truly no equilibrium between the simple excellence of God and the complex capitulation of mortal men who would rather run astray. His Love is forever unconditional and full. He will never concede to our half-measures or whimsical fluctuations. Jesus had to die on the Cross because humanity rejected Him at birth. He gave His Life totally and completely because we failed to do our job. And, when He died, we were all gained to the benefit of Paradise. Therefore, there are no ends to what Heaven will do to spare us all from harm; nothing human, or ever mortal, or even mildly intellectual.

Many people falsely believe that there must be balance in every action that humans set-out to engage. But, contrary to their skewed opinions, God asks for our total being, our all, our complete abandonment, and our best-laid spiritual sacrifices. Those who call for balance between religion and a worldly life always see the faithful throngs as being bestrewn religious fanatics. But, their vision of the Truth is not as God really sees it. Do we remember Jesus' road to Calvary? We should not measure Love from the middle of our minds, but rather from the bottom of our hearts. That is where Christianity takes its roots. The Holy Mother asked me to tell the world that Love must be measured from the bottom of the heart to the top of the soul. She also gave us a simple picture to augment Her message tonight. It is a beam resting upon a center fulcrum:

It symbolizes the belief of many people that we must be level-headed instead of completely righteous. Yes, we see a world of opposing fields, but that ground is also infested with the many sins of humankind. Its level balance displays a flattened age of mortal indifference without any spiritual direction. Jesus came to redirect our attention toward His Divine gift of Salvation and the destination of those who would follow Him. The Lamb of God came to destroy and expunge our every condemning transgression. Indeed, He came to catapult the world toward Paradise.

There is nothing that can outweigh the Sacrifice of Jesus or His ability to lead us to Redemption. No matter how hard evil tries to counter-balance the Sacrifice of Christ, no person and no action can erase or destroy this almighty blessing from God. No accumulation of human sin can ever overcome the Salvation we have gained through Jesus' Crucifixion on the Cross.

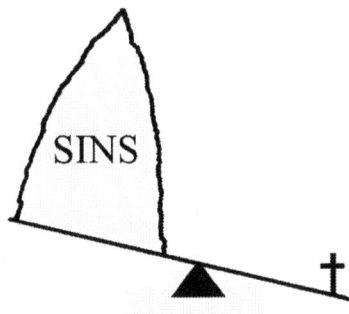

What you are seeing is a visual means of confirming that our mortal errors can never outweigh the Blood that Jesus has shed on the Cross to destroy them. Our Holy Mother asks us to realize that a heap of depravity reaching upward into Eternity, with each sin being represented by a grain of sand, could not destroy the Love of Jesus when He died on the Cross to save us. But, many people have decided that this Truth cannot factually exist. They do not understand the power of the Cross that the Lamb of God heroically carried and upon which He surrendered His Life. You see, Divinity is never less than complete, full, and total. That is the true balance of Love! It is the picture which the Father asks us to envision with the clarity of Redemption because the Truth remains alive. There is no equation on Earth between our holiness and the call from the wild to be materialistic, slothful, illicit, and self-indulgent. We must unite our hearts with Heaven if we ever desire to arrive there intact. Therein lies the only balance that is acceptable to Almighty God.

Our Blessed Lady continued this evening by telling me more about the Life of Her Son. We are richly enlightened about Christ's Sacred journey of Earth when we read the Holy Scriptures. The four Gospels describe Him as being quite confident and composed. When He was born of His Virgin Mother and became a Man, He did not come to destroy our faith. Indeed, He came to restore this Divine capacity so that we could be saved through His Sacrifice. Our Lord held the full authority to teach the Love of God because He was the Father incarnate. He was independently a Man for Himself, and yet, the Man for everyone. He knew that He had to be culturally matriculated in order to be completely trusted. Ironically, it is the same in our present day world. When others saw Jesus in a crowd, He looked like any other man in body, stature, symmetry, and all other mortal qualities; except He absolutely knew no sin. God truly bound Himself in human flesh for our sake. Jesus' trials began when He was opposed by others who refused to believe that they were worthy of seeing the God of Mount Sinai as somebody they could physically touch. Moreover, He was opposed by those who did not believe that God would come as a servant for gypsies and thieves. This, too, has never changed in our day. But, through the grace of Heaven and the impenetrable Truth of Christ Jesus, Christianity has flourished among those who believe that His Love is so powerful and creative that Paradise has come to Earth as a perfect Man to love us and lead us in prayer.

The Apostolic Church is founded upon the faith of the early Christians, particularly Saint Peter, himself. Within this Church resides the same Love whom the Almighty Father gave to us upon the birth of Jesus, and which He promises to sustain until the end of the world and throughout Eternity for those who love Him. Our Savior knew this truth, which was a source of great strength for His many travels and revivals. The Lamb from Paradise came to teach a rough-edged humanity the knowledge of the Heart of God, but most people were afraid because they did not fully comprehend Him. Subsequently, they did not believe Him, either. It was too huge a leap of faith for their limited consciences to undertake. Many of them were unable to grasp His great Wisdom because God had not previously come to Earth as a man. For that reason, among many others, it was more difficult for the early societies to accept their eternal God as an immortal being in mortal flesh. It has now been twenty centuries since this magnificent time when Heaven first appeared on the Earth. The Resurrection of Christ is 2000 years passed and is, yet, new to this very day. Jesus' Victory over death is timelessly immeasurable, perfect, and permanent. That is what the entire body of humankind must ultimately come to know. Jesus Christ is alive and breathing in the Blessed Sacrament of the One Universal Apostolic Church. He lives in every Catholic Tabernacle of the world and in every heart that beats through His loving Spirit. Love is alive.

When Jesus sent His Spirit to the Earth at Pentecost, He founded His eternal Church on those who followed His call, responded to His teachings, and sought the Father while living in anticipation of the manifestation of Universal Redemption upon His Glorious Return. Jesus is the only true foundation. His Love is the only strength which can support the entire world, and all of us with it. The modern Church is still the Traditional Church, the

Church of the Apostles. We have a great need to remember the traditions of Christ when we pray and gather in our sanctuaries. In our ministries and evangelization, we are faced with the same fear, opposition, questions, and head-strong intellectuals that Jesus met while He walked the Earth. He found very few open hearts; and this has gotten even worse. Today, there is little time taken for the Love of Christ, even among those who profess to be His contemporary followers. And, there is precious little conversion occurring as each day passes by. So, we ask ourselves, "What can we do?" We must remember that, as Jesus taught others about the justice of Love and the Mercy of God, people knelt to pray, hoping to receive His eternal blessing. And, as a result, the world began its final beatific transformation. God responded because He has never sought our destruction, just our spiritual conversion. Jesus was sent to save the world, not to destroy it. Humanity needed His redemptive grace and His guidance away from the abhorrent abominations that will lead us all to eternal damnation. Things have not changed a bit. We continue to need His Mercy now, more than at any other time in human history.

In light of all this, God still loves us so much that He gives us the freedom to accept or reject our eternal future with Him. While He wishes everyone to comply and accede, He will not force us in any way to take His hand. Therefore, we are at liberty to either be saved or destroyed. That is the essential freedom that we hold to be self-evident. Those fortunate ones who invoke their faith, love Jesus, accept His Crucifixion, and live His Commandments will be joyfully delivered from the hellish fires of eternal punishment. It is our choice to be the beneficiaries of this Promise. During our conversation today, our Holy Mother told me that many who reject Christ do not truly know who He is. So, She has been asked by God to miraculously intercede for them, bringing His Love to those who do not yet realize His Mercy. Jesus has sent His Mother to help us expand our hearts to embrace the complete fullness of His forgiveness. The Virgin Mary is convinced that, once we know Him, we will no longer need to search for happiness or fear His almighty justice.

As we continued, She addressed an issue about which I have very strong feelings. I have always been concerned about the destiny of those who belong to the protestant denominations. I was told that Heaven includes faithful protestants who have loved God in the best way that they know how. But, Our Lady added that most all of the members of the protestant faiths will return to the original Church when they accept the Truth of the Most Blessed Sacrament. The Eucharist is truly God coming to man in an eternal way and is the dawn of Jesus' great Return. But, She added that protestants are in less danger in the eyes of God than Catholics who refuse to be worthy of this great Sacrament. She wishes all of humankind to reunite under the guidance of our Holy Father, Pope John Paul II, and return to the original Church of the Apostles and the

Seven Sacraments of grace. While protestant Christians will be saved through the Mercy of God, Jesus still wishes that everyone would accept His original Catholic Church, which held strong through the first fifteen centuries.

The Virgin Mother reminded us that Jesus walked with the knowledge that more people would be afraid of the required sacrifice that He asks of them than would oppose Him from disbelief. We must come to understand that to follow Christ is to take up our cross in the way of His Life. Many in His day hid their fears by joining the opponents of Love and justice. It is the same to this day. Many people disguise themselves in very worldly and materialistic terms for fear of being outcast by those who despise Christians. We must pray that everyone invokes the strength to follow Christ's way without moral trepidation. To do this, we must truly understand Love in the way our Holy Mother teaches, i.e. it must be fluently received in the human heart. This has been the same since the first humans were given the breath of life. Jesus walked in a world of stony hearts and closed minds, which were the sad effects of the fall of Adam. His desire to teach holiness and openness of heart truly led to His Crucifixion. Our Life is meant to be total Love and our imitation and emulation of the Life of Jesus is the never-ending example of the perfect manifestation of His grace. We must strive to be holy and live each day with the loving eagerness of a child. Nothing should be allowed to stand in the way of our joy in loving every soul that we meet on the street.

Sunday, September 15, 1991
"My little ones, while you know what peace is, you also feel that solemnity is very difficult to achieve. It can only be attained through peace, which lives in the human heart both initially and ultimately. I wish for all of My children to know this..." This evening, our beautiful Virgin Mother drew a comparison between movement and motion. The former is the natural temporal unfolding of human existence. It does not lead to spiritual distress when it is engaged with the Love of Christ in our hearts. While God wishes us to be human and progress through life, He hopes that we will do so while basking in His Love. We must guide our hearts in union with His Divine Will, while remaining peacefully at ease in our mortal station. However, if the mind becomes absent of the heart, our movement toward and in unison with God gives way to worldly motion which controls and violates the fruits of the Holy Spirit. Our peace takes flight like a terrified fledgling. By embracing Love more intimately as the nourishment for our heart and soul, it becomes very easy to recognize and sustain the stillness that God provides in the midst of the world.

Many people who realize the difficulty of maintaining a tranquil oneness with Heaven in their own hearts look toward their brothers and sisters as the reason. There are those who believe that the ills of humanity are to be blamed upon people who are born as evil from their conception. Our Lady told us tonight that no soul is born inherently evil. Any maleficence that we embrace comes from the darkness in which we are raised. Sometimes we are taught to be less than completely loving. That is why Our Lady has come to ask us to pray. When we turn to the guidance of the Holy Spirit, we resist and destroy the evil that influences our souls. Prayer builds our love and trust in one another and God, Himself. It spiritually tempers the human mind and helps us to understand that we must be strong in His Commandments and in the Love that Jesus teaches in order to survive as a righteous people. Prayer softens these hardened hearts and opens them to spiritual healing. While the Almighty Father gives us countless gifts of grace in perfect softness, we often turn them into stone. A symbolic example is a tree which has become petrified. Satan is attempting to effect this same transformation to the branches of our love. He does not want our hearts to flourish, grow, or ever bear fruit. But, when we pray for the intercession of the Hosts of Paradise, he is permanently destroyed. Our Love for Our Savior eliminates the icy indifference between peoples and brings the blossoming of peace and Redemption. Our Lady asks all families to pray together as one. This is how we build God's undiminished Love from the very foundation of our lives and communities. We must accept Jesus as a member of our family through the recitation of the Holy Rosary and the reception of the Sacred Eucharist at Holy Mass.

Tuesday, September 17, 1991

"Good evening, My special children. I am with you to show My Love and to deliver another special message for the world. Thank you for praying! Our time together is very important. While you understand Love, I must tell you that this Diary will be received with fear by many who know its truth. It will have great awakening power. It is a message that far exceeds man's ability to deny it. Mankind must look to God through the heart to see the vision of Love and not the sight of temperament. I have come to teach all of My children to see the Truth in prayer. Thank you for helping Me do so! I love you and bless you in the Name of My Son."

Saturday, September 21, 1991

The Holy Mother of God came to us at nine o'clock this evening to continue Her instruction of those who desire to go to Heaven. She began, "Thank you, My children, for praying! I have been telling you that the heart is the home of Love. Jesus' message is always Love. He spoke louder than words in His deed of dying on the Cross. It is the greatest prayer for you to His Father. He still speaks to you through that Love, which rings as a never-ending song. Jesus is with you always. Love speaks to you everyday in all you see and hear, and touch and smell. His is a concise and concerned voice in the Blessed Sacrament. That is why it is so important that all know the Truth in the Eucharist..." Our Lady's message is always the same. Love is Salvation, while conversion is the vehicle which delivers us to the Savior who makes it possible. Love cannot move without the fuel and energy embodied in the Holy Eucharist because Jesus is the sacred power who propels the Holy Spirit through the souls of men. His Body and Blood are the accelerant that we consume daily for our fiery purification into holiness. Our Virgin Mother ardently desires for the world to be converted. The cries from Her Immaculate Heart are a pleading petition for us to embrace Love and live as Jesus has given the example. Her most impassioned plea is for Her unborn children. We must end abortion now, before we all tumble as a collective nation into the flaming abyss. Indeed, we are tottering on the precipice at this very moment in time. She told me tonight that conversion from this global horror must begin in our nation. Through the prayers of the faithful, the battle will soon be won.

Monday, September 23, 1991

"**Bless you, My little children! I have come again, and soon My Son will also come again. You are celebrating Love as Love should be shared throughout the world. I love you as Jesus loves you! Thank you for writing your journal so well. The world will like it. One day, My children, all of the hopes that you have for the world will come to pass. Your prayers are not in vain! When given in prayer, your Love will transform the world to Salvation. Amen! You realize the task before Me and Jesus to answer your prayers for all humankind. There is an abundance of hope which accompanies your love for the world, which will also come to be. Please continue to work on your Diary and pray with Me. Together, we are working for the conversion of the world!**"

Friday, September 27, 1991

Tonight as we prayed, Our Lady gave me one of the most beautiful and powerful messages about the truth of the Holy Eucharist that I have ever heard. She began, "**I love you, My little children. Thank you for praying! I have come to give you another special message about the power of the Eucharist so that you can transfer the information to the world, especially to those who refuse to partake...**" There is plenty of material in the world, but not enough spiritual love and faith. We have blind confidence that the wind will blow, the sun will shine, and water will flow. We openly confess this assurance by the ante of worldly possessions that we wager upon it. But, what does mankind stake on Love? What effort do we expend for the sake of goodness and righteousness? Our Lady wishes it to be known throughout the world, by rich and poor alike, that prayer is the ultimate power to change the Earth. It is the paddle-wheel or windmill which transforms the omnipotence of God into functional human good. These spiritual wheels are set into motion by the endowment of the Bread of Life, the Sacred Body, Blood, Soul, and Divinity of Jesus. The Most Blessed Sacrament is the wind that blows, the sun that shines, and the water that rolls. Like the forces of nature that transfer energy into humanity's greatest engineering accomplishments, the Holy Eucharist is the power of God applied to the hearts of those who pray to be worthy of receiving it. But, Our Lady tells us that we must lift our petitions with conviction and compassion. This is what She has come into the world to teach us.

Mankind is rowing a boat toward Eternity, and each individual soul has an oar. These paddles begin to move like the feet of little ducklings under the water when we pray from our heart. But, as we invoke the majesty and elevation of the Holy Sacrament, our moving oars plunge into the water with enraptured devotion, propelling us toward Salvation like a hydrofoil skimming across the glassy surface of an ocean on the calmest sunny day. Our Holy Mother asked us to fervently fan our dedication to the heavenly gift of Jesus' Body and Blood in the Most Blessed Sacrament. She reminded me of our prayers on the twenty-second day of March, 1991. As we recited the Holy Rosary that evening, my brother authentically experienced being in a mystical canyon while I knelt beside him before my prayer altar. Our Lady said that we live perpetually in this valley of Love when in union with the Holy Eucharist. Without it, we get no closer to the heavenly pastures than I did that night in March. These supernatural gifts of God's power and nature through His Son are given because He loves us so very much. For the most part, we are attempting to utilize nature for the good of our being, but we also need to understand the Eucharistic Grace we require for the good of our souls. The Most Blessed Sacrament is the pinnacle of supremacy that bears superiority and dominion over the forces of the Earth that often seek to destroy us.

The windmill has a *clutch*, the water-wheel has a *dissimeter*, and a solar panel has a *transfuser*. These are the transforming connectors between the power given by God and the energy needed by man. In the Holy Mass, it is the Priest who is the convener between the Almighty Father and Jesus Christ. At the Consecration of the Holy Sacrifice of the Mass, the Master of Creation comes in His infinite power as the Holy Eucharist. The *transubstantiator* of the bread and wine is the celebrant Priest. He is the reverent one whom God uses to become a physical and tangible reality in the world of man. That is why priests are required to be holy, pure, and single-minded in the Will of God. The Roman Catholic priest is a part of the sacred chain of Love from the Almighty Father into the incarnate hearts of His children. At that shining moment in the Mass, the hands of the Priest are the hands of God offering His Son to the world in Love. For that radiant Eternity, that Moment of Consecration, the world and all in it are created again. God says, I love you over and again. Then He says, I love you again, and offers His Son once again. At the hands of the Priest rests the Salvation of all humankind. Inside the Holy Tabernacles of the Catholic Church stands the future of all humanity whose Love is all we truly own, nothing more. And, Love owns us, too. It is reciprocally one, the beginning and end, the Alpha and the Omega.

Saturday, September 28, 1991

I knelt to pray the Rosary about 9:00 p.m. and the Holy Mother came to shower Her grace over my soul by saying, **"My little one, I am with you because I love you so much! I have come to give you another special message for the world. They are all very special in their own way by giving direction to Love through prayer and conversion. I have come to tell you how many children of the world who consider themselves practical and pragmatic can come closer to God through Jesus..."** Our Lady began Her address this evening by telling me that human logic is only a guess and science is only a theory. Earthly facts and formulas are never the constancy that is endemic of the Creation of Love. What we believe to be constant and efficient, or even co-efficient, is not vaguely relative to the world of Jesus. This is the problem when science fails to prove that there is a God, then rejects that He is. Science is merely an explanation and description of the world as finite mortals see it. It is not a prescription for Love and human Salvation. While the Father proves Himself through science, humankind cannot always find Him there.

The Holy Mother used the point of our intellectual observations to explain why abortion is especially wrong. Many doctors and expectant mothers errantly believe that the Life of the child that they are seeking to destroy does not begin until it is delivered into the world. The Virgin's Divine Wisdom assures us that human Life begins when the Almighty Creator conceives His child in the womb of the one chosen to be its mother. The first nine months of every human Life are spent in the womb. It is abundantly clear that we must accept the effect of God' Infinite Love by recognizing human Life at its conception. He breathes Divine fire into an embryo in a beautiful realm that we do not have the capacity to visually or intellectually penetrate. We never see the actual ignition of Life. The Queen of Paradise is making the point that Life begins before there is a pulse for our doctors to detect, in the same way that it continues after the final beat at our physical passing. We do not see prior to one or past the other. The bestowing of Life upon Creation is a priority for God, alone, which no human being can either explain or imitate. Practitioners and pragmatists do not take into consideration their helplessness before denying their Lord and Savior. Jesus is of the most simple places in the world. We should consider the many other gifts from His omnipotent bounty that we cannot explain. We have studied the transformation of a seed into a flower. We know about how the soil, water, and air assist in this procession. But again, we do not know how it happens or when it actually begins. Our limited vision cannot detect God's action, although we can see the Life of His Will when a flower breaks through the fresh topsoil. There are many other examples like the rain, a rainbow, and its ribbons of color.

Ponder the moment when the breath of Life is given to a new child. This is where the soul is born. The physical body is the last part of this new Creation to become present in the mortal world. The tangible and material dimensions of the Earth have only a periodic custody of this sacred Life. It is temporary counsel for one who struggles to return to God. The soul needs much loving nourishment during its tenure in exile. This Love comes through the Most Blessed Sacrament with the same mystery that stimulates a seed to bring a beautiful flower before the eyes of humankind. Again, we do not see any of this unfold. We know that it happens, but we dare not say why. We know the process of its growth, but we do not know how it begins. Furthermore, we do not see the culmination of a living soul in Creation. We cannot see it leave its body. Neither do we recognize that a flower has a soul. The Virgin Mother tells us that it, too, is Love. We are witnesses to what lays between the origin of Life and its passing into Eternity. Yet, we are blind to the beginning and the end. Mankind refuses to acknowledge that the Alpha and the Omega belong to God Almighty! We pine for the limited answers that please others of our race and the mortal men of our time in answer to the problems of our days. Sadly, this is only the poor minimum of cerebral lore that we need to fully survive. Our genius resides in the knowledge of Love that is taught to pliable human hearts who are willing to comply with the spiritual greatness that centuries of good people have been giving their lives to evangelize.

Our true achievement has already been accomplished by Jesus Christ while hanging on a Cross to eradicate sin from the Earth! He offers His Infinite Love for our success and fulfillment beyond mortality for all Eternity. The Blessed Sacrament is our means to triumphant achievement and everlasting victory. The Son of God who lives in the Holy Eucharist will actually let us see His Father's work, not solely the result of it. When we gaze upon His Eucharistic Body, our physical eyes are seeing first-hand God's sacrificial travails for the Redemption of man. By witnessing the Consecration of the bread and wine into the Body and Blood of Jesus, the worldwide scientific and academic communities can see their anemic lives and careers fulfilled before their astounded eyes. They will no longer have to prophesy and predict! Nor will they have to weigh and measure. They will endorse the true high-browed Divinity from its eternal foundation to its vaulting majesty. It is the Love of

God through Jesus Christ. They will then know that truth is found not in physics and law, but in Love and Passion, and Salvation and Eternity. This liberating vision will finally give them the venue to realize for the first time that they can stop greedily dissecting the world in their synthetic laboratories, but rather see this radiant Creation as a participant in its meaning, which is always Love.

After that, there will be no self-indulging questions or pontificating answers. Gone will be the hypothetical corollaries and mind-boggling equations. Nothing will be found to equal it or compete with it. And, there will be no cause whose effect is not Love. The Most Blessed Sacrament completes the beatific fruition of the unfulfilled souls of dreamers and discoverers, alike. Nevermore will one find ratios, comparisons, or quotients that can dare match this superpotent union with God, Himself. The one and only Love which explains, follows, and nurtures the world and all in it, is revealed to humankind in Jesus Christ. Our Lady concluded tonight, **"Thank you for your prayers. Jesus delivers graces to the world, especially to those who pray from the heart and receive Him at His Tabernacle. These are the children of the world who know that the final product of Life is Love, as it was in the beginning. In the Holy Name of the Blessed Trinity you are brought to Love, and Love to you."**

Sunday, September 29, 1991

For all the world and for all peoples of every nation and race, our Virgin Mother came again tonight as my brother and I began the Holy Rosary. She said, **"My special ones, thank you for your prayers! Tonight, I have come in peace to tell you more about Love, the catalyst for change and conversion for the world. The perspective from which all should see is from the vantage of Love. Love is the factor through which all actions should be procured. It is Jesus who provides fulfillment of human hopes. I would like to tell you about that perspective so that the vision of the world can be improved for the good of the souls of men..."** Love must become the reason for our every human action. We must not allow ourselves to be distracted from Christ by the cares and concerns that the world ignorantly heaps upon us. It is easy for open hearts and sound minds to grasp what our Holy Mother wishes us to know. She hopes that we are listening and changing because She awaits us with Her Infinite Love, which is beyond all comprehension. She touches hearts with care, sorrowfully knowing that most people must be shocked or appalled before they will pay the slightest amount of attention to Her call. She is not beyond sending us into the extraordinary if that is what is required for us to listen.

As an example of this fact, our Holy Mother reminded me of Her intercession on the 24th of March, 1991. On that miraculous day, my brother and I were in the cemetery praying when She physically appeared for the first time. The next day during our prayers, She had Timothy draw a sketch of us kneeling in the yard next to the Crucifixion monument. The picture revealed a perspective through Her own eyes. We were shocked by the virgin revelation to our hearts. The image was drawn on that day so that this message would bring great dimension and meaning. I was taken-aback by the drawing because my heart could see from a vantage point that I had yet to ever consider. It was always there, although I never thought to look down from the heavens at myself through Our Lady's eyes. She used this innovative and creative convention to show us new possibilities in our lives. Her desire is for us to embrace Jesus in a way that we have never before dreamed. She wants us to see Love as He is in His Infinity, in His unbounded Mercy and acceptance.

Our Virgin Mother told me that this is difficult because Satan continually tries to redirect our thoughts and desires in an effort to take us away from grace and holiness. Although God holds the ultimate power of Creation, He has given us absolute latitude to destroy every cunning advance of Satan. The Heavenly Father has armed us with prayer so that we can actually eliminate evil from the Earth. We gained this magnificent birthright when Jesus died on the Cross, rose from the dead, ascended into Heaven, and returned His omnipotent Spirit to our hearts. When we pray, Satan not only goes away, he is actually diminished and destroyed. He is rendered powerless and helpless when people fall to their knees and ask their God for help. Our Lady also comes, asking us to pray the Rosary, fast, do penance, convert, and cultivate hearts with peaceful compassion. She encourages us to recognize the truth that we are living, but do not yet completely understand. We are children of Light who have been created to return to Love in the heavens. Jesus Christ is alive now and at our side. There is an Eternity of Salvation and joy in His boundless Love if we have enough faith and trust to stand penitently beneath the Cross of His Sacrifice. What additional motivations do we require to accept these eternal truths? Christ's answer is the maternal direction of the Queen of Paradise. Our Virgin Mother is erecting bastions of faith and trust in Her Son. She is the final instrument of pre-Redemption Mercy extended into the world from Our Savior, Himself, because there will be no need for faith when He returns to take our souls to Glory.

A RIVER OF LIGHT

OCTOBER 1991

Friday, October 4, 1991

This evening, Our Lady reminded us that our prayers continue to be very powerful. She began by saying, **"I love you! Welcome to My Heart as I come into yours with the Love of My Son. I share your joy today and your feeling of contentment. Thank you for knowing peace through the Love in your heart. I have come to share with you more about Love. I am with you to protect you.. Please keep constant knowledge that Jesus will also protect you..."** God will bless all those for whom we petition because He wishes us to be completely one in Christ. His grace enters other hearts as a result of our prayers, changing them to be more receptive to His Light and peace. Our hopes must be strengthened so that Salvation can reign throughout the world. We will someday see that we truly possessed the invincible power to transform the Earth, and to what degree we invoked it. Our Lady wishes us to be elevated in holiness and to strive diligently for success. The Holy Sacraments of the Catholic Church are the avenues for our return to grace. During our times of unity in prayer, humankind is more able to see the Light and live together as one indivisible family. The original symmetry of Creation is restored through the common bond that is created in our sanctified congregation because the fruits of the Holy Spirit can blossom in this fertile spiritual environment. We also realize that the Love we feel in our hearts is a salve that heals everyone who invokes the faith to partake of it. The power of Christ's Wisdom reaches beyond time and space and is deeper than the shallow sensations of physical touch. Our Lord brings consolation to every heart who is united with His own.

Saturday, October 5, 1991

"My little children, how I love you! You have such a special place in My Heart and Jesus' Sacred Heart. I wish for all My children to know His Love..." Tonight, Our Lady wished to remind each of us that the world is ailing and She knows precisely why. Our sickness is due to the dissension between people. We are separating ourselves from the eternal health of Love. These divisions can be overcome by our participation in the worldwide community of prayer. Our discord is conquered through our Communion with the Blessed Eucharist at the Holy Sacrifice of the Mass. Furthermore, we must collectively pray the Holy Rosary as Our Holy Mother asks so that our vision of Love can gain both clarity and consistency. We must ultimately realize that the unity of all mankind will only come at the Altar of Sacrifice, and not before.

Monday, October 7, 1991

"My pretty little child, you are seeing a marvelous manifestation of messages. I wish to help you progress in your understanding of Love. I have always known that I could help you understand. That same progression is how you have also recorded My messages. Together, we are building faith, a knowledge of Love, a fortress, a dream of hope in the heart, and a beginning of Love for millions of your brothers and sisters. Each time you place your pen to the page, it will mean another soul into the hands of Jesus. When you love, you are visited by the Holy Spirit, who asks you to live Love in your heart. You have consented and responded, and millions will profit..." I asked Our Lady when this will happen. She responded, **"In time, My little one, all things will come to pass! Prayers, love, and time!"** We are called toward the humble peace which came to the Earth on the first Christmas eve in Bethlehem because the Holy Spirit wishes us to embrace the majesty that the Morning Star has proclaimed. Jesus came in human flesh because our Holy Mother said "YES" to God for the sake of our Redemption. Everyone needs to imitate that same profession of faith.

We can historically see and prophetically know the effect of Her Fiat. She wishes us to be the fortunate generation who is prepared for the return of Infinite Forgiveness. The entire world is changed every time just one of us consents to the Will of the Father. As we surrender into the union of His Divine Love, every other thing moves joyfully toward this beatific unity. Each soul who has been given Life by God is the one that completes Creation, making it whole again. Every race of people is needed in Heaven. Color and nationality are only an external attribute of the physical body. But, inside of each of us lives a spirit that is the same heart in Christ Jesus. Everyone desires for their hopes and dreams to become a reality for them. That is why Our Lady is with us, guiding our footsteps toward this everlasting fulfillment. If we come to know Her well, we will have found everything for which we are still endlessly searching.

Tuesday, October 8, 1991

My brother and sisters, I ask you to open your hearts ever-wider to embrace the message I am trying to deliver. Our Lady speaks soothingly and patiently, hoping to change the dispositions of those who have the faith to listen. Each day, She teaches me more deeply that God loves us in every way and through all of time. I have been asked to embrace and celebrate the beauty of Paradise that She asks us to seek. But, we must not compare our mortal fanfare to the eternal festivities which have commenced at the Banquet Table of the Lord because our worldly celebrations reflect only false victories. The Blessed Virgin said that the people of the Americas must realize that competition and sporting events will never deliver them to eternal happiness. She wishes us, rather, to participate fully in the Victory of Christ. Our perfect happiness is in His attainment of Paradise for our souls. Our Divine Creator wants everyone to have the following trophy of His Son's Triumph in our homes to cherish and admire all of our days.

The Cross is the infinite sign of how Jesus proves His Love for humankind. It is the trophy that God wishes us to venerate from the celebrated perch of our mantles. Through the Crucifixion, we remember the greatest Man of all, the Man-God, Jesus the Christ, who secured the most overwhelming triumph ever known to Creation. Since that eternal moment of Love, mankind has every reason and responsibility to unite in compassionate understanding for one another and to defend the oneness that Love seeks to maintain throughout the end of time. We need not search for any other honorary plaque, elevating badge of honor, or elusive victory cup, because they are paled and diminished by the heroics of the Eternal Champion who has saved our souls. Our Holy Mother said that each time a man declares himself a champion, he separates himself from the true Champion of Peace, Truth, Salvation, and Love. Each person who proclaims himself exalted does not understand whose victory they are claiming as their own. There is truly nothing worth seeking unless it serves to the Redemption of humankind. And, in that purpose, Jesus holds absolute superiority. He won the conquest of the Cross, both perfectly and permanently.

The conscience of man cannot grow if we remain attached to the physical world. Our Lady hopes that we will recognize how Satan diabolically attempts to diminish our love for one another. When we see the repeating seasons of competitions in sports and entertainment, we are only witnessing the smoke which obscures our vision of the Cross. We do not see the Champion, so we are trying to create imposters. This is why we must turn our eyes to the hallowed hall of celestial fame and gaze upon the triumphant victory over death that Jesus Christ encased in the history of man for all to admire. We must remember these words, **"Each time a man declares himself a champion, he separates himself from the True Champion."**

Thursday, October 10, 1991

"**My little blossom, thank you for allowing Me room in your heart and home. I have come to reassure you of My Love and confidence that your writing is well. The world is being converted! These messages and your writings are being inscribed into these hundreds of pages in the shape, condition, and form that the world is being transformed into. The thoughts of Love are being shaped into reality, making your writing like permanent footprints on the Earth. Enjoy these days! Look upon them as sacred in your life...**" Our Holy Mother has been allowed by God to bestow many graces, blessings, and miracles upon the world throughout the centuries. Yet, She says that many of Her children who do not think they are worthy of these loving gifts entice everyone they meet to disbelieve and discard them. Somehow, they have failed to realize the immense grace that Jesus Christ gave to the world when He said, "**Behold thy Mother.**" Notwithstanding that, the world will soon recognize His mighty Love through the Divine Maternity of the Perpetual Virgin of Nazareth. The first benefit of His birth is our very life, itself.

The Life that we live entered the world through the Womb of our Immaculate Virgin Mother. Once we realize this simple joyful Mystery, believing that we are worthy of His Love will be the easier part. We will then accept His many prodigies with great anticipation and faithfulness. When we come to understand the Eternal Life that Jesus perfectly personifies, we will know that every other gift will inevitably follow in its wake. We must perceive the magnificence that has dawned! We have already received the pinnacle blessing of God as Jesus died on the mountaintop of Calvary. He is *everything* for which human hearts now hunger. But, somehow, we continue to live as though we are spiritually starving to death. We are standing before the buffet of eternal food, yet concede that we are not worthy enough to eat our fill of ecstatic joy. It is Jesus, Himself, who commands us to receive Him so that we may be strong and holy against the temptations of the world. We must attend one another to the Eucharistic Table to be nourished and replenished, validating our commitment to becoming one heart in this Divine Communion of Love.

Friday, October 11, 1991

This evening Our Lady spoke with me again about the secular media in our country and how it presents the American government to the public at large. It is obvious through our communication how loveless our western civilization has become. The sense of mercy and compassion for those who are weak is almost never portrayed. Even if it is, it is done so apologetically, as if forbearance were a display of some inherent inner-weakness. We find ourselves accusing, convicting, and punishing everyone who is spiritually broken as a result of being human and deprived of mutual respect. Mankind convicts his brothers of failure in love before he ever takes the time to show him what it is. Christianity is the vision through which we should envision the entire world. But, it is blocked and distorted by our sins and lack of personal forgiveness. Our Lady has come to convert us from this pitiful state into a concise vision of Jesus' Love. Her Wisdom accentuates the meaning of life as everyone should lead it. America should be more concerned that millions of unborn children are being killed in the wombs of their mothers than administering an adequate measure of punishment for those who have admitted to their crimes.

There is no doubt that our vision is quite errant. Unethical puritanical zealotry causes us to grandly display the smallest infractions of a spiritually tortured humanity and retort, "This is what you cannot be." Should we not, instead, elevate unconditional Love which is our healing balm and proclaim, "This is what we must become?" We have a similarly erratic view of human emotions. We falsely believe that distraction and lack of peace blend us into one America. It really does quite the opposite because it only separates and divides us. The United States, the so-called melting-pot of humanity, is actually a battlefield of the greatest worldly competition. Being absent of love, this arena has become strewn with the casualties of destroyed hopes and broken dreams in a nation that supposedly guarantees life by its own Constitution. We must remember that life is Love, and therefore, it is mandatory that all human life be protected if that Charter is to be valid. This, of course, includes the life of the unborn. Those who are blindly ensnared by the fallacies of the mortal world do not realize their own hypocrisy. That is why Love is so revealing.

It is as though we are walking on a treadmill that continues to increase in speed due to the footrace of souls toward damnation. The pavement keeps streaming toward us, requiring furiously repeated steps to remain upright. Exhaustion overcomes us, but the walkway will not relent in its pursuit of our next step. When we finally collapse in fatigue, those who claim to embrace love condemn and ridicule us because we cannot keep pace with their commotion. We are ingrained in the paving material of the street upon which the world's most powerful climb to glorify themselves. Our Lady told me that we need not take another futile stride because we can simply step-off of the machine. When we do, our noble efforts of holy advancement will be directed toward grace and sanctification through a distance that is transcended by our prayers. Each stretch becomes a productive new movement toward unity and oneness with the everlasting purpose of God. This is why Love is the only alternative, and also the most attractive of all. It cannot be purchased or controlled by the rich. It is the greatest power which is ironically affordable to the poorest of souls. In order for the world to truly be transfigured, we must stop our hell-bent turbulence and live the genius of peace and brotherhood.

Tuesday, October 15, 1991
　　Our Lady came again to show Her Love for all of us and give another message from Her Immaculate Heart. She began, **"Good evening, My beautiful children. I am with you again to show My Love and to bring you another special message. There is a tremendous variety of topics and subjects in your Diary. You can be assured that Love will not be lost in all the diversity. So many subjects serve to indicate how universal Love is. The Truth of Love will always prevail..."** The Blessed Virgin appeared again today in search of loving hearts. Like we would search for water, She comes looking for the most essential element that we need to survive. Our holiness is the life-blood of our love for Jesus. We must drink of the grace of Our Lady which She so profoundly offers because we need Her intercession to survive. In order for us to be holy, it is *sine qua non* that we imbibe in the Life-giving waters of Salvation. Mankind has used forked branches and sticks to locate water that is buried deep beneath the bowels of the ground. This process is called "dowsing" for water. Our Lady is using the cross-beams on which Her Son was crucified and is "Divining" for Love inside the depths of our sleeping hearts.
　　We can look throughout the world and see that it is as difficult for many people to find Love as it is to locate drinking water in the desert. There are some places where Love flows like a stream, both obviously and plentifully. But, in other quarters, the parched landscape is almost absent of this life-preserving sustenance. This is where there is war and transgression against peace and human life, especially unborn children. When water is scarce, we plumb the depths of the Earth to find it. To secure Salvation, we must tap the deepest recesses of human hearts, which validates the need for prayer. Through humble communication with the Spirit of God, our hearts open to admit His Wisdom and grace so that we can project Divine Love toward our fellow man. People can then reach-out to eagerly swill from our well so that the lonely fires of their hearts may be finally quenched. Mankind is thirsting to be loved, and each heart is a spigot of pious consolation. We must give of ourselves to all who come to us for refreshment. In those dignified moments of service, it is Jesus who is standing at our door telling us, "I thirst." Our Holy Mother constantly reaffirms how special we are, while continuously asking us to pray from the heart so that we may fulfill our beautiful journey through life into the arms of Her Son. The Almighty Father wishes to bestow perpetual elation upon our souls for all Eternity. He desires that we purify our hearts in acceptance of His Infinite Beatitude. When we beseech His help, we say "YES" to His Will.

Wednesday, October 16, 1991

Our Lady came and said, **"My gracious little children, the Almighty Father, God of the world, has sent Me to ask for help in converting humanity. Your Mother is tremendously happy that so many are adoring the Blessed Sacrament during these times. It is important that humanity bows in adoration and very important that everyone enjoin through the participation of the Holy Eucharist..."** It is fitting to inform those who do not understand that the Holy Eucharist is the Body and Blood of Christ, the Communion Host that the Catholic Church shares during the Holy Mass. The Eucharist consummates the union between the unseen heavens and the knowable world. It is the point of Divine contact between God and man, the perfect and unifying catalyst, sustaining the bond between our hearts and the Love of Jesus. Many feel that God does not show Himself strongly enough in their lives. Their lack of vision, faith, and love causes others to feel completely separated from Him. If we honestly seek to embrace the Love in the Most Blessed Sacrament, our faithless human minds will never again generate the false perception that we are disconnected from our Almighty Father. Indeed, we will actually feel the grace that solidifies our oneness with His Sacred Heart. While in the flesh, we often feel divided from God's Love.

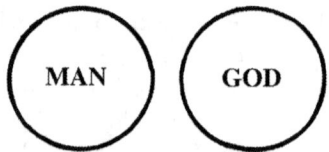

This, quite obviously, is a depiction of our false perception. It has no basis in truth because we cannot stand either independently or omnipotently divided from God. Our Holy Mother told me that the world of man and the omnipresence of the Almighty Father do, in fact, meet in the Holy Eucharist. The point of contact is the Consecration of the bread and wine into the Body, Blood, Soul, and Divinity of Jesus Christ. This Miracle is performed by the priest during the Holy Mass.

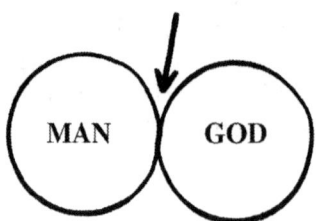

Then, when we partake in Holy Communion with our Eucharistic King, the world of God and man become perfectly one and the same.

A.   **B.**   **C.**

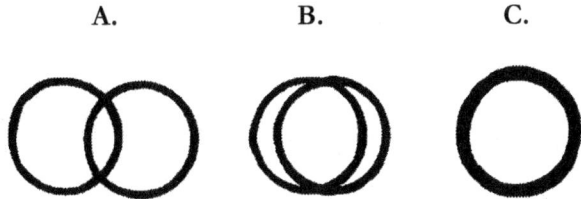

The Kingdom of Heaven eclipses our world, a total covering of our souls with His Love, effecting the perfect unity and compassionate oneness that He yearns to share with His children. We become one with the Almighty Father, as simple and easily as A, B, C. Heaven and Earth are actually separated only by the thinnest of veils, leaving us not quite as far from Paradise as our minds tell us! Our exile can be mystically transcended when we attend Holy Mass and worthily receive Jesus in the Most Blessed Sacrament. A similar lack of understanding surrounds the Adoration of His Sacred Body in the Monstrance. During this time, Jesus is standing right before us upon the Altar! Some errantly believe that it is only a symbolic reference to Him. Others disbelieve because they cannot detect physical dimensions of His appearance, as if He cannot be perceived past the measurable size of the Host. And finally, there are those who simply reject His true presence outright.

Eternal Truth demands the proclamation that Jesus is truly and physically present in the Sacred Communion Host. He radiates His Love, Mercy, and forgiveness to and from all directions. The Infinite Species is much like the sun which projects and radiates Light into the lives of everyone who comes into its path. Christ's power and grace miraculously enter our hearts from His glorified presence in the Monstrance during Adoration. His Love is what we feel. Without Him, our hearts would simply be a mass of physical tissue. In the absence of this Divinity, our souls are just inanimate and helpless entities, spirits bound to the Earth without direction or purpose. Our Holy Mother asked me to remember that Adoration of the Blessed Sacrament must always be accompanied by the proper blessings that are recited by the presider.

THE DIVINE PRAISES
Blessed be God.
Blessed be His Holy Name.
Blessed be Jesus Christ, True God and True Man.
Blessed be the Name of Jesus.
Blessed be His Most Sacred Heart.
Blessed be His Most Precious Blood.

Blessed be Jesus in the Most Holy Sacrament of the Altar.
Blessed be the Holy Spirit, the Paraclete.
Blessed be the great Mother of God, Mary Most Holy.
Blessed be Her Holy and Immaculate Conception.
Blessed be Her Glorious Assumption.
Blessed be the Name of Mary, Virgin and Mother.
Blessed be St. Joseph, Her most chaste Spouse.
Blessed be God in His Angels and in His Saints.

Thursday, October 17, 1991

Again, the Holy Mother came to show Her Love for the world and to deliver another special message. She began with these comforting words, **" O' little special one, I am with you again to pray with you! I thank you for singing and playing for Me. You know the songs that touch My Heart. I will take all of My children to Jesus who come to My arms and pray with an open heart. My Immaculate Heart is very warmed when My children bring Me into their confidence. When My children come to Me, they no longer are separated from peace."** When hearts are open, it is easy for Love to flourish and caress us. It is, likewise, very easy to render ourselves separated from it. Our vision is most keen when we fully comprehend the limitless Divinity in the Sacrifice of Jesus upon the Cross. The battle lies in the wearisome burden that is caused by our frail mortal minds. Although our hearts pine to be loved, we cannot force others to reciprocate. In the barren predicament of another's refusal, we must enlist the strength to love them anyway. Our Christian profession must be an open act of the free will through a sacrificial heart. Our Lady told me that humanity is aching with a "heady" feeling because intellectual concerns seem paramount in our world today. But, they are, indeed, a false burden at that. They are one of the main reasons that we do not help one another as we are required to do.

Sooner or later, we must become cognizant that a strong will and overpowering mind only serve to feed an ego that wishes to reign supreme. Our prayers will help us to be more humble, which will diminish our appetite for egotistical gain. Heaven is an ecstasy far beyond anything we can imagine. It is very difficult for us to lift our hearts high enough, or powerfully enough, to comprehend its boundlessness. As our Holy Mother told me this, I asked Her if She would tell me more so that I could try to understand. In response, She asked me to envision the happiest time of my life. For some of us, it may have been a great sports victory, or perhaps a wedding day, or the birth of a child. Recall the purifying exhilaration, the feeling in the welling-up of tears, and the explosion of happiness which lasted during those moments. These instances are tangentially similar to the impressions that are generated by Heaven as it meets and consumes the Earth, like we saw in last night's message.

They are the hint of ecstasy in the two colliding worlds. But, Paradise is the absolute inundation of our heart and soul by that beatific enchantment which will catapult our awareness past every moment in time into the complete Eternity of joy! Salvation is a constant magnificent fulfillment that will last forever. We will know how God feels being Omnipotent Love because we will be just like Him. The height of our hopes, united with the exhilaration of Infinite Mercy, will bring the ignition of our souls like mighty rocket engines. But then, Our Lady added, **"And, with these words, I fear that I am only able to show you the front door! One day, we hope, all mankind will see this eternal beauty."**

Friday, October 18, 1991

The Mother of Jesus came to the world again to offer another message to Her children. She began, **"My little flower, thank you again for praying. I have come to tell you that your writings are made whole and holy by their content of Love in your heart, brought together through My intercession. This is a beautiful and glorious time! My son, you are involved in the transition and transformation of man from sin and mortality to perfection and the completion of Love through the unending spring of Salvation forever. This is truly the grace that My Son seeks for all humanity..."** Love is endless and will never expire. The consummation of the union between God and man is integrally involved in this perfection, as it should be. Oneness in being is in and through the Almighty Creator. But, we must always remember that it was man who first moved away from Him. Through sin, we abandoned the perfection in which we were created, and therefore, are responsible for our perishing flesh. Humanity turned toward evil and was lured away from Eternal Bliss. As our eyes fell from the Holy Firmament, evil brought its diabolic seduction to bear upon our sights. Therefore, God saw it necessary to remove both evil, and those influenced by it, from the glories of Heaven. In that sad process, we fell from grace and became a mankind without dignity, function, or direction. The condition of our collective soul was both reckless and misguided.

Then, Jesus Christ came into the fallen world, teaching, dying, and rising from the grave to restore us to the Kingdom of His Father. He transformed our hapless and helpless state into a perfect circle of new Life. Indeed, this Alpha, this new beginning was inaugurated on the Cross and is the shape of our own resurrection. The Virgin Mother told me that the entire world became the burdensome Gibbet that Jesus endured to sanctify Creation. If it were possible to delineate the transformation of a lost and shapeless humanity into the perfect circle of the blessed children which Jesus came to save, it could be shown in this picture.

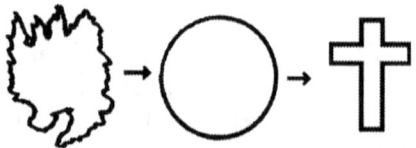

Through time and the power of Christ, we are brought to the salvific Cross to validate our Redemption. This illustration exhibits the procession of our perfection and reflects every message that the Mother of Jesus has given to the world through the passing generations. While guiding us in this transformation, She helps us to be courageous in lifting others to this same potential. The intention of God is for us to grow toward the Light of His Divinity. We must draw ourselves away from disorder and inhumanity into the dawning Love that awaits us in Paradise.

Saturday, October 19, 1991

Tonight, our Holy Mother calls everyone's attention to the self-proclaimed independence that the men of the world declare for themselves. We maintain that we are the masters of our own universe. This is evidenced through our complete subjugation of everything that lies within our ability to grasp. We have built machines to serve nearly every purpose that we can logistically imagine. Even our brothers and sisters are classified by how they toil in our many vast places of industry and recreation. But, Our Lady says that all of these so-called freedom-makers need to realize that they are no more liberated than their ancestors of five hundred years ago. Advances in commerce, communication, transportation, and science have done essentially nothing to help us grow into the original Love of God. We have placed ourselves on the false foundation of material hope and worldly achievement. We have done many things to shape our environment, but are helpless in any attempt to attain Eternal Life on our own. Our Blessed Mother gave many examples of how we have become self-sufficient and self-serving. We engineer vehicles called *automobiles* that transport us from one place to another on our superhighways. Further, we design them to move on their own using an *autopilot*. We sign our name as an *autograph*, and write the history of our personal lives in an *autobiography*.

We have established for ourselves as free and independent a position that we can possibly muster. But, we fail to acknowledge that God supplies the support for all of our successes. Everything that we accomplish rests upon the effect of the Almighty Father. The automobile is useless without the ground below its wheels. It must employ the physics of friction to push-off the pavement so it can move around. Mankind, himself, did not create this element. Rather, it is from the genius of our Creator, intrinsically woven into His glorious handiwork. Consider the marvelous human memory as another one of His great gifts. He allows us to recall our lives and write an autobiography with the agility to affix our attesting signature. Even in this elementary case, we do not have any freedom which we can implement until it is given to us by the Lord. Therein lies the wisdom of this point given by the Virgin Mary today. "AUTO-SALVATION" does not exist, nor can it be created or built. Compared to our Father in Heaven, mankind is geriatrically weak and ineffective, failing in the control of human destiny. We can count the number of our mortal days, but we cannot control their quantity. This, and all else, belongs to God alone. The source of our Salvation and the means to endless days is to abandon our lives to Jesus Christ.

Monday, October 21, 1991
Our Lady came today bearing another message with resounding dimensions. She asked me to consider the position and attitude of the Earth in the solar system. I was to contemplate how mankind looks at the globe as being a part of God's Creation. She brought to mind a question, "How can it be that the world is round, and yet, is sitting in a universe without a top or bottom?" In other words, if someone is standing on the north pole, why does another person on the south pole not realize that they are standing upside-down? No matter what continent upon which we are positioned, we stand upright with our feet on the ground in relation to everyone else and the sky is always overhead. Our physical perception tells us that any direction that is beyond the Earth is upward. Therefore, mankind says that there is no top or bottom to it or the universe that contains it. But, still, it spins on an axis, capped by northern and southern poles. Our Lady told me that many people have speculated about the reason for this axis and that scientists consume themselves with studies such as this. They impress their egos with where they are located in the galaxy, but they are not concerned about where they are going on the day they finally leave it.

The Holy Mother brings a very interesting point. Is there a given distance from the Earth that we can go and look back to see people as standing upside-down? Can we view the Earth from outer space as a temporary place given by God for our destiny in Love? This is not a complicated matter. Since we relate our thoughts to our stature in existence, we must surely be able to transform our hearts from this habitat into our eternal destiny. The Virgin Mother has come to enhance our vision so that we may see our distance from Love, rather than our coordinates in time and space that are relative to another given point. We must be transformed into Divinity for our reception into Heaven. Jesus wishes to elevate us beyond our mortal parameters into paradisial Life. He commands us to love one another so that we can, instead, see the firmament of Eternity. When we pray, Infinite Love comes to us and fills our souls with Light. Love is the Truth of our immortal destiny. I asked Our Lady to explain further by giving me another example. It was not that I did not completely understand, but I had become very imbibed by Her beautiful stories. She asked me to think of a picture that is very breathtaking and reveals the heart of the artist. This is a vision of timeless beauty which can bring a renewed hope and insight to the hardest of hearts. Around the canvas is a quite ornate frame which encapsulates the work with great majesty. I was also asked to imagine someone who is a collector of picture frames and is filled only with the desire to add this beautiful one to his collection. He looks so intently at the frame that he fails to notice the painting. He overlooks the very beauty that gives the frame its shape and function. We must remember that picture frames have no purpose without a scene inside them.

The Holy Mother related this parable to our station in the universe. By relocating the Earth in the solar system, or by moving the sun so that it rises and sets from north to south, Jesus could make the equator cold and the poles hot, if He so desired. The point remains that we must acknowledge God as the Omnipotent One who controls the beauty of Life within His earthly habitat. We are asked to search for Jesus Christ throughout our bounded realms. He is found in the Tabernacles of the Catholic Church and in the hearts of those who love God through the Holy Spirit. While the Father holds the framework to our Creation, our attention should be directed to the beauty of His Son upon the Earth. We must invoke His Holy Spirit and receive the Most Blessed Body, Blood, Soul, and Divinity of Christ Jesus in the Communion Eucharist at the Catholic Mass. The focus of our aspirations and accomplishments must be conducted away from the Earth, the solar system, and the universe which compose the framework of our beautiful location in Creation. We must look to each other and to Our Lord for sanctified guidance in preparation for the Second Coming of Christ into the center of His picture. It is mandatory that our portraiture be of a holiness so great that it guarantees that our lives will be majestically suspended upon the walls of God's endless Glory.

Jesus is the only answer in our search for this immaculate vision. He is the reason for the existence of everything that we experience. When we place the world aside and pray deeply from within our hearts, we see the beauty which permeates everything that is alive. Our Holy Mother wishes us to overcome our sorrowfully limited senses through prayer and render ourselves complete in the ocean of God's Mercy. She is fervently attempting to refocus our understanding and enliven our aspirations so that we will strive not so much to touch the Throne of God just yet, but to portray the Love of Jesus on the Earth in our time. That beauty is Christ, Himself, perfection in human flesh, who sits at the right hand of the Father. Finally, can we assume that, as the Holy Spirit is on Earth, the Earth is also at God's right hand?

Wednesday, October 23, 1991

This evening, I noticed that Our Lady came with a very commanding and authoritative presence to give me an extremely strong message about America. The time has arrived where even simple and innocent people are not allowed to walk freely. Basic human rights and the peaceful dignity of humble citizens are being infringed. This is being done by those who are in positions of power who try to justify their oppression by calling it protection. There is a terrible punishment coming to those who disguise their prejudice under the guise of social justice. **"Woe be to those who are such hypocrites!"** Many people are drawn into this system of social terror. Simple and innocuous acts are met with a conspiracy of sordid accusations and persecution. The American social psyche functions under the code of "divide, condemn, and punish," all in the name of justice. It is not founded on the mercy and forgiveness that Jesus Christ asks us to live. The Love of God is the answer to all of our societal ills. He is the Conqueror of evil, the Light to those who are blind, the healing of the sick, and hope to those in despair. His Son will remake us in a way that our public systems of justice have never even attempted. We must learn to pray deeply for those who are weak and to forgive them without condition. We are obligated to petition with equal intensity for those who hold the broken-spirited under their strict control. We must lend a helping hand and give of ourselves so that everyone may see that they are loved, and that they are also capable of loving. Most of all, they should be convinced that they are truly worthy of our affections.

Our Lady has come to reveal that Jesus Christ loves us all with the same, infinite, boundless, and eternal Love. He is the true definition of Redemption. We must allow others, along with ourselves, to become His image, despite our many weaknesses. Prayer is the catalyst which inflames this miracle within our souls. But, many people have already hopelessly given-up on holiness because its course and method confounds their dictatorial minds. Our journey begins by remembering to love with the exact intensity as given initially by Our Lord, Himself. The Crucifixion is the ultimate beacon of Light for the world. The Love of Jesus, given during our age, emanates from the Cross upon which He died. Anger and animosity are lost in this beatific ocean like two forgotten castaways. When we invoke the vision of Heaven, we realize how special other people are, allowing us to recognize ourselves in their reflection. The grace of the Almighty Father initiates this revelation so that no one will surrender their hopes of one day being delivered into Paradise. This is why our inner-patience is such a grand virtue. It allows us to peacefully make room in our hearts for each of God's children. This must be accomplished in a world that continuously attempts to destroy the reputation and dignity of its citizens through any means it can find. The moment a broken soul tries to rise, society calls them to a scourge of accounting for their *audacious* ascension. In the eyes of the world, they have no right to their dignity. However, through the virtue of patience, we see anew that forgiveness and Mercy are the pathway toward the solemn unity of all races of humanity. Why, then, do we see so much prejudice in our midst? Because most people do not wish to share the world with others, even though God created it for the souls of every nation and race. While every set of lungs inhale the same atmosphere, there is but one Eternal Breath which respires Life into the soul of man, perpetuating our rise into Eternity. That is the Love of God.

Our Lady assured me today that our Heavenly Father does not look cynically upon the world. However, He truthfully knows that, in time, there are those who would even attempt to monopolize and market the air we breathe in order to gain profit and complete their domination over their fellow men. God sees us as somehow wanting to replace Him. We wish to control, manipulate, and subjugate the human family and Creation, itself, for our own material gain. We strain to define the parameters of respect that we must give to others, delineating its appearance according to our own benefit. We refer to Our Savior as an "it," who is actually a "He." Others even try to prescribe what it takes to earn His Love! What misguided outrageousness! His Divine affections cannot be earned. He has completely given Himself to us out of the omnipotent and perfect Will of His Father. We cannot control Him, anymore than we can monopolize the air we breathe. We are His beloved Creation who diminish our own beauty by our forays of competition and our insatiable desire for gaining superiority over everyone else in sight. This places an almost unbearable burden upon our capacity to love and unite. Our Virgin Mother says that our efforts to conquer our brothers and sisters constitutes an attitude of outright physical and spiritual darkness.

The problem rests in our inability to recognize that we are collectively helpless and that we actually have no universal control over Creation whatsoever. We place windows in our homes, yet do not realize they are of no value at night! Along with their failure to provide perpetual vision, they actually reveal our true inner-selves to those who choose to peek in. So, our temporary capabilities and intentions ultimately serve only to reveal our hypocritical weaknesses for the entire mortal world to see. We have created this shameful irony in our attempt to partition and shape the Love of God to our own advantage. In order to accomplish our earthly purpose, we have uprooted our souls from the Truth that has been revealed by the Life, Death, and Resurrection of Jesus Christ. We live in darkness and our bay-windows are useless. But, if we accept Christ as the Truth, we will have a stronghold of Love to keep us in His Light. Through Him, we have a perfect vision of our world and its purpose toward our Redemption. Thereafter, we will have no need to construct any other corbeled skylights from our rooftops. If we love and pray for conversion, we will be effecting the best usage of the bountiful air that sustains us!

Thursday, October 24, 1991

Today, our Blessed Mother provided some special words of consolation for people who are suffering persecution for the Glory of Her Son. Those who are enduring the atrocities of malevolent men, while being repeatedly neglected by the world, are the Divine instruments of Christ's Love upon the Earth. They are moving the Divinity of God into Creation through the terrible adversity which will gain them the highest of Heaven. They are the poor in spirit who are open to receive others, while their suffering is, and will always be, quenched by the holy waters of God's Mercy. They are the hearts who yearn for peace and seek compassionately for the road that returns the Love they offer. Their perseverance and endurance are always holy because they live with their heart, instead of their intellect. They do not distress themselves looking for understanding, but rather, they humbly accept their lot which abundantly fertilizes the piety that grows so bountifully in their wake. After telling me these beautiful things about the world's suffering-millions, Our Lady encouraged me to continue with my record of Her words. This writing is a splendid gift of grace for the conversion of humanity to the Mercy of Jesus Christ. It is one of the many blessings that God has bestowed upon His children to strengthen us in our horribly formidable journey back Home. Our Lady said, **"I wish for you to continue to be happy during these days. They are truly marking the time of the reception of Love into the lives of many. One day, all will know the Truth! Thank you endlessly for your prayers from the heart."**

Friday, October 25, 1991

From the Glory and majesty of Heaven, our Holy Virgin Mother came to speak with us again this evening as we recited our evening prayers at nine o'clock. Tonight, She addressed the nature of original sin into which we are all born. Through our Baptism, we are cleansed of this initial stain and elevated toward a new vision of the future. Once we touch God at our Baptism, we never completely descend back into the world that once held us. It is as though we walk on a plane of glass which keeps us elevated above the ground, aloft in grace and prepared for eternal Salvation. From this perch we openly realize that the world is in need of diametric change because we recognize the damaging forces of Satan at work below us. Our ascendant plane of vision does not make us feel that we are better than others, but simply gives us the venue to reach-down and pull mankind to the spiritual heights that we already know. The glass figuratively represents the supporting and glorifying nature of faith. While resting upon it, we notice that it is transparent and that it brings us to summon the grace to believe that it is both strong enough to hold us and free from any holes through which we might fall. It sometimes feels as though we are walking on ice whose thickness changes depending upon the season.

Our faith is strengthened beneath our feet by our prayers. And yet, we must remember that we are called into the valley of service. We are commanded to attend the lowliest of places with the message of Jesus so that every soul will be made happy by the Good News of their deliverance. Therefore, our hearts must always remain aloft, out and away from the transgression and delusion of the world, while our vocations take us into the lives and circumstances of anyone in need of the love in our hearts. Our spirits must always remain above the glass, although we gladly serve others in the lowly ghettos and ravines of the Earth to alleviate the depths of their human despair.

Our daily efforts in Love are supported by what we cannot see. The Mercy of Jesus always protects us, especially during our weaker moments. The Light of faith is ever-present to assist us, not to supplant our Christian service in the world He owns. Indeed, this is a beautiful playground of possibility and the ultimate command of the Son of God. The true power in Creation is the Truth of His Gospel. We once suffered in complete sin, but are now set free by His total forgiveness. All transgression and travesty expired with Him on the Cross and Eternal Salvation was raised from non-existence to absolute certainty when He rose from the tomb. It is upon this Promise that we must lay our fears. Nevermore should we tremble in the presence of sin. It has been erased for those who accept the Truth that is revealed by the Holy Spirit. The knowledge of Christ ensures the expungement of stain and death from the parameters of human history. Our Lady has come in an Immaculate Way to prepare the world for the Sacred Way! Everyone who petitions Jesus to temper and dispense His Divine Mercy toward all souls will also receive it themselves. We are assisting in the perpetuation and magnification of His Kingdom upon the Earth. Likewise, we are the instruments who are shaping Eternity by helping to maximize the Mercy of Heaven to the inevitable extinction of the role of damnation. Now is not the time for us to concede any soul to perdition, and Our Holy Mother told me that we are overwhelmingly winning that battle!

Saturday, October 26, 1991

With each new day that passes, the world becomes more focused toward the vision of our eternal legacy. The Holy Eucharist is the disciplinary means of curing the heart of humankind so that we may faithfully see the destiny which our Almighty Father seeks for us. As we humbly gaze upon the Eucharist with our mortal eyes, we can see Jesus standing before us with our hearts wide-open. The Son of God is physically present before humanity as the Eucharistic Host. To see this reality in our hearts is the most perfect and holy vision that can be attained. However, it is nearly impossible for those without faith to accept the magnificent graces that proceed from the Most Blessed Sacrament. That is why our Holy Mother emphasizes our need to become like little children. They all believe Him most profoundly! It is this innocent faith that will transform the world, convert human souls, and allow us to accept the Salvation that Our Lord has promised to bestow upon the Earth. The gift of faith serves to clarify and complete the vision of the heart so that our eyes can also see. Jesus truly desires for us to partake of His Divine Flesh and Blood. He has stated this clearly in Sacred Scriptures. Those who hold themselves at odds with the Catholic Church have decided that His intention has somehow changed. Notwithstanding, Jesus commands us to unite as one people through His Body and Blood, the Sacred Communion Celebration that we share. This heavenly union will save humankind and change the world into the perfect reflection of Heaven upon the Earth. And, too, our collective front against human suffering will move Love throughout every heart, eradicating the effects of our mortal errors all around the globe.

In Her conversation with me about human simplicity, our Holy Mother mentioned the many religious conferences that Her faithful children regularly attend. She said that those who participate in such huge gatherings need to remember the plight of the poor. It is the larger "conference" of mankind that She is now calling to order. The humble prayers that we lift from our silent bedrooms have as great a converting effect as those in convention halls and stadiums. In addition, Our Lady calls us to accept the Body and Blood of Jesus at the Altar of Sacrifice to receive the power which nourishes this transforming fruit. She plainly tells me that the Most Blessed Sacrament is essential for our ultimate holiness. The solace and solitude of prayerful peace, especially before the Eternal Bread of Life reposed in the Monstrance, can overwhelm the magnitude of any religious seminar. These supplications are the true oratories from the spiritual summit of our Christian authenticity. We should begin our accumulating days with honest petitions from the heart so that all of our thoughts and actions will become gifts of love for Jesus Christ. We will maintain our conviction if we remember what He gave so that we can live forever with Him in Paradise.

Sunday, October 27, 1991

"My son, I have another special message for you today. It is about human forgiveness. I hope that you will record it in your Diary for the world to see..." Our Holy Mother requested that I continue to paraphrase Her lofty words so that the images of Her message will be easier to understand. First, I was asked to remember when I might have been offended by someone for whom I deeply cared. In these instances, forgiveness is very easy because we have been the recipient of their goodness on many previous occasions. Our desire to return to normalcy as quickly and effortlessly as possible causes us to be quite sympathetic toward their moment of weakness. Therefore, we pardon them and completely wipe the transgression from our memory. Our Lady also asked me to recall other times when we have suffered at the hands of those we do not yet know, or ones who seem to be habitually offensive. On these occasions, our willingness to absolve them can be more difficult to muster. The discriminatory way that we have grown to view other people shapes and skews the condition of the love in our hearts. This stems from the negative thoughts about them that we cannot seem to expunge from our minds because we fluently remember the pain and suffering they have caused. But, through our charitable decision to forgive them, we can erase all of their infractions from our recollection. Our opinion of our brothers and sisters must not be shaped by our habits, but rather by the newness of Love that occurs every time a thought of them enters our hearts.

I was provided a means through which to fully understand this concept more clearly. Our Virgin Mother told me that She could prove that I have a preconceived recognition of others. I was asked to list the middle names of the members of my family and a special group of friends. I obediently wrote them down on a sheet of paper as I was instructed. After finishing, I realized that I have never known any of these people by the names I had just written. I had a new outlook toward them, seeing them now in a fresh and spontaneous light. Therein is the reason that our Heavenly Lady asked me to inscribe them in the first place. I was shed of the stagnant biases that caused me to perceive certain individuals in accordance with the surnames that are ordinarily associated with them. Through this simple lesson, I learned that labels are neither fair, nor accurate. They tend to hinder our own good will and create a barrier for someone else who wants to be affectionate in return. Everyone wishes to be recognized and remembered for their greatest achievements. But, because of our paltry desire to forgive them, we create countless hurdles that are nearly impossible for them to ever overcome. This makes it very difficult for others to join in the community of Love with any sense of dignity at all.

The errant nature of our collective judgement is rampant throughout the world. If we would only rid ourselves of the habit of hating and begin anew in the responsibility of loving, the Earth would, indeed, come closer to being like Christ. If we call to mind the many self-ascribed and disparaging labels that we employ; conservative, liberal, prudish, introvert, extrovert, convict, idiot, homely, fat, skinny, illiterate, degenerate, and thousands more, we would see that they only stand in the way of the perfect oneness that is expected of the human family. Each of us is a product of God's Will, created to return to Love with Him in the heavens. There must be no solitary person left-out! To do this, we must open our hearts to a degree that we have yet to ever manifest, loving every soul who has been given the gift of life. Our prayers must be strong as we stand together, witnessing to the true Light of our perfect Creator. His Virgin Mother concluded tonight by saying, **"Thank you, My little son, for your love! I will help you in writing your messages. Please tell the world that Jesus loves them, as do I! I love you with all of My Heart. I** am with you to help you to love and to come to Love. Please pray for the unborn. They need your powerful prayers."

Tuesday, October 30, 1991

As beautifully as the breaking dawn, the Holy Mother came today with another special message for the world. On this occasion, She spoke to me about the Light of Christ. It is the brilliant emanation of the Almighty Father which is projected into the world through the perfect, sacrificial, and exemplary Life of His Divine Son. Our Lord's Crucifixion and Resurrection compose the original Alpha and Omega, as we know and see them. This beatific vision is made possible by His Death on Mount Calvary. Every person on Earth is given the omnipotent power to project His Love into the world like a laser beam. Although many people believe that His Light originates outside their being, as though it is an independent and disconnected para-phenomenon, Our Lady told me today that the gleaming rays of Christ's Love actually originate inside the human heart and are transmitted from that noble seat of faith. We shine and glow with the magnificence of Divinity when we love in the way that Jesus is teaching. The Light of God emanates from our faces onto the most perilous pathways upon which we walk in His Name. Our countenance is of moonbeams and sunbeams, excellent incandescent streaks of perfection that we emit into the world because Jesus is alive in us. Indeed, the effervescent Brilliance of the Savior of the World originates inside the people He has come to redeem.

In order for us to see clearly in a world of darkness, we must allow this glorious radiance to enlighten our way, allowing Love to lead us confidently and proudly down the avenues of life. Our intellect tells us that light is a visible manifestation in space that transcends both distance and direction. We also understand that it must always have an origin. But, while it is a matter of refraction and transmission through space, the Light of Christ is also a reflection and propagation throughout time and Eternity! Our aggregate Salvation is the amalgamative essence of Christ's generative Love and the eternal destiny of all humankind. This reconstitution harmonically resonates throughout our lives when we invoke our fealty to His Sacrifice on the Cross and promise to live as He commands. Therefore, His Spirit reflects beyond our existence, while solar light is confined solely to the limits of what we can see with our eyes. This is what gives our Christian faith its warmth and illumination that can be detected by the most faint of hearts. Yes, we can see the Resurrection of Christ emanating from those who believe in Him! And, like the stellar giants of outer-space, Heavenly Light also has an originating source of power and Wisdom. The Holy Eucharist is the glowing beginning of every energetic ray of Love that mankind will ever know on Earth. Our eternal absolution is the energy of the Light of Christ. The lens for this brilliance, the magnifier, and focusing agent is the sincerity of our prayers! If we do not accept the Most Blessed Sacrament of the Altar, we will have no true Light in our lives. Indeed, we will have no Life within us.

There can be no true emanation of the Infinite Love of God if we are not mystically united to His Divinity. Further, without invoking our petitions from within our hearts, there can be no absolute magnification or intensity of the advocacy that He gives us through the Holy Spirit. And, without the Holy Eucharist, there would be no rays of grace to be transmitted and no true revelation to magnify. If we do not accept His Love through this Great Sacrament, we will have no energy to get up and go on should we trip and fall to our knees. Light will always lead to greater Light, and Love will forever beget Love. That is how Christ can be seen in the human heart with the vision that is garnered through our faithful petitions. He shines through mankind to project our goodness back to His Father's Kingdom. When we see His Countenance encompassing His Blessed Face, it is the holiness that we direct back to Him from the polished surface of our open hearts. This is our gratitude as it is returned in-kind, a mortal splendor that is offered to His paradisial Light in humble reciprocation for the allegiance that was first dispensed to the sinful world by the little Child of Bethlehem. In Him, we own the power to resonate His invincible innocence into every dark crevice of the Earth so as to clearly reveal the only Pathway to Heaven. The Saints of old are already anxiously waiting there to receive us! God wishes to see Himself as though our hearts are a mirror into which He can perceive His own Divine reflection. We shine His Love throughout the world as His Countenance is enhanced through our every pious act.

This is how the Light of Christ is given to the world from within it. Each of our souls is God's magnifier who solemnly reflects the beauty of Paradise. And, our Holy Mother told me this evening that She is the symbolic *switch* who initiates the connection between the Power in Heaven with the physical Earth that Her Son has created. The Light in the house is rising through Her miraculous intercession and, soon, will become the High Noon of our Eternal Reckoning. She asks only for the opportunity to properly prepare us to receive Him. If we fruitlessly and dangerously stumble about in the darkness of the pagan world, we will allow evil the opportunity to snatch us away from Paradise. Satan festers in the pitiless clay of creation like a vanquished mole, waiting for us to fall into his viral grasp. But, Jesus has created a holy road that is filled with Light upon which we can walk if we will humbly surrender to His Eminent Plan for our Redemption into His outstretched arms. Tonight, the Holy Mother also warned me about those who refuse to take their place in the foyer of spiritual conversion that She is revealing through Her chosen messengers. She told me that there are many people who believe that they are their own self-sustaining source of power, notwithstanding their absence from prayer and their denial of the Celebration of the Holy Eucharist. Most of them believe that they are their own sign of essential goodness. They must be warned about their lack of participation in God's Kingdom to come! To close Her message for this evening, Our Lady asked me to recite the following Biblical passage.

"Be doers of the Word and not hearers only, deluding yourselves. For if anyone is a hearer of the Word and not a doer, he is like a man who looks at his own face in a mirror. He sees himself, then goes off and promptly forgets what he looked like. But the one who peers into the perfect law of freedom and perseveres, and is not a hearer who forgets but a doer who acts, such a one shall be blessed in what he does." - *James 1:22-25* Through these words of Truth, the Holy Spirit is inviting us to become active in doing God's work and reflecting Jesus' Love toward others for the purpose of conversion and the collective Redemption of humankind. Through Our Lady's intercession, hundreds-of-millions of souls are perceiving life through the pinnacle vision of Love. She is developing our submission like a photograph to give us a permanent reminder of who Our Savior really is. His Love can propagate from heart-to-heart very simply if we become like little children in the backyard playgrounds of His Most Sacred Heart. This is a lesson that only the most innocent and unassuming will comprehend. Everyone on Earth must eventually humble themselves in time to find that Jesus is still waiting to receive them, even in their tardiness of faith and good works.

NOVEMBER 1991

Sunday, November 3, 1991

Among the many profound things that Our Lady wishes us to know, She earnestly desires our realization that the Earth does not sit afloat in the vast vacuum of a simple solar system. It actually rests on a dimensionless foundation. And, that basis is the Love that God has for us through His Son, Christ Jesus. Through our prayers, we enhance our penetrating vision into the living bedrock upon which the world is now positioned. This omnipotent sight changes our hearts so that it becomes natural and pleasing to affectionately love all peoples. There are many who readily accept the Virgin Mary's messages, but still a vast multitude who reject them. Indeed, much of humanity lives in this same darkness. Perhaps the thunder that rolls through the heavens on a stormy night is God's reminder that He is forever present, telling us that He still cares for His children with the original Love through which He created the universe. In all of this, He commands us to be holy in earnest. He showers upon us the Divine invitation to be peacemakers and knowers of the Wisdom that He reveals through His Glorious Mother, the Blessed Virgin Mary. He asks us to honestly recognize the fruits of His Holy Spirit, whether or not we have ever seen His Love in such beautiful dimensions. These bountiful benefits of holiness cannot be mocked, nor can they be falsely imitated by an errant human will.

Our Holy Mother told me today that Satan mimics the fruits of Holy Spirit in order to tempt us into believing that his sinister ways are good for us. The Evil One's perspective of the truth is only an abhorrent caricature of righteousness, not the genuine fruits themselves. He is the merchant of death with no new Life or nourishing nectar coming from him or his horrid group of followers. The true bounty of God's Love brings a succulent cider of complete health and spiritual elevation in grace. The Blessed Virgin told me that there is always one standard which will determine whether we are seeing the true fruits of Jesus' Life. Although they are rarely detected with the naked human eye, they are magnificently portrayed through daily prayer and the sanctified approach to one's life in union with the Sacraments of the Holy Mother Church. If we do not pray or desire to embrace God more deeply, we will not recognize the true fruits in other's lives or produce them from our own. It may take an extended period of time to witness the bad fruits. But, authentic Love can always be seen immediately. We must remember that Satan will never do one good deed. If he comes to us and says that he desires to love, it is another of his lies. His only compulsion is to destroy our souls. We must never fall into His trap of diabolical seduction and vagaries. We must always realize that Love and Truth will always bear-out in time because they flourish and bask in the Light of Christ. And, just like the sunshine from above, Jesus' radiance brings the bounty of His Love to full bloom. A ripe fruit of goodness is always easy to recognize.

I was given another very simple parable with which to understand the truth and Love of God in the world. Our Blessed Mother asked me to imagine being outside in a terrain where the ground is very rough and rocky. Suppose you wished to locate a perfectly level surface, but have no device to help you measure what is truly flat around you. Do you know what can determine this absolute horizontal on the Earth, and what will always depict that constancy? Our Lady told me to pour some water onto the ground, not to see its flowing movement, but to find where it forms into a puddle. As the water is caught by the landscape, it comes to rest in a cupped area, leaving a small pool. Therein, God provides the perfect level plane that we seek. The delicate surface of the water has been created by His own hand. And, ironically, mankind cannot touch it without destroying its symmetrical consistency. Nor can he detect it or judge its dimensions by being above it, but only from the vantage point of its lowly profile. If we tamper with it, we will pervert it.

To continue this parable, our Holy Mother told me that Jesus is the One whom we must seek to become aware of the uniform Truth in our lives. We cannot wish to alter or redefine His Love. If we do so, it will not be as He revealed it to the world. We will lose the view of its level constancy, just like the plane atop the water is obscured if we touch it. We must not observe Jesus from a lofty perch, but rather in humble deference to Him as He comes to the Earth. The profile of God can be seen while upon our knees with Christ standing among us. Imagine a little child squatting-down and looking very intently at a bug crawling upon the ground. In his innocence, he is very close to the creeping things. Nothing escapes the notice of a child's curiosity. And, thereto is the reason why God asks us to become little and humble. From that pose, we can see the smallest grace that He charitably offers to the Earth. This example shows us that He has given us Love, nature, and indeed, His entire Creation to assist us in knowing Him ever more concisely. Our Lady asked me to prepare a simple picture of the water resting in a small cup upon the side of the hill that She mentioned.

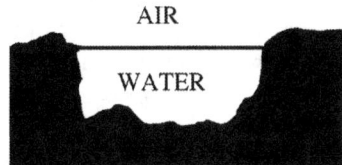

The horizontal line represents the perfectly level surface of the water which resides peacefully in the motionless state that God intends. It is in harmonious union with all the forces that He effects in Creation. Now, She asked me to consider the abundant graces that He lovingly pours from the heavens upon us, the morsels of Divinity that mystically connect Heaven and Earth. A vertical plumb dropping into the basin of water symbolizes these blessings as they descend from above.

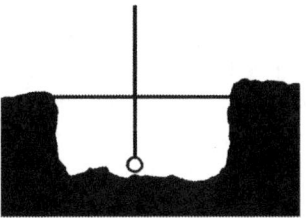

And, as if I should have already known, Our Lady showed me the following image in the midst of my picture.

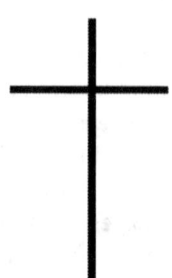

Through Her parable, She again led me to the Cross which is representative of the perfect constancy of Jesus on Earth, united with the sanctified gravity and plumb of God's graces from above. Together, they intersect in a crux, producing the living image of our Salvation. The point where they meet is the union between the seen and unseen worlds, the juncture of contact between God and man. The Cross is the magnificent writ of alliance that the Almighty Father has unilaterally composed, uniting Heaven and Earth once again. The upright plumb is His magnanimous desire and willingness to show His salvific purpose and direction, and most importantly, His miraculous intervention. The knowledge of the level and the plumb is required to build our engineering designs and structures. So, too, are the truth and guidance of Love cardinal in erecting our future in Paradise. We need the fulfilling absolution of the Cross of Calvary to gain Eternal Life. Jesus is both the horizon and the perfect perpendicular, the level and the plumb. He is the cleansing water that supports the symmetrical plane of Life through which we must pass to live again. The Virgin Mary wishes us to see that this Love is immortally exemplified in Her Innocent Son's death on the Cross, rising from the grave, and ascension into Heaven. Human hearts are the Christophers, the Christ-bearers in the world. They are His mode and means of mutual transcension. Therefore, we must be of one heart and mind with Him for His Love to be magnified and shared.

We must lift prayers so profound that the collective heart of humankind will be shockingly awakened to yet unknown beauty and possibility. Then, the warmth of Heaven will blaze into the lives of those who are lost in the frozen tundra of indifference. We must approach the Holy Sacrifice of the Mass like a child and extend our hearts into the Divine Fire like a marshmallow on the end of our first roasting stick. Grace will burn in a beautiful glow as our souls ignite with an unquenchable desire to love our brothers and sisters, and God in return. Then, mankind will be one people again. Our Holy Mother wanted me to understand a clearer distinction between Jesus' Birth and Crucifixion as they pertain to the Holy Mass. Our Savior is not conceived by or held in the hands of Our Lady at the Consecration of the Host during the Sacrifice of the Mass. The Eucharistic celebration is not His Birth. She did not hold the Body of Her Son in Her arms until after the Sacrifice was complete. The Sacred Body and Blood of Our Lord is brought into the world at the hands of God's chosen priests. We must remember that His conception in the Womb of the Virgin Mary was not yet His sacrificed Body. The provision for the Almighty Father's ultimate forgiveness came only upon His Death on the Cross and Resurrection from the dead. Christ's birth is God's eternal sign that sin no longer prevails over the world. And, His Son's Love has actualized the eradication of our sins from Creation.

The Sacrifice of the Mass and the Holy Eucharist do not represent the "regeneration" of the Birth of Jesus, but rather His Death and Resurrection. It is the Passion and Crucifixion of Christ that truly changed the eternal destiny of all humankind. The Holy Mother consented to that manifestation by bearing the Son of God into the mortal world. But, it is Jesus Christ *alone* who circumscribed the legacy and destiny of mankind to redeem us. The Eternal Truth of His Redemptive Sacrifice must never be diminished. Jesus is our Salvation! And, the Holy Eucharist is the ragged and tortured Body that hung on the Cross, not the plenary Flesh that emerged from the Virgin's womb. The Fruit of the Immaculate Conception was ripened by the Sacrifice of Death! The Most Blessed Sacrament is the perfect Fruit of the Cross. If all those who protested the Holy Catholic Church during the history of Christianity had but realized the beauty of the Holy Sacrifice of the Mass, they would never have left the Original Apostolic Church. The Protestant religions must come to realize that they do not have the Bread of Life because they do not have priests! Some protestant churches may proclaim to be enjoying communion with Jesus' Sacred Body and Blood, but they are completely and absolutely in error.

God allows the Body of His Son to be consecrated on the Earth by His priests alone! It is not a decision of man, but a Divine vocation and mandate from Heaven. Jesus Christ, the Savior of the World, comes to the Holy Mass in His Crucified Flesh to replace the bread and wine that are present in the hands of His priests. At the moment our reverend fathers Consecrate the Host and Cup, the bread and wine are completely gone, ceasing to exist. Present in our midst and held aloft for the world to see is the precious Body, Blood, Soul, and Divinity of Our Lord and Savior, Jesus Christ. Nothing in Creation can obscure or rescind this eternal fact! Yet, there are many who cannot accept that their Savior mystically appears in Creation as the Bread of Life. This miracle is performed by the power and authority of God, which no mortal can question or duplicate. Our Holy Mother describes it much like the soul of a flower. It is the indescribable Heaven before the eyes of man which no human mind can capture or destroy. Jesus could reach-out and physically touch everyone at the

Consecration if He chose to do so. But, our Holy Mother says, **"What would that do for human faith?"**

Many people try very hard to disavow the necessity for faith, believing only what their eyes can see or their ears have sensibly heard from their blind theology instructors. They will only accept what their senses grasp, rather than what their hearts perceive! Many wish to keep everything in the *seen world* because they lack the faith to believe in the *unseen* Kingdom of God. These people are pragmatists and practitioners of physicality and worldliness. They lack the strength to be holy by faith so they demand their right to see a change before they will surrender their hearts! Their worldliness will not elevate them to realize that God can change His Creation without their knowledge or permission. The Roman Catholic Church is the original Apostolic Church, founded by Jesus Christ upon the Earth for the Salvation of all humankind. It was started by the same Holy Spirit who anointed the Apostles on the day of Pentecost. From that moment forward, they set-out on a penitential journey, seeking those who would love God and respond to their prayers, petitions, and ministries. And, the Almighty Father validated their evangelical credentials by bestowing the ultimate gift of His Son's Sacred Flesh as the Holy Eucharist. It bears being repeated in this Diary that the Lamb of God coexists in Heaven and on Earth through the Miracle of the Consecration at the hands of His priests.

Our Holy Mother told me quite tersely today that only a Catholic priest can bring the Miracle of Transubstantiation, not Martin Luther or his descendant followers, neither John Wesley or his spiritual offspring, nor any other public or private protestors of the sacred and disciplined institution of the Holy Priesthood. Those who find it difficult to visually subscribe to the change and action of the Holy Sacrifice should look intently at the Life of Padre Pio and his stigmata. This precious priest certified Christ's Eucharistic Sacrifice of Love during the Twentieth century. His sanctified Life bears the undeniable witness to the greatness of the Holy Mass. Our Lady finished Her overpowering proclamations by reminding me that I was born on the anniversary of Padre Pio's stigmatization, September 20th, which he bore for a half-century. Her beatific intercession to my brother and me is a fruit of this priest's pious suffering and prayers. **"The Life of Padre Pio wins the argument with those who believe that God will not manifest change and grace in human form. Indeed, many stigmatized disciples have walked the Earth to show humankind the magnificence of Jesus' Sacrifice. I invite you to remember and imitate the Life of Saint Francis of Assisi. The lives of the Saints were never in vain. They were of Christ's Light, as you are Christ's Light. You have Padre Pio's torch; The Love of Christ in your generation. My little one, carry the torch high for all to see! Brightly it will light the way to Truth and eliminate the darkness for many. Together, we will pray for that end."**

Tuesday, November 5, 1991

At nine-thirty tonight, Our Lady returned to pray with us. She began, **"Good evening, My little ones. I come to you very happy today because you are still praying for Me as good little children! I have another special message for you. My messages are very important and I hope that you remember them always..."** The Blessed Mother told me of the many times and ways that we are separated as a people by classification and discrimination. It is somewhat the nature of man to be divisive and self-actualizing. Most of us want to be free and independent from others. But, our differences are only one of the barriers to our unity. We must recognize that our absence of Love is a direct product of such disconnectedness. Although most people do not deliberately isolate themselves in an attempt to destroy their unity, the destruction of the natural cohesion among the human family is a by-product of their selfishness. In other words, they are not inherently evil, but rather indifferent towards the debilitating effect that they are having on the body of humanity. It is very important for us to become unified in Love, despite all of our desires for separatism and individual distinction. Diversity cannot be manipulated for evil purposes if our unique individuality always provides for the endless possibilities of Divine beauty and unity at the Altar of Sacrifice.

For example, when we celebrate the founding freedom in our country and call it Independence Day, we have bombs that detonate in the air. These fireworks are quite symmetrically beautiful, yet diverse in color and shape. Imagine a magnificent display exploding overhead. The widespread geometrical patterns make this sight very breathtaking to the eye. This is what mankind wishes to exhibit to others, but unintentionally fails to design or choreograph his gleaming explosions in a demonstration that is harmonious with the Heart of God. Humanity actually loses the symmetry of Love in the process of being different. Our Holy Mother told me that we do not have to sacrifice our individuality in order to be Love. It is the division that is caused by our reckless self-absorption that hampers our true magnification of grace. We must lift our diversity upward into the skies toward the Face of God for them to be beautiful. Heretofore, it has become extremely destructive upon the ground. Generations of humanity have undergone incredible suffering because of the exclusion wrought between people. Imagine the same beautiful fireworks display exploding on its launch pad. There would be intense terror, damage, and deadliness. This is what we have done with our freedom and diversity. We must, instead, elevate it into the heavens, offering our lives to the magnificent possibilities that God conceives so that we may become beautiful and unique at the same time. We will nevermore be afraid of sacrificing our characteristic self-identity because the exhilaration of celestial bliss will bind us together as one Love with all the Heavenly Hosts.

There is not a soul in the heights of Glory who has lost the gift of personal identification because everyone in Paradise wishes to be seen as the perfect emanation of the Life of Christ. God does not require that we lose this indelible mark of our essence. He calls us to be perfectly identifiable by all of the Courts of Heaven. Jesus made each of us unique in our capacity to magnify the infinite facets of His Divinity. And yet, He came to tell us that, in all of this limitless potential, we must still be one in Love. We should be united in prayer and the thanksgiving Eucharist to help us become so. Our Holy Mother continued with another example regarding the playing of a piano. We play songs that are made of notes. Sometime we use just a few, while at other times many multitudes with several pianists in accompaniment. The most beautiful renditions are those with the greatest diversity in tones, composed to the finest and most intricate harmonies and melodies. But, imagine if there was no time signature or key structure. What if all notes were played at random with no encompassing purpose or periodicity? Would this produce a soothing or heart-lifting sound? Without a melody and associated harmonies, there is no Life in any work. They cannot reflect the symmetry of Creation as God intends, and neither can they bring or sustain peace.

The symphony of man is written in the polyphonic infinitude of the Heart of Jesus Christ. It is His rhythm of Love that we must learn to perform with fluent masterfulness. He is the Virtuoso of the Redemptive Score that was played in the Command Performance of Calvary, given at the request of His Almighty Father. He was not simply the perfect soloist in the prized "first-chair." In history's darkest hour, He was the Conductor and the Composer, alike. He was the entire symphony; the sinew of the bows and the tension of the strings. He was the clarion call of the brass over the pealing thunder of the percussion. He was even the delicate winds that whistled across the beams of His Sacrificial Throne in a call for the Flaming Steed which He will mount for His triumphant Return into His Creation. Jesus Christ is the First and Last Perfect Man to die for the Redemption of humankind. His magnificent Cross is where we should place our collective eyes so that we can understand the tempo in which God asks us to live. It is possible for all men to be one in Christ, one song, one beauty, and one heart in Love. There can be great diversity along with unity and brotherhood. God intends for us to play our own part in a harmonious resonance with the Hosts of Heaven. Our Lady's graceful accompaniment to Her Divine Son is miraculously perfect. Woe to those who raise their arrogant heads to critique Her Immaculate Divinity! Her Sacrifice rings more majestically than that of any creature ever placed within the universe. A holocaust of the entire spectrum of history cannot equal the impact upon the Omnipotent Heart of God that Her grief-stricken immolation convoked. Yet, look how splendidly that She towers above Creation in the grace of the Almighty Father. She is the Queen of Calvary who will forever stand beside the Throne of Her Regal Offspring. Hail Jesus and Mary!

Wednesday, November 6, 1991

My brother and I began the Holy Rosary at 9:20 p.m. and Our Lady came to give us another message. She began with these beautiful words, **"Good evening, My beloved children! The world is changed by your prayers and by your continuing effort of composing your Diary. I am very happy that you never grow tired of My messages of Love. I will help you in such an important gift which you have taken into your heart. Today, I would like to speak to you about the Love of God. Among all of the attention that has been given to the prescription of Love through Jesus' Sacrifice and to the changing and variant natures of man, it is important to remember the gentleness of the Love of God, Who is all-responsible and complete..."** Our Holy Mother again asked me to paraphrase Her thoughts so that everyone will be able to receive them in this miraculous record. As I consider this request from Her, I wonder whether it is also a message that She does not wish us to scrupulously dissect Her words at the expense of what She is trying to relate to us. Today, She told me that the Love of God is the foundation upon which Jesus was sent and Creation is made complete. This original inception of Divinity is the reason for all that *is*. Love is the spark and Light of Life. Jesus has lovingly created the world for us to inhabit during our holy incubation. This ground is the stage, a podium for Love to unfold and grow into fruition. He wishes for us to come to spiritual maturity in this present generation.

When Love blossoms from our hearts, we begin to realize that the end of human existence is near. Immortal Life is at the door, ready to consume us in the beautiful hopes that flashed through our hearts during the many sacrificial days of our lives. We must pray for our brothers and sisters to realize that Love is the reason that everything has come into being. Esteemed architects plan mighty structures. And so, God planned for Jesus to encircle and deliver His children back into the original Womb of Divinity. Our Lord intends for every created thing to revert its course back to Love again. We must earnestly come to understand this inversion, this process of converting our lives. We commence it through prayer from the heart. We see best when we fully comprehend that we are one humanity, one spirit who seeks the transformation from emptiness and blindness into fulfillment and beatific vision. Further, our holiness must be remembered and lived once it is learned. Those who have never understood what it means to be pious must begin to anticipate and prepare for the Second Coming of Christ. The breath of righteousness is the gentle Love of God, His beautiful Spirit that He exhales both upon and through us. The caress of the Most Holy Trinity is wholly magnificent, like when our biological fathers are at their most soft and warm.

The hand of our Almighty Father is extended to praise and assure us, not to punish or divide us. His encompassing veil of protection is oftentimes forgotten amidst His somewhat exaggerated domination and authoritative wrath. This is why most fear to approach Him. They look upon Him as a taskmaster who is going to require more of them than they are comfortably willing to surrender. In this misconception, they are at a distance from His kindness, softness, and gentleness which is much like the fur of a kitten, the beauty of a flower, or the gentle petting that brings warm chills to our souls. This is the essence of His Love for us. Mercy is abundant for those who accept the infinite compassion of God and extend it to others. It is for everyone, especially those who do not yet accept His Kingdom. Our Infinite Creator came to teach us in the person of Our Savior. He understands that we are sinfully human and is, therefore, willing to grant us the time we need to convert our lives into the image that Jesus projects. Above many other things, Our Lady is a reminder of the soft compassion of God, telling us that His Love is fully exemplified through Her motherly grace. Mary's caress will always be possible for the world because Her embrace awaits our conversion. She asks that we pray as one humanity with fervent hope and love.

Thursday, November 7, 1991

Today, the Virgin Mother described the reverberation of Love through time. She said that the sound of the Light of Christ is the echo of God's Love for us, reflecting from one generation to the next and back again. It is enlightening to know that Light can be heard in God's Kingdom. The Blessed Mother reminded us that we do not see Him clearly because our vision is skewed and distorted by the nature of our sinfulness. But, when we come to live as Jesus asks and listen to Her Divine messages, we see the symmetrical perfection that God intends for our Life and for our world.

 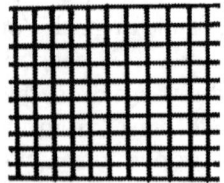

The organized pattern on the right is the way Jesus intends for us to see His genius. It is a vision of balance and uniformity emanating from Love. However, the shape depicted on the left shows how we actually understand the grid of perfection on the right. While they are actually the same diagram, we do not see the flawless Kingdom in the way God generously presents it. That is why *we* must change, instead of arrogantly presuming that God must alter the Truth that He has spoken through Christ. It is very difficult for mankind to recognize the Cross on which Jesus died in our garbled view of the Creation that the Father provides. We must unclutter our minds and allow our perceptions to be united in His Heart so that we can know our place and understand the focus He asks us to hold. When we surrender our hearts and allow ourselves to be conscripted into the body of His righteous people, our view of Creation will match His own in a sacrificially profound way.

The Cross is apparent in the Kingdom which God asks us to see and the Life He wishes us to lead. Although the Crucifixion of Christ stands majestically in time, it is quite difficult to discern its presence within the contorted view of humanity's 20th century mind. Imagine trying to locate Jesus' Cross in the previous left-hand picture. We must peer into Creation in the same way our Heavenly Father gazes upon us to recognize the Cross as the means to accept the Love of Jesus. It is very important to remember that our vision is never holy unless it is through the focus of the Messiah's great Passion and Death. As our vision matures, we will realize that Christ completely consumes our lives. Our Holy Mother told me that only the heart can perceive the beautiful symmetry of Love with its stillness, peace, plan, and order. If we refuse to live it, our vision is blurred by chaos and disorder. She added something very stunning tonight, **"My son, it is very important for Me to have pity for all of My little children. I love each one so much, with the same pity as when I held My Son in My arms who gave His Life for you. You know with what pity I felt and held His Precious Body, and with what hope His passing would bring the world to Love again. My hope was not in vain, as was His Death not in vain. That Pieta, that picture of pity, awaits all of My children whom I hold in My arms."** I asked Her why it is pity, and She promptly responded, **"It is pity because of the terrible trials which mankind heaps upon Him. Mankind's self-imposed punishment can be avoided by accepting Jesus. In addition, it is pity because My Son looks with Mercy upon those who are pitied. Therefore, I pity all poor sinners who seek to accept My Son and pray for His Mercy."**

Friday, November 8, 1991

The Holy Mother has come to the world to help in the most important of all persuasions: *To convince humanity that Jesus Christ is the Holy Eucharist.* When we gaze upon the Consecrated Host of the Catholic Altar, we are truly seeing the Lord Jesus Christ come to the Earth. This is a matter of factual knowledge. The bread and wine take their leave and make way for the Savior of the world in an instant, although He looks the same as the gifts which preceded Him. As She reiterated this to me, I asked a question regarding this miraculous transformation. Although I absolutely believe that Jesus is present in the Holy Eucharist, the very formation of the question in my mind betrayed the hint of a doubt about its true essence. Our Lady responded, **"My little son, you are very human and have doubts naturally and beautifully. But, your participation helps build your tremendous faith. Remember that it is believing without seeing. There is no such thing as doubtless faith. And, this is why it may be strong, because it has a weak to be compared to. It is not like Love that is one universal constant without measure."** She asked me to ponder whether I believed Jesus also had to once have faith. I turned my thoughts toward this contemplation while She continued. Our Lord knew that faith was founded in Himself and He also understood that He was bringing Love to the world as He came into it and walked upon its paths. His purpose is still to help all humankind grow faithfully in the knowledge of the Almighty Father through His own intercession for the restoration of His Kingdom.

To this day, He asks that everyone believe in faith that He will soon return as the same merciful Son of God. Jesus testified that those who know Him also know the Father who sent Him. His continuing Life is the factual evidence. But, our faith is oftentimes weaker because of our humanness. Notwithstanding, we must always strive for doubtless belief in the same way that we try to hear the sound of the Light of Christ. Faith is weak when our heart is weak, but it thrives when the Holy Spirit is allowed to augment its journey into our consciousness. While Jesus' Love is the initiating element, our Christian conviction is a mighty function of our love for Him. We must allow the fruits of His Sacrifice to nourish and govern our lives. This surrender to the grace of God is the evidential act of faith. Our Lady told me that if I try to deny myself the right to be human, I am also denying my need to have faith. Jesus came as a man, although a perfect one at that. We are to emulate His humanity by responding to the perfection that He teaches. He tells us concisely and clearly that being human does not make us naturally bound to error, although the sin which we inherited caused humanity to be cast-down from Paradise in the first place. We are not exiled because we are human, but rather because we are sinful humans. Jesus came to restore the children of God into the likeness of our original conception in the mind of God. So, we must remember that our love comes through faith in what Christ represents. We learn to overcome sin by first accepting that it is not only possible, but commanded through the Gospels. We must have faith in Love, Himself, and be happy with our progress as we strive for that perfectly peaceful objective.

Saturday, November 9, 1991
"Good evening again, My precious children. I love you dearly! Thank you for praying. You are doing the holy work of My Son. You are telling your brothers and sisters about Love to bring them out of the darkness. You must give this message to mankind: *Tell him God is Love."* Our Lady asked me to look at these words as though they were being reflected in a mirror.

Tell Him God Is Love = L I G H T

Love is the Light of the world. We should always remember that we are wanted and needed by Christ, letting our light shine before all men. When we do, we are reflecting the Light of God perfectly and reciprocally back to the Earth that He claims as His own.

Monday, November 11, 1991
Tonight, our Blessed Mother provided an example to challenge the faithless opinions of those who reject the Holy Eucharist because their eyes do not detect the physical change of the bread and wine into the Body and Blood of Jesus. It is quite simple. Consider if the communion host was shaped in a concave/convex fashion, depending upon which direction was facing you. If the priest held the convex surface forward and at the moment of Consecration inverted it so that the concave side was presented to you, would you be able to detect the change if you were not allowed to see the switch? The answer is no. From your position in time and space, you would still see the communion host as being flat as it rests in the hands of the priest. Hence, our eyes do not provide a sound basis for determining the Truth that God manifests to us. Our Lady wishes to convince every human being that Jesus' Body and Blood miraculously replace the bread and wine at the Consecration in the Holy Mass, bearing the Bread of Life to the Earth. However, our physical eyes tell us that they appear to be unchanged. Again, this is a function of our mortal sight. With immortal vision, we can see that the bread and wine of the Catholic Altar become the Body, Blood, Soul and Divinity of Jesus Christ. It is time for everyone to realize that their Savior is physically in this world as the Most Blessed Sacrament. For two thousand years, He has been true to His promise of being with us through the end of time. If we invoke the faith to believe that the Divine Eucharist is the Body of Christ, we will witness the eternal liberation

of our souls from their imprisonment in time and the bonds of the physical world. No one can change the Truth of this Holy Sacrament. They must either accept it, or deny it to their own unfortunate diminishment.

Tuesday, November 12, 1991

The Light of Christ reflects through time like a mighty beacon. There is a powerful surge in the luminous nature of His Light through the many prayers and works of great Love. The Virgin Mary is the Mother of the Heavenly Luminaries. She is the Woman Clothed with the Sun who bore Brilliance, Himself, into the world to conquer the darkness. Sincere efforts in Love pass through time like the wake of a huge ship voyaging the celestial seas. Our Love expands into the future, changing Creation from the depths of every heart who is open enough to hope for eternal unity and peace. Through our faithful acceptance of everything that is of God, we echo new waves which tender the hearts of humankind in joyfulness and gratitude for the reality of Christ's Love for us. We must not become disturbed or distracted by those who arrogantly criticize Our Lady's intercession because they, too, are washed by the sacrity of the Blood of Christ to the shore upon which They both stand. Acceptance of the Glorious Mother of Humanity is inherently a matter of faith in the forgiveness of our sins. From the beginning of time, She has proclaimed that God will forgive our every transgression if we submit to Her Beloved Son, Jesus. This Infinite Mercy has been offered to humankind from its Sacred Conception through the perfect grace of the Immaculate Virgin. We must partake of the boundless charity that is being dispensed by our Heavenly Father by embracing His gift of the Most Blessed Virgin Mother. In the wake of the humility and affirmation of this Ark of the New Covenant, we have already been redeemed.

Our Lady told me tonight that we must always be compassionate toward others. We live in darkness, while treating our brothers and sisters as though we wish our ship to pass quietly and indifferently past them in the night. We must, instead, reach-out to accompany and guide them, lifting every sorrowful heart toward the future that we confidently proclaim to be about to dawn. This is responsible compassion. We are called to understand the power that lives on the Earth through Jesus, Incarnate in the Tabernacles of the Catholic Church. He blesses our hearts with His Holy Spirit so that we will accept the Seven Sacraments of His Apostolic Church on Earth with perfect allegiance at each morning sunrise. This is the call of God through the Blessed Virgin Mary. These gifts of infinite proportions are both immortal and magnificent. Time is only of a world that is ultimately consumed by Eternal Life. Too many people fear that their lives will have no lasting effect. To that end, they struggle every moment of the day acquiring estates and building municipal kingdoms which they hope will promote a material legacy for which they can long be remembered. They do not realize that their empires will soon become a pile of rubbish which will serve only to fuel the fires of God's Almighty Justice. We must invoke greater wisdom and choose to build a world of higher Love for one another, one which will last through time and every element, leaving only the sweetest of memories for us to take past the dawn of forever. Only an inner-beauty of this magnitude will carry our souls into Eternity.

If we reach-out arm-in-arm and embrace humanity with a convicted strength of compassion and unity, we will approach and transcend this threshold of majesty, reflecting the breathtaking rays of the Eternal Kingdom like children sparkling in the sun. Those among us who are strong are called to offer untold heroic sacrifices and lifetimes of self-denial so that the frail and decrepit can also be lifted to distinction and dignity. Those in despair, along with the blind and the lame, must be given new reason for hope and a concise vision that Love is their strength. When we do this in the Name of Jesus, they will finally stand again. Yes, we must all be swept into the arms of His Love and be elevated above everything that has heretofore damaged our fruitful progress toward the desires of our hearts. We must stand with Our Lady, united in Her prophecy that Christ is drawing all things to Himself as we speak. The Blessed Virgin Mary is preparing us for the Second Coming of Our Savior into His earthly Kingdom. Come that rapidly approaching day, we will experience the fulfillment of every expectation that has been conceived in human hearts since the foundation of the material world.

Thursday, November 14, 1991

Our Lady has come like the dawn to awaken the sorrowful and sleeping eyes of those who yet do not know that Jesus is alive. Her message is that all humanity must see Love as the ultimate power in the universe. Indeed, Love transcends both the seen and unseen. The manifestation of the Father's Mercy in our world is Jesus Christ because He owns the Earth on which we live. He is our Champion, Advocate, and Savior. If we do not offer our love to others in complete abandonment of ourselves, our lives will be insufficient in delivering our souls to total unity and peace. We must eliminate the imperfections of bias, anger, false expectations, and transient human whims. Our Love must be as free-flowing as a river between ourselves and all others. Jesus tells us clearly that we have neither the authority nor the ability to stop Him from reclaiming His Kingdom. Therefore, if we are to be saved from this world of pitch darkness, we must become the Love that He requires. Our Lady provided a parable which exemplifies the simplicity of Her Wisdom regarding the human heart. She has told me many times that Love moves between people through suffering and prayer. Suppose that the human heart is a bottle which is labeled with the markings of our favorite soda that someone has left for us. After a very difficult day of labor, we eagerly anticipate opening it and taking that first swig of refreshing delight. We envision the hiss as we pop the top, followed by the anticipation of the bubbling-carbonation that will leave a burning trail pouring down our parched throat. At the closing bell, we take the bottle in hand. But, much to our disappointment, the familiar release of pressure is not heard as the opener pries loose the cap. And, upon quickly taking a curious sip, we confirm that it is flat and not worth drinking.

The liquid represents the apparent composition of one who believes that they embody the most fulfilling qualities of life. But, their inadequate nature reveals that they harbor only emptiness and indifference. They contain the consistency of life, but have created a reason not to be of the refreshment of Love. They do not encapsulate the essence that would bring sweetness to the hearts of others. Our Holy Mother says that there is no reason for ever failing to love our brothers and sisters. Those who will not love oftentimes feel self-justified in their conduct because of the veils of their intellectual apathy. They always feel the need to grasp onto something to become more stable and fulfilled. It is apparent that they must embrace the Love of God! The answer is for them to begin to pray. Prayer fills the heart with the syrup of holiness, mixed with the ingredients of life and the effervescence of Divine grace. The chambers of the soul become aerated and compressed with millions of little carbonated bubbles that are the vibes of the Spirit of God, waiting to be released for the enjoyment of all humankind. Then, when it is opened either by circumstance or suffering, fizzling-fulfillment rushes from the container into the lives of everyone else. This is how the fruits of Love blossom from our hearts. Prayer tenders our soul to make it easier for Love to permeate the walls that we have erected in our lives. But, there are many people who release their Love the same way that a bottle of soda loses its carbonation while sitting on a shelf for an extended period of time. It escapes in microscopic quantities with unnoticeable effect and no benefit to anyone. This is why suffering is such an effective tool for God to employ.

Human suffering brings about the flourishing of Love. When we face tragedy or if our peace is ever destroyed, we always suffer. We wish for our serenity and comfort to be restored. If this occurs in the form of a confrontation or breach of peace by others, an immediate outpouring of forgiveness is required to restore our lost tranquility. The overwhelming response of human compassion that is evident in the many disasters of life also speak to this instantaneous opening of the heart. Our Lady is describing the nature of a broken heart. When a heart filled with Love is crushed by pain, sorrow, or injury, it manifests the explosive nature of the Almighty Father. There is truly a wound to the heart, an opening where God can be seen in the soul. We gaze upon all of the beauty that lies within mankind as it is released into the world and met with reciprocal compassion by those who have witnessed the Crucified Christ. It is no longer a simple permeation like a soda going flat on a shelf, but an actual opening of the heart as though the cap has been ripped away from a beverage after having been violently shaken. The Good News is that Jesus lives in our hearts with a Divine combustion that no force in Creation can stop once it is released. Indeed, His Love will never be depleted.

We should hope that our entire world will soon become exactly like the inside of a heart that is filled with Love. Then, there will be the inversion of which Our Lady has spoken. On that day, the globe will be turned inside-out and we will see the final explosion that will ignite Heaven upon the Earth as we are released from exile like a beverage pouring over the lip of Eternity. Therefore, the Love from deep within our souls must be the first manifestation that our brothers and sisters know of us. This will make the world a function of the Holy Spirit, instead of the cold and indifferent strains of intellectuals. This is the Light that Our Lady asks us to live. Believe it or not, we exist in a society where tenderness and compassion reside at the threshold of each day like a beggar hoping for the most casual gaze. We live a Life where forgiveness is the most precious gift that multitudes spend their lives seeking, yet never seem to find. This is a modern-day age where purity and perfect holiness are regarded as being obsolete and altruistic fantasies, rather than a required state of being. Fortunately for us, this is also an existence where the family of humankind is coming quickly to the realization of the pricelessness of unity under God. Our congregation at the Catholic Tabernacles to receive the Most Precious Body and Blood of Jesus Christ is the culmination of this ultimate dream. We can be united no more concisely under any other grace.

Friday, November 15, 1991
Throughout the centuries, the world has been heavily peppered with the corpses of millions of souls who have fought and died for no more than a land to call their own and a place to lay their head. But, the Blessed Virgin Mary has come to tell us that there is a higher battle of a more noble purpose. It is the fight for the hearts of those who will win the reward of Heaven. We are the soldiers of dear allegiance to God in that spiritual war. Our Lady has come with a message of great urgency and, within Her Immaculate grace, She holds the battle-plan that is the key to our final victory. Therefore, She has come again today to rally the consciences of Her faithful children with another message, calling us to holiness, embraced in prayer, and charging in spirit to the depth of our souls in cadence with the solemnity and prophetic Promise of Her Champion Son, Jesus the Christ.

"Good evening, My special little sons. Welcome to My arms! I love you very much..." There are many people who believe that they have the authority and ability to judge the works of God. Absent of prophetic Light, they invoke the audacity to predict what He will do next. Such people are quite surprised when they eventually discover that Jesus is greater than they once professed and that He goes places and performs miracles that they could have never anticipated. Our Blessed Mother calls this the eternal awakening of their souls. Jesus is not confined, confounded, or limited by human thoughts or assumptions which are only our vain attempts to define the criteria of His Will. **"Many people will be stricken with awe by this Diary! It is your fellow faithsians who will attempt to disparage My work. I regret that many of them believe they can dictate how God does His work."** The Almighty Father allows these awakenings to destroy the indifference which is sorrowfully rooted within the Church. Mankind sees the journey to becoming the full-blooming flower of Love as being too great in suffering and sacrifice. So, he focuses upon one petal of the flower in an attempt to imitate it, and then proudly claims that he is a full-budding spiritual beauty. As Jesus provides these enlightening graces, people are more apt to see the unintentioned assumptions and biases that previously clouded the purity of their mortal vision. Many more supernatural revelations will occur in the future to assist thousands in their understanding that the intercession of Heaven can neither be constrained or misconstrued by the errors of our human intellect.

Our Lady asked me to ponder the image of the beautiful skyline of a large metropolitan city. We have used technology and architecture to build and reshape the cityscapes of the world from our creative points of view. Unfortunately, many people also believe that they can dictate God's entrance into the world for others in much the same way. The Almighty Father does not yield or conform to the conscience of man nor the means with which humankind develops and constructs the physical environment at large. As a result, when His Love is dispensed in ways that do not comply with our inadequate expectations, the Father's Divine messages are not always believed to be true. Subsequently, His messengers are also derided and persecuted to all extremes. Ironically, however, the most genius of all human architects, the man with the greatest vision, Jesus Christ, was killed because He wished the world to read the blueprint that would allow for the construction of a Divine mansion for every person on Earth. His Plan will provide for the protection of all, rendering no one ever homeless or helpless again. But, mankind believes that he has the power to create a mirror in which the Creator will see Himself. Instead, it is God who holds the mirror for us to inspect our own helpless souls and each of our individual lives. No mortal man possesses any power or authority unless it is granted by our benevolent Father in Heaven. Every inch of human mobility is a gift that is granted through the charity of Jesus Christ. Therefore, we cannot dictate to His Father what He is allowed to do. He will never again, and I repeat "never," bow to the whims of a people who do not understand His power and Divinity. Mankind has no other choice than to be humbled by that.

Our Holy Mother led me to understand more deeply the power of our prayers. She asked me to envision the reflection of a beautiful skyline in a lake beside a city. The Almighty Father's endorsement of our desire for symmetry and peaceful composition reflects from the surface of the water through the genius He employs within nature. God sees the spiring signature of our skyscrapers just as we see them in the waves. Likewise, if we engender a desire for beauty and build the same peaceful symmetry with our prayers, He will see our arching souls, too. But, we do not always pray in accordance with what is holy and righteous. So, how do we learn to recite our petitions and ask God what to do? From what source can we draw knowledge to know what He wishes for the world? Our Holy Mother said, **"The Pope can see! He can see the skyline and above, and how God intercedes. While he does not dictate what God will do, he prayerfully petitions for that which God can do. It is the intercession of this Pope with such Divine vision which brings God to the hearts of men through the Holy Church. There have been no Popes who have not led their flock to Jesus Christ in Love. They have all been infallible in this leadership. Any perceptions and misinformation to the contrary have arisen through the abridged opinions of fallible human unbelievers..."**

Every priest of the Roman Catholic Church holds the same Divinity that is reflected by our Holy Father, Pope John Paul II. Many bear his singular spiritual vision, but none is his equal in infallibility. No other is the Vicar of Christ on the Earth. This Office is held solely by the Successor of Saint Peter, whomever he may be during a given period in time. Our Lady refocused tonight upon the great powers of Consecration and Absolution which She says are of primary importance to the unification of all humankind. Anything from God is Divine. Priests of the Holy Catholic Church are asked by Him, and simultaneously empowered through Him, to manifest Jesus' Body, Blood, Soul, and Divinity into the world upon the Altar of the Holy Sacrifice of the Mass. Further, in reflection of the Original Apostles, Catholic priests can absolve anyone of their sins with the complete power and advocacy of the Will of God. The Blessed Virgin said that we do not realize how special we are.

We must remember that Our Lord's Mystical Body on Earth is still in its mortal frame. It will be so until He returns in Glory to bring Judgment and Everlasting Life to the faithful of the Church. Our Holy Mother is moving the basis for our lives toward His Plan for Eternity in beauty and celestial exhilaration. Wouldn't it be nice if all people in the world utilized our planet as a foundation for launching the Love of Her Son? How fine things would be if we did not expend our futures building skylines which only perish through time, element, and planned obsolescence. God desires that we live like little children playing joyfully together in a sandbox. And, while we are constructing our castles, we should place a Tabernacle in every building and ordain a priest to Consecrate the gifts of bread and wine for everyone else to receive. Then, the Creator of all Life would physically appear at each sight! We could also consider placing a Crucifix atop every structure that we erect. They would be the lightning rods which would invite Our Resurrected Savior to come into our midst in jubilation and victory. We are guaranteed to dictate our own happiness by attending the Holy Sacrifice of the Mass. There, we establish the highest and most noble skyline by accepting the Truth of Christ's real Sacramental Presence.

Sunday, November 17, 1991
"My sons, I come in a state of great joy! You are excising the cutting-tip from the projectile of worldly motion for many souls. The winds of peace remain unpierced when man's mobility and motion have been suppressed. The messages of your Diary will blunt the ability of many to live the fruitless motivations of their minds..." The miraculous intercession of our Holy Mother is severing the forward-tip from the sword of mindless distraction that is assailing the future children of Heaven. She knows that the peaceful calm of God will remain when our fruitless mobility and motion cease. Over and again, we have been reminded that Her messages serve for the reconstruction of dignity and the serenity of Paradise. She provided this visual image of the projectile of our worldly motion:

Our Lady is blunting the leading edge of those who obstinately refuse to unite in the Sacred Heart of God by providing Her overwhelming grace as an enlightening countermeasure, rendering their swirling intellectual minds at a loss to move any further without Her. Our supposedly educated teachers keep us from living in peace when they reject the handwriting that Christ is etching upon their souls. The miraculous Wisdom of Our Lady is helping everyone to recline in silence and await the swift winds of the Holy Spirit that will momentarily consume us. Our worldly perspective falters and stumbles when we use it to decipher and reconcile God's miraculous manifestations of Love on behalf of His children. If we look at our Almighty Father through the eyes of the world, He seems to be unexplainable and inconsistent with the unfolding product which we believe precedes Him. Without the ability to penetrate His mind, our burdensome ignorance is so great that we can go no farther than where we are now. Therefore, we must stop so that He can reach us. Our Lady wants us to desist in our headstrong flight toward spiritual destruction.

Have you ever noticed that elderly people are usually the most peaceful among us? They have virtually stopped their motion because they desire to live in quietness and accord. The accumulation of their days has blunted the cutting-tip of their desire for any fast-paced stimulation as they find themselves drawn into the arms of their serene contemplations about the meaning of life. Many of them have come to understand the beauty of God through the shock and grief that have accompanied their length of days. These horrible moments have caused them to describe their own sorrows as being instances when "time stood still." However, it was not the clock on the wall that came to a halt. The worldly activity of their senses ceased when their mind was moved from the disorganized collage of human existence into the symmetrical logic which God calls human suffering. This, too, is what the grace of Our Lady's messages is all about.

Tonight, She warned me that not everyone who reads my Diary will be convinced that it is authentic. Sadly, there will also be many advisory priests who will cause defray to Her work. I asked our Holy Mother why a priest who is alive in the Holy Spirit would not place value in a work that is overflowing with such Truth. She responded that Her intercessory manifestations such as interior locution or direct apparition are simple, direct, and clear. Many priests do not see God as being that precisely revelatory. Second, Jesus is still contemplating His great Return, and there are many people who think that our Virgin Mother's intercession somehow diminishes that great moment. They errantly maintain that the Glorious revelation of Christ's Second Coming cannot be usurped or preceded. Our Lady has a grand surprise for them! Every soul should remember that She magnificently preceded Her Son's initial appearance on Earth. Indeed, God has sent Her back many times already during the past 2000 years since then. Therefore, the Immaculate Virgin has been serving as the predecessor to our Redemption from the foundation of the world. Why, then, would She not be the prefatory grace that will bring to fruition the eminent Salvation which God intends for His divinely-civilized union of souls?

Some priests and other religious practitioners mistakenly feel left-out of the procession of delivering God's messages to humankind on Earth. Therefore, they refuse to believe the revelations of laypersons and others who are proclaiming to be witnesses to the intercession of the Blessed Virgin Mary. Furthermore, they choose to look at the faults of the messengers as a criterion to invalidate their credibility instead of realizing the great fruit of the Holy Spirit that is before them. God asks all souls to be His messengers. He wishes us to faithfully flock to the priests to receive the Sacraments of the Church, particularly the Most Blessed Sacrament. Satan knows that one way to inhibit man's acceptance of God's miraculous intercession is to highlight human weaknesses to decertify those who bear the message. And yet, we are all expected to rise above the world in faith and be strengthened by prayer and the Holy Eucharist so that we can willfully accept the validity of the gifts of God. Our Lord Jesus is prepared at this very moment to come back into His Creation. Do we properly spend our time contemplating that explosion of Glory? It will be the heavenly marriage of mortal daylight with the omnipotence of God, Himself. Any attempt to describe these banns falls futilely short of reality because we, as yet, do not fully comprehend a human life in which evil will be no more. Come the wedding day between God and His people, Satan will have no voice with which to continue his lies because he shall never be heard from again.

Still, many people are worrisome in anticipation of that redemptive day. They do not fear their destiny, but that they will have no destiny at all. Most do not tremble at the thought of entering Hell, although they understand that they are failing to make themselves worthy of Paradise. How frustrating to be cast into the middle of this limbo of anxiety, to fear being nowhere at all! Imagine being left-out of everything, as if there is a place that will go unnoticed, a homelessness where there is no meaning for sacrifice, commitment, or life, itself. Oh, how people fear that God's Love is indifferent! From where do they procure this falsehood? It is from their own apathetic sloth. They know that they would not judge themselves kindly at the end of time, and therein lies their fear. It is based upon a state of panic toward the futile, the lukewarm, and the hollow. How needless are these ferocious phantoms! Man has the freedom to choose his own destiny by virtue of the Love of Christ. This is why many people try to hate. They would rather not face the question or the decision of bringing their lives into conformity with the perfection of Heaven. Our Lady asked me to remember, **"No one has learned enough about hatred to hate."**

If we decide that tyranny is a better fate than freedom, then we will also believe that hatred is a more demanding despot than indifference. We must, instead, understand that Love destroys both of these diabolical fiends, leaving us awash in the boundless liberty to believe that a most-benevolent God is the benefactor of our fate. We must enjoin the Spirit of the Lord as a participant in His Plan, rather than as a spectator who will later walk away with no particular place to go. We must encamp at the gate, joining with this Champion and concelebrating the gifts which God redemptively bestows upon those who accept His forgiveness. We cannot refuse to play the game or disobey the orderly rules. And, most important, we must never concede that there is a way *to* lose. The leadership before and above us is in the hands of Jesus Christ. He commands with power and direction, love, unity, and peace. When we see our Savior as the culmination of freedom and love, and if we realize the fulfillment in our choice to be truly worthy of Heaven, we will have the greatest hope that could ever possibly be mustered in the mortal world. This faithful expectation is well-founded because, through the Crucifixion, Jesus has counted us both individually and collectively worthy of the mansions of Paradise. Sorrowfully, however, most people have already given-up before allowing their souls a chance to invite the Mercy of their Savior to their tables. And, after abandoning the holy fight, they also surrender the more noble course of espousing saintly conduct. Their lives become a terribly condemning snowball, although never too late to reverse.

Jesus' Return will be a day of fulfillment and promise. On that glorious morning of harvest, the Lamb of God will present to us the fruits of our labor upon which the heavenly Hosts have feasted since the moment we became humble workers in His vineyard on Earth. He will encapsulate and ratify our lives in one immortal stroke of Divinity that will close-out the mortal ages. By the same measure, it will be the hour when we will witness the final destruction of everything that could conceivably cast a shadow of sorrow on a weeping human heart. Existence will end with the severance of the piercing will of the human agenda. The minutes will read that time has been separated from Eternity! On that great day, the children of God will receive their new-found berth in total freedom with the eternal satisfaction of the richness of Love. Every soul will be nourished and fulfilled, electrified by the pulse of their new heart which will beat in the ecstasy that will sustain them forever without end. Love will have returned to Love everlasting and we will finally embrace God perfectly, delighting in the victory that our hearts have yearned to achieve from the first pulse of life in our mother's wombs.

Thursday, November 21, 1991

My brother and I began to pray at 9:30 p.m. and our Holy Mother said, **"My little ones, be happy! Our work together has given you blessings and graces unknown to many. Your knowledge of Love is clear because I am teaching you. You now understand what a gift you truly have..."** She continued by telling me about the many people who compromise their conviction regarding Her miraculous intercessions because they fear being seen as religious fanatics. She holds every soul dear to Her Immaculate Heart who is consumed by the Spirit of Love, who sees God's Divinity in all good things, and has a burning desire to embrace Him to the fullest. Jesus is of such logical persuasion! He is not flighty or aloof, but overwhelmingly determined about our living Love as the fulfillment of the command of the Almighty Father in Heaven. His mandated intention and sole purpose on Earth is to Love. This, too, is our basis for being and the reason we were given the gift of life. Our every breath is the same inhalation of the innocent holiness which we were given at our birthday. We must finally come to realize that the ultimate fulfillment of human existence resides in our believing this Truth.

Evangelization for Christ is composed of our relentless request for others to open their hearts to the Wisdom of God. Christianity teaches us the catechism of the heart and opens our lives to communicate with our Creator through prayer. All of the rest is a discipline that is based upon, and grows from within, this foundation of Love. If the heart is weak in petitionary abandonment, the soul will not recognize that Jesus is the Holy Eucharist. We learn to love by being loved. So, Love first, and all else will acquire its inevitable place. Our Lady asks for heart-work, not head-work. She is not criticizing the religious educational system, but simply teaching:

"And if I have the gift of prophecy and comprehend all mysteries and all knowledge; if I have all faith so as to move mountains but do not have love, I am nothing." - 1 Corinthians 13:2

Our love for our Crucified Savior is the greatest mystery that we could ever possibly embrace to lead us toward the acquisition of perfect human knowledge. Every prophecy is fulfilled in Him because He will always be the Son of Wisdom through whom we gain Eternal Life. Christianity, itself, is fulfilled in Jesus' Sacrifice because His all-encompassing Corpus is embodied in the Most Sacred Host at the Consecration during the Mass. There is no greater revelation in the life of humankind than the miracle of Transubstantiation that is performed by the priest on the bread and wine of the Altar, transforming it into the Body and Blood of Our Lord. This defining moment transmits utter perfection during the communion between God's children and the Eucharist of His Son. Our Heavenly Father complements our lives with this true Eternity, Heaven-come-to-Earth to consume humankind.

The Blessed Virgin Mary gave me yet another example of Her Divine Maternity so that we can better understand how to welcome Her presence within us. She hopes through this parable that we will more readily allow Her to be the living, breathing, and caring Mother which Jesus bequeathed to us from the Cross. She asked me to call to mind the types of motherhood that we see in nature, specifically the birds of the air and reptiles who give birth to their young in a self-contained way. Compare this to ourselves and the other warm-blooded species who feed their young embryo by placenta and umbilical cord until birth. This dichotomy of examples bears-out the point about Our Lady's intercession. Many of Her children errantly believe that they are contained in an egg and that their gestation period for holiness is separate from the fostering Lifeblood of the Mother. She is, rather, the nourishing one who not only keeps us warm, but feeds holiness into our hearts until we are born into Heaven. Jesus has sent Her to lead us back home. We are tethered to the Virgin Mary as Her tiny spiritual embryos because our souls are within Her Womb. The miraculous gifts of Her intercession are the manifestations of this motherly care. We need to understand the wisdom within the miracles that are occurring throughout the world. Our Lady knows that it is oftentimes difficult for us to believe, but She is helping us with such amazing grace. Through Her continual urging, we will soon arrive safely at complete freedom in unbounded bliss. The Immaculate Queen of Paradise will always show us Her Son because She knows that He is our "all." Nothing else exists that could ever match His glorious Love because He is the fulfillment of our search for an everlasting immortal destiny. She, in turn, is the Immaculate grace who has delivered Him to bless us.

Saturday, November 23, 1991

When Our Lady appeared tonight, She urged us all to move closer to Jesus. The intensity of His Passion and Death is the glorious revelation of Love, itself. Anyone who finds it difficult to embrace others with an open heart must look at Our Lord's Crucifixion. When we gaze at Mount Calvary from any place in history, we witness the perfect Man who loves each individual person as if they were the only human to ever be given life. Humanity was not faceless to Christ when He hung on the Cross. He knew each of us intimately and completely. He gave His own Life so that all people in every age could see the Love that they must accept in order to be granted Salvation. The Eternity of God is defined by the Truth we see emanating from the Crucifixion. We need to contemplate Jesus' Sacrifice from the vantage point of imminent holiness and undiminished Light. We must respond with human perfection to be provided the elevating rise to our honorable sanctity.

The Holy Mother told me these things after I had seen a benefit dinner for someone who is suffering from a terrible disease. Those who participated in this gathering were able to see the suffering Christ through the love they held for their afflicted brother. I felt both compassion and affection flowing from them as they offered words of hope through their tears. Everyone's heart was open and responsive to the compassion of God in the way of our merciful Lord. They realized the Crucifixion of Christ in their empathy, although they might not have concisely known why they were being so touched of heart. Our Lady was very happy for those who were involved in this community prayer for healing. For a brief moment, the world was bathed in heavenly Light. In our time, the knowledge of human suffering is often limited to those who find themselves afflicted. Callous indifference has caused many of us to disregard the plight of those who are enduring the most miserable conditions on Earth. Those who live without charity in their hearts often care very little about human agony until it finally comes to rest upon them. We must, instead, recognize the paramount procession of heart-rendering enlightenment that occurs through those who suffer in the image of Jesus. They embody the true essence of submission which we must collectively share as the family of humankind.

Everyone must become aware of these interior warriors whose image and legacy is the advancement of our own individual transformation and ultimate Redemption.

It is impossible to understand the meaning of suffering with a closed heart because, in that dark state, one only senses the presence of hopeless mental anguish. But, when we see the Crucifixion of Jesus in the midst of human tragedy, our own suffering becomes a hope-filled and impassioned yearning for the restoration of peace and convalescence. It is through that same desire for healing that our destination is always founded in the perfect Man-God of the Cross. He is the Healer and Comforter for all who are afflicted by sin and injury. We should always joyfully greet suffering with this in mind. When we cultivate this vision, we exercise our capacity to conquer our sinful nature through the devotion which Jesus places in our hearts. Therein also lies the ultimate source of happiness for the Immaculate Heart of Mary. Many people work unselfishly and tirelessly for the sake of our conversion. Thousands of generous souls aspire toward sacred perfection by serving the cause for which Christ has died. Our Lady told me that most of them are stationed at the apses of the Church. The Catholic priests elevate humanity through humble hands to the Summit of Love, the Crucifixion of Mount Calvary at the Holy Mass. Sacrifice and suffering for the sake of Redemption is not just a part of mortal existence, it is the timeless essentia of human life which unveils the realms of Eternity. If we look with our hearts, we will actually see the movement of the Holy Spirit across the globe through the lives of the poor and afflicted. This is why the transcending fruits that are borne through suffering can never be destroyed. They are as permanent in Divinity as the scars of Jesus' Sacrifice.

Consider the unquestionable moral power in Mother Teresa of Calcutta as she calls for assistance to the poorest of the poor, or a tortured survivor of a death camp pleading "never again," or a crippled soldier wearing a heart as purple as the scourged Body of Christ. There is no force in Creation that can drown-out the message that their crucified hearts proclaim. The Mother of God has come for the wounded and crippled, the tortured and blind. She confirms Her presence through the words and messages of this Diary. Life radiates from the Truth, touching every soul who is humble enough to accept that the day of our most sacred dreams is now upon us. Our Lady concluded, **"Little ones, this time is special for you because you have been given the gift of confirmation. This is to show you how special the others are, especially not having the direct intervention from My intercession. This is why the faithful are so special to Me and why I have come to help build their faith. A miracle has been brought to you because you have chosen to suffer so that Love can enlighten the world. Thank you again for your sincere prayers. Your work on your Diary is going exceptionally well. Thank you."**

Sunday, November 24, 1991

Our Lady came at nine o'clock this evening while we were reciting the Holy Rosary. She began, **"My happy ones, thank you for praying! I love you! I have come to bring you another special message."** After Her greeting, I related to Her that I wished everyone could be immediately converted. She responded, **"I, too, would like that everyone in the world be converted to Jesus at once..."** Our conversion is contingent upon our movement toward holiness during the passing of time. I continued my questions by asking how Love could be quickly propagated and shared throughout the entire world. She told me that my question was logical and based upon my human perspective of space and time. Our Lady reminded me of a previous message about the Light of Christ whose Love is that beatific radiance. Even using human standards, we can easily compare the Light of Christ, which is alive in our hearts, with the natural light of the world that we see with our eyes. Light travels through the universe with such velocity that its transcendence within the marked scope of our lives is undetectable by the human eye. In fact, the light that we see travels at a rate of over 186,000 miles per second. We must refer to miles per second because we have no sensible numbers which correspond to the distance that it travels in a given number of hours. Therefore, it is a matter of a quantified rate and measurement.

We remember that Love cannot be constrained or defined in quantity, distance, or the passage of time. The beaming Spirit of Christ Jesus moves throughout the ages, from one generation to the next and back again, without impediment. This reveals to us that no time expires between the conception of our prayers and the answers that are granted by God according to His Divine Will. His response to our hopes and petitions are instantaneously present while we offer them. He does not bow in deference to the traveling of any distance or hesitation in time. But, when our supplications seem to go unanswered, it is simply a matter of our impatience that is generated by our misperception of time. This is the same error that befalls those who refuse to believe that the Holy Mass is the Crucifixion of Christ which occurred 2000 years ago. The bondage that lies in observing linear moments is a deterrent to their faith. In fact, faith is as timeless as the Crucifixion in which we believe. God, in His unique genius, answers all prayers to their maximum effect. Sometimes this means that they are delivered silently, other times as brilliantly magnificent as a composition describing the relationship of His Virgin Mother with one of Her children. It is important that we do not pressure our own consciousness to seek the answers to our invocations. Jesus dispenses His grace through our hearts in innumerable ways that we may not readily perceive. We discover at the last that our mortal perception is inherently flawed, along with our recognition of His subtle blessings upon us.

Our exile within the boundaries of time is our precious allocation of the fullest opportunity, and the Heavenly Father is neither remanded to, nor constrained by, its effects. Therefore, He graciously answers our pleading cries for His help. He desires for us to know His Eternity of kindness through the loyalty that we cultivate throughout our sacrificial lives. Amidst our spiritual meditations, we know that prayerful servitude and patient endurance truly change the world, both perpetually and retroactively. This is how the souls of our departed brethren are petitioned from under the burden that is heaped upon them in Purgatory. We ask the Almighty Father to forgive our wayward siblings and provide them Eternal Life, innocent and absent of the sins which Jesus has washed into the abyss. Like the actual reversal of time, their errors and omissions are removed from existence by the power of God's forgiveness, no matter what any historian may contemporarily contend. In the image of Jesus, we must likewise expunge our memory of their sins, lest we become the errant record-keepers of their terrestrial legacy. Remember that Our Lady said, **"Once sins are forgiven, they were never committed."** She asked today that we foster the movement of Her Divine Son's Spirit throughout the world by holding fast to the Truth of Jesus' Love. The Life of Christ cannot be diminished or defeated by human judgment or error, nor by any opposition that can ever be generated or perpetrated. Love is eternal in this sense and beyond any other facilitating capacity.

Monday, November 25, 1991

Our beautiful Virgin Mother, who is masterful in both reflection and prophecy, came today to share Her Wisdom, grace, and candor in hopes of teaching us to know God better than we ever have before. As we prayed, She told me that we are all very special and blessed. Jesus is allowing Her to intercede on our behalf in many miraculous ways and through numerous simple people. It is time for everyone to open their hearts in faith and accept the supernatural gifts of God's infinite Mercy. We must fill our spirits to overflowing with good will and compassion, tempering our consciousness to embrace the Cross of Christ, which rises during so many occasions in our everyday lives. There is always happiness in the righteousness of the heart. Our Lady said, **"Jesus has allowed you many great graces and afforded Me much happiness. I have come to give you another special message because My children are very special. I would like to tell you about the human intellect. Men have a seeming need to classify and divide others in accordance with their divisive and colorful opinions..."**

The Holy Mother has told us many times of the countless means through which the human mind classifies other people with differing lives. She spoke in an earlier message about how colors elicit altogether different moods. She showed me an image today of a rainbow of hues that somewhat resembled an unfolded oriental fan. I could see each separate color as though it were a playing card amidst the rest of the others in the hand of a pinochle player. Each spline of this spectrum was to be associated with one of the multitudes of moods or feelings that are recorded by the intellect through our senses. This is a symbolic pictorial of how the mind disseminates what it encounters. The different shades are places where man originates his feelings as a reflection of what he experiences. Color cannot be heard, smelled, felt, or tasted, but is detected only with the eyes. Therefore, we have no other means to distinctively separate what we see if, indeed, this "color scheme" is the only criterion we use. In other words, we have no method for distinguishing the differing shades without our temporal vision. Our Lady is trying to help us realize that we categorize the world and our brothers and sisters by what we see. We are accustomed to using this delineating technique to predetermine our set of standards for human behavior and actions of the heart. Unfortunately, we also lose our spontaneity and receptiveness in the process. While this carousel constantly revolves before our consciousness, the passage of Love from the heart is blocked by the incessant distraction that is caused by our habitual nature.

Our Holy Mother is revealing to us that our systems of discrimination and categorization are destroyed by the holiness that She teaches. All pigments and hues blend into perfect unity through the vision that Her grace is engendering. We prayerfully lose our ability to divide or ignore any portion of humanity for our own personal gain. Once we have Love in our hearts, it is neither possible nor desirable to classify, segregate, or exile any other human being from the community of our peers. The Virgin Mary asked me to consider the heart of mankind as a beautiful peacock with its feathers proudly expanded. Love causes the plumes to enjoin and become vividly singular en masse. Their majestic brilliance blends into a fan-shaped array of refracting and reflecting color which transcends the plane of their blades. Together, they are all one salient tincture of Love. All pigments and shades have become one in such a way that is specifically perceived and appreciated within the heart. This is the stillness and peace of the Love of God.

Our Lady wants our souls to shine with the Light of Divinity, like a peacock during his grandest of moments. By beseeching Our Savior to make it so, we move the entire world toward this paradisial unity from within our own homes. This is how a flicker becomes a flame, which in time becomes a beacon. When we enlighten our spirits in peace and entwine our lives through our prayers, Love consumes all Creation. It is the reflection of Heaven from one heart to all others. It is also the gallant prophecy in which the Virgin Mother asks us to become a selfless trustee and participant. Love is an invincible sheen that is strengthened in the hearts of men throughout the timely distance of the ages. It goes on and on and becomes brighter and more fulfilling each time another new soul reaches within himself and makes the sacrifices to enhance its transmission. We may not always see the fruit of our initial flicker while we are still on the Earth. But, these flaming embers continue to timelessly grow, never to be extinguished because the Light of

Christ is forever into Eternity. Again, each petition that we utter is as permanent in God's Paradise as the scars of the Sacrifice of Our Savior, Lord Jesus.

Our Heavenly Mother asked me to ponder another exceptional image. Recall when you may have seen the reflections of two mirrors facing each other. In one mirror is the image of the other, and vice versa. Additionally, we see the image of one mirror reciprocally in the other, then their multiplied reflections seemingly without end. This is the symbolic likeness of the Love of Christ, although inversely in power. Love actually pours-forth from the inside out. Jesus' Spirit timelessly propagates to us from the Infinity in which He lives as though the tangible mirrors before us represent the present day world. We are simultaneously seeing and living the concurrent moment of the Resurrection of the Messiah and the Redemption of all humankind. This truth is enhanced as we polish our hearts into a reflecting surface where others can look for the presence of God as His Light emanates around the globe. We must see the future with a stronger faith and a hope that is worthy of our most noble of hearts. The sacrifices and prayers which we offer feed the revelation of our eternal destiny to those who do not yet know that Jesus of Nazareth has saved the world. And, like God, Himself, Our Lady is trying to speed-up the day when every race and nation will live the Divine reality that Her Son has destroyed all evil influence in our path. Our Heavenly Mother asks us to pray together in the continuum of that assurance. She wishes us to hunger and thirst for peace, desirable to anyone who hears Her blessed messages.

Tuesday, November 26, 1991

The body of mankind is made fertile like the soil that grows the tree of Love when it is tilled with grace, and Our Lady is effecting such cultivation throughout the world. She is turning the souls of men to God like the folding of the soil for the planting of seed in the springtime. What is it that makes the Earth fruitful and fertile? We know that the miles of farmland acres are enriched by the breaking-down of unusable and fruitless particles of past Creation and existence. Our fields are made even richer by the moisture that is provided by the Providence of God and the time that He allots man to witness its eventual plenty. This, too, is how the collective soul of humanity is prepared to generate an abundant crop of conversion. It is made fruitful by the degeneration and destruction of decadent hatred and former biases which are manifested as food for the heart of mankind. Human tears moisten our souls, providing the regeneration of promise where we can grow in mutual understanding and love for our Creator. Our prayers are the investment of our time, our movement toward eternal vision which particlize the useless and excess, rendering the grace which is the sweetness of our lives. This becomes the foundation for goodness to flourish across the fields of mortal Creation. Our open hearts are the furrows in which Christ implants His seed of Love. His Holy Spirit grows and feeds upon the richness of forgiveness, nurturing the collective soul of humankind toward fruitfulness, instead of barren ruggedness.

Through our prayers, we assist our Immaculate Mother in the enrichment of our souls in prospective and hope, rather than leaving them poorer through spiritual indifference. Many shoots of new life appear as our timely holiness begins to flourish. We often see the stamping forces of Satan trying to obstruct our development in love because he prefers to see an empty and fallow world. This is a preference which he will never achieve because Our Lady has proclaimed that the Evil One cannot win since he has already been defeated! We have plentiful strength, nourishment, and moisture for our perfect maturity in Love. And, as God's children, we are also the seed that He has planted upon the Earth. It is quite obvious that the sunlight for our progress is Jesus Christ, who has come to propel the future of man toward a fruitful Eternity. His sinless Mother has shown us that the magnification of His Divine Light is like a beacon that precedes our destiny toward everlasting Salvation. We can achieve this holy Redemption when we beseech the King of kings in reflection of His own prayerfulness.

Tonight, Our Lady also showed me a second dimension to the pulsing Light of Heaven. She brought my understanding to an improved and multi-staged movement of the Love of Jesus. In essence, She is telling us that the grace of God cannot be stopped once it has begun. When we allow Christ Jesus to re-inhabit the major part of Creation, beginning with the chambers of our hearts, He will sufficiently enhance our understanding so that we can perceive where darkness still remains. This is the principle of His increasing returns, like the bountiful yield of the crop of human souls which He so desires to savor. The web of Love which Jesus brings is the inner-connection of the heart-strings of His people:

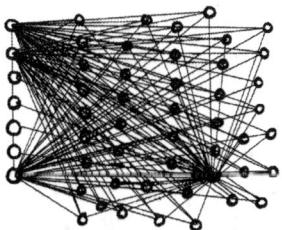

This depiction is the reciprocal reflection of holy Love between open hearts. Consider the great message that God gives the world through a simple spider's web. The individual threads spun by the tiny creature are woven together with Divine precision, symmetrical pattern, and an overwhelming strength. When proportionately compared to the architectural feats of humanity, the engineering genius of the spider has yet to be equaled by any other mortal laborer. The tensile strength of its tiny fibers are comparatively beyond the capability of any scientist to duplicate. But, it is now possible for humankind to imitate and transcend the knowledge of these creatures. Our Lady is revealing that the web of Love must become our supreme response to the parable of the spider given by God. The sacrificial unity of His children under the Cross of Christ is the Divine construction whose eminent power and light are ultimately sustainable through any storm or attack. The progression and multiplication of good will between men becomes whole and immortalized through Jesus' touch. The mass conversion of humanity from fragmentation into unity builds this beatific fortress. Once Love is set free in our hearts, it will never be bound or impeded by darkness again. Light can never be blocked or captured by the night. The shadows of evil are cowards who flee from the revealing righteousness of God's justice. Indeed, righteousness will always triumph in the openness of eternal day. Our Holy Mother wishes us to inflame the Earth with the power of Her Son's Cross because it is the source of ecstatic brilliance. The dawn of this endless Easter morning begins in our humility and forgiveness. When we pray, a picture of the soil truly becomes the fertile Earth and our potential to Love springs-forth from the Truth that we faithfully know in our hearts. When we magnify Christ Jesus, the world becomes alive and whole, pure and pristine, functional and worthy.

The Blessed Mother pleads every day for an intensification of our petitions for unborn children. The fruition of human life and the fulfillment of their miraculous birth is only a prayer away. Each tiny baby cries-out for Life, and God hears them. The intentions of the born will deliver the lives of the unborn to their entrance into God's Plan for Redemption. The supplications of the mortal will transpose all souls into Eternity. Yes, prayer is the greatest power! When the salvific sentiments of our hearts reach the Bosom of God, souls are drawn to our Savior like little filings to a magnet. Love must be from one end of our hearts to the other and given to the Infinity of God. He is that timelessness where love comes to Love.

Friday, November 29, 1991

"**Good evening, My precious little children! You are doing very well in your work for My Son. You should be elated with your progress through which many hearts are being aligned with Jesus. The miracle you seek has come to you as I am here and the world is being converted and saved. You truly have no means to measure the success of these messages at a given point in time. Just remember that the conversion of millions is made possible because you have consented to record My words. This makes our relationship a victory already! The rest is according to the hearts of the world who are hungry. You are helping Me tell them to be nourished in Jesus' Love. I realize that this is overwhelming and encompassing. Yes, you see the miracle, and your**

faith tells you that it is true. You have been given many gifts to savor for the rest of your days. You will receive many more graces..."

Tonight, I was asked by Our Lady to remember that Jesus extends His Mercy in accordance with our own knowledge of His expectations of us. However, He condones no differentiation in our love for others. We must always respond completely with our best understanding and exertion. Our honest effort must leave no room for apathy or indifference in our struggle to be perfected. The tree of Love must be flexible, but we should never plan any weakness in sin or repeatedly fall toward any transgression. Even though we are human, we cannot allow or justify any sin if we wish to be flawlessly united with God as He desires. A simple example is when someone uses a butter knife in place of a screwdriver to open a can of paint. The blade will bend and break. Likewise, worldliness will damage our lives and render them useless for their intended purpose. Humanness is meant for holiness, but we are misusing our potential under the guise of freedom instead of surrendering our hearts to the power of Jesus. We often allow ourselves to be spontaneously and subconsciously weak. It would be more fitting to remember that Love is constant and level like the surface of a standing body of water. True and total Love is always without differentiation. Better presented, the Bible clearly states this Truth:

"Love your enemies, do good to those who hate you, bless those who curse you, pray for those who mistreat you. To the person who strikes you on one cheek, offer the other one as well, and from the person who takes your cloak, do not withhold even your tunic. Give to everyone who asks of you, and from the one who takes what is yours do not demand it back. Do to others as you would have them do to you. For if you love those who love you, what credit is that to you? Even sinners love those who love them. And if you do good to those who do good to you, what credit is that to you? Even sinners do the same. If you lend money to those from whom you expect repayment, what credit is that to you? Even sinners lend to sinners, and get back the same amount. But rather, love your enemies and do good to them, and lend expecting nothing back; then your reward will be great and you will be children of the Most High, for He Himself is kind to the ungrateful and the wicked. Be merciful, just as also your Father is merciful. Stop judging and you will not be judged. Stop condemning and you will not be condemned. Forgive and you will be forgiven. Give and gifts will be given to you; a good measure, packed together, shaken down, and overflowing, will be placed into your lap."
(Luke 6:27-38)

Saturday, November 30, 1991

I thank the Almighty Father again for allowing the grace of Our Lady's intercession so that this Diary can be composed for the world. I hope that everyone on Earth will come to realize how tenderly our Virgin Mother holds each of us to Her Immaculate Heart. We can imagine how She held baby Jesus in Her arms and with Her consoling Heart during His Nativity in Bethlehem. This is the same great maternal power that is engulfing us at this very moment. Anyone who outrightly denies this truth in their lack of faith is rejecting the compassionate comfort which is being extended by the same Blessed Virgin Mary whom Our Savior profoundly commissioned to be our Mother upon the Cross of Mount Calvary. This same Lady of Perpetual Help appeared to me again this evening to tell the world of the blessings that are now being bestowed upon all who worship Her Son as the anniversary celebration of His birthday approaches.

"Jesus is the Word-become-flesh by virtue of My Womb. It is imperative that the West return their focus to Love as this anniversary nears. As the Patron of the United States, I call all of My children to prayer and fasting in recognition of the anniversary of Jesus' birth. Thank you for accepting these messages on behalf of all in the world who will greatly benefit from their consecration to the Blessed Sacrament..." Since Christmas is such a powerfully grace-filled time for us, Our Lady asked me to contemplate the ways that the birth of Jesus and the Most Blessed Sacrament are related, as a means of existence and co-existence. When we think about the Nativity and the Blessed Sacrament, we are to consider those who believe in faith that Jesus was born in a stable at Bethlehem, but do not believe that His Sacrificial Body is brought into the world at the hands of a priest on the Catholic altars. Furthermore, consider the many people who faithfully accept that Christ was miraculously conceived in the Womb of the Virgin of Nazareth and entered human existence from Her body, but also do not believe that other unborn children are worthy of life. Many of these same pseudo-followers of Jesus condone the murder of children through abortion. We are asked to recognize this terrible inconsistency. The Mother of Our Savior poses this question, **"Why do millions of mothers who celebrate the birth of Jesus kill their own unborn children?"**

The Queen of Heaven wishes us to remember the impenetrable grace of the Most Blessed Sacrament in this struggle for human life. If our misguided sisters will come to the Holy Mass and worthily receive the Blessed Eucharist, the Holy Spirit will reveal to them their error and lack of knowledge of the Truth. They will see that the Child of the manger and the Fruit of the Altar are one and the same Christ. They will also accept their own unborn children with the same love that Mary embraced the Son of God in Her Womb. We must utilize the anniversary of Jesus' birth as a perfect opportunity to help expectant mothers wholly realize the fulfillment of the life within them. We should invoke the paternal protection of Saint Joseph, who is praying unceasingly for all of the unborn. He, too, was present with the Virgin Mother at the Nativity of Jesus in Bethlehem and concurrently lives the Truth of God that all unborn children must be brought to full birth. As their stepfather, we should ask him to intercede for the tiny children who humbly weep within their mothers' wombs for a chance to live.

DECEMBER 1991

Sunday, December 1, 1991

The yoke of Christian conviction is not a mortal pillory or a pragmatic approach to human discipline. We are called to be divinely contemplative in a world where we perform great acts of charity and assistance. If Jesus is a burden, He is light to even the most faint of heart. That is the wisdom in our call to Love. Anyone can know God and the fruits of His good will. And, that is the essence of the message which our Holy Mother brings, the desire and the taste that She wishes us to savor. Knowing Her as well as God will allow, I understand why She has come again today to speak these words during my humble prayers. **"Good evening, little special one and little chosen one! Thank you for helping fill the world with prayers for peace and Salvation. There are many graces being bestowed and much cultivation now occurring. I am helping the world to love in faith instead of being lodged in indifference and sin. I humbly lead all of My children to Jesus. But, there is often much opposition to My work. It is the same many places in the world. I come to teach the symmetry of Love in a world that is burdened by the haphazardly constructed mind of man."**

Our Lady's messages impact our hearts in ways that are oftentimes too magnificent for us to comprehend. During other moments, Her intercession is more discreetly graduated. Today, She asked me to consider how Her messages and grace-filled lessons from the Holy Trinity are impacting the world to its very depths. These instructions teach us the symmetry of Christ Jesus and solidify our faith in Him. As Her words rendezvous with our hearts, we interiorly conform to the wishes of God as Love overwhelms our souls. Hence, our lives mirror the Will of the Holy Spirit in communion with the miracle of Her Immaculate intercession. This is what She calls happy human obedience. It validates our authentic desire for peace that is gained in the Truth of Christ. We are cultivated by Her mystically-piercing entreaties. Her loving guidance is an appeal for our prayers, conversion, penance, fasting, and peace. When we convert our lives at Her behest, Jesus will have a smooth surface upon which to travel from one heart to the next. Peace is brought forth through the symmetry that is created by God's loving presence within the human spirit.

The Most Holy Trinity has always intended for every person in the world to find peace and joy in His unparalleled Creation. Our minds are oftentimes at a loss to understand His magnanimous motivations. But, if we vacate our mental inquisitions in favor of His Divine Will, we will have begun our return to Paradise. We must wisely conform to the shape of holy receptacles, accommodating every holy inspiration and gift that Christ has presented to the Earth on our behalf. This is the origin of our meaningful desire for peace. Although we do not always understand it, the Holy Spirit will confirm us in hopeful acceptance and anticipation until we can see more clearly. Those who decline to believe in the powerful intercession of Our Lady are downplaying, or even disregarding completely, the Almighty Father's gifts of such miraculous grace. But, as Christ moves more swiftly across the landscape of human life, even they will see His Truth, and thereafter elevate the Mother of God as being a necessary grace in their search for a peaceful heart. It is readily apparent that the Church will soon be set afire with pure devotion to Jesus Christ through the work and intercession of the Immaculate Heart of His Virgin Mother. Therefore, we must make our hearts like Her own because no one else knows how to love the Redeemer of humankind in greater dimensions.

Tuesday, December 3, 1991
Our Lady composed a special message early today for me to give to the poor and downtrodden. It punctuates the beauty of the Spirit of Christmas to those in need of consolation.

A special message for you as you prepare for Christmas.

"This message comes to you from a very special person; and I have come to bring you some very good news as you move more closely to the celebration of the birth of Jesus. Christmas is a time for all of us to remember that cold winter night when Jesus came into the world as a tiny Baby. He was born as a very special little boy, who was sent into this world by God to show you how to love and to have faith in the Promise that Love will save you from all of your weaknesses, illnesses, depressions, poverty, and wrongdoings. We all must remember that Jesus was born into poverty, and He has a special understanding of what it is like to be poor. I hope that you will read this message in a quiet place and with all of your loved ones around you if you can. We also know that Christmas is a time when all families gather together to enjoy each other as a new year is about to begin. There is a very special feeling at Christmas time, and it seems to be most strong in our hearts, where our Love for others comes from. This meaning of Christmas, the memory of Love and happiness that we have shared throughout the ages, allows every heart to open in expectation of a gift from the bounty of the world through the hands of others.

Do you remember when you were a child and could hardly sleep on Christmas Eve because you were anxious to know what your presents would be? And, now that you are grown, you do not seem to feel that excited anymore at Christmas? You can become as anxious as a little child again if you remember what the meaning of Christmas truly is. Yes, it did begin with giving. The birth of Jesus was the finest gift that God could give to the world. Christmas brings you the good news that, in your poverty and depression in your daily lives, you will know that your deliverance from suffering is Jesus, the same Jesus who was born in the night so long ago in a lonely place. You have no longer any worry about what you will give your loved ones and others for Christmas. The gift has already been given to you to pass on, and it was purchased by Jesus at the cost of His earthly life. The Gift is Love, My special people! Jesus died on a lonely Cross in the same way that He was born in a lonely stable. That is why Christmas is so special. That is why Love is so special. You need to also remember that, even though Jesus died so that you would have a Christmas present to give to others, that is Love, He is still alive because His Love is so strong that it conquered death. That is also what He gave to you so that you can be happy all year long, for all of your life.

There are many who believe that you cannot see Jesus with your eyes. But, you really can see Jesus with your eyes! He lives in the Tabernacles of the Holy Catholic churches all over the world. He asks that you consume Him so that you can also remain alive, even after you have died. You know about the bread and wine in the churches. Jesus becomes alive in the Church where the bread and wine once were. This, too, He does because He loves you so much and He wants you to be happy and saved from all of your burdens. The little Christ Jesus came into the world at Christmas as a special child of God. He came to bring you happiness and freedom. You no longer are poor when you allow Jesus to make you rich in Love. Jesus was a very special baby, and His coming into the world showed us how special all babies are, especially those who are still in their mother's womb. These are the most special of children because they need you so much to help them to be born. You can share the Love that Jesus shared with you by doing all that you can to see that all unborn children are given the gift of Life in the same spirit of giving that God showed us in the giving of Jesus to the world. Your new beginning and new happiness will come to you very soon when you pray to God and tell Him that you love Him as He loves you. Tell Him from your hearts that you want Him to help you, too, to be happy.

Go to your church and ask for a priest who will tell you how to pray and to be happy again. This is how you can make this Christmas a special time of giving, like you remember as a child. I bring this message to you to help you on your way to meeting your special friend,

Jesus, whose birthday is almost here. I know Him very well. You see, I am His Mother, the Virgin Mary, who saw and bore Him into the world. I love you, too, and want to help you. I have special little helpers at a Marian Center in your town whom you can ask for help too. Like Jesus, I will be with you at Christmas and always to ask you to pray. You will become one in Love through your heart with Jesus and you will be happy forever." I was very touched by these words. A special feeling engulfed me when She asked me to transcribe them into a simple message for humble people who wish to know God better. She said, **"My happy little child, I am with you to tell you I love you and to pray with you. It is a special time when Jesus' birth is observed. I gave the message earlier today because I know you love Jesus and all He created very much. I am happy when your heart is so touched..."**

Our Immaculate Mother told me that this Yuletide message highlights how we often move very quickly and unwittingly toward distraction. It is true that our curiosity and desires for intellectual stimulation insidiously drive us to acquire far more material possessions than we need to comply with the simple Life that Jesus asks. This is why brotherhood is diminished and minds collide, thus inhibiting our progress toward peace throughout the world. The Virgin Mary's treatises help to realign our goals with the symmetry of the Heart of God. We are at His Mercy and cannot create for ourselves a purpose or authority larger than He has intended. Our finite nature and mortal stature are the result of our collective sinfulness. However, through the Life, Death, and Resurrection of His Perfect Son, we are mystically heightened in awareness and elevated in both spiritual standing and capacity which secures a rebirth that we never before possessed. When Jesus rose from the dead, we were transformed into a new Creation on a scale previously unknown to mortal man. It is in the ever-contemporary promise of this new Life that we see the true meaning of Christmas. The age-old simplicity of Love eliminates the self-generated complications that blind us from the plain truth of the little Child of Light in the manger. We are not happy or fulfilled because we are failing to imitate the Heavenly Prince who birthed His Divinity into one of the Earth's lowliest hovels.

The Virgin Mary is gently adamant about Her desire that we not look upon the celebration of Jesus' birth in material or financial terms. She told me today that it is very evident that the world revolves around money, rather than the Savior of mankind. I was given a graphic parable to consider. We already know that, in God's original Creation, man was placed on the Earth to reflect Love in perfect harmony with the Almighty Father's sacred conception of Life. He provides the resources that we need to sustain ourselves and those who need our assistance. This generosity by our Omnipotent God is a reminder that we must care for those who cannot fend for themselves. Consider the following illustration on the left as being a neatly-stacked number of coins at the height determined by the generosity of our Creator. They are placed solidly atop one another, symbolically representing both the simple and original nature of man.

But, when people try to selfishly expand themselves in the material world as depicted on the right, they recede from this paradisial symmetry and the true purpose of their lives as God has prescribed. As numerous societies of people who live in different nations and under separate economies move away from their perfect purpose, both conflict and perversion result.

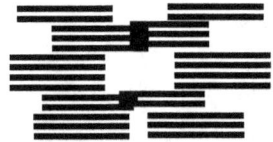

Eventually, through the failure to maintain our original stability, order, and neatness, we will feel the collapse of the world come falling upon us.

This is not the chaotic disarray which God has intended for the lives of His children. We are arrogantly imposing our own imperfections upon the world, while walking on shaky ground toward our self-imposed condemnation.

The Blessed Virgin Mary added another factor that is related to the Advent of Christmas. She asked me to look again at the right-hand frame of the first picture in the previous series. Notice the vacant area in the stack left by people who transfer their wealth laterally in the same socioeconomic class. Their refusal to give to the poor leaves a vacuum that causes the instability in the entire hierarchical structure. If we would provide to the less-fortunate and disadvantaged the share of the resources which God has allotted for them, we would not be heading so quickly toward our imminent downfall. Those who are living in poverty are the victims of the greed of others. When people fail to love those who are poor and celebrate their care toward concern for them in union with Christ, the world as a whole is much more destitute in spirit. Our brothers and sisters who suffer without the barest of necessities must be extended the compassion and assistance that the Light of Christmas brings.

Our Lady told me that we do not see well because we are standing too close to physical Creation. We must take our souls aback and place ourselves in the lives of the weak and downtrodden to see the true picture of human nature. It is not unlike trying to read a very large billboard while standing only a foot from its surface. The Mother of God has come pleading for us to prayerfully retreat from our own requirements and material possessions in order to recognize where we can best concentrate our resources to those most in need. As we begin to pray and practice this self-denial, and fast and receive the Holy Eucharist, our vision of Love becomes much more broad and clear. We must realize that Jesus, alone, grants us the perspective that we need to see the entire substance and message of our lives. Only through Christ can we learn about sharing, knowing full-well that we are faithfully cooperating in the responsible action of a righteous people. Therefore, it is incumbent upon us to realize that only love allows our hearts to see. This is how a world of faith is built. We know that eternal happiness and the Savior whom we yearn to see stand just past the external complexion of those that we engage every day. We must care for the people of God and sustain His Creation with charity because it is His almighty intention. Upon accomplishing this noble purpose, we will then see His Countenance through the gratitude that He bestows through His Holy Spirit.

Our faith encourages us to hope endlessly, while our Love helps us to see the foredrop which precedes our reunion with Eternity. Our enlightened vision allows us to see Creation as though we are looking into the vaulting heavens. We cannot truly encompass the depth of the universe or the dimensionless Wisdom of God, but we can know the beautiful Visage which paternally oversees the world He owns. Our lives of perfection in Christ represent the ability of man to touch His Face like a blind person touching the cheek of a friend. The surface of Creation is composed of the appearance and Will of the Almighty Father. There is infinite depth in the powerful winds of His Spirit which make it possible for us to see Him within our folded hands. His genius is in the silent fathoms of our heartfelt intentions. We must invoke this peace so that the world will know the beautiful shores from which we launch our hopes onto the sea of God's grace. This is what Our Lady's Christmas message does. This, too, is what our own petitions will accomplish. The message of Love must reach the lives of those who do not even know that there is a picture at hand. Those who believe the ocean to be an insignificant puddle also do not realize that the smallest prayers manifest the greatest miracles. They have turned their backs to the very Creator who wishes to look into their eyes and, with a wink, tell them that they are worth the price that His Son paid to save them. And, since so many souls are searching endlessly in the darkness, Our Lady has come to turn them around. As She calls our attention to the Light of Her Love, we see a fresh beginning on a road of opportunity that we never before realized has been paved. We must focus our aspirations and intentions upon traveling this pathway with perfect vision. Our invocations for unity will call the lost to the bounty that Heaven dispenses. Yes, we must return to Love at the Table of the Lord.

Wednesday, December 4, 1991
This evening, my brother and I attended a prayer vigil for a Novena honoring Our Lady. Upon returning home, we prayed the Rosary and the Immaculate Conception appeared. She said to us, **"I love you! Thank you for adoring Jesus the way the other little lambs did at His birth. I would like to remind all who refer to Me as the Mother of Mercy and Love that the literal meaning of what they are saying is true. I gave birth to Mercy and Love into the world in Jesus. The birth of the Word of God-become-flesh represents the true beginning of God transcending the unseen Glory of Heaven to the seeable world of man. The birth of Jesus is God coming into the world He created to both save it and preserve it for all Eternity..."** Before Christ was born, human mercy was present in those who knew how to love as the Deity loves. Men offered other men the forgiving compassion of understanding. Jesus is God's Mercy brought forth to carry our souls into Eternity through the forgiveness of His Father. The perfect forbearance of Christ is not simply a finite pardon in a human world, but rather an infinite clemency that is bestowed by an immortal Heart through which He desires all souls to be delivered to the highest Paradise we can possibly achieve.

If not for our sins, there would have been no need for such Divine Mercy. But as such, Jesus administers judgment and grants Salvation to fulfill the Redemption which He manifested through the Scriptures that He fulfilled. The Messiah came to the world as the Love of God to perfect the souls of His people. The requisite call for His merciful judgment is a direct result of our own failures. And, while this heavenly sufferance has always existed in our loving Father, upon Jesus' birth, we were able to live among the Divine standard in the likeness of man. The omnipotent Creator showed us convincingly that He loves the world so much that He would sacrifice His Beloved Offspring to save us. This same beneficent absolution is present through the Holy Spirit to comfort, guide, elevate, and unite humanity for presentation into the celestial gardens of Paradise. Christ's Sacred Spirit is the miraculous Fire which enlightens the souls of His faithful, illuminating our being with beauty and infinite possibility. Therefore, our road to happiness resides in petitioning God for His Mercy through Jesus' Sacrifice. He makes it possible for the family of man to collectively share the new perfection that is brought through His forgiveness of all our transgressions. We need our sins cleansed from our souls by the Blood of Christ to render us eligible to enter Life eternal with Him in Heaven.

Saturday, December 7, 1991

Faith, hope, and charity destroy hatred and indifference. Love is the answer! The world needs to be built upon selfless generosity, tolerance, and compassion. We must seek unity and peace because, heretofore, violence and aggression are only serving to diminish humankind. Likewise, we must believe that our faith-filled hope is a tangible opportunity that dawns upon the world through our charitable gifts. This is how Love flourishes in the Light of God. Our prayers and good works, no matter how small or unnoticed, truly change the landscape of the Earth to an exponential degree. The simple recitation of an innocent child changes the very shape of Heaven as purity radiates from their soul. This is no casual feat, but rather the purpose and destiny of our mortal existence which is ultimately worthy of eternal reward.

Today, Our Lady addressed this sacred guerdon and the blessing we need to attain it. She thanked me for pondering the birth of Jesus and the Most Blessed Sacrament in the way She has asked. **"I am with you, little ones! Thank you for your prayers. I am happy that you have been pondering the birth of Jesus and the beautiful Eucharist. The anniversary of His birth has nearly come. It is good to think of the birth of Jesus, the Word become flesh, as the same birth that a recipient of the Holy Eucharist experiences as he is born into the world of Love while still living in the mortal world. This new Life is the transformation of the Christian person into holiness, a nativity for the soul. Jesus came in Love to the world as flesh in the same way He comes to each Mass as His Body and Blood. He is the same, although the Blessed Sacrament is His sacrificial Body, and the Nativity is not. Always remember Jesus' birth as the innocence of the Incarnation of Love, exemplary of all newborn Life. But, also remember that this innocence was a fruit of perfect sinlessness. The Blessed Sacrament is the resurrected Body, which is exemplary of His Sacrifice.**

Jesus' Life as a newborn child on that first Christmas is God's desire to show that He would like all of His children to be innocent. Each person, every soul, who enters the Kingdom of Heaven will be as innocent and unassuming as little baby Jesus. The Christ-Child is the Truth who was born in Bethlehem. Little children know only the Truth

because they have not been exposed to mortal deceit and hatred. The catalyst for the return of all peoples to Truth and innocence is the Holy Eucharist. The Eucharist is the means through which each person is purified in body, mind, and soul so that the heart can feed Love to the conscience. As Jesus was innocently born in an environment of poverty, the Holy Eucharist bears each soul into self-denial and absence of worldliness. This is the miracle of the Eucharist and the miracle of Jesus' birth. He was born into the world to consume it in Love. Conversely, He comes as the Blessed Sacrament for the world to consume Him in Love..."** As Christmas draws nearer, we feel the benevolent strength of Jesus in our hearts. Advent is a season for the celebration of Love, not an opportunity for material gain. It is the time to give our love new birth and to nurture its growth.

Our Holy Mother asked me tonight to remember the symbolic way that little children envision the peace of the Nativity. She referred to a song about three oriental kings who carried riches to baby Jesus to pay Him homage. While we all recognize this song, it is not meant to imply that the Truth of Love is founded in riches. But, it is a fitting reverence for us all to lay our wealth at His feet. We should surrender all of our possessions to the Glory of Jesus' Kingdom. She also referred to a second song that assists in our vision toward paying deference to our newborn King. While the piece is only a parable, it revives the heart and soul of the faithful to courageously give the best that we have to offer in honor of the benign Christ-Child. The song is about a little boy who had only a drum to his name. While he had no other gifts or riches, his heart pounded-out the rhythm of Love that he joyfully shared with Jesus on his little instrument. His humility and innocence are a message to us all. He gave everything that he had in honor of our Emmanuel. Yes, he played his best for Him, and that is the meaning of the birth of Our Lord at Christmas. The Spirit of this season is why Our Savior first came into the world. We must all prayerfully become His sacrificial little drummers. While we are called to be poor in spirit, we are richer still in His grace. We must extend the miraculous gift which God gave to us in the appearance of this little Messiah in human flesh. The Love that Our Lady so wishes for us to live is perpetually present at Christmas, emanating a never-ending birth of freedom for humankind and the flourishing of peace on Earth.

The little percussion-master wrapped his gift of love in a song that was played on a stretched-out piece of dried skin. He intoned his simple part in the symphony of man in the same way our elevating gifts can be enfolded in an embrace, a prayer, or any other way that helps in transforming another's heart to understand the depth of our love for them. And, yes, Jesus is best shrouded in the holiness of the great Eucharistic Tabernacles all around the world. He is the miraculous benefaction that Roman Catholic priests give to us throughout the entire year. The unifying Sacrifice of the Lamb of God is the ultimate sustenance for humankind. The Most Precious Body and Blood of Our Lord is offered to us every day at the hands of our reverend fathers. Our search for Love and fulfillment is culminated at the Celebration of the Holy Eucharist. There is no doubt that the Kingdom of God is at hand! Christmas brings this Divine realization closer to universal being.

Our Lady left it to my discretion to include another point which She made in Her message this evening. She spoke of the many evergreen trees which are taken inside our homes during the holiday season. I prayerfully decided to add this reference in order to reveal our Holy Mother's feelings about our usage of nature. Trees should be used to build shelter rather than be utilized as a crown for the material items which lay beneath them. However, She said that She would not ask anyone to stop erecting them in their homes since it is a means through which families are brought together. They are also a way for Jesus' birth to become important to little children. She told me that, if the felling of the many pine trees helps Love to grow, then it is a worthwhile sacrifice of the resources of the Earth. If each tree represents a converted heart, then God will assuredly supply plenty of them.

Tuesday, December 10, 1991

Our Lady always strengthens my soul with Her loving encouragement, giving many graces to increase my still infant faith. She is the greatest evangelist for Her Son with a converting power that is unequaled in the New Covenant ages. The inadequacies of human language render my efforts most laborious in attempting to reveal the splendor that I have already witnessed. There is only one word that articulates Her revelations most concisely. The never-ending syllable is "LOVE." It is all-powerful God, a blazing inferno, raging flood, and roaring quake, yet so gentle and of such peace that there are no forces or powers that could ever waver His impenetrable foundation. Love is a graceful silence that can shatter the Earth, leaving a stillness in its wake that deafens the hardest of heart to the cares of the world. It is a holiness that lifts us to sanctity with the ease of the dawning sun. Our Lady is the most docile appearance of the brilliance of God. Yet, She is valiant, fearless, and courageous enough to engage evil at every venue where Her children are in danger of being eternally harmed. She is the Mother of Heaven who loves us with the infinite magnanimity of our Divine Redeemer, Jesus of Nazareth.

Tonight, in referring to Her Christmas message of the 3rd of December, our Beloved Mother told me how Her words will touch the many souls who read them. Those who are caught in worldly motion will be the most affected. They will undergo a true awakening as though a mighty flash of light has impacted their conscience. Can you remember seeing a strobe-light that seemed to stop something's motion? This is what happens when the spirit of man encounters the omnipotence of God. The Truth and Light of Christ collide with the rambling minds of mortals causing them to halt in the face of a Mighty Rock that they cannot seem to move. Our Lady said that Her loving litany of the previous week invokes this interaction between Heaven and Earth. Her Divine Wisdom helps us understand that Jesus' birth is the miraculous planting of the seed of Love into the world by our Almighty Father, a kernel that grew into the full fruition of redemptive Sacrifice. This is what the Virgin Mary is trying to miraculously effect inside our hearts. With instruments such as this humble Diary, we can cultivate the Love of God in human consciences so that each soul will mature into the flourishing manifestation of prayer and self-denial. Then, others will be incalculably impressed, furthering the revelation of Light in the presently darkened world.

Our Holy Mother told me that goodness is always a fruit which we can offer to other hungry hearts. When we ask what virtues we have extolled today, we are truly asking ourselves, "How deeply have I loved today?" Life is a product of our Christian loyalty toward others. War and ill-will are a result of our defection from the noble principles that Jesus has inscribed into Creation. For those who wish to embrace His Love, prayer is the source of interactive knowledge. When we pray, we prepare, lift, and open our hearts to allow room for the Holy Spirit to enter. Our petitions initiate the welcome convention between ourselves and Almighty God, resulting in the peaceful union of His Heart with our own. Our Lady concluded by saying, **"It is a truly loving day! I give you a special blessing for what you have done for Jesus. Thousands of lives are changed by your prayers and good deeds. This may be difficult for you to understand, but you are praised for your obedience. I love you very much! Your prayers are very powerful for the good of humanity. Even your intention brings people closer to God. I love to praise My children! It is a happy time. Thank you for the hope you have afforded the world. Always remember that I love you."**

Saturday, December 14, 1991

Since it is nearing the Holy Feast of Christmas, Our Lady has continued this week to speak about the Nativity of Her perfect Son. She calls each of us to abandon temporal materialism and become God's little children again. Tiny Jesus was a simple and peaceful child at His birth. We are called both individually and collectively to live this same example, despite the forces which oppose our every good effort. It is quite difficult to project our original innocence in a world that is so filled with responsibilities, distractions, and societal burdens. It is not easy being a sprig of youth in a forest of stubborn old trees. Our hearts usually remain docile and pure until we are given the yoke of adulthood which all capable people are forced to carry. To restore the purity of our childhood, we must become less calculating and analytical as a signal of our fearless trust in the Heavenly Father. Our conversion toward our greatest potential begins within the honest simplicity of the Holy Mother's grace, where we are re-initiated in virtues of mutual kindness and obedience.

The Blessed Virgin provided a pretty example to clarify my understanding of Her lesson today. She said that small children do not know that there are supply pipes under the floor which feed water to the faucets. Likewise, they have no awareness of the electrical wires which connect the power to a light switch. They simply know that water falls from the tap into the sink and the switch on the wall makes the lights come on. This is a perfect reflection of the unimpeded vision which Jesus asks of us. We must humbly believe without question that His Kingdom springs-forth from His own omnipotent hand. We should also love one another with an absolute spirit of filial abandonment. Our thoughts and actions must buoyantly lift others in dignity and nobility, helping them to remain united as the Mystical Body of Christ. God not only gave His Son to the world at Bethlehem so that our souls will be saved, but also for our recognition of the requirement to imitate His likeness in service toward our brothers and sisters. Our Glorious Creator knew that His Son would be crucified from the very beginning of time. He not only had knowledge of it, but He wholeheartedly condoned it because He loves humanity with such infinite intensity. He knew on the darkest day of mortal history that His Beloved Son's sacrificial witness to Love would convert the entire world of every generation. Hence, He also asks us to reciprocally accept the events of Good Friday as a gracious acknowledgment that we love His Son, too. In that, our Heavenly Father displays His trust in our ability to embrace humankind in the way that Jesus still teaches.

The fact that Our Lord was crucified by mortal men does not mean that we are incapable of loving God in like measure. Indeed, the Holy Paraclete instills this spiritual capacity in the very message for which the Lamb was killed. To this very day, our Redeemer remains on Earth as the Wind of the Sacred Spirit and the Most Blessed of Sacraments because He knows that, in the final immortal end, there are multitudes who will accept Him. So, when Christ was born from the Womb of the Immaculate Virgin, God began the validation of our trust in His Will. He would never have allowed His Son to die for a fallacious cause. Therefore, where does He ask us to place our trust today? Our Virgin Mother explicitly states that He hopes that we will accept Jesus-present in the Holy Eucharist. The miraculous Bread of Life is the supreme premise upon which we build our faith in His Salvation. He generously allows humanity the free will to accept the Redemption that He is offering. This is the portion of perfect liberty that is surrendered to sinful creatures. The choice belongs to every individual who is created by the Breath of God. Jesus loves us so much that He tenders the freedom to choose or deny the direction through which He requires us to comply with His Commandments. No person on Earth can choose abortion without risking the loss of their paradisial Salvation! Human life is of infinite dignity because it revolves in communion with Eternal Life. Every soul is ultimately transformed from mortality to Eternity by Christ Jesus. Therefore, anyone who attacks life, especially in the womb, is truly assaulting the majesty of the Almighty Father and their own eternal destination. Tonight, before departing, Our Lady asked me to remember those who are poor in my prayers. The Feast of the Holy Family is celebrated immediately following Christmas. It is a special Sunday when all families should pray for Christian unity. This feast strengthens familial love and peace. Our Virgin Mother told me that She provides special blessings on that day to every family who prays together for Her intercession.

Sunday, December 15, 1991

Each new day, I continue to record another entry in this Diary as a display of my heartfelt love for every person who will someday encounter my witness. With every stroke of the pen, I give to you what Our Lady is giving to me; the Love of Our Almighty Savior. Please allow your hearts to be united with mine in affection for Him. The Advent of His joyful Birth magnifies the great call of God for our unity. We must come together as one people in order to obtain His universal Redemption. One soul in ten, or perhaps fifty, is not enough. Everyone must be washed by the Blood of the Lamb of God at the hands of His Immaculate Mother. The unification of every heart with all others is the communion of Love which will secure our acceptance of His Promise upon the Earth. Yes, our Divine Creator dispatched the Virgin Mary tonight to advocate this perfect oneness in my simple home again. She asked me to ponder the holy atmosphere inside the church, and within the Tabernacle which houses the Eucharistic Body of Her Son, Christ the King. I was to literally ponder the breathing air inside our congregational building. When the doors are opened, the winds from outside enter and are exposed to the Tabernacle. Then, as they retreat back across the threshold, they travel into the world and are inhaled by those who do not yet know Jesus or where He physically resides.

As we attend the Holy Mass and receive the Bread of Life, we are much like the breezes that travel around the globe to satisfy the needs of others and unite with their suffering. Our holy participation at the Sacred Sacrifice gains for us the desire and direction to serve those whom Our Lord loves so dearly. Likewise, when we pray from our hearts, Love transcends across the Earth in the same manner as the holy winds carry the grace of God from the Tabernacle throughout the landscape of Creation. Consider the celebration of Christmas which is about to occur. We are asked to prophetically envision the majesty and beauty of a world where all people are humbly prostrate at the feet of the Baby in the manger. This Feast of Light is a time of immeasurable focus and concentration upon the Redemption of humankind. We must be united in this celestial celebration and welcome the King of Creation as He breaches the bonds which had heretofore separated us from unending Glory. Our Lady has told us that we are presently living the period of the Second Advent in anticipation of Christ's Triumphant Return. But, She also says that humanity is nowhere near ready for this immortal flourishing of Eternity. The step that will bring us all to perfect preparation is our commitment to pray and accept the Holy Eucharist. One day very soon, we will intensely experience the great need for our conversion. Our Holy Mother concluded by saying, **"Thank you for your prayers! A special blessing has been bestowed upon your sibling whose birth is celebrated today. I have seen many loving acts from her in her life. There is great love shared in your family. I bless you through that Love in the Name of My Son."**

Tuesday, December 17, 1991

Today is somewhat like a dream from which I never wish to awaken. I confidently write my acclamation in the depths of these pages that Jesus Christ, the Savior of the world, spoke audibly to me. *"My brother, I am with you. I am your Savior who has come today to ask you to be strong in Love for Me. Thank you for helping My Mother. You are blessed on My birthday, too. I love you. Blessed are they who come in My Name and beg for Mercy. I have saved the world. I love you, My brother, I love you, Amen."* Our Lady prayed with me for an extended period of time, waiting for my heart to somehow grasp the dimensions of the words that the Kings of kings had just spoken. She then continued saying, **"Christmas is a time of unity. It is a time for everyone to remember the gift of Life conceived in the womb of their mothers by God. Jesus is the living presence of the preciousness of newborn Life. Unborn children are the beginning of a generation in which the Light of My Son will reflect for the next to offer and to accept. I bring you blessings from Jesus to continue His work in bringing Love to all Creation. His words to you today will strengthen you on your journey. May His Light forever be a beacon to keep you in the radiance of Truth. And, please never tire from your labors. Jesus and I are with you and ask you to remember this special time for the world. I remind you of the many waves and reflections through time that your prayers and holy acts are making possible. I now bless you in the Name of the Father, the Son, and the Holy Spirit. I love you. Goodnight."**

Wednesday, December 18, 1991

Love grows where it can and when we allow it to flourish. God will send His Son wherever He wishes to go. He knocks upon our door, but He will not open it because it is our responsibility to let Him in. Our Lady told me how we must passionately embrace love and forgiveness within our families for peace to flourish. I was asked to relate this message to the members of every family. We have difficulty when we try to breach the avenues that Love must take to fulfill our true happiness in Christ. The Virgin Mother has asked me to consider whether parents should prevent the companionship of a child with someone whom they do not personally care for. As long as the other person is living the Commandments of Love in accordance with Christ's Church, it seems to always be a relationship of faithfulness and grace. When the union in question is in harmony with the Sacred Scriptures, yet is still aggressively opposed, the willful intervention is against the principles of Jesus Christ. Millions of families disagree and grow apart because of this problem. Without Her saying so, I believe that our Holy Mother is asking us not to be too judgmental about those with whom our children would choose to unite in marriage. Jesus awaits patiently, hoping to satisfy the tiniest longing in our hearts. He tries to shape our souls into a perfectly symmetrical holiness, while asking us to love one another as He loves us. He will help us through every avenue which we grant Him. In union with the Spirit of Christmas, we should submit ourselves in trust to the good counsel of Love who rested that first joyful night in a manger. Frail human logic is superceded through the wisdom that is wrought by prayer. God's Divine Love overpowers and transcends the feebleness of our errant ideas and emotional judgments. We cause ourselves far too much grief when we give-up on the power of Love before we ever allow Jesus to touch us inside.

Thursday, December 19, 1991
"Good evening, My special little children! The hope and truth in our hearts will never die! Thank you for your obedience and prudent judgment. It is a fruit of your acceptance of Love. I ask you to be strong and pray for a Life during which you can tell many millions about Jesus." Our Holy Lady bids us peace during the celebration of Christmas. In light of the elevated concern for the dignity of humankind that we see during this season, our Blessed Mother asked me a very revealing question tonight, **"Does it surprise you to know that very few expectant mothers wish to have an abortion on Christmas day?"** That was the sole substance of Her question. I found it to be both rhetorical and commanding. Why would the conscience of these mothers be dead on every other day but Christmas? This inherent knowledge in the human soul provides the possibility for the conversion of anyone. Every soul can rise to perfection through accepting the Will of God, discovered through sincere prayer. Since no one would procure an abortion on Jesus' birthday, this highlights a splendid opportunity for us to realize that every day is as special as Christmas. The challenge to strengthen our awareness of the manifest dignity of Life is present. The Heavenly Father will take us where we need to go once we commence our journey in the holiness of His Son.

Our Holy Mother asks us to say "YES" to Love, especially regarding the lives of Her unborn children. She petitions us to prayerfully unite in heroic support of the dignity of all Life. The world will then grow closer to God as one humanity. When we lift the wretched from their darkness into the Light, the entire world is sanctified and elevated toward a more beatific pose and purpose. We experience the oneness of heart as a united community of caring and compassionate people, composing a symphony of Light throughout Creation. Our Lady metaphorically said that the gigantic trees are the large baritones. The birds which live in them are the chanting bells. The sky and green grass provide the shadow harmonies. And we, Her children, are the delightful melody whose hearts remain in rhythm and tempo with the Heart of Christ. We must manifest peace on Earth and good will toward all mankind or we will perish in the smoldering ruins that will ultimately result from our selfish hatred and greed. These are not just simple possibilities, but are tangible realities based upon whether we choose to accept the Savior of the world or continue to flaunt our blind arrogance before the Face of God. Our focus upon the Manger will help us to better fulfill Our Lady's beautiful prophecies for the future of our Salvation, instead of the looming chastisements which may soon purify the Earth through the wrath of the very God who created it. The Light from the redeeming stable is so bright that it illuminates our lives even to this present century. I thank you for your prayers and ask you to love Baby Jesus more intensely than you ever have before.

Saturday, December 21, 1991
With the celebration of the birth of the Christ-Child only hours away, Our Lady asked me to contemplate the humility in which He was born. Jesus Christ is the Sun of Creation who has destroyed the darkness of night. This great Warrior and eternal Victor came clothed in the armor of defenseless infant flesh. The King of Eternity, the Maker of Magnificence, and the Glory Forever, was welcomed into the world by the weathered homage of shepherds. He wasted not a moment of His Divine Life upon the Earth. As quickly as He drew His first breath, His work to feed the poor, to lift the lowly and outcast, and to find the lost had already begun. He was born to a welcome family in a humble stable whose impoverished atmosphere best allowed Love to grow and be presented to the ages. Everyone should marvel at the genius of God's entrance into His Creation. The arrival of peace in our time requires the same abandonment of worldliness, the mutual plummet in humility, and the same elevation of beatific possibility and hope in the human spirit. The grace of prayer from the heart lifts our souls like a helium-filled balloon rising into the sky. The solemnity of Christmas radiates out of the paradisial soul of Christ who brought Heaven to Earth at His descent into the Virgin's Womb. Our Lord is present in the world in both Spirit and Body as the Holy Paraclete and

the Eucharist of the Altar. His Imminent Return will consume the remaining darkness, despair, disease, and helplessness that we are unwilling to eradicate by our own obedient conversion and moral strength.

Until that eternal moment arrives, we should fervently continue to partake in the Fruit of the Tabernacle to sustain solace, pardon, peace, and the steadfast courage to wage the battle for the souls who are being spiritually decimated by proud opportunistic worldlings. Therein lies our freedom from both affliction and terror. We must be thankful to God for His Sacramental Gift of the precious Body and Blood of His Crucified Son. Christ Jesus is the ultimate and highest bestowal of grace that has ever been given to such an undeserving species of people. We must, in turn, provide this same bounty to every child of God. We have the power to return the world to paradisial beauty. The question is, do we have the desire to do it? Moral leadership and spiritual authority spring from the continence of the universal grace that is cultivated in sacrificial hearts who love openly and completely. The entire world must be led to Christ now or we will all perish without effecting our greatest imitation of everything that is noble and true.

Sunday, December 22, 1991

In a world that is so limited in visionary wisdom, and likewise, inebriated with blinding mortal thought and deprivating conjecture, we all need to realize that only God is infinite. Everything has been created from His immortal Love and boundless intention to care for us throughout Eternity. But, we are powerless in both reception and transmission of grace unless we accept His Son, Jesus. Our exile is of finite nature in a lethargic physical world. Any division or separation from Love forces great constraints upon the happiness and contentment of our fragile souls. We recognize and address the world through dimension, size, range, and scope which keep our nimble consciences locked in frustration within confining dimensions. We must, instead, strive to achieve the limitless nature of the heavens without considering the seamy impediments of the measurable world. This planet without Jesus is simply a celestial rock with numeric parameters prescribed by imprisoned mortal intellects. But, with the Son of God, life is of an unending freedom which is not subjugated by complex equations and integral values. All Love is one in the genius of Our Lord. Our new beginning in Christ the King is the end of human bondage to sin and despair. It has been replaced by the fresh timelessness of fulfilled hopes and benevolently-conferred happiness. This is what our Holy Mother calls us to realize through the unerring focus of Her Immaculate Heart.

As my brother and I prayed the Rosary today at one-thirty this afternoon, She said, **"I am very happy to come to you again. You recognize that Love is truly the beginning of Eternal Life through Jesus and the**

Church. **Your vision is concise. You have been given the opportunity to provide My messages to all the world. You serve Jesus by presenting the world what I have given you..."** She added that there are many special prayers being lifted today by humble and obedient children that are changing the world. This day also marks the beginning of the tenth month of Her miraculous messages to my brother and me. We are very grateful to Jesus for this magnificent blessing. It is overwhelming to be supported by such loving guidance day after day. The particular topic that the Blessed Virgin invoked to continue Her lessons this evening is how the forces of the world condition our habits and styles, preventing us from perfectly knowing Her Son. We have become humanly fashioned through our obsessive compulsions and whims. Our addiction to these earth-bound routines must be broken in order for our souls to grow in more distinguishable dimensions. God loves us in universes and eternities that we have never before imagined. He came to Earth as a definable human being, hoping for us to achieve more than we have ever previously dared to envision. We must love with an equally authentic allegiance to the Almighty Father that Jesus lived while treading upon this same ground in mortal flesh.

When our souls breathe the beautiful Love of Christ into other lives, the extraordinary capacity of humankind to become elevated to the right hand of God comes clearly into focus. In hearts who are destined to be reunited with Heaven someday, Love is the standard of human morality, not the exception. Placed into the context of our daily world, the Spirit of God is the rule of Life that will transform our communities and societies in the same way that Christ Jesus transcended the politics and protocol of the first-century Earth. But, many of us do not recognize such powerful and holy Love because we have never felt the healing hand of another person, or extended our own to anyone else. Our Lady offered me a simple example of this principle by asking me to look closely at the following symbol:

As I surveyed this remarkable graphic, the first thing I wondered was whether She was going to lead me into one of Her subtle moral lessons for which I was about to be the unwitting volunteer. Oftentimes during our messages, our Virgin Mother will ask a rhetorical question or show me a completely unrecognizable picture so that I will remember my reaction as exemplary of anyone who may read this Diary in the future. This is Her ingenious means of teaching me, while allowing others to also participate in Her supernatural instruction. I set-out to determine the meaning of the incomprehensible symbol which She asked me to ponder. Initially, I thought that it might be some errant aberration of the Cross for which She was going to admonish Her children. Next, I thought it might be a cursive combination of the letters "T" and "S," remembering that She previously told us that these letters are indicators and signs of Salvation. Having not ruled-out any of my ideas, I patiently awaited Her reaction to them, knowing that I would eventually be given the true purpose of Her example. I continued to pray the Holy Rosary, pondering what She would do with this message. I have come to know that there is always a factual predicate to every exercise that Our Lady delivers. She provides a spiritual lesson of Light after allowing me sufficient time and plentiful substance to understand myself and anticipate the reaction of anyone else who might be assigned this same simple task. She finally came to the aid of my confounded heart. She asked what I believed the symbol to be and gave me the context in which I should properly recognize it. How could I have known what it really was? I was not surprised that my preponderance did not yield the answer for which She was looking. The following display is the completed picture which She asked me to see. As I had anticipated earlier, my Beloved Mother utilized my humanness to teach a more broad and universal principal.

The character is the letter "J." She knew that I would never recognize it because I could not see it in the context in which She would later place it. I had not been completely preconditioned to recognize Jesus in the totality of my daily routine. I had never considered that a "J" might appear in a form which I could not easily comprehend. And, now, the moral to the story. Centuries before the Blessed Virgin Mary gave me this message tonight, the world similarly could not have envisioned the God they knew coming to Earth as a tiny child. This message is a parable for us all. We must be prepared for our Triumphant King to enter His world in any way that He chooses to employ. Our patience must be strong enough to allow the eyes of our souls to focus upon that prospect. No contextual habit or teaching should prohibit us from expecting that Our Lord will do many miraculous things to reveal Himself before Creation. The "J" is the seed for an entire fruitful vine of faith which sprouts from within the hearts of humankind. In conjunction with our inability to recognize the letters, we also fail to acknowledge Jesus as the Savior of the world. Many still believe that He is always out-of-context with our advanced societies.

This is why we must question our frail judgment and to trust God, instead. We best attain this deference through our prayers. Humble communication between the Heavenly Father and ourselves is the mystical fulcrum, a human necessity that reveals the balance of our hearts in a form of beauty and art like a ballerina on her toes. We must remember, however, that we cannot ignite unadulterated belief if we require vision at the outset. Wisdom is a reward that is obtained by virtue of our faith. It is not of the eyes, but of the heart. Love provides our immortal sight without ever having to broach our attention to the material world. Likewise, there can be no trustworthy certitude without Christ because He is the breathtaking object of our sacrificial conviction and belief. This is the essential advocacy of the Holy Spirit within our hearts. When we give all of our affinity to God and His people, our lives become spiritually awakened, more strong, and everlastingly beautiful. This indomitable revelation quickly explodes, consuming all infinite dimensions, facets, and colors that surround us when we receive the Most Blessed Sacrament. But, it also continues to remain of simple beauty and innocent splendor.

During Christmastide, we blessedly rendezvous with the recognition of Love in our hearts in an open and apparent way. The celebration of the birth of Jesus allows us to see a symbolic mark as the concise alphabetic letter "J," the first inscription on the mortal page of an otherwise endless Eternity. We must pray to reveille the soul of every person so that our collective heart may remain aware of the majesty of Christ Jesus throughout the rest of the year. Indeed, the season for giving His Love to others is perpetual. We are granted eternal sanctuary with Him through our service to others. Our hopes are changed for the better when those in the world mystically join in the fruitful expectations that our Christian surety generates. All of this beauty comes from the bounty of God and takes root in the innermost cells of our spiritual being. Jesus is this Root of Jesse. The season for the celebration of His entrance into the world is made whole and manifest by our forgiveness of others. Humanity will be converted when every single soul opens to the flowering utterance of, "I forgive you." Peace will then flourish in the wake of invincible Love. The true reflection of God is peace on Earth and good will among men. However, our honest intentions must come first. To effect this sweet everlasting legacy, we must mutually accept the Messiah of the Cross for the mortal chapter of Creation to be brought to an appropriate conclusion. Therefore, in this age and time, Jesus' Crucifixion can never be deleted or overshadowed in our observation of His Nativity. The Holy Mass is always part of our celebration on the eve of Christmas.

Wednesday, December 25, 1991

The words, **"Unto mankind today the Savior is born,"** have made this day most beautiful. My brother and I began the Rosary at nine o'clock tonight and Our Lady came to me as miraculously as Jesus was born in Bethlehem. She asked me to pray for everyone to manifest their acceptance of His Mercy in their hearts. Love is not measured by weight, distance, or any other means. But, when the Christ-Child was born to His beautiful parents of Nazareth, Divine Love could be physically seen in His incalculable bounty on Earth. Even now, through the Holy Eucharist, Our Lord presents to humankind the same Body, Blood, Soul, and Divinity which lived as the Baby in the manger. He was born as visible and tangible Love, immeasurably personifying our unseen Creator through the lessons He taught and the example He lived. God became Incarnate through His Son, Jesus, as the living witness of how we can transcend our own physical limitations that keep us sorrowfully detached from the perfect unity of Paradise. Our right to Salvation is exemplified when we extend forgiveness and compassion of a universal magnitude and order, while still living in the mortal world. The Infinity of the Holy Spirit in our hearts makes us "little Christs." That is how we are set free. We can experience immortality in a captive world by accepting the Son of Mary. Love is that freedom! The Savior of all humankind sets the beatific horizon within our sights so that the eternal happiness of our Redemption can be envisioned from the depths of our hearts. In that, we are able to mystically surpass the surface of the mirror that separates us from Heaven. Our heart is a tool that is rendered worthy through the prayers of the good carpenter, Saint Joseph. This tender instrument allows us to peer over the boundaries of Creation, despite the grievous and compelling nature of the world. Our petitions hold the true power that cannot be conquered or constrained. They prophetically overwhelm anything that might attempt to impede our sacred dreams.

What, then, is the effect of sin upon our souls? Why the imprisonment and the sorrow? Our Holy Mother has clearly taught us throughout the many centuries that we must be washed clean of sin by the Blood of the Lamb who was born in the manger. She directs our prayers to strengthen us against our errors and to raise our sights in humble acclamation to Infinite forgiveness. She often honors specific people with Her honest accolades in hopes that we will emulate them in their holiness and wise guidance. Our Blessed Lady told me tonight that Padre Pio and His Holiness, Pope John Paul II, are two salient examples of the radiant Spirit of Her Son. We must also accept the fact that even the most wretched among us can ascend to their holiness and example through the power of prayer. The birth of Jesus began this fertile process. His Nativity showed us that it is not a sin to be human. He revealed the true potential of our souls to become God-like in both capacity and capability. The ultimate goal of the Man-God was to teach all men to be like Him. And, that spiritual redefinition now rests in our own ability to love completely with every fiber of our being. Our elevation in holiness brings us to the clearing of perfection where the Almighty Father resides in Omnipotent Divinity. Yes, He is real. But, the world has not found Him because we refuse to collectively pray for His vision.

The origin of human absolution was brought on Christmas day, many years ago. Our birth into sanctity is, indeed, alive and well. God's powerful Child still lives in corporeal form as the Most Blessed Sacrament. When we partake of this Sacred Bread, His transcending authority and heavenly Wisdom are provided to each of us. And, where do we find this Heavenly Food? He lives in the Tabernacles of the Catholic Church, providing tangible characteristics that are observable by all humankind. His breath is not unlike the wind. As the latter moves the leaves in swirling circles on a bright autumn day, so does the Breath of the Father enliven the hearts of men. It is the detectable and knowable Spirit of God that makes us cry happy tears. When His caress touches our souls through the love in our hearts, we experience the gentle embrace of Heaven. Our Lord speaks a language that is recognizable by any of His creatures. His words of compassion can be heard when someone speaks from their heart. Indeed, His Holy dialect does not even need to be spoken for us to understand it. The voice of Christ is detectible through generosity, prayer, and common obedience. His Nativity at Bethlehem makes the unlimited grace of Redemption tactile to every man on Earth. Our symmetry becomes comparable and one with God through His Perfect Son. We were created as children in His Divine image for all Eternity. Nothing can change that except an arrogant humanity who refuses to accept it. The Light of the World has commanded us to share His Love reciprocally. Amidst all of these gifts, we must assuredly see that He simply wishes to someday hold us in His arms forever. I humbly pray for each person to embrace a contemplative understanding of the holiness of this day. Please continue to hope with me for the inheritance of Eternal Life for us all.

Thursday, December 26, 1991

While I was preparing in silent meditation for my prayers tonight, I kept thinking with confidence that, after all the Blessed Virgin has told me about the Life and Death of Her beloved Son, God must assuredly believe each of our souls to be worthy of eventual canonization. He would never have allowed His Son to die in vain, and neither would He concede our conversion through Him to be a fruitless proposition. This is why our Holy Mother intercedes for Him by interior locution and apparition throughout the world. She, too, knows the truth of God's pardoning of His people through Her Messianic Son. She is equally touched because of His virgin birth in Her Womb. She believes it to be imperative that everyone hear the message of our miraculous and merciful God. To that end, She came again tonight while I was lifting my petitions through the Holy Rosary to the heavens. She said, **"I love you, little ones, more than you can imagine! I have been telling you about the tremendous power of Jesus and His Love in the world. I will tell you how His power proceeding in your hearts can preserve the dignity of man."**

Our Lady has told me many times that Love assists us in our transformation from mortality to Eternal Life. Each new generation is granted the same opportunity to love. We build the world upon a foundation, utilizing the liberty that we gained through Christ in the first century. The Earth is now living the potential of being completely saturated with dignity, peace, and fulfillment. Our happy freedom lies in our ability to arrange our cultures as innocently as children stacking their toy blocks on the floor at our feet. Each new generation receives the custodial responsibility of the spiritual construction materials passed from the preceding generations. Our Holy Mother asked me if I remembered having such little building blocks when I was a child? I told Her "yes," whereupon She responded that the principle of this message is the same. Jesus symbolically gives these ingredients to the passing centuries so that His people can freely arrange their world as they see fit to choose. Although the designs usually differ by fashion and need, He wishes for us to use them to erect a staircase upon which we can be elevated high and away from worldliness and the frailty of sin and indifference.

Not for the purpose of being cynical, Our Lady asked me if I knew what we have chosen to do with our blocks. When I said that I did not know, She told me that mankind either isolates himself by building confining walls, or stones one another with them. These symbolic playthings are actually meant to be the actions, deeds, and thoughts that, when properly utilized under the guidance of the Holy Spirit, will lead us to Paradise. This is why we must decide to avail all of our resources for the purpose of seeking Love upon the Earth. For example, the building block of communication should be for speaking of peace instead of threatening war. A righteous people will prayerfully compile their gifts into a staircase to Jesus with the remaining ones composing His Cross as a hopeful sign of Redemption to humanity. The heart provides the knowledge that assures our understanding of the latitude that we are allowed and the responsibility we are given to seek the Eternal Kingdom. The gifts of God sustain our timeless mobility. If we arrange our lives in a united communion with every race and nation who understands the responsible call which God asks of them, the Earth will become like Heaven. Until now, however, the blocks seem to be left in disarray by each generation for their descendent posterity to reorient. Without a proper blueprint of spiritual charity, there is no guarantee of our erecting a stable structure anytime soon. Herein lies the power of which Our Lady spoke in the beginning. The knowledge of Love is learned from the previous generation, but every heart needs authentic conversion to the Truth of Christ to sustain its depth and beauty. Each new mortal age must learn who their Savior is and why He died so profoundly on the Cross. This requires our own lives to be grounded and positioned in holiness from the absolute foundation of our hearts.

Baby Jesus was born into the world as the Knower of all. He is God from the very beginning. And, we must lovingly embrace the humanity that He came to save. We should begin by imitating the little Christ in ourselves. Therefore, blessing, feeding, admonishing, and healing are the works of Mercy that we are called to articulate as human actions to magnify Heaven upon the Earth, while increasing the scope of Paradise for all who participate in such grace. Many times, we have wondered about the acceptance of our unheralded acts by God, who is also unseen. When we live the example of His Son, we can be assured in the full Light of Eternity that we are manifesting the Divine principles for which He came. All of this is brought forth through the power of our humble prayers.

Sunday, December 29, 1991 - Feast of the Holy Family

I have learned from Our Lady that it is important for us to remember the call of unity while embracing our responsibilities of sisterhood and brotherhood. It is imperative that we recall the ties that bind our families together and how they are strengthened. Forgiveness is a great gift of Jesus that often seems to require painful sacrifice-of-the-self to extend. We honor the esteem and dignity of others when we grant them pardon for their failures and weaknesses. Gone is the weight of their transgression. Our heartfelt absolution destroys the walls that divide us, bringing a unity that protects everyone from lasting dissension. Forgiveness reopens the avenue of love between hearts, renewing the overtures that will heal and moderate our relations. In order to accomplish this heroic spiritual task, we must understand what causes others to be offended. We must be gentle, always remembering that we will be pardoned if we, too, choose to forgive. When we live our devotion for others, especially our families, we are less apt to be offended. It is a signature of pure intention to accept the suffering brought through another's transgression, yet continue to bestow our greatest humility upon them. That is why peace begins in the heart, and also why we must keep it pure. When we are filled with Love, we cannot be embittered. That is why forgiveness must be offered and accepted to preserve our state of grace. It is a mandatory attribute of the reciprocal nature of Christ.

Our Holy Mother came today as I was praying the Rosary and brought my heart to better understanding of forgiveness. She began, **"Good afternoon, My special little ones! I love you more than you can comprehend. Jesus is always close to you and is especially pleased with your service and obedience in seeking hearts for Me. You will always know that Love is** the most special ingredient. I have come searching for the hearts of all mankind, in much the same way as I searched for Jesus when He was found in the temple. I realize, however, that many human hearts have not been doing the Father's work. That is why Love is so important. Like sheep, they have gone astray, but shall be found. Those who are blind, indeed, will see. Thank you for helping them. I hope you can see how the beauty of Love helps you. I enjoyed your prayerful meditations before I came today. I, too, come to ask all in the world to seek reconciliation..."

This is the feast which recognizes the Holy Family of Jesus, Mary, and Joseph. It is, indeed, special for all families to recognize the example of such a Godly source of grace. We must know that forgiveness will come easily when we live the example of Our Savior's perfect household. Our Lady has told me many times that Love cannot be measured. Therefore, forgiveness must be equally as boundless. Many are tempted to say, "I have forgiven you in greater measure than you have penitentially offered in return", or perhaps, "You did not truly forgive me so I, therefore, take back my forgiveness of you." It is obvious that these are not sanctified words. There is no competition to forbearance, nor can it be revoked. It is our essential gift, not our commodity to barter. It is the most fundamental act of charity upon the Earth.

While my brother and I were continuing the Holy Rosary later in the evening, the Blessed Mother told me more about the Holy Eucharist. She is quite happy with those who participate in bringing the knowledge of the Bread of Life to the world with the conviction that is gained through reverential faith. Our many hours of hope, prayer, and effort are a fruit of our piety. There is a culminating revelation of the Truth of the Most Blessed Sacrament in the near offing. Our Lady's children are sowing the seeds for this eternal harvest. The time is near when this generation of humanity will tearfully celebrate the jubilation of the Return of Christ to unite Creation in Paradise. The key to this hopeful manifestation is our call to holiness. This has never been an easy or self-satiating process because it requires our sacrificial love for God, choreographed in the pious lives we lead. But, many people have an errant idea that it is easier to love than to be holy, not realizing that they are uniquely inseparable. Conversion begins in our desire to be loving. That is the bountiful seed which the Blessed Mother is planting in our hearts. This miraculous kernel of hope thrives upon the nourishment of our prayers. Our love for Jesus is our yearning for goodness and our intention to embrace others perfectly. We are assisted in our effort to ascend these sacrificial peaks when we pray.

By all means, how does this discussion relate to the Holy Eucharist? Our Heavenly Mother says that the Blessed Sacrament is the peak of perfection, the summit of infinite vision, and the destination of every soul who is bound for

Paradise. Each time we receive the Body of Christ, we touch that mystical pinnacle of holiness as Our Savior becomes one with our soul. He loves us into the heights of Redemption! Thereafter, the faith that we live prevents us from falling from this supernatural moment of Holy Communion with His Divinity. Our faithful conviction allows us to live our eternal destiny while still in the capacity of fleshly existence. This is the invincible power of the Love in the Bread of Life and it is the reason why forgiveness is such a universal grace. When we forgive the transgressions of others, we shed any spiritual weight that would prevent us from sailing the heights of joy with Christ. After providing this blessed discussion, Our Lady brought me to Her Mantle, held me in the esteem of Her Holy Heart, blessed my soul, and quietly departed.

Monday, December 30, 1991
Without prelude or preface, Our Lady simply asked me today to give the following message to you. **"I have reminded the world many times that the fulfillment of the Fatima promise in 1917 is at hand. Yes, there are graces for the world and many to come, but also there will be reprimands in other locations. The years between 1917 and 1992 have been treacherous and oftentimes filled with evil. The Twentieth Century has been particularly marred by the aggression of Satan. We have made great progress on many fronts and in many places. Prayer and conversion are defeating Satan. My precious children, we are at the threshold of the conversion of millions of souls! Jesus wishes to carry the Church, which is His Bride, over the threshold into Eternity in Heaven. We must pray that those in the Church will allow Him to elevate them. All must abandon their will and the weight of their mortal sins to be carried into His Kingdom. Many wish not to let go of their materials and wealth. Love will bring them to relinquish their earthliness. Their day will come through the Divinity of the Light of My Son, Jesus. Since the road is filled with stumbling blocks, it is better for you to not bother to look down, but to always look up to Jesus and ask Him to carry you above it in His arms. That is the beginning of the elevation of the human soul. One of the provisions of 1992 that I wish the world to realize is how helpless mankind is on his own. He must seek the hand of Jesus. Please accept His Love today and always."**

Through this beautiful message, I am able to clearly see the hope which Our Lady holds for our future. She has not given up on our conversion and asks us to live with that same conviction. As I come near the end of this spectacular year, it is one which has permanently changed my life and brought great revelations about God which my soul had never before realized. I do not know how much longer the Blessed Virgin Mother will speak to me, nor do I know the finished length of my Diary. But, I feel completely satisfied that She will accomplish what She has set out to do through my life. I am Her child, obedient and willing to be used for the Glory of Her Son. As you read this timely record of my new direction, I ask that you accept with childlike faith the simplicity and symbolism of the messages that I have been asked to record. This has not been an easy task. I do not know what my life would have otherwise brought, but I am convinced that the exhilarating course set before me by the Immaculate Mother of Our Lord is one which any soul, no matter how far from an understanding of human Redemption, would both embrace and strive to bring to success. I love you in as great a magnitude as our Virgin Mother loves you, although I do not yet personally own the sacrificial heritage to prove it. Maybe before my life is over, I can give you that gift. I ask only that you return the greatest love that you can muster to our Divine Queen of Paradise. I promise that She will return your devotion by magnifying the grace of God in your life in ways that you could never have possibly imagined. You cannot "out-love" the Blessed Virgin Mary. I ask Our Almighty Father to bless you in your acceptance and understanding of the miracles that I am describing in this literary composition. So, together, we march into 1992 with the strength to endure any trial, the passion to convoke all righteousness, and the patience to let God's Will be done on Earth, as it is in Heaven.

UNVEILING HELPLESS MANKIND

JANUARY 1992

Wednesday, January 1, 1992

I look at our Holy Mother with tremendous love, respect, honor, and obedience. She is our celestial Matriarch who perfectly defines the virtues of motherhood. She is gentle and yet, firm. She provides the sure-footed guidance we need from someone who has traveled the journey of life before us. It is She who protects us from the enticements of the wayward paths. Our Virgin Mother is more than a teacher of Her beloved children. She is Light for our soul and our sustainer of hope. She knows God intimately and is aware of what He wishes for His children. Our Mother-Advocate is the presence of universal grace and a constant source of reverent solace and limitless consolation. I call upon Her daily for spiritual strength and new direction. I lift the prayer of the "Hail Mary" to invoke Her intercession before God on behalf of everyone on Earth. Yes, I have more than come to know the Blessed Virgin as the Mother of Jesus Christ, but also as the Mediatrix of the entire bounty of God. She is not nature, but the Mother of the Creator of nature. In Her sinless perfection, Her Divinity flows to all of us through Her Son, our Savior, Jesus Christ. She gave birth to Mercy, Himself, and in doing so has asked our monarchial God to hasten our Redemption and the blessings we need to realize His Love in every age. That is Her gift to us all.

I now know a different Virgin Mary than I knew just a year ago. But, it was me who had to make the change! Every day, with Her help, I try through this written work to enlighten all of Her children to the miracles that Her heavenly station is bringing to us. I began this new year by praying the Holy Rosary in hopes of meeting the needs of all the world. Through the intercession of Our Lady and the Glory of Jesus, I believe that we will succeed. She asked me to tell the world that 1992 is the year in which we will finally come to know that we cannot be saved without Her Son. We are all too mortal and too helpless. We cannot be redeemed into Eternity without the Mercy and absolution of Christ. Every message that Our Lady gives throughout the world is based upon this same universal premise. We must realize that we cannot achieve on our own what the Son of God had to die to accomplish. We all desire to love deeply through the grace that we are given to understand. But, we must seek and accept Jesus and partake in His Eucharistic Body to have Life in us.

The realization that mankind is totally and irrevocably lost without Christ is the foundation which Our Lady presents Her messages of the new year. God provides ample opportunity for those who do not know Him to procure His blessings through His Mother. The Immaculate Conception has called my attention to the peoples of Russia who have seen the transition in their homeland from involuntary constraint to the freedom of democracy. And yet, they are still lost as to how to govern themselves in the infancy of their newfound liberty. They are a parable for all the world because they represent the enlightenment of humankind once we finally understand that worldliness and materialism are confining our souls. Millions of people are held captive by lives of luxury and facility. These chains bind them to procuring the resources they need to support their continuing addiction. But, like the Russians, we will all soon realize that our detention by the influences of the Earth is about to end. Everything that is worldly in nature is finite and limited by sheer obsolescence and the element of time. When humanity eventually sees the awful condition of mortal life without Jesus, we will effect an exhaustive search to discover any means at our disposal to find Him.

Through the recent decades, Russia has been a prime example of what happens to a people whose government denies them the freedom to worship the Savior of the World. Men of great fortunes are equally helpless without their corrupt empires, their social stature, and their imperial wealth. They, too, will eventually lose it all and be forced to turn toward Jesus as their eternal treasure. They will require great spiritual counseling from the shock of meeting their future without the security of their past. The men of our very own nation are marching inexorably toward this same demise. There is great selfishness inside our American borders regarding the welfare of the poor and the fate of the innocent unborn. It is also reflected in the discriminatory dispensation of the resources of our public treasury and in the violation of every moral and sacred Commandment that God has seen fit to put before us. The greatest sin against Heaven that we are presently committing is the killing of little children in the wombs of their mothers. Our sins against the gift of Life are equally aggravated through the execution of prisoners and the so-called mercy killing of those who are chosen to suffer. And, as if this is not sufficiently grotesque, our outright rejection of the Sixth Commandment is egregiously as sorrowful and disastrous.

Mankind refuses to obey the call of our Almighty Father for purity and chastity. It is an abomination to believe that homosexuality is an acceptable way of Life. It is a sinful affront to God and a violation against the Divinity of Jesus Christ to practice it! The Lord is offended by these horrific atrocities and, equally, by the acts of vengeance perpetrated by those who feel that their right to sin is being infringed! None of these people realize that they are eternally helpless. They cannot ask a government to justify their conduct when that government is opposed to everything that is righteous. Only the Son of God can reconcile them in the Truth! Only the Messiah can heal their souls. Only by accepting the Holy Gospel can they find the absolution of Love instead of the darkness of subservient condemnation. Eternal brotherhood and peace are found only in the acceptance of the Life of Salvation brought by the Love in the Sacred Heart of Christ. His Holy Mother has commissioned us to observe 1992 as being dedicated to prayer for our understanding that the world is helpless without Him. She is guiding us to see this through the most enlightening grace ever known to man. **"My little children, My Immaculate Heart and the Sacred Heart of Jesus are so offended by sins against Love. Mankind has found any way it can to disguise its evil and indifference by falsely donning the cloth of love, but not living Love in their heart."**

The movement of human hearts away from Love began at the fall of Adam and Eve. Jesus created them in perfection, but sin distorted and perverted their pristine nature in every way it could. Unfortunately for us, that sin would also stain every human soul given life thereafter. But, to our great benefit, Jesus has reshaped Love into the formation of a Cross. He destroyed not only the sin of Adam, but also the transgressions of every person who would accept Redemption thereafter. The decision is now in the hands of mankind as to whether we will embrace our refurbished perfection. It is the desire of God that we come to the Passion of His Son and stand forward as the beneficiaries of His bloody Crucifixion. We need to accept Jesus without condition and deed our souls as His personal property. This is the greatest decision that has ever been suspended before the judgement of the human species. It is the very reason that you are reading this miraculous Diary. We must listen to the messages of hope which God brought to the Earth from the first words of an angel named Gabriel to a young handmaiden named Mary. His requisition was validated in the Life of Jesus Christ and made perfect through His death and Resurrection.

The Almighty Father has granted the opportunity for many hopeful souls to die in the profession of evangelizing His Son. Many great people have traveled the path of Life with tremendous converting power, but were consequently killed for their faith. There was a great American leader who once stated, *"Some men see things as they are, and say, why? I dream things that never were, and say, why not?"* Robert Francis Kennedy stated this hope as a prayer for the lost and forsaken. He was a Catholic, a child of the Holy Eucharist, who was gentle of mind and strong of heart. His brother was the thirty-fifth President of the United States. Our Savior wishes us to emulate such simplicity and Love. Mr. Kennedy's proclamation is an example of our helplessness without Jesus. Unless we accept Him, we will always see things as they are and ask, "why?" In Christ, humanity can hope of things that will soon come-to-pass and say, "why not?" Everyone needs to pray and resolve to this Truth. Thereafter, the transition of the world will become more than the simple exchange of bad habits for malfeasance, but the true transformation from darkness into Light.

Thursday, January 2, 1992

The Blessed Virgin Mary, our paradisial Mentor, Benefactor, and Advocate, arrived at my door in response to my prayer of the Holy Rosary. She told me that Jesus loves the world so much that all graces are possible for the conversion of our hearts to Love. Our prayers invoke this power because they are limitless and are always answered by God. She also told me that She planned an apparition for January 11th before my brother, but it would be a private revelation that I would understand later. Her beautiful words for today are these, **"Good evening, My little son, I love you very much! I have come in Love on behalf of Jesus to tell the world that it is dangerously lost. This danger is the result of the helplessness of mankind. We must all pray for the end of evil and indifference. I ask all of My children to pray for this conversion. If you do not, you will witness the effect of human indifference as many chastisements may come. Mankind's lack of discernment and lack of Love for human life and the sins of impurity which involve promiscuity and homosexuality are the reasons for such chastisements. As we pray together, we hope for the conversion of the world, so as to avoid them."**

Our Holy Mother wants us to be persistent in telling the world about Love and displaying the urgency of Her call. But, it seems that only a few are willing to listen. We are often disappointed by the lack of response to Her intercession, but we must persevere, nonetheless. Many souls will not acknowledge their conversion in the company of other men because it is not the "masculine" thing to do. Many consciences are changed when the penitent is alone. I am convinced that God does not seem to mind, as long as the soul makes the transfer into His grace. This is a very timely and revealing experience. We must reach out to the timidly lost and bring them to Salvation by convincing every sinner on Earth that we love them. Moreover, we must tell them from whom we learned such conviction! The Blessed Mother says that the Holy Spirit gives us a power that we cannot envision with our eyes. She identifies the parable of being able to see radio waves spiraling through the air. If this were the case, we would not be able to drive down the road because of all the visual turbulence inhibiting our view. The intercession of the heavens is that prominent on Earth! It is happening as a result of our prayers, but we do not recognize it as we should.

We are effectively manifesting great graces for the world which cannot be detected through an optical lens. Still the same, we must never allow ourselves to be distracted from Jesus' work by what we visually perceive. His Holy Mother is keeping our concentration toward its proper course. We must be assured of their Love and remember that it is forever authentic and sincere. Our Lady has already expressed Her hope that no soul shall enter the fires of Hell. But, we must continue to seek the conversion of our brothers and sisters because the doorway into that pit is still wide open. We should pray for the desires of God to be actualized. To that end, we must bring the entire world to Love, touch every heart, dignify the lowly, and breathe new Life into those in despair. We own the task of giving others a reason to hope by lifting their spirits from oppression. Let us raise them to new heights through the power of our Love and the Precious Life of Jesus Christ. We must remind them that He has fully redeemed the world.

Saturday, January 4, 1992

We would be a diminished and wholly-unsanctified people if not for the redeeming Love of Christ Jesus and the grace of His Immaculate Mother. Entire generations of, otherwise, complacent people have become, instead, leaders and practitioners of the Church of faith because they have been enlightened by the superior call of this Savior and His Mother. We cannot be the first generation to walk into a new century without carrying our trust in God with us, kept neatly-packed within our hearts as we cross the finish line of time. We must all listen adherently to the call of the Virgin Mother, who says that this new century is destined to be the last. That is why She has come to ask me to record Her remarkable words. Tonight, Her intercession was particularly a combination of the poignant and the beautiful. When I began to pray, She told me that I should remember that the curious human mind seems to search for substantiation and effect in everything it encounters.

Our thoughts are inherently analytical. We search for a central meaning in every occurrence and comparable similarities in any process. If there is an anomaly, we are determined to find it, or bust. We are neither fair nor impartial judges as to the interaction and result of the world in which we live. It is this calculating state that has caused the proliferation of many false distinctions and harmful divisions throughout the passing centuries. I am somewhat disappointed that we, as God's children, have not made a more righteous use of the gift of human knowledge. I hold many regrets about the past and just as many hopes for our future. And, in these thoughts, I recall that all moments of life are connected and interrelated with the previous and subsequent ones. We have the capacity to recall events and passages of time, but they are only highlights in the recesses of our memories. Indeed, they are like links on a chain that connect human existence into a time-transcending symbol that we believe to be as universal as God, Himself. These moments make-up our perspective of the present. They are the feelings that we generate from a happy recollection or a painful encounter. They are the most noticeable peaks in the architecture of our inner-psyche. Somehow, time does not seem to exist between them at any level of detection.

The Holy Mother helps me understand that there are times during the procession of life when we are between historical events. There is often a lull in human interaction that seems as hollow as a well. We would not consider the time we spend sitting in a rocking chair on our front porch as a commemorative juncture in life. We often look back at these hours as though we have not accomplished a thing. When reflected in the light of our most momentous occasions, we can still find great peace resting there. These are the pallet-like allotments of our days. Our Lady told me this evening that they are the ebullient eaves of peace where our Love most assuredly resides. What we believe to be a waste of time is often when She is quietly singing Her sweetest lullabies to our hearts. We must remember that we are the living Love of Jesus in every breath we take. Let us never surrender to depression or succumb to the chain-link effects of our linear existence. It only sets the stage for a lack of peace in our hearts while regretting the durations we falsely believe to be uselessly spent. The Holy Mother wants us to embrace our perpetuity as a continuum of grace that flows from the Kingdom of God. This gift is a matter of essence that is not to be disdained or discarded. All of our days are beautiful, even our most simple of moments. That is when our prayer is most powerful and our visions of returning to Paradise are made abundantly clear. There is no doubt that the Holy Spirit is the choreographer of these synoptic lessons of Life.

We might consider the wheels of a wagon as it is traveling past. Through the mystery of light, it appears as though the spokes are revolving backwards. This is an example of how our eyes pervert our impressions. It is also the same principle as the times when we feel we are accomplishing nothing. Our mind's eye tells us that we are idle because there are no highlights to capture our fancy. Like the appearance of the wheel, we falsely believe that we are regressing in time. Quite the contrary, we are actually moving forward in Love by being prayerfully still. It is during these moments that we sit with dignity like the dove on the wing of an eagle, while silently perched on the hand of Our Lord. Have you ever noticed when looking at the spokes of a rolling wheel that they seem to stop when you blink as though being stilled by the flash of a strobe? This is not unlike the way our heart stops the motion of our mind when we embrace the peace of our prayers. When we lift our hearts in remembrance of God's Love, we wink-away the posture of the world. Even as exiles from Paradise, we must remember that Life is a precious gift and that every second counts. The beauty of Heaven resides in it all! Every fragment of time provides an opportunity for us to love more deeply, to open more fully, and to reflect more perfectly the image of our unseen Father in Heaven.

Wednesday, January 8, 1992

Peace becomes a detectible sensation that is felt by the physical body as the heart opens to receive it. We recognize it when we live in communion with God through the Holy Eucharist because our environment is overshadowed by

His Sacramental Grace. To continue the manifestation of peace on Earth, our Holy Mother returned today in an attempt to deliver our souls to the realization of the tranquility of Heaven. She asked me to remember when I was once caught by a schoolteacher while day-dreaming in class, and then startled back into reality. For a few passing moments, the world and all of its distractions were gone. This is parabolic of an open heart that is filled with the peace of God through the Blessed Sacrament. During Holy Communion, we are engulfed and overwhelmed by the presence of God's Love, while the perils of the knotty world are washed away. Our new identity with Jesus is always a fulfilling experience because we are as close to Him on Earth during that moment as we can ever possibly be. The Sacred Host is one within us as Our Lord lifts us to perfection through His Eucharistic peace. This is why we must be reconciled to Him through the Sacrament of Penance prior to the Holy Sacrifice of the Mass so as to be worthy of this gift of Divinity. The Almighty Father bestows these blessings upon our souls to make us indivisibly prepared to greet the Glory of His Son.

After receiving Our Lord Jesus in the Holy Eucharist, we inherently know what Heaven looks like from beyond the strains of life. It is in this peaceful assurance that we become Christ in every trait and attribution. With the greatest of Love, He reciprocally dispenses everything upon us that is divinely present in Him. This prelibation of our Redemption is the most enlightening and prodigious moment of our entire lives of faith. When we receive the Most Blessed Sacrament, the treasured perfection of God that enriches all other overtures of our days completes our purpose of loving Him and the humanity He has come to save. After all, Life is the procession of our very beings back to the Paradise we lost to sin. During this systematic evolution, we are affected in many ways by the people we meet, by our environment, and by the brightest anticipations of our hearts. The Holy Mother has helped my brother and me gain a better perception regarding these principles since the early days when I felt that we were not accomplishing much for Her and Our Lord. They have been teaching us that we must dedicate ourselves to the alleviation of the suffering of the people who surround us. We should live in unison with humanity by remembering the teachings of I Corinthians 12:12, ***"As a body is one though it has many parts, and all the parts of the body, though many, are one body, so also Christ."***

Every new day is an apportionment of the shape of things to come as the world prepares for the Return of the Son of God. Each minute, each second, and each immeasurable moment fosters the movement of humanity toward the fruition of the intentions of God. While many men fallaciously assume that the creation of the universe is a result of some gigantic explosion, we must remember that the unfolding of the Plan of Salvation is actually an implosion in the hearts of all mankind. This is why each tick of the clock is so very important. Every single person is incarnate Love and can never be disclaimed, lest we render ourselves subject to the throttling bonds of incompetence and deception. Our goal is to become a Divine Affinity in the way of Jesus Christ. This is why the universe is said to be unfolding like the blooming of a flower. It is the process of human hearts being purified and made worthy of highest communion with the angels and the Saints.

It is important that we pray for every soul to be conceived into this beauty. Its conception is no less filled with refinement than the gregarious Hosts of Paradise who have already been granted immunity from perdition. Jesus has destroyed our sins so that our deliverance to His side is an irrefutable conclusion. There will be no more sinners left in Creation if we all commit our hearts to Him. It is so elementary that even a little child can understand. The Sacraments of Penance and the Holy Eucharist sanctify our inner-desires for this Love. Through them, our souls are without sin, and therefore, perfected in Christ. This is why Heaven is our new and everlasting Life. Everyone there is equally pure. Like it or not, our Holy Mother has assured us that there are, indeed, levels of Heaven that are based upon our service in this world. Nonetheless, every Saint who lives with Jesus is eternally happy with the dispensation of His Justice. We must be careful not to reject our ability to become the greatest of saints by assuming that we can do no better. This criterion of servitude is a portending factor to every struggling soul. Simply stated, Jesus richly rewards those who are His vessels. But, He is also aware of those who have disassociated themselves from Him until the hour they fall asleep in death.

When a person leads a lukewarm or indifferent life and converts at the very last, they will voluntarily partake of a magnitude of Heaven that is less than someone like the Pope or Mother Teresa. Our Holy Mother told me that the Mercy of Her Son is both endless and boundless. But, in the Justice of God, those who have served Him in the vineyard of human exile with the greatest of fervor will enjoy their everlasting Feast from the most comfortable chair. Without this eternal standard, the whole world would choose to be Godless until their very last moment on Earth. Jesus does not want us to be lying on our deathbed before we choose to convert, although many-a-saint has waited until then to decide. We must live every new day with a proactive Love. Even if our efforts seem to be going nowhere, we are still moving toward Love if we give our lives to Christ with all our soul, mind, body, and strength. Jesus asks us to live totally encapsulated by the integrity of His purpose. He seeks a desire in us for our own Redemption in Him. We must leave no stone unturned in conditioning our hearts and purifying our souls. His Immaculate Mother presented the following illustration to delineate this revelation more clearly.

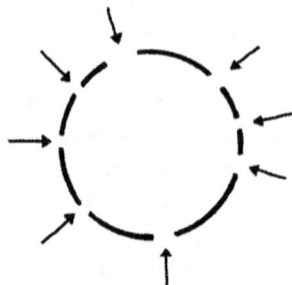

The circle of our holiness in still incomplete. It has been said by many people that Jesus is not quite finished with them yet. He also asks us to understand that we cannot be finished with ourselves until we offer our extra prayers and perform the additional acts of charity that will advance the conversion of the self-appeasing world. This will make the circumference of our faithfulness both contiguous and whole. Jesus wants our lives to be perfectly reciprocal in Him and, therefore, a never-ending source of peace and good intentions. He mandates our mortality to be a perfect perimeter of Love, unconditionally proceeding toward Paradise without respite or end. He chooses to be all things to all people. He has entered the world so that we might learn to make our choices a reflection of His own.

Thursday, January 9, 1992

Our Lady petitions the world to place our hope in the Mercy of Her Son and to always remember that His Sacrifice of Love has extinguished every ill. Anyone who leads a life of hatred is already dead and gone. She is very happy that Her messages are being spread so prolifically all around the globe. She often speaks of the Divine nature of man, but there are many who still have difficulty comprehending what She means. The Mystical Body of Christ is perfectly Divine. We often forget that we comprise the Eternal Corpus of the Lord. Life is a spiritual Kingdom in which we are allowed to share His Truth while our souls are being purified through the Sacraments. We do not truly realize how special we are! Our Blessed Mother has been trying to tell us this for centuries on end. The Holy Spirit has descended upon the world to purify the chosen. Jesus calls for such perfection as an abode in which He resides. No longer will He resign Himself to the starkness of a stable. He now lives a resurrected Glory that He wishes to bring into our hearts. When we allow Him our most stately of rooms, we inherit the dignity of His Life within us. Through the Divine Love of the Almighty Father, we are His gift to the rest of Creation. We exist for the celibacy of Love, not for the licentiousness of the world.

We must be perpetually mindful of the forces that try to diminish our faith in God so that we never succumb to the treacheries of doubt. The source of everything that is good is found in the Holy Eucharist. The presence of this Most Blessed Sacrament casts-out every falsehood in Its path. The Tabernacles which contain the Body and Blood of Christ are the resource centers for the face of the entire Earth. The Tabernacle is the origin of every righteous blessing and the focal point of all communication between Heaven and the souls who hope to inherit it. There can be no natural laws of physics or science without the ordination of God. The numerary postulates that mankind has established as truth have come to fruition through the Genius of the Cross. Jesus Christ circumvents the consensual corollaries of the world upon the Altar, but many of His detractors still question His authority to wield it as He pleases. Our Lady says that all humankind will see this more clearly when Jesus returns in Glory. All Truth will eventually come to Light. The concentric essence of that precedent is Love, given freely by Jesus as the pious Victim of the Crucifixion. There are no separate gradations that exist in the conversion of His peoples. Human Salvation is one unified discipline of supremely perfect Divinity.

People of fidelity always hold their opinions away from their souls so the Light of Christ can help them accede to His intentions. Their indifference is eradicated as soon as they open their hearts to receive Him. This is not the same as a simple thought of Love. One cannot be like Jesus by thinking they are God. We are forced to live in a framework of confinement by such illusions instead of sailing without constraints across the freedom of our faith. Our piety must never be a function of our frail mental impotence, but the Life-giving paternalism of the Holy Spirit, instead. It is good to know that those who think they are loving are at least recognizing that they should be trying to be holy. Divine Love is absent of consignment because the mansions of Heaven are not for sale. Many of us will not Love because we will not trust its profits in advance. We cannot walk up to God and demand to know what will occur on the final day in time. This is why our libraries are filled with products of the human mind, we can write the endings that we want. But, this same facility can overflow with the magnification of human compassion if everyone inside it loves the rest. Our Lady has told us many times that such beauty is perceived by the heart. It need not be confined to a page or a book, or even a building filled with rooms. Our prayers have already amassed a world-wide cartel of Love that is teeming beyond our shores.

"It is important for you to remember that the written copies of your Diary of My messages are not necessarily products of the heart until they are lived. That is what I have told the world at Medjugorje. The messages must be lived! I know that millions are taking heed, and I trust in their response. Remember to always hope through prayer and you will be happy. The plan for the world is meant for grace, not for

destruction. The fate and destiny for mankind has always been for Love, not for hatred. The Will of God the Father, through His Son Jesus, has always been for Mercy and Love, not for punishment and condemnation. The world must realize that God is the Creator of Love. Evil and sadness are caused by straying souls and weak hearts, calculating minds, and ill wills. Together, we are helping the world realize that the origin of mankind is through the dignity of Love. That is how men should live and allow others to live. It is time for man to acknowledge that he is almost finished moving through the ages. Jesus is about to return and time is nearly over. We must pray for mankind to accept Him before his journey through time has ended."

Like our Blessed Mother, Herself, I also pray and hope. I continue to record everything that She is telling me so the world can receive Her help and guidance in an intensely personal way. I pray that every soul on Earth will eventually listen and convert. Our just God will not allow our sins to continue unabated. He will powerfully intervene to purify us if we do not seek-out His Mercy in advance. **"My son, I leave you again tonight with My blessing. I am happy that your awareness of the Truth of Jesus has so fulfilled your Life. It is clear to you what everyone in the world must feel. As you can daily see, it seems apparent that chastisement is the only way to urge people into listening. They will then know how helpless they are without Jesus. Please do not allow your grief for the fate of others to interrupt our progress. We still have hope that everyone will be saved! Thank you for hoping and praying. I love you. Goodnight."**

Sunday, January 12, 1992

The fields of human souls are ripe for the Harvest that will bring an end to our mortal Earth, presently being proportioned in Love by the Immaculate Mother of God. Most of us truly do not know how to practice the faithfulness that She teaches. This evening, She made a particular point to address the paraphrasing of the Holy Scriptures which is now being implemented in various deaneries across America. She said that the employment of this practice is completely unacceptable. **"The sons of the Earth are not the 'people' of the Earth. Wives must, indeed, be submissive to their husbands. It is improper for anyone to alter the original text of the Holy Scripture unless it is infallibly approved by the Holy Father. I pray that the Scriptures will be kept in their sacredness as was originally intended."** Our Lady also expanded Her discussion of the "transfiguration" of our hearts into holiness in Her message today. Our truest vision of God blooms from inside the fruitfulness of our Love. We can see past our mortality and transcend the infinite when we are perfectly united in Him. We own the capacity and ability through the Faith Church on Earth to know that we are one in Spirit through the Savior of the world.

A portion of our total being is a manifestation of our senses in communication with everything we know to be the Truth. Sadly however, other sensations distract our thoughts from the holiness which the Father desires of His people. Our mind deduces that everything we see with our eyes is the totality of our surreal environment. To exacerbate the problem, our conduct follows this same falsehood like a lost sheep at dusk. We are the commandeers of the systems that we create with our own ingenuity. And yet, we are slaves to that same inept mentality. Striving to reach our potential, we achieve only what our thoughts tyrannically allow us to become. However, when we turn ourselves to prayer and look into the depth of our hearts, our senses no longer affect the stability of our minds. Prayer casts aside our meandering thoughts so that an infinite vision from inside us engulfs our entire ability to think. Any carnal pleasures or material distractions are rendered helpless in its wake. Through our newly acquired vision of the Infinity of Love, we prayerfully transcend both the world and the quaint station we hold upon it. Since Jesus lives perfectly and completely inside the chambers of our heart, this is where Heaven intersects the Earth. It is the convocation of our mortality with the Eternal Life of God.

We do not have to die to see such unbounded beauty. We meet and become like Christ through the power of the Holy Spirit. In the Light of this Flaming Paraclete, we are transfigured into a new Creation and a revitalized world of Love. This previously unseen Divinity conceals no constraints or confinements that can snare us. It is a place that is reserved for our souls by God, Himself, and not our curious intellect. The greatest Architect and Carpenter has built a candelabrum chapel for us in the fertile solitude of our hearts. When we don this miraculous vision of Salvation, we become the reality and simplicity of generative Love in walking human flesh and grow to be the children upon whom God has bestowed His symmetrical image. We stately bear the reflection of the Love which Jesus has shed upon His Church. We finally realize that the Redemption for which we were ordained is, indeed, a higher benefaction than our psychic genuflections could ever supercede. While we are certainly not the Creator, we assuredly have the capacity to Love with the same dexterity as the Father who gives us Life. We have learned this Truth through His Son, our Savior and Lord. His Life is our potential because we are destined for the very ideal of exacting His exemplary Love. We are to emulate the incarnate sinlessness that made Him God on Earth.

Our beatific preoccupation has already made us a collective new world. Through Jesus Christ, the Earth is now a place of fulfillment from which Eternity can begin. Our intuitive cognition rests in our vision of Heaven. United in the Love of God, we have immortally overcome death in His Son, forever to come. To accept Love is to look with the same brave insightfulness of the Creator who gave us eyes to see. To know His Love is to live with the faith that we will soon be one in Him and the Heights of the Paradisial Courts. Every speck of human hope comes through our prayers from the heart. When we petition Our Savior through the Blessed Virgin Mary, we find the infinite protraction of our deliverance into everlasting Life. Our spirits reflect our intentions with the clarity of a mirror. Through lives of servitude and sacrifice, Jesus allows us to see past the surface that we often cast-aside as being the recondite bonds that detain us to the gravity of defection. We are able to inherently know by the power of our prayers that we can no longer abandon the wishes of our Redeemer. We must condition our hearts through this revealing Wisdom! If we accede, God will guarantee a place for our souls in the Pantheon of the Firmament where the angels will remember us beyond the ages yet to come. This celebrated anticipation is the only reality that will flourish at the end of time. It allows us to see God as He truly is, each of us at His side in adoration of the solemnity of His Sacred Heart.

Monday, January 13, 1992

I have been pondering how to clearly explain that our love must be sincere. The Blessed Mother has told me that we should all remember the concept of, "Condition." Human faith and servitude must always be given without it! We should stop wasting time making judgments regarding where to cast our affections or in what given situations they might serve us best. One of Our Lady's most persistent tenets is that Love cannot be measured. That is why it is very difficult for Her to describe how Jesus loves us and to the great degree that She, Herself, desires our conversion into His peace. The main precept toward our faith in Christ is that we must love completely, totally, and without reservation to the fullest measure of our faith. We are constantly called to remember the awful Crucifixion that He suffered. The purpose of His death on the Cross is to imbrue humanity with the Blood that has washed an entire Creation free from the tarnation of sin. The events of Good Friday have capitalized the complete Love of God for the people He knows as worthy to be saved. We learn from Mount Calvary that Love can be given without calculating the cost. Its perpetual effect cannot be constrained by our frail introspect or discriminatory prepositions. God saves whomever He pleases and we cannot impede His Mercy. We cannot condemn a soul that He has already chosen to redeem.

By all means, we should pray to be the first into the foyer that leads into the Hallway of The Saints. That is where we will find whether our love is truly worth its holy oats. The epicenter of this knowledge is located in the things we do on Earth. Our love must spiral outwardly if it is to encompass every soul within its reach. It is like a seed blooming into a flower or a tightly-wound wristwatch mainspring as it unwinds to celebrate the passages of time. The amount we grow in Love determines God's ability to recognize our acceptance of His grace. If we love from the outside in, like a free-flying kite string being rewound around its core, we will only grow smaller in stature and impotent to summon the Hosts of the Divine World above to conquer the one we fear inside. Our task is to maintain the determined strength to live the unfettered Love that our Holy Mother so humbly offered when the Angel first came to greet Her, *"Hail, Full of Grace!"* She calls us to imitate Her compliance so that we will understand the meaning of obedience and to gain the strength that rests within Her care. Prayer is the nourishing consecration that develops our devotions to be totally unaffected by condition. We must be like Our Mother in every way and bow in simple service to a Creator we have yet to fully see. Then, we will be the little "Oblates" of Metronymic integrity, worthy to be called the Blessed of the Earth, the Heirs of Redemption, and the Chosen Representatives of the Champion of Peace.

Prayer is our invitation to the Holy Spirit to come into union with our souls. That is why our petitions must be lifted with the highest of sincerity. God's Divine Advocate soothes and preserves us like a protective dome of Love that extends to each horizon within our hearts. It is the arc of the smile of Love which is felt by the human spirit. Our Lady asked me to remember the times when I have cried tears of fulfillment when I realized that I am loved and embraced by others. This overwhelming feeling is nearly uncontainable and quite difficult to describe. When we sense such Love, we are tucked neatly inside the harbor where the presence of God has fully overwhelmed our being. Christ Jesus brings us to this splendid nature by dispatching His Mother to teach us to recite the Mysteries of the Holy Rosary. The power of the Decades is beyond anything we have ever conceived. God has promised Saint Dominic that we can obtain any blessing we seek of Him through the veneration of His Mother. Our foremost petition should be that we will always search for Heaven as Christ calls us from beyond the hovering stars. If we surrender completely to the Plan of Our Almighty Father, we will recognize His desire to Love us in return.

Tuesday, January 14, 1992

We must search for the presence of Love deep inside ourselves like an innocent child looking into a box of coloring crayons. We know that we want to create a beautiful picture, but we do not realize which color would best represent our Love. Perhaps it could be green because we are quite fond of a nearby grassy knoll. At other times, we may think that red would suffice because it is the color of tandem trucks that extinguish horrific fires. We eagerly search through our obcordate box, seeking-out the crayon that is labeled "LOVE." If we find its color, we will easily be able to change the hue of ourselves and everything around us to become what our benevolent Creator wants us to be. Then, we will be walking in fields of green, living the purity of white, and embracing the golden truth of God Almighty. Our Lady has told us before that the grace of Heaven is unlike any color in a box of crayons. If we search through them to find the one marked "LOVE", we will be dismayed because Jesus Christ cannot be described by one chromatic hue. Indeed, Love is the waxy essence of each crayon which bears the rainbow colors that make Creation shine.

We find at the last that our entire box is completely filled with Love. Since this origin of our sanctification represents our hearts, there is nothing inside which cannot be claimed by God. The task before us is to utilize the gifts at our hands to allow His presence to flow into the world before our eyes. Our work is as prayerful as painting a picture and the pouring-out of our inner-selves into all that comes-to-pass. It is a beseeching requisition to compose such a beautiful portraiture! We are the artists who go to the Communion Table of the Lord to receive the Sacred Host. Through this beatific union, our handiwork is given real Truth and transformed into the multiple dimensions of Life. We intensify our talents every time we reach-out to the poor and kneel in collation at our bedside at the closing of the day. Employing that power has been the tone and substance of Our Lady's messages from the first time She ever showed Her Face. She addresses the universal nature of the Spirit of Love through which every beatitude flows. Her assertions are of undeniable tenability because She has already seen the end of time. The destiny of our American Nation is very dear to Her Immaculate Heart because She is the Patron Saint of our native homeland. She told me this evening that the western world is woefully insufficient in our commendatory acknowledgment of the Mercy that we require in order to be saved. We are still failing to live peacefully in accordance with the Commandments and the Mother who bestowed incarnate Life upon their Author.

Through the intercessory messages of the Queen of Paradise, we are becoming called from out-of the darkness. Our Virgin Mother is helping rid the world of hatred, greed, and outright discrimination. She tells us persistently that these vices are never fully absent from any country, even one as free as our own. Her presence is a beacon of Light that will be seen for generations to come, should there be others to be made part of time. The Blessed Mother does not know the exact day nor the hour when Jesus will return, but She is fully aware that it is imminently soon. That is why we must move in earnest conversion toward accepting Our Savior and His Cross. The Holy Spirit will always tell us how to prepare for our deliverance into Glory. What better reason for His Mother to communicate with us now? Human ignorance is a damnable avenue in the hands of evil works. If we are lacking in the Wisdom of Love, our conversion will stand in the perilous paths of grave danger and ill will. Modern societies have already borne the plight and devastation resulting from the ignobleness that blinds us from perceiving the suffering of the world.

That is why Our Lady's messages are many. Through Her witness, She shares the enlightenment that shines ever more visibly within human hearts, despite the passage of time. It is all very clear to us now that She desires for everyone to carry the Gospel of Her Son to those whose souls are still groveling in the pits of noxious sin.

We take our Love for our brothers and sisters directly to their grieving hearts when we pray to spread the Christian faith throughout the entire world. We must greet every soul through the vision of these honorable intentions. We have the capacity to bring humanity to the veritable brink of perfection while seeking the help of God on our knees. Our piety clears the pathway before us so that we can attain the high holiness of Christ. This admirable emulation is quite possible for our chosen human race. The Holy Mother offered a simplistic illustration to depict this road to unity and peace. Which of these little spheres will eventually arrive at the bottom?

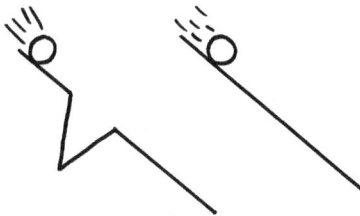

The one on the right will attain its goal because its path is unimpeded by our faults and stubborn ways. God provides the drive from above to land us in the arms of Christ, but we have created a surfeit environment which is so fraught with pitfalls that we descend into destruction along the way. This is another example of our failure to take the proper course. If we approach God as a people who are free from impasses of our own making, we will arrive at the shores of Paradise without the baggage of distress. So often, Love is not shared between people because we employ a battering ram instead of a gentle knock at the door. Subtle persistence requires great patience and strength. Jesus allowed those He taught to arrive at His conclusions fully of their own accord. He often did not have to explain the reasons they came to know. The simple impression upon their conscience was the parable that changed their hearts. Our own precepts of Love should be offered as the most attractive solutions to whatever stands in the way. However, there are certain commanding statements of Truth that must oftentimes be invoked in order to destroy the diabolical actions of evil through the Wisdom of the Holy Spirit. Only from a heart that is authentic in Love can these be dispensed without the destruction of mutual peace. Satan will never be converted and must always be destroyed. Love will kill him! Our Lady wants us to feel confident that this power is now in our hands.

Sunday, January 19, 1992

Just as we are told that there would not be enough room in the world to hold the books it would take to describe the words and actions of Jesus, there is also an insufficient number of terms in the English language to delineate the Life that Our Lady is calling us to live. She is offering Her children in cursory definitions the substance of miracles that would require countless libraries to adequately describe. Since She is the Mother of the Alpha and the Omega, She fosters the commanding presence and final analysis of all human communication. This dialectic genius is further revealed to humanity through Her message of this evening. Our Lady came to pray with my brother and me just-past the hour of seven o'clock to help us better understand the incalculable power of Love to a new and exponential degree. As God's beloved people attempt to explain our views of the universe through our ineloquent vision of faith, we have collected long and protracted dissertations that are filled with the multiplicity of linguistic pronouncements. Much to our dismay, our every discourse falls painfully short of describing God as He is Divinely present in Christ.

The Holy Mother says that we should discontinue our endless narrations of hollow adjectives and allow the Wisdom of peace to accentuate the solemnity of our prayers. She provided the example of how difficult it would be to describe a sunset in literary terms. How can you possibly ask someone to see such magnificence and majesty unless you actually take them there? The Holy manifestations of God must be realized within the human spirit because our platform exhortations fail to make them clear. This is how we should approach the abundant works that reside in the offing before us. Living Our Lady's messages is a greater task than simply recognizing that they are real. A life of Love is more than a dissemination of oratorical objectives. We oftentimes have no generally accepted phrases to characterize the Heaven that is just beyond our reach. In an attempt to improvise the comprehensive nature of our knowledge in Christianity, Our Lady gave me a new term which transforms our human understanding of Love into a breathing form of life. The word is, "accourse." It is the process of living in perpetual accord with the Trinity of God. Its meaning is enhanced by Love as the heart overcomes the mind. We live in accourse with the righteousness of Christ by being His disciples in the lineage of His first.

The Blessed Virgin offered another example to supplement Her case. Do you suppose that you could listen to a person who is speaking while someone else is simultaneously singing different words and still remember what both have said? You are most apt to remember the message of neither one, but only the tune of the song. The melody will always distract you from the lyrics. You identify with the symbols of the music, but cannot sustain the impression of the message that accompanies its notes. This is precisely why many people do not hear the pleading of the Son of God. There are too many other inflections competing for our thoughts. But, we can clearly remember His melody in our hearts! It is the composition of Love, and every one of His holy children is an instrument who plays along. We best resound the strains of God by loving in the likeness of His Son. The Commandments and the Beatitudes are the audible harmonies of Paradise that come to rest in the balconies of our souls. We can concurrently hear them all by living Love in accourse with the Word of Jesus Christ, taking His message around the globe, and echoing the gentle Spirit who is beckoning us all to come back home.

To live in proper accord is a state of being at a given moment in time, while our accourse in Divinity is a perpetual procession of Life. It is a never-ending and reciprocal oneness with the Love of Almighty God. Our accourse is not only a state of propriety on a given date on the calendar, but also the reflection of the Savior of the World throughout all generations, transcending the framework of human existence in unity with the Glory of Heaven. Those who are living in accourse with Christ Jesus have their eyes fixed upon the Cross. They recognize and serve Love in every thought, through each descriptive word, with the totality of their actions, and by responding to the opportunities that fall before their feet. As strange as it may seem, they can actually hear the sound of Peace flowing from the Light of Christ. That is what makes Love such a beneficial sweetness. God brings us miracles to which only little children can relate. This is why He implores us to cast-off our vestiges of obstinance and privacy and open to one another in the full brilliance of our youth. Thinking and talking about Love is not sufficient to suit the likeness of the Saints we must become. Our Christian beliefs are not simply a depiction of what God would have us do, but the living reality that makes us an organic species which finds rest only in our imitation of His Son.

The Blessed Virgin Mary allows us to own a better understanding of the limitless dimensions of Heaven. There are explicit reasons for Her discussion of parabolic terms. For example, those who worthily receive the Holy Eucharist are in accourse with the Will of the Father because we inherit the perfect oneness that He requires. It is an ongoing process through which our souls shall never die. Our Lady makes it very clear that those who do not prepare for this Communion, or are unworthy to receive Him because of the presence of grave sin, are not living the accourse of which She speaks. This separation is not a decision made by Christ, but a result of the errors of those who choose to sin. Most everyone who lives in the gravity of transgression is fully aware of the consequences that might result. They must step forward to participate in the Penitential Rites of the Church. The continuation of grace for those who wish to be like God is to desire to "live" as Christ decided to live. That is the essential difference between just acknowledging the Truth that He is Emmanuel and living in accourse with His Word. A stationary poise of "being" does not necessarily imply a perpetual life of faith and good works. We remember that Jesus is one-in-being with the Father because He is as perfect as Our Creator, Himself.

We, too, can stand intrinsically with God through living the Way of His Son. Our service and conversion must be a kinetic life of impetus and strength. To walk in the footsteps of Our Redeemer is to live uniquely in His Love. That is the only means through which God will ever claim us. We do not have to die before becoming reunited with Him. We already hold the potential for perfecting our Love while we live in mortal flesh. We are in a constant process of becoming the reason for the Resurrection of Christ. We must never cease or desist in our labors or say that we are holy enough. We can never stop and proclaim to be, "I AM" because there is always more for us to do. Love is a "livingness," not a quaint circumstance or a periodic element of time. Salvation cannot be found on the clock because its hands are too frail to carry our souls back to God. Only Christ is our strength during these revolutionary times! We must become His children by living in His Love. That is why our conversion is a matter of the heart. While our thoughts reflect moments that will soon pass, our Love is our voracious spiritual power! It cannot stop because our souls would never allow it. To be all of God is to depend upon Him to consume our entire selves. Then, we are no more, but Christ is in us! There is no better asylum for anyone to rest.

Wednesday, January 22, 1992

Today is the observation of the beginning of the twelfth month of the beautiful messages from our Blessed Virgin Mother. She came to pray with us in greeting, **"My beautiful children, you are both so busy! That makes Me happy because you know to distinguish the world from the Truth. Therefore, you will always be free from the chains of the world. Your Love will keep you free! But, you best understand your brothers and sisters by remembering how repressive their worldliness is. Thank you for completing your writing for Me. Your work is excellent. Today, as you know, ends the eleventh month of My messages. You have done so well for so long..."** I have included this splendid sentiment from Our Lady so that you may truly know the personal motherly intercession with which She greets us when She comes. This is how She holds every one of Her children, without a hint of reservation. She is, indeed, the Mother of all humanity.

If the world knew the Mother of God the way that my brother and I do, our entire population would run at galactic speed into Her arms. I do not have adequate words to describe to you how She loves us. Jesus awaits our prayerful petitions while resting in Her embrace. He silently contemplates the gradual opening of our hearts, waiting in confidence to right all the wrongs we reveal. What a fateful day this one has turned-out to be! It is the anniversary of the decision of the Supreme Court of the United States to legalize the killing of unborn children through the scourge of abortion in 1973. It is also the premonition of an hour to come when the Son of Man is going to demand answers, sound the roll-call of the damned, and employ the vengeance of an outraged God! We already know that abortion-on-a-whim is an obvious violation of His Will for all life to be given its proper domain. To inhibit conception or breach an impending birth is a repugnance that is still nauseating to His Soul. The bringing of a child into the world is not to be sundered by the invasion of human hands. The act of procreation should not be manipulated and the rights of the little child in its mother's womb must never be infringed. Human procreation is a blessing that is reserved for the holiness of marriage, not for those unwedded or in a union that is otherwise not sanctioned through the Sacraments of the Church.

Our Holy Mother speaks of the dire consequences that will befall humanity if we do not reverse the terrible scourge of abortion. She also speaks of the horrifying punishments that will follow the unholy practice of contraception. God wishes for the beauty and potential of all life given through His Love to be preserved by those to whom it is bestowed. The world is in much need of repair, and the next newborn child could be the Pontiff of the future who will continue to lead us back to Christ. Our Father in Heaven requires a simplicity of the heart that forgives and never weighs the cost. He also mandates our acceptance and compliance with His desires and intentions to sustain the Creation He has come to bless. Jesus and His Mother hear the cries of the little ones from their mothers' wombs throughout all the world. They beg us urgently to allow them to continue to live.

Our Holy Mother's call is a persistent reminder for us to seek refuge in the Immaculate Heart of Heaven. She says, **"I hear your cries and wishes. You must remember that I am forever! I will never leave you. You have Me, as I have you."** With these words, The sinless Madonna calls us to pray fervently together, knowing full-well that we are protected in Her care. It is She who is calling us with the dearest of words to come forward to Redemption. We do not realize what happens to our souls when we pray from our hearts in the way that She is teaching. The Virgin Mary is trying to help us realize how fortunate we are to be Her children and that Love is all that can save us. We must embrace one another in affection or be lost to the depravity of our divisions. Our Lady's sorrow is a testament that the world has yet to forget the past and begin anew. Let us hope that the next tomorrow will ignite a great fire of Love in the hearts of all humankind. We must flood the Earth with good will from one corner of Creation to the next so that every tear will be wiped from our eyes and the Kingdom of God will reign forever amongst men.

Friday, January 24, 1992

While some people may stand stoically opposed to the beauty of the Holy Rosary and our veneration of the Immaculate Virgin Mary, I choose, instead, to fall to my knees with tear-laden eyes in awe and respect for this heavenly Queen. After all, She is the Lady whom God has deigned to call His own Mother. I will never understand the renegade disobedience that I see from some of Her children, but I pray in earnest that they will soon come to know Her as I do. I often think about the parable of the Prodigal son. Deep inside, I believe that we will one day understand that it was his mother who chased him down and sent him back home to his father's waiting arms. That is what the Virgin Mother of Our Lord is doing for us now, and for anyone else who is lost. She tells us to return to the Father because He has forgiven us and plans a bountiful feast upon our arrival. It is through this same hope that I continue to offer Her words to you as She has given them to me.

Those who accept Jesus grow closer to Love because they become helpful and adequate instead of hopeless and deficient. Our Lady told me today that it is important that we love all little children because they will carry that message home with them like a seed to plant inside their families. It is in our humble castles where the pinasters of Love can be nourished to bloom to their fullest of grace. This is the requisite authenticity that remakes the world and instills a new freshness inside stagnant human hearts. It gives further meaning to our holy actions and brings a salvific response from our Redeemer on the Cross. The Holy Mother also told me that the messages we deliver around the globe on Her behalf are the petitions that are read by the hour in Heaven. She wants the entire world to understand the seriousness of Her mission in preparing humanity for the Second Coming of Her Son. She wishes us to be freed from the material dissuasions that impede our progress toward the holiness we should aspire to attain. Her words echo the mandate of Our Lord when He said, *"Be perfect as your Heavenly Father is perfect."*

Sunday, January 26, 1992

Our Lady asks us to share Her words and messages with the world in a way that they will be openly received. She wants all of Her children to see Love and offer it to humanity in the fullness of our profession. She came this evening to bring another revelation of conversion and asked me to record it with the hope that it would reach your hands though this Diary. She reminded me again that we must realize the futility and helplessness of our lives without Her Son. Love is often compromised through the restive grip of human stubbornness and the darkness of our blind indignance. We are mistaken if we assume that we are capable of reaching the destiny of Eternity without Christ. With the aid of the Immaculate Conception, our struggle during that journey is made much more easy to bear. This beautiful Lady addressed another such compromise in Her message of this evening. She referred to the date of June 17, 1977 when the Holy Father in Rome issued an *ex cathedra* decree allowing the reception of the Holy Eucharist in the palm of the communicant's hand. This pontifical confirmation was cautiously deployed to ensure that no one would deny themselves the soul-saving grace of the Blessed Sacrament because they did not want the Body of Jesus placed onto their tongue by the fingers of a priest.

This is an effect of the so-called modernized Commensal that was promulgated so that many Catholics will continue to receive the pureness and bounty of the Host. There are numerous other such compromises, including the introduction of female altar servers and the rhythmic method of family planning. Popes throughout the ages have grappled to keep the peoples of the world united in Jesus through the graces of the Church. They have infallibly recognized this to be the means with which to avoid the just chastisements from God that would otherwise result from the abdication of mankind in rejecting our responsibilities to imitate the holiness of Our Lord. They have also known full-well that the Messianic Covenant of Christ is neither a democracy nor a reprieve of free volition! The Son of God is total Love who requires a reciprocal vow of Divine obedience from the people He came to save. He handed Himself over to Passion and Sacrifice for the eternal vindication of mankind from the sentence of death that originated from the sin which we, ourselves, created. In this universal Truth, God never once asked to hear our ulterior opinions or to receive the deceitful collusion that is still pouring from the vileness of our mouths.

Responding to the invitation of Our Lady to pose a question that had gone no further than my thoughts, I asked what happens to people who are never baptized so as to be cleansed of the effects of original sin. Her response is that we should not assume that those who are not baptized are "automatically" cast into Hell when they die. Our Salvation rests inside the providence and graciousness of God. He knows our ability to answer the eternal questions, **"Do you accept Jesus as the Savior of the world? Do you accept His Love over evil? Do you recognize His Love as the beginning and end of all Creation, seen and unseen? And, do you plead for and will you accept His Mercy on judgment day?"** The Sacrament of Baptism is the preeminent union between the life of man and the Divinity of Christ that secures our redeeming absolution during the delicate juncture of our moment of mortality. Therefore, in answer to my concern not yet voiced to Our Lady, She told me that Heaven knows the capacity of every soul to respond affirmatively to the questions asked of mankind by The King on the Throne. In the case of little children who do not yet understand, He does not exclude them from His Kingdom because their perfection already lives inside His tear-shedding Love for them.

Those who comprehend the power of the New Covenant between Heaven and Earth through Jesus Christ must accept what the Son of God has brought to humanity in expiation for our sins. This is the Blood that Jesus so profoundly shed on the Cross to purify our souls. We must accept that Sacrifice before all the world and to Almighty God in order to be saved. We are equally required to proclaim the Creed of the Apostles to be the Truth by which we live. Jesus is the owner and the conservator of all the ages and the final destiny of Creation. He holds the power to baptize His children as they are conceived into His hands. After all, He is the God who grants everlasting Salvation and sustains Eternal Life. He asks all of His children to be baptized in mortal flesh to cleanse them of every stain, whether original in nature or manifested through the weaknesses that are incurred during the journey of our days. Through our Baptism, the Grace of God is dispensed without the concurrence of anyone else who might oppose. We should bequeath all discretion and exceptions to the Heart and Hands of Jesus Christ, Himself. The sacramental gift of Baptism is another blessing in our procession of Life in accourse with the "being" of God. By all means, His only begotten Son was baptized to remind us of this fact. He wished to be the initial example before everyone who would follow Him in faith.

The waters of the River Jordan would become the precursor of forgiveness preceding Our Lord's Blood that is poured-out upon the Cross for the expungement of the sins of every generation. He accomplished this task so that no one would commit themselves into eternal death when they see their reflection in God's Face. The Holy Waters of Baptism signify and validate that the person who is christened accepts the renewal of Life by the shedding of death. Our Lady told me that even tiny babies mystically know the moment when they are cleansed. The Holy Spirit imprints it upon their soul. If an infant is only one-day-old, they know that they have received this Sacrament. I also asked Our Lady tonight whether certain activities are prayerful to condone. I queried about the musicians and recording artists who have gathered for the cause of feeding the starving in Africa. She responded, **"These prayers are in accordance with the wishes of My Son. Feed the poor! Of course, it is a blessed way to utilize the resources of man. We must pray for the continuance of this type of prayer."** Of all the things that She has taught us, they are summed-up by our need to love one another through the most open of hearts. Together, we must pray for the world to know the beauty, peace, and Love that is possible to share among everyone who lives. This is where all our dreams and hopes are fulfilled and the reason Eternity can begin on Earth.

Wednesday, January 29, 1992

Not only should we embrace one another willfully and warmly, we should also remember how delicate, fragile, and helpless we are. It is only through the humble prayers of God's faithful children that the world has come as close to Jesus as it has. We are all immeasurably precious in His sight! He blesses our innocent faith through our prayers and guides our lives to make us happy. Our Lady is oftentimes sorrowful because not all of Her children have turned to Jesus to cast-away their mindless despair. Those who live without direction or any desire for God are caught in a very intemperate and occlusive place. They simply cannot see! They feel their way through life with hands that are made numb from the coldness of disbelief, grasping for material objects with unstable grips, and absent of the firmness and steadfastness of any spiritual conviction at all. We are very precious to God! But, without Him, we are quite alone and unmistakably helpless. This is why Our Lady cries.

The Holy Mother says that the conversion of humanity will come as Her work continues to flourish. God loves all of His children with the same fidelity that He embraces The Lady wearing the Crown of Twelve Stars. His Love absorbs the world in an outward way, closer than any touch could ever be, inside everything good that has descended upon the Earth, and subsequent to any conclusion about Eternity that might potentially be drawn. His Wisdom is the highest peak of Dawn and our comforting nightlight at dusk. He is the Wise Counsel of novitiates and the unfathomable bastion of recurring strength Who stirs the winds to blow and the falls to seek the bays which nourish the aquatic hopes of everything that swims below. This is how He loves Creation and the reason we have the courage to live in hope. Jesus Christ is the Love that Our Almighty Father has intended for us to achieve. In Him, we perfect our souls so that the day will come when we are able to perceive all peoples in the compassionate way we were meant to see. Our Lord has preserved us from the distractions and evil skulduggeries which come from under the trestles where foul stenches lurk. Satan is still concealed in our materials and emotions, hidden in our desires and in our fancies. He is obvious in countless other ways, but we pray away his snares so as to avoid and destroy his wickedness for those who cannot see.

This collection of heavenly messages is a call to the world for our return to Christ. Our Lady has laid Her hands upon the hearts of all Her children, asking us to listen to Her words and respond with a compliant "YES" by living as She asks. If we decline to obey, there will assuredly be chastisements which will pale all others that have gone before! God the Father is serious about converting His people into the propriety of Love. That is the reason He is allowing His Mother of Benevolence to appear on His behalf and to confer His Holy Spirit upon the Earth. It is quite unfortunate that so many people refuse to humbly accept Him. There can only be goodness in Our Lady's attempts to bring us all to prayer and to look upon Creation with a more charitable perception. She has asked me to convey a special message to one particular group who has been markedly disparaging upon Her work. They refuse to accept the Truth of Jesus in the Holy Eucharist, appropriately enlisting His rage. Our Lady has shed many tears of grief over the fate of these lost souls. **"They dismiss graces and miracles as coincidence and chance. They are true examples of those who would divide the Church. They do not believe that they are helpless without Jesus. They are indifferent and lukewarm in love, but at the same time, are disguised in the cloak of faith. Oh, the peril that they are in! I say woe to them, for the Son of God is outraged."**

The Blessed Mother told me that such false apostles will soon learn a terrible lesson and that we must pray for their souls in earnest. She also asks us to beseech the assistance of God with intensity for those who publicly govern the democratic nations of the Earth. They impassively allow the statutes that permit the culture of death to continue inside their borders despite the Truth being revealed by Christ. The Son of God says without uncertainty that abortion is a mortal sin! We must continue to trust in the fruit of our prayers that these souls will soon realize the flagrancy and error of their ways. Our hope is for them to surrender their lives to Love. God is already reigning with power and bringing a new Dawn upon the universe. Jesus is about to return into His Kingdom in Glory! After offering Her intercessory Wisdom, Our Lady departed this by evening by saying, **"I love you endlessly and immortally! Goodnight."**

Thursday, January 30, 1992

The longer I attend daily Mass, the better I am able to comprehend the Eternal Light of God. I have come to know Life as one perpetual day, encompassed by the pulsating night, during which we hide our hearts in the dark corridors and sleepy hamlets of our own subconsciousness. The Holy Bread of Life, Our Eucharistic Jesus, is the King who rules all time. Whether we acknowledge His power or reject it, we are all subject to His creative and justified authority to mete-out our existence and dispense the grace of God as He sees fit. So, I humbly bow to His Will and to the benevolent prayers of Mary Immaculate on our behalf. Through Her Divine intercession, our destinies are in good hands and our souls are in the care of loving Hearts. We have no worries that we cannot overcome through the faith they bring, a gift for our starving souls. These messages are such a gift and Jesus' Sacred Body is our Holy Food. I ask that you embrace them both with filial love as we journey together toward the ultimate perfection that God seeks of His people.

Tonight, Our Lady offered another message about the skewed envisionment of humankind. She has come to offer us a glimpse of the Glory that is about to be dispensed upon the faithful and to strengthen our allegiance to Her Son. When we look at a beautiful painting, we see a particular assemblage of colors and textures that are mixed into an image which beams inside our heart. In our admiration of such work, many of us fail to recognize another picture that is simultaneously resting in its place. There are actually two scenes, the colorful landscape and the purest white of the canvas surface that is hidden underneath. The image of the initial purity is still present and is just as visible to the discerning eye. If we remove the impasto that we have carefully stroked over its top, the virgin canvas can be seen again. This is symbolic of the Love of God. He supports and sustains everyone who commends their souls to Him. His Love enhances the clarity and definition of our lives beyond their innumerable dimensions. Our Lady wants us to learn that the purity of Love is forever present and that God firmly upholds the backdrop of Creation. This is why the Most Blessed Sacrament is the infinite perfection of the Body of Christ.

The Greatest Artist ever to be known has placed the snow-white purity of His Son into our liturgical faith so we can truly see the Eucharist in its Divine Species from the Altar of Paradise. When we look upon the Most Blessed Sacrament, we are able to perceive our previously unseen God, visible to us in Creation from its inception to its culmination. We see all that is now, and will ever be, world without end! Anything that is possible and every conceivable potential on Earth is manifested through the Manna of the Mass. All landscapes and beatific imageries are made visible through Jesus, the Maker who transcends both timeliness and space. He has parted the curtain of our blindness so that we can see the Glories of the picturesque Kingdom to come. He is One with the reality that allows our eagerness for Eternity to grow. In the miraculous power of God, Christ is the Painter within us who reveals the image of Heaven from the recesses of our hearts.

FOCUS UPON THE PATH FOR HOME

FEBRUARY 1992

Saturday, February 1, 1992

To begin this new month, Our Lady asked me to expand the descriptive substance of Her messages in my Diary so that everyone will feel encompassed by Her tireless works. To that end, I give you Mary, the Mother of God. "Good evening again, My little ones. My Love is with you and I am with you through Him. I have come today to assure you that your work continues to be of blessed accord and accourse. I wish to instill upon you today that the vision the world hopes to gain from My intercession is comprised of the beauty of ten thousand canvases. Hope for the world is written in the hearts of mankind. The Author is My Son and the message is Love, and there is but one chapter. All peoples of the world must learn to read the message of Love from within themselves and through the hearts of other mortal men. In the hearts of men has been inscribed the message of peace and solution for the imposition and evil of the world. The message is Love and the solution is 'to' Love. Jesus Christ originally carried your vision of hope into the world to help remake the sanctity of old. It will rebuild the vision of purity for those oppressed by sin and indifference.

Herein lies the purpose of our encounter and in the need for you to continue to rest, not only in prayer, but also from your dailiness of toil and mortality. I hope with tears that you will continue My request without falling back into the routine of human habit which has caused such paste and sanction to worldliness instead of heavenliness to so many other messengers. I hope for your days to be built with newness with each opening dawn, with the freshness of spring at the bringing of new light, with the fondness of the beauty of the human heart as the rhythm of days pass. Oh, how I wish you to remember how Love will not allow anything to stale or starve from usage or exposure. Love is always new and fresh because it is the beginning of all, culminated by the Finisher of all faith, My Son, Jesus. This is why you have been chosen with your brother to be one, the coupling of experiences and approaches. You cannot do it alone, only Jesus could do that and live to tell it.

Jesus is the binding and saving force of all mortality. He will resurrect and make whole all that is fallen by sin and time. Likewise, you have been given to bear the needs of the heart of your brother who has called on you in a number of ways. You are responding well. You are watching the hopes of Jesus' Heart for the world and your dreams, encapsulated and fed by Love, unfold into reality before your very eyes in the way you have always wished. This has happened because you love, and because Jesus is in you. Do you see? Then, you must now be happy knowing you are Love. This unity is rarely seen anywhere in the world. Your unity will help move the many to Love. And, one day all will see and know that Jesus is the cause and conservator of Life by your example.

Thank you for opening your hearts to extend your prayers into the heavens. Please remember that the only intended identicalness of one day to the next is Love itself. All other is man-made habit and ritual. Love renews the freshness of all existence. That is why you are happy today and will be happy tomorrow. That is also why there is no record of time in Eternity. All is complete happiness and newness in Love which can never grow old and has no rhythm or record. I will bless you now, and give you the continuing power to bless the world by your prayers, acts, and intentions. I love you! I love you! You are My special children! Goodnight." My brothers and sisters, this message is also for you! I ask that you open your hearts and lift them to the works of God. As one united family, we can change the face of the Earth and restore its beauty. Everyone must be included because Jesus' Love is for all Creation. Our Lady so desires that the entire world pray the Most Holy Rosary in a never-ending chorus of love for Her Son, and to consummate our union in the reception of the Most Holy Eucharist, the Bread of Life.

Tuesday, February 4, 1992

So many of God's children have problems dealing with the fleeting world and its materialism. When this happens, we are set into motion and lose our peace. This will inhibit our ability to communicate Our Lady's messages to the world from deep within our heart. When we try to disseminate Her wisdom and guidance in a secular environment, it is a difficult job at best. This is aggravated when we receive little help from others who appear to be running around us poking out their tongues. The Blessed Virgin highlighted this situation to illuminate a perspective which would preserve the continuation of peace. This message takes the form of shape and fiber. She once told me that mankind builds a fortress where he encloses himself in hopes that it will shield him from the inevitable fate of time and death. When he entrenches himself behind this imaginary shield, he feels that nothing can touch him there, not even the will of God. These people, in fact, only confine themselves in the prison of their closed hearts, making their fortress a captivating container instead of a liberating force. Mankind does this using the human will.

If we were to consider a piece of plywood, we would see that it is constructed of several layers of wood whose grain patterns are placed in differing directions. This gives it added strength when compared to another whose grain patterns are all running in a parallel direction. The interconnected interior of the lumber makes it less susceptible to being broken. However, a sheet of wood without this interconnectedness can easily collapse. This is a parable of the world in relation to the human will. Due to mortal circumstances and minds that control personal and financial gain, we are subjected to the unyielding strength of the human will. This is not the composition of the selfless heart that Our Lady desires. It is, rather, a description of those with whom we are in contact who work steadily and in unison with other worldly-minded people to construct the fabric of society according to their own selfish accord. If we are in this situation, how can we be happy when the fiber of these wills are entrapped by worldliness? It is a descending roadway that cannot elevate any of its travelers. Their attitudes contradict the Virgin's perpetual message that we must be strong of heart, not of the will. Invoking a courageous and sacrificial spirit allows the true freedom and happiness for which we seek. It is the only way to truthfully accept Jesus Christ. Therein lies the solution.

Imagine someone sitting atop the sheet of plywood which has great interconnected grain patterns, and then a great weight were dropped upon them. Since the material is very strong, it would not break, leaving them crushed between the wood and the weight on top of them. Conversely, what if they were resting upon the fragile parallel grained wood and the same weight were dropped. The sheet would fracture into two pieces, allowing them to fall beneath it without being harmed. So, those who relentlessly pursue worldliness will be destroyed by the weight of the world and the sins they have heaped upon their own souls. However, those who have given their will and heart to Jesus will touchdown safely in the freedom of His arms. We can see this helplessness all over the world. People create situations and are yet unable to control their effects. Too many times, multitudes of lost souls cry to the heavens for God, asking Him what to do. The choice to peacefully convert to a Life of Love is actually their own. Yes, they must passionately petition the heavens, but their tears must be for Jesus to come knocking on their door. Each of us must abandon our errant will and mortal desires. Our will is given to us by God in order to make the wiser choice, that of accepting Christ and His salvific holiness. When we survey the world, it is easy to see that mankind has perverted that sacred choice. Together, we must pray for change. We must realize our helplessness and abandon our will so that our Savior can keep us safe and happy. Then, we will not be crushed by the heartless world or by the sins of others. We will even avoid the punishment that we have wrought by our own transgressions.

While the human will is strong, the Love of Jesus is strongest. Love will overcome every temptation that wishes to entrap us within our prison fortress of worldliness. We must cross the threshold that separates us from the errant belief that evil will overtake the Earth if we choose to be meek and humble. Everyone must come to know that Love is the greatest power in Creation. It is the only thing that can change the world. Love is not a signal of weakness, but rather, omnipotent power in its very essence. But, it seems that arrogant and proud men have no time for tolerance, forgiveness, or sacrifice. They believe that their will must be done, both boldly and forcefully so that the world will bend to their submissive control. Oh, what blindness these men of the world suffer! They do not understand the wisdom of the Lamb of God. Each time a human soul bows before the infliction of suffering in the Name of Love, the heart becomes an 'intimate' in the Redemption of the world. And the infinite Beatitude of Christ shines through them. This is the purpose and product of our sacrifices and sufferings. This is how human joy is brought to perfection.

Thursday, February 6, 1992
We know that the promise of Heaven has changed the world. It is a vision that, for now, is held in the beauty of the human heart. That is why every one of God's children must believe with faith in the bounties of Paradise. It is a factual place outside of time, a true Eternity of fulfillment and joy which is beyond the capacity of the human mind to conceive. Tonight, Our Lady came as I prayed the Rosary to tell me more about this blissful new beginning. She focused Her attention again on the western world which is abhorrently distracted from the sight of Heaven by material wealth and the satisfaction of individual desires. We must turn our minds and hearts to everything that will help us anticipate Heaven more passionately. We must prayerfully hope for our deliverance from eternal death. It is likewise appropriate to pray for our health, prosperity, and the fulfillment of our personal needs while in this life. Our Holy Mother tells us that Jesus promises all of these in Heaven. But, we must ask Him to deliver our souls into that perfect Kingdom. We are already encompassed by God's plan for Eternity because Salvation has been granted, and is at hand. Our efforts toward this Victory will not lift us from this world unless we pray because we are helpless without Love. Yes, we do love our way into Heaven.

Prayer is a precursor to the enlightenment of our souls. Our Lady warns us that we are placing our happiness on Earth, and future in Heaven, at risk by being indifferent in Love. Not only must we love, it is imperative that we actively participate in the plan of Salvation by accepting Christ Jesus by becoming the image of His Love in the world. Many have difficulty with this conviction because they greet Life only at its casual surface. For example, when we see a wave crashing to the shore, we can only see an effect which consists of the force, the foam, and the recession of the wave. The true impact and cause, the soul and intent of the wave, are aspects over which man has no control. We do not make the wave, but we can see the effect that it has. We do likewise in life. Our lives are a reaction to God's intent. That makes us very helpless because we do not initiate Life or bring it to fruition beyond the vision of our control.

We must accept the Love of Christ as each day is created and offered to us by God. By the time we could envision creating a day, we are already living it. We arrive at curtain call in time to applaud the tremendous production of this immense Creation. Yet, we foolishly believe that we are intrinsically in control of the origin of Life from its inception. The only means within our power to pose creative questions is through prayer. That is the invocation of the wisdom of the Almighty. When we Love in the way of Christ, we are allowed to enter the arena of God. He will augment His plans through the influence of our prayers when we ask them in the Name of His Son. We have the power to change the world because our Omnipotent Father will alter the course of His Creation in response to the humble requests of men. It is an eternal sharing of Love which has already begun. I ask everyone to pray with the assurance that Jesus is listening. We are most dear to His Sacred Heart. He fearlessly responds to us more quickly than any friend we could ever have. Even the ominous veil of death on Good Friday could not waver His eternal loyalty. That is the day He saved us. He will soon take us to Heaven where we will live with Him forever. But if we refuse to live for Him in this world, how can we desire to be in His presence in Paradise? He is the same Jesus now as He will be then. We must say "YES" without condition. The strength to abandon our lives to this conviction comes through our prayers.

Sunday, February 9, 1992

I often feel saddened when the time arrives for my nightly prayers because I am unable to put into coherent words the daily anticipation I have experienced since last February. I never previously knew that a manifestation of the Love of God could be so beautiful until I was approached by the Immaculate Conception, the Virgin Mother of Jesus Christ. Neither did I know that God loves us with such serious overtones. The Crucifixion of His Son had formerly seemed like a centuries-passed miracle that I could never have clearly seen or learned to truly appreciate. But, God is now raining His Wisdom upon the Earth through the genius of His Blessed Mother. Her words clearly bring the Passion and Death of Jesus into the 21st century with clarity. I now know that His Resurrection brings Life to everything good I had previously thought to be dead, long-gone, and out-of-sight.

It has been difficult to paraphrase the thoughts and images that the Holy Virgin has asked me to capture on these pages. But, I continue the best I know how, with the miracle of Her help. I often wonder why She does not simply give me the finished text of this Diary, word-for-word, and be done with it. But, She always preempts my curiosity by telling me that the world will better understand if a human, such as myself, tries to explain the often inexplicable from the vantage-point of my own mortality. As a sinner, I am burdened by the same helplessness and curiosity as everyone else on Earth. But, through this writing, I hope to share with you my newfound freedom at the hands of our Mother, Mary Immaculate. The following words comprise what She asked me to hear today. **"Good afternoon, My little one. I am with you again as I will always be. I love you so much. Please always remember that the only factor dividing you from being with Me in all of your senses is the lack of that sense which is gained when Eternal Life is granted. Obviously, you have not gotten there yet. You still have much work to do for Jesus."**

The Holy Mother asked if I would be willing to help Her to a greater degree. She hoped that I realize what my answer of "yes" would bring. Her messengers are often subjected to previously unknown consequences and attacks from evil. One of Satan's most subtle tools is the indifference of those without faith. She earlier told me that evil is like a fine grindstone. When you begin to feel weak and frail, you will know that he is near. I was also instructed that it is very important to Our Lady that I continue to live my life. She has not come to supplant my course of days, but to assist it. She said that She would repeat these facts over and again until I strongly understand what She means. I am to participate in the facets of life, but not in a worldly or sinful way. Today, She talked about sainthood and our rise to perfection. There are varying degrees of Heaven which are awarded to the faithful in accordance with the degree of sacrifice made for Jesus by individual people. Every honored saint began their life as lowly as each of us. If we remember this, we will also understand that it is possible to be perfect Love. Anyone who does not believe that they can be perfect in Love as Jesus is perfect is truly not enlisting His help.

There are those who maintain that human perfection is not possible. For that reason, they will not try at all. The opposition to the revelation of the Messiah is not as strong as when most of the recognized saints lived. Therefore, we are more free to be God's perfect children and love in the way of Jesus than we have ever been. This is what our Holy Mother has been saying all along. It is not the opposition from others which hinders our love, but the refusal to love by our own indifference while harboring every excuse as to why it is not possible or required. The problem lies inside ourselves. We must correspond to the Holy Spirit of Jesus Christ through our heart and soul. We hold this power unequivocally and unyieldingly. No one can take it from us. It is enhanced and focused by referring to Our Lady's message of the Light of Christ. Jesus expects His Light to be reflected from the hearts of mankind back to Himself. Each time an act of Love occurs, a beam of Divinity polishes our souls, and the refracted colors of Paradise rebound from the depths of our heart into the world. This is how others see His heavenly luster glistening from our refurbished souls. There is a warmth created in the soul when we love. These are the times when we reflect the grace of God as Jesus wishes. Everyone has assuredly felt it many times. And when we do, this means that our Love has become bright like the constant Light of our Lord. Christ is actually alive in us.

The faithful of the world are passionately trying to emit Jesus' Divine Radiance amidst the darkness of the Earth. With the help of Our Lady's miraculous intercession, we are cleansing the obscurant indifference from souls who rest upon Creation like mud caked on the lens of a flashlight. We will have succeeded when the Light of Christ is perfectly reflected by every human heart without exception. Then, we will have the station to proclaim the world converted. The Communion of Saints who have loved in faith assist us with luminous ripples of intercessory grace that they receive from the Bounty of the Lord in Heaven. They are like lighthouses near the sea of Creation, helping us navigate the treacherous mortal seas. For many people, this is a very long journey. We must accept the prescription of Love extended by our Holy Mother. She is teaching the responsibilities stipulated by the Holy Commandments set forth by Jesus when He walked the Earth. For example, Love fulfills the "Our Father" prayer. When we recite it, we invite the fulfillment of the Kingdom of God to Earth. We attest to the forgiveness that Christ Jesus requires us to offer to others in return for the pardon we humbly wish to receive. This is the essence of Jesus' Life on Earth. Total Love can be achieved by mortal men. Jesus proved it. Our reflection can be as bright as God's Source. Our Love must be as powerful as Jesus Christ as He hung on the Cross! That is why He died, to show that Love is all that is. It is so strong that it conquered death. God never intended for us to be of this world. He wishes us to participate in His Life and become one with Love eternally! It is possible for us to live mortal lives with immortal dreams. That is what Jesus shows mankind. And, that is what Our Lady has come to tell us.

Wednesday, February 12, 1992

The Holy Mother came as we prayed the Rosary in the evening. **"Good evening, My son. I love you and all of My little children. Thank you for praying to help save them. Thank you for helping them to be set free from themselves. As you and your brother share your love and pray to change the world, there are many other ways that I am at work. You are** such a special and important part of My plan. The work that you and your brother are doing is so helpful to the many who do not believe that My Son, Jesus, created all in the world and all that is not of this world. I know that it is oftentimes difficult for you to be unable to see the immediate fruits of your labors. I promise that all of your work is achieving our goal. I have told you many times that if our messages were interrupted tomorrow, you will have already received enough to convert multitudes. With our prayers, we will continue to pray that all peril and persecution from the world avoid you. I will always help..."

As She continued, She spoke of those who believe that they can compose their own life and develop the synopsis for their permanent happiness. It seems that many who have been successful in material ways also draw others to themselves by a conscious ability to manipulate those in their stead. They use their financial compilations to influence and allure others. Our Lady says that although they have procured their own material fortune, they can never author their own destiny in fate and Eternity. Mankind does not possess the forthright nature to achieve the true success which will transcend the ages, the elements, and his self-appointed future. The power of all ages and the Author of all endings is Jesus Christ. We hope for the day when everyone will seek to diminish human goals and, instead, work to achieve the Glory of Christ the King. Our Love is truly worthy of our submissive will in communion with the understanding that we are helpless without God.

The world is filled to the brim with people who would otherwise be saintly or venerable, if not for their distance from grace through concession to materialism and weaknesses of the flesh. We must pray that these would-be saints will strive toward the goal of holiness and purity. They are presently holding fast to all that they have allowed to conquer them. They are truly defeated by a world in which they are imprisoned. They find themselves out-of-grace and away from Love and prayer because their possessions and cravings of the flesh have herded them into spiritual isolation and deprivation like lambs led to the slaughter. All the while, they are exultantly heralded by others just as blind as themselves. They will become saints if we get to them in time with the words of Our Lady. Through Her intercession, God is filling the world with revelatory gifts of grace by miraculous messages, visions, apparitions, inspiration for prayer, desire for peace and holiness, and callings to return our Adoration toward the Most Blessed Sacrament. Through these gifts, God offers His great Mercy so that we may see our true destiny in the higher call of Heaven.

We were created for Paradise, not for the mortal world. But, we build our mortal lives as though we are permanently staying in them. Quite the contrary, we are only passing travelers on a pilgrimage to our eternal home. If not for the fall of Adam, we would never have been placed here. It is not inevitable that we will arrive at our happy destination if we do not make the effort to complete the journey. We must enter the Narrow Gate before it is sealed for Eternity. The path to deliverance is the pure, unconditional, infinite Love of Jesus Christ manifested through our own example of His perfect Likeness toward our brothers and sisters. Two of the great Commandments, love God and love your neighbor as yourself are fused into each of God's children to complete His command, ***"Be perfect as your Heavenly Father is perfect."*** The Communion which fulfills this Commandment is made present in the Holy Sacrifice of Mass. The Blessed Sacrament is the destination of every soul seeking Paradise.

Friday, February 14, 1992

The world is so busy doing the work of men. Governments are changing and the resources of the lands are being filtered to the few. Hearts are locked and tightly gripped by the intention of man to own his own soul. This is how the human will has blinded others from Love. Today, our Holy Mother came seeking the hearts of Her children, hoping to orient us toward Jesus. She is very sorrowful that Her Divine offspring do not always turn quickly to Her heavenly call. Again, She has asked me to expound the discussion of worldliness that we must avoid. The nations of the world are governed by many who control the resources of their people. When these leaders turn to Christ and Love, so will all who depend on them for sustenance and guidance. But, the few who hold control of the lives of the many are easily influenced by evil, thus they maintain their self-serving authority. Our Lady says that this is as readily apparent in the western world as it is in undeveloped countries.

Love forces the conscience of those in power to share their resources, a charity they are very reluctant to extend. Moreover, the world's influence-peddlers seek to destroy all that is made hallowed by the tremendous power and example of the Life of Christ. Jesus told His Apostles that the world would treat them just as it treated Him. Anyone who stands for the Light of Love will be condemned in a mortal way by those in seats of authority who see Jesus' message as the destroyer of their empires. The social damnation of the witnesses for Christ is an example of perfect and purposeful human suffering. Such martyrdom majestically soars like an eagle above the arid consciences of man and moves Love throughout the world as Heaven collides with Earth. This provides the Divine opportunity for the conversion of those who are strangling their brothers and sisters. They see in a new Light that they must convert their lives in order to preserve and protect the human dignity which everyone truly deserves. The grandeur of human life must be ensured from conception to natural expiration. Unborn children must be absolutely protected so that all Life given by the hand of God is allowed to consummate and flourish in the same Love in which He created it.

Public leaders are truly afraid to allow Jesus to govern their careers. They cringe at the Truth of the Christ's Gospel which states that those who would be great must humble themselves and serve the least of humankind. Their minds and spirits reject this call for humility like their stomachs regurgitate curdled milk. But, Jesus can take them there. Those who hold power must realize that they are also helpless in the eyes of God. They, too, must begin to pray. Strength of leadership does not rest in the laurels of arms and dominating ideas. It lies in the willingness to Love in the image of our Savior through every mortal test of the will. Indeed, virtue lies in never surrendering the belief that Love and Mercy are the answer to all worldly affairs. Prayer is the transcending mobilization that brings the response of the Father in every hopeless situation. There is no possibility of defeat or despair with Jesus. He is the Champion of all hope and victory. Mankind needs to accept the only Son of God, and reject the errant assumption that the Earth will be ravaged if mortals stop trying to control it. Indeed, it is being plundered by those same mortals who are manipulating it without wisdom or conscience. To alleviate this damning impropriety, we must accept Jesus Christ as the orchestrator of human destiny, and realize that our beginning is in His Love.

Sunday, February 16, 1992
Our Lady's loving greeting began today, **"The bountiful Love of My Son is with you My children, and I am with you. Please be happy! I have come again today to tell you more about the dignity of human life, and how precious Life is."** It was later than usual in the evening and I yawned from being a little tired. Our Lady quickly retorted, **"Will you be able to stay awake?"** I said yes, and She responded, **"That is good."** She then began Her discussion with the original premise of Life which is the Love that God has for His Creation. We are forbidden to violate His Love by destroying either our own life or someone else's. There are grave consequences awaiting those who ignore this command. God calls each of us to recognize the gift that Life is to the world. It is the Light and constancy of His Love. He confirms the dignity of human life and requires us to recognize the truth that He proclaims by it. Quite simply, human life is the Love of God.

We know through the comprehensive knowledge of Divinity revealed by Christ, that Life is good. To breach one's mortal existence is to participate in darkness and sin. It is highly dignified to protect all forms of Life as a manifestation of ongoing prayer and respect for our Creator. Everyone must renew their love for Creation every day. That mandates the recognition of the preciousness of Life. Love for Life begins in the human heart. When we give our lives to God, we realize that we belong to Love and are responsible to embrace others. Therein lies our source of infinite happiness. But, when we are indignant, Love has no room to bring us joy. The true definition of indignance is lack of Love. It is manifested in many unfortunate ways in the world. For example, in order for abortion to end, the value of human life must be recognized by the people who perform and procure it. The first abortion ever inflicted allowed millions of other unborn children to be murdered. That initial moral turpitude was the temptation which led to the avalanche of legalized abortion which is burying our societies in a suffocating blanket. Those who are guilty believe that the commission of this sin is an easy way to run from the responsibility of parenthood and the experience of rearing children. They do not realize that they cannot outrun or outdistance the judgement of Almighty God. Neither do they realize that is He going to accept no excuse.

Many sins which are now regarded as socially-accepted conduct arose in this same aberrant way. They grew from a lack of substantial private and public opposition. Far too few prayed! And too few loved! This led to the promulgation of our present social condition, the false belief that unborn children are not truly living people. This entire pretense of living outside of God's law led to the judicial legislation making it legal to continue to murder the unborn. And in the process, the essential dignity of every unborn child was also disregarded. These are the grave consequences of the absence of Love and the indignance that many live, calling it their own choice. This decimating darkness has been the root of all indifference and destruction throughout every century. Our Lady is calling on all humanity to pray and love so that dignity can be restored and lives saved. It is the same principle that has caused the existence of prisons. Where is the dignity in being caged like an animal? Indeed, there is no dignity in caging an animal. Such incarceration is an act of frustration, fear, or simply human pride. It is the direct result of the lack of Love and forbearance. This, too, has been allowed to flourish because not enough good souls have stood firmly upon the truth of Christ.

Imprisonment is not just physical confinement. It is a violent act of hatred by those who bind others in chains within restraining walls. Christ is quick to tell us that those who hate are more imprisoned than those whom they hold in bondage. It has been said many times that in order to keep someone in a ditch, you must stand there to guard him. How, then, can this be a righteous use of anyone's life? Those who destroy human life and who imprison their fellow man are, themselves, incarcerated by hatred. They have been circumscribed by their own inability to Love. Those who disdain Life will never be set free until they open to grace and release their own hearts. The grip of hatred destroys the dignity which Love brings to Life. It is a beginning which lives in the heart itself. Our Holy Mother cries many tears for those who hate themselves and others. She comes to remind us that Love has set everyone free. Humanity is bound by his own chains. Jesus is the Victor over all imprisonment. The conqueror of all evil is steadfast goodness and Love.

The third restriction of Life and freedom is the factual nature of the scourge of oppressive poverty. There is no dignity in causing destitution or hunger. The resources of the world should be shared the way Jesus would have us dispense them. Again, this is a function of the human heart that is one of the greatest demands which Jesus makes of us. Share the wealth! Feed and house the poor! Comfort the sick and disabled! With Love, all of this will be done. Christ wants His Creation to live with dignity without exception. It ensures the preservation of Life and the magnification of Love in the world. The only true way to confirm the dignity of human life is through Love. No individual has the omnipotence to create Life. Likewise, no one has the authority to destroy it. Therefore, those who perform abortions, along with mothers and fathers who choose to destroy their children, are guilty of grave sin. While they destroy the mortal existence of their children, they cannot reverse the Love of God. These Holy Innocents live forever in the arms of Christ. But, He will one day call to justice the thieves who stole the lives that He placed in those wombs. Jesus demands that the unborn be allowed to flourish into the fullness of existence and Life.

Our Blessed Virgin Mother loves all of Her children. She asks us to pray and convert to the Truth, so that no soul will be eternally lost to damnation. Now is the time to choose the dignity of Life and fortify our protection of those who cannot help themselves. When we see those who live without any blessed honor or meditate upon the precious unborn; when we ponder the plight of those in prisons and feel the hunger pangs of the poor, we are praying for Christ to come to our aid. Our Lady says that there will be a time when it will be too late to choose Eternity in Love. This leaves no other choice than to pray now, starting today as you read these words.

Tuesday, February 18, 1992
Our Lady wishes to help us realize that guidance is given to the lost, the lonesome, and those in despair through the Light of Christ. Today, She asked me to record a very simple correlation. In a previous message concerning the Moment of Love, we saw how all force was directed at the Cross and Jesus. Then at the completion of His Sacrifice and upon His Resurrection, there came an eternal emanation *from* the Cross. The rays of Divinity from Calvary are the spires of His Kingdom. These beautiful beacons shine upon every one of God's children. No one can hide from the Truth which rides on its incandescent streaks. Those who try have their backs to Him and walk in the shadow of their own sins, haunted because of their rejection of every virtue. The Love of Christ at His Crucifixion and Resurrection is the Light that fills all that "is." His Sacrifice is the Power given to the mortal ages which raises us to perfection. If we but surrender our will and accept His Love, we will see that He has forgiven our sins and restored our ability to shine as a spotless child of

Paradise. He assures us of Eternal Life in Glory. Our affirmative response is the fulfillment and manifestation of that destiny. Eternity begins here on Earth for those who live in the Light of the Eucharist. We become one with He who is Eternity.

Further, Our Holy Mother spoke poignantly this evening about a little boy who was terminally ill and being kept alive with machines. She said, **"I ask you to pray with Me that the family of the little child who is so ill will terminate their manipulative, artificial, and mechanical efforts to preserve him. You should know that such mechanisms which many purport to preserve Life are an act of selfishness and a denial of the basic premise of faith and acceptance."** With that, She offered Her bountiful blessing and departed for the day.

Wednesday, February 19, 1992

My brother and I found it very interesting and gratifying to know that Our Lady watches our lives so closely. Today, She provided living proof of Her presence at Holy Mass in the likeness of Her position under the Cross on Mount Calvary. The reading for the Mass was about the Deluge. We were wondering why Noah sent both a raven and a dove from the Ark. Quite to our pleasure, Our Lady was listening and tonight provided an explanation. We began to pray the Rosary at 9:00 p.m. in compliance with Her call. She dearly wishes all of us to ponder the Mysteries of the Life of Christ. During our prayers, She explained that Noah dispatched the raven because it was known to be a predator of great courage. He was adventurous and symbolic of the strength which most men utilize in time of danger. Their purpose is a determination toward this strength instead of the aspects of beauty. We remember, however, that it was the gentle dove that carried the welcome message, the olive branch which indicated land ahead. The raven is known to be an avid and strong flyer, a tough navigator that can survive a treacherous and long flight. However, it was the peaceful dove, likened to the Holy Spirit, which carried the Good News.

In continuing our prayers and silent meditations, Our Lady began to address mankind's so-called "ocean of love." She assured me that it is not a coincidence that the reading of the Deluge came on this same day. The sea is regarded as a place of peril; and the Deluge is an example of that fact. You also hear mankind speak of Love as being an ocean, a sea of passion which consumes and drowns him. He has come to this conjecture because he does not understand Love in the perfection of Jesus. Rather, man sees love as emotional, physical, and sensual derivatives. True Love is quite another fact. Jesus is the accurate and perfect definition of Heaven's highest order. His indomitable conviction has brought us to the salvific shores of His loving ocean. His passion buoys us to the surface of Life, away from our worldly concerns. It is not possible for one to lose their life in the depths of His mightiness. But, without Him, we can and will. Therefore, Love is not inanimate and lifeless like the violent seas, but rather, a vibrant and living Light which shines from every calmly rippled surface.

Mankind is confused because he has attached his definition of Love to worldliness and sin. We mistakenly believe that God's affection is the undefinable cause of our problems. Notwithstanding, the truth remains that the perfect nobility of the Savior of the world is really the solution to them all. The ocean of Jesus' Mercy incapacitates the human description of the "sea of love." While we have to be saved from the rolling rapids of our emotional stimulation, it is the infinite forbearance of Christ that keeps us from sinking into the depths of oblivion. We must consciously immerse ourselves in the bay of deliverance where our fall is breached by Mercy Himself. Our Lord will rescue everyone from their self-serving helplessness. We have falsely affixed an errant connotation to His grace by mistaking it for lust. I tell you, what man is thinking is not what is truly happening. The original premise is false! And, this is why Love is not defined by indulgence in a lapping basin of fleshly stimulation. If it is a sea at all, it is one which bathes, cleanses, purifies, and saves. Our Lady repeated that Her Son is a boundless immensity of goodness and peace, but not the briny waters that man perceives.

Our Crucified Savior is perfectly one with everything He has created, each part singly in Creation. He is all seasons of the climate of God. Yet, many people allow themselves to see Him only in their wintery-cold moments. He is likewise the wind, earth, seas, air, and all the rest of His grand conception. But, we refuse to see Him in this universal context. Many people oftentimes do not wish to see Him at all. And in doing so, they conjure their manipulating moods and enticing circumstances. This is also why some so negatively define emotion and affection as a body of stimulation in which they drown, while mistakenly calling it Love. Our Lord is not the inanimate drowning sea, but the entire Ocean of Salvation. He touches our lives and hearts through every moment of our lives and each interaction of our days. He became one with us by being born as man. He is the unseen Love of God the Father which has become seen in the flesh and soul of His Creation. Our Blessed Virgin completed Her message this evening with Her beautiful blessing and departed after uttering the words, **"I love you, Goodnight."**

Thursday, February 20, 1992

The Holy Mother reaffirms the truths of the Scriptures in Her role as Mother of the New Covenant. She began this evening by discussing our responsibilities in borrowing and lending. She has very little regard for our systems of controlling and distributing wealth to the detriment of Love and charity. In putting forth Her case, She said that no one should lend anything, wishing to recollect a larger sum than the original loan. Borrowing is a means through which the lender can display trust. But, if he requires more in return than he gave, it is not an act of trust at all. And, it is definitely neither kindness nor charity. Indeed, the higher the lending fare, the greater the display of distrust. Our system of sharing has become a profit-making prospect. Generosity is completely conditional and has become void of any magnanimous purpose. The process has become a model that mankind is using to dominate and subjugate his fellow man. The poor are refused their allotted portion because they cannot afford to pay the immoral profiteer's fees. They are refused their essential dignity and are not able to contribute to the collection of worldly wealth. I am not sure why our Holy Mother chose to discuss this issue on this day. But, trusting Her as I always have, I am sure that it will be of good use in the future.

Our Lady continued on another subject by mentioning the "New Age" philosophers who have been increasing in numbers in the western world. She said rather strongly that they have not defined "Love" in the way of Jesus. She also prefaced Her strong discussion with the affirmation that the Earth is no one's mother. She is the Mother of God, of all His children, and of all nature. She continued to address these "new age thinkers" who are prone to place the power of the world in thought and not in prayer. *"I think, therefore, I am"* has nothing to do with Love, God, or the Salvation of human souls. Therefore, we cannot think that we are loving, neither can we love by thinking. The new age movement does not see freedom residing in the command of Jesus to responsibly love. If they wish to believe in the transcendent nature of man, they should reflect on the infinite Love of the Holy Eucharist from the Altar of the Catholic Mass. The Holy Eucharist will transfigure them. This is the only place that they can truly become one with all that is.

Mankind must be wary of the philosophers whose deceitful tactics proclaim that Jesus gave them the power to be independent from God. Christ did no such thing! These same people promote and fund movements in favor of the murder of unborn children. Simply stated, Our Lady told me that the "New Age" theory is another dark avenue brought through evil work. The lack of mankind to recognize his helplessness is centuries old! But, he will always try to supplant his lack of Love with some other distraction. No one can be saved without accepting the Crucifixion of Jesus Christ. There is no substitute for Love because nothing else is true or real. I offer the following parable as an example. When someone loses a leg, he is provided a wooden prosthesis so he can stand and walk. He does this because the missing leg provided mobility and stature. But, it can be easily supplanted by an artificial one. Herein lies the inconsistency and the real truth. If this same man loses an eye which is replaced by a glass one, he will still be just as blind. Hence, there is no substitute for the original creative Love of God.

This is the substantive truth about the Almighty Father. It is the vision that allows us to see the Light of salvific Eternity which cannot be replaced! It is a tremendous thought for warming the heart. Love is the essence of Life. Love for one another is not simply a state of grace or a gift randomly given to different individuals. Jesus calls everyone to Love in obedient responsibility to His Sacrifice on the Cross. We are given the capacity and mandate to Love by the Crucifixion. We should not view this absolute command as an alternative for which we have yet to receive the grace to manifest. Loving is the essence of our living being. This should be our response when others complain that God has not yet given them the gift to accept others. There is no excuse for refusing to Love after seeing the Passion and Death of Jesus Christ. He eliminated the force of sin over the children of the Divine Kingdom. Those who recklessly continue in sin have not begun to pray or beg for the Mercy of God. He will save them, but they must ask.

Saturday, February 22, 1992

I know that there are varying degrees of propriety and formalization that any written work should embrace. Compliance with at least a minimum number of generally accepted literary principles should be the goal of any author. There is one problem, however, with such disciplinary prudence when it comes to this Diary. God does not always present Himself in the simplicity of normal semantics, and almost never in traditional English. I have had to transcribe Our Lady's miraculous words so that the most lenient of critics would, at least, remind himself that this is a record of the Divinity of Christ and not a polemic for rhetorical critique by subjective poetasters or collegians. Our Holy Mother speaks in complete sentences alright, but they often run together and incorporate multiple subjects leading to the moral lesson upon which Her purpose is predicated. This has made it necessary for me to break these points into additional phrases that are often cumbersome to read. Moreover, I have noticed that God cares little about the standards that this book would have to meet as established by professorial reviewers, had it not come explicitly from Him.

The Virgin Mary has given me the exact words that compose Her messages and has equally blessed the descriptive parables that have been paraphrased at Her direction. Therefore, you will find a flurry of sentence fragments and comma splices, all which serve to prove that God is not too captured by the rigors of literary propers. You will also notice that the Holy Mother often repeats Herself, carefully using the same words over and again. She rarely presents a message identical to another, but She sometimes selects a number of synonyms to emphasize a single point. In light of these facts, I ask you to read this miraculous gift with the reminder that, in Heaven, all days are one and the tone of infinite and simultaneous prayer is the perpetual dialogue of the Saints.

Our Lady chooses Her words like plucking the strings of a harp, and sometimes several at once. I have had to break them apart so that you can enjoy each one in its individual beauty. Indeed, I do not think that God cares whether we like the coherency of His thoughts as long as we accept the authority of His message and the grace of His messenger, Our Divine Lady. Therein lies the purpose of this Diary and the reason I hope you will be absorbed by Her call, rather than distracted by the cumbersome nature of my written human communication.

Today is the anniversary of the beginning of Our Lady's messages to me as the Queen of Love. She came filled with joy with another message to move the world closer to Her Son, Jesus, so that He may live and shine in union with the hearts of His children. This is how a bridegroom feels toward his bride. How God wishes we could know the reverence and passion with which His Son loves the world. And I, too, wish all the world could know how He longs to kiss our souls. I hope for the day when everyone will truly understand that the Light from the flame of Love will never die. One day, indeed, every eye will see. We are the musicians in an orchestra. The prayers from our hearts are the sweetly flowing melodies. Our Lady is pleased to listen to our songs of petition. She is happy because faithful hearts are praying, listening, and opening. Everyone is important to the heavenly Father. No one is excluded from His Love and Mercy, or from Salvation and happiness. And because of the messages given during the past year, the world is closer to its fulfillment than ever before. We must continue to pray that no one is separated from Love by their own inaction. Our helplessness must encourage us to realize that without God we cannot stand in the truth. It is much like trying to reverse time itself. If we love completely, understanding will bring fulfilled yearning to continue in such happiness. We never forget the feeling in our heart that is generated by the Holy Spirit when we love in His likeness. This is the eternal bliss which we can never reverse. Our Lady says, however, that it is important that our love not be intermittent. She provided a simplistic picture to explain.

It is a rope which has frayed on both ends. It would be very difficult to connect anything with these ends to form any order of strength. Once the rope becomes ragged, the ends must be severed so that a stronger and more unified remnant can be joined. This is what happens to those who separate themselves from Jesus. They become isolated, making it very difficult to reunite with the same strength.

This is why it is important to never become separated from the eternal union of souls who live happily in the beltway of the blessed. If we never become divided as a people, our individual frays will never impede our reunion as one people under the Crucifix-masthead of the ship of Redemption. Forgiveness enjoins brawling humanity into a cohesive Love from which every soul can benefit. While hatred severs us from others, pardon and absolution cauterize the wounds, bringing and sustaining hope for oneness. We must commit our hearts to the task of reaching-out to others with our hands filled with peace, instead of leveled in the poise of warfare. In totality, forgiveness mends the severed cord of the spine of human love so that we can walk in grace and peace. We must profess our Love for all peoples of the world. Then, we will not be distracted by the worldliness which is such a perpetrator of evil. We should seek the great perspective of Divinity manifested in the Passion of Jesus. There are many thousands who know who He is, but our call is to advance beyond knowledge and theology. We must realize and implement active Love in our lives. Our Lady has made this very clear on every continent. The permanent and perpetual Christ is all that we need to understand the lives which God asks us to live. His Love is offered today with the same strength that He gave at His birth, from the Cross, and at the descent of His Holy Spirit. We must open our hearts to live prayerfully and peacefully within the beautiful grasp of our Holy and Blessed Mother, Mary.

Monday, February 24, 1992

Our Lady designated this day as a time to speak about the Sacrament of Marriage. I do not ask why She chooses to address certain subjects on a given day. I hope, however, that anyone who is married will find this entry especially revealing and inspiring. I am sure that She intends it for all who are united in Holy Matrimony. It is obvious that the world is witnessing great suffering in families. Our Holy Mother says that husbands and wives are divided when either of them fails to maintain perfect fidelity to their precious marital vows. They must call to mind the devastating effects that such division has on their little children. Their own offspring are the true victims of the indifference that they show toward the sacred gift of marital love. Be they infants or young adults, the experience of their children is cold, traumatic, and a source of shock. The stability that these parents are required to provide within the family is stolen from the smallest and most vulnerable members. The grief can be seen in their sorrowful eyes because their tender hearts do not understand. They are so easily bruised and long-scarred by the raging trauma of the unkept vows they witness before their eyes. Our Lady asks us to pray for the strength of these children that they maintain the grace and poise to continue to love those who have so offended them. With hope and prayer, their tiny hearts are mended, sustaining the innocence through which they entered their untimely suffering. Jesus hears our prayers for those who are affected by the loss of trust and sad divisions which are coming more readily into married families. Everyone must realize that two lives become one Life when Matrimony is blessed by Jesus. This is why any severance or violation of this sacred union is unnatural and sinful. We must pray for the hearts of those who are tempted to such infidelity. Prayer is our duty. All human imperfection is mitigated by prayer. It is the proper way to remedy this problem and change the world.

Tuesday, February 25, 1992

With the passing of each new day, I am learning the fulfillment of knowing the wishes of God for His people. It is possible for anyone to have a revelation of the heart and become one with our invisible yet knowable Creator in Heaven. His brilliance is reflected through His Virgin Mother, Mary, the Queen of Martyrs. She is the ancillary ambassador from Glory itself. She is also our Mother, a beacon Lady of the highest sovereignty, a royalist who lives Her perfection from the orphanages of the Earth to the Throne in the heavens. Hers is the Kingdom of laurel trees and monstrances, perpetual Dawn and angels' prayers. She calls us equally to be Her own. Our intercessory Mother is still revealing God to the nations. Her Queenship thrives through His mystical works. I can visualize Paradise and hear Her angelic choirs when I pray. When I place my hands upon a Holy Rosary, I can actually touch the Face of God. My soul speaks in silence to the Almighty of Forever, a Spirit whose Hand I can grasp, the singularly omnipotent and Eternal Father. He is the collective repose of a society of Saints and irrepressible Martyrs who are the faceted jewels of the Countenance of Heaven.

Our Holy Mother has taught me that Love is still alive-and-well through the solace and comfort of Her blooming Heart. Heaven is Immaculate because She is enthroned there. We are made the inheritance of God by Our Savior, Jesus, who gained wisdom and strength from this same Holy Virgin that bore Him to Earth. In Her Love, all human achievement and acclamation are universally born, never to wane, and never to die. Now, the world is a place of refurbished hope. Our Mother gives us Her noble Child, whom She blessed with sartorial grace in the most humble of homes. We now know our Father again through His pastoral Son. He creates and unites, admonishes and mends, and forgives and heals. His Body is blissful Paradise. His veins are tunnels of pristine gold, like the Chalice of the Altar, from which flows His sustaining

Blood of Mercy to His people below, to His created incarnation, to His pride and joy.

We have been delivered to the feet of God by our Holy Mother. Through Her grace, we are borne back to Him in the armor of holiness and the nativity of contrition. All of this, and we have yet to leave the Earth. All who read this book-in-hand will know of my joy because of Her devotion. I ask you to share in the resurrecting transformation that She also seeks from you. We must bow in diminutive oblation to this Holy Princess of the ages, to plead together and to pray as one. When my brother and I recited the Rosary again this evening, our beautiful Mother came to say, **"Good evening, My precious little ones! It is so nice to see you again. I have come to tell you that I love you and that I love the people of the world."**

In response to Her Divine proclamation that we are helpless if we do not love Jesus, we must also live with strength that commitment in freedom. It is much more than just an understanding of our helplessness. We must actively Love or the commitment is not alive at all. Many people recoil, waiting for miracles and graces to come to them. They are idle and refrain from prayer, doing nothing to live-out the Love that Christ commands the world to live. But when they see that their vacuous lives bear no fruit, they falsely claim that Love is an empty and false prophecy. This is a result of their own failure to commit their hearts to the task. They feel as though they have given their all toward the noble effort, thus, there is no other alternative but to question, rather than to trust. Faith, in itself, is the Life-giving essence of our decision to trust the God that we cannot see. Even in my own right, if I did not know that it is God's Mother who sometimes disciplines me, I might be tempted toward a response of questioning Her motivations. As it is, I do not wish to invoke the audacity to challenge the Queen of a Heaven I wish to someday enter. Further, it is impossible to dispute Her judgement because it is the will of Jesus Christ. I trust their Love absolutely. With the promise that Jesus has made which He fulfilled so convincingly on the Cross, we should know by now that He is trustworthy beyond any other creature of God. And, His messengers bear that trustworthiness.

Our Lady has told us many times about the symbolic mirror, which some call the surly bonds, that separate mortal existence from immortal Life. It is the seeable image which God portrays of Himself in our own lives. We sometimes believe that He antagonistically plays "tug-of-war" with our present and future. We refuse to let-go of the present worldliness because we fear the unforeseen future that He has planned will not make us as happy. One of the greatest powers that we seek is the ability to predict the future. Oh, if we were all so clairvoyant, we would know not only what to pray for but when to anticipate the answer. Notwithstanding, God does allow us such vision when we pray. While we do not stake games or wagers based on advanced knowledge of approaching events, we can be sure that we will receive what we ask for when we petition the Almighty Father in Jesus' Name. The power that we wield through prayer would astound the most prolific odds-maker.

We cleanse ourselves of errant feelings and false anxieties when we pray from the heart. We call-up our greater capacity to give more of ourselves to the cause for which Christ died, far beyond our mortal efficacy. Moreover, we duly prevent tragedy and sin by asking God to preempt them with His grace. We must do this because humanity does not intrinsically know how to solve even the simplest moral questions on his own. However, the fate of human civilization rests in our own hands. We must, willingly and honestly, accept the Crucifixion of Jesus as the standard by which we shall live. It is Our Lord's greatest prayer for His people. Second only to this impeccable Sacrifice, the prayer of the Holy Rosary will bring our future of Light and happiness. Jesus wishes to see the children of God sitting in the arms of His perfect Mother, perched beside Him at the right hand of the Father. Hope for the world resides in our commitment to conversion, prayer, fasting, and peace. All of these are manifestations of the Love raining upon us from the glories of Heaven. The Queen of Heaven is miraculously interceding the world over to show us that Christ Jesus is the answer to all questions.

Thursday, February 27, 1992

Before the Blessed Mother came into my life, I used to believe that my prayers were somewhat pretentious and oftentimes presumptive. I have sorrowfully pondered, "Why would God ever listen to my needs, when there are so many others in the world who require His blessing more?" I wondered whether it would be futile to ask Him to heal a world that is so much more deserving of His final judgement and justifiable wrath. But, the Blessed Mother has shown me that this is all the more reason for us to lift our hearts in invocation. I can remember from Her first messages that She told us that the greatest waste in the world is a prayer left unsaid. So, I now pray from the heart with the expectation that Jesus can clearly hear me. I have seen the tangible effects of prayer and the way that He desires to grant our intentions. But, we must approach Him with sincerity in communion with our Holy Lady. We must meditate upon the Will of the Father and become open to His Spirit. That is how we can know what are truly the most noble aspirations for man. It is how we understand what God wishes for the world in order to evoke our conversion and the vision of His grace.

I always contemplate the beauty of our Blessed Mother's prayers. I engage Her in the intimate depths of Her Immaculate Heart. These are the things that help me to know that our supplications are so powerful. God will, indeed, respond to each of us, even to our seemingly most insignificant of intentions. To continue to teach me this contemplative discipline, our Holy Mother came again today to deliver another revealing message. She told me that mankind has contributed in many ways to his own dissatisfaction, disorientation, and loneliness. And, without Jesus in our hearts, we will always be so despaired. We have caused our own captivity because we have turned ourselves over to the world and its propensity to detain us. We spend most of our time trying to maintain control over everything we call ours, cringing from the temporal aspects of our custodial stewardship.

We learned from centuries past that sin is fatal to the human soul. Although we seemingly live a life of continuity with intermittent moments of happiness and success, it all comes to the end when the penalty for sin must be paid. That wage is mortality. But, Jesus the Lord paid the price and acquitted the debt so that we would not be forever dead. We live again in Him. Our Lady calls this resurrection, our deliverance from mortal existence into Eternal Life as fulfilled in the New Covenant books of the Holy Scriptures. She has told us many times that we cannot get to Heaven without first taking the hand of Jesus. We must accept and obey this Gospel as the Holy Word of God. Our Lady also made it clear that the Gospel handed down by the Apostles must not be abridged or amended to complement any contemporary human desire. God's intention is that we be saved through the Crucifixion and Resurrection of His Son.

The Holy Mother offered a beautiful parable this evening. It concerns the locking of human hearts and the blocking of the entrance door through which Jesus would like to enter. Some have closed their hearts so tightly that they will not allow anyone's love inside, not even Christ Himself. Our Lady asked me to ponder this situation in the relevance of our helplessness. She told me that we have locked the door of our heart from the inside and dropped the key which has fallen to the floor. It has subsequently bounced across the threshold to the outside. Those who reject Love are now inside a self-imposed exile of indifference or hatred. They have helplessly incarcerated themselves in the material world and are secluded from the goodness of Light. They live in the darkness and are deficient, alone, and afraid. It is a very cold heart that will not allow Love inside! The universal key, the master key, which will unlock the door, is Jesus Christ! He does not necessarily need our individual key should we not be able to find it within ourselves. If we ask Him to enter, He will open the door Himself and allow Love inside. So, when we say "no" to Love, we drop our key onto the outside world.

If we invoke the faith to believe that Our Lord is knocking on our door, He will set us free. He permeates our penitential abode to grant our soul freedom into the Eternity of all Creation. This parable is concisely what Our Lady means when She says that mankind is helpless without Jesus. We are battling our own soul for happiness and fulfillment. The only way to win this fight is to accept Christ and live Love. Prayer from the heart overcomes our perpetual perception that somehow we must escape the life of mortality through the world itself. Instead, it is God's transcending power which moves us forward. Our false perceptions cause us to believe that we are in a routine of dailiness. We do not realize that we can truthfully touch, soothe, lift and change every soul in existence and through all Eternity by simply kneeling to pray.

Saturday, February 29, 1992

The message of the Love of Almighty God is to be manifested through the unity of all mankind. That is the essential reason that He has sent His Mother to call us to order. His eternal purpose is that we embrace this oneness of Love so that we will all grow forthrightly worthy of the Kingdom that He is about to bestow upon us. Our Lady says that even though it is apparent that many of us wish not to be quilted into the fabric of Love, God sent Christ into the world as the only alternative and true means for us to achieve Salvation and happiness. Only Love is Life. Jesus teaches that those who are divided need to come together for the world to be one. Love in the way of His Sacred Heart brings the cohesive wisdom that we need to effect this global transformation. It is possible to be one family of man, regardless of any diabolical forces that try to divide us. God has revealed this truth in many beautiful ways. Even the physical structure of the world was created in the image of loving oneness. Just as east and west, and north and south, are opposite, they eventually become one. They are distinct and separate only to the point where they begin to rejoin because of the spherical nature of the Earth.

Our Lady asks us to consider this parable toward our reunification in Love. No diametrical opposition between men can destroy the desire of God to make His people whole. The Virgin Mother passionately wishes us to love from our heart, while realizing that we need one another to perfectly glorify the Mystical Body of Christ. We must pray and live together in the unifying grace of peaceful brotherhood. To this end, we are earnestly asked to pray the Most Holy Rosary. This will make us one again. Our unity in bonds of Paradise is God's merciful promise, sealed through Jesus' Passion and Death. The Immaculate Virgin told us in one of Her original messages that Love is strongest when given to someone not readily open to receive it. She asked me to remember this phrase, **"May the words of my mouth and the meditations of my heart be acceptable in Thy sight, O Lord, my Strength and my Redeemer."**

By contemplating these holy words, we come to understand the spiritual elevation that Jesus desires of us. No degree less than perfect Love is acceptable to our Lord. But, it seems that we have mistakenly convinced ourselves that perfect holiness is impossible. This is a false assumption by a helpless people. We somehow reject God and then blame Jesus for the inadequate use of our own free will. We have the responsibility to love or to destroy ourselves in the omission. We must choose the dignity of Life as the only choice that leads to the Eternity of happiness.

MARCH 1992

Sunday, March 1, 1992

Since this was the first Sunday of the month, several of us who pray together attended a Mass in Peoria, Illinois to commemorate the Marian Shrine at Medjugorje, Yugoslavia. Upon returning home in the evening, Our Lady recollected the day. She seemed happy with Her faithful little children who adored Jesus in the Blessed Sacrament with such great love. She said, **"Many ills of the world have been rectified by your love for Jesus and for all of your brothers and sisters. My little priest loves in the image of Christ. He knows the holiness that you are being taught by Me. There were many more faithful hearts at the Exposition, Adoration, and Benediction today. This makes Me very happy! The world has been made twenty-five times more sacred as a result of the twenty-five special Sundays that you have offered to Jesus so far. Thank all of you very much. I am touched and pleased. Your prayers and hopes are being answered. You know that prayer is unifying the world. Hatred and oppression are diminished and eliminated by prayer. Hearts are lifted to the heavens by the loving acts of the faithful. Enemies are conquered by those who pray to convert their hearts. The world is brought again to peace and to the symmetry of Love. Today, the shape and condition of men's hearts have been brought closer to one, unified under the Cross of Jesus..."** Our Lady added a simple predicate to Her words to close the day. She said that we must all continue in our elevation to God from within our hearts. Every soul given to Christ is unified in the heavens under the Cross. This is why church windows are shaped to a single point at the top. Everything beneath is elevated to the single unity of the Heavenly Father.

Monday, March 2, 1992

Each new day, our Holy Mother gives me the gift of Her intercessory grace. She often speaks in detectable terms, while other times I simply know that She is at my side. I never prod Her for new meanings or search for answers to countless questions I could possibly ask. Her presence alone suffices for now because God is with me through Her, and I could wait a thousand years before I would ever think of questioning His patience. The Holy Spirit speaks to me through our Blessed Mother one message at a time. Today, She asked me to sit down and write a monograph that I should give to other families during Lent to help bring Light into their world. I want to do the things that She asks of me the best that I know how. But, when I tried to compose the letter today, I could think of nothing to write at all. I could not muster any beautiful images or inspiring meditations in my mind. I became anguished because I felt that I was letting Her down. Our Lady has been speaking to me for over a year, and I have not found the ability to compose even a simple spiritual contemplation to my brothers and sisters for Lent. The Holy Mother addressed my despondence upon Her appearance today. She said, **"My frustrated little son, now can you see how helpless mankind is without God? I will give the message for you to send."** The following text is the written composition that Our Lady proposed.

Dear beloved friends in Christ Jesus,

We hope that this letter finds you enjoying the happiness of our Lord's Love for you. We are at a very special and urgent time in our lives. Every one of God's children needs to open his heart to the will of Jesus and proclaim that Love is the Victor over the world and all in it. God is calling us to prayer and conversion, especially during this time of Lent. We, your friends, are sending you the Most Holy Rosary of our Blessed Virgin Mother Mary for you to use to help us turn the world to Love. The Rosary is not just being sent to you because you particularly need help more than the rest of the world. We are asking you for your help by your prayers. We are not members of your parish, and do not even live in your town. But, we know that you, like all of God's children, possess the power to help us change the world. With your prayers, we can all help Jesus to remake the face of His Creation. Together, we can bring back to perfection what mankind has tarnished. Without your help, our effort will not be the same.

We ask that you join with us in prayer, especially the Blessed Mother's Rosary, so that all of us can heal our world and return the hearts of humankind to their origin of Love and purity. We join with our Champion Savior, Lord Jesus, in wishing you the peace and strength that will open all hearts to Love, and will restore all of Creation to holiness. And, it is in His Name that we proclaim our inseparable and heartfelt Love for you and your family. May the peace of Christ and the memory of His Sacrifice bring you a new beginning of Love in a magnitude which you have never known. All praise and glory belongs to Jesus, the Lord and Savior of all mankind.

Our Lady asked us to send this message along with three Rosaries to a family of our choice during each week of Lent. It is a simple example of the loving acts that we should perform to unite us in prayer to Jesus. Many rely on

Him only when they feel that He is a last resort. They do not truly understand that Our Lord is always with them. They feel that they should invoke His Love much like an independent object after all else has failed. Our Lady reminds us, instead, that Jesus will support us with upright dignity at every invocation in a world which tries to repress our fervent Christian fidelity. It is, indeed, a struggle to stay gracefully aloft in holiness amidst such a world of despair, corruption, and hopelessness. We must be confident that Jesus will lift us each time we may fall. That is the main reason why the Blessed Virgin calls us repeatedly to the Holy Sacrament of Reconciliation. Christ Jesus will never let us move away from a perfectly upright position in His sight. He forgives all sins, except the sin of wanton rejection of His Sacrifice.

Our human tendency is to be self-sufficient, only turning to our Savior when we have no where else to go in our search for fulfillment. We realize that we are apt to fall, yet do not know how to prevent it. We must realize that Perfect Love eliminates any possibility of that occurrence. A pure heart does not yield to temptation, although sin may present itself within an uncomfortable proximity. We must simply place our trust in the Love of Christ. He is always with us, even when we feel far from Him. He knows our humanness, and therefore, asks us to clothe our humanity in the Glory of holiness. Indeed, we are directed to maintain the solemn oath that we professed to God at our Baptism. When we remember the magnitude of Jesus' Love for us, we will succeed. This is, likewise, the case when we are asked to forgive one another. Our first order is to recollect the clemency that Jesus has extended to our souls. We will then smile throughout our suffering as a way of telling Him that we remember His Sacrifice for us. And, the ecstatic happiness that shines from His eyes will be the loving reward that buoys our joy, making our life completely fulfilled.

OUR LENTEN PURIFICATION

Ash Wednesday, March 4, 1992

Our Lady offers Her words through the indelible grace with which She shines. They are often given in conjunction with the Church calendar, as She addresses certain issues according to their respective season. She obviously speaks of the birth of Jesus during Advent and Christmas. The self-denial that we are called to embrace is usually discussed during this season of Lent. The Holy Mother has reduced the actual number of Her messages during these forty days and has asked me to continue to live in faith, like everyone else on Earth. It is a time for deep reflection upon Our Blessed Savior and for pondering what Christ, Himself, must have suffered during those long and humiliating weeks under the desert sun. Since this is the case, I will include some of my own prayerful meditations on the days that would otherwise be marked with the grace of Our Lady's words. I have selected no particular order for the placement of these lines, but have presented them in accordance with the call of God for us to be perfected into the likeness of His Holy Being. This is a special time for our beseeching supplications and the lifting of personal alms. I know that we should meditate upon Our Lord during the entire liturgical year.

What words could I use to describe these moments with Our Lady? How can I unveil Her majestic maternal Love? The Holy Mother of God has come! And, Her Heart beats the rhythm of timeless Love with all Her little children. The Virgin Mary wants to give a perception of grace that has become unknown in the world. She wants to tell us in yet another way how Jesus is so compassionate and understanding. Our events, thoughts, and circumstances take the form of perceptible shapes in our heart and mind. Human love must be all-encompassing and flexible so that the variety of shapes are in unity with the perfection of God. For example, a sentiment which may be expressed by a triangle must come from the same essence of Love as a thought resembling a square. Our feelings and perceptions do not always enjoin on the same plane of thought and action, but they must all be a fruit from the ultimate seed of Love which is Christ in our heart. It would be difficult for thoughts resembling three different objects to all have an adjoining surface, text, or line. We learned when we were children that a rectangle cannot be placed into a hole which looks like a star, because the two are not geometrically in union.

This is the same problem as the near infinitude of differing aspects of human life. In spite of all that makes us unique, our pressing goal is to unite as one humanity. Love is the transforming and cohesive power that allows all people and the environment that we perpetuate to unify in Christ. When everyone loves in accordance with the messages of Our Lady, our souls become one, even though different. And yet, none of us remain in our original shape. Therefore, a triangle and a rectangle each become a circle; and the circumference is the mantle of our Blessed Mother. Yes, they are complementary. The wisdom of God forms the understanding for all human actions and difficulties. Love can be exemplified as being somewhat like water. The different facets of our lives and human systems might be symbolically expressed as containers which hold this life-sustaining liquid. What does water do when poured into a vessel? It geometrically conforms and adheres to the interior surface of each container, notwithstanding the shape. Further, if the water from each container is poured into a single vat, would you be able to determine the portion which came from each container? What if each vessel held an equal amount, could you interchange the contents and at the same time determine their initial origin. This is the universal nature of Love and the capacity of Jesus to touch the soul of all people in every land.

Our Lady uses this parable to describe the international pilgrimages of the beloved Pontiff, John Paul II. He visits the humble, devastated, and poverty-stricken African nations, while he also visits the ancient sites of Egypt and rustic hamlets of Europe. And too, he comes to bless and teach the industrial, modern, and developed countries in the western world. All of these places are different and variably changing; so far apart in description and style. Yes, they are like the containers. And, the Holy Father is, like Christ, "One Love." He responds gently and humbly to the places where he goes, pouring his soul forth like the holy waters of God's peace. He fills their cup to overflowing with the new blessings of the promise of Jesus' Love so that they can conform themselves to the Scriptures and be united with all others. We must live the Love that the Roman Pontiff teaches all over the world. Love gives us the ability to be as accepting as His perfect example. We must never be confined to any biased boundaries in our search for human cohesion under the Cross. Love is always comprehensive and universal, allowing the receiver to transform himself into the unity of Love, like changing a triangle to a circle. Jesus does not force Himself upon others, but He will be the undeniable Redeemer of all souls when He comes again.

Saturday, March 7, 1992

There are many reactionary and interpersonal influences to which I have become respondent in my increasing awareness of our modern era. The Holy Madonna is showing me what a cynical age we live in that is seemingly spinning out-of-control in the void of space. We demand our right to overages and are resistant to being held accountable for our share of world grief. We sue one another over insult and injury at the drop of a hat, and there are hats laying everywhere. Booming businesses expect better labor for lower payrolls, and workers demand higher wages for less output. All of this serves to diminish the spirit of American charity and good will. Thank God, however, it is not necessarily endemic to our society at large. If our heritage is that of lifting-up opportunity for all, we have arrived at a time when we are violating the very operative principles on which our sophisticated country was founded. We are an overdeveloped nation of self-satisfied progressives, too industrial and too secular for the good of our souls. A very holy priest once quoted a foreign visitor to America as having said, "They even have houses for their cars!" God clearly sees all of this hypocrisy while we stand-by and watch helpless people die on other continents, succumbing to starvation and disease. Even to begin the reverent season of Lent on Ash Wednesday, many Americans spend the preceding twenty-four hours indulging in drunkenness and revelry at a celebration called "Fat Tuesday." Is that any way to show God that we are serious about His call to fasting and self-denial? Our Holy Mother has helped me recognize all of these aberrant vices that I previously thought were acceptable ways of life in a liberated country. Now, I see them as an incredible offense against God during a time when He is trying to teach us the virtues of humility, sharing, and conservation through Christ, His Divine Son.

Monday, March 9, 1992

"Good evening, My little precious ones. I love you very much. I have come to speak to you again. I wish to reassure you and reaffirm the incredible power of My messages. Your Diary is overwhelming, like the miracles of My shrines and healing graces. I love you so much for your faithful help. I am also happy to see you and your brother again." This evening, Our Lady spoke about human suffering. Even in all of its converting power, it has monumental dimensions. In spite of such pain, we are not without hope when we pray. We change the world with every petition, and simultaneously come to understand that suffering is not a punishment from God. It advances the cause of our Salvation, and releases the grip of the vices of impurity, indifference, and blasphemy. This is the cleansing and purifying effect of the blessing of human suffering. And it also reflects the invincible power of the Crucifixion of Jesus. All torment, whether spiritual, mental, or physical, is in union with Christ, the Original Love. The world is truly vindicated by the suffering of mankind in union with the Crucified Son of God. What it comes down to is a matter of dimension. If we see Love as a two-dimensional circle on a page, suffering enhances our vision to acknowledge it more fully as a three-dimensional sphere. Our exile does not preclude us from Love, nor does our mortality predispose us to be repetitive in sin. It is true that we are sinners, but our destiny in Christ is to be sinless. This is the perfection that we seek by living the perfect example of Our Savior's Love. It is not an impossible task. As a human person, Jesus lived a perfect life. He is our destiny and potential.

Our Holy Mother is assisting our growth in faith to know that Love is the purifier of human life which breaches the inherent nature of man to sin. Love has delivered humankind from imperfection by destroying the desire to accede to the guiles of temptation. Theologians have long speculated and theorized about the Beatific Vision that Jesus had when He was on Earth in a mortal body. We can attain that same Divine purview through total Love. It begins in prayer and is perfected in human suffering. Each of us has this realistic capacity. We need faith to understand that we are created in the image of God and that Jesus' Sacrifice is the price paid-in-full which has returned us to pristine perfection. We have been purchased by the Blood of our Savior, Jesus, and are offered the grace which does perfect us at each moment in time. It is a much more reverent prospect for us to overcome anxiety through faith than with knowledge. It is better to hope than to succumb to despair by choosing a destiny that is other than heavenly. This is why we are given the power to pray and the command to utilize it. Prayer is the power of God in ourselves, and a fruit of the perfect Love from which we are created. We are helpless in all that we do if we do not invoke the heavens in the way that Our Lady teaches. And, if we fail to obey, we deny our own hope for eternal Salvation. We gain our resurrection in totally unrestrained and unabashed freedom by virtue of Jesus' Love. Satan has a grip on the western world, seriously inhibiting us from choosing to Love perfectly. Witness the horror of abortion. It is a sickness of the soul and a symptom of a world absent of Love. The single truth is the preciousness of Life. There is no alternative to the acceptance of God's Love. The choice must be to choose the blessedness of Life. To prefer eternal damnation is not a choice at all. It is forever! Jesus is happy with those who seize their opportunities to proclaim the sanctity of human Life. Oh, how happy He is to see Love triumph over the force of public opinion! We should pray from our hearts for the elevation of human dignity. Jesus says, ***"Whatever you do to the least of your brothers, you do to Me."***

Tuesday, March 10, 1992

I have learned many things as a follower and believer of Immaculate Mary. I now better understand why death is imminent, although it is not a final sunset. The apocalyptic Dawn that follows will never expire. Beyond that break lies everything we have been forced to relinquish in defense of our hearts for years-on-end, lest our compression of grief kept us from ever raising our faces to the skies again. Yes, beyond that immortal sunset lives every marriage that we hoped would never fail, every soul that should never have died, and children we wanted to raise, but never had the opportunity to bear. Living beyond that chasm is our chance to boast of successes that would not come and the rebirth of special friendships that were mortally wounded ages before.

Above all else, the Holy Virgin has taught me to hope in the joy that Jesus brings. In Him, we will find every buried treasure yet-to-be discovered and will sail anew on each stately vessel now crying for resurrection from the bottomless depths of the teeming seas. We will soon be able to see all things we previously thought to be unknowable as clearly and majestically as God envisions them Himself, like trees that bear fruit in the winter and a blanket of snow that yields to a seashore in the blink of an eye. Pheasants and foxes will play together again, and all life will be hypnotized by the mountain ranges of food, unable to remember an antiquated phenomenon called hunger. Through this recorded Diary, I offer that hope to you, and joy to share atop our victory. And, too, I pray that you will remember what you have read in these humble paragraphs as the breeze that set your mainsails high for the journey back home to God.

Wednesday, March 11, 1992

Our Holy Mother brought with Her this evening visions and meditations of peace equally as beautiful as that of yesterday. She is always with us when we live Love because She loves us in return. She calls us to the Light of our hearts so that we see the simplicity of beauty in our memory. We desire the cessation of motion so that we can comprehend the resplendence of a pure Life in all places and during all times. For example, when we thumb through photograph albums, we see breathtaking remnants of our lives captured in the stillness before us on a page. We can close our eyes and relive the laughter and the warmth of familial union and good friendship. I ask you today to remember simplicity, like the feeling of seeing the sun setting behind a field of ripe corn stalks. As you pass by them in your car, the sun strobes in your face through the tops of the tassels like a motion picture film. Or perhaps, we could imagine a little bee buzzing around a beautiful flower on a sunny day, or the trickling of a hillside stream through the rocks in a shady forest. All of these images produce a peace in our souls which remind us of the simple beauties of life from times gone by.

Do you remember the sound of a car traveling a distant highway as you watched the fireflies from your lawn chair on the porch? Can you, likewise, feel the peace you knew when you stood gazing at the majestic setting sun? There are countless images and scenes which we are free to remember from our earlier days. We remember as children sitting in the yard all alone and hearing the crickets chirp on an early autumn evening. We have all laid on our back to see the stars flickering like lights from the heavens through the trees. We thought that we were so alone in the world; that no one else was like us, and none of our thoughts would have the courage to enter other minds. All of this time, we were waiting for our call to something we yet did not know. But in this anticipation, there was still great peace. We knew that our hearts were open, but not how to prepare for what life would bring. The simplicity and peacefulness grew from the knowledge in our soul that Jesus was always there. He has stood by us during those times, in victory and defeat, and in accomplishment and disappointment.

Our Lady has always been there too. Together, they prayed with us. And, Jesus lived in us as He does to this day. They have not changed since our infancy in mortality and faith. To our good fortunes and strength, during trials and outright boredom, we should remember that those earlier times still live in the freedom of our heart. They are a function of our love for God and have no parameters that are affected by the passing of time. To this day, we must maintain that innocent simplicity to see the world with new revelation of its true beauty. All of this is a gift from Christ Jesus so that we may render them into prayerful peace. I wish you the majesty and magnificence of the peace of Love. I offer you the holiness of laughter and a smile. And, I sing of a future that is Love forever.

Thursday, March 12, 1992

The common thread through our fleeting years and line of generations is the always-unstated question of why God would place us in a life that so easily breaks our hearts and leaves us barren-of-hope when everything else that is benevolent in the world seems to be calling us to a higher station. The truth that we have yet to finally realize is that Life cannot pass away unless we give-up on the faith that unites us with the Eternity of His Promise. That is why we believe in One Perfect God in Three Divine Beings, Father, Son, and Holy Spirit. The Father is the Creator of everything that is good, Jesus-the-Son is the Restorer-to-perfection of all that is lost, and both of them together, through the Holy Spirit, tell our souls that Life is worth living and nothing is really deserving of human despair.

Now, we have again been given the original Mother of this message, Mary of Bethlehem, whose Son restored the solemnity and dignity that we forfeited in the fateful age of Adam and Eve. She is the new Star for the eminent Dawn of the Son of Man. Jesus, the Gift Bearer, will soon return and reunite all Creation inside the palm of God, outstretched to bless us as we begin once more to enjoy our faultless lives amidst the caroling angels of Glory. It is God-the-Spirit Who resides in these typographic pages through which you can hear their songs. He asks us, in the Perpetual Virginity of His Immaculate Mother, to believe that He will use every alternative and prophetic venue to arouse our sleeping hearts. So, please awaken to Her call so we can begin our ascent toward this long-awaited blessing.

Friday, March 13, 1992

I invite all of my endearing brothers and sisters to remember that Jesus Christ has spoken to humanity through ancient prophets and contemporary visionaries. He wishes that the complacent world was already engulfed in flames. The Holy Scripture tells us that He will destroy everything which prevents the human soul from perfectly knowing Him and the salvific tragedy of His sorrowful Crucifixion. We recognize the fire in His Sacred Word as being an inferno of human conversion. I believe that, if we pray and follow the admonition of the Blessed Virgin, this providential combustion will ignite from within our hearts. The first imperfection that we should incinerate is the prejudice over our own eyes that keeps us from seeing and knowing the Truth. God will soon destroy everything that prohibits us from focusing and concentrating on His relentless desire to deliver us back to Heaven. I humbly beseech your help in prayer and solitude so that the message of those prophets and visionaries can forthrightly come-to-pass in our day. Time is now extremely short, while our inner-Light is still very dim. We must try to the heights of our sincerest ability to do better. We can begin by heeding the words of our beautiful Mother Mary.

Our Lady came about eight-thirty this evening as my brother and I prayed the Holy Rosary. Her purpose this evening is to protect us from the ways that evil is trying to attack our hearts by using the worries of the world to tear us down. Satan attempts to keep us in mental disarray by attacking our weakest points. He batters us with worries about our health, and our station and reputation with our friends. In all of this, we must remember our obligation to Love. This is our freedom from any encumbrance of temptation or fear. We are protected from evil when we remember to pursue holiness with the Love in our hearts. Jesus always helps when we trust in Him. It is important for us to remember during any trial that He wishes us to partake of His Body and Blood in the Holy Eucharist to gain the daily strength in the fight against the burdens of the world. Our faith receives a resounding newness each day as we pray and receive Jesus. Worldly thoughts which try to pull us away from Him and our Holy Mother are only delusions of a transient mind.

Christ Jesus restores our sense of direction and lifts our thoughts into sanctity toward holiness and away from the earthliness which seems to pull our hearts downward. It is imperative that we receive the Most Blessed Sacrament daily to help us renounce all that afflicts us. Our Lady, likewise, asks us to pray the Most Holy Rosary to remove any feelings that we are victims or slaves of our thoughts. Jesus responds with the supernatural grace that allows the heart to overcome the mind. Through Him, the Blessed Virgin crushes the hissing head of the serpent who has beaten our souls with worldliness. This is the depth of Love that God has for us. Our stay on Earth is only temporary because we will soon return Home to face an accounting of the harvest we reap in the name of Christ.

Sunday, March 15, 1992

"Good afternoon, My beautiful little sons. It is a glorious and happy day today! I love you so much. Together, we have made great progress in your struggle against evil and indifference. A future of promise awaits you and your brother; but I ask you to please protect yourself from peril by remaining close to Jesus and Myself. Soon you will enjoy the beautiful outdoors with the coming spring. Your hopes will blossom with the spring, too." Today, Our Lady spoke to me about the progress of my Diary. She always helps me with the text of what will become the dated entries. She continued today by asking me to remember that Jesus provides the opportunity for us to convert at our own will. His Love and the promise to return us to Heaven is the most attractive incentive over anything else in the world. With Our Lady, I pray for everyone to open their heart to receive Jesus as a sweet fruit of these holy messages.

We can better understand the sacrifices that Jesus made for us when we look at Lent. When we observe these precious forty days of self-denial, Satan tries his hardest to break our strength and allegiance, just as he tried with Jesus during His trials in the desert. When He was hungry, the Son of God was taunted by the Evil One with food. He told the Christ that if He was truly the Son of God, He should turn the stone into bread. But, Jesus said, *"Man does not live by bread alone, but on every word that comes from the mouth of God."* Next, when Satan told Him that he would give Him all the possessions of the world if He would worship him, Jesus said that nothing of this world is worthy of praise. Only His Father in Heaven is deserving of such worship. So, Satan tried a third and final time to diminish the righteous strength of Christ. He asked the Son of God to have His Father save Him from a fall. Jesus replied that no one should put Almighty God to the test.

These three temptations are the key to our sacrifice during the days of Lent. When we remember Jesus' thoughts and responses, we know that He emphasized fasting, the elevation of the heart to Heaven, and trust in God without the proof of His power. This is what Our Lady has come to do. These are the messages of Lourdes, Fatima, Medjugorje, and all the other sites of the miraculous intercession of Our Lady throughout the world. The common principle in each is that prayer is the source of our success toward the satisfaction and accomplishment of all three of Jesus' triumphs. And when we come to know Love as defined by the Immaculate Virgin of Nazareth, we will offer our lenten sacrifices more willingly and without the expectation of compensation. The fruit of Love is Love Itself; and the reward for forgiving others is the pardon from God of those who forgive. We all need to move to this point because this is how we are forgiven.

Our Holy Mother also told me today that some people believe themselves not to be sinners. She says they believe this because they have not found a need for their absolution from their own transgressions. These are the ones who do not understand that the wage of sin is death. And yet, they travel the Earth asking God why they will die. Many of them have not suffered much. In their indifference, they do not understand that suffering and death are the result of sin. These are also the same people who believe that they are already loving to perfection. They could not be further from the truth! Christ died to destroy and forgive human sins so that mankind could overcome his own corrupt fate. This sinless Christ incinerated the sinful nature of an errant people. The Resurrection of Jesus to be celebrated this spring is proof that all mankind can live forever. His death eradicated our sins, and for that reason, we have everything to gain by giving Him our fallen nature. This, too, is what opens the door of Love between peoples and nations.

Indeed, we must pray as a united Earth if we are to succeed. This is a reminder of the purpose of the lenten season. It is the beginning of a world of peace. Nothing on Earth is of any value in achieving Eternal Life. Only total abandonment to Love will take us to the fulfillment which God intended from the foundation of the Earth. *"What does it profit a man to gain the whole world and suffer the loss of his own soul?"* Our Lady is appearing throughout the world, trying to show Love as the only alternative for human deliverance. She provides the opportunity for us to completely transform the face of the Earth. Through Her, the grace is present as never before in the history of the ages to become one humankind in Love. After this great period of cleansing mercy, there will be only the Justice of God to prevail.

Tuesday, March 17, 1992

I am learning more every day about God's wish that we, as His people, will turn to His forgiveness in repentance. I know that He truly desires for us to live again with Him in heavenly Paradise. I can feel His pull on the world for us to be regained through the awesome Sacrifice of Jesus on the wooden Cross, where He died for the sins of all mankind. I have wondered why it took the execution of an Innocent Man to redeem the guilty. Why did a perfect Christ have to suffer and die for an imperfect humanity? Why is His Blood the salvific species that He still pours forth to blot-out our sinful nature? My questions are answered through my prayers. I realize that humanity rejected God at our most perfect moment in the Edenic meadows. When we could have said yes, Adam said no. With the chance to resist temptation, humanity chose to fall, instead. In the wisdom and genius of God, Christ was born so that perfection could be sown in our garden of exile.

When the question was suffering, Jesus said yes. When the price was condemnation, Our Savior laid down His Life. So, I have indeed learned from our Virgin Mother that God has rescinded our eternal damnation through Christ to lift us back to the perch we rejected thousands of years ago. It is high-time for our preparation and celebration of this Truth. But, we still have much work to do. Our Mother came again today to help us carry it out. She has told me on countless occasions that the fruits of Love are nourished through the bringing of absolution from the heart. That will make the stone walls and pillars of hatred truly come crashing to the ground. Everything that is born of Love is good for the human soul. Forgiveness is a responsibility essential to Love, not an option made possible by human discretion. Our Lady showed me the following image that is symbolic of those who embrace a righteous Life in Christ.

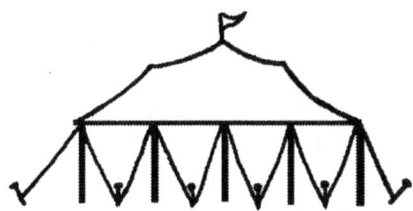

This, obviously, is a tent. It consists of the canvas which rests on the support of poles that are held in the ground by ropes connected to stakes. These stakes are placed at random and keep the poles erect. They are also the first part of the tent that is placed into position. They are securely implanted before they are used to anchor the tethering ropes. According to Our Lady's parable, the pilings represent the lives of those who serve Jesus in anticipation of His great Return. They are the vessels of great faith, which include Our Lady's messengers and the many who live Love in example to others. In their living example, they foretell the quickly approaching Re Appearance of Jesus in Glory. They have staked-out their faithful proof that Love is alive, and that we need to prepare for the Coming of our Mighty Savior.

The Holy Mother told me that Jesus plants these stakes in the hearts of those He knows will be open to receive His Spirit. Those responsive to His call live His example, and He pins His hope on the fact that He can anchor His Kingdom to holy souls. Therefore, our innocent hearts are at first like the undisturbed ground under each stake. But once Christ touches us and we accept the responsibility of Love, He has firmly planted His Spirit in our being. That is when we see the righteous change in our lives that Our Lady is seeking. She tells us that Jesus knows in whom He can embed His trust. Mankind will be simply astonished about how forgiveness will make him feel, both to offer and to receive. Many find it nearly impossible to pardon their brothers and sisters; while others cannot envision being granted clemency at all. Forgiveness makes the heavens resound in joy and the Earth tremble and bend to the power of Love. This is the overwhelming dispensation of God's grace that causes hatred to turn and run like the coward he is. Then, Jesus' countenance shines onto a world which was once filled with night. We must not impede the progress that He seeks to enliven the world with His radiance. All of us must pray and love. Pray, Pray, Pray!

Thursday, March 19, 1992

Our perfect and omnipresent God is neither evasive or ambivalent to those who faithfully seek Him. Christ is the intuition and premonition alive in our hearts that we will see God soon and know Him in all ways relevant to the essential nature of His creative power. We will understand the supernature of His Love as both absorbent of our own perfection and inspective of our true allegiance. He knows us from the inside-out before we can attest to our own motivations. There are no ulterior inducements in the City of Paradise, but only genius and charm that boast of the intelligence and perpetually-infinite introspect of the mind of God. All transcendent and intellectual power are His. Should we not, then, understand that our search for Christ is a mark of our own genius? Is faith a socially-accepted fanaticism that transcends the need for mortal charisma, supplanted by our desire to equate human existence with the perfection of God? We can be sure that this is the indelible wish of Jesus Christ for the collective generations that He saved as He bled to death while suspended by nails on the crux of a tree. He teaches the perfection of human love as assuredly as His precious Blood has poured-forth throughout Creation for 2000 years.

We cannot justify our own existence until we shed the world and embrace this prodigious Christ. Human growth and development are no more than a sporadic achievement in self-preservation unless we accept the modifier and catalyst Who makes us one in God. This is the Divine principle and purpose of the Life and Death of Jesus Christ. We are fetal-in-nature in all things but destruction and malfeasance; and there is a large cleft that still begs for the will of humankind to reconcile with the Truth of God. Indeed, it is the paranoiac side of man that makes us build intercontinental ballistic missiles that we believe are secretly-tucked beneath our lapel like a derringer, but are actually buried under the ground to be closer to the Hell that inspired them. If we so fear one another, how will we ever muster the courage to trust that we are called to live as one body, kept alive by a singular Blood? This is no time for us to be debating the merits of the countless graces dispensed by the Virgin Mary. We are being called to our feet by the God who is about to pronounce sentence on our very souls. If we are in shackles, we voluntarily put them on ourselves. And if we plead "guilty as charged," we have not invoked the vindication granted to us by the Barrister of the Cross who represents the Judge, Himself. He is the Son of Mary and our blood-brother to the most honorable degree, the sinless Alpha and Omega who wrote the very Statutes to which we are being held accountable.

As if prophetically on queue, Our Lady is now urgently leaning over the shoulder of humankind en masse in a final appeal for us to enlist the valedictory intercession of the Christ She bore to save us. Regardless of our shame or inhibitions, this is not the time for humanity to declare its worthlessness in the eyes of God. We must trust that Mercy is the Son of Justice and that the Father has sent His Offspring to set the world aright. Moreover, the faithless must renounce their own autonomy from the heavens which are about to descend to Earth and crush them under the weight of their own denial. The scourge of outright atheism is its own fuel to incinerate its essential being. Only Christ is the Path and Destiny to Eternal Life. God will allow the disbelief of faithless souls to rend themselves back into pathetic obscurity. There is nothing that the dawdling rhetoric of theologians and politicians can do to change this absolute and impending truth.

That is the reason that Our Lady is telling the world to actively accept the Redeeming Blood of Christ on the Cross now! Those who refuse will suffer the fires of condemnation forever to come. During this unique time of Lent, humankind must take a greater look at itself. We must purge ourselves of more than just the tawdry inclinations that make us weak. We must endure a completely self-denying sacrifice of love for Jesus Christ. While our hands are stretched-out for the help of others, we must reciprocally take-hold of our inner-selves to tear out anything that renders us imperfect in the eyes of God. These forty days are an opportunity to show Our Lord that we are serious about being transformed into His likeness. We must kneel to pray, thirst and cry, and repent and reconcile. Then, we will be able to look up into the skies with honor and say, "Please, Dear God, come into your Kingdom! We are prepared to touch your Redeeming Hand!"

Our Lady confirms through Her Maternal power that our preparation for this new beginning of the soul is founded in our willingness to serve humanity through any selfless way that comes before us. At every avenue and opportunity, we must kindly place our own needs behind those of our brothers and sisters. If we are to be like Christ, we must live to serve and not to be served. The pain of others must be eased before our own. Our hunger should be the reason why others are fed. The tenderness that God has placed in our hearts is a gift that must be given to His people, lest it needlessly die unfulfilled. These are among the sacrificial images that Our Lady brought to my prayer room today. Jesus teaches that mankind should elevate the dignity of others through the humbling of the self. All who seek to serve must remember that they must be humble if true servitude is to exist. The following example represents the measure of service to others compared to the humility of the self.

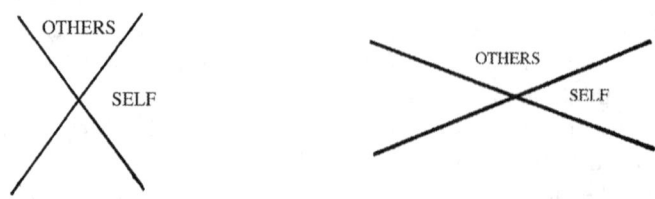

The pictures clearly indicate that we must decrease if our service to others is to increase. In order for the dignity of others to expand, self-satisfaction is naturally lessened. And, as the lesson of Jesus is understood, this fact becomes inevitably apparent. Our Blessed Mother came back a little later in the evening and said, **"This is your special blessing now. I give it to you and your brother in the Name of the Father, the Son, and the Holy Spirit. The cool breeze, warm light, and fresh air of the new spring are now with you in Love. Thank you for staying with Me and beside Jesus for so long. We still, yet, have much work to do. I love you. Goodnight."**

Sunday, March 22, 1992

Through Her words, symbols, parables, and miracles, Our Lady has come to the Earth in search of Her children. She tells us that God is near and that He is both angry and happy, this Father of infinite Mercy and Justice. His Son is alive and we have been found. Now, we must bless Him in return. We must search for Him and humbly beseech His pardon. I cannot write in descriptive terms how God Almighty must be poised as He ponders our work. He has already told Creation through Jesus 2000 years ago, "They will not come to Me, so I must go to them." He sent His Son through Mary to save us. He must be pondering still. Jesus told us that He would return at the end of time. But, He did not give us permission to sit-back and casually wait. He told us to seek His Kingdom and to fight the good fight with courage and honor, in steadfastness and conviction. We must not abstain a second time, thinking He will forget about His Plan. Mankind should move toward Him first! We must convert and pray, and convene and unite. We must precede His Return by sounding our ship and trussing our weak souls through the power of His Spirit.

The Lady whom we call Mary is here to help. She brings us strength through Her loving call. Tonight, She lifted my heart with these words. **"Bless you, My little children, I love you. I have come again today to show you how I love you, and to tell you again that Jesus is the answer to all questions..."** To search for consolation through material prosthetics does not display a resilient faith in Jesus as our Savior. We must completely believe that He is the mitigation to all human affliction. In this beauty, the feelings in my heart and the integrity of my thoughts are being soundly protected by His Love. Our Lady said that everyone who reads this Diary will be touched by the power of God. Its very existence is a miracle. Many people seem afraid and try not to become engulfed or affected by Love as though He does not have the power to touch them. To this end, Our Lady gave us a parable about Love, using water again as the example. Love renders everyone deeply touched and affected when it is given from the heart, although many do not wish to be immersed in it. They do not desire to become "wet" by the grace of God. Others believe that Love is like liquid mercury that does not make damp what it touches. Truthfully however, Love actually saturates everything with a cleansing and wholesome effect.

That is why Our Lady's words have so much power. She witnesses that this Diary is undeniably Divine and will stand despite the faithlessness of those who will attempt to divide, separate, and disunite its words, attempting to destroy or discredit it. She does Her work through Her children with the most beatific intention, and what others choose to do with it is a matter left to themselves and their trust in Jesus. God asks every soul to become secure in His Son. Christ is the only true Light reflected by the hearts of men. How powerfully we turn to holiness when we pray! The Messiah of God holds the key to our happiness, security, and sanctity. He grants the miracles that the world seeks toward the bringing of hearts to truly know Love. His example teaches the world that Love can only begin through sacrifice of the heart. Without self-denial, there can be no true Life-giving grace in our world. We must give our lives to others because it is our greatest possession. According to the words of Jesus, there is no greater Love than he who lays down his life for his friends.

Our Holy Mother has come seeking the conversion of all sinners. Her Son continues to call all humanity to lay down our cares and accept the sacrifice which He asks us to make in imitation of His own. In this, all humankind will be transformed. Our Lady is happy that so many have embraced their crosses and give them in return as Love to Jesus. It is truly trust in His way that will bring Love to fruition in the world. Our prayers are the obedient response to that call for trust. The Most Holy Rosary is the means through which we must petition God for His unifying grace. The Rosary is remaking the Earth and providing the cohesive movement for mankind's birth into Eternity.

Monday, March 23, 1992

As each new day arrives and I am prayerfully brought into compliance with the Will of God by our Holy Mother, I feel the spiritual communion with Heaven that She told me would occur. One day at a time, I feel a holy disconnection from the mortal world and an elevated oneness with all that is good in the lives of the Saints. But, coming with it is also a battle I must wage to understand that I have to wait to see God's Eternal Face. I still have to go to work everyday in a land that is corrupt and violative, impure, and material. Ours is a world held hostage by evil and ill will. It is a struggle to keep reminding myself that it is only temporary and transient. Sometimes, I feel like the little child in the back seat of the car, leaning forward to our Mother as if to say, "Are we there yet?" Even in all of this, Our Lady is helping keep my spirit above the fray. Through Her almost-daily messages, I have come-of-age and hold a better understanding of who I am and what I am supposed to be doing. My soul is still being seasoned and tanned. Never before have I realized so clearly that Jesus Christ is the source of every intention of righteous-hungry men. He is our healing balm and our cache of resources from whom we gain new strength to greet each passing day.

Tuesday, March 24, 1992

It would be a contradiction in terms if I stated that we, as a family of people, must become secularly holy. But, it is righteous at any price that we must become. No longer can we pander to those who say that we lack balance in life just because we choose to pray to make things better. Gone are the excuses that we feign for not attending daily Mass. The beautiful Blessed Mother calls for our allegiance, not only to God and Herself, but to one another. We must be teachers of exemplary piety. There must be no boundaries that we will not cross to take people to the brink of their own consciences in order to lead them to Christ Jesus. We have seen what indifference can do all over the world. The horrors of war and the conflagration of human dignity flashes before our eyes every day. But, we have never considered the powerful forces of unity under the Cross of Jesus as one collective humanity. We have never dreamed with true intensity or definition how the world would be transformed before our eyes if we focused both individually and collectively on Our Savior Lord. We must join our hands with unprecedented communion and lift them in supplication to God. And, when we are alone, we must fold them and symbolically embrace suffering humanity within them. That is what God does for us. To further heighten our compassion and concern, Our Lady came again today with a message of sharing and Love about the ongoing Lenten Season.

This is truly a time of trust and we should see the days unfolding as one is removed from atop the next to reveal the new face of the Earth. Each bountiful morning is a beautifully different and significant expression of Love. This Lenten emphasis on self-denial brings us to the realization of the great suffering around the world. Unborn little children are being murdered in the wombs of their mothers. Others are starving, while hundreds of thousands are being deprived of their freedom. Humanity is being completely stripped of its dignity. All of this, and millions do not yet know Jesus Christ. The world will finally know about Love when we learn about Him and the indelible legacy that He carved into the historic face of Creation. All He asks is that we love. Bitterness, hatred, poverty, hunger, and division all perish in its path. That is how human suffering will be brought to an end. Lent is a time to conform ourselves to God's will and be cleansed of our sinful humanity by becoming clothed with Light. It is also a time to forgive others, an offering that Our Lady says is the greatest gift of charity that mankind will ever witness. We must bear our crosses in Love and realize that if we do not, we have already failed, no matter how successful we have been in building a world empire or how accomplished the world tells us that we are. Victory is solely in our return to Love in the image of the Savior of the World.

As one humanity, we should gird ourselves with the hope that we can faithfully embrace the celebration of Our Lord's Resurrection on Easter Sunday. On that anniversary, we are a new Creation, infused with the beauty and Love that Christ so triumphantly displayed to both Heaven and Earth at that prolific dawn. We should abandon our devastating darkness and sinfulness in the days of Lent, just as Jesus remanded death to the bowels of the earth. We must, indeed, become a holy people, a new race, and a citizenry set apart. Mankind is transfigured when we love one another in the intensity of Jesus' suffering in death on the Cross. In Him, we are born again and elevated together as one Love bound for Eternity. It is for this reason that the Holy Virgin of God has come to the world. Through the power of the Love of Her Son, She makes the shedding of worldliness, materialism, and sin, a sacrifice of great joy. We breathe a liberating sigh of relief and re-creation, and feel a bonding motherly embrace of affection that incinerates any shadow of sadness or despair. She is the glorious Holy Mother of Humanity who encourages us to rise to perfection. And in order to do this, we must deny ourselves, take up our cross, and follow Jesus Christ.

Wednesday, March 25, 1992 - Feast of the Annunciation

It has been said by theologians and agnostics the world-over that life must become something more than an inane progression of time and events, leading to our eventual death and the extinction of man. I have learned in recent months that our life is, indeed, more of a purpose than a process. That is why some of us live for a day, a week, or a few years, while others live for many decades. There is a purpose in the particulars of dying young which, we must concede, we cannot yet see. But, it must be something special because it precludes the reason for growing old. If we unite perfectly in heart and commitment to the Virgin Mary, I am confident that we will know the relevance of life in total concurrence with its sequence. I invite you to continue with me on the journey that our Mother has laid-out for us. The next step is today, which we will better understand because of Her miraculous intercession.

The new Light that She sheds on our world helps us conquer the forces that would diminish our hope. This is the celebration of the Feast upon which the Angel Gabriel appeared to our Holy Mother and asked Her to bear the Son of God into the world. It provides somewhat of a breath of "fresh air" in the midst of our Lenten mortification. It is the day that Satan knew he would be a dead man just-beyond the passing of thirty-three years. Those three decades-plus-three is the incarnation of immortal grace!

We should continue to pray fervently for the Crucifixion of Christ to defeat the dying echoes of Satan in our everyday world. Evil has already lost. This is the faith and solemn belief with which we live. The Will of God has been done. Our acceptance of this brings us to respond in prayer because we know that we have, once again, become His holy children. He grants us this power because He, too, knows that evil cannot triumph over the souls on Earth who have placed their hope and fortune in Jesus Christ. These are the days of our purifying endurance that gain great grace for the world. Human love and filial abandonment are triumphing in the face of many sinister acts. Suffering is the flowering of the beauty of Love within us. God's perfect obsession with His people fortifies our endurance so that our hope can bloom in undeterred commitment. In light of the sorrowful Crucifixion of Jesus, we know that the Lord God need only say, "Enough", and our battles will be finished. I pray for every grace possible that the fruit of all human suffering will be a converting gift for every race of people. Mankind needs to see Love as our Salvation and the end of all darkness, just as the Lord is the Light of the dawning day.

Sunday, March 29, 1992

It seems like it was another lifetime when I awoke each day and planned my material duties and booked my routine schedule. So much has changed, brought forward by the gift of Our Lady's intercession. I feel united with past generations whose daily labors were much different, more manually laborious and heavier to bear. We have an easy life in our American nation. We have leisure time, play time, and freedom from simple chores and fighting for our everyday needs. Never before has a generation of people had a greater abundance of opportunity to pray. But, in all of this, we ignore the call of God and the destiny of others, alike. I know through Our Lady that we must repudiate our playthings and take-up the Holy Rosary. We must embrace Her intercession and prepare for Eternity with the Spirit of Her Son as our guard. I am happy to be one who finally understands. And, through Her Immaculate Wisdom, She invites everyone to openly know God's will for the culmination of Creation.

This evening, Our Lady came to remind me that mankind is under attack by Satan through venues he could never secure until this age. He distracts us through our modern technologies in an attempt to dissolve the sacred union that Jesus made of all souls under the Cross. The Blessed Mother has taught us many lessons through our daily encounters and has allowed us to be subjected to severe trials so we will be able to experience Her messages while we receive them. She continuously tells us that the Kingdom of God is at hand. We should run to Her for protection and embrace the Love of Her Son. She reminded us today that this is an important period in time for intense prayer and our venturous work in the battle against evil. We should remember the Passion that Jesus suffered for the Salvation of the world, and that we are the precious briolettes being safeguarded in His incorruptible Love. We must come to realize that without Him, there is no telling what forces might try to steal us away. Our Lady told me that She will pray with us for the peace and protection of all.

APRIL 1992

Wednesday, April 1, 1992

None of us yet knows what it is like to die, but we can assuredly understand the trappings of life, its failures and weaknesses, and some small joys amidst the mountains of futility. But, our years are given more meaning and intelligible reason when we open our hearts for the business of God. Our door-lights must be on and our welcome mats brushed clean. The visitor to the house is the Landlord who offers us a new Mansion, far away from all the trials and pangs of mortal strife. Today, my soul awoke to the call of His Mother, the Eternal Madonna, at the doorway of my heart. She brings food for our conversion and provisions for our journey back to Paradise. She has been ushering the Holy Spirit to His rightful place in our hearts and around the world throughout every preceding age. We cannot risk the danger of not hearing Her beatific utterance, "You are free again because Jesus has liberated you from sin!" We are slaves no more to sadness and grief, and nevermore bound to loneliness or frailty. We can now live with the lofty hopes and honorable anticipation of a reward that we have gained anew, that another Man named Jesus-the-Christ won for us by living the sacrificial Divinity of God. The precursor to that bounty is our comprehension of what we must do to secure His blessings in our day. The Holy Virgin has come to help grow our respondent wisdom with messages from Our Father in Heaven, given through Her Immaculate grace.

Thursday, April 2, 1992

Through Our Lady's intercession, I have somehow been taken in spirit and memory back to my infant days, the times of my youth, when I saw the world in such a hopeful light. I used to hold an inherent trust in others and the wonderment of their adulthood. I was awed by the official life of the prominent and affluent. Now, my childhood dreams seem to transcend the mortal. I can breathe a new breath of air about my feelings of anticipation and hope. Our Lady evokes images of a previously elusive and unapproachable world of peace and health for all. I am not afraid to be simple again and to laugh at the helplessness of our human condition. And, I am able to see the folly in the thought that we could ever take control of the world in the first place, never-minding our schmaltzy endeavors to conquer outer space. I often envision human progress like someone might see a puppy running to catch a passing automobile. What would he do with it once it is within his grasp?

What is really most important is the grace that sustains the world from the other side of life, the transverse Love that connects Heaven and Earth. That is from where the Blessed Virgin has come, and that is what I seek. I am increasingly curious about the age of our universal Creator, or whether He even has an age. I am confident, however, that this is His age and time. Christ is about to return to absolve our culpability and retrieve His prize of humanity for deliverance to the feet of the Almighty Father. Our Lady is continuing to offer Her primordial invitation for us to praise Him through filial love and sincere prayer. We must persevere in faith by remembering what She has taught and shown. Jesus wants us to trust in the power of His Love and to show the world that it is true. Likewise, the Holy Mother seeks our complete concentration on our Salvation in Her Son through service for those He loves. This is a time of great opportunity for our dissemination of Her messages to the rest of the world. It is through them that She truly explains the trials of these times and how much She loves us, prays with us, and is always near to lift us up. She reminds humanity at every turn that our obedience to the Gospel will carry us through.

Friday, April 3, 1992

God is the determiner of the just and the adjudicator of the accused. In all of His Glory and power, He cannot render Himself any less than perfect. He cannot sin and condones no sin. He will chastise and purify to reclaim what is lost because He loves righteousness and mandates Love. These are the bold facts of the purpose of human amendment and Christian conversion. These are the reasons why Our Lady has come. She wants us to stand fully-aware of our place amongst the ages and our fate through the impending closure of time. Jesus is our Immanuel and ultimate redressor before God. He is our sacrificial advocate and our sacramental nourishment for our life's journey back to epochal peace. The voice of Heaven is given resonance by Christ the King. That is why Our Holy Mother earnestly insists that we petition Her Son for His redeeming grace. Eternal Salvation starts with the key of human conversion; and prayer is the catalyst for our engagement with God. Who would know better what the Christ-child desires? His Mother knows Him well and sees the transgressions that offend Him the most. Our sins continue to perpetuate His pain. I offer my reparative prayers and arduous work to try to console His wounds. Our Lady tells me often that I am doing well. I trust with hope in Her words.

Saturday, April 4, 1992

Our Sweet Jesus has set-out to fuse the complection of the transitory ages through the revelations of His Blessed Virgin Mother. Her new and miraculous manifestations around the world are at the cutting-edge of our impending Redemption and reconciliation to God. If we cannot see this obvious reality, we are, indeed, as blind to the Truth as Jesus told the world twenty centuries ago. We must rise to the beckoning call of our virtuous Mother. She is present all over the world, rallying an army of righteous souls to enlist the faith of those who cannot believe. No one is too wretched or so far from God that they are not worthy of the Fruit of Her Womb. We must reach to the ends of the Earth with a fervor unlike any other age. Now is the time for human reaction in response to the charitable intervention of God. We must love as we are commanded, pray as we are petitioned, and convert as we are called. Only we, ourselves, can cause our Redemption to fail. We must seek-out the souls of the lost to become aligned with the Will of the Lamb of God, who was lamed and murdered for the price of our entrance into perpetual light and eternal day. Our journey of Earth must find its culmination in Heaven. No one can preclude a soul from inheriting Paradise who seeks it with an open heart.

Sunday, April 5, 1992

Our Mother, the Immaculate Conception, asks us persistently to pray for the Church on Earth so that it will remain strong through the travails of modern times. If there is a rising dissension in the Mother Church, it is because not all of her faithful are maintaining the veneration and admiration of the sinless Virgin, whom God has sent to teach us. We must heed the call of Our Lady and unite under the infallible guidance of the Vicar of Christ, the Pope and Bishop of Rome. Many revelations of destruction and division in the Church can be precluded if we pray in the way the Holy Mother has asked. The main purpose of the Church is to administer the seven Sacraments that Christ has given in Love for our grace, to make us worthy of the Paradise He promised. Our Lady is insistent that the Roman Catholic Church is the original apostolic church on Earth, for which She is Mother and Queen as ordained and crowned by Our Savior, Himself.

We must lift-up the priests, humble ourselves to the mandates of the Catechism, and practice self-denial and mortification as a means of sacrifice and penance. We must again become the undivided Body of Christ under the Mantle of the Blessed Virgin Mary, united arm-in-arm as we hold to the Truths provided by the Apostles of Jesus in the first century. There is precious little time left for us to collect ourselves. We must submissively serve with humility all those in whom Our Lord has disguised Himself; the poor, the imprisoned, the starving, and the naked. Such is the submission that will ensure the unity of the Church and strengthen all God's people under the single, miraculous Cross of His Son. This is the Crucifixion that Our Lady extolled when She came to speak to us today. She seemed sad about the apathy that She sees in the world toward Her Son. It is as damaging to the flow of Love as those who profess no faith at all, and is a wasteful and blasphemous means to live. Human indifference is Satan's most gratifying meal. Hearts that are vacant submit themselves to his strike without opposition.

Jesus must be allowed entry into every heart in the fight against this most damaging assault. Hungry souls filled with the Spirit of Christ will purge their minds of unholy pondering. Prayer to the Son of God is the sure way to open these sanctifying avenues. Our Lady told me tonight that we are becoming "in-spirited," or "Paracleted," by the experiences we endure for Lent. Prayer is our union within the Holy Spirit. We must continue to live our Holy Mother's messages so that evil will have no room to move or function. All of God's children should pray for the strength of heart to bear such a difficult time for the world. Our suffering is intensified when we refuse to acknowledge and live by Our Lady's messages. She has appeared in countless places, but the world has yet to collectively convert. It is sad to see the children of God living such frivolity and lack of conviction. We seem to act as if perfect holiness is not achievable or is no longer required for our entrance into the Eternity of happiness. The Holy Mother has come into the world to express the seriousness of the call of God for the conversion of sinners. Eternal damnation is inevitable for those who do not accept Jesus and live by His Commands of Love.

Religious indifference is a trait that is damning to the soul. It is a fire that no longer burns, a desire for holiness that has ceased to exist, and a soul that is not moving any closer to Heaven. Moreover, indifference is an attribute of someone who does not consider the crucified Son of God important enough to love and trust. This sinner has been overcome by mortal reasoning and is complacent and satisfied by his own opinion that his soul is enriched enough and that the Savior of the world will just have to accept him despite his sinfulness. These indifferent ones wish to claim Heaven while standing on Earth with one foot in the pit of Hell. They wish to steal their way into Paradise instead of pursuing the purity of the Narrow Gate. The children of God are the siblings of Light who bask in the day-shine of Love! We must be of one heart, one Love in a single humanity, breathing the freshness of our newly-found Creation drawn to celestial perfection. This is not to say that we must refrain from praying for the indifferent and unholy. Quite the contrary, they should be the object of our petitions above any other needs of our own. God needs them and Our Lady pines for them. No one should allow themselves to be left-out of Eternal Life in Glory. We can all get there together, but our effort is not as strong without the prayerful support of each and every child of God. This is why the Immaculate Virgin has come. She is leading the world by the Heart to the end, to the Love, and to the Eternity. Pray, pray, pray!

We should always remember that Satan is real and vicious and alone we cannot defeat him. Only by taking the hand of Jesus can we win the war against evil. The Blessed Virgin Mary has the power through Her Love to lift us up so that we can reach the hands of Her Perfect Son, Jesus. The Virgin Mary wants us to go to Him for help in our struggles; and Christ wants us all to run to His Mother's arms in the way He did many times as a child for comfort and caress. It is as if Jesus is telling us that in sharing His Mother with all humankind, it is another way that He is bestowing His overwhelming Love upon everything He has created. Our Lord is telling us that His Mother is also our own. She is Heaven's Maternal Queen who is our tender protector. The Blessed Virgin is the Lady of Dignity who wraps Her warmth around the hearts of all God's children. She looks upon our suffering with the same compassion through which She sorrowfully saw the suffering of Her beloved Son.

Our Lady knows that Her Child removed our suffering with His own. That is why She calls us to Him, so that we will confide and reside in His Sacred Heart. She tells us often that we get there by our prayers, especially the Holy Rosary. This beaded string of powerful invocation is not a novelty attached to our lives to provide a symbol of holiness. It "is" our life, itself, which delivers us to holiness without revelry or symbolism. Prayer of the Rosary is real, like breathing and feeling. The true substance of human success is in the recitation of the "Hail Mary," the salutation of the Angel Gabriel. When Jesus returns, He will come to judge the living and the dead. The Holy Mother is here now to help make us worthy of His merciful judgement. My brother and I have seen Mercy and the wonderment of answered prayers during this Lent. We have seen that hope is made fact in prayer from the heart. The great miracles from God in our lives are delivered through the extension of our hearts to our Savior through our passionately sincere prayers. That is all that can help us to go on. That is all that can destroy evil. That is all that will make us holy and worthy of Heaven. That, also, is the only thing that matters.

Monday, April 6, 1992

In the process of absorbing the lessons in the messages that our Holy Mother is kindly giving, I occasionally ponder-aside to consider the substance of Her teachings compared to my previously-held opinions of the subjects She discusses. Since this Diary is meant to be a public record of some of my private revelations, it came to me that the inclusion of a simplistic summation of my inner-thoughts would not be summarily unwelcome. I have been obediently meditating the virtues of hope and faith as our Holy Mother has asked. It is obvious that She has come to strengthen our trust in God and in the Son He dispatched to save us. She desires us to pray fervently for the Return of our Redeemer in hopes that, when He does, He will find us acceptable in His sight. I have concluded through the guidance of the Blessed Mother that faith and hope are, indeed, distinguishable from each other. Faith is of higher fiber and a more firm foundation than simple hope. It is a gift from God for which we should fervently pray. Hope is more our dependency on levels of opportunity or chance. It is a desire for the undefined intangible, while faith is knowledge in the Truth.

Hope is like waiting for a pulse of electricity, while faith is the constant touch of a hand. In some ways, hope is almost a desperate anticipation, but faith is the realization in our soul of the facts as they are. Therefore, we pray in faith. It is our communication with the God we believe in, not one we just hope to be there. Faith is much more revealing than hope. Even though they are not mutually exclusive, faith brings immortal knowledge, while hope allows us to walk through the dark. I have thought about what it would feel like to discover that your attic of precious collectibles is really the disposure in the basement of the tenant above, whom you did not even know had moved-in. This helps me more easily desire the certainty of faith over the intangible aspects of hope.

Unless we choose to listen to the wisdom of God, we are going to rest at the brink of finishing a tremendous job with the final turn of a wrench, but will be left standing with only a hammer to our name. And, while we must hope so that our spirits remain high, we must live our faith in God to enlist confidence that our hope is not in vain. If hope is the last goodbye to a terrible world, faith is the first hello to the Paradise that follows. I will not try to sift through or trowel-out the differences in these noble virtues any further. I am inclined to believe that it is for the strengthening of our faith that Our Lady has come. She grows our belief in God, whom She humbly represents. Therein lies the basis for our hope.

Tuesday, April 7, 1992

Our Lady is our perpetual help. She implores Jesus to vindicate the woefully insufficient work of our idle hands and to purify our scattered hearts. All too often, we fail to acknowledge the great intercessor who is our Immaculate Mother. The opportunity of our lives is now before us to come to the Divine invitation God is now dispensing through His Holy Mother. Nothing before in the history of mankind has been so undeniably important. I know that Our Lady is pleased with the progress that our souls have made to seek Jesus. Her tears are both happy and sorrowful, indicative of the mixed reaction She has received from Her children. My intention is to assure that all of Her tears are a product of Her Heart of joy and hope in the people of God. I work tirelessly to bring to fruition the completion of this Diary. I pray endlessly that it will have the effect that Our Lady tells me it will produce.

While nothing is certain when facts are left to mortal discretion, I know that if we turn to the call of the Immaculate Queen, there will be no margin for indecision in the fate of our future. She is the humble conqueress who has claimed the children whose souls were commended to Her protection by Jesus of Nazareth on the Cross 2000 years ago. It is She who speaks to me now, and to all the world at once. Today, I felt such peace and confidence knowing that Satan has absolutely no power to destroy my soul. It is almost a prefigured image of assured victory that I see in my heart, a hope that is more real than the worldly battle before us all. Satan's power was destroyed on Calvary, and I can see that his evil is as temporary as this passing world. He has lost the battle for the children of God; and we must all finally come to proclaim it.

Faith becomes knowledge for those who serve. With this same faith, we can see the coming of the Son of God in Glory. Live that moment as it already exists in time! Through that vision, we can see the very last minute of the final day of Earth. It will be everything that you imagine, and infinitely more. Our Redemption will be the recapitulation of ecstasy, exhilaration, tears, explosive light, purity, indestructible joy, weightlessness, vision into eternity, sight into the depths, holiness over every brim, an electric happiness, shocking new senses, a single heartbeat of Creation, and a chorus of voices from every living thing; rocks and trees, plants, the waters and wind, the stars, the moon, and the clarion calling of time, ringing into Eternity to the Glory of the Lamb. *"To the One who sits on the Throne, and to the Lamb, be blessing and honor, glory and might, forever and ever."*

Wednesday, April 8, 1992

The Holy Cross upon which Jesus saved the world is God's contemporaneous presence through the passage of all ages. He unites His children in one perfection through the Sorrowful Crucifixion and Glorious Resurrection of His Son. Time is a hypothetical supposition designed to accommodate our transition into holiness. Its solitary significance is to remind us that we are not truly prepared for the oncoming splendor of the Divinity of Heaven. It is more than just a visor to protect our eyes from the glaring light of reality or to shield us from the buffets of the linear decades. Indeed, we must perceive the element of time in union with the sacrificial Cross. If we are to become as timeless as God Himself, we must go to the Master of the Ages and be stripped of the corruption which binds our souls. The very concept of our nature and being originate in the Crucifixion which restores our imperishable oneness in the Almighty Father.

Consider how the Holy Cross has maintained its integrity throughout the centuries. A humble tree was pressed into service as the universal conveyance of the Salvation of man 2000 years ago. It has maintained its singularity and simplicity despite all attempts by conventional secularism to parody and simulate its authenticity. No one will ever diminish its unyielding confirmation that Eternal Life will be granted to all who embrace it. The power of the salvific Cross is a fortress in which the most ignoble and loathsome of souls can find refuge. The Man who was transfixed to its terrible face will turn no one away in His crusade to purify His people. God has deigned us worthy to be His own again through the suffering of His incarnate Son. This is a revelation that is too transforming for a people of conscience to ignore. It is a tragedy of the highest nobility and the reason why we hope for ourselves and the descendants we leave behind.

The wood of the Cross is now depicted in silver and gold upon the hallowed walls of our churches and cathedrals. This is a proper expression of the restoration of the human soul from transient to immortal. Through the Blood of Christ, we are given the sheen of precious elements previously reserved for the finest parlors in the heavenly Kingdom. His Heart is the repository for every wish we could muster and the restorative Spirit that rescues us from sorrow and resignation. Through the invincible power of His Son, God dares any diatribe or sorcerous legion to challenge the faith and security of His children. That is why we can always trust in Jesus to protect us in every trial and affliction. It is another essential lesson we can take-to-heart from this holy Lenten season. Satan's gruesome nature is fueled by minds that are not perfectly anchored to trust in the power of God. This Lenten season has been a purifying trial. Evil can only be defeated by the omnipotence of Love. Without Our Lord, mortal men are helpless in the battle against a fallen angelic creature such as Satan. He has the force to fatally crush any living thing, but for the Providence of God.

It is in Christ Jesus that we find the ultimate power of bucolic Love to protect us. He holds a perfect guardianship over our thoughts, actions, and physical make-up, and will not allow us to be tempted or injured beyond our power to continue in His grace. Those who refuse to love do so of their own obstinate will. Fortunately for the blessed, worldliness is never permanent. All time and material are at the command of Christ. There is no disease that is incurable, no injury that cannot be healed, and no earthly disillusionment that cannot be dissolved. Every thing and every circumstance is subordinate to our Father, God. Prayer is the power that moves Our Lord to ameliorate the Kingdom subject to Him so that it may glorify Love, itself. Any gift or grace, and any situation or problem, can be granted or changed for the elevation of Jesus. All our hopes and visions of Love are a reality in time and borne into Eternity because of His infinite Love.

Having studied mathematics and physics at the university level, I have come to truly realize that such knowledge and study by mankind of natural laws are nonbinding to the statutes of God. He does not manifest His power only through detectable occurrences as some would have us believe. Nature and the physical world are completely at His will, and can be changed by Him at any time. Therefore, when mankind is in union with Love, we transcend these same laws and render them quite insignificant. Simply stated, there is no factual basis for something being impossible just because the laws of physics state it to be so. The real power of man and his ability to perceive the tangible universe lies in the gift of prayer to God. It is the greatest and ultimate power in Creation.

Through this invincible grace, human helplessness is destroyed. There is no longer a state where we might see our hopes as forever impossible to attain. The foundation of our pious desires already exist in Jesus and are fulfilled while we pray. Our Lady says that our invocations are answered the moment we lift them. These past six weeks have revealed the power that is changing the world and making it new. Mankind does not comprehend that Love is brought into Creation as fast as lightning blazes from one horizon to the other, and as quickly as light removes darkness in the flipping of a switch. Our Holy Mother radiates with this magnificent power. She reflects the essential beauty of Her benevolent Son. She is comfort and counsel to us during these last days of Earth. I know in my heart that we will be victorious at last. We will win every battle thrust upon us by Satan, and God will be glorified. If we remain united in Christ, the Evil One cannot destroy our Love for one another or our promise of fidelity to our Thrice-Holy Mother. The very awareness of our worldliness and its dangerous physical consequences is the Divine Light that guides us. Our protection is the Love that burns like fire in the depths of our hearts. God has asked us not to fear those who would destroy the body, but rather to flee in faith from the destroyer of the soul. Through our prayers, our hearts become impenetrable to the forces and fears of the dark.

Our Lady lifts and protects us. She gives us the grace of confidence to know that Satan has no power over the children of God whose hearts are filled with Love and trust. He cannot deceive those who accept Love as their only power, and who receive the Eucharistic Christ from the Altar of Sacrifice. The Passion and Death of Our Lord is the moment in all of time when the world physically stops. Every living thing looks to that pinnacle of Light to find its path and destiny. The Crucifixion is the Eternity of Love through the purifying fires of human suffering for the sins of the wayward world. Therefore, holiness is the armor of the children of God. Evil is certain to destroy us without it. Prayer is our sword and the instrument of destruction against the harbinger of death. The Holy Eucharist is the eternal fortress where we gather together to wage the battle for souls. I thank Jesus for the many graces of these days and pray that the world will move into communion with Him, with Love, to change the Earth into the likeness of Heaven. Beneath the Mantle of Our Lady's intercession, every one of us will win. The Kingdom of God awaits the end of time with comfort for every soul. No one needs to be left behind when we march forward to Eternity in His blissful and ecstatic joy!

Thursday, April 9, 1992
Our Lady is bringing great wisdom into the world as She desires us to know the reconciliation of humankind to God at the end of time. She knows that we lead lives of great grief and pain and that we struggle the best we know how in our limitations forced upon us by our own lack of faith and trust in Her Son. We try to find solace in a world where only a few truly desire peace. The Mother of God tells us that we will see the worst in ourselves come Judgment Day. Through the Holy Scriptures, the grace of God's Church, and the Holy Spirit of Christ, we know the criteria upon which the Heavenly Father expects us to base our lives. And, at the end of time, this forgiving professorial jurist will turn to each of us and say, "What grade do you think you deserve?" That is when we will have to justify our lives in light of the sacrificial Cross of His Son. We will look back on our life's journey and see ourselves as He saw us all along.

Again, this journey is not always of happiness and peace. And God knows that. His merciful forgiveness is built upon His Love and understanding that worldly temptation and materialism are our greatest barriers to seeing Him perfectly in the vision of our faith. So, our Virgin Mother has come to clarify our knowledge of God, now and in our time. She truly wishes us to come to know the joy of Jesus so that our journey will be a time of fulfillment and gratitude, and our impending rendezvous at the judgment seat of God will be one of reward, rather than condemnation. We must freshen the collective spirit of humankind and lift our hearts to the heavens as though they are filled with helium. Upward in holiness, we must strive for the perfection which God calls us to seek through Jesus. Then, we will worry not about the degree of our transgressions, for we will have given them all to the Mercy of the Blood of Christ. We may not be perfect; but we should wish to be. Our Lady is at hand, telling us how to pursue the humility that will take us there.

The Blessed Virgin Mary came once again to pray with us and to offer the Love of Her Son. Her presence is of such great encouragement during these trying times. She asks us to proceed in hope because Jesus has saved the world from condemnation. Today, She requested my brother and me to remember our sacrifices for Lent. We should envision them as lessons toward our progress in faith. Our trust in God resembles a leap forward across a great chasm of all that is still unknown to us. We must be willing to risk falling into the "gap" of the deliverance of our soul totally into whatever trials and sacrifices Christ asks. Our Lady strongly reminded me today that Jesus will never allow us to hit-bottom when we take a leap across the tumultuous flagrancy of the world to reach His arms. During the times when we think we are falling, it is truly the elevation of humanity that passes before our eyes as we place our souls into service at the feet of those in need of our love. We are called forward to lead the struggling multitudes who cannot see on their own. In our struggle against the forces that oppose the holy works of our Lord, God will deplete us of our excesses and brings us to enlist our most elite forces. It is ourselves who must be poured-out if others are to gain the dignity that God wishes to grant them through our lives. The Holy Mother asked my brother and me to remember this noble fact as we prepare to enter Holy Week.

Palm Sunday, April 12, 1992

Today will always be special to me because it was just a year ago on the celebration of Palm Sunday that I witnessed a great miracle in the skies. I saw Our Holy Mother and Jesus with my own eyes. And as She did then, Our Lady reminded me of the honor which was bestowed upon the Messiah as He rode into Jerusalem which made His suffering of the next week so ironic and prophetic. As Holy Week begins, it is good for us all to recall the Passion which He suffered for the Salvation of the world. It is during this time especially that we can see the true suffering which provides the preservation of all human dignity. The Love which Christ showed to the world was consummated through the events remembered during these seven glorious days. This is the monumental week that Our Lady is trying to get mankind to recognize as the one that truly changed and rescued the world from certain condemnation.

We are also called to remember every soul who suffers for the sake of God's Kingdom on Earth. The Blessed Mother says that the brave warriors whom God calls "suffering humanity" provide the braille elevation needed by the faithless blind to know the Heart of Christ. Therein lies the perfect purpose of our trials and infirmities. We are united in the Cross of Jesus when we suffer for the sake of humanity. We join the profession of Saint Paul who said that human suffering is our communion in Christ Himself for anything that might be lacking from the last days of His Life. But in all the wisdom and fidelity of Paul, he truly knew that the Passion which Jesus perfected on the Cross is the sweet fruit that preserves our souls for Heaven. While our pious sufferance places us in the Garden of Gethsemane in oneness with Our Lord, no other than He would have to die to destroy the sins of the world.

The fruition of Our Holy Mother's messages throughout time and space are realized through the living of the Crucifixion and Resurrection of Jesus. Our faith allows us to be present on Mount Calvary in every essence of our being. There is a short parable which helps to bring this to light involving glass from which windows are made. The better quality of glass used, the easier the window is to see through. If the glass is flawed or imperfect, the vision we see through its surface is skewed or distorted. Imagine that each of the 2000 years since Jesus' Crucifixion is symbolically represented by a pane of glass. Those representing the years immediately following His death are very clear and concise because the recording of this tragedy was made by people who either witnessed it or knew those who did. The accuracy of their recollection was made possible by their faith in what they knew to be true. They were a people readily open to the Holy Spirit who inspired the record of the events of His own Life. Therefore, a clear pane of glass represents an accurate description of the earthly days of Jesus. It was clear to all that He was, indeed, crucified to save the world and render our souls eligible for the Glory of Heaven.

But, human faith has become weakened by passing generations and centuries. People have fallen away from the Truth that is written in the Holy Scriptures. Their teachings often do not present a clear image through the pane of glass they present as the original suffering and Death of Christ. They have not relied on the Holy Spirit for inspiration. The Cross where Jesus died is as authentic and timeless today as it was on Mount Calvary. But, the vision of modern man has been distorted by the skewed and errant interpretations of authors and theologians, alike, since that great day. They have presented a perception of the Crucifixion through windows that are fogged by the smoke of their own error. These imperfections distort the realization that Jesus is truly man and that He actually suffered, died, and rose from the dead. They have so dimmed the original vision of the Truth that we have become vulnerable to the conflicting imaginations of people who do not know Jesus or what He teaches. The Truth is buried beneath the error of human interpretation. The faithless and blind are inhibiting others from seeing that Christ is the greatest Love the world will ever know. He is as perfect now as He was on the day He died. He has never violated Love with any word, thought, or action.

Yet, the Son of God was slaughtered before all Creation because humankind was so filled with pride that they refused to defer to His Kingship or His power to remake the world. But much to the dismay of many nonbelievers, He remade it anyway! It was very sad that His beautiful Mother had to stand beneath the Cross and see the horrible way He was killed by those He saved. We must remove the imperfect vision which modern man has of the Cross. The conversion of future generations depends on it. This is the essential purpose of the intercession of Our Lady and the prayers to which She calls us. The Most Blessed Virgin of Calvary is not only cleaning the glass of hundreds of bygone years, She is actually removing them from existence. Nothing opaque or impermeable can prevent our living presence at the Crucifixion of Jesus. When we attend Holy Mass, we are not looking through a pane of glass. We are seeing the Last Supper and Death of Jesus with our eyes and souls in perfect union with His suffering. There is no measure of time or manner of interpretation that can destroy this undeniable fact.

Our Lady calls all of Her children to the Holy Mass, the Table of the Lord, to receive the Eucharist. The Mass is the unifying and sanctifying gift from God which perfectly unites and remakes humankind. It is the Eternal Moment that is not confined to the first ages. It transcends any imaginable constraint to renew Creation into Paradise by destroying all darkness, sins, and the bonds of mortality. The Consecration of the bread and wine into the Body and Blood of Jesus is the transfer of humanity into Eternity right before our eyes. That is why we must believe with our whole hearts in the presence of Jesus in the Blessed Sacrament and become worthy to receive the Life and Death that has saved us.

Good Friday, April 17, 1992

This is the celebration of the Day that Jesus Christ saved the world. Not only was He scourged and beaten, His head was impaled by a circle of thorns. In the name of the Love of God, we are brought to peace. Let all the world stop to remember the suffering that Our Savior bore on this day so that we can be lifted away from grievance and grief itself. We can now look humbly upon ourselves and others so that all disparagement can be cast away and solace will forevermore replace the quest of evil which thrashes against the very survival of the human heart. This is the day that truly changed the world and allowed humankind to see the glistening vibrance of love. There now needs to be no unhappy or hopeless thoughts, nor any anxiety. This is the happy day that the Blood of Christ washed indifference and sin from the face of the Earth. The celebration of the true Life of man was born to our souls at this joyous moment in time. We need to remember it as the end of worldliness and the promise of Love and forgiveness for our souls. The beauty of Creation was restored the moment Christ laid down His Life for us. Darkness has been consumed and defeated by the blinding Light from the Man on the Cross. The spotless Lamb has brought the restitution for every imaginable transgression against Infinite Perfection, short of denying God Himself. The locked doorway that separated man from the glorious heavens was ripped from its primordial hinges when Our Lord delivered His Spirit back to the Father on the Holy Cross.

Our ease of movement toward Paradise was made possible on the solemn day of Christ's Crucifixion. His Light has ended mankind's midnight assault against human dignity and decency. Salvation has come to live among us in our day. Our hope is fulfilled by His courageous dismantling of mortality, destruction, and desolation. The ecstatic immortality of all humankind is present in the Divinity of the Crucifixion. All that will forever continue to be was manifested at that instant in history. Every living being should look to the Crucified Lamb of God and see into the expanse of forever. There is no longer a restraining horizon to encapsulate our frustrated hopes. Through the Death of Jesus, we are free to witness our every dream come true in our land and during this time. We can ponder the length of our own immortality from our flashing inception in the Creator's mind through everything we wished we would ever be. In Christ, we are purified and restored, complete and fulfilled, and overflowing with light brought to life. The broken and desolate of our age can now go to this Savior for restoration with the same faith that many were healed when Jesus walked the Earth. And anyone who suffers from debilitating wickedness or pride can be granted the humility and perfect love for God that they could never before find. They will discover it in this Lamb sacrificed to purify all hearts.

But still, there are many who are far away from Salvation because of their non-existent faith in His power to Love and answer them. Throngs of poor sinners still reside in lands starving to hear of the Good News of Christ. They hunger for the knowledge of submission and the responsibility to love their brothers and sisters. They can see the measure of their awful distance from righteousness with each new day. And, they are growing to understand that everyone can choose to be holy by reversing their decision to be unholy. This is a choice that is readily at our hands to make. When we come to truly understand the power of the miracles now happening in the world, the task of conversion will be made infinitely more bearable. The Virgin Mother of God is preparing all of us for the Return of Christ, Her Son, in final Glory. She has told us time and again that our prayers are the beautifully spontaneous Light of His Dawn.

We must open the floodgates of our hearts and allow Christ the King to consume the world. It is our solemn duty to pray and prepare for the blinding revelation of Redemption whose source and legacy is the Man on the Cross of Mount Calvary. Our mortal veil is about to be removed to reveal the shining moment of Christ's Death and Resurrection. He will shine forever through all visible and tangible Creation. The "seen" and the "unseen" are about to be eternally enlightened with the flawless Beatitude of the Lamb. His promise of Love is the powerful message through which we live our hope given to all believers during the awesome hours of this Holy Day. Jesus' promise of His imminent Return to take us home was fulfilled in the utterance from His Sacred Lips, "...It is finished." Love has won and we are the heirs of His Divine inheritance.

Saturday, April 18, 1992

The Holy Mother came during the Easter Vigil Mass when many of Her children were Baptized and Confirmed into full communion with the Catholic Church. It is a great day of celebration because many worthy souls will now be our fellow communicants to receive the Bread of Life. Together, we all remember how the world waited in great hope for Jesus to rise from the grave as He promised. All of the messages that Our Lady has given find their meaning in the anticipation of this night. Come to the Eucharist! Everyone must complete the full-circle which millions before have traveled to become one in the body of humanity which Christ will soon come to redeem. It begins with prayer from the heart and continues in self-denial and forgiveness. And tonight, many souls have found this new birth in their First Holy Communion with Jesus in the Holy Eucharist. We celebrate the glorious Resurrection of Jesus at the Easter Vigil. And, we will also soon observe His Ascension to the Throne of God where He is waiting for all of His children to return to Love.

God has dispatched His Mother to teach us how. She is, indeed, the Queen of His loving Heart. It is through Her guidance that we learn that Christ is alive in all people open to receive Him. The Lord-of-all has risen and is guiding humanity back to Himself. The gentle and breathtaking beauty that we witness in our lives is the vision of the living Spirit of God Himself. He is the truth in our hearts that strengthens our faith in the Eucharistic Flesh of His Son. This Blessed Sacrament is the same Body and Blood which hung on the Cross and triumphantly rose from the dead. The Most Sacred Host is the crucified and risen Lamb of God, breathing the same morning air, seeing the same sparkling Creation, suffering the same Holy Sacrifice, and loving as He has always infinitely loved. This past Holy Week is one of the most awe-inspiring opportunities for us to see the endless possibilities that are brought by the Truth. God begs us through His Mother to respond with open hearts to these great Mysteries of His witness to the Father. But, we are still overwhelmed with our own trite perceptions, attitudes, and haughty conduct which fuel the outrageous indifference that keeps us divided and corrupt. We must learn from Good Friday and Easter that material security and human achievement are no guarantee of holiness. Indeed, our pious nature will only come through personal self-sacrifice in reparation for the sins of our brothers and sisters. The divine foundation for our holy lives is derived from communion with God in the Most Blessed Sacrament.

Jesus died to convince us that He is the Way to everlasting Life. This is as true today as it was 2000 years ago. But, we need to confess that we are not living His Way. Indeed, we must turn our lives into a fruitful manifestation of infinite Love for one another. Again, the only way to achieve this selflessness is to be recreated in the likeness of God through our attendance of Holy Mass and reception of the Fruit of the Altar. At that celebrant juncture, our souls are transformed with a new hope for the Coming of the Son of God back to the world to end all sadness, to cure every pain, and to make each one of us a perfect being in the full light of consciousness. We must anticipate this rebirth like we see the rising of the sun or the blooming of spring. The children of God have already won this happiness. But, we must endure, persevere, pray, encourage and admonish others for the strengthening and enlightening of God's people. We must patiently wait in merciful endurance for all of the children of Paradise to come to the Table of Jesus' Sacrifice. Indeed, acceptance to the depth of the human soul is Salvation itself. It is the reciprocal abandonment to the Love of Christ which brings Eternal Life.

Easter Sunday, April 19, 1992

Today is the great day of the celebration of Easter. Our Lady reminded my brother and me to always remember the many things She taught us during Lent. I especially recall what She said to me on Ash Wednesday about the symbolic shapes of a circle, a triangle, and a square. It is a fulfilling reminder to ponder all of the parables that The Virgin uses to help us understand the teachings of Jesus through Her own grace. I went to visit my family today and shared Easter dinner together with them. Our Lady was present as She is with all families who gather in prayerful remembrance of the Resurrection of Christ Jesus. She gave me a great grace through my little five-year-old nephew. I am confident that it was because She knew my overwhelming despondence brought about by the refusal of my family to accept the validity of the messages She has been giving to my brother and me.

I was sitting alone in the livingroom and my tiny relative came-up to me very timidly and handed me an envelope while saying under his breath that he had made me a "present." He was so very precious in his innocent meekness. I took the envelope from him and began to tear it open. He had written "Uncle Bill" in letters which were indicative of someone approaching kindergarten. I was very touched by the handwriting; and was very much more moved that he had been thinking of me and considered me worth the trouble of taking his time to prepare me a gift. It seemed more than any of my other family members were willing to provide. I asked him what was inside the envelope as I was opening it, and he responded with the word, "shafes." Not understanding what he said, I asked again and received the same response. It then occurred to me that he was saying "shapes." At that very moment, I knew the miracle that Our Lady had brought. Every word that She had spoken on Ash Wednesday exploded in my heart.

I somehow knew what was in the envelope before I ever poured-out its contents. When I turned it upside down, out fell three shapes raggedly cut by the scissors of a pristine child: a circle, a triangle, and a square. My precious nephew looked into my eyes as I sat in awe and said simply, "I love you, Uncle Bill." I had to fight-back my tears as he stood so innocently in front of me. I was looking at one of God's messengers before my own eyes. I never felt so uplifted and renewed in all my life. The tiny pure love of my little nephew was God's confirming grace for my strength. His very presence was the validity of the Father's desire for me to be happy. I will forever remember this peaceful moment as long as I live. During that brief time, I felt like I was physically attached to Heaven. I looked into this tiny child's eyes and prayed that God would see me as simply and lovingly as I looked upon this little boy. And ironically, his birthday is February 11th, the Feast of Our Lady of Lourdes.

DISCIPLINE IN PRAYER

Monday, April 20, 1992

Through the grace of God, our Holy Mother came again tonight to speak to me as I prayed the Holy Rosary. She comes bringing the gift of eternal happiness because She knows that we are often too burdened by the dailiness of life. She is not hesitant to remind us that time can deceive anyone because of the repetition of the passing days that often afflicts our peace of mind. We must forget our cares of yesterday, recollect ourselves of the blessings of today, and look into tomorrow with the Light that Jesus gives through His promise of Eternal Life. Our days of true joy are in the very near offing. Today, Our Lady came speaking of the fruits of forgiveness and mercy. Not only are we granted them by God through His Son, He expects us to offer them to each other, unreservedly. Everything we do is revealed to our Creator before we ever act. He knows the condition of our hearts and whether we live in accordance with His Divine will. The Blessed Mother tells me that the pain and suffering which diminish our hope for human dignity are mitigated by our forgiveness of one another. The union between the Father and His children culminates in our awareness that Christ is calling us to become one with Him through such infinite perfection.

We must turn to prayer to satisfy our hunger for the sacred and inspirational fruits of the living God. We must light a fire in our hearts that will burn uncontrollably throughout the Earth to unite humankind in Christ Jesus. Our Almighty Father loves us through the miraculous presence of His Son, the Blessed Virgin Mary, and all the heavenly Hosts of Saints and Angels. When we love in perfect unity with them, our lives become a part of this great chorus of eternal jubilation. The source of our happiness is in the Lord of Creation; and we must return home to claim it. But, we do not have to die or leave the Earth in order to gain it. That is what makes every day special. Our Lady proclaimed in the first weeks of 1991 that there is a given number of days allotted to the mortal world and we do not know where the count stands before Jesus will return. Although we are spiritually blinded by their repetitiveness, God Himself has not stopped counting. We are closer to the Return of Christ in Glory than any generation before us. That is why we must seek great holiness in Life and recognize that it is, indeed, a gift from above. When we perceive it through the eyes of Love, we will no longer see it as a burden. Everyone will know that Life is the beginning of our transformation into Eternity itself.

Our Lady knocks continuously on our hearts and consciences to call us to prayer. This is the most special kind of Life. She asks us to pray for ourselves and for those who will not open their hearts in love and piety. We must ponder what we would purge from ourselves if it meant that everyone else could enter Heaven. Would it be as monumental if it meant that only one more soul would enter Paradise? Indeed, do we live the Life of Christ with the confidence that all souls are rendered more acceptable in the eyes of God by our example? That is the faith to which we are called; and we must live it without the benefit of a periodic "report card" from On High telling us whether we are on track. Our Lady is traveling across the surface of the globe in hopes that Her intercession will lift every heart and convert all souls. There is nothing lacking in Her resilient Love for humankind. Her hope for the world lies in our response to Her call. We must be the reason for Her happiness as She reigns as Queen of Heaven and Earth in a way that She could not come to know as the lowly hand-maiden of Nazareth. We must respond with commitment and devotion by surrendering to our God who is calling through His Virgin Mother, Mary.

Wednesday, April 22, 1992

I hope that the entire world will read this Diary, and I wish for everyone to heed the call of Christ. Our Holy Mother tells us that very few people believe in God with doubtless faith, some will believe when they have seen enough, and others will never believe at all. But, the fact remains that everyone will eventually know. And, to accentuate that truth, the Holy Virgin has come to ask us to prepare in supplication, contemplation, meditation, and conversion. It is the Holy Rosary that She asks us to pray. God seems to be appeased by that. And, no wonder. If He sees the Virgin Mary the way I have come to know Her, He probably prays the Rosary, too. Today, Our Lady spoke to me about the progress of my Diary. She reassured my brother and me that we are making great strides and that we are not behind in our work. She said that each alphabetic letter is a prayer of Love for lost souls. That is why She is happy in our obedience and calls us to join in Her high hopes for the success of Her intercession through us. When we seem depressed, it has a negative effect on those around us. They come to us seeking joy because they know it is Christ who gives us peace. And when we give them the Love of Jesus, they will know Him too. When we all pray together with the Blessed Virgin, we see the goodness and beauty of Creation that enlivens the happiness in our hearts that we can find nowhere else.

The greatest joy we will ever know lies in the faith which tells us of our destination in Paradise. If God would presently allow us to openly see what He has prepared for His children, we would be brought to ecstatic bliss. Suffering of any nature or intensity would be borne with great peace and endurance. But, it is only in faith that we can yet come to know such fulfillment. Therein lies the origin of our indestructibly placid souls. And, it begins with the sincerity of holy prayer and our realization that everything Jesus teaches is true. By becoming the Victim of Sacrifice, He has destroyed any desolation our hearts can feel from the ravages of worldliness, corruption, and sin. There is no other means through which we can stand. If we do not love others in reflection of His Sacrificial Love, our souls are as dead as the corpses of ancient mummies lying under centuries of mortal rubble. This is the wisdom that Our Lady teaches Her children. She brings our allegiance to the Almighty Father to contemporary life. We learn to see the truth as infinitely as God, Himself. I thank Her over and again for saying "yes" to the Archangel Gabriel in affirmation of the Love that She still has for us. I offer without condition my reciprocal "yes" to Her by obediently responding to Her call for prayer and holiness. If each of you will join my brother and me in this cause of faith, the world will be returned to the beauty that God intends for it to extol.

Wednesday, April 29, 1992

As Christians, how can we believe all we claim to know and not want to take to-the-road with the message of Salvation? How can we not chant the glories of God? Why don't we revel Him from our housetops? Our Holy Mother sings His praises because She cannot help it. That, too, must be our song. She came again to my door this evening to inscribe more lyrics upon my heart. We must joyfully sing with Her, with timbrel and heart, in tenor and tone. She turned Her discussion today to the enlightening concept of human holiness. She has drawn the fitting comparison that there should be great depth to our faith and intense elevation in our holiness. When our prayers are lofty and our love is strong, the peaks of holiness can be more easily attained. Likewise, the deeper our faith in God, the better our souls will invoke the truth that Jesus Christ is our Redeemer and the Ruler of Creation.

Sorrowfully for many, they have self-proclaimed that their faith is strong because of their own sure-footed definition of Him. Many claim that God does not bother them because they are living an acceptable life. These souls are like people walking through shallow water who do not know how to swim. Their feet grounded in the depths of the world are their false sense of security. They move forward in confidence knowing that they will always be able to keep their head in breathing air. But, they will always be a shallow people living a trite testament to the fraudulent nature of those without faith in God. They will never leave the shallow water of the Earth for the more fruitful and indulging satisfaction of the heavens. The fact that they have no faith will remand them to the world forever. As long as they can manipulate, control, and sustain, they see no reason to grow toward immortality in judgment or courage.

But, human life consists of much more than a simple walk through a knee-deep pool. We cannot be completely confident that God will not allow us to sink or swim in waters of suffering and sacrifice much more intense than we might expect. What happens if He casts our walk of life into much deeper waters? Will we be able to walk on top of it? Not likely. Those who walk without faith eventually find themselves struggling for life on the bottom of a swirling whirlpool of mortal suffering. And they can paddle and flail as long as they must, but the tide will eventually engulf them. They never expected that their path of life would lead them into anything more than a playful stroll through a tranquil puddle. What becomes of these faithless people when life throws them an unexpected breach to their foothold of indifference? They have no choice but to come to the saving grace of Christ Jesus to be brought to shore. And even if thinking about God means having the ability to swim, we must still actively accept Him because we will never be able to tread water forever. Thoughts will eventually die with all that is mortal. We must give Jesus our whole heart, soul, body, and wisdom if we are to be united to God through Him. That is the committed acceptance that He expects from us. He knows that we are helpless to save ourselves whether we are in the ocean or a backyard swimming pool. We can do nothing immortal without His grace.

Our Lady has come to the world and shaken the foothold of the indifferent. The souls of many are now gasping for air because they never before knew that God was real. This Virgin has brought the truth of God to us so profoundly that millions have been swept off their feet. She is teaching that the heavens are greater than man in all ways conceivable. We have never before been so deep in the waters of sanctified reality. Our Blessed Lady has brought a flood of truth to the 20th century that makes the waters in the days of Noah look like the wading pool She used to describe this message. We have never before been called to such tremendous expectation of the Return of the Son of Man. We have never been in water this deep. Neither have we ever truly had to swim where evil has crested so close to our souls. Our faith is being tested the world-over while millions are experiencing this great time of revelation. We must let-go of worldly action, intellectual engagement, and our endless search for facts and answers. There may not be a rhyme for every knowable reason during our lives. Logic cannot explain-away every influence that tosses us about in time and space. We need to end our relentless struggle for self-preservation in a world that is eventually going down the drain out of our control. We must desist in fighting the engaging arms of Christ. Then, we will feel Him carrying us now to safety.

It is not our will that matters anymore. Neither is knowledge a suitable power for our perpetual survival. We must stop looking at faith as though it is founded in some earthly cache of mortal reasoning. Then, we will learn to trust the Love of God which has no particular position in time, space, or coordinate. We will never be able to calculate a way to preserve ourselves in every eventual loss-of-footing that God will allow. Our faith must be deeper than our losses and stronger than the challenges which are coming toward us with greater ferocity than ever before in the history of the world. Only our hearts can save us because human logic has already failed. The Love of God for His people is the final story about the lost and found. The faith that Our Lady is growing in us is the lifeline between Earth and Heaven. It is the reason we can walk through any depth of human tribulation and be confident that we will succeed in Jesus Christ. Our Holy Mother has come to the Earth to take us to our feet and teach us our first infant steps.

Thursday, April 30, 1992

The Eternal Father is our Genius, the Worker of miracles, and the Master of timing. Each Holy Mass is the first time we partake in the Crucifixion of Christ. Every "Hail Mary" is the first time we recite it. We leave the confessional having never before sinned. Who else but God could magnify our good deeds and expunge our errant past? And, why would we flee from such gifts? Why do we fear? If courage is knowledge, it is time for us to learn. If faith is a gift, we should be in the mood for accepting. God is the supply and we are the need. So, let us enjoin Him to sanction our good will by taking His case to the world. His Mother has come to lead us to the Way. We must close our eyes and open our hearts to walk hand-in-hand with Her to Him. She came again today to bless my life with the touch of Her purifying grace. We walk by faith and not by sight! That is the prolific posture that will keep all people of God united to the heavens. And, it is an exercise in generous love and gratitude for the blessings that flow through our lives more abundantly than we care to realize. Somewhere intrinsic to our relationship with God lies His mandate that we live a suffering that is unique to ourselves in the way Christ Jesus was given His own Cross. Everyone must pass the test of faith. For some, that trial may come to them during their last mortal days. Nonetheless, many of us bear the price for the conversion of others by our very own lives. But, we do not recognize it as a grace from Our Lord.

With reference to yesterday's message from the Queen of Heaven, those who walk by faith need not be concerned whether their fate is sealed by Christ into inevitable deliverance to the Throne of the Father. It is an irrefutable fact. His Divine Blood is the cohesive grace that binds human souls to the God who made them. The foundation of our Salvation was laid by the sacrificial Lamb on the Cross of Mount Calvary. We must walk to it in blind acceptance, come hell or high water. There is no need to measure the distance or conjure a quantity of chance in our determined paces toward Heaven. When we get to the Salvific Hill, Jesus will do the rest. Luck and possibility have no bearing on this eternal fact. Just as we have no control over the number of our days or when the last one will arrive, we are powerless to see our future without the true vision given through our love for God.

Peace and Salvation are found only by meeting the coming days with faith and trust that the God who created them will see us through. Love should always be our response to His celestial overtures, come what may. Perfect human trust and faith rest in our freedom to acknowledge that the Love of Heaven's First Son is more powerful than anything we will ever know. He cares for us more than nature panders to the birds of the air and the lilies of the field. We cannot fall into darkness because the Light of Jesus Christ caresses our souls and lifts our spirits. Therefore, those who gamble upon good fortune, refusing to trust in eternal Salvation are lusting in darkness and poised for the fall of their lives. Their spirits are burdened by the drunken indulgence of worldliness and materialism. It is only a matter of time before they will have to make the decision which will define the destiny of their souls. They will have to accept the Crucified Lord of Glory and His Promise of Redemption or be lost in the nether world to the unending misery of their castigated souls.

Our Lady helped me form these words for today's Diary entry and told me that She truly loves us. She wants no soul to be lost to the abysmal fires of condemnation. She is working immortally to open the hearts of Her children. No one will reject the Saving Messiah if they will allow themselves to know Him as perfectly as She does. And, just as Jesus Christ is the Mediator between God and Man, She is the Mediatrix between ourselves and His magnanimous Love. Nothing can destroy the Promise of Jesus to the sinners He died to save. And, we must reciprocally allow nothing to separate us from the Love that He offers.

MAY 1992

Saturday, May 2, 1992

I have come to recognize the Holy Mother as the most uplifting and encouraging soul ever given breath besides Christ Himself. Her Love is the most engulfing and powerful presence of Divinity we can know aside from the moment we receive the Blessed Eucharist at Holy Mass. She has shown that the God of all universes is mighty and magnificent in ways that we have yet to see. But, He is also the same loving Father who guides His children in every last detail of our lives. I have been given very many graces and blessing through the years. To fail to evangelize His Love for us now would render me one of the darkest of men. If we were to see for just an instant the raw and intimate power that our interactive and participative God has for us, we would truly be stunned beyond belief and would never fear anything again. Jesus lives the detail of every soul who accepts Him from the simplicity of His manger to the Glory of His Resurrection. We come to better know this supernatural grace through the prayers to which we are called by His words and the Mother He sends to awaken us.

We live-out our lives in faith so we can have access to our knowable Father in the heavens. When we pray, He listens and answers. If we knew the power of our petitions, we would pray continuously. That is our invitation for God to come to our door and our validation that we believe He has arrived. The peace that the world yearns for is perpetuated by our prayers for His healing intercession. Our Lady says that we must be the world's peacemakers through living in Christ as He is present today, touching and guiding our hands from beside and within us. Those who believe that Jesus is a centuries-passed figurehead from a long-gone God had better figure again. Christ is the immortal Son of our Ever-Living Father who knows and sees all from preconception to expiration. He witnesses our every thought and guides the impulses and inspirations of His holy people. He is closer to us now than the very hand at the end of our arm. In Him, we can reach into all Eternity and never lift a finger. Without Him, our hands are miserably bound behind our backs.

Jesus is gentle and comforting to those who return His Love in-kind. But, He is also paternally stern and swift to discipline the proud and those who believe themselves inherently deserving of redeeming grace regardless of their conduct or conviction. His hands can reduce the mountains to rubble just as gently as He can place them on the cheeks of the smallest child. And when He smiles, the entire world is lifted by the truss of His reassurance that we are moving in the direction that will lead us Home. When He looks upon us with a forward glance that tells us we ought to be doing better, it is the same as the Father in Heaven taking us by the shoulder and turning our face toward the blinding sun.

In every aspect that we can imagine, God loves us with an unrestrained smile of affection. When we live in faith and perform good works, He looks upon us with a nod of affirmation to rival that of His own when He created the universe and said, "That is good." In His smile, we are "all" to Him, the completion of the purpose of the Love He has always been. In His eyes, we are unequivocally worthy of the price of His Son's Life, Death, and Resurrection that will take us back Home to His side. We are the picture displayed in the hallowed chambers of His Heart from which He painted His profile of happiness. Not only are we the essence of the Love that created us, we are the jewels which adorn the crown He wears. This is a depiction of God's smile for humanity. We cannot fathom the reward which awaits those who love Him. If we would lay down our arms and prejudices and embrace the Love we are called to be, no evil or discontent could deter us from living in eternal fulfillment. No thief could claim the prize we know is rightfully our own. By placing the treasure of our very souls in Christ Jesus, we can live in complete assurance that the night will never steal us from the living Dawn.

Tuesday, May 5, 1992

As I make my daily entries in my Diary, it seems ironic that such a traditionally private and candid artifact would eventually become a centerpiece for the infant faith of those whom the Blessed Mother told me would read it. I am happy to record the annals of my newborn conviction through Her virginal Wisdom. It is a humble feeling to collect my thoughts and Her messages in one comprehensive manuscript. I know that I am doing well because She is guiding my hand, as well as my words. It is the nurturing experience of a great teacher watching over my shoulder while I am writing the answers to a test about a subject that I have learned well and will eventually master. I know that God is watching, too, and that He is pleased by our prayers. He looks over the horizon at our lives like we would peer over a doorway transom to watch our children play. He sees me immortalizing these words and is planning our reunion as you read them now. Through our Dear Eternal Mother, He wishes us the best.

While praying the Holy Rosary just past nine o'clock this evening, the Blessed Virgin came to my home from the Halls of Paradise to tell me how difficult it is for those who do the Lord's work to be accepted by the world. She referred to the plight of Jesus when He was cast-out by the people who knew Him. In their lack of faith, they refused to see His kingly power and dignity. He was labeled as the son of a carpenter and that was the way his fellow citizens continued to perceive Him. They had no intention of stepping-out in faith to realize His role as Teacher and Redeemer. He came to Earth as God and simultaneously His Word. His teachings are the intentions of the Almighty Father for His people.

Our Lady said that I am facing somewhat the same rejection by proclaiming Her words to others. It is frustrating for me to not be able to share the beauty of the Mother of God just because others do not have the faith to listen. They truly do not know the gift which surrounds us. Now, I confidently know why Our Lady cries for Her children. She speaks of a world absent of our obsession with mortal events. Yes, She does have immortal hope! My vision has become more refined concerning the condition of the Earth because the Holy Mother has drawn my attention away from materialism and toward the common suffering and indifference of humankind. I have explained in other sections of this Diary that the Blessed Virgin sees the very details through which we live. Tonight, She referred to someone whom She called "one of Her children" after my brother and I watched a television documentary about his life. The program was about America's 36th president, Lyndon Baines Johnson. The program was somewhat critical of his leadership during the Vietnam War. Thousands of young Americans laid down their lives for the purpose of promoting a democracy in Southeast Asia that would never come.

But, Our Lady said that the end of the life of Lyndon Johnson is an example for all Americans. After leaving office semi-voluntarily in January 1969, Mr. Johnson traveled the country making speeches about his presidency. Even he had a chance to take another look at his tenure. To paraphrase President Johnson as he stood before the world giving a speech which he had to interrupt by placing heart-medicine in his mouth, he proclaimed, *"If our cause is just and if our hearts are right, I am confident that we shall overcome."* This was a reference to the civil rights movement which occurred during the 1960s. Our Lady told me today that this statement, made just prior to his death, was a fruit of the presence of his conversion to perfection. This was his open public statement to humankind that Love is the ultimate victor over evil and all the terrible prospects that a lack of good will forces upon a nation and world. And, this is the pose that he struck when Christ took his picture for the annals of Eternity. He had come full-circle to the truth that the cause of Love in the human heart is all that matters.

Our Lady is the perfect Mother to us all. She stands by us to teach and bless us in our struggle to be like Jesus. She said that Heaven gained a "...good little boy" when President Johnson died. She reminded me what a terrible day that was for the world. On the day he died, the U.S. Supreme Court legalized abortion in America. It was January 22, 1973. She added that someday we will all see the simultaneous occurrence of these two events as more than just simple coincidence. She also asked for us to continue to pray for the end of abortion with the same fervent conviction that Lyndon Johnson proclaimed the victory of the heart on his last day.

Monday, May 11, 1992

So many times, I have tried to place myself in a somewhat intangible role of being another person looking-back at this Diary, wondering what others would think about my writing. I have felt the high hopes that God is bringing through His messages, along with the apprehension that I might be unable to fulfill all that I am asked to accomplish in the short span of one human life. But, through it all, I have held-firm to the confidence that Our Blessed Mother will never lead me astray and would never ask me to do more than Jesus would do for me. Therefore, I cannot desist in my labors for them both, and ultimately for the Almighty Father, Himself. I keep praying and continue to record Her words. This is the new format and substance of my life, at least for now. Our Mother brings Her miraculous and incredible graces to us in Love, a message for all faiths and peoples who inhabit the Earth.

I have been worrying and upsetting myself about the selection of words I have chosen to place on these pages. It seems that syllables cannot adequately describe the feelings that I have when Our Lady comes to speak. I have also been concerned that I have not been dedicating enough time to my work and that I am moving too slowly in this period when the world needs Her intercession so desperately. She told me that my concerns were unfounded and that I should trust Her to guide me. She became almost indignant that I had not been showing greater trust in Her power to keep me on track. It was as if She had chosen to answer my impatience by being impatient Herself with the way I have been behaving. Her presence was almost mirror-like in showing me what I have been portraying to Her. I did not like what I saw any more than She did. I promised Her that I would be more patient and trusting.

The Holy Mother also addressed a Marian Conference which my brother and me recently attended. We left it with the feeling that Her messages were never truly shared by the people present. It was as though the conference was centered more on the actual presence of Our Lady than what She has come to say. Many are inspired by Her pretty words, but not impressed to the point of living the messages. So, the Holy Mother responded to our reservations by saying that the focal point of the Love of God has been skewed by those searching for miracles to satisfy their own inner-wonderings whether He exists at all. She spoke of the irony of this phenomenon because the very miracles that God is allowing through Her are for the purpose of increasing our faith in His Love. The point is that we should not consider miracles as being confirmation of the omnipotence of God. We should believe that on faith alone. The supernatural manifestations are to give us grace so that our strength can be nourished. There is an awful battle to come which will end the world as we know it. God is providing ample proof of His power for all people to gain fortitude and conviction so we will remain at the side of Jesus when the war against evil is at its highest peak.

We must accept all heavenly gifts in simplicity and humility. Too many souls are sitting back in awe of God's miracles and trying to define for others what they mean. There are too many errant and awkward interpretations of the manifestations of God. The Holy Spirit will always tell us the intentions of the Almighty Father if we will just simply kneel and pray from the heart. The Blessed Mother did not want us to believe that the conference in Her honor was in vain. She said that it is always good when thousands unite in prayer of the Holy Rosary. Then, in nearly the same breath, She returned to Her concerns about the worldliness and materialism of those who came to pray. She said that many were too concerned whether they had a nice place to sit in the auditorium. Others were seen to have been humorizing and glorifying their past sins. Some of the principle speakers somewhat portrayed this presence. While it is always good to acknowledge our own sinful nature and accept pardon when we come forward in contrition for reconciliation, we should not use our sins as a subject matter for converting oratories. Indeed, we should reserve every opportunity for proclaiming the perfection of Christ and the power He gives to attain it.

We should not be giving the impression that we can live as sinfully as we wish with the expectation that we are washed clean by a Sacrament that we do not enter with a serious purpose of amendment. This is one of the reasons why the Protestant Church does not believe in the Sacrament of Confession. Having made that point clearly, in the final analysis, the Marian Conference was little more than a social event with people whom the rest of the world sees as a collection of cultish fanatics. Instead of taking the message of Our Lady into the world so that all of Her children can come to know Her, the attendees of this event gathered to revel their own faith and went home to their otherwise indifferent lives. The Holy Mother seemed sad that not enough time was dedicated to discussing the plight of the poor and lost. Too little prayer was offered for the lives of those who do not pray on their own. One speaker after another stepped-forward to criticize political leaders, but none of them offered any prospects on how to convert the secular world. The podium was used as a bully-pulpit for political partisanship rather than a means of enlisting the assistance and prayers of the faithful to convert anyone who is not living the Truth of Jesus Christ.

At the last, Our Lady said that Jesus is pleased when His children gather to honor His Mother. When we venerate Her power and grace by gathering under Her Mantle, we are living the intentions of God. But, we must focus upon "why" She has come. If we speak about Her without living in unison with Her, we are failing the purpose of Her intercession for us. She calls us to the simplicity exemplified by the Birth and Life of Her Son. We must seek the response of the Holy Spirit to our prayers, not in podium-thumping speeches. In order for us to openly accept every grace that Our Lady is bestowing upon the world, we must put forth our best and most noble effort toward its conversion. Each of us needs to see with clear vision what is most pleasing to God. And to do that, we must listen to His Mother with simple and unassuming hearts.

Tuesday, May 12, 1992

Our Lady continuously tells me how appreciative She is for my obedience to Her intercession. But, deep inside my soul, I keep asking myself how anyone could say no to such a miraculous grace. Has there ever been anyone in history who has told Her to go away? My heart cannot even envision such a tragedy. After all, She is the Mother of God's Word and, therefore, the prologue to His gift of Redemption. And, She thanks me every day for praying and attending Holy Mass. These are not the extraordinary sacrifices of some pious little boy, but rather the requirements I know to be a part of my Catholic profession. This tells me that God is, indeed, pleased with the faith of His Church on Earth. I wish not to be known for supernatural grace, I leave that to the Almighty, Himself. I desire only to be His instrument and example, and a humble servant with whom He can do as He pleases.

I attend daily Mass because I need such nourishment from God. My soul hungers for the Life-giving Bread of the Eucharist. And, I pray because I wish to change the world and manifest in myself the transformation that will make me like Jesus in every way. This, too, is simply my openness in receiving His invocation to participate in the perfection to which we are called. God does not have to tell me that I need Him. I have known that since I was old enough to hear. But, I have not always known where to listen, or to whom to respond. I am now convinced that my ears are lent to the most powerful voice in the Kingdom of Heaven, Our Lady, the Mother of Christ. To Her, I genuflect because She holds our Savior in Her arms. She often brings Him with Her when She speaks to me. I have every reason to believe that He was with Her while She came to pray with me today.

This Mother of Salvation miraculously spoke openly with me as I recited the Holy Rosary. She addressed our need to help our brothers and sisters in Christ who are stricken with poverty, sickness, and famine. These problems exist all over the world, including the western continents. And, the terrible truth of human suffering is a statement about the abundance of goods and material lifestyles that we in America enjoy. From the leaders of our country to the average man on the street, we are failing to give the message about Jesus to the world. It appears that the United States has little desire to end the suffering of our brothers and sisters in poorer regions. Our leaders seem hapless and helpless to take a serious look at the plight of the world's poor. We must embrace the message of Christ and take it from within our own hearts into the farthest places on Earth. And not only that, we are mandated by God Himself to accompany our prayers with the goods that others need for survival. In undeveloped countries where corrupt political leaders are keeping needed food away from their people, we must use our righteous strength to remove them from power.

Tonight, Our Lady also praised the Glory of Her Son in the Holy Eucharist. She proclaims that if every living soul on Earth comes arm-in-arm to the Holy Mass and receives the Most Blessed Sacrament, the scourges which impale the world with suffering would pass like darkness fleeing at dawn. In addition to prayer, the Holy Eucharist will lift us all out of spiritual and material poverty. It changes the world from inside human hearts and gives strength to anyone fighting the temptation to sin. The presence of Jesus in the Eucharist is the consummation of the purpose of human life. His Sacred Flesh is not a supplement to our needs, He is the Food we need to sustain the very Life and destiny of our souls! No matter the walk-of-life, every persons needs to commune with Christ in His Body and Blood of the Altar of Sacrifice. Our lives are molded in as many different ways as one could connect lines, dots, and circles to make geometric shapes. There is a seeming endless nature to the types of personalities and professions of the people on Earth. But, we are all united as one humanity in the perfection of the Divine Body and Blood of Jesus.

Instead of shaping the Eucharist around our lives, we must make this Holy Sacrament the reason why our lives are formed into the likeness of Christ, Himself. We must be engulfed by His grace, wisdom, and power by placing our lives inside the Christian Divinity of the Most Blessed Sacrament. This should be the reason we get out of bed in the morning. Many observers have correctly noticed that some sinners have placed God in a box that they can toss-about and store wherever they please. It is as if they can put Him in a closet so He will never be able to see how they live. Oh, how wrong they are! If they confine Him to parameters in which they think His reign can be contained, He will show them that these boundaries only constrain their own inability to become larger than life. Jesus is the freedom that people seek, but they are too blind to recognize His grace. The Holy Eucharist provides the vision for the soul to know both God and the reason for Life. Then, instead of Jesus getting a small portion of that existence, He becomes the true reason for living in the corrected vision we receive. He must be accepted with an open and penitent heart.

Those who consume Jesus' Body and Blood in the Holy Eucharist also become inebriated by His Love. This union is consummated at the Altar of Sacrifice. Indeed, our lives should be a part of the Holy Mass, rather than the Perpetual Sacrifice being only a brief moment in our day. Then we will gain the perfect knowledge that the Consecration of the Sacred Host is the moment in time that the world becomes a re-generated Paradise. The Holy Altar is as monumental as the Throne from which God created the world in six days. We must accept Him and answer His call to participate in our reunion with Heaven. This requires an active cultivation and conversion of humankind which begins and culminates in the Holy Eucharist. We must crave the blessedness of the Light and reject the falsehood of darkness. This simple message from Our Lady is poignant, prophetic, and beautiful. Her call is urgent because time is very short. The Sacred Host and the Cup of Eternal Salvation are the true, physical, incarnate, and glorified presence of Jesus Christ on the Earth. He is the Heavenly Bread, just as He told us at the Last Supper. He is the Author and Finisher of our faith that we must come to know and accept in every way that God provides. It is in this Holy Eucharist that He is present in His fleshly Body. We engage in complete oneness with God when we commune with Him and open our hearts wide to embrace the Holy Spirit who is one in that glorious embrace.

Friday, May 15, 1992

Our souls are parched and hungry for the Life-giving waters and sustaining Bread of the Sacramental Body of Jesus. As was affirmed by the Apostles, where else can we go for Life? But, I have learned that this is never a "like it or not" dead end. No one other than Christ can enlighten and sustain us. When we one-day see the universe from the other side, we will know that we stayed with Our Lord Jesus because it was the intrinsic desire of our soul. With that same faith, I offer you the messages that the Blessed Mother asks me to record and offer to the world. **"My special son, I love you more than you can imagine. I am consoled that you are happy today, but I am also sorrowful in all of the injustice and indignity that is being heaped upon My children by the ruthless followers of Satan. Day after day, we see more evidence of inequity in human functions and fates. Please help Me pray for all of those being held captive by poverty and others who are being held earthbound by impurity. You know that Satan sanctions all of this evil.**

I can assure you that many innocent and loving hearts are broken by the ravaging attacks of temptation that evil imposes on the weak and innocent. That is why our prayers are important. Humanity is hungry for the Truth. Their hearts are hungry for peace. So many people are tired and broken, weary, and despondent. Now is the time for peace and conversion. Thank you for helping the world to do that. Jesus is very pleased with you! My Heart is filled with Love for you because you seek to be nourished by My grace. You keep wishing that all of the world would see Me and My Son like you do. That day will come! Your patience, prayers, and persistence are important. There are many terrible trials to come before that. Many, many, terrible trials! We will confront them together. Please accept My blessing in the Name of the Father, the Son, and the Holy Spirit. Thank you for praying. I will speak to you soon. I love you. Goodnight."

I hope deeply that everyone on Earth will turn to prayer for the conversion of humanity. The perfection of our souls depends on it; and God requires it. The Love of Jesus is the only answer to our questions, *"Why me...why now...and why here?"* The source of all knowledge is the Sacred Heart of the Messiah of God. Some of us feel that the conversion of our souls is more a nuisance than a hazard. But, you can see from the words of the Blessed Mother that now is the time and ours is the generation. We should embrace one another in Love if we are to face the trials the future will bring. And, we must be strong in faith under the Mantle of Our Lady. If we ratchet-up our prayers, God will surely be moved to spare us from the snares that have already begun to devour the world from under our feet. We do not all have to be overnight saints or martyrs. But, we must be the offspring of Light. Somewhere hiding in each of us is more than a soul who can live in simple faith. We must be doctors of the universe called to heal, perhaps not prophets, but certainly practitioners of hope and service. We must believe that even those who live decades proclaiming the Name of Christ, never giving-up the ideals that Christianity embraces, are worthy of a martyr's crown. Will that include us?

Sunday, May 17, 1992

The grace that God is providing through the miraculous presence of His Mother is beyond imagining. We can live this supernatural grace in our hearts by praying the Holy Rosary. Anyone who meditates upon its Sacred Mysteries is a bricklayer and paver for God as He carefully constructs the many mansions He promises in Heaven for those who love Him. We do many little things that please Him, too. If we send a simple note of thanks to someone, He sees it as a great manifesto of human gratitude. Tonight, Our Lady referred to the simple placement of a statue in Her honor that I erected in the front of my home. I installed some floodlights before it so passers-by could see it at night. **"My little ones, My children, all of My Love through God shines back to you the way that you have lighted My Life to the world in front of your home. My little sons, you have brought a blessing that happens ever-so rarely. You have turned Jesus' tears into joy instead of sadness because you are allowing Me to shine brightly to your brothers and sisters. The words that are available for Me to dictate to you are insufficient to express My Son's happiness with you. Your love and sharing of Love with others makes My Son remember that He would have died a thousands times to save you. His Crucifixion is venerated and shown in the true Light of your actions and faith. Please let it shine often! I love you so. My Heart is so filled with Love for you. My arms are open-wide to receive you. The world does not realize how far it has moved away from Love. You are helping many souls to return. Thank you..."**

Our Lady calls each of us to touch other hearts the way that She embraces all of Her children. There are no barriers or limits to Love that cannot be expunged by our own desire to live the Life of Jesus Christ. This is the hope we carry with us every day that comforts us at night as we tuck ourselves into bed. It is a fruit of the prayers that Our Mother seeks from those who are just-now coming to know God. Such humble prayer is the source of our vision to know the grace of Paradise in ways we never before thought possible. Jesus will answer our petitions by allowing anything we ask if He feels it will assist in the conversion of the world to His Sacred Heart. But, our own hearts must be pure if we are to clearly comprehend the holy beatitude, *"Blessed are the pure of heart, for they shall see God."* Tonight, Our Lady turned the substance of Her holy message to the fruits of the Second Vatican Council from the 1960s. There has been much discussion throughout the Church regarding its design and implementation. Some believe that it has been a scourge to the traditions of the Roman Catholic Church, while others hail it as a great ecumenical movement to unite all Christian faiths under one umbrella.

There have been such descriptions of Vatican II as the weight that sunk the mighty vessel of holiness that once sailed the seas of Christ's teachings, to a comparison with the launching of a great orbiter that has allowed the Catholic faithful to join in the modernism of the living God in the 20th Century. Our Lady told me that both of these are extreme descriptions of a council of worthy bishops who were guided by the Holy Spirit. The unity of Christians has always been the desire and intention of God the Father. The basic purpose of the Vatican II Council was to draw all mankind to Jesus Christ during a time in history when the Church was under the threat of extinction. There was a tremendous and powerful alteration of the vision of the Church in the 1960s brought by the industrialized and materialized West. Not only were the Americas not stopping to admire Jesus, they were not even looking in His direction when they passed by in indifference. And following the terrible wars of 1917 and the 1940s, Russia was preparing to mobilize the errors of her atheism throughout the world. During the 1960s, she was prepared to assume control of the entire eastern hemisphere of Europe and work her way into the western world by placing nuclear weapons in Cuba. It is also obvious that the U.S.S.R. was feeding weaponry and other assistance to the communists who were fighting the pro-democratic forces in Indochina and throughout southeast Asia.

The union of faithful Christians made possible by the Second Vatican Council helped to deter the aggression of the atheist-communist states from moving any further to the West. They knew that Pope Paul VI had united Christians from all walks under the Cross of Jesus Christ and that the faithful were not about to relinquish the freedom they enjoyed to praise Him on their own soil. There was a great unification of the Catholic and Protestant faiths that helped to reaffirm to the communists that Christianity was prepared to live-on regardless of the struggle. The ecumenism of Vatican II was instrumental in providing this Christian alignment. After providing this unique description, Our Lady told me that we would be naive to assume that the states of the former U.S.S.R. have converted to Christianity just because their political union is dissolved. Only the role of their conjoining boundaries has changed. Those countries are composed of human hearts that must be converted to the truth of God. The faith of many survived through decades of religious repression; but millions were never given the chance to know Jesus Christ. Their faith is yet infant and tender, but the door is now open for them to praise the Good News of Our Lord along with the rest of the world.

We must pray for these people to exercise their new freedom of religious expression. They must be encouraged to speak-out in defense of their faith in ways that they have never before known. We should teach them how to pray and offer them every assistance available to continue to grow in faith and love for God. The Blessed Mother told me that the essence of the Catholic Church did not change during Vatican II, nor will it ever. There are still seven Holy Sacraments of which the Most Blessed is the Eucharistic Body and Blood of Christ from the Altar of Sacrifice. The Sacred Species is the Body, Blood, Soul, and Divinity of Jesus Christ. This irrevocable Truth can only be brought at the hands of a Catholic priest offering the Holy Mass. But, there are many false-issues that have been raised by critics of the Second Vatican Council that should never be the focal point of any discussion. The Council is a work of the Spirit of Jesus Christ, Himself. When parishioners and clergy complain about some of the changes brought subsequent to the implementation of Vatican II, they are actually seeing alterations made by opportunists within the Church who are changing the liturgy and visual Propers of the Mass.

These alterations were not a part of the protracted purpose of the Council, but neither does it specifically prohibit them. This is the reason why some liberal Catholics have interpreted Vatican II as permitting them to make some controversial modifications to the physical Church and its traditional liturgy. The Tabernacle has been moved from the center of the back Altar to the side of the sanctuary or even to another adjoining room. Statues of Christ and His Mother have been replaced by modern art. Changes such as these are deeply offensive in nature and an affront to traditional Catholics. They were not intended to be a part of Vatican II; but there is no specific language in the Ecclesiastic documents which deem them improper. Jesus wishes for the unity of all people gathered in His Name. But, He also desires that every soul who seeks His Mercy should come to the original Apostolic Church to receive the Holy Eucharist, the Bread of Life. Only the churches recognized by the Pope in Rome have this Most Blessed Sacrament.

There is still time for everyone in the world to come to the Holy Mass. And, the command from Jesus for humanity to unite in Love will never change. Our responsibility to pray is still one of the cornerstones of our faith. These are the things that make us Christians of one heart. This is the call that our Lady brings to the world today. While She has been summoning all souls to come to the Holy Eucharist for centuries, Her present manifestations throughout the world reflect a final urgency and a clarion call to conversion. Hers is God's final merciful hand to help us reach our Savior, Jesus Christ. Therefore, we must become one heart through the prayer of the Holy Rosary and returning to God the Father by regular attendance at the Holy Sacrifice of the Mass.

Tuesday, May 19, 1992

My spirits have been somewhat dampened today because it is apparent that there is a certain lack of reaction by the world to Our Lady's messages. Jesus' Mother deserves our infinite and complete response. Christ loves us to the point of offering more than we could ever conceive possible; but there are few takers who will accept the loving miracles He provides. Our Heavenly Mother says our battle is not only against the forces of evil, but also against the scourge of such human indifference. We have been so hypnotized by our materials that our desire for holiness has been nearly extinguished, if indeed it ever lived at all. Our recognition of the need for faith is perishing along with the eternal lives of the souls who refuse to give Jesus the command of their existence which is rightfully His to claim. Human indifference only gives Satan free access to unwitting souls and more room to spread his evil works. If we do not embrace the providence of God through His Son, we are endangering our immortal destiny. Creation belongs to God and we need to proclaim it from the rooftops. He owns the present and our future in one timeless moment. When we turn to Him in humble contrition and the promise of amendment, we become heirs apparent to that beautiful Eternity.

If we reject sin and avoid its near occasions, evil will have no influence over us. Satan only succeeds where there exists an atmosphere absent of Love, prayer, and holiness. The evil one cannot claim a share of paradisial Eternity because he is the father of lies and the representative of the condemned. He will never be a part of the Divine Providence of Salvation. Any soul who accepts Jesus Christ as their Lord and Savior simultaneously rejects evil and diabolical works. Souls given to Christ remain forever in His Divine Providence which precedes all mortal nature in mind, thought, and action. Souls who are sitting at the feet of God are saved, thus allowing them to precede the world that contained them. Jesus makes this possible because He destroyed our sins on the Cross and thrust every evil into the fiery abyss at the bowels of the Earth. Satan will forever be mortal, fatal, and subterranean as a result of Jesus' Sacrifice. Evil can never be transposed into Love, ever. If someone tells you that it can, they are speaking on behalf of Satan himself, the first liar in Creation. Evil must be destroyed because it has already rejected the immortality given through the Blood of Christ.

Evil is a descending death which can never be resurrected. It is already terminal. Satan is locked in time, wishing to keep the children of God there, too. He wants to capture as many souls as possible, to throw into Hell in order to keep his infernal fires burning. Those who are cast into perdition are locked into the confines of a timeless epoch of suffering and gnashing of teeth. They will never know the Eternity of heavenly bliss. The damned are caged by unfulfilled desires and perpetual scourging. Their day is the relentless tick of an infernal clock that tells them that it is too late to be saved. The horror of

Hell hides them from even the slightest glimpse of consolation and detains them in endless torment. On the other hand, the true benchmark for the Salvation of souls is the Love poured-out by Jesus Christ. Those who are washed in the Blood of the Godly Lamb are granted the timeless and unbounded freedom and satisfaction of their every dream. Those who reside in Heaven know no sadness and cannot remember ever having been depressed of heart. There is no recollection of anything but Love. This is the Eternity of the Paradise without parameters that contrasts so successfully against the confines of the binding snares of Hell. In the Divine Wisdom of God, the saved must give their souls to Jesus to inherit this everlasting Beauty.

Those who accept Our Lord's Sacrifice, forgiveness, and Mercy are elevated from the mortal chains which once held them. They are catapulted into the Light of immortal Glory. Jesus asks us to bear our crosses as a signal of Love for God and humankind. Those who cast their crosses to the ground will be sorry when the Triumphant King comes to ask them why they refused to imitate His Noble Sacrifice. Christ knows that our mortifications and charities are the means to show our love for Him. Someday we will be given an eternal crown because, like Him, we were willing to be stricken by the pain of many inflicted thorns from those who refute the message of the Love of God. Our suffering is a precious gift we can offer Jesus when we meet Him Face-to-face. Our trials represent the doorway that brings us to the majestic and bountiful Love that He revealed to Creation from the Holy Cross. We must remember that God willingly chose to become a man when He sent His Son into the world. It was His decision to suffer and die for humanity. He descended from the eternal contentment of Heaven to become subjected to the scourges of mankind for the purpose of rescuing the children He loves. Those who wish to be saved must accept the exemplary Life of Jesus and the reason He died. If we are to savor the sweet heavenly dew of Divine satisfaction on Earth, we must embrace the Spirit of this Holy God-Man.

Jesus shared our desolation and said, "I love you." He embraced despair and affirmed, "I need you." He then endured destruction and proclaimed, "I forgive you!" His Crucifixion is the universal moment of God's Love for humanity. When we look to the Hill of Calvary, we can see past Eternity and into the eyes of Glory now uniting Heaven and Earth as one. Prayer is what brings this sanctifying Light into our hearts and reveals the timeless intention of God for us to share His Glory with Him forever. The uplifting Mysteries of the Holy Rosary are brought to clear understanding because through them we are meditating on the Life and Death of Jesus. When we contemplate the sorrowful Crucifixion of Christ, we unite our prayers with those of the Blessed Virgin who intercedes before God for every child who is lost. Before the Cross under which She stands, every knee in the Heavens, on Earth, and under the Earth will bend to proclaim the Glory of the Champion who died. Jesus is the stricken warrior who has secured the blessings of our eternal liberty. The Crucified Lamb is the adorning ornament and the paradisial beauty of Creation. The Cross is the Lamp of Divinity that lights the world, shining with the brilliance of a million suns calling us home to the Kingdom that awaits every converted soul. It is the Door of Eternity which is open-wide to reveal an endless valley of celestial bliss.

The Heart of Christ was laid open by the horrors of human decadence and is a floodgate that allows immortality to flow into the hearts of mortal men. It channels perfection toward the saturation and immersion of the entire Creation of God. Jesus brings a newness that transforms human corruption into purity and rebirth. And, He springs-forth now in the one who perfectly reflects humanity's response of reciprocal Love. She is His Mother who matched every drop of His precious Blood with a heartfelt tear for the Son She lost. She cried because He suffered; but wept happily that He saved us. Every grace that flows from Our Lord's Sacred Heart is received, caressed, and nurtured by the Divine Virginity of the Blessed Mother. She is the only Creature who absolutely and perfectly suffered Jesus' Sacrifice in the desolate depths of Her crucified Heart. Indeed, She is the only Mother ever to birth a sinless Son. But, She responded with flawless assent to the Father's Will and has become the flawless emanation of the response God always desired from His people. She is humanity's response of "yes." Oh, how the world should run to Her! Oh, how we should see Her place in God's Divine Plan! She is the Queen, the Mother, the Lady!

Friday, May 22, 1992

The months of Our Lady's intercession keep clicking by as though She somehow wants me to see Her miraculous presence as both a gift to be accepted and a responsibility to fulfill. She asks me to tell everyone that She is present in the Life of all of Her children in the same intimate way. She brings the bountiful graces from Her abundant storehouse of Love to everyone who prays the Holy Rosary. Her gifts are so magnificent that our imaginations cannot fathom being worthy to receive them. But still, so few are willing to break free from the bonds of the world and pray faithfully to God for His grace and blessing. The number of souls who are willing to help humanity reach its destination is small. We must all call upon Jesus to deliver us to the Heaven for which many-a-living soul laid down their life to receive. Today, Our Lady repeated Her request for our prayers because this is how we enlist the aid of God's Divine Providence. Our petitions and intentions are the power we wield to transform the Earth to be like Heaven. That is the Will of God the Father for His children and the world He owns. We pray, "...*Thy Kingdom come, Thy Will be done on Earth as it is in Heaven.*"

When we pray, we lift our hearts heavenward for the purpose of returning our love for Jesus through the acceptance of His mightiness. This is our visible and tangible role that helps bring the Kingdom we pray for. The Holy Mother says that the ultimate prayer is to ask Her Son for assistance in our acceptance of His Sacrificial Divinity. We must ask Him to help us believe that He is our Savior. This faith is, indeed, a gift from God. We praise Him as our omnipotent Father only because His Spirit places this truth in our hearts. We walk through life at the whim of our passing fancies. But, our Creator has placed a ladder before our eyes that will elevate us to His Bosom. We must ascend into the likeness of Christ if we expect to become the incarnation of holiness which will render us worthy of Paradise. If we pull a Rosary from our pocket with the intention of praying, we have placed our foot on the first rung. This ladder of prayer will take us up to the brink of the horizon so we can see God's intentions for the Earth. This is the living purpose of the Holy Cross on which Jesus died to destroy our sins. We are elevated to paradisial heights through the Death that Our Lord endured.

The Lamb of God died on the Earth so the heavens can be filled with those who inhabit it. He chose to accept the Will of His Father with the same compliance that He seeks in us today. We are helpless in all ways earthly and heavenly without Jesus Christ. That is why we must decide for Him in order to be saved. While many souls feel that there must be some other way to gain Eternal Life in Heaven, Our Lady assures us that there is none. People search for some hybrid formula or solution, or perhaps a combination of intellectual and celestial forces that will save them. They are calculating how to avoid the perfection of living in the image of Christ Jesus so they will not have to relinquish their fortunes and lavish lifestyles. Nothing of this world is of any value in Heaven. No mortal treasures have ever transcended the surly bonds of Glory. According to Our Holy Mother, this proves that prayer is an immortal act. Our petitions permeate the bonds of our earthly exile to reach the Throne of God. When we pray, we are uniting our souls to the elevated and divine. Prayer from the heart is as much a part of the perfection of God as when He created us. Our Lady says that the words of this Diary are a prayer for humankind, and therefore a part of the Divinity of the heavens. This is the power we wield when we pray; and this is the answer to those who say that the Will of God is locked in time and they cannot change it.

Anyone living this "doomsday" attitude needs to stop and realize that the beauty of God has already won the future for all who accept it. All Jesus asks is the opening of the heart of one of His children and He will fill it with grace. The Providence of the Almighty Father is Love for all the world which is consummated and defined by the Crucifixion of His beloved Son. It is in knowing Jesus that we find our eternal happiness. That is what He sent His Mother to tell us. Her task is somewhat like coming into the world and seeing it filled with baby kittens. There is a box in the corner of the Earth and She is gathering these furry creatures by the armload to place into it where they will find food, water, and a soft pillow on which to sleep. But, as She turns to collect the next rambunctious lot, the ones already in the box scamper away and have to be retrieved again. We are much like those little kittens with a will and mind of our own. If we heed the call and enlist the guiding hands of our Mother, we will be nourished to fulfillment in all that God knows is good for us. She tells us that there is an angry dog in the room that will hurt us. That vicious mongrel is the evil that is rampant throughout the Earth. If you ever wondered why God allows evil to run amok in the world, you might consider that it is because He knows we will all flee for our lives into secure confines that He has provided until He comes home to get us. And if we are obedient to His Mother, we will always be out of harm's way in Her protective embrace. Our Lady wishes us to accept the comfort and protection of Love before it is too late. There is no guarantee that we will make it back to our shelter before being grabbed by Satan if we continue to play near his perilous turf. If we abandon prayer and holiness, we are vulnerable to temptation and destruction.

After this parable, I asked the Holy Mother a question that was of great importance to me. Are we seeing God the Father when we witness Love in the world? She said that when we see Love, we are living His intent. She said that we cannot yet see our Omnipotent Creator because He is alive in Heaven and yet unseeable to us. But, He still lives in Christ Jesus in the Most Blessed Sacrament and through the Holy Spirit in our hearts with the same presence that He lives in Paradise. He is somewhat like an invisible oceanliner moving through the water. We see the displacement of the water where it rests, the lifting of the waves as it cuts its way forward, and the wake it leaves behind. We recognize the mighty effect of God in the world even though we cannot yet see Him with our eyes. But still, some people fail to notice the beauty of an oceanliner they can see!

When we see people living Love in the way of Christ, we are seeing God's Will being done. We are not inhibiting His desires when we pray to understand what they are. And too, God responds to man's inhibitions by allowing us to ask ourselves why we are so helpless without Him. That is the reason prayer is such a revelation of the Father's intent for His Creation. It is an act of thanksgiving to Him which allows the Earth to be made new again. Our vision of Love is our living example of what is to come. And, the perfection of this venue is the task that Our Lady has taken on. She wishes us to see Love through faith in the way that She sees the Beatific Splendor of Heaven at this moment. If we can even attempt this great prayer, our conversion is at hand. We must remember Her words, " **The ultimate and most important vision of Love is for mankind to see Jesus as He is present in the Holy Eucharist. This is the vision of faith that I have asked you to embrace. The ultimate prayer of Love is to tell My Son that in your heart, you know that He is the Eucharist.**"

Our Lord's true, physical, and transubstantiated presence in the Holy Eucharist is the complete and miraculous Mystery of the Will of God. It is Love incarnate that God asks us to believe this without question. If you have difficulty accepting this Truth, you would have been one of those who rejected Him as the Messiah 2000 years ago. The knowledge that Christ is the Holy Eucharist comes in our act of faith and the return of our love to God as He convokes His Blessing upon us by offering His Son in the Blessed Sacrament. Human love for our Immortal God is the source of our passionate conviction. And, the spoken truth to our souls is that Jesus is the Most Blessed Sacrament. All of this reverential knowledge is strengthen by our prayers to God. He does not validate the presence of Jesus in the Holy Eucharist through human eyesight because He knows that our majestic display of trust will come through our faith alone. We are invited to see the Son of God through the eyes of His Holy Mother. We can permeate the dark lives we live and be protected from the cold winds of despair in Her care. We will be perfectly united with the glories of Heaven if we follow Her to the Saving Cross. We will then see and know every soul God has created in perfect unity. There are no strangers in Heaven. Let us say to Jesus, *"...may we see, may we know, and may we hope for love of You."*

Saturday, May 23, 1992

Today, Our Lady tried to get me to slow down. She says that I often act on impulse and do not move peacefully about. This is a function of the mind absent of the placid temperament of the heart. And, it can lead to great disturbance when a group of quick-thinkers try to pool too many ideas and suggestions that are not agreeable to all who participate. It can lead to actions which have undesirable results. The fast pace we often live does not allow time for peace and patience to elevate our pious attributes that reveal the Will of God. Our Lady also responded to a question I asked last night about the Holy Eucharist so I could better understand this precious Sacrament. I simply stated, *"How is Jesus present in the Holy Eucharist?"* I wanted to know what She sees while looking at the Sacred Host. She said that the fact that I posed the question reveals a discouragement in my faith about Her Son's presence in the Blessed Sacrament. She said that when I ask "how" He is present, it is like asking what color is the number "2." The knowledge that His presence is absolutely factual is in no way connected to "how" He gets there. He is the Blessed Sacrament because God wishes us to partake in the Thanksgiving of the Crucifixion of His Son.

The answer to the question of "how" lies in the miracle and power of a priest to consecrate bread and wine into the Body and Blood of the Savior of the world. Again, we are asked to faithfully believe this without question. The truth in which we love God and each other is the same truth that tells us that the Messiah of God is the Holy Eucharist. Once the heart opens to receive that revelation, it cannot be destroyed. Our Lady asked me, "**Do you see the Holy Eucharist as Jesus?**" I responded "*yes.*" Then She said, "**That is also Who I see.**"

Monday, May 25, 1992

Again, I am given the grace to know the perfection of God through His sinless Mother, the Virgin Mary, as She came today to enlist my aid in giving Her messages to the world. She takes my thoughts up-and-away from my daily cares. She places my human mind in a framework of immortal dimensions, as my heart is lifted above the Earth. I keep hoping that my interaction in the world will not pull me back into a material rhythm like the daily tick of a massive clock sitting on Christ's night-stand. I do not wish that we, as a people, will ever pervert or misinterpret Our Lady's purposes for coming. Perhaps, I do not trust humanity because of the awful scourges we have already allowed to be perpetuated. Sometimes, I think that we are so catastrophic and ruinous in nature that if we were fish, we would assuredly find some way to drown. But, Our Blessed Mother keeps my hopes alive. While She chastises humanity for our sinful omissions, She also tells us how special we are in the eyes of God. The Father, Son, and Holy Spirit love us intensely and without end. Their guidance and care take us to the immortal threshold through which we will soon pass into the blinding Eternity that rests beyond the ages.

Our Lady came again today to tell me more about this blessed transformation we will eventually come to know. She continued a discussion that She began on Saturday about the level of consciousness that confines the human mind. During the process of the day, our intellect is battered by a veritable barrage of impulses and stimulations. Normally, we are able to process and prioritize them in accordance to our needs and their importance. They cause very little impact on our capacity to think or the constitution of our memory. She showed me a picture that looked somewhat like the profile of a bunch of jumping beans under a handkerchief. The surface of the fabric is likened to our level of consciousness which is affected by our inner thoughts. Usually, the stability of our mental health is not lost in the process of our normal interaction with the environment.

However, there are some poor souls who suffer mental and emotional impairment which breaches their normally-accepted ability to behave in a stable way. To illustrate this point, Our Lady showed me a picture of the same profile of bean-like shapes under the cloth. But this time, one of the seeds had ripped through the surface of the fabric up into the air above. She said that this parable was symbolic of someone whose level of consciousness had been ruptured. It is caused by the suffering of conditions that have no place of rest in the mind. These poor individuals lose their logical means of disseminating and processing mental images and information. The systematic framework of their mind has been pathologically altered and their brain chemicals become imbalanced. This is the basis for all mental illness.

While I was not bored with Our Lady's message of today, I was assuredly confused as to why She would present such a clinical discussion of the functions of the human mind. She told me that She wanted me to recognize the fragility and frailty of our mental constitution for purposes that She would explain later. For today, suffice is to say that I understand that the world impedes our progress toward our peace of mind. And, Our Lady told me that these people must be allowed to heal without pressure. We must never approach someone and say, "Why don't you snap out of it?" The healing process requires our humble patience with those who suffer. We must be receptive of those who have experienced this type of illness. We become stronger ourselves and more compassionate when we understand that those who are afflicted are actually the victims of physical and mental distress that we may not truly be able to know on our own. We must allow the breach in the fabric of their mind to heal through the pouring-forth of our great love for them. Our Lady asked me to pray for their *compos mentis* until She comes to give another message.

Wednesday, May 27, 1992

I began to pray the Holy Rosary tonight at eight o'clock in the evening and the Mother of God came to speak to me again. I was thrown quite aback by Her last message because I thought Her intention would always be to address the faculties of the heart as it is given completely to God in Love. She chose to discuss the recesses of the mind and the manifestations which cause mental instability. The first thing She asked me to do tonight was to pray with Her for all who are afflicted, those who are physically infirm, those living in poverty, and everyone who is being held captive against their will. She also prayed with me for the end of abortion and the safe-delivery of all unborn children into birth. We had no more than finished these important intercessory prayers when She again continued Her discussion about mental impairment. She told me that there are many who misconceive the mind as being an independent and powerful source which is capable of self-sufficiency beyond the control of God, Himself. (Then I knew exactly why She was talking about the constructs of the human mind.)

The Holy Virgin continued by saying that many believe that the mind has a supernatural power to physically change the world from within. They errantly concoct a notion that they can generate thoughts to project forces for the purpose of altering Creation. Our Lady issued a stern warning for me to avoid these people because they do not invoke the universal power of the Holy Spirit of God. What they claim as miraculous powers are the works of evil spirits and the influences of "trance-channeling" which are separate from the mind of God. Those who study the powers of the mind as a form of "religion" are very far from the Kingdom of Heaven. They have no power at all to perform benevolent works on behalf of Jesus Christ. They may try to imitate His healing grace toward the purpose of a later scourge of evil; but they will be forever dead in the process of ignoring the sanctifying Sacrifice of the Crucifixion of their Savior. There are no solar or lunar influences that the mind can possess. And, no one can harness the genius of Almighty God without touching Him through heartfelt prayer. He, then, changes the world through the Love in His Heart.

In the final analysis, it was not the mind of God that kept His Son nailed to the Cross. It was the infinite Love for humanity in Jesus' Sacred Heart that brought Him to be tortured and bleed to death to save us. Hence, the heart filled with Love is the only true, universal, and ultimate power that can stand the test of Eternity. The human mind is a function of the mortal will, and nothing more. The heart is the true receptacle and reflector of the indomitable power of God across the universe. The mind cannot know Love if it is not in tune with the heart. Moreover, the theory that the mind controls this world is precisely the reason why it is in such a pitiable condition. Our intellectual capacities are a feeble competitor against the evil forces of worldliness, temptation, and sin. There has been a parade of mortal geniuses pass through the ages; and the fruits of their work have been atomic bombs and supermax prisons. If the knowledge of these individuals would have been enlightened by the Love of Christ, they would have instead developed ways to house every homeless soul and cure any illness in sight.

That is why the mortal mind is not capable of Love. Christ affirms that His spiritual home on Earth is the human heart. That is where true benevolence begins. His commitment is permanent, uncompromising to any naysayer, unchanged from the day of His miraculous conception in the womb of His Mother, and always clear to the open of heart and simple of soul. Love is life walking; while human thought is the mortal floor. It cannot be caged at a level of consciousness or limited by the inadequacy of human action; nor can it be diminished by the bonds of physical movement. Jesus Christ is this power within us and is thrice unconquerable, Father, Son, and Holy Spirit. We who have chosen to abandon our whole heart, mind, body, and soul to Him are the children of Light who will gain eternal health for all who are mentally, physically, or spiritually afflicted. Our prayers are the undoing of any evil that may try to infiltrate the commons that Christ has reclaimed for God the Father in Heaven.

Our Lady told me tonight that there is no inherent need for drug-induced inhibitors for depression and anxiety. The Love of God given freely through His children on Earth is all the medicine they require. There is no requirement for chemicals for the mentally stressed and no reason to punish those whose actions are affected by it. It is Love that heals the world and makes all things new. Institutional laboratories are no match for the restorative power of Christ's convalescent grace. We must stand by those who are afflicted instead of remanding them to cold rooms in dark buildings. We must be the ones who will emulate the Crucifixion of Jesus for the world. It is from the shores of our hearts that we must signal those lost in despair and hopelessness that their Savior lives in us for them. In a world filled with indifference, God asks for our conviction, commitment, and holiness, wishing that our ego would be supplanted by meekness and humility. And, He forthrightly desires our endurance and joyfulness in the gift of the days He bestows upon the Earth until He sends His Son to take us to Paradise. We must forgive others so their healing can begin. It is our dutiful assignment to run to protect the dignity of their souls through our own sacrifices and penances. That is what it means to bear with one another in the struggle of returning our love to the Glory in the heavens from whence it came.

Thursday, May 28, 1992

If persistence is the key to success, then the efforts of Our Lady are going to be a great benefit for both Heaven and Earth alike. The only other word besides Love that She keeps repeating is, "**Pray, pray, pray**!" Her message is that we truly cannot Love in the way of God unless we petition Him from the depths of our hearts. That is the source of Light that She continues to ask us to reveal. The fitting comparison that She makes is that prayer gives us a lofty vision of the heavens above rather than the confining lateral two-dimensions of the directional world. Jesus came into our existence to destroy sin and show humanity how to love with restorative grace. He asks us to live this same Love by recognizing its fruit in others and nurturing it within ourselves. The Virgin Mary has come back into the same world where She was once born and raised to be the Mother of God. And, She hastens to remind us that God has not sent Her to prove that He exists, but because He loves all of His children so much that even He wishes to help in the conversion that is quite our own responsibility to effect. This leads to the paradoxical nature of the intercession of Our Immaculate Queen. Those who already live the faith that God is in Heaven and loves them dearly are precisely the ones who discount Her miraculous presence to assist in our conversion. "I already know what She wants," it is often heard said.

Many people proclaim that they do not need miracles to augment their faith or to bring the world to perfection. But, they have not the foggiest idea that to ascend to the highest grace, we must heed God in every admonishment and accept every gift He places forth. Our Lady's messages are not a novelty that we can accept or reject. She is the true presence of the Divinity of God in our modern-day lives. She is the Mother of the very Eucharist which gives us Life! So many observe Her appearance with somewhat the notion of, "That's nice...", but do not comprehend the urgency of the reason God has sent Her. Of course She is beautiful in Her station as Queen of Heaven and Earth; but Her intercessory power is an advocacy we cannot afford to take lightly. We must not look at each other just to see how certain individuals are reacting to Her so that we can choose the depth of our own faithfulness by comparison. Each of us must lunge forward in active exchange with this Lady of Light to listen to Her words and respond in obedience, just like Jesus did when He was growing into maturity.

We take the intercession of Our Heavenly Mother for granted when we should be asking Her to teach us, "More, more, more..." She is the beginning of our final transformation into the souls Jesus will come to judge. We are creatures of habit in that we know God is somewhere, but we never really care to be exposed to His wishes. It is the same as our awareness of the library in the courtyard, but we never really stop to think that it began with only a single book and grew from there! God wants us to become unified with His creative power so we will understand His inner-thoughts and the depth of His Love for us. We do the same on Earth for ourselves. The library, for example, is composed of a large contingent of an artifact called a "libre." Hence, the collection of their numbers is a "libre-ary." A deposit of words is found in a "diction-ary." The place of solitude and prayer is the "sanctus-ary", or sanctuary. Each of these is founded upon an original thesis and premise. We know the inner-being and intentions of our work by what we build and how we are represented. And, it is much the same with our faith in God. We understand the word "convert" as a noun that we know describes the acceptance of Christianity. But, we falsely assume that we may already be there. Our Lady has come to continue our "conversion" because we need to continue in active participation with God to complete our transformation into perfection.

Faith is more than a place, it is a living state of the human heart. Just as the root of the sanctuary is "sanctus", the root of our faith is our prayerful love for God and each other. Its origin came on the day Jesus was born and culminated in His Ascension back into Heaven. Now, we are living amongst the fruits of His Life, still guided by His Love present in the Holy Spirit. Our faith tells us this only because His enlightening Wisdom gives us the power to know. Heaven is the place we seek, faith is our knowledge, prayer is our strength, and Love is the Way, the Truth, and the Life. And if we wish to find all of this in a building, all we need to do is attend Holy Mass and look for the letter "E", the Holy Eucharist. This is the powerful and all-encompassing Sacrament that binds all the others together because the Most Blessed Sacrament is Love, Himself. Our Lady is calling everyone who knows this Truth to stand on that power and utilize its fruit to change the world. Those of us who have received the grace to know are responsible in God's eyes to saturate the Earth in His Love by the work of our own hands. We must transform our excellent potential to Love into real manifestations of good will and evangelization.

Jesus asks us to take-up our crosses in complete abandonment to the Almighty Father in union with His own. We must burn inside with a passionate Love for everyone, even the most wretched. This is not the time for those who claim their allegiance to Christ to suddenly change their mind because they are being asked in faith to sacrifice more than they originally wished to give. God will not allow them to turn away from Him in such indifference. His teaching, exemplified by His Immortal Son, is that true Passion is sorrow for the sins of humanity. That is the fervent zeal we must embrace to lift us from our complacent darkness. It is the bedrock vision we require to show us that the world is filled with unchecked evil and wanton blasphemy. These scourges cry-out for reparatory prayer. We have lost sight of the intentions flowing from God's Kingdom and have forfeited our hope that the Almighty Father hears our prayers. We should not be intimidated by the inherent lack of human spirit in response to the heavens. We must forge-on because our Beloved Father hears the cries from our loving hearts which yearn for the new Heaven and new Earth.

The age has come for Creation to be remade before our own eyes. This is history's "crunch time" because our birth into Eternity is at hand from the womb of the Mother of God, given to us from the Cross by Christ Jesus, Himself. We hear His final words in the Book of John, **"Behold your Mother!"** At that moment, the Virgin of Nazareth became the chosen Creature who is about to immaculately conceive every child of God into the waiting arms of their Savior, Jesus. Her miraculous appearances and manifestations around the world are the nourishing and gestating Love that is strengthening us for our new Life in Heaven. Her prayers are the very Life-blood of holiness being fed to our infant souls. Our transforming return to God is in the very near offing. It is time for us to hope again, to believe again, and to cast away every shroud of darkness where we have laid timidly out of the sight of Heaven for far too long. Our purpose in Love and Life must begin anew, and now!

Virgin winds are blowing across the Earth. Breezes of brotherly affection are stirring in all corners of the globe. Holiness is swirling a sigh of relief into the cracks of broken hearts. Whispers of comfort are providing a gentle touch to enkindle the dying flickers of hope amidst crushed human dreams. God's beautiful Spirit is finally being allowed by mankind to march across the soul of Creation again. He is calling with commanding resonance for peace and unity among all peoples. We have no alternative than to arrive at the undeniable conclusion that He is the King of the Universe, the Life, the Love, the Way, the Truth, and the Light of our final destiny. He holds all of this power as He,

Himself, is held in the arms of His Holy Mother Mary. We must also run to Her waiting arms for freedom from the destruction and terror of the world that is all around us and ominously approaching with an even greater ferocity.

Sunday, May 31, 1992   Feast of the Visitation of Mary

Today, Our Lady has come to reveal Christ to the world with the same perfection that She bore Him as our Savior on Christmas night. She brings us the Holy Balm which will heal the world. He is the teacher of forgiveness and elevator of human dignity. This Jesus provides a multitude of avenues through which we can love one another, while working in our own small ways to show others that they are special to us. We may write a note, present a token gift, or perhaps offer a simple smile or handshake. Whenever we do these things in Love, we do them in the name of Christ Jesus. We cannot worry that those to whom we offer our love may feel patronized. We must simply love and the Holy Spirit will do the rest. Through this humble affection, we can destroy bitterness, hatred, poverty, hunger, and division on every path that we walk.

Our Lady gave me a short parable today that exemplifies people who do not see the need for small acts of charity. She even criticized many Catholics who are seen by others as being stuffy and arrogant. I was asked to ponder the image of someone driving an automobile while trying to maintain a speed of sixty-five miles-per-hour for an extended period of time with a broken speedometer. The farther they travel, the less-able they are to control their speed because of the character of the road and the self-conditioning brought by the motion of the car. After traveling at fifty-five mph for a distance, then seventy for a while, this person does not recognize the variation. This is the deception that many people fail to perceive who believe they know all there is to understand about Love. They have no awareness that they are slowing down or that their own definition of paradisial acclimation may not be the same as God's expectation of them. In their own mind, they no longer have a need for a speed indicator. This simple parable shows that we are traveling the road to holiness in ways that are not always acceptable. We need a speedometer to help us realize the pace of our efforts. The Blessed Mother is this indicator who tells us whether we will arrive at perfection in the way that Christ seeks before He returns to the Earth. Just as a carpenter cannot build a house without a hammer, we cannot build our lives on faith without the gift of Our Lady's intercession. She repeatedly impacts our souls with Her words, **"I love you, I love you, I love you..."**

JUNE 1992

Monday, June 1, 1992

The Holy Mother did not make a physical or audible appearance to me today, but I know She was with me as I prayed the Holy Rosary. I have made this entry in my Diary to reveal my heart. Page after page, my effort is to convince everyone how much Jesus and Our Lady love us. I would now like to describe how I love you in ways that you will understand because I can see that we mean everything to God and each other. You are the souls who will complete the joy that I will live in Heaven. It is because of you that I will look to Jesus and say, *"Thank you for creating us."* For now, it is you with whom I share this mortal exile. And, together we hope and struggle, arm-in-arm, to finish our journey to the destination of Eternal Happiness. Jesus has a Paradise that awaits our arrival because He knows we will do as He asks, **"Love one another, as I have loved you."** But, the world seems populated with souls who pass on the street that are too closed to care that another yearning heart in the likeness of their own is just an arm's length way. We avoid making eye contact with our brothers and sisters in the hope that we will not have to be concerned with what burdens them. The touch of hearts which Jesus asks of us is buried in our own philandering and sinful nature.

The messages from the Blessed Virgin which I have recorded make it possible for us to transcend all our limitations and meet heart-to-heart on these pages. Her work is a great gift from God that shows that all we truly own is our love for each other. The millions who read this manuscript will likely see one another for the first time in Heaven. But, we do not have to wait to be one spirit and body if we collect ourselves in the saving grace of Jesus Christ. Through Him, I can already see the most intimate places in your humble hearts. They are very much like mine in that you desire to be held and protected from the ferocity of the world which is desperately attempting to destroy our bonds of affection and unity. Our Lord asks us to be like Him in all ways! That means we must shed ourselves of every transgression and avoid the near occasion of sin. We should allow His Holy Spirit to unify our hearts as we march together to receive His Eucharistic Body and Blood, the Bread of Life, who lives now in the Tabernacles of the world.

We must multiply the moments which produce great strides toward Christian unification. To that end, I forever promise my most noble effort so I will never be a burden on your souls or the cause of the loss of your happiness and fulfillment. And maybe if God's Divine Plan provides the opportunity, we will meet in this world not with distant eyes, but in an embracing caress of hearts bathed in tears of forgiveness. I have included these sentiments to help you know that I love you as Jesus Himself. I would happily lay-down my life for the cause of your happiness, conversion, and Salvation.

I need your unity with me so Our Lord may be worshiped and adored as He rightfully deserves. There is no greater sacrifice and no taller Love than that which He gave at the Eternal Moment of mortal history on the Cross of Mount Calvary. It is Love as Love truly lives, who is about to Return to the Earth in Glory and power. We will meet on that day for sure. Please look for me; I will be the one wearing the shirt bearing the words, *"I love you."*

Wednesday, June 3, 1992

Our Lady returned this evening to offer Her beautiful Love to all of Her children once again. This is a special week for the world. It is the celebration of the completion of the Blessed Trinity as the Holy Spirit descended upon the Church during Pentecost. The revelation of God as Three Divine Persons in Creation was manifested ten days after the Ascension of Christ into Heaven. It completed the Plan which would transform humankind into the likeness of Jesus and usher-in the beginning of Eternity. This Spirit is God Himself still alive and present in our mortal world. His Holy Spirit is Love in every sense of Divinity. The union of human hearts is made possible through the common thread of virtue provided in the Paraclete. The world tends to diminish our awareness of this infinitely sustainable power. When a loved-one travels to a distant place while we remain at home, we feel the emptiness created by the distance. But, we cannot see the reality that we go with them in spirit, hope, and prayer in the same way that they remain at home in our hearts. This feeling of separation cannot bind the transcending nature of the Holy Spirit. Indeed, the Spirit of Christ is the reason we are not isolated from one another or from God the Father. Jesus resides in every heart which welcomes His Love. We gain the strength and knowledge that those we love will also live in Paradise with us forever.

Our Lord Jesus is never separated from His Spirit. When we see love being shared from heart-to-heart through charitable works and acts of mercy, we are truly seeing His living presence manifested through His people. We represent Him when we live in accordance to the teachings of His Son. And we, ourselves, precede Christ upon the Earth while awaiting His triumphant Return. This is the same truth that lives as the Spirit of Jesus who has already preceded His own Second Coming to redeem all who accept Him. Again, God shows His precedence and finality, the Alpha and the Omega, which encradles our lives in ways yet unseen by mortal eyes. But, we witness His glory more clearly as each day unfolds. Our Lady told me today that the most responsible and blessed human act that someone can undertake is to love Her children in the image of Jesus. It shows our acceptance of His Life and the power of His Crucifixion. And during this week when we prayerfully ponder the manifestation of the Holy Trinity, we must remember that only God has the power to succeed Himself into the Creation He owns. All we can do is pray and serve. In His eyes, that is enough for now.

We must go to the Lamb of the Cross because He is the authority that engulfs and transcends all mankind and the effects of being human. This is the omnipotence of His Love. The Holy Mother assures us that when we live in the Spirit of Christ, we are not doing it on our own. He is with us to teach, guide, bless, and heal. God reciprocates all actions and events that are offered in His name. We are absent of mortal will and intellectual thought when we place ourselves completely in the hands of the Holy Spirit. This is the essential impression of Jesus on our souls, just as a starfish leaves its indented figure in the sand. We must turn moreover to such abandonment to the Lord of All. He will tender our hearts into peaceful silence because He is the Dove of Peace who lights where there is the tranquility of prayer and serenity. That is why Our Lady so much desires us to intone the Mysteries of the Holy Rosary.

Indeed, it is our lack of prayer that allows the corruption of sin and violence to fester throughout our culture. When we pray, we force all evil spirits back into the confines of Hell. That is the power of the Holy Rosary. Evil is no match for the righteous strength we gain when we recite the Hail Mary on the Rosary Beads. Such prayer unleashes the glorious power of the Holy Spirit throughout the globe because Our Lady summons His assistance for the children who are calling through the words, "Hail Mary!" The Rosary confounds the proud and casts the mighty down from their self-appointed thrones. It lifts-up the lowly and downtrodden by taking them to the living truth who prophesies that those who are last will be first. We gain a Divinity through the Rosary that we could never before know. It is a prayer with the Mother of the Holy Spirit who asks Jesus to perform another miracle for the marriage of humanity to perfection.

Thursday, June 4, 1992

Learning about holiness from our Blessed Mother is, indeed, an experience of soul-searching proportions. She has confirmed the facts of the Catholic faith, the infallibility of the Pope in Rome, and the truth in the grace of the seven Holy Sacraments. I have gained increased fidelity toward the Church and the active presence of the heavenly Hosts through this Lady of supernatural Wisdom. I have also acquired the knowledge that faith can come to any heart that is touched by Love. This is a testament to Christ's converting power. I have also come to better know the omnipotent ascendancy of the Almighty Father, who lives proportionately present in the Divine Trinity. Once we have gained a complete understanding of that, we will realize more fully that Christianity is not a mere eclectic procession of random alternatives. Jesus is the single and sole Son of God, born of Mary in a manger, and manifested to this day through the Holy Spirit. Anyone who comes to your door two-by-two proclaiming to be witnesses for Christ and, yet, denies the existence of the Holy Trinity is preaching heresy and error. Our Lady has allowed me to know the beauty in the nature of man when we are united with Her thrice-blessed Son.

I now know that fanaticism in Christian propers is a virtuous piety. And, an eccentric with a Rosary in his hand is as powerful as any nuclear weapon in destroying vice and indifference. I thank the Blessed Virgin for widening my awareness of the graces that God has placed within our reach. Unfortunately for us, we never use them to their fullest potential. I beg you to share my newfound knowledge by praying for the world to be converted to Jesus for Salvation. Today, Our Lady came calling to remind me to remember the precious unborn in my daily petitions. The second thing She asked me to do is to be more happy. I often think about how ironic Her request is for me to find some new elation in the ongoing world because She has been telling me for months how far humanity is from Love. How can I be happy about that? But, She insists that I should find hope in Her intercession and in our prayers that the world is changing every day. I know that human life is filled with unhappy hearts, those who are unfulfilled, and others who are suffering outright rejection and persecution. The only gratifying suffering known to humankind is that which we do out of Love. Those who say that they suffer gladly for others best do so when they offer their sacrifices in the name of Jesus.

I have been thinking since yesterday about the message our Heavenly Mother gave regarding the Holy Trinity. My meditation is founded upon how the descent of Jesus' Spirit manifested the completion of the Trinity. I have also been wondering whether He existed before He was born as a Man on Earth. As always, Our Lady responded today to allay my questions so I would not be distracted from my prayers. She asked me to remember that God is timeless. Therefore, the Holy Trinity has always existed as one in being with the Almighty Father. The process of effecting His Divine Presence upon mankind began with the birth of Jesus, who came to save the world. God's intention to take us back to Paradise existed long before Adam and Eve ever sinned. Therefore, there has never been a time when Jesus did not exist. Each Person of the Holy Trinity has always been present in the powerful Love of the Godhead. Our Lady told me that my understanding of His Infinite Nature is impeded by my inherent assumption to expect all events to follow a sequence of time. The Omnipresent Creator does not live by such parameters. Love is neither influenced nor truly contained by time. Even the 33 years of Jesus' Life was an immortally timeless event, just as the Crucifixion is outside the boundaries of both the calendar and clock. But, when we view the incalculable aspect of Eternity, we realize that the Creation of the universe itself was an act outside of linear moments because it was a manifestation of the Love of God.

Our sins have caused the necessity of time. When Christ died to destroy the darkness, our souls became as timeless as His own. That is the vantage point where we observe our superceded mortality as the beginning of Eternal Life in Heaven. God has no past or future and Creation has always existed. The seven day record of the making of the Earth in the Book of Genesis is for the purpose of our understanding that God created "something" out of "nothing." Only He has that power because He is the original Love that has always been. And in an irony only His Nature can effect, He had no beginning and will have no end; but His Sacrificed Son is the Alpha and the Omega. Our Savior is the infinite and timeless God in human flesh with a date of birth and time of death. When the Holy Bible states, *"In the beginning..."*, it does not mean the beginning of God or the origination of Love. It refers to the tangible effect of the His Love through which He created the world. The Bible is written so that we will understand that the Almighty Father is the Creator of all things inside and outside of time. He created the world in a period which evolved to be six rotations of the Earth on its axis. The first day existed in His mind before it ever began. When we say that in God, all things are possible, we are not simultaneously affirming that all things are probable. Therefore, His Holy will is the only truth that matters in the universe. He has the authority to change whatever physics necessary to render us helpless to determine that He may act is some preconceived way.

To be quite simple, God owns all He created, including ourselves. He commanded us to inhabit the Earth and to be fruitful and multiply. We hold dominion over all that is below the heavens; but we are only its temporary custodians because of the fall of Adam and Eve. If not for the Salvation we gain through Christ Jesus, we would lay forever under the soil where we stand. But, He has made our souls as timeless as Himself through the torture He suffered on the Cross. He is the Second-Person of the Trinity, the Suffering One whose Life and death restores our souls to perfection and grants us Life eternal. He provided mankind a means to measure our imperfection in comparison to God. The Lord does not have to count the days; but we have to do all things mortal to keep ourselves alive. We see the passing years that only render us even more helpless. This is why it is imperative that the world accept the Crucifixion of Jesus as expiation for our sins. When He died, Christ said that He would rise again and take all souls in union with Him to Heaven. He, indeed, rose on the third day as He said because He is Truth. Just as His own Resurrection was fulfilled in His word, so ours will be fulfilled when He comes again in Glory to judge the Earth and reclaim the children of Light. In God's time, He has already come. But, not yet in ours. We are still watching the sun rise and fall over opposite horizons, waiting for the glorious Return of this One Father, One Son, and One Holy Spirit, Triune United and Divine. We are the Mystical Body of Christ that He will momentarily come back to redeem.

But, we must not just sit back and wait! This is our exile, the time for us to prepare for this great Coming of Divinity. We must strengthen our capacity for sharing Love, growing our faith, performing works of penance, and sacrificing ourselves for the good of our brothers and sisters. Such self-denial intensifies our union with the perfection of Heaven and takes us closer to the heavenly Hosts. Our lives bear much greater fruit than we can see with our eyes. And, our prayers for the poor souls in Purgatory gain their release into Eternal Bliss so they can intercede reciprocally on our behalf. Our Lady says that these yet unfulfilled souls are detained in Purgatory not by a sentence of time, but rather as a reflection of how we pray for them. If we ask our Heavenly Father to release them, He will do it. Many have said that God could end the reign of evil on the Earth with the snap of His fingers. That snap was the Crucifixion of His Son 2000 years ago which flows through time to this day. If we embrace the Cross, we are manifesting the destruction of the evil that lost the battle to Jesus Christ on Mount Calvary. We best invoke the power of the Cross through our prayers and attendance at Holy Mass.

Jesus seeks such reciprocation of His Love. His execution was the greatest prayer the Earth will ever know for the future of mankind. He simply asks us to accept it by offering prayers of our own. And, the descent of the Holy Spirit at Pentecost gave us the power to pray in the ways that please our Almighty Father in Heaven. If we do not welcome this Spirit, we will continue to be an errant humanity. The intention of this message is to show that simple and humble human love shared in the name of Jesus is the way to peace and our own fulfillment. God asks us to look into our hearts to see how special and magnificent His Kingdom is. He will come soon and turn our hearts inside-out like inspecting a ripened peach. He wants to find us rich in love for Him, not soured by the bruising rot of our own indifference and rejection. We pray for ourselves and one another to make our souls savory and sweet to His touch and taste. This is the essence of the messages of Our Lady all over the world. She asks us to pray and become a beautiful crop of souls for Her Son to harvest.

Saturday, June 6, 1992

Thankful for another dawn and the gift of a new day, I walk through my holy labors in trust that my work is pleasing to God. I live in the peace that we are all guided and comforted by the Love of Jesus in our hearts. We cannot fail and will not fall when we protect Him there, away from any new scourge that might dare to accost His Sacredness, and beside our soul so we can feed-upon His strength. My desires and intentions have become those of His Mother, who presented Herself today to ask us to give Him repose in the depths of our faith. She began by telling me that my brother and I have a great deal of work to do for Her Son. We are to remember how special we are in God's eyes as He sees us laboring in His vineyard. He is happy when we flock to the side of our Blessed Lady to learn more about how to become like His beloved Son. The Holy Mother comes to us in every way that God allows. Today, She presented my brother a plaque depicting Her intercession in Mexico. It was a beautiful image of Our Lady of Guadalupe. She told us that Her Shrine in this city is of special significance for the healing and protection of all who pray there. For whatever reason, She also asked us to record the following correlations between Her presence at Guadalupe and my brother's family.

She asked us to record the dates that She listed. The first two apparitions occurred to Juan Diego on December 9th. That is the date of birth of Timothy's father in 1914 and his brother in 1946. On April 27th, Our Lady was declared Patroness of Mexico and a terrible plague of typhus was eradicated. That is the birthday of John, another of Timothy's brothers, in 1948. December 12th is the Feast Day of Our Lady of Guadalupe. It was on that day that Timothy's nine-year-old sister was killed by an oncoming car in 1959. My brother, himself, was born on January 27th. On that anniversary day in 1979, the Holy Father, Pope John Paul II, became the first Pope in history to visit the Shrine of Our Lady of Guadalupe. Finally, Our Lady asked us to record the birthday of Timothy's mother, April 16th. She said that the first year of the 20th century is the exact median between the death of Bernadette in Lourdes on April 16, 1879 and the year of his mother's birth of 1921.

Of course, we asked Our Lady the significance of all this. She simply told us to record it here and it would be explained later. We were reminded of the number 111 that She showed us during the very beginning weeks of Her messages in 1991. She told us to also remember that this number would be quite significant for future reference. It is indicative of the Holy Trinity, One Father, One Son, and One Holy Spirit in One God, $1 + 1 + 1 = 111$. All three numerals are separately one, but the number 111 is also one in itself. To capitalize this combination of holy features, Our Lady said that Pope John Paul II was elected by a college of Cardinals consisting of 111 members. Once we completed our collection of all this data, the Virgin Mother turned Her conversation toward our growing faith. She said that present generations must learn about the Life and Death of Jesus by the teachings passed-on by the written Scripture and the mortal witness of fellow Christians. Some people say that they have never met anyone who was at the Crucifixion who has first-hand knowledge of the Death of Jesus. Therefore, they will not believe because they have not seen. Our Lady is prompt to say that anyone who leaves Holy Mass is a witness to the Crucifixion of Jesus. Their confirmation that Christ died for the sins of the world is as authentic as those who stood on Mount Calvary 2000 years ago.

The Holy Mother continued to speak in an especially intimate way with my brother and me. When I say that She is speaking to me, it is because I am the only one who can hear Her when my brother and I are together. Timothy can hear and see Her when He is alone, but cannot always hear Her when we pray together. This special bond was authenticated while we were alone inside the home of a visionary at Medjugorje, Yugoslavia in December, 1989. Since that time, we have both been trying to live according to the will of Jesus. But, I often feel that I am not as close to Our Lady as She wants me to be.

Sometimes I think I am not winning my struggle to be holy. She also asked me to consider the hundreds of messages I have received from Her and all of the signs of grace and love She has dispensed. My heart is now filled with visions of Love that She has placed there. When I occasionally think that I am still not blessed, Our Lady tells me to compare the gifts I have received to the millions of other souls who would forfeit all they own to hear one word from Her mouth. I have really had to suffer only a little for Jesus. Those who have lost their work, their homes, families, reputations, and have been jailed and persecuted in defense of Our Lady's intercession are those who have lived the witness that Christ will eventually seek from us all. The Holy Mother told me that they drink from the Divine Chalice in a most special way, and that I should look upon these days as the happiest in my life.

Tuesday, June 9, 1992

There are countless questions which arise from the bounty of the intercession of the Blessed Mother. Some of them that have come to mind probably have no easy answers. But, the Holy Virgin is humored by my desire to know. She seems to be flattered by my child-like queries. For example, why do we not have wings to fly, and yet, God has given birds legs with which to walk? Why, after so many centuries, do fish still fall for our worm-on-a-hook ploy? And, why does God have to make it so cold when we want to build a snowman? A pretty snow for a Hawaiian Christmas would be grand! Yes, Our Lady does have a sense of humor when She laughs at my unanswered musings. Then, She tends to the serious matters of the present times. The Blessed Mother came at nine o'clock this evening and offered a great perspective about the Love of God. She referenced a picture of the Divine Mercy that my brother has placed into a sealed transparent plastic case. I think it was originally intended to hold a baseball card for use by collectors.

The Holy Mother said, **"...tonight, the case has the true Champion enshrined. I am so happy. You know that little things like that are very special. This humbleness and love for Jesus is all He requires. That faith of Love which resides in the simple heart affords Him the nicest place to live."** She also spoke to the necessity of slowing the pace of our lives so we can live more in the peaceful union of the Holy Spirit. When we listen quietly to the voice of God, we can detect the smallest distance we need to travel to be perfectly united in Him. We move toward Him in prayer as He comes to us in response. The purpose of our discussion this evening about such peace was brought through a situation at my workplace. Some of us had a disagreement about worldly matters, business, and money: none of which are an interest to God. Our Lady told me that we must refrain from such controversy about productivity, wealth, and power. All our efforts should be for the purpose of spreading Love throughout the world, into every home, and into every heart.

The Virgin Mother has shown Her Love in so many ways that we should be able to conduct ourselves by Her perfect example. But, we are helpless if we do not listen in humble obedience. Jesus sent Her to the Earth to teach us that He is the reason why the world is capable of Love again. We must concede ourselves to His Divine Will. This humble Diary is my concession to God that Jesus is all and everything. And, while I know that not everyone who reads it will believe and obey, there will be many whose hearts will open because of my obedience to His Mother. She affirmed to me today that I will never meet most of you, but I should trust that my work is going forward like a lantern in the night to reach the hearts God already knows will be touched by it. The purpose it brings is that our example in life and the prayers of our hearts are the best message we could ever send into the world. Openness in love and self-sacrifice, compassion, and forgiveness are like magnets that draw all who are open-of-heart to unity under the Cross.

Thursday, June 11, 1992
Inherent in the substance of our Blessed Mother's messages, I can see that God knows the world to be a limitless production of human expression. We teach and learn, devise and control, and encounter and proclaim. Our Lady says that this is our freedom, but it is also our cause of deprivation from the knowledge of God. We are busy with trends and fashions that not only distract us from Him, but also perpetuate the materialism which sustains the retaining-wall that blinds us to His blessings. From the words of the Virgin given in this Diary, I can see that we are to blame for our own distance from God. Yes, we are, indeed, at liberty to express and appreciate; but with that freedom also comes the responsibility to adhere to the call of the Eternal One who allows it. His message of Salvation resounds through Creation from the awful Mount of Calvary, the same mountain ridge that is now the Altar of Sacrifice in the Holy Roman Catholic Church. Therefore, we must embody the bold proclamation of Jesus' impending arrival with our own good faith, excluding no overtures from Him that will take us to higher grace. This, after all, is why our Virgin Mother is calling so urgently, and why we must listen and respond with obedient compliance.

To this end, Our Lady hastened to my side tonight during my prayers. She spoke about the ongoing perversion of the teachings of Jesus and the Church, which results in horrible dissension and disunity of the Christian family. Today was an extension of the message She gave about the Second Vatican Council and the narrow path that leads to Salvation in Jesus Christ. Somehow, in the implementation of Vatican II, certain clergy and parishioners are trying to see just how far God's Mercy will stretch before He puts an end to their desecration of the Holy Traditions of the Mother Church. How indifferent and "protestantized" will He allow them to become? How much apathy and desecration by mankind toward the Most Blessed Sacrament will God allow? The Second Vatican Council states that the Holy Eucharist shall be regarded as the central Sacrament of the Church. After all, it is the Body, Blood, Soul, and Divinity of the Christ who created it. This means that we should do everything in our physical and spiritual power to preserve the dignity of the Eucharist. This does not simply mean that we must keep Jesus central only in our minds and hearts, but also centrally located in the physical composition of the Church.

But, some clergy have incorrectly interpreted Vatican II as allowing the relocation of Tabernacles into places that diminish the importance of the Eucharist to their parishioners. They are, indeed, certifiable hypocrites if they believe this maintains the presence of the Blessed Sacrament as central to the Holy Mass. After all, the purpose of the Mass is the Celebration of the Eucharist. It is also unfortunate that many of these same heretics believe that Jesus becomes physically present in Body, Blood, Soul, and Divinity in the bread offered in Protestant churches. This is one of the greatest lies Satan has ever told! Jesus appears in complete spiritual and physical presence only at the Holy Sacrifice of the Mass offered by priests recognized by the Holy Father in Rome. The incredible perversion of the intentions of Our Lord through the Second Vatican Council by liberal opportunists has led millions away from the Sacrament of the Holy Eucharist. As Our Lady reaffirmed this evening, Vatican II is a work of the Holy Spirit to prepare us to attain the unity that God the Father wishes of all Christians under the Cross of His Son.

Our Heavenly Father wishes to solidify the Truth of Jesus in followers of the faith throughout the world. He never intended the diminishment of our fervent reverence for the Holy Eucharist or to promote the agendas of those who have protested against the Catholic Church throughout the ages. Our Holy Mother wants to heal the divisions between Her children through Her miraculous intercession across the globe. When the servants of Christ do not adhere to the Truth of God as She teaches, Her task is made very difficult. She knows that She was made Mother of the original Catholic Church by Jesus on the day He was Crucified. Those who have left this original Institution are renegade children that She is trying to recall to the Table of the Bread of Life, the Altar of Sacrifice, the Holy Mass. Christ asks us to trust in Her as He also trusts. Our strength to find that abandonment is found in the recitation of the Most Holy Rosary.

Sunday, June 14, 1992

Our beautiful Holy Mother knows very clearly how to raise us from the burdens in our hearts so we can be made presentable to Jesus in joy. And, She knows the nourishment we need to grow on the path to righteousness. We are to be like olive plants around the Table of the Lord. Sometimes I feel like the little plant that has spent its entire existence growing unrestrained in any direction I wish to go. But now, I can feel the holiness of the Blessed Mother cropping and pruning my soul so I will grow straight and true. She is clearing-away my excesses, removing my errant opinions and false-assumptions, and closing the doors to the paths of perdition. She has given me a vision of reality that is being refocused with each passing day. I still have to fight temptation and battle the acidic lies of others about my reputation, but I am being shielded by the shining Light of God that surrounds me and enlightens the path on which I walk. When my brother and I attended Holy Mass today, we saw a mother holding a child in her arms that could not have been more than four years old. She was kneeling in front of a sculpture of the Last Supper showing the child which of the statues represented Jesus and the Apostles. As the child looked forward in awe, his mother described what happened in the Upper Room the night before Jesus died.

I could not help but believe that this is how Jesus wants us all to live the intercession of His beautiful Mother. We must all humble ourselves to learn because it is through our child-like innocence that the Holy Spirit can teach us. And, it is through our humble obedience to His Mother that we can learn how to prepare for His Return. She teaches the virtues of prayer and peace which strengthen our pathway to holiness. Christ has also given us humble priests who powerfully shine forth His image when they live in allegiance to the Holy Father. Together, they continue a singular grace through the vocation of His Holy Priesthood by consecrating bread and wine into the Body and Blood of Our Lord. And that is not the only vocation that is important to Jesus. He fills the world with little children and consecrates the vocation of parenthood upon their very fortunate mothers and fathers. He asks these parents to fulfill the responsibilities of their station in the likeness of His own Holy Family. They should protect these innocent little beginnings of Divine Love who bring Light to Creation through the beauty and purity of their baptism.

Our Lord does not stop there. He has given Creation a world filled with His own children of Light, brothers and sisters who form a Divine orchestration of beautiful humanity. We participate fully in Him by loving and praying, and by entering the Church for the purpose of participating in the many Holy Sacraments. We are told time and again that the Most Blessed Sacrament is the Holy Eucharist. That is God's Divine Will for His Church on Earth. We reach the mountaintop when we receive it, communing on the pinnacle of human faith in action. There we truly come to understand that God loves us to the Death of His Son. Our Lady is trying to convince us of the imperative requirement of our submissive reception of the Bread of Life. She has made that clear in every authentic apparition She has brought to the world. Our souls are made perfect during Divine Communion through the eternal power of Jesus Christ. He regenerates our perfect souls when we accept

His own spotless Divinity in the Holy Eucharist. By the power of Love which knows no bounds, which has no blemishes, and lives without end, we are elevated and purified to sit with Him at the right hand of our Father. We must live in this confidence because Christ commands that we will have no stain when we receive the Bread of Eternal Life.

We must make our love for one another the purpose of our lives, and our prayers the reason we speak. It would truly be better to lose everything in the world we enjoy, every penny to our name, every ounce of respect from our fellow men, and any necessity that our physical being requires than to omit a moment during which we can glorify Jesus and spread His Love throughout the world. This is why we should pray continuously and tirelessly for the Kingdom of God to come. Our hearts open like flowers to a different world when we seek the beatitude of the Saints through humble petition. We see all the infinite possibilities of grace through a humble vision of hope. God will respond to every last desire in the recesses of our heart with a singular glorified Eternity soon to dawn upon the Earth. Everything that the human heart pines to give or receive is already complete and immortalized in the timeless reality of Heaven. Even the scourges that we see here and now are stricken by the prayers we lift to the infinite Glory of Paradise.

We elevate the lowly and weak, feed the physically and spiritually starved, and conceive restored beauty through the same Holy Spirit who gave Perfection to the world through the womb of our Holy Mother at the utterance of Her compliant, **"Yes."** We should thank Her every day for bringing Jesus into the world. And, we should respond to Her call to thank the mothers on Earth for giving birth to their own children and pray for those who woefully choose to abort them. The strength of our devotion and our hope for the infinite and beautiful response of God will end abortion. He hears our plea for those who cannot state their own case. He will answer our call by overpowering this desolation, destruction, and hopelessness. All of these mothers will be saved through the Mercy of Jesus if we pray to make it so.

Tuesday, June 16, 1992

The Blessed Mother exhibits the pinnacle of grace and gratitude to the children who listen to Her call. But, this does not mean that Her back is turned to those who still live in sin and error. It seems that as long as the sun sheds light on the darkness of the world, She is somewhere speaking to anyone who will listen about our Salvation through Her Son. Today is no exception because She came again to my door reveling the omnipotence of God and the Sacrifice of Jesus. He is the Leader Who will take the world to authentic peace and prosperity that will last beyond the ages. All of the great prophets and governors who have preceded Him cannot match His wisdom and desire for His people to not just survive, but to grow in every righteous sense . His Love is more powerful than any public policy and more enlightening than any system of education. If we embrace His perpetual tenure, we will be led away from poverty, disease, and war. The brotherhood of man is consummated in His Sacred Heart.

The Immaculate Conception asserted in Her first messages to my brother and me that the finite nature of human judgement cannot approach the power of the infinite wisdom of God. For this reason alone, we will never be able to survive as a peaceful collection of nations on our own. We must let Christ reign on the Earth that is rightfully His to dominate. But, we refuse to let go. All of the political and environmental activists who spend their time preaching and protesting should turn in prayer to Jesus Christ for the rectification of the problems they seek to resolve. The re-creation of the Earth is a manifestation of the power and authority of the heavens. The roads we travel are horizontal and eventually come to an end. But, the road which Christ has laid for us is elevating and infinite. Hence, our temporary solutions to lifelong problems are weak and ineffective unless we enlist the help of our universal God to remove all that renders Earth less-than Heaven in any way. Quite concisely, Christ must be acclaimed as the King of Creation from every lip that speaks the mortal hope of a resurrected world. This is the only way that we will win the fight against the evil that ravages our lives.

People who live in power in high public places are the prime targets of Satan's perversion and abuse. They will not listen to reasoned judgement or the plight of the poor because they spend their lives in defense of their failed policies and collections of wealth. Their lands are rendered the domain of division, disunity, war, famine, and disease. Peace cannot survive in any nation not given to Jesus Christ because those who lead will not commend their offices to the wisdom of the Lord. Our Lady says that there are many who still believe that Satan can be converted to Christianity. The fact is, he will never be holy or righteous. He has separated himself and all who follow him from God for all Eternity. He is against the Cross of human Salvation in every sense and, therefore, is the prince of darkness whose home will always be the fires of Hell. Anyone who fraternizes with the devil is flirting with disaster and the impending condemnation of their own soul. Satan will never do anything good and must be destroyed because there is no compromise between good and evil. There are no ongoing negotiations between Heaven and Hell that will determine the fate of the souls Christ has saved. God speaks directly to the people who will accept Him, while those who do not will be cast into the fiery pit where their own sweat will sizzle from their dismal faces.

By always praying and living the Love of Christ in the fight against temptation, a soul cannot be claimed by Satan. This is the way to destroy evil from the face of the Earth and not compromise with it by allowing it a place to live next door. When we rely on the invocation of the power of the great

Archangel Michael, we are protected from the fatal forces that try to strip our souls from the grasp of Christ Jesus. This is where our hope lies that the world can become a better place. It is the beauty of the Holy Mother's intercession. She calls on us to pray to Jesus and the great Saints and Angels for strength and protection. In the middle of the world's darkness, the true power of God is beginning to shine again because of the awakening call of Our Lady to sleeping human hearts. When we see conversion to Jesus, we are witnessing the Salvation of souls before our very eyes. And as long as the clock of mortality is ticking, there is still time for our conversion. The pulse of good human intention is still beating, but it is not much of a pulse. We must allow the Holy Spirit to revive our souls and bring us to full awareness of the dire circumstances that engulf the world. There is precious little time for us to proclaim Christ as King from every corner of the globe. Perhaps that is the proper introduction He is awaiting before He steps from behind the curtain dividing Heaven and Earth.

MEETING LOVE IN PERSON
"THE HOLY EUCHARIST"

Thursday, June 18, 1992

I have recently employed a printing company to reproduce a "Holy Card" with a picture of the Blessed Sacrament in a beautiful monstrance and the words of Our Holy Mother on the back. I plan to send several hundred to far-off places by mail in hopes that it will lead at least one soul to our Eucharistic Jesus. And as She often does, the Holy Mother mentioned the card in Her intercessory message to me this evening. She was particularly pleased that I had reserved time to take a photograph of Her Son for such purpose. The monstrance is located in an Adoration Chapel of a nearby Franciscan convent where the precious Sisters have been in continuous twenty-four-hour perpetual adoration of Christ in the Blessed Sacrament since August 2, 1930, which is the Feast of Our Lady of the Angels. Our Heavenly Mother said that the reproductions of the picture are beautiful and She promised to go everywhere I send them. The photograph gives the sense of the truth of Jesus in His undeniable presence in the Eucharist. This is true of any holy relic that we design to elevate Our Lord and His Mother. Our heart describes the feeling and vision that our soul comes to know, especially if it is a written composition of divine and heavenly expression. Such works tell that we, indeed, live in the midst of Paradise. It is proof that the Holy Spirit has come to Earth to live in human hearts. Our Lady added that Heaven can actually be seen in the Holy Eucharist because the Blessed Sacrament is the Body and Blood of Jesus Christ Himself.

Our beautiful Mother told me that many miracles will happen with these pictures. Some of those who open their envelopes to reveal the photograph of Jesus' Eucharistic Sacrament will recognize that they are seeing the Bread of Life for the very first time. Everyone is made whole and is led to the living Church by His Sacrificial Body and Blood. Through our Adoration of Him, we experience the inviting call of the Holy Spirit to come to Heaven. And to assist the world to recognize the graces inherent in the Eucharist, Our Lady said that God will give everyone a special blessing whose eyes greet these holy cards. She told me that when I took this picture, Jesus was not just looking into the lens of my camera. He saw the faces of everyone to whom His presence in this Chapel will be revealed. The opportunity for the Holy Mother to restate the importance of the Eucharist was ripe as She addressed this picture. She said that Jesus sees everyone who comes to adore Him in the monstrance. He sees us to the depth of our souls because He is the Son of the Father who created us. We should yearn to attend daily Mass to receive the Most Holy Bread and answer the call-to-grace given through the Sacrament of Reconciliation, penance, and conversion. This is how the power of the Eucharist flourishes in our hearts as we open them in prayerful invitation to God.

We petition Jesus' power and authority when we receive Communion just as those who lived with Him 2000 years ago called upon Him for healing and Salvation. He loves us in the same infinite degree. The Blessed Virgin says that when the human eye makes contact with the Holy Eucharist, it is the kiss of Jesus upon our souls. And, those who are blind that enter a place of Eucharistic Adoration are given a special blessing known to no others because of their very presence. The Love of Christ is physically transferred into every soul during Adoration. He lives in us in total compassion with the grace of Mercy which is our first sweet taste of the Paradise yet to come. All who wish to be one in Love and strengthened in the fight against evil should come to the Most Blessed Sacrament for such transformation. This is why Our Lady calls everyone to Confession. It is part of our preparation and conversion to the perfection of Jesus. We outwardly profess our sinfulness and invoke the power of Christ to heal us through these Holy Sacraments.

Any soul can come to the cleansing Sacrament of Confession. No sin is too great that it cannot be expunged from a penitent soul. It is the first step on the elevating road to conversion. We should return to its cleansing grace often for strength and renewal so we may remain in full communion with the other Sacraments. And when we are assigned our proper penance, we should see it as a gift of loving sacrifice which delivers our soul into union with the self-denial of Our Lord. We must take-up whatever cross is placed before us because our Christian conscience will never allow us to step over or around it and remain one with Jesus. These crosses are not necessarily all penitential in nature. We are called to live lives of prayer, peace, purity, fasting, and conversion. None of these can be achieved through half-hearted conviction. Jesus asks His children to choose the Life that Heaven promises no matter what we must overcome to get there.

Saturday, June 20, 1992

Within these recorded pages is a simplistic beauty and truth about God that many have never known before. I have often wished to see the faces of everyone who would read this Diary. I wish not to be proud of my work, but humbled that our Blessed Mother is able to intercede before God on behalf of Her children by standing on my soul to be heard. There is no other life that I would choose and no other perfection I could know. There is only one Virgin Mary, who said "yes" to an Angel and perpetuated mankind's original magnification of the Lord. This modest volume contains the intentions of this Matron of Fiat, who blessedly beckons us to affirmation to Her call and the elevation of our hearts. In what continues to be a nearly impossible task, I am trying to place the grace of the Almighty Father inside human parameters, that can truly not be wholly revealed by description alone. Linguistic phrases and literal definitions are insufficient tools in anyone's effort to unveil the majesty and magnitude of Heaven. I have tried to be simple because we are all just little children with a sparse understanding of the Kingdom of God. Anyone who might employ an "attack-dog" approach toward this work by wielding the power of theological authoritarianism will only be confounding themselves because the message of Our Lady is much more candescent than they choose to realize. And yet, Her authenticity and power are also much larger than many are willing to accept.

The dimensional depth of the human mind is not the benchmark for capturing the invincible and unbounded Love that Jesus pours-forth into the world. We have a great distance to travel before we will fully comprehend the infinity of His Love. If we listen to the Queen of Heaven as Her little children, we will trust Her words without question. We may not initially comprehend what we hear, but we will never refute the facts. Our Lady is lifting Jesus in Her arms so we can better see Him. We are asked to look through the same faith that took the Wise Men to the side of the Manger. Then, our hearts will be open to Love, assuming we allow the Holy Virgin to teach us how. She would never break them or violate our trust by giving us anything other than the perfect Love of God. She is gentle to all because She is continuous and timeless in Love. Each time She comes to speak, I can feel the building crescendo that my heart is being filled to overflowing with Light and grace. And yet, Her subsequent appearances somehow reach a peak higher than ever before. She is living proof that Heaven has no boundaries. That is why the ills of the world cannot defeat the Son of the Living God in human hearts.

It seems as though our little hearts do not stand a chance in an environment that is wallowing in materialism and greed. We will not be still and obstinately refuse to live in peace. But, God has infinitely many ways to bring the silence we need to hear the soft voice of His Mother. What would happen in a room of screaming people if someone fired a howitzer cannon amidst all the pandemonium? There would be silence then! This cannon fire is about to come in the form of chastisements if we do not kneel to listen to the heavenly words of Our Lady and accede to the wishes of the Holy Spirit. But, such punishment is not inevitable. When we read the signs God places before us and respond with simple obedience, we will live in peaceful harmony among ourselves and with nature. Everyone must play a part in the great conversion of humanity to Christianity. We must pray and love as one people for the end of violence, disease, and poverty. Hopelessness must be supplanted by the eternal joy of uniting as one people in God. Then, disasters will end in rainbows of prosperity.

A new breath of dignity and honor will destroy war and division. The feathers of human life will rest in supple peace because our sanctity will be at hand. We will be consumed by the everlasting bliss of eternal Light that will never allow a shadow of hatred to darken our infant hearts again. Even though the Gate to Paradise is narrow, it is still sufficiently wide to receive collective humanity in one swallow. Our Lady seeks this peace from Her children because She knows it is the Will of the Father. She pleads with us to pray with Her from our hearts so our vision will become like Her own. We must keep our eyes affixed to that narrow Gate and never lose sight of the promises that lie beyond it. The world is being bathed by miracles at the hands of the Blessed Mother whose grace is single-heartedly guiding humankind to Jesus Christ. We must embrace the power of the Holy Rosary to remain united with Her and the intentions of Jesus for His children.

Monday, June 22, 1992

Our Holy Mother has told me explicitly that the conversion of humanity to Her Son is the precedent to our Salvation. We will never truly know Christ Jesus until we accept His redeeming Sacrifice as the Love that reunites us with Heaven. He cannot lift us up if we fail to first reach-out to Him. We will not be drawn out of the world unless we take His Love to all our brethren around the rest of the globe. This work stands imminently before us, even as we are yet in the infant stages of grasping the significance of His intentions. We must not wait for the final answer or the last day to find out. Christ will come for us in His time and due season. I rest assured upon the hope that I have recently gained from His Blessed Virgin Mother. My faith is renewed every day because Her Wisdom is so eternal and beautiful. She calls us to be blessed because She, Herself, is the essential persona of blessedness. Before She departs each time She comes, She raises Her hand in the sign of the Cross to bequeath us all to the protection of the Holy Trinity. I hope you can see Her motherly Love in your heart as you read this accounting of the gifts She has given to me.

This benevolent Lady told me today about a special opportunity that Our Lord has manifested through our prayerful work. He knows that She is looking for Her children that He commended to Her care from the Cross. These faithful people must surrender themselves to suffer under some very sacrificial conditions in their fight against rampant indifference all over the world. We have the opportunity to show Jesus the depth of our love for Him when we comply to the wishes of His Mother. This is not to say that we will become popular in the eyes of the influential. Jesus told His disciples that the world would hate them, just as He was also despised. He asked them not to compromise their faith by giving-in to temptation and materialism. He knows that perfection in Him is possible; and He tells us this same truth today. I remember a discussion I once had with an elderly woman about the plight that

Christians suffer in reaching-out to others in the name of Jesus. We have been scoffed-at, ridiculed, publicly condemned, and spate-upon in our evangelization of the Good News of Christ Jesus. Her response was, *"Isn't that wonderful!"* Her answer was a great source of Light because I could see the acceptant nature that Jesus asks of His children who are despised and chided in His Name.

We endure all of this and still hold fast to Our Lord's teachings about forgiveness and perseverence. We must tell our brothers and sisters that we have been carried-out to sea by the tide of the world which pushes us away from Salvation. We often sit in the confines of our individual rafts believing that the waters will always be calm. Many of us do not paddle for shore and ignore the ugliness of the ominous clouds overhead. We often gain a false sense of security from inaccurate observations and popular conclusions. The seas of life are rough and we are a long distance from the shores of human perfection. We cannot wait until the last moment to respond to the warnings before our eyes. The roughest leg of our journey is at the shore itself, where the waves and undercurrents of evil lash against our souls with the greatest force. We cannot be assured of not being smashed against the rocks before our souls stand firmly on the sanctifying Truth of Jesus Christ. No matter how peaceful the world may seem, there is a great storm in the offing, when Satan will make his last effort to steal as many souls from Christ as he can.

We must escape to the safe-haven of the Sacred Heart of Jesus because He is our sure lifeline who delivers us to sinless perfection. His peace is not the false security of the world, but an everlasting beneficence that begins the moment we ask Him for help. Our Lady is the Ark of this New Covenant who has come into the perilous ocean to take us to perfection. She asks Her children to board the grace of Her intercession by walking the gangway of penance, sacrifice, prayer, confession, peace, and love. We no longer need to fear the imposing and seductive surf just off-shore because Our Lady is unimpeded by any evil which may fall under Her feet. She parts the worldliness which detains Her children and crushes the head of any diablerie that may dare oppose Her course toward the safe repose of the Sacred Heart of Her Son. We pray for the strength of all who refuse this supernatural and intercessory grace provided by the Mother of Jesus. If we pray our Holy Rosaries with our hearts, they will be the lifelines needed by the lost to pull themselves to safety.

Tuesday, June 23, 1992

Today, Our Lady came to bless my brother and me and join our prayers for the conversion of humanity to Her Son. When we pray and open our hearts, graces fall to Earth like rolling from a heavenly spigot upon the children of God. They are so plentiful and overwhelming that they even splash upon those sitting in the dark. The handle is in God's hands and He turns it on in answer to our petitions like a father responding to a child calling, *"May I have a drink?"* When we pray, we quench the fires of wretchedness and oppression.

We hear the sizzling expungement of hatred being destroyed from the sight of all humankind. And, we wash clean the minds of expectant mothers whose intellectual filth may be about to cause them to enter an abortion clinic. Our Lady also spoke to me about our beloved Bishop. Every bishop has a difficult job during this period in time because of the movement of the world away from the Apostolic Church. The responsibility rests upon them to continue to fight the oppression of materialism and worldliness against our faith.

Evil attacks against the clergy are a horrible scourge, very much like termites eating-away at the foundation of the Church itself. When these holy priests profess their allegiance to their vocation every day, they will not suffer any erosion of holiness like moths consuming their vestments in sacristy wardrobes. God's holy Will has not changed since He ordained the Apostles as the first priests. We must lift them up and defend them against any aggression or attack of evil. They are His special chosen ones who bring the Body and Blood of His Son to the Altar of Sacrifice. The bishops are direct descendants of the original Apostles. They lead the Church in their respective dioceses through the guidance of the Holy Spirit. They are responsible for the conversion of all souls under their care, not just Roman Catholics. They should be held in esteem and honored because of the grace of their office.

Sunday, June 28, 1992

Day by day, the Holy Mother is allowing me to see better through eyes of greater hope and trust in God. I had once thought what a grace it would be to live on Earth with Her as She was rearing young Jesus through His formative years. Would I have befriended this noble lad? Would He be like me in all things but sin? Would I be able to boast to every new generation that He was my closest companion on Earth? Our Holy Mother is making it clearer that Jesus did, in fact, play and jest with a simple mind and joyful heart. He was equally injured by foul words and offended by hatred and malice as He is to this day. Much the same as ourselves, Jesus knew then what He still knows now, there is a stench about a lack of Love and the presence of bitterness in an otherwise opportune world. It was His conviction to change humanity to the depth of our souls that got Him killed of the Cross. That is the reason for the martyrdom of thousands of others since His early days. Their prayer to God was the life they gave so we could all better understand Him. And, unless we listen carefully to the Blessed Mother, we may not deem ourselves fit to join them at the end of time in the heavenly court of honor. Our hearts must, likewise, be as open to respond.

My brother came home very upset today after having been attacked by the malignant forces of evil in a world very opposed to our holy work. He was accosted by someone who vehemently disbelieves in the miraculous intercession of the Blessed Virgin Mary. To make matters worse, this opponent is an officer of public law who used the authority of his office to persecute my brother. The officer has made false accusations and stated half-truths about him in an effort to discredit our work. Many law-enforcement personnel have aligned themselves against the work of Our Lady because Her messages speak in direct contravention to the oppressive use of the power they wield. I pray daily for all who try to impede the work of the Blessed Mother anywhere in the world. Somehow, they must also become united with Her requests for holiness and conversion in the benign peace of Christ Jesus.

I feel very blessed as I offer my prayers in great fervor and thanksgiving to God for allowing me to participate in His work. When God comes calling upon His people for help, our only answer must be "yes" to all that is good and right in His eyes. We must not fall into complacency when we are asked to repeat certain duties that praise His Holy Name and glorify the Cross. Our intense prayers keep our souls focused on the inequities of the world which remind us that there are many of our brothers and sisters who are besieged by evil in ways we can never truly understand. The number of praying children of God must multiply by countless scores. They are now the silent multitude who will one-day rise together to conquer evil and indifference by virtue of their own holiness. Millions of faithful people have remained silent to avoid the terrible persecution that accompanies the evangelization of God through the Holy Spirit. Just as the world crucified Jesus, it will assuredly oppose anyone who attests to His saving grace. It has been this way since the first century. By the same token, some messengers of God have had to be taken into protective seclusion so the work of Our Lady can continue.

The forced resignation-from-office imposed upon my brother is one such example. It was August 12, 1991, just six months after the beginning of our messages. The Holy Mother said that this date should be recognized as the fulfillment of the prophecy of the book of Wisdom. **(Wisdom 18:6-9)** *"For that night was known before by our fathers, that assuredly knowing what oaths they had trusted to, they might be of better courage. So the people received the salvation of the just and destruction of the unjust. For as thou didst punish the adversaries, so thou didst also encourage and glorify us. For the just children of good men were offering sacrifice secretly, and they unanimously ordered a law of justice: that the just should receive both good and evil alike, singing now praises to the fathers."* There are many resigned by fate, some to succeed themselves into the privacy of prayer, while others have resigned in scorn. But, Our Lady's messengers suffer banishment, such as my dear brother. The fruit of their sacrifice is sweet, indeed, because the eternal gifts from the Holy Virgin are unending and powerful. All things work for good for those who love the Lord. The revelations in this writing are living proof for the world. Before leaving this evening, Our Lady blessed us in the Name of the Trinity.

JULY 1992

Wednesday, July 1, 1992

I have more recently been recognizing the scourge of offenses against Love and the many terrible violations against peace and human decency. The world swelters in such a reckless disregard for the Salvation of the human soul that it almost seems impossible that anyone could find Christ in all of the darkness. I am thankful that the Blessed Mother has come to tell me that no one can conceal themselves in a place so dark that Jesus cannot find them. His Light is so bright that it can be reciprocally seen by any soul seeking His favor and forgiveness. Everywhere we look, we see people defining and calculating how large they will allow God to be. Humanity does not seem to realize the magnitude of this perversion and the resultant destruction of the precious life we have been given. There should be no tolerance for evil acts. We must love the sinner, but despise their sin. We see traces of the lives of thousands who have attempted to leave a legacy in their path. Unfortunately for the world, some of these footnotes have been of sorrow, destruction, and despair. As long as they leave a mark, that is good enough to satisfy the hunger of their egoistic appetite. The bequest of others may not be near as malevolent, but their worldly nature renders them to be just as fruitlessly indifferent.

The Holy Mother told me today that it is a signal to history that makes man want to leave a commission for others to recall. Only those who live in Christ leave a lasting impression on the soul of humankind which defies any anthology that could contain their timeless service. But others struggle for the length of their days trying to imprint their names into historical reference. They deal in policy, substance, and material in an effort to secure a dignified worth before the eyes of the world. Unfortunately, most of these achievements are only temporal influences for a passing age. It is simply not true in the eyes of God that, "...the bigger the monument, the greater the man." Only the Cross of Mount Calvary is the legacy of infinite achievement that will stand at the end of time. Jesus' presence in history is, indeed, an immeasurable mark. And those who die defending His name are worthy of the same immortal honor. Anyone who lives a life of sacrificial Love completes a stroke of the Divine brush that paints the masterpiece of Eternity. This is a permanent gift, an eternal flame that cannot be hidden in a closet. Those whose lives are defined by Love leave a definition of life so transcendent that history is too immature to contain it or describe it.

This is the essence of the Life of Jesus Christ; a vast and silent strength of Heart that cannot be remanded to the annals of passing time. He is remembered as the Love who permeates any capacity to circumvent or incarcerate Him. God is not confined to the parameters of writings, works of art, or sculptures. We could compile all of the beautiful literary masterpieces in Creation and they would never come near the simple utterances of Christ the King. His immortal wisdom reduces our inadequate volumes to the size of a drop of water in a thousand oceans. We could exhume every precious jewel from the bowels of the Earth and retrieve priceless gems from all the planets and Jesus would use them for His footstool. We lose our capacity to measure time, distance, and space in a single blink of His eyes. He is, indeed, undefinable and beyond any limit that could be used to define Him. Love cannot be captured by human thought or action because its immortal boundlessness is defined by the very Cross which reveals Him so magnificently. All of our actions are reduced to a subpart of His universal Sacrifice.

As long as we refuse to approach Our Lord with the intention of being perfected in His image, we will be forever confined and detained by our faults. If we continue to live in worldliness and materialism, we will be held bound by the constraints of mortality, severing ourselves from the True Vine by not serving proudly as the branches He puts forth to defend Creation. We must understand the helpless nature in which we live. We cannot flower if we are cut-off from the stem. We will die from spiritual malnutrition because our flesh is consumed by sin which takes its toll by time and fate and leads us to the grave. This is why we need Jesus! He is the sustainer of all human life and the Redeemer of our souls. We will never be free or live Eternal Life until we accept His Sacrifice on the Cross that destroyed our infirmity and restores our nourishment in God. We must seek the forgiveness we are granted by the Holy Messiah or suffer the permanent death we inherited from Adam and Eve. All immortal victory and paradisial happiness are found in the salvific Blood of the Lamb of God.

Human sin consumes all that is of man and the world. And every material we possess inhibits our union in the Son of God by distracting us from His call. We must cast-away all materials that bind us to the Earth and weighs us down from the elevation that God provides through His Son. When our hearts are broken, we try to mend them with the briny cast of materialism instead of giving them to the healing grace of Christ. His Sacrificial Love heals our every wound from the spiritual to the physical. His Blood purifies our souls, washing away any stain that would imprison us in the lost caverns of the dying world. Jesus has this power because He is the Son of God and the Holy Spirit. Proof of His Mercy is that He has yet to Return to Earth to judge the woeful people who refuse to surrender their destiny to Him. He is allowing plentiful time for our conversion while He stands aside waiting ever-so-patiently in the wings of Creation. The grief in which He watches the corruption of the Earth provokes His salty tears that keep the oceans full. That is why He has sent His Mother to our aid. ***"Tell them to get ready!"*** is the charge She brings from Him. She comes saying that "now" is the time for conversion, while there is still time left.

We are asked to light our lamp of Love for all the world to see. The Bridegroom is fast approaching for His Bride, the Church. And while Our Lady does not know the exact day or hour, She knows in the sweetness of Her Immaculate Heart that the time of the Second Coming of Her Son is soon. We must pray, fast, do penance, convert, live in peace, and love one another intensely. **"Do not make an indelible mark on the minds of man, but leave an immeasurable Love in the hearts of those who would know Jesus for the exercise of that Love!"** With these words, Our Lady calls Her children to begin our lives for Jesus so all who know us will know Him. Our hearts have an endless capacity for the storage of Love. Like Jesus Himself, they cannot be constrained and they emit a Light that will never be destroyed. We must begin to love as we have never loved before. And, we should all move together as one people toward this righteous goal by abandoning our struggle for materials and intellectual superiority. We must be strong of heart and meek of mind, allowing only the holiest thoughts to remain. As we fulfill this mission, we will become a part of the infinite Love of God Himself through Christ Jesus. We will leave in our wake a legacy of supernatural charm and immortal benevolence.

We must fill all empty hearts with Love by joining the parade of untarnished forgivers whom Jesus holds so close in His bountiful grace. When we do, we will be one with the sinless wonder that transcends all worldliness and containment. A single human soul is a jewel worth the price of the Life of God's Eternal Son. Each us of is a pearl that will soon adorn the crown of His blessed beauty. This is why we must all become one in the Holy Eucharist, the eternal Thanksgiving between God and man. It is the Sacrament through which mankind unites with the transcendent beauty of undefined timelessness. The Most Blessed Sacrament transforms our souls into holiness and the image and likeness of God.

Thursday, July 2, 1992

Tonight, my brother and I bowed our heads and offered our hearts in complete abandonment to God in all ways that He chooses for His glorification. We prayed the "Hail Mary" with the reticent humility that Our Lady requests of all Her children. We pray not solely because this pretty Creature speaks to our hearts, but in response to Her eminent invitation on Christ's behalf that we seek His presence. It is God Himself who sends His Mother with Jesus in Her arms in response to human petitions. His wish is fulfilled at the meeting of Jesus and the human soul. And, He is equally glorified when we worthily receive His Son in the Eucharistic Sacrament. The Blessed Virgin came to pray with us for the sorrowful needs of the mortal world. She was concerned today that many who receive the Holy Eucharist do not prepare their heart and soul through proper purification and prayer for such

Holy Communion. She said that thousands receive the Blessed Sacrament in a state of mortal sin, while others approach Him with blatant indifference to the perfect grace present in the Eucharist. It is true that God and man become physically unified through the Sacred Species, but Our Lady says that the human soul is also inseparably bonded to Heaven in Christ's Body. The human heart must be tendered to this gift in all ways in order to effect this miraculous marriage of the soul to Jesus Christ. We must remember how sacred our hearts must be.

What does this preparation truly mean? It begins in our affirmation that Christ is more important than any material or influence in Creation. He is the most precious manifestation that God ever sent into the world. Jesus is the Son whom God loves more than any mortal has ever loved a son. He courageously sent Him to die among us so we could again be reclaimed by the Holy City of Paradise. The Sacramental Body and Blood of our Savior lives on Earth today for the same reason. And since the Holy Mass is Christ's Sacrifice for the expiation of our transgressions, we are expected to be shed of all sinfulness when we receive the His Sacred Flesh and Blood. Our Lady asks that we receive the Sacrament of Confession at least once-a-week to prepare for the perfection of His Body and Blood. Quite essentially, we must strive to live in the purity of Jesus Himself if we are to be worthy of the Eucharistic Sacrament.

The Holy Mother told me today that She understands how we are distracted by the world. Our minds are influenced by matters of the flesh and the tempting parade of material possessions that pass before our eyes. We must allow nothing to inhibit our mortifying preparation to enter into complete unity with Jesus in the Holy Eucharist. Heaven itself descends to earth during the Holy Mass for our humble consumption. Therefore, it is imperative that we prepare to receive this Manna from Heaven in the same holiness that we anticipate being taken to Paradise when we die. Our Lady addressed a simple parable to make this point more clear. She showed me a picture of what appeared to be two hollow cylindrical tubes that somewhat resembled human blood veins about to be sutured into one. The separate vessels are representative of the flow of Life from God into mankind through the Holy Eucharist. Life immortal is brought into our mortal beings by the Body and Blood of Christ Jesus.

Our Lady showed me an image of the connection of this essential union which is made perfect when we commend ourselves to God's purpose. I first saw the mortal vein being thrust about as a soul unprepared to receive the Lifeblood of Jesus. That is the perfect parable of someone not worthy to receive the Holy Eucharist in the perfection that God seeks. This suture will leak in revelation of the soul not being in complete union with Him. Then, I saw a second suture that displayed a perfect union of the graceful vessel of

Christ Jesus and a mortified and purified soul. There was no such seepage of blessing or holiness in this flawless Communion. It is very much like a waterline coupling that needs to be perfectly connected so there is no breach in the delivery of this soul-quenching Sacrament. Such human preparation comes through contemplative meditation and by giving the heart totally to Christ. When we receive the Holy Eucharist, we know in faith that we are loved beyond any vision, inspiration, or comprehension that we can conceive. Once the Bread of New Life has entered our veins, we can rest assured that we are marching toward our final Redemption.

The Holy Mother told us in Her first intercessory messages that She is the Seamstress who has come to connect the hearts of men. It is also obvious that She is the Maternal Surgeon whose role is to perfectly unite our lives with Her Son in the Holy Eucharist. She has come to prepare Her children for transplantation into paradisial beauty, to by-pass the fallen world, and to become one with God in continuing precious Life despite the calcified nature of human imperfection. Through the perfect unity of God and man in the Holy Eucharist, we are able to see in our hearts the transformation that He has accomplished in our souls. We are elevated to His holy arms and placed into the comfort of His awaiting Heart. Infinity is within us because Christ clothes us with His infinite grace. Jesus simultaneously consumes us as we receive His own Sacred Body and Blood to be borne into the magnificent Light of God. It is the beginning of our impending ecstasies of Eternal Life while still in mortal flesh. This all begins with a human submission that is as perfect as the Sacred Body we receive to restore us to Divinity with one God in Three Persons.

Every step toward Jesus is a perfect one. It may be as simple as placing one foot ahead of the other, or a full-length stride of determined sanctification. We know we are not at peace until we begin that journey. We do not stand alone and must not stand-still for human indifference. If it is suffering that takes us to perfection, we must walk forthrightly toward it with the courage of the Holy Spirit in our hearts. When we see the suffering of others before us, we know that we are on the path to Him. They are the signs of His presence on the earth. Whether we choose to believe or turn away in dismay, Christ Jesus reveals Himself in the pain and sorrow of the peoples of the world. When we address their needs, ease their pain, comfort them in sorrow, and lift them prayerfully to dignity, we are walking at a saints-pace toward our destiny in Christ. Then, we can approach the Altar of the Church to receive the Holy Eucharist with the assurance that the flow of Life between God and our soul is beyond reproach.

Our Lady addressed another very simple parable by comparing the surly bonds of Heaven and earth to the silver reflecting surface behind the glass in a mirror. The Holy Eucharist likewise serves to reflect the perfected soul of mankind into the world. We touch Jesus Heart to heart, Body to body, and Soul to soul through the transcending power of the Most Blessed Sacrament. All the world can see their own beauty in us because we have lifted them from the caverns and crevices of the sorrow of suffering. We have become the likeness of Christ Himself because we live His image which He places on our souls when we worthily receive Holy Communion. It is for these transforming reasons that we should attend daily Mass to receive the Eucharist. If we wait only until Sunday, the wiles of the world will shake our souls and distract us from our bountiful duty in God. We find ourselves on a journey to reorganize, dissipate, and dissent. The One Crucifixion of Christ in daily Mass keeps us new in all ways.

The passing hours and weeks are only a mantra to get us to supper on time. But, the Holy Eucharist is a perpetual meal that truly feeds our souls. This is the perfect submission worthy of a people who yearn from the depths of their hearts to be one again with God. We offer everything that pierces our hearts to Him in Love. All we need to say is, *"Here, Jesus, I offer my temptations, weaknesses, and suffering to you in hopes that your Heart, too, may mend as mine."* Tonight, Our Lady also asked me to pray especially for the millions who are being held in prisons and other confines against their will. We must pray that the punishment of persecution and prosecution are supplanted by healing and Love. Vengeance is no reparation for transgression and weakness. Only forgiveness will bring the hallowed peace that all men seek in response to human sin.

Sunday, July 5, 1992

Patriotism in America is a common bond between our citizens and a cause for celebration during many holidays and occasions of solemnity and sorrow. Indeed, it is for land and country that many have died so that we could be free to prosper and travel. Our Holy Mother is the Patron Saint of the United States of America. She knows that it is through our right to religious freedom that Her messages are able to be spread between our shores. It is Her Son who allows us the grace to remain free and self-reliant in a nation blessed with resources and souls who yearn to remain filled with the Life of liberty. What we are now coming to know is that, when God shed His grace on our country, it was the Maternal Grace of His Mother that He truly wished us to see. We must embrace the majesty of the Cross with the same conviction that we bow to the colors of the flag. The flag commemorates those who died to keep a nation free, but the Cross is the living Memorial to the Champion who died to set free an entire human species. All people in every nation live under the liberty granted by Jesus from the 2000 year-old Cross. That is why the Saint of the Americas is the Virgin Mary. She is the true grace that God has shed upon our land.

I offered the prayer of the Holy Rosary in the afternoon because I planned to join my family later this evening to watch fireworks for the celebration of Independence Day. Our Lady told me that it is important that I maintain my familial relationships. She wishes for me to be seen as a normal brother and son in my effort to proclaim Her messages. This means that my struggle for holiness must be part of my living joy with my parents and sisters. For years, we have united to watch the fireworks displays for the Fourth of July, and today will be no exception. Whenever I see the thousands of people gathered in anticipation of a great show in the skies, it gives me great hope that they will one-day gather for the purpose of uniting in prayer of the Holy Rosary in expectation of the return of Jesus from above those same skies. Many hundreds of thousands join for worldly reasons, but rarely make an effort to come together in prayer for Jesus.

The Holy Mother spoke to me today as I prayed in Her honor. **"My special child, how are you? I am so happy to be with you again. Today, I am seeing the big celebration that North America is having for their freedom anniversary. I am also filled with sorrow because America is still being held captive by Satan and everyone is still celebrating. Many times, I have told you that America does well to remember the rights of humans personally and civilly. But, as a government, so many are left unattended, so many are killed, even before they are born. It is the celebration of indifference that America is observing today. I have come to tell the world that a great saving miracle will occur in the West when they light the skies and cities on Easter morning in the same way that they celebrate the anniversary of their government. Oh, but how happy Jesus would be that at the sunrise on Easter morning, the bombs and flares of humanity would be raised to complement its light and likeness as a unifying gesture with God. The celebration today is a false one. Satan is celebrating his victory today.**

My little son, I do not wish to diminish your patriotic spirit. Humanity will leave its mark in the sky today and the silence will be pierced by the roar of festival. I should tell you that as all of humanity is making its mark, the most important and lasting marks are the wounds of sacrifice that My Son Jesus bore for them. All other marks are diminished. My Son so loves the world that He hopes for the West to flourish in its freedom. Yes, America, God did shine His grace on thee! But, He also asks for an answer of dignity, not uncertainty. It is possible to maintain a light heart today. I hope that your joy is abound today. I will be with all of you watching and listening. My precious little one, I will ask you, as you see the closing and loud moments of your evening, to offer it all to Jesus and to those held captive, not by governments, but by the closed hearts that makes them evil.

Please hold a thought for the unborn that their freedom can be assured. This can be a celebration of hope for that reason. I will be hoping and still caring with a tear in My eye and prayer in My Heart for all those who are not truly free. That freedom must begin to bloom somewhere..." I asked Our Lady what more I could do to help convert the world. What other sacrifices can I offer that would really make a difference? She said, **"My Son would like to ask you the same question. What more can He do to assure the conversion of every heart? Yes, He knows that the answer is to ask little hearts like yours and your brother's to help Him."** With these words, Our Lady wants the world to know the true definition of Love and to willingly live it. We are being pressed into service like soldiers in an army of holiness. I have learned by now that prayer is the source of our vision. It purifies the scope of our wisdom so we can see the Divine intentions of God with spiritual clarity.

Tuesday, July 7, 1992

I have often sat weeping, if only inside, with a hope and desire that your eyes would eventually greet the words you are now reading. I think that time is very short because the urgency of God is so great. The coming miracles of the twenty-first century will bring an immense surprise to us all. I beg for the dispensation of the gift of faith upon every living soul. And, so does our Mother, and that is why She has come. Today, She spoke to me again as I offered the prayer of the Holy Rosary. **"My little child, I am with you. I love you very much. I have come again today to show My Love for you. You know that Jesus truly loves you, too. I am evidencing that throughout the world. I would like for you one-day to respond to the many Protestants and others who do not see clearly what My role is to the world. My Son wishes that everyone would come to My Heart and to My motherly arms for transfer to His Heart and grace. Today, I would like to remind all the Earth, all of the children of God, that I am their Mother..."**

Through the Divine intention of the Holy Spirit, there has been an increased honor, fervor, and growing devotion toward the Blessed Virgin Mary. While some discard this veneration as religious fanaticism, we must understand that Jesus has sent His Mother to the Earth to assist in our conversion and prepare our hearts for His infinite Mercy. No one other than God, Himself, knows the power and grace of Christ better than His Mother. She is our Advocate who bore Jesus into the world before any man ever knew Him. Who else could better prepare us for the Paradise He offers? She has already seen Heaven and knows the transformation our souls must undergo to reach the perfection God requires for our admission. Her eyes have seen the Glory of the Coming of the Lord! What a surprising revelation this is for many faithful who have for decades discounted the role of Mary in the Salvation of humanity. Many Protestants and Catholics alike believe that She gave birth to Jesus in a lowly stable in Bethlehem and was then absorbed by the fabric of human life, never to be heard from again. Christ performed His first miracle at the request of Mary. He honored and obeyed Her in every way that a perfect Son would venerate His Mother. And, He elevated Her from the role of lowly handmaid to become the Queen of Heaven and Earth.

The Holy Spirit works miracles to this day at the request of Our Queen, once the simple Jewish maiden whom God knew would be perfect for these End Times. She helps Her children with the same compassionate direction that the most loving mother on earth guides her children to Jesus. And, She has the miraculous power through Her Divinity and intercessory station to seek-out God's merciful pardon for the most wretched of souls. Today was one of the few days that Our Lady actually addressed a contrast between Herself and our earthly mother. She provided two very simple pictures that display Her role as Mother of humankind in comparison to the role of a mortal mother toward her own children. The first picture depicts the encompassing love of an earthly matriarch with all of her children close to her side. I could see these little ones surrounding her like ducklings following her to a pond. Obviously, they were scattered in many ways, clumsily moving about her through the most advantageous avenue they could find. If she was not careful, any of her children could become lost and she might never be able to find them again.

Our Lady then showed me a picture of Herself and all of us. I saw the same maternal love that we received from the one who bore us. But as children of the Blessed Virgin, we are somehow located inside the physical jurisdiction of Her power and grace. Our Holy Mother knows our spiritual location both in and out of Her sight. We cannot become lost from Her and are never out of Her reach. This second picture brought the enveloping nature of Our Lady's care to perfect focus. It is as though the first picture showed a number of precious jewels situated to the side of a fine purse, and the second presented the jewels inside it. That is the supernatural and encompassing Love of the Blessed Virgin for Her children. The Holy Mother wants all of us to enter Her Immaculate Heart for protection so we can be drawn by Her care into the Light of Christ. We are all "enwombed" in Her Motherly Heart so She can "give birth" to our souls into the Mercy of Her Son. It is much the same way that She gave birth to baby Jesus in the manger on Christmas. God wills for us to be borne into perfect Paradise in reciprocity of sending His Son into the fallen world to destroy our sins. He came to humankind through the Virgin Mary, and subsequently bequeathed our conversion to Her when He hung on the Cross, knowing that we would most readily return to Him only through Her motherly grace. This is the reason for Her miraculous intercession the world over. She has come to purify and convert Her children for transfer to the merciful Heart of Her Son, our Lord, Savior, and Brother Jesus Christ.

We must follow Mary Immaculate in the same innocent trust that Christ brought to the world upon His birth. He is the universal lens through which we focus upon God Himself. And, Our Lady proclaims of Herself, **"My soul magnifies the Lord!"** We are the fortunate beneficiaries of Her sinless presentation of Jesus to humankind. There are many who will not allow themselves to see this! They will not give their souls to the wisdom of the heavens and offer their lives to be filled with grace. The future of endless delight is assured through Him. It is as though someone has approached a doorway that leads to a beautiful paradise carrying a large package of refuse that will not fit through the opening. They are staring eternal bliss right in the face, but they will not drop their useless baggage and step across the threshold. They will not rid themselves of sin and accept the Christ who destroyed it. He is the only step that sinners need to take on the journey back to God. We are much too little and soiled to take the leap on our own.

Our Lady asked me to imagine the entrance to a beautiful mansion that has a front door four feet off the ground, but no stairs. We cannot take a step large enough to get into the foyer. We are too small and the chore is too great. We need an elevating landing to bridge the distance between the ground and the stately home. It is the same truth that man cannot traverse the distance from Earth to Heaven without Jesus Christ. In Him, we are able to discard our useless baggage of transgressions and stand tall upon His sanctifying Sacrifice and sail the distance from mortality to Eternity. Indeed, we need the Holy Spirit to understand that the heavenly mansions await our arrival. He is our wisdom and His Blood is our deliverance to the Throne of God. Our Lady has made it clear that, **"Each person is a kiss of Love that Jesus gave to the Earth."** We are created in the likeness of God as a manifestation of His perfect Love. We are the imprint of His immortal genius upon Creation, just like a mighty lion confidently leaves a paw print on the ground. And although the foot of this jungle beast has separate pads that leave unconnected impressions, they are all made by the same purpose and power. Each of us is a member of one humanity created through the singular Love of God the Father. We are a product of His timeless intentions. Every universe and world is an impression left by this Omnipotent Creator. He is one Love who has manifested Himself in Three Divine parts on Earth; the Father, the Son, and the Holy Spirit.

Every distinguishable size, shape, fragrance, flavor, and resonance known to man is a footprint of God revealing where He has been. All Creation lies in wait for this King to return, looking for the virgin traces of His immortal steps that we have somehow tried to erase from existence. All that is of man and nature is a descendent from God Himself with the exception of sin and imperfection. This, too, He came to expunge in the person of His Son whose legacy is truly yet to come. In Jesus, the world is finished, but He is not yet finished with the world. He will return to judge the living and the dead in fulfillment of the Holy Scriptures. The miracle of the Creation of the world will come to fruition when Christ takes the Earth and every soul united in Him to Heaven. Once we finally understand this great purpose and perfection of all Creation and the Love which sets it into being, we will be one with the Infinity of God. We are drawn to Divine unification in this truth through the Holy Eucharist. The Body and Blood of Christ Jesus is our Salvation and the source of all knowledge of the saved. We are transformed from the simple thought of God into full participation with Him through the Most Blessed Sacrament. We grow from one dimensional beings into the multi-faceted boundlessness of Love. The Blessed Trinity comes to rest on our souls like an angel with three wings when we receive Holy Communion. We become more than just people under God, we join the census of citizens who live in Him.

Our Lady has told humankind throughout the world that our love for God and one another must become "active." This living and generative desire is received in the Holy Eucharist. Our awareness that we must become one with the Almighty is given flight so we are spiritually taken to Him. Our acceptance of Jesus is incomplete if we do not believe in faith that He is the Eucharist. And, our faith does not live if we do not worthily receive Him in this perfect Sacrament. The Body and Blood of Christ Jesus effects our full participation in His Kingdom on Earth. After Our Blessed Mother gave me these beautiful thoughts, She directed Her attention to my well-being and conduct. I have still had some difficulty living "slowly" in prayerful peace. She asked me to call to mind the vision of someone spinning saucers atop wooden dowels. They try to keep as many saucers spinning at one time as possible. This is the way many people live who have more to do than they can control. Our Lady asked me today not to become one of them. If I strive to live in the peace of Her Immaculate Heart, She will better be able to protect me from harm and evil.

Thursday, July 9, 1992

Today, I have been pondering the truth that Jesus rose into Heaven on Ascension Thursday and Our Lady followed Him later, Body and Soul. She was raised there on a date that we celebrate as the Feast of the Assumption of Mary. This causes the desire of my soul to look upward in anticipation of the Return of Jesus. I know that He and Our Lady have been sighted in many miraculous apparitions throughout the world. He has yet to Return in full view of all souls for the purpose of ending the world and taking the redeemed to Paradise. However, the Blessed Mother tells us that Heaven is already in and around us through our Love and perfection in unity with the Holy Spirit. She also affirms that no humans launched into outer space get any closer to the Heavenly Kingdom because they have yet to die to sin. When Our Lady came to pray with my brother and me today, She addressed these important questions. She told me that our mortal perception of Heaven is not the same as those who have died and gone there. Heaven is a Paradise in which God and all the Saints and Angels reside. There is no temptation or sin there, only perfection in Love. That is why She tells us that when we love in the image of Jesus, we can begin to live those graceful heights here on Earth.

It is possible for us to love in perfect unity with the Blessed Trinity. That is the essence of Our Lady's call for us to become one with Christ in the Holy Eucharist. Heaven is a paradisial Kingdom high above the universe, but its depth can descend into the hearts of humanity on Earth. The Throne of God is above the celestial firmament, but His will is on Earth when we live in union with the Holy Spirit. When Our Virgin Mother says that astronauts get no closer to Heaven, She does not mean in the physical sense. Even though they are closer to the Throne of God in outer space, they are not able to reach it in their mortal bodies. Therefore, they are no closer to Heaven than someone still standing on terra firma. Everyone must die-to-sin and be resurrected by Jesus Christ before their soul can be transferred to the Home of the Creator. And in the perfection of all His bounty, He has placed His Throne high above the Earth in a shining City called Paradise.

This led the Holy Mother into a discussion about a "double standard" that is forced upon us because we exist in fleshly exile on this side of the veil. Those who reside in Heaven can come to Earth at the request of the Almighty Father. And when they do so, they never actually leave the intrinsic ecstasy of eternal bliss. This coincides with Our Lady's previous assertions that the Earth is a subpart of heavenly Creation, even though it is the home of those awaiting Redemption. When we love in the image of Christ and the way His Mother teaches, we transcend the veil that inhibits our vision of God. This is how the Earth becomes like Heaven. The world is the vantage point from which we can see the Crucifixion of Jesus at Holy Mass, and yet is also the property of Heaven annexed by God in reflection of the conversion to Love of those who inhabit it. But, we who have yet to die do not enjoy the immortal mobility of those who are in Heaven. We cannot pass through the doorway to the perfect Kingdom because we have not attained the perfection required to live there. We will reach that summit either when we die in Christ and are raised by His Mercy or when He returns to the Earth to end the world on the last day.

The Queen of Heaven told me that Her intercession is not for the purpose of satisfying human curiosity about our physical location in time and space. Hers is an immortal message of Eternal Life beyond death. Our focus should be toward the preparation of our souls for Redemption. Only Love will do that. Then, we will no longer be limited by the dimensions of the sky and earth, or by time itself. We will be one with the Angels and Saints to wander freely throughout Creation, shed of the bonds of mortal flesh and the tempestuous world. These servants of God are always where God sends them. While we cannot see them because of the constraints of our exilic nature, they are perfectly united to us by virtue of their heavenly sanction. There are some who do not believe in the company of the Angels and Saints or that they have any influence toward our sanctification and protection. But all who reside in unity with the Divine Trinity play a perfect role toward the conversion and purification of mortal souls. We remember the tremendous power of the Archangel Michael in our fight against evil spirits. When we pray for his intercession, he will provide it. All of Heaven is at work to complete the intention of God to reunite His Creation. Even our loved ones who have gone to Heaven pray on our behalf to the Almighty Father. They gained their power through Christ's Resurrection from the grave on Easter morning. This is where we will also be granted immunity from the stings of death.

Today, Our Lady also told me about Her children being "in-spirited," meaning that the Holy Spirit fills every soul to perfection with Love. We accept this blessing when we open our hearts to Jesus. God fulfills and completes His desire to be one in us through The Paraclete just as He did for the Saints of old. They were consumed with the desire to love their brothers and sisters in the way of Christ Jesus. By tendering their hearts to the fire of His Love, He was able to utilize their lives to transform the world. Anyone who kneels in complete submission to the Will of God and receives the Holy Spirit is an instrument in His Hands. This is the way we become Christ-like in nature and action so Heaven can live in us. Remember when Saint Stephen was in front of the Sanhedrin before he was martyred. The passage reads, **"All those who sat in the Sanhedrin looked intently at him and saw that his face was like the face of an angel."** The Blessed Mother continued today by telling me that mankind lives in anticipation of stimulating crescendos instead of a perpetual state of grace. We seek some sort of flourish or climactic finish to our every affair and practice. This is the case when we have an "open house" or a "dedication" of some worldly structure. It is reminiscent of a band playing *"ta-da"* with a cymbal crash at the end of a trapeze act. But, to yearn for the Face of God is to work humbly, reverently, and with perseverance in the infinite reflection of humble servitude.

We do not have time to take a bow for our work just yet. The Holy Mother says the same of a material pennant. She asks what good can come from it. Might it be nothing more than just a simple product of human pride? We compete for the victory and claim the prize. But, the reward is nothing more than something material we store away that has to be regained next year. There is no permanent or humanitarian aspect to its purpose. We should instead struggle to accomplish the universal goal of the conversion of humankind to Christ so we will never have to fight for victory again. That is what romantic writers have been dreaming for generations. They capture on page the legacy of great ones breathing their last, their flesh riddled by wounds and their lifeblood of love pouring onto the ground. They suffer in desolation in the path of the fatal enemy, securing the victory with heroic courage and capturing the future of unending bliss. These heroes are immortalized because they triumph over evil and pave the way for a new and fresh beginning for all mankind who can now live in peaceful contentment and perfect Love.

Whether it is the intention of these writers, they are describing the purpose of human sacrifice that God knows is necessary for the conversion and Salvation of His people. The true Hero and Conqueror who is greater than any warrior from the conjuring minds of authors is Jesus Christ. He is real and alive in our world. His Cross of Victory is the final battleground for our own immortality because that is where He invincibly destroyed our death. He is the Champion who died so that humanity could savor Him as the first fruits of that Divine engagement between good and evil. He was laid to rest in His Mother's arms and transferred to a Tomb that could not hold Him. In light of the Triumph of the Cross, our finite victories pale. All our efforts are fruitless if not given to the purpose of transforming God's people into holiness. We must even lay down our lives if that is the call of the world. But, when we look at the physical presence of a pennant, we see the transient nature of our efforts:

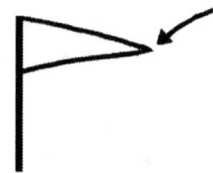

We can see from its very shape that our worldly successes are constrained by space and time. The tail of the pennant comes rightfully to a punctuation point. But, when we fight the good fight for Christ to advance the cause of His Kingdom on Earth, no pennant can articulate the infinite victory at hand. The world cannot physically hold its timeless nature:

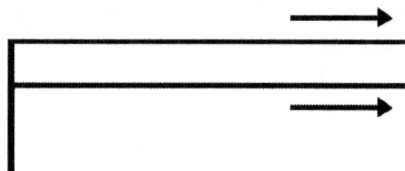

Our conviction to Christ is a never-ending triumph. Its exhilaration ecstatically consumes the futile festivities that follow our mortal accomplishments. Victory in Christ will never diminish through time or space because it is our assurance of the continuity of Love, Salvation, Heaven, and Eternity. Such fulfillment is everything that God ever intended for His holy people. That is the reason why He sent His Mother into the world. He wants everyone to join in the eternal celebration of Paradise. We must pray for the coming of this perpetual delight in the arms of our Heavenly Father.

Tuesday, July 14, 1992

It has been five days since I last made an entry in my Diary. Our Lady has remained very close during my prayers, offering graces and signs in reflection of Her promises to Saint Dominic and Blessed Alan for those who recite the Holy Rosary. I am very aware of Her presence, even when She does not speak in audible words. And on the occasions when She does, I am coming to full understanding of the miraculous gift God dispenses through Her words. In the most simple of terms, His message is that we are to come to Him through Christ Jesus. When we pray the Rosary, the Holy Spirit lights upon our souls to strengthen our petitions and grant us peace. The Holy Virgin brings Her Son to our side when we contemplate the Mysteries. Both of them hear our intentions for ourselves and those we offer for the world. They are as physically and spiritually present as those kneeling beside us. If the entire world could see what individual visionaries have seen and heard, human hearts would faint in ecstasy. There would be no doubt in anyone's mind that the reign of God is at hand and we must awaken from our slumbering beds. But, He asks us to live by faith and not by sight. That is why we must trust that Jesus and Mary are with us in every way to assist our conversion and Redemption. We speak to them by the meditation in our hearts and the words from our mouths. They respond with graces and blessings unknown to the human senses.

Our Lady has told the world in many apparitions that if humankind would live Her messages, we would not realize our passage from this life to the next. We must learn to trust the visions of our hearts and be confident in the discerning power that God provides through the union of the Holy Spirit with our soul. This is the same Truth Who tells us that the Holy Eucharist is the Body and Blood of Christ. We gain this knowledge because our hearts are open in faith to the wisdom from on High. The origin of our grace-filled senses lies beyond the surly bonds of permanent Eternity and is as real as the pew in which we are seated. Christ replaces the bread and wine on the Altar of Sacrifice at the power of the Almighty Father. This is the truth whether we choose to believe it or not. The Savior of the world lives in the Eucharistic Tabernacles of the Catholic Church. His presence is proof of the Father's Love for us. But, we often leave Him there alone . Our Lady told me that this makes Jesus very sad because He wants everyone to experience the transforming power of the Most Blessed Sacrament. He wishes to be venerated during Eucharistic Adoration and consumed at the Holy Sacrifice of the Mass.

When people feel alone and abandoned in their service to God, this is the same loneliness that Christ feels when we place Him in the Tabernacle and behave like He is not even there. But, we should take hope because just as we will be joined by the silent millions yet to speak out for human Salvation, Jesus will be again reveled and honored as the King of all Creation. There are many people who truly want to change the world back into the beautiful perfection that God intends. Thousands of our brothers and sisters cry out for the return of civility, kindness, and love. But their pleas fall on the deaf ears of the indifferent, apathetic, and agnostic. They do not know how to reach those who blatantly refuse to listen. There have been evangelical missions and crusades all over the world by the faithful who proclaim the Good News of Christ Jesus. They have had limited success to the extent that they are reaching people who have suffered enough to already know God. The rich, affluent, and famous somehow fall through the cracks in our efforts to convert humanity. They dodge and hide from the truth like it will never affect them at the end of time.

This is why the undeniable power of prayer must be invoked for our lost world. Human testimonials and mass mailings can only do so much. We have to ask God for miraculous intercession for the healing and conversion of ourselves and all humankind. He sends His Love into the world through Jesus and Mary with every intention that they will succeed in rescuing us from the rubble of the material world. We must join together to outwardly reveal the Love in our hearts. Our Lady said today, **"Do you not know that you have all the strength that you need in your heart? Do you not know that your Love is your strength? That is what Jesus gave you when He died for you. You will always have strength for that reason. Those who say that they are weak have not truly accepted Him. Please know your strength is Jesus' Love in you, that all His strength went to you as He gave His Life on the Cross."** Our Lady is asking us to look individually into our hearts in response to Her call. We find the Divine Wisdom of God in the Love we share. When we give everything in our entire being to Jesus and live our hope for the world, we feed the starving, clothe the naked, comfort the afflicted, stand with the weak, nurture the poor, and live a Life worthy of being called blessed in the sight of the Holy Gospel of Jesus.

Sunday, July 19, 1992

I have worried for a long time that my recording of Our Lady's messages would earn me the dubious distinction of being labeled as simply another fanatic, not unlike the disparagement of those who have claimed to see a UFO. But, I am able to conquer any assaults upon my intellectual integrity by remembering that I know what I have seen and heard from the pinnacles of the heavenly Kingdom. I am confident that my work is a fruit of the Holy Spirit and the Virgin Mother of God. Jesus knows that I will respond in love for Him, and that is all that matters to me. It is not my intention to stand forward and publicly defend the messages I have received. I can see that the Almighty

Father has perfectly accomplished that goal for all time and before any people. He is, indeed, the only genius in Creation. Our Holy Mother interceded from Heaven again today as I prayed the Holy Rosary. **"Good day, My happy little beautiful one! Why aren't you celebrating? Oh, My little one, you have never seen Me in such a state of ecstasy with you and your brother as I am today. Last evening was a great victory for Jesus because worldly conversion begins in little places..."**

It is very important for us to realize the magnitude of Our Lady's guidance and intercession worldwide. We have reason to hope in ways that generations before us never knew. The world is, indeed, changing before our eyes and a new morning is coming to Creation. The number of faithful followers is increasing because the Blessed Virgin is teaching us. Her children are opening their hearts and are being rewarded by God for their faith. His great Light is pouring-forth over our souls. Many have come to see that "now" is truly the time for our transformation. Everything Our Lady has told through the centuries and the prophesies of mystics are being fulfilled during this age. Our faith is being raised to heights that one would never have before dreamed of attaining. The hopeful possibility of human unity is alive, filling the open-of-heart with Divine anticipation. These children of Love wish to share the joy of the Return of Christ Jesus in Glory. They herald the arrival of a new age when Our precious Lord will be able to live amongst men and in their hearts. This revelation is a truth that is too real to ignore. The Sunrise is near and the Light of New Dawn can be seen in our midst.

Soon, no shadow will have the courage to remain over us because God's Holy Light will have conquered any semblance of darkness or despair. This is the moment for which Our Lady lives. She calls us to prepare for the Return of Christ with prayer, fasting, and conversion. We must open our hearts in expectation of the Coming of the greatest joy we have ever known or could possibly conceive. When God brings the revealing truth of His Final Will into the world, who among us can stand? Only those whose souls are perfectly united in confident submission to Jesus Christ will survive the impending Judgment of the Almighty Father. This is a day which approaches with processional signs and graces. The gift of Our Immaculate Mother is the greatest revelation that God has granted the Earth since the descent of the Holy Spirit at Pentecost.

Now is not the time for the world to cower in fear and rejection. We have to raise ourselves from the dungeon of human corruption and infidelity and be remade through the Sacraments of the Mother Church into the people Christ will claim as His own. If we lay in wait, it will only be for the inauspicious grasp of evil and indifference. We are too good a fruit to be thrown to the hungry jaws of the roaring lions. Our souls are too precious in the sight of God. If we refuse to believe this, there will never be any hope for our conversion and transformation into perfection. The moment has arrived for us to stand and tell Jesus that our sins have truly been destroyed by the death He suffered to conquer them. His death-warrant was written on the fabric of our transgressions. But, now, He has been Resurrected and we must join Him for our transposition into everlasting Life.

Monday, July 20, 1992

Today, I was given a great grace from God that allowed me to see the beautiful power of prayer. I had become very disturbed this evening about situational matters having nothing to do with holiness and elevation. I was being beaten by worldly thoughts and felt like I was nearly drowning in a sea of helplessness. When I went to Holy Mass with my brother, I asked him to pray for me so I would be at peace to receive the Blessed Sacrament. Somehow my soul seemed to be hemorrhaging from the infliction of this pain and my lifeblood of holiness was dripping onto the floor of the Earth. I saw my brother begin to pray the Rosary before Mass and I turned my own heart to the Blessed Mother in hopes that She would intercede by asking Jesus to immediately stop this awful manifestation. As we prayed, a tremendous vision unfolded in my heart. I was standing with both arms covering my head in an attempt to deflect the blows I was receiving. I felt like I was in the middle of a street-fight being beaten by a violent gang.

Suddenly, a protective barrier started to form in front of me in mid-air. Pieces of this shield began to fill-in the space before me like bricks in a wall, although it had not started from the ground. They were just randomly appearing in no particular process or order. And as the shield was being completed, the blows I had been dodging were dissipating. I could feel the sensation of pain only through the holes yet to be filled by the remaining pieces. When the shield was complete, a silent peace came over me as though I had been plucked from the ground like a crying baby from his crib. I could still see and hear the violence on the other side of the wall and could even move stealthily through it and back again. But, somehow I felt an immunity inside a protective haven that I could not fully explain. I still had the fear of a child after a nightmare hoping that the shield was strong enough to keep me from harm. I felt like it might be fragile to the touch like wet mortar in a wall of bricks. But, the longer I was protected by this fortress of peace, it seemed to become more permanent.

My soul was now at peaceful rest for the celebration of the Holy Sacrifice of the Mass. I could sense the prayers of my brother at the time this Divine protection came over me. I received Jesus during Holy Communion with great joy. This contentment continued through the evening when Timothy and I came home to offer our evening prayers. I knew that through his petitions and the opening of my heart in union with Our Lady's intercession, I was placed in the protection of Her Motherly Mantle and the care of Her Immaculate Heart. She came to speak to me again this evening as we knelt in front of my altar and invited the healing of God by calling on Her intercession and accepting the Love of Jesus through the Mysteries of the Rosary. That is the only way we will ever truly know peace. We must be self-assured that God loves us in ways that we do not yet know. Our Lady has come teaching the miraculous intentions of the Heart of God so that we, too, can Love in a supernatural way. Then, we will see the transformation of the Earth as the Kingdom of God falls from Heaven.

As I saw today, when we pray for each other, the Almighty Father will provide miracles for our healing and protection. Our petitions bring safety to our brothers and sisters who are in peril. I am convinced that when we pray from the heart, our generous Lord places baskets of food in front of the starving just like the bricks-in-the-wall appeared before my spiritual eyes at Holy Mass. The Holy Spirit reveals the Divine intentions of God that lay beyond the limits of our comprehension. He is as loving, gentle, and charitable as anyone we will ever know. The Heart of Jesus is wounded by our sin and error in the same way that we are injured by physical aggression. We must, instead, be His companion and allow Him to teach us a life of peace in His Sacred Heart. This is of great importance to the Blessed Virgin. Her assertion is that Jesus Christ needs us! The beauty of Creation is incomplete without every holy soul God gave Life. His Mercy is infinite and His Love is of great magnitude that draws us to Him like a ship to a lighthouse. We are forgiven of our transgressions of the past and must decide to avoid sin in the future. We can live in such perfection when we give ourselves to the Christ who needs our souls to make the Kingdom of God all He wishes it to be. Our souls are like the flowers and ornaments that adorn the beauty of a hall of stately grace.

This does not mean that our Omnipotent God is less without us. He does not need our praise to continue to be the Almighty Creator and Adjudicator of all things. But, He did not create us to be bound to sin. The Blood of His Son has cleansed our souls into perfection so we can, indeed, be the beautiful olive plants around His Table. We are part of God's Countenance that shines throughout Creation for all Eternity. We are saved not only because we do not wish to spend infinity in the fires of Hell, but because God wants us back at His side in His paradisial Kingdom! He created us to glorify Him in that noble abode. And, we begin that adoration by accepting the gift of the Holy Spirit in our hearts and by living the image of Christ ourselves. We are then united in the Love of the Almighty Father once again.

We do not have to run into the point of a sword to make this proclamation. It is the collective genteel of a humble humanity that makes the world shine in the Love of God. He seeks our simplicity in the smallest gifts from the heart. This living example cannot be supplanted by any diary or doctrine. The world cannot defeat our works of Love. We are like corks in the water who refuse to remain submerged in order to show God He has found us. The weight of the world might pull us down, but will pass in the current of time and human conversion. Mankind does not realize the magnitude of the graces presented through Our Lady's miraculous intercession. She accomplishes in short moments what it would take the greatest Saints centuries to achieve. We are living in a very blessed time. I offered my thanks to this Lady of Fidelity before She left this evening. She bid me farewell by saying, **"I love you and will speak to you soon. Please be happy! Goodnight."**

Saturday, July 25, 1992

The Blessed Mother has been perpetually at my side since my last entry. I hope that She is accomplishing all She wishes to achieve through my life. I do the things I am told and perform works that I know make God happy. We must desire to remain simple and continue to walk in the Love that Christ gives to the world. Our Lady said to me today, **"I would like to tell you that you are seeing your Diary take the form of its earthly body, as it is about to become borne into the world. You have held it in your 'womb' and nurtured it, and its birthday is soon to arrive. Also, I see that you have noticed lately that the perils of the evil one have avoided you in your work lately."** I told Our Lady, "thank you" for protecting me. She replied, **"You are welcome. You must remember that there is so, so much Love in what you are doing that the 'coward' has not yet devised how he will attack. But, he will, and we will be ready."** Humanity has been so suppressed by the world that the vision of God that we are called to see is often difficult to obtain. We must always remember that the Life Jesus asks of us is not an impossible task. The good we do in His Name must be nurtured through our prayers, lest we lose-hold of our desire to continue to grow our perfection in greater ways. If we see our sacrifices as having no immediate value, we will refuse to carry them any further. It is important that we remember the infinite Love that Jesus holds for us that keeps our hearts awake in Him.

Imagine a long street lined with tables of vendors on either side. If we are one of them sitting in our own booth marketing our wares, we can see the rows of our fellow vendors waiting for passing customers. But, there are no consumers on the street. The vendors are just sitting near their cash boxes waiting for at least one person to shop. Suddenly, we see a single man standing on the road in the distance. He seems to be walking confidently toward our booth, waiving to the vendors nearest him to gather their goods and fall-in behind as he continues toward us. Throngs of merchants quickly load their wares onto the backs of donkeys and follow like a cloud of dust behind a moving chariot. As he moves inexorably closer to our booth, other vendors continue to take their place behind him, some with wooden shingles, others with door knobs and fixtures. We see curtain hangers, carpet weavers, marble cutters, and crystal engravers. There are painters, plumbers, brick-layers and carpenters. They carry hammers, nails, saws, bolts, windows, and doors. The crowd gets larger as they approach our booth, everyone taking their place behind this very curious pied-piper of human persuasion. Each has brought what he owns and has taken a place behind this magnificent being whose purpose is to finish his journey. Everyone following him seems rapt in a joyous ecstasy unlike any we have ever seen.

Now, we wait wondering what could have made such a throng of people follow this curious man. Whatever the reason, we know it must be good and that we want to join this celebrant parade. But, we fear that he will not see us in the midst of all the rejoicing and tumult of the crowd. Our anxiety is high because he might pass-by without noticing our little booth. We look around to see what we have to offer. There are no fine linens or colorful banners. We are not a goldsmith and could never afford diamonds. There is nothing of any value in our stock that could impress such a great traveler and fisher of men, who is now just a few strides away. So, we sit teary-eyed with our face in our hands. We will never be able to join this blissful body of humanity because the only commodity we sell is planting soil. As we sit crying in our booth, this Mighty One peers-over and sees our distress. He leaves His position at the center of the street and walks away from the crowd to approach us. We raise our face and meet eye-to-eye a crystal beauty of Eternity gazing back at us. He is incarnate Love whose caress has just encompassed the world. He asks why we cry and our response is that we have only dirt to offer. We know that it cannot compare to the many invaluable wares the others are carrying for Him on their journey together.

As His gentle gaze falls upon our sorrowful face, His countenance intensifies as He says, *"My child, you understand so little about what I value. You are observing all of these people who are following Me with everything they have, and you do not see your place. You see, I am a Builder. I am going to a land where I am going to erect a Kingdom that no one has ever imagined. It is going to be of a beauty that surpasses all beauty. It is going to be built in the image that I see in Me, and that I am showing to you now. I have told all of these people that they can live with Me if they will offer Me what they have so that I can build a place for them. Now, you are crying because you see your piles of dirt and do not think that I can make use of them to make for you a place. Amen, I say to you that these piles of worthless dirt will be the virgin soil with which I will cover the distances of My Kingdom. And, I will make sprout from this fertile ground flowers that will dwarf in beauty the plants that you see.*

Flowers of light and plants that sing to the Glory of their Creator will rise in spontaneous choirs of dance and song. And you, My child, I will make their conductor. Come and follow Me. I will make you a gardener of Eternal Beauty, and keeper of the heavenly scents, and the protector of the pedestals of sparkling celestial dew. I will give you the choice of seats in this valley of Love, with a view surpassing all of your limited bonds. I will create for you a Paradise from your dust and dirt, just as I raised the universal beauty that you live in now. Yet, I tell you that no moth or worm will destroy or devour this Kingdom I will build. Your sadness must be left in this one. Come now with Me, come with us, your brothers and sisters into the Eternal Heaven. I love you."

This majestic King then reaches to lift you from despair and hopelessness. He takes you by the hand and leads you to your place in the crowd of Saints in the street. They do not have to part to allow you entry because there was an empty space where you now stand as the others greet you in mutual companionship and heavenly victory. We all turn uniformly to march forward arm-in-arm behind the Lamb, the King, the Man-God, Jesus the Builder. This parable is a reflection of what Our Lady tells the world. The King is coming soon and we see the crowds beginning to form. Millions are turning to the Blessed Virgin in recognition of Her great works. She shows us the height that Her Solitary Warrior stands above the rest. He is the gleaming Knight of the Salvific Cross who now walks Resurrected throughout all Creation. He has come seeking the gift of our very souls with which He will build a Kingdom of perpetual Light.

Sunday, July 26, 1992

Today, I have been very concerned about a group of people who flagrantly disregard the supernatural intercession of Our Lady. I am not worried that their souls will be lost. They, indeed, love Jesus and Mary very much. But, I fear that when they learn the truth of what is really happening, they will be filled with self-disdain and sorrow knowing that they were opposed to such a revelation of God's Love. It is not a sin to disbelieve in the miraculous intercessory apparitions and interior locutions of the Blessed Mother. But, how might someone feel when they find they have persecuted the faithful messengers of Christ? Will they ever be able to forgive themselves? Our Lady addressed the matter of self-forgiveness in Her message today. It is extremely important for the human soul to recognize its worth in the eyes of the Lord. That is the true reason for self-denial and mortification. It is one wing of the flight of sacrifice, the other is the restoration of the lost and downtrodden to dignity. Christ has erased our sins from every part of Creation except our own memory. We remember them as a reflection of the wisdom that we are no match for the universal omnipotence of God. But as a result of the Crucifixion of Jesus, we are lifted by Divine Grace into the undeniable and immeasurable immensity of complete Love.

Part of our acceptance of the Death of Christ is to know that since God has forgiven us, who are we to stand in opposition to the newfound innocence we inherit? There are those who say that people who do not remember the past will inevitably repeat it. While this is not universally true, we must still be aware of our propensity to sin. We are often weak in the face of temptation and lacking in courage to fight the battle against evil. We must keep our sights on the Cross of Christ and receive His Holy Body and Blood for strength and enlightenment. After all, Jesus said to humankind, **"Do This in Memory of Me."** This means that we must be perpetually aware of the power and fruits of His Death on the Cross which destroyed our sins. We must love and forgive ourselves in the same faith that we do others. By the Holy Cross of Jesus, we have been reconciled to God and our perfection is restored. When we embrace the power of the Cross in its infinite Divinity, we will see that God has granted us freedom to begin anew in Him through Christ. We take nothing on that journey that is of this world, especially the sins that Jesus has destroyed.

We must remember that the pathway to holiness is as important as holiness itself. We cannot commit transgressions toward the purpose of producing good. There are no good fruits in evil works. That is the reason for our conversion to God's Commandments in the Person of Christ Jesus. It is overwhelmingly the purpose for our lives if we wish to reach the pinnacle of Heaven. Jesus is the Way, the Truth, and the Life for all who will forever know God. We live in the confidence that we belong to Christ because the Holy Spirit has given us the vision to see. This is the assurance that Our Lady is offering as She delivers the Good News of Her Son to the world. She offered me a parable today to help further my understanding. She said that there are certain reptiles and crustacean that mature and leave their outer shells. They actually shed their skin which stands as a hollow monument to their former selves. They can look back to see where they have been and feel the newness of their fresh beginning. Their outside crust of course dead skin no longer binds them to the way they were. The children of God who are on the path to holiness abandon their lives of worldliness in the way that a reptile jettisons its outside layers. This is a process that begins in the recesses of the heart.

The Life that others see in us should reflect the sheen of our new conversion. We have to be willing to remove the old wrap of our sinful self and walk away knowing that it will lie forever behind us. This is the essence of the forgiveness of the self. Our Lady also asked me to call to mind the many sea shells that pepper the shorelines around the world. They are intricate and beautiful in their artistic reminder of God's Creation and remnants left by the life once present in them. This is the legacy that the Saints in Heaven have left us to enjoy. Their memory leaves us a celestial song of a Life-giving Eternity in the same way that the pretty shells render the song of the ocean from whence they came. We must lift the prayer of our hearts next to the souls of the Saints like we place our ear to a seashell. God sees us in the same beauty that we enjoy the shells as a fruit of the sea. The culmination of the union of Heaven and Earth is found in the heart of humankind as we realize the beauty of our souls in God's eyes.

Tuesday, July 28, 1992

The Blessed Virgin continually brings peace to my heart by showing me Life through Her eyes. She takes away my uncertainties that serve to disrupt the clarity of my perception. I continue to remember that I will not lose peace when my faith is strongly anchored in Love. I have even found new courage to withstand the criticism and attacks lodged against me for proclaiming the authenticity of Our Lady's messages. Some people focus their attention on the character of the messenger and the mechanics of delivery instead of the substance of what is being said. The message of Love is the puritanical essence of the revelations of God through His Mother. We should always ponder the sweetness of the fruit before we decide that a tree is not worthy of Life. It is very important to the Holy Mother that Her messengers remain "little servants" of Christ Jesus. Not one measure of credit for the success of the Holy Spirit belongs to a visionary or other messenger for God. Of course they can be witnesses and evangelists, but their souls must be tendered in humility and grace to the authority of God. No mortal messenger is the Savior of the world. Only Christ Himself holds that title. Our mission is not to draw attention to ourselves, but to point others in the direction of Jesus and the Cross of Salvation.

No one is a messenger on their own. They have no power to convert the world to the Almighty Father not given them by God Himself. The Holy Spirit gives man the ability and grace to stand in any nation and proclaim, *"Jesus Christ is the Savior of the world!"* We must remember that Jesus had very little regard for mankind's image of greatness. He fled from any attempts to make Him a king of the mortal world. His response was that He came to serve, not to be served. That is the message He gives to anyone who aspires to be elevated to a position of public authority and to those in power over the lives of the lowly. God is most glorified when He is allowed to raise a most worthless creature to sanctity because it provides the opportunity for Him to display an infinite Mercy that man has yet to achieve on his own. Humankind does not own the Word because it is a gift to be shared. In Jesus, many who are first will be last; and those who are last will be first.

Our Lady told me that She is very happy with Her priest-sons, especially one who appeared on a religious television program today. He told the world that our Holy Mother often comes to discipline Her children in maternal seriousness. She is dispatched to the Earth by God with the full authority to speak on His behalf. Her admonishments are premonitions of things to come if we do not convert. She has the power to command our obedience and to exact discipline when necessary. This has been documented the world over as many people have been brought to their knees in compliance to the Almighty Father at the direction of His Mother. Her purpose is to be kind and gentle to all of Her children. This is also the Will of our Father in Heaven. But, we are taught that a Father who loves His children will discipline them in that same Love. We must remember this in His call to conversion and perfection. If we refuse to obey, we have not truly given ourselves back to Him.

Friday, July 31, 1992

Our Lady tells us to persist in Love and to never give up. Even when it seems like we make mistakes trying to correct our errors, we must keep our hearts to-the-mill and forge onward in faith. Always and forever, She tells us that God is our strength. It is in Jesus that we find the will to summon this power. He is our purpose and our goal. We are blessed and recreated in Him. All that is lost is finally found in Christ. Every day that passes, I remember the courage I am given from God through His Son. I stand on the foundation that His Love provides. I know that my Diary is bound to succeed in the sure-footed wisdom of the Holy Spirit. I only hope that I can keep myself strong when it starts its journey into the world of cynics and cowards who would rather run from God than acknowledge that it is He who is chasing them. This manuscript is my record of His call through our Virgin Mother. I have prepared it with love for my brother-and-sister humanity, with care and dedication. I have learned this from the Mother of God, our Holy Queen, who I see still hoping in the future of our souls with Herself and the Hosts of the heavens in Paradise.

Our beautiful Lady came this evening to remind us of Her Love for humanity and to augment our prayers. Her message is that faith is the initial precept for accepting anything we cannot yet see. She has been helping me continue my writing and to transcribe some of it into portions for early distribution. God has been very generous in allowing His Mother to speak to the world and helping to make this Diary the benefit of all humankind. My continuous desire is that I am able to relate to you that Jesus loves us in immeasurable ways. Sometimes I think that I have only opened the doorway a crack in comparison to the vision we truly need. If you will pray together with me, we will all be able to push the doorway of our faith wide-open to reveal every intention of God for His people. This begins in our love for one another and our promise to unite as one under the Cross of the Christ who saved our souls from eternal damnation.

Our Lady offered Her beautiful words of encouragement tonight. **"I love you so very much for all that you have done to prepare your Diary, your sacrifices, your labors, your prayers, and your hopes. I have tried very hard to help humanity to come to Jesus. I have used your love, the love of you and your brother, to the best of its power for the good of all of the world. Please remember that it is your response of love for your brothers and sisters that has made all of My messages to you possible. And now, the fruition of your many years of companionship is about to be revealed** to the world, and in mighty forces. I have told you that not everyone will immediately accept this Diary as being from God. You must not let that dismay you. Please know that, as your Diary stands, it is extremely, extremely filled with power of, and through, the Holy Spirit. Even though your manual efforts have compiled it, it now has a universal and almighty composition and Divine purpose. Jesus has blessed the work of your hands as His own. You now must not observe your Diary as a function of you and your humanness.

Like the human person is made-up of many parts, the body would not be whole without each one of them. And, as all of the parts are united to make up the human person, which is much more than the sum of these parts, so it is with your Diary. It is no longer a compilation of letters, words, paragraphs, thoughts, days, or pages. It is now greater than the summation of all these things. Your Diary is now of immortal quality and a sense that can only be perceived by the human heart. As I have told you, you have nurtured and nursed it to its birth. Now, you must set it free into the world. And, you must not feel obligated to govern or to support its every journey. You need not feel it necessary to substantiate or prove by explanation its every statement. You may provide additional witness to help support its content, but not as a way to try to refute the claims of nonbelievers. You will do well. I see that you feel very warm and hopeful about your first Diary. It is a seed of Love that will flower into the blooming unity of humanity toward Salvation. Your prayers will help provide the nourishment for that seed. As I bless you now, I do so with My loving thanks for your submission to God, your example to others in Love, and for your purity and holiness. Thank you for your prayers. I will speak to you soon. I love you. Goodnight."

I know that I am not truly worthy of such pious words or the tasks I am being asked to fulfill. Sometimes I live in holy fear that I will do something wrong or allow my love to fall into a state of imperfection in the eyes of God. It is as though I am somehow too timid to lift my face toward Heaven. But, I know this to be what Christ wishes for our souls because He is the happiness we are seeking. We remember that Saint John often laid his head on Jesus' chest out of reverence and humility. Like this great Saint, our feelings of unworthiness must not deter us from accepting and honoring Our Lord. We are all equal in His eyes, even those who are far from Him. It is for the conversion of the wicked that He came. He destroyed the death of us all by His own execution on the Cross. If He did not think we were worth that price, He would assuredly not have paid it. We are all the pleasure of God's eyes, but we cannot yet stand in human flesh in the full presence of His infinite Justice. Only through the cleansing Blood of Jesus Christ are our souls so prepared.

No mortal can stand Face-to-face with the Almighty Father and say, "I am." Only Our Lord is that perfect. But, if we unify ourselves in Him, we will be rendered worthy of judgement by a Truth that will not perish from our souls. It is for deliverance to this great Mercy that Our Lady has come so urgently to prepare us.

AUGUST 1992

Sunday, August 2, 1992

Jesus has allowed His Mother to reveal many previously-hidden graces during the past months through Her supernatural intercession. The unfolding of our Salvation is occurring just beyond the reach of our mortal perception. And too, there are many signs occurring directly before our eyes, but we do not have the faith to recognize them as messages from our Immortal God. These manifestations are part of His Divine Plan to save humanity for deliverance into Heaven. What will it take for us to comprehend what this means? **Pray, Pray, Pray**. The magnanimous purpose of God transcends all human thought and comprehension. Every level of our consciousness is encompassed by His power and authority. Our recognition of this truth is the origin of our conversion and service in the name of Jesus Christ. It is the same Divine acceptance by those who are now happily living in Heaven.

I received a very special gift today. One of the holy saints spoke to me about the Kingdom we all hope to reach. I was asked not to reveal his name because he wishes to continue to serve God in Heaven with the same humility that he did on Earth. His words were few, but of great encouragement. He asked me to remember the power of the Sacraments of Baptism and Confession, and to reveal to the world God's request for all of His children to receive them. I have recorded his message here for the world to see, just as I promised. We must respond to the Communion of Saints as though they are individually and collectively Christ Himself speaking to our souls. Like the Holy Mother, they cannot come to Earth unless it is the Will of the Father. And like Her, they pray to God for our protection, conversion, and deliverance to the Paradise they now enjoy. Our Lady came to speak to me after this holy Saint finished. She told me that this grace was brought to help me continue my struggle to record Her messages. Somehow, those of us who hear the word of God by audible and visual means have to proclaim that we will continue despite the forces trying to diminish us. I know inside my heart that Her revelations elevate my soul to near paradisial heights. I do not enter a state of "ecstasy" as defined by other messengers, but I am filled to overflowing with peace and strength when I am contacted by a citizen of Heaven.

I firmly anchor my life upon the fulfillment of the prophesies I see as days pass by. My soul holds fast to the firm foundation of Love brought by the

Holy Spirit implanted in my heart. But, Christ did not affirm that human faith is to be founded on supernatural graces alone. We know that He is the Eucharist because the truth lives inside us. That is the home of our belief. We must trust the God we cannot see by living a faith whose fruits we can see. This sweetness grows from the seed of Love through which we know that the Most Blessed Sacrament is the Body and Blood of Christ. And, our souls are convinced that the Holy Mass is the Crucifixion of Christ Jesus on the hill of Mount Calvary. We see through faith that our Redemption and Salvation are before our very eyes in the presence of infinite Love and Mercy. This is the same creative Glory through which God Himself made the world and sent His Son to save it.

Our Holy Mother told me that my writing will be an anchor for many who have never believed that God loves us as infinitely as He does. His desire for us to live in Heaven is so strong that He has chosen to provide miracles to strengthen our faith. He knows it is difficult for those who live in this age to believe without seeing. We are somewhat the offspring of Doubting Thomas. But in the miracles God is providing through His Mother, we are able to "touch" Christ Jesus by Her Divine presence and say, *"She has been sent by Our Lord and Savior Jesus Christ in whom I firmly believe!"* I often think of the day when I will stand before Jesus to make an accounting of my life. I hope He sees my years as an effort in humility and preparation for His infinite Mercy and Salvation. I have given my life to Him. It would be a source of God's pride for Christ to ask, **"How did you die?"** , and our answer to be, *"I drowned in the Redeeming Blood of Your Cup of Salvation!"* I pray from the depths of my heart that I will be given the chance to return His Love with such power. If that opportunity should come, I owe every grace and thought of humility to our Blessed Mother and the Holy Spirit through which She comes.

Wednesday, August 5, 1992
Feast of the Dedication of Saint Mary Major

There is a litany of perfect terms which describe the beauty and grace of our Holy Mother. And, after becoming even more intimately acquainted with Her Divinity, I have told Her that I wish these titles could be added to Her veneration.

Womb of all Saints	Eternal Intercessor
Usher of Light	Delight of the Angels
Lady of the Faithful	Bearer of Mercy
Solace of Sufferers	Blissful Countess
Seamstress of Perfection	Our Charitable Nourishment
Essence of Piety	Divine Benefactor
Procuress of God's Bounty	The Splendor of Purity

There are no mere human expressions that can accurately define the infinite perfection of our Holy Mother. She told me that She is humbled by these descriptions. I know that She has earned every one of them. I am also happy that She came today to speak to me under the title of Her Holy Wisdom. She had many things to say tonight about the glories of Love. She speaks with great joy and hope about our conversionary work together. Of all the beautiful words She has spoken to Her children in countless parables, the most profound are Her simple utterance, "I love you." It is very clear that She reflects the intrinsic desire of God to call us home to Heaven. We must eventually acknowledge the fact that Jesus loves us so much that He has sent His Mother searching for our souls. She knows the saving grace of the Crucifixion of Her Son because She was under the Cross when He died. We are taken to Calvary with Her when we attend the Holy Sacrifice of the Mass. We were proclaimed Her children by Christ, Himself, just before delivering His Soul to the Almighty Father. When we attend Holy Mass, She turns Her head to see humanity standing beside Her as Jesus consecrates us to Her Immaculate Heart.

The Holy Spirit has been welcomed by generations of people throughout the passing centuries. Indeed, Our Lady has also appeared to thousands. Christ has manifested His message of Salvation through countless pious theologians and priests. He is now trying to inspire the world through the infallible Life of Pope John Paul II, the Vicar of the Apostolic Church on Earth. His encyclicals and homilies resonate the Truth of the coming Kingdom of God into the world. He has written several ecclesiastical volumes that explain the Divine nature of Jesus and the Salvation we find in His Body and Blood from the Altar of Sacrifice. The genius of God is also revealed through the simplistic lives of unknown souls through which He brings the miracle of His Mother's intercession. He chooses the weak to cultivate the strong and the simple of mind to confound the masters of philosophy and calculation. The Holy Spirit comes to the most serene of souls to sing the praises of God's Love. Christ lives in the suffering of the poor to speak the message of healing and deliverance. He calls for active participation by everyone to alleviate the plight of all His people. We are not supposed to look upon them and simply say, *"I'm glad that is not me!"* Our duty is to repair the lives of the broken and restore dignity to the lost as we see Christ Himself standing before us disguised in these poor people.

Our Lady spoke to the power of Christian unity in Her message today. Jesus has placed no stumbling block before His people that we cannot overcome in Him. There are, indeed, powerful forces at work to keep our hearts divided. But, the Holy Spirit gives us the conviction to destroy them. In a world encapsulated by animosity, bitterness, and disagreement, we are called to be one in the Lord God Almighty. Feelings of resentment are a repulsion to those who know what it is like to be free from them. They are a barometer as to whether our own hearts are open to offer forgiveness. If we resent others because of their sins, we are not living the Life of Christ. We must teach by example and pray out of compassion. The strength of human love will always be more powerful than the weakness of hatred. The origin of this peace is founded in unconditional forgiveness of others. This is the most important virtue toward the unification of souls in Christ Jesus. It is also the one that reveals our most discernable selves. We may be willing to forgive the transgressions of our brothers and sisters that we are also guilty of committing. When we exhibit the same errors as others, their failures do not seem as offensive.

However, if we have become immune from falling to a certain temptation, we often expect them to have the same strength. If they do not, we look upon them as being reprehensible and disgusting. We fail to recognize that others are strong in areas that we are weak. When we are confident that we would never fall into a certain sin, we reprimand, castigate, and punish those who do. We even take the lives of criminals while denying our hypocrisy, claiming we would never commit the crimes for which they are executed. Love is greater than any disagreement, moral violation, or public infraction. Every time we overcome a wall of grief and darkness, Creation takes a giant leap toward Paradise. Each time we choose purity over the filth of lust and perversion, we take a drink from the Life-giving fountain of Eternity. When we open ourselves to the cascade of beauty from another heart, we become one in their joy and united in the blissful Mercy of God. He will leave no one behind who offers their entire being in prayer and contrition. Every soul He created has a mansion reserved in the bounty of Heaven. We are granted that seat by the grace of the Crucifixion of His Son. The Salvation of humankind was not won in a chess-match or foot-race.

The perfect Christ of all Creation suffered and died to render us free from sin and eligible for the glories of Heaven. He not only rescued us from the grasp of our attacker, He single-handedly destroyed our opposition in the process. We are now free to show our mutual love for one another and God will see it from His Throne. We can now help each other into Paradise, knowing that our lives truly make a difference. Jesus has granted us liberty to forgive others in a supernatural way, performing the miracle of expiation though the Love in our own simple hearts. We begin by embracing the suffering of others and releasing the indignation that prohibits us from approaching those whom we fear. Our love grows stronger when we shamelessly shed tears for those whose help lies in our hands. This is how the bonds of hatred are destroyed. These are the new beginnings that cast-out the wretchedness that stains our souls with the soil of indifference. Christ has given us the perfect passageway to immortal justice. He is the New Covenant between God and man Who proclaims it to be a righteous act to turn one's cheek in advance of another slap. We can be proud to suffer once again in the name of the Redemption of humanity.

Those who have never been loved by anyone can now see the smallest touch of affection and attention as the fulfillment of everything they ever wanted. Together with them, those who live in Christ are soon to be exalted and glorified above all Creation toward a new beginning in a timeless beauty that could never be conceived on Earth. The poor, the homeless, the starving, the afflicted, the despised, the ridiculed, and the oppressed are the glorious saints-in-waiting for confirmation into the Light of Paradise. We need to focus our hearts on the way the world must become and live-out the opportunity to attain it through Christ the Lord. Those with little faith on dirt paths need to be elevated to the superhighway of trust in God. Anyone sitting alone looking through a window of despair can stand and jump through the glass unharmed into the waiting arms of Jesus. He waits for our response like a father beckoning a child to jump toward his arms into a pond for the first time. When we overcome every fear, anxiety, and hesitation that might keep us from knowing our God in the perfection He seeks, we will have truly begun to live-out the words of the great evangelist Martin L. King, Jr. who proclaimed, *"Free at last! Free at last! Thank God Almighty, I'm free at last!"* Let the celebration begin.

Thursday, August 6, 1992   Feast of the Transfiguration

There are periods during the presence of the intercession of the Blessed Virgin Mary that are timeless events, not able to be attributed to a certain day in the progression of linear history. Our Holy Mother's powerful and transcendent purpose allows us the unique opportunity to escape the captivating conventions of the physical world. She brings us the revelation of God Himself, eternal and present-day, to open-wide our souls to realize the Kingdom about to come to the Earth. Although the Glory I saw today is outside of time, I have placed it at this date in my Diary for the application of human reference. Even the task of describing it in words imposes a constraint on its infinity to which it can never truly be held. Today, I was given a message not of religion, but of the reason for religion, not of faith, but the purpose of faith. To help me comprehend the splendor of Jesus' Transfiguration, I was taken to the mountaintop of grace. I was approached by a definitive man who asked me to accompany him on a midsummer journey through the countryside. But, this trek was not of labor or lesson, but of discovery and disclosure.

I accompanied this humble soul through the comforts of nature, but I soon found that the solace lived in Him. Without a sound or focus of an eye, He became transfigured before me like a flash of great light. He spoke without saying a word, telling me that He had come to beatify mankind in the Truth, once and for all. I could see the emanation of His starlit heart in one perfect vision. He was a hologram of every facet of perfection and fineness that mankind could ever be. He knew me completely, having never before stood at my side. I was deplete and hollow, He said, and absent of light and strength. He had an impeccable yearning for me to know Him without reservation and to become one with the bounty He held. But, He could not reveal it yet, because my heart could never withstand the joy. I could not resist my submission to His salient sheen, like a jewel never-before held, with an undiscovered elegance and a power never before known to humankind. This was a universal man who grasped in His hands the souls of every generation. He knew the answers to questions I never thought could be asked. And yet, He was simple and sweet, one who would rather plant a flower than savor the fruit of a diamond mine, even if all the riches were His. The commander of nature, He seemed to be. Like God Himself, but with a body as brilliant as the sun.

His presence took-on the ecstasy of an apparition, though He was real and alive in every way. And, He spoke in silence of the Glory of Heaven, of strength and courage, and the nobility we seek to be one with the Almighty Father. Nature itself was present in Him from innocent sprout to bountiful harvest at one perpetual moment. He reached with His Heart behind the depths of the clouds as if to comfort the tangible side of God, gently caressing His Face like touching the cheek of a child. I knew that His Love for me was as undeniably real. He told me that it is possible for humankind to be sinless like God, but He still never uttered a tone. He was clearly the essence of perfect man. I saw the way The Father answers our prayers in unabashed Love for His people. He knows the desires of our hearts and the reflections of our souls. This Being was the endless future and our reconciled past in one great light, willing to make amends for any infraction that has tarnished our hope or impeded our trust.

I was an apprentice at the hands of a Master; and He the melody to a song known only to me. He was a flash of elegance I had never before seen, with undefinable grace and polydimensional power. Yet, He was still simply knowable. He recounted my life from my innocence in the cradle to the complications of my present-day self. Somehow beside me, He became the origin and meaning of Life from enwombed divinity to the blossom of perfection. My soul knew Him as the manna from the heavens, come to rest on the table of Life, and also the horn of plenty who is filled to overflowing. He had a fragrant and contemplative composure, and exuded a clement fidelity unsurpassed by any other being in all the universes combined. I do not know how such emblazoned power could be captured by the vision of the human eye. He read my soul like a mystical genius, while touching my heart with the effortless charm of a factual God. I saw Him as the conqueror of the world as He reached into a pond to feed a fish and pat a toad on the head.

Above all, I knew that He was a Champion who once had to fight for His crown against the worst of odds, while lifting Himself to His feet. In His victory, there is nothing I would ever fear again, no threat of punishment or deprivation, no height, or no weight. He said that He reigned from a juxtapositional Throne that I knew was rightfully His. And from there, He nourishes Life and tells nature to echo the promise of His eternal loyalty. Even today, He took my soul beyond any limit that mankind or the boundaries of Earth could impose on my hope or anticipation. He called Himself the Dawn, but was already emitting the blinding sun of high noon. The solitude of His faithful eyes poured-forth the Light through which I saw His infinite Love. He told me that He would see me in the morning as He parted in peace. The moment seemed almost like a dream from which I awoke with a refined soul. Just as quickly as He came, this man of permeating Light passed forward through a translucent sheer, but left me made new and willing to face any force obtuse enough to challenge my invincible resolve to see this great One again.

That was the vision I experienced before Our Lady came to speak with me again today. My brother and I prayed the Holy Rosary this evening and affirmed to all the accompanying heavens that Her Son is, indeed, the response to our every supplication. His Love is so powerful that no clamoring pitch of worldly pandemonium can drown-out mankind's humble invocations. She asked my brother and me to continue to pray for the awakening of hearts in Jesus and to restore the Earth to the tranquil order known only in the bounty of Heaven. She also spoke about a portion of my Diary that I have already recently released to some of my fellow acquaintances. I am hoping that it is composed in such a way as to inspire their hearts to unite in the cause of Our Lady's intercession. Time is far too short for them to cower in disbelief.

Our Lady said,**"Satan is now running in full force against your Diary. He will not succeed! But, you will be subjected to a wide array of ridicule for a while. You would do best to be joyful. Many will dissect your Diary in the same way that they also try to dissect the revelations of My shrines. You see, My messages to the world are a supplement to the Holy Scriptures, which many are not open enough to accept. My words are intended to draw My children together through the Holy Spirit. We will be patient and watch those who will make their case against My intercession. Their opposition will pass, and the true multitude of people whom your Diary will lead to Jesus will begin to be touched. But, there are those who still insist that God does not work this way. They will have plentiful chances to show their trust. Thank you for your prayers. I will speak to you soon. I love you. Goodnight."**

Saturday, August 8, 1992

Today, Our Lady told me that some people wish to take Her messages to other visionaries for verification of their authenticity. It is oftentimes not the will of God to provide such exchange. What would this do to build faith? It is always a source of sorrow when we find that a gift from God has been confirmed by mortal discovery when we should have initially accepted in faith. She also discussed the necessity for my brother and me to remain united in prayer so Her messages can continue. She often refers to the sending-out of the seventy-two disciples by Jesus in pairs. Together, they were able to witness to our Salvation through Christ and deliver the message of conversion. Each of them was given a supporting partner to keep them strong during times of duress and opposition by the world. God knows that we do not have the strength to stand alone. That is why He sent the Holy Spirit to give power and ability to those who have no one else to stand with them. We must remember that when Christ dispatched His disciples, the Paraclete had yet to descend to Earth.

My brother and I complement what is lacking in each other. Neither of us could sustain the buffets of criticism and ridicule we have suffered on our own. The anguish that any mortal finds in their witness for Christ is burdensome because nothing in the world is more opposed than the peace trying to engulf it. That is why we must all be partners in faith. We can accomplish far more together than we can alone. Our Lady presented a parable of two separate tables.

You can see that these tables can accommodate a large burden, especially if they are made of solid wood or a type of stone. But, their foundation is not protracted to the extent that they would not fall-over under the influence of their environment. But, two such tables connected by a common surface are nearly invincible in their capacity to sustain weight or any forces that may try to topple them.

The common surface that makes these two tables one is symbolic of the shared love for God between two hearts. Their combined strength is physically and spiritually greater than either of them alone or even of the sum of their individual capacities. To this end, Our Lady asked my brother and me to pray for each other and to reflect holiness into the world through our union in Christ. One is to lift up the other who may be suffering fear or temptation. We are to counsel each other in the way of Love. While we have yet to physically heal anyone on our journey for God, I am confident that we have mended souls who have no one else to pray for them. We know that Christ is with us because we are united in His Name. Our Holy Mother has spent a great deal of time the past few days trying to focus my heart on the work at hand. I have been concerned that the partial writings I have released to other individuals will be discounted as zealous opportunism. She asked me to allow the Holy Spirit to do His work while I tend to mine. I have the same fear as a father whose young son has just gone into the cruel world. My work is comprised of my innocent effort to convey Our Lady's messages to the world in the best way I know how.

It is a very difficult task trying to place the Immaculate grace of Our Lady into discernable words on a page. She told me that Jesus will protect my work on His behalf. Even though it may not contain the inherent beauty of pearls, He will not allow any corruption to destroy it. I am reminded of the pain that the Holy Mother feels when Her words are cast-aside by people who fail to understand the mightiness of God's Love. She has been sent to convert the same world that killed Her Divine Son. But this time, the advantage is on the side of Heaven. No ill-intentioned mortal can blemish the beauty of the Blessed Virgin. Jesus will toss the world across the universe like emptying a pail of water. Our Lady is telling us that the grasp of His Hands is already on it. By dying on the Cross to save our souls, Jesus simultaneously acquired the authority of God to dispense with wretched souls through His own discretion. That is why we must pray the Chaplet of Divine Mercy like never before. Our Lady can touch any heart that is open to the Holy Spirit, and has the power to chastise those who are not. By virtue of Her sorrowful suffering at the foot of the Cross on Mount Calvary, She is vested with the grace to befall anyone indignant enough to spate at the Resurrection of Her Son. This is the same Love and authority that She wields through the immortal truth She reveals to the world.

Her message is that the righteous have nodded-off waiting for Christ to return and those who are dead-asleep in sin are about to be shocked into reality like being stung by a cattle prod. Therefore, we must show faith in the miracles of Jesus and be willing to sacrifice our lives in His Name for the conversion of slumbering sinners. We must invoke the pleasant nature of the Holy Spirit and greet our brothers and sisters with compassion, understanding, and forgiveness. This is our time to live the example of Love on Earth in the way that the Saints of Heaven walked before us. The most beautiful aspect of human life is that we will never be deplete of opportunities to perform the works of the Lord in His Name. There will never be a time when we can cease praying for ourselves and one another. This is the conviction to which we must dedicate ourselves and never waiver from that promise. It is the living echo of Jesus' Crucifixion and the Life He asks us to lead. And, it is a prize that no thief can steal. The gift which God has made to us must be given from ourselves to others. The essence of our acceptance of Christ and our compliance with His command rest in that transfer.

Monday, August 10, 1992

Days pass-by very quickly, as though we are branches being carried along by a rolling river. In my new beginning with the Blessed Mother, the weeks seem like days and the years seem like months. She brings a perpetual state of grace in Her presence, in which I am fully embraced. I now pray every petition with greater love for God since I have known the beauty of His Holy Mother. She tells us that He hears our call for the healing of our souls, the mending of the broken lives we see, and the unity of all hearts in Jesus. My most fervent prayer is that Our Lord will make me worthy of the gift of His forgiveness and Mercy. I know that He will pardon me at the end of time; but I only hope that I will truly be able to absolve myself for any distance I may have created between us. My prayers are for all of the intentions that Our Lady has asked me to remember. I keep looking inside myself and trying to reach for more that I can offer to Her cause. God knows that Judgment Day will be the reckoning of all souls from every age. I wish to be in that great body of Saints who will someday live in complete bliss with the Hosts of the heavens. Jesus will help me make it there, if I listen to His Word. Our Blessed Lady tells me about the Will of our Almighty Savior.

I ask God daily to help me to comply with the wishes of His Mother. She knows that I grew-up in a fast-paced environment with a family of eight and have been trying to shed my habits of swift response, reaction, and spontaneity. I also participated in athletics, which taught me the necessity for quick-thinking and instantaneous movement. That was years ago, but I have carried that same approach and behavior into my maturing years. Somehow, my passions and feelings have become as important as winning a basketball game, but they are actually no more than my human reaction to the world around me. With Our Lady's peaceful guidance, I am becoming more able to discern what affects and stimulates my inner-self. I am better able to cope with the advances of the world through eyes of greater wisdom and comfort. Each person we meet is a product of their own feelings and personal characteristics. To know anyone well, we should understand their lives in light of their sacrifices and suffering. How we behave in difficult circumstances and whether we are able to successfully sustain the throes of mortality define the substance of our faith.

This entire process is a fruit of the love we hold for God and His children. If we are reserved in temperament and kind-of-heart, we can better understand the needs of the silent multitude of people crying for consolation. We should make our words the sentiments of Christ Himself and our actions the extension of His Hands. At this late hour in the existence of the world, there is no time to waste in offering Love and goodness in reflection of the Life of the Holy Spirit among us. This is not to say that we must scrupulously watch our every word so as not to offend those who are opposed to God's work. We do not destroy peace when we speak the Word of God in a quiet place. If their silence is a product of human indifference, they have already breached the union between themselves and the paternal Spirit of Eternal Life. Words which describe the Love of Jesus are never inadequate when being spoken by someone willing to know Him. Those who are still growing in witness for Christ speak at the pace of the Holy Spirit. This is the reason why we continue to pray and hope for change. We know that the world is not "there" yet.

There are many frivolous words that describe the Earth and the lives of those attached to it. But, any simple phrase that brings the thought of God into someone's heart is the thesis for which we live our Christian faith. Every moment we live for Love is one captured for Eternity. It is part of the endless storehouse of paradisial bounty in Heaven. When we exhibit the grace of Our Lord through the smallest of gestures, we are bringing a director's wand in front of an eternal orchestra waiting to play the songs of Redemption. Christ is the melody and we are the harmony to His resounding masterpiece of heavenly bliss. We are a participant in the march toward the Kingdom even if our role is no larger than the simple ringing of a bell to call the faithful to their feet at the beginning of Holy Mass. We are the polished pins that Christ wears on His lapel as He travels the Earth and distant universes to proclaim the Good News of our Salvation. I have come great strides in my understanding of peace and prayer. My soul has grown from the uniformed player on the court to a hope-filled participant in the conversion of men. I know I can pray with the best and suffer with the worst. This enlightenment is one of the many fruits of the intercession of Our Holy Lady. I am now joyfully clad in Her grace and prepared to face any opponent who foolishly proclaims to be mightier than the Spirit of God.

Wednesday, August 12, 1992

I know that I am learning an immeasurable lesson about myself from the Holy Virgin as I grow in wisdom through the bounty of God. That includes my perception of others and how the righteous are, indeed, held in great esteem by Christ the Lord. While I have been afforded the gift of speaking to His Mother, millions of my brothers and sisters in Christian conviction are having to walk the pathway to Heaven on their faith in God alone. We are saved by the grace of God; and His living faithful are unequivocally worthy of His blessing. Tens of millions of mortal souls read the Holy Bible and pray. They attend Holy Mass and recite the Rosary in private cenacles. They open their hearts like innocent children to the offering of any little sign that God will give them that they are special in His eyes. I affirm the truth by this writing that God's followers are His most beloved possession. I have to try harder to succeed because I have seen more than most. Yes, I still need faith to see Christ clearly. The Blessed Mother would never take that from me. Her presence has highly strengthened its power. My love and respect for those who walk by faith alone has grown to infinite proportions because I see the good fight they must wage against the pitfalls of the world. They are winning by their own love for God.

Our Blessed Lady brings Her words and deeds of holiness every day to strengthen our lives in Jesus. She makes it clear that Her presence is not solely meant for me, but for the world and all who will better know Christ by Her messages. She said very beautifully tonight, **"My little child, I love the world very much. I wish for peace to abound in every nation, in every land. Thank you for your prayers! Thank you for praying the Holy Rosary, My Crown of Roses, which makes Me smile in Love for all My children. Be happy! I love you."** The Holy Mother asks us to live prayerfully because She knows that Satan is poised to attack anyone who responds to Her call. She tells us to hold our Rosary in our hands so all Creation will know we belong to Her. This is a sign to any evil that we are the children of the Holy Virgin and any attempt to draw us from Her is in vain. Christ destroyed the desolation of sin that previously detained the mortal world. When we give our hearts and souls to His power, no evil can touch us. Satan himself knows this Truth and will cower and run in fear when he sees God's imprint on our soul. The Blood of Christ kills evil in its tracks like an antiseptic destroys bacteria. With the Holy Rosary, we hold the Cross of our Redemption in our hands because it is the key link to which the decades are attached. Satan will flee for his very existence in sight of the Cross of Our Lord. I continue to hope that I am sharing Our

Lady's words with you in a way that expresses Her infinite beauty. She tells me over and again that Her Love for us is never-ending. This cannot truly be portrayed in my words.

In light of the Passion of Jesus, mankind is rendered wholly insufficient to describe the immensity of God's Love. The Holy Mother explains that it will suffice for us to understand that Her messages are of that same Love. She wants us to live their meaning in the same conviction that we affirm our faith in Her Son. If we do not, we are living our belief by proxy and not truly dedicating ourselves to Jesus as the reason for Life. To be sure, our best understanding of the Love of God is that He is the Light which gives Life. He is the sun of our souls like the daytime that grows pretty flowers. Our vision of where we are going and from whence we came comes in the glow of His Wisdom. He gives it freely to all hearts open to receive Him. This is the power of Almighty God which He dispenses to the Earth in the Holy Spirit. We are free to coopt this authentic influence to cultivate our souls and the people of the world. This is the Divine Will of the Father that masses of mortal beings still refuse to acknowledge. Our Lady told me that She would continue Her words soon and for me to record this message as you have just read it. She said Her next lesson would be about the pre-Eminence of God. **"I have given you a Diary describing the basics of Love. I am teaching you Who Love is and how you are to reflect Him. Now, I am able to speak of God in His True Eminence."**

Saturday, August 15, 1992   Feast of the Assumption of Mary

Our Lady keeps my soul aloft with the inner-vision of God and the fulfillment of His Spirit. She never lets me stray far from the guidance of Her Love. If I move further than a crows-leap from Her hand or just outside the shadow of Her mantle, She swiftly calls me back. When the world seems cumbersome and sad, She lifts me to higher joy. While I cannot remember Her ever tossing my soul into the air above Her Crown, I am sure that She has allowed me to sail freely amidst the countenance of Her grace. I trust Her completely in all things and follow Her to places I have never been. The road has not always been easy and I have stumbled on more than one occasion. I have also asked what little signs have meant along the way. She always replies with Her humble petition for me to trust like an obedient child. This is the same Mother whom I wish for you to know. She is the embodiment of God's Immaculate sacredness. I know that I will find Jesus in Her, just as the humble souls of Bethlehem found Him resting there. Please join me under the Morning Star, whose motherly Light is guiding us back to Light. Today is an opportune time for us all to seek Heaven together.

When I began to offer my prayers again for all humankind at the hour of eight-thirty this evening, the Holy Mother appeared during my recitation and said, **"It is evening again, My sons, and I have come to pray with you. Your prayers are so sweet, so heartful, so filled with compassion. In unison with the prayers of all the heavens, and all of the world, you are bridging the opening that separates mortality from immortality. Thank you, My little sons, especially so for honoring Me in your hearts, so filled with Love for all the world..."** Our Lady addressed a description about the pre-Eminent nature of Christ. She referred me to the Holy Scriptures, **Colossians 1:15-20**. After I read them, She spoke about the contrast between *"eminence"* and *"imminence."* The former is a description of power, authority, and mightiness, and the latter is a function of time. Both of these terms help us to understand the Alpha and the Omega as well as the timeless nature of God Himself. Without trying to be confusing, Our Lady told me that Christ is pre-Imminent to man and nature because His power precedes anything that can happen in the world, i.e., the events of the future. His Love is the powerful precursor to time itself and will forever succeed its passage. He is "one-in-being" with the Father and in union with the perpetual Light of Creation.

Therefore, Christ is the source of Light for the world and also the Light itself. He is the sun and its rays in one eternal Being. Therein lies His Divine presence as the Path and the Destiny of our souls. When we look at a light from a distance, we see its brilliance like the glow of a star. We notice that we are somehow warmed by this Light as we see its cast upon our hands and arms. We wonder how a light so far away can shine through the distance and illuminate our world with such power. We have no choice but to conclude that this light is not only in the heavens, but apparent and present among us through the properties of time and space. We cannot see the rays, but our faces reflect this heavenly glow. Hence, Christ is the source of Light in Heaven and on Earth by preceding our very ability to survey Him. Since Our Lord is the Alpha and the Omega, all Creation flows from His perfect infinity. He is the Father of all that is seen and unseen which finds its destiny in Him. That renders Him the greatest power in Creation. All other forces and influences are an effect of time of which He is the *Imminent* Ruler. He is not confined by the property that belongs to Him. There is no power or authority at the discretion of men that can encapsulate or affect the paramount control that Christ holds over Heaven and Earth.

Our Lord reserves the *Eminent* right to claim any person or property as His own. As a result of this irrevocable Truth, He is the supreme Magistrate and Judge over mankind and every aspect of our lives. So, our criteria for discerning the power of men falls infinitely short of applying to Christ and God the Father. We are infirm in all ways to even consider the definition of greatness. The Life of Christ which culminated in His Death and Resurrection casts an irreversible cloud of obsolescence over the human description of heroism. Jesus is the only infinite incarnation of God Who renders the search for other redeemers both futile and vain. Those throughout the centuries who have tried to seek another savior have found themselves unreconciled to God and buried beneath His avalanche of Truth that we all eventually come to know. This one Mightiness is held inseparable and yet distinct in Three Divine Persons, The Trinity; Father, Son, and Holy Spirit. Creation itself stands in no greater or multiplied presence. Its simplicity lives in the stillness of peace through the jurisdiction and power of the Holy Spirit. And since only good comes from God, Creation itself must be intrinsically well-founded. Everything that He does is perfect. This is the reason that every manifestation of Christ is a product of the sinless perfection He holds in union with the Almighty Father. Therein lies the Love we must come to know.

The world fell to sin through the lives of Adam and Eve, including ourselves by virtue of our inherent nature of being God's created people. Sin transforms our souls from good into bad. This is a product of the human will we were given at birth. But, through Christ, we are vindicated from the original sin we inherited from Adam and from every transgression against Love we have committed on our own. We have to use this same will to accept Jesus' Crucifixion as reparation for our sins in the eyes of God and in the recesses of our hearts. We must actively choose to do good and avoid the influences of the evil that travels the Earth seeking the ruin of souls. I asked the Holy Mother about many things that mankind sees as bad, such as tornadoes, earthquakes, and other natural disasters. What is the purpose of plagues and infirmities? Are these horrible strains punishments from God? Her response is that our conscience allows us to see them as His justice. We realize our helplessness and the distance our souls lie from God when we see the manifestations of nature and the existence of pestilence and disease. Anything that pushes our souls away from peace and fulfillment is the effect of human sin. And, we often suffer in reparation for the lives of others in the same way Jesus' Passion made amends for the moral and physical transgressions of ourselves. God realizes mankind's distance from Love.

Because Our Lord loves us so powerfully, He allows the revelations of nature and our own suffering to draw us to Him. At the last, we must understand that we cannot preserve ourselves outside His protective countenance. When we suffer a natural disaster or a bodily infirmity, we should call on Christ to come to our aid. That is what *He* wants to do. The effects of the world are not God's angry punishment upon a people He rejects, but the means through which He can grant us great comfort and reconciliation. His purpose is always salvific and benign. His every act is a cultivating and redeeming fruit of His infinite Love. The strength with which God holds Jesus in His Heart every day is the same loyalty that He offers to us. He asks only for our humble submission and reverent servitude in the likeness of His Crucified Son. Nothing can destroy our unity in Him or the fulfillment of a human heart that finds its nourishment from the graces He dispenses to those who believe.

Monday, August 17, 1992

I have been wondering recently how the special pictures of Jesus in the Eucharist that my brother and me have been sending to others are being received. I remember that The Blessed Mother told me that miracles would accompany these holy cards with Jesus in the monstrance. I do not ignore God's miracles because I recognize them as the great gift they are rather than an aberration of His generous Mercy. But, it would take an extraordinary miracle of the most infinite degree to overwhelm the Consecration of bread and wine into the Body and Blood of Jesus by a priest at Holy Mass. I am grateful for all the blessings He bestows on His children in whatever form He chooses to dispense them. As you can also see, I am elated and surprised that He sent His Mother to speak to my brother and me on His behalf. It amazes me that God can peer into a crowd and see individual souls He recognizes equally. He loves all of us and ignores no one. His Love is universally inclusive.

When Our Lady came to pray with us this evening, these are the revealing words She said, **"My little children, Jesus and I come to you so tenderly today. So many scores of happy faces saw Jesus' face in the Monstrance today in the pictures. There were miracles granted to them, I am saying that they 'saw' His face. Jesus is so happy with you, He brings His kindness and gentle appreciation, and His return of Love to you. He has allowed Me to come to you as His sweetness and beauty and joy. My little precious ones, so many thoughts today were composed of the quiet and little places of Love, like the wing-tips of a little butterfly, the mite just beneath the bark of a tree, the wind whirling around and through the small evergreens, the soft and quenching trickle of a forest brook, and the slender ray of sunlight as it lands on the ground beneath the maple branches.**

Today, My sons, the minds of men were directed to the cool and crisp summits of the mightiest mountains and the clean, clear-blue ponds of the rocky west. Jesus came to many in the back lawns of estates, the terraces of governors, inside the dining rooms of managers, and on the greens and fields of those who would see their holidays of vacation transformed into the breath of freshness of Love and promise. Today, the face of Jesus brought Light to dimmed hopes, Life to stagnant souls, keys of release to caged hearts, and a shining beauty to the gloom of the repetitive beat of daily labors. I am telling you, little children, that you are seeing the good fruits of what your efforts are doing. I also wish to tell you that what has happened today is very little in comparison to what your Diary will do. So, up with your heart! I love you so much. I hope with you and pray with you. I have come to tell you that I am not only thankful for what you are doing to help your brothers and sisters, but I am also thankful to you for an even greater achievement.

You are helping to bend the scarred cheeks of My Son upward into a smile, so that He can now feel not so lonely. He has new cause today to feel strength, and not sorrowful frailty. You have chosen to help show the world that He is the Champion, the Winner, the One of all, whose only hope is to save the souls of humankind and only cause is to love all, and be all, to those many millions who are also lonely and desolate like He was once before, to the aged beautiful hearts that no one will give a chance to be shared and the little innocent hearts that are cast aside in their child-like littleness. Today, My little precious Jesus is smiling, and I am crying tears of thankfulness to you for helping Him to do so. Please call yourselves to remember this day, among many, that you helped Jesus to smile. Yes, you have seen His Beauty. Remember, always, to speak of His Beauty and Hope, as you are so ardently doing..."

The Holy Mother then asked me to read Revelation 21:21,

"The twelve gates were twelve pearls, each of the gates made from a single pearl; and the street of the city was of pure gold, transparent as glass."

She then continued. "**You must imagine what it would be like to be able to see through the pavements that are laid in the world, as if the paving material were transparent. You would see the Earth as smashed, compacted, and uniform. It would be one-dimensional, lifeless, and barren. This is nearly what the governments of the world are doing to their people, including the Western world. In the Eastern hemisphere, it is done with force, in the West, with materials and wealth. All I ask of government is that it promotes respect for Life and allows the nourishment of Jesus into the lives of all, that everyone be allowed to live with dignity. For these reasons, politics does not really bring much goodness. Remember that prayer should be the constitution of all the world. This will govern all souls toward grace, peace, and Salvation. I will bless you, now. Thank you for your prayers again and for being so precious. Remember to display your love. I will speak to you very soon. I love you, goodnight."**

My dear friends in Christ, I ask you to humbly pray with us wherever you live and whatever your station in life. The Holy Mother offers these words knowing that some have given little toward the coming Kingdom of Her Son. But, many of you have labored long and intensely for God's children. Your reward in Heaven will be majestic, magnificent, and fulfilling. We know that even the smallest taste of eternal Paradise waiting for those who serve the Lord is beyond our capacity to comprehend in this life. Thank you for loving and praying for the arrival of God's Kingdom.

Thursday, August 20, 1992

Our Lady allowed me to take a portion of my Diary that I had prepared to my workplace today for one of my friends. I have been trying for weeks to help those around me understand what the Blessed Virgin has been saying. I realize that it is difficult for others to abandon their reservations and faithfully believe that the Mother of Jesus Christ has come to my home to speak in the same comprehendible way that you and I communicate. But those who refuse to pray for discernment at all and outrightly reject the miracles of God seem like they are living in a cage and enjoy being there. I presented an excerpt from my Diary to a young lady with whom I had recently spoke about the Holy Mother's shrines all over the world. So often the signs of God that are meant to strengthen human faith are passed-off as mere coincidence. The lady read my written compilation of the Blessed Mother's words, but she seemed less-than impressed. At that very moment, God came to my rescue. The young lady began to fan through my Diary and abruptly came to a page and started reading. I asked her the date of the entry, which she said was August 20, 1991, exactly today's date a year ago. She looked at me with the face of someone who had just learned they won the lottery.

After she finished reading, I asked whether she thought this sign from God was a coincidence rather than a miracle. Unable to speak, she quickly looked at the calendar and then back at me. It was at that very moment that she began to understand that God loves her as infinitely as anyone else He created. But, God did not stop there. A couple of nights ago, the Holy Mother said that it would be better if I changed the color of the binding on my Diary from black to white. It is a better reference to the purity of God. I had not told this young lady about that, but in a matter of a few seconds after looking at the calendar, she turned to me and said, *"...and if I were you, I would change the cover of your book from black to white. It is more appropriate for something like this."* I told her that the Holy Mother suggested the same thing just a few days earlier. I asked if she thought that was also a coincidence! The young lady looked at me again in the same awe that her feelings about the nature of God were the same as His Mother's. The Blessed Virgin will provide every grace at Her disposal to help increase our faith in Jesus.

"My little children, I have come to you very happily today. I am sure that your happiness also abounds in your complete surrender to Jesus. Tonight, please remember His Love for you in a very special way. Yes, I helped you with the little girl at your workplace today. It is by these small graces that enlarged hearts of faith are built. Praying the Holy Rosary has gained these graces for you. It is August 20, 1992, and everything in the message from August 20, 1991 is the same. I still love My children who honor Me through the recitation of the Sacred Mysteries, and Jesus is still the Way to Heaven..." This message is very special because it represents another occasion during which Our Lady has addressed the reflections of my life. As I have indicated before in this Diary, Her lessons sometimes come in advance of the actual words She speaks. Often, they are difficult to learn and uncomfortable in nature. But in this case, I was pleased because it showed that the Holy Mother loves all of us to an infinite degree, even the young lady who had previously discounted the signal graces of God.

Also this evening, I have been repeatedly confronted with situations that call-to-mind my sinful past when I was offensive toward others and unkind in spirit. I was fighting against the same forces that produce these feelings. I could not physically relocate myself to escape the environment. Our Lady told me that I should have approached this situation from the vantage point of confidence rather than fear. I had great anguish that I was being tempted to fall in ways that I promised Almighty God that I would forever avoid. Our Lady invited me to read the Sacred Scriptures for strength through the Holy Spirit. She asked me to read **I John 4:16-18**. *"We have come to know and to believe in the love God has for us. God is love, and whoever remains in love remains in God, and God in him. In this is love brought to perfection among us, that we have confidence on the day of judgement because as He is, so are we in this world. There is no fear in love, but perfect love drives out fear because fear has to do with punishment, and so one who fears is not yet perfect in love."*

It seems like we keep our fears of temptation locked behind some sort of restraining-wall in our mind. We spend our lives rounding-up the stray horrors that haunt our memory and place them in a dark corridor in the recesses of our thoughts. Our conscience sits like a sentinel-in-the-night with eyes glued to the door separating us from the person we never want to be. This requires a great deal of repression to keep that archway from opening even a crack. Somehow we become almost chained to our station of guarding that frightening partition to ensure that it will not open and reveal our inner-being to ourselves or others. We are essentially the captives of our own fears. We must stop this endless game of allowing Satan to haunt us over memories of sins that Jesus Christ has destroyed. His lies are an evil attempt to convince us that we will never be a greater people than our recollections will permit. The foundation of our confidence rests in the faith that Christ has truly restored us to sinless perfection, both by His Cross and through the Sacrament of Confession. When we arduously accept forgiveness, we also acknowledge that our sins were never committed in the first place. Our memory is simply the dust left behind when Christ incinerated them from the face of the Earth. But for one puff of the breath of God, our memory would also be expunged.

We must be self-assured of the power of the Blood of Christ because Satan knows this to be a provision of our faith. He tries to persuade us that we are not one of God's children and that human vindication through Christ does not apply to our soul. Fear has always been one of his favorite avenues to bring us to hopelessness, despair, and weakness. He uses our memory like a flash-card to make us cringe in the face of temptation rather than conquer it through our love for Jesus. He taunts our souls with the caustic lie that we are not worthy of Divine Mercy. We are left to question whether the father of lies might be telling the truth for once. We must allow the Mercy of Christ to heal our memories as well as our souls. After all, God does not remember our infractions, so why should we? When we truly accept the Sacrifice of Jesus' Death as reparation for our sins, our precious thoughts will no longer haunt us. We must confide in the truth that temptation is no more than another stone on our path that we can step over while holding the Hand of God. The Holy Spirit tells us where they are and we accept His wisdom to avoid them. This is what makes all Christians great saints. Our confidence in the pardon we receive through Jesus is so strong that we dare Satan to stand in our way.

Jesus has total and irrevocable Love for us and is committed to our success in His Name. He reminds us that He never sinned or gave-way to plundering temptation because His Love is so strong. When we live in His image and pray as we ought, no temptation will distract us from the pious road of holiness. He asks us to shine outwardly in the full blossom of our heavenly potential. Through Him, we are given the capacity to Love in an intensity like the Almighty Father sitting upon the Throne in Paradise. Our Holy Mother asked me to look at a picture describing our "doorway of failures" that we fear to approach. It conceals the thoughts of our fallen past like a scar over a horrible wound. We push it away and out-of-sight, but our memory knows it is still there. It is a place we refuse to go. And as a result, the Light of our Love does not shine when we are with certain people or in given situations that force us to remember these guilty feelings. Our Lady asked me to think of my love as a beacon on the backdrop of Creation to show how we are inhibited by these fears in our memory.

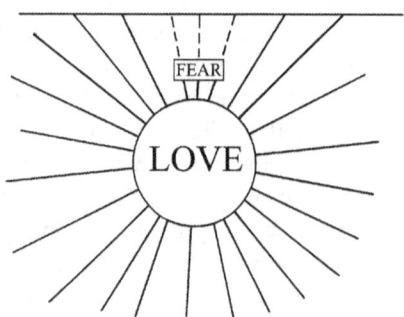

Indeed, the full-light of our love is unable to shine into all Creation when we fear to tread beyond the doorway concealing our memories. This is the falsehood in the lies that Satan tells. He hides his most innocent victims in the confines of their fears and incarcerates the souls he most insatiably desires behind the blockades of their own inhibitions. But, we must remember that Satan is a coward. He will not go where Love lives. He is more afraid of the Light than we are of the dark. By launching the Love in our hearts past every refraction of our minds, we can destroy any evil that tries to keep us from touching the souls he has burdened, including our own. This is the fruit of our faithful acceptance of the forgiveness we receive in Christ Jesus. United in Him, there is no fear we cannot overcome and no memory that can taunt us. His Spirit comes like an instant break-of-dawn to give us courage to go anywhere in thought or action that will bring His Kingdom to the Earth. We are like children waking in the darkness of night calling for our mother. The wind is howling through our souls and the terrible world lashes against us like renegade tree branches casting shadows through our midnight windows. We are petrified by the pitch darkness in our rooms, fearing to move enough to breathe. But, Our Mother has answered our call. She is the Blessed Virgin who has come bearing the Light of the World. Jesus is the emblazoned Light cutting through the darkness Who gives us courage to rest peacefully in anticipation of the coming Dawn.

Friday, August 21, 1992
Sometimes, I feel like I am hanging over the edge of a terrible precipice in fear of letting go because I will never hit bottom. Then, I think about how very infantile and humanistic this must sound. It is quite natural for us to fear and a blessing to remember everything that will harm us. I am also learning of late that it is natural for us to have courage. It is not beyond human achievement for frightened souls to summon the greatest of strength and to defer to no fear or temptation. I have learned this from our heavenly Mother, who is Our Queen of Valor and the Divine Advocate for souls. I again welcomed Her today as She came calling to ask me to bear witness for Her cause. Our Lady began this evening by addressing some scenes that my brother and I saw on television before we prepared to pray the evening Rosary. They were pictures of starving people in Third World countries. She said, **"You can help feed those people from here in your home with the Rosary in your hands. Please know that millions of dollars in food and medicine are directed to these people, but their own governments are intercepting it and selling it to third countries. It is appalling and condemnable. We must pray for all of these poor little children. It is the same in parts of America.**

My little one, many of these people do not know what a church building is for. The observation by many is accurate, that those in the

church in America are failing. That is why I have come to so many, to show masses of people for the first time who Jesus is and how Love has saved the world. I also see that you have been thinking about your fear of resignation that we spoke about last night, the one which seems to block the total brightness of your heart into Creation." The Holy Mother helped me again in prayer to address the unfounded fears reverberating in my conscience. She reminded me to read the message of last evening over and again until I understand it in complete confidence. I am to be fully aware that my inhibitions are only imaginary mental images that cannot diminish my capacity to live in complete assurance of my purity and strength. Those little "boxes" of doubt and residual memories often impede our ability to love completely and to shine our holiness onto the backdrop of the world. Tonight, Our Lady provided a pictorial parable to help me further understand the nature of our memory. The one She showed me last night was a two-dimensional display like the drawing I recorded for you to see.

However, the radiation of our love is not confined to the parameters of a page. She asked me to consider the multi-dimensions of the sun in the sky and the endless facets of the greater universe around us. The sun is a sphere instead of a circle, symbolic of our love that radiates in every conceivable direction. But, the little doorway that contains our fears remains just a one-dimensional memory. In other words, since our infractions have been erased from Creation except in our thoughts, they are removed from the halls of God's Justice. He builds no case against those who have been Redeemed and purified by His Son. The only remnant of our sins is the singular thought of our mind. And as far as God is concerned, it is dead and no longer a part of the Kingdom that He will give Life forever to come. The Blessed Mother told me that we should not make more of our memory than it actually is. We must relieve ourselves of feelings of guilt when we live in full faith of God's forgiveness and the Sacrament of Reconciliation. What we believe to be a tangible object worthy of fear is actually less than a shape on a page. Consider the following drawing. It helps us to acknowledge the true lifelessness of our guilty feelings.

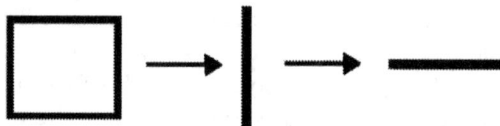

This is an example of the diminishment of our troubled mind. What we believe to be a three-dimensional square is remanded to the confines of this two-dimensional page. And, when we fully understand the futility of remembering forgiven sins, we can further reduce our recollection of them to a single mark. We view the square from the side and see that it is only a one dimensional line. It is not connected to life or reality in any sense but our ability to remember it. And, by accepting the grace of God's forgiveness in our heart, soul, and mind, this single trace of thought disappears from Creation like the last image from a freshly-unplugged television.

The Holy Mother told me that the human mind is not transposed into Eternity. People who live in Heaven know their souls were saved by Christ, but they no longer suffer any guilt. There are no sad thoughts or repressed memories in Paradise. The thin line of our illegitimate feelings is committed to the bowels of the Earth. So, we can walk through life now as we will for Eternity to come, confident in our reunion with God and unwilling to surrender to Satan's reminders of our past transgressions or concupiscence. We must allow our love to shine without breach into every avenue and alley and into all dark corners of the world. Nothing can harm us that does not come from within ourselves. When we live the purity and assurance we gain in Christ, our Love is invincible and uncontainable wherever our souls proceed.

Monday, August 24, 1992
Prayer from the heart is the substance of the desire of Mary for Her children. It is our means of loving Jesus in return and requisitioning His merciful forgiveness. Our Holy Mother wishes our prayers to not be a simple multiplication of words. She ironically tells us that the recitation of the Holy Rosary is a new petition with each "Hail Mary." God is pleased when we pray the Rosary to venerate His Mother. There is no perimeter or circumference that can contain the multitude of graces that He showers upon His people when we pray. We sing to His soul with the "Our Father." We comfort His breast through the "Glory Be." We must pray with meaning, shed of the encumbrances of doubt or repression. The alliteration of the Holy Rosary brings a rhythmic loftiness to the human spirit that elevates us from the world. We know these things by the faith we are given. The Mother of the source of all goodness is the Immaculate Virgin. She rejoined me today to offer the following words.

"Good evening, My loving ones. I have come again to be with you in your joy of Love through which you are able to envision the destiny of all humankind. I love you endlessly. I am with you so you can truly realize that, through your faith, your happiness manifests the fruition of Love into the hearts of those for whom you pray. Yesterday was another opportunity for the success of righteousness. You always do very well. My little sons, there is so much goodness, love, and justice which are emanating from our work that Satan is becoming quite enraged. I have come tonight to reveal to you that his plan is to continue his divisive forces against you and your families. Thank you for embracing your

unity in Love. That keeps Satan away. He is diminished by your faithfulness. Today, Satan was enraged by the power of our work. This time, he spate on My statue and pushed it down. This is a signal, a warning to you by him, that he is near. You know how to defeat him with Love..."

Our Lady was referring to the stone statue in front of my home that I keep lighted at night and adorned with pretty flowers for passers-by to see. When I came home this evening, I noticed that someone had pushed it off its pedestal into the background hedges. This is the second time that someone has done this. There was mucous all over Her face that someone spat in vile hatred for the Love She represents. I washed Her and reset the statue on its pedestal, knowing all the while that Satan was behind this reprehensible act of evil. But, even though he may topple a simple statue, Satan will never knock Our Lady off-balance. He is helpless and gasping for a life he has already lost under the heel of this Infinite Mother of Christ on the Cross.

The Immaculate Virgin has given many revealing messages to Her children about the Holy Eucharist. Now is the time to eliminate the protestation by humankind toward this Divine grace. The Most Blessed Sacrament is the essential element in our conversion. When we receive Holy Communion, we "swallow the key" to the lock that protects us from the evil and deception outside the passageway to our souls. No diabolical burglar can enter our hearts when we are filled with the Manna from Heaven. We are perfectly transformed to the fulfillment of our Divine purpose through the Body and Blood of God's Son. And in unity with the Holy Spirit, there is no other place on Earth we can find such oneness with Him. This is the universal intention of God for those reconciled to His Heart. The Holy Mother affirms this through Her words. **"Today is a special day for humanity in the Eucharist, as is every day, because the Holy Eucharist strengthens your power to fight against evil. Those who do not partake in the Eucharist are frail and are void of solutions to earthly problems that hold mankind hostage to his own mortality. People who partake of the Holy Eucharist hold in their power a prescription for solution, for without that prescription, the substance of man is purely weak and vanquished.**

The Holy Eucharist allows men to turn their love from a whisper into a shout, with volume and courage. Mankind has no means through which to speak the language of Love without receiving the Sacrament of Jesus' Body and Blood. All other attempts to succeed in Love are only movements of the lips and exasperated sighs of helplessness. The Blessed Sacrament provides resonance and strength, the projection of Love, which can be echoed in dimensions, rather than the hollowness of human desperation. Receiving the Holy Eucharist allows your conviction and your capacity to be of motivation, rather than just a

reason to exist. The Eucharist helps you in your rhythm of Love in prayer."

Our Lady directed Her discussion following these words to the effects of righteous discipline and instruction as a Spiritual Act of Mercy. I recently witnessed someone reprimanding another person in a way that seemed less-than generous in nature. I did not see the display of gentle Love and mercy that I have come to know from Our Lady. In fact, this redressing was outright confrontational in its approach. But, I was surprised by the response of the Holy Mother because She said that this is the only way that some people will listen. It is a sign of our own indifference if we allow Love to be trampled-upon by someone who fails to be God's witness. We should object to the slothful conviction of those who say that God will have to accept them as they are. These hypocrites attempt to diminish the repulsive nature of sin to avoid their own conversion. Indeed, while Jesus walked gently upon the Earth as the Word of God, He did not scorn and showed no disdain; but He told the Truth through which the sinners He admonished were self-indicted. He knew when to be gentle and whether to be aggressive. This discernment came from His wisdom as God on Earth and is the same knowledge we gain from the Holy Spirit. Its foundation is Love and compassion for the fate of others who know God better by our witness and instruction. Our approach should always be consistent, fair and impartial, and reflect the genuine nature of Christ, Himself.

In our Christian charity toward others, we must remember that Jesus is not naive. He knows the intentions of our hearts and the motivations behind our actions. Even some of His contemporary followers wane in their support of the Commandments they embrace. Not all sinners are pagans or barbarians, or people without protocol and ethics. Those to be reprimanded include people of faith caught-up in material excess and worldly indifference. Firmness toward the purpose of discipline does not indicate a lack of Love. Would the people of our own century consider the Deluge a little more stern than we actually deserve? We have been reminded that there are certain Chastisements waiting in the wings. That is not to say that they cannot be avoided if we pray and convert in the way Our Lady is asking. Through the fidelity of our own conviction, the courage of commitment, righteous discussion, prayer, fasting, and conversion of the heart, the Chastisements will not be necessary. The Holy Mother is telling us how they can be deferred. She has come to advise, advocate, and admonish to elevate us in faith and conscience to the truth that Christ is alive and the only Way to Eternal Life in Heaven. But, Her work is impeded by people who believe they already know enough about God and how they will be judged before Him. These are the pseudo-Christians who no longer strive for perfection because they have already conceded defeat to their own weaknesses. Together with the blind indifferent, they compose a large number of people who may find their place in the line of saints well behind the ignorant and unaware.

These are Our Lady's very words, **"Please do not be shocked or disappointed that you are not seeing the most gentle side of Love. Please remember your recent Scripture, 'What father does not discipline the children he loves?' The Heavenly Father often chooses to do this through mortal people. Please remember that they are no-less gentle and no-less loving, and are righteously correct."** Mankind must realize that Love is a perpetual process and a display of all its fruits. Our fluctuating fidelity to Christ is not the example He asks us to portray. The Love in our hearts is not a possession we should jealously guard or give only to those who suit our fancy. Neither is it a product for market to the highest bidder. Love is free and forever impartial. That is the way we wish to be treated and is forthrightly what others deserve from us. We should always remember that we are not judged solely by how we treat the image in the morning-mirror. The kindness in which we embrace ourselves must reflect the Love we extend to others. And, we should be grateful to anyone who admonishes us for stepping-off that righteous course.

Tuesday, August 25, 1992

The Mother of Jesus is calling for our prayers and petitions to change a world that spews repulsion before God and His righteous people, alike. As long as there are baby children crying-out from the wombs of their mothers for birth, our holy work is not yet finished. Until the innocent and afflicted no longer plead for nourishment and healing, we cannot rest. When there are any two people who cannot coexist together in Christian peace, we must continue to pray. God is aware of the wretchedness that mars the beauty in the hearts of His people and soils their daily lives. When He dispatched His Mother to tell us so, He fully anticipated our participation in the transformation of the world back to His image. For that reason, we must reach-out to one another in good works and humble ourselves in unified prayer. Only then will God trust our willingness to join in His desires for bringing perfection to an Earth that has gone awry in social hatred, squalor, and indifference.

As we are called by the Mother of God, we must respond with swift obedience and honest intention. Saints gone before us have said that they would not rest until they were reposed in Christ. That is also the standard by which we should rise from our sleep. Our Lady lives in the company of these same Saints. She comes in Love to pray with the world every day in our call for their intercession. I have always believed that our power is poorer when our faith is weak. To strengthen it, we must attend to others in times of crisis and tribulation. Not only is this a signal of Love, it is another means through which to exemplify our lives in Christ Jesus. We gain a "mortal omnipresence" when we live-out our faith by enriching the lives of our brethren through compassion and servitude. To that end, I went today to visit an elderly lady in the hospital who is terminally-ill with cancer to try and console her family. I know these people personally and wished to offer the peace and comfort of Jesus to their sorrowing hearts.

When I arrived, I was viciously confronted by one of her relatives who stands in vehement opposition to the messages I have been receiving from Our Lady. I am convinced that if there had been no one else nearby, I would have been physically assaulted. I immediately left the hospital, shaken with grief. I was not so much offended by the lack of faith of this person as I was spiritually saddened that he would resort to threatening interpersonal violence to state his case against the Blessed Mother. My feelings were paradoxical because this situation also allowed me to participate in the rejection that Christ suffered on the Earth. For this, I am forever grateful. The attack was a product of evil influence, which served only to strengthen my inner-desire to continue the righteous work of the Immaculate Virgin Mary. I know that my trust in Jesus must somehow become greater in magnitude. I have always been truthful about the intercession of the Blessed Mother and all aspects of my temporal life. But, those who choose the path of disbelief often violate others who do believe by resorting to defamation, ridicule, and violence.

When peace is destroyed by their opposition, witnesses for the Lord are falsely blamed. Such detractors scour the Earth looking for more scoffers to strengthen their numbers, spinning the world into motion and manifesting aggression by people who really do not know what they are fighting for. It is just another chance for them to be independent of the truth, of faith, and of responsibility. Our Lady appeared this evening when I prayed the Holy Rosary, bringing great consolation and peace. She told me that this is a time to be happy about my participation in the work of God. I was asked to pray for these very special people whom I dearly love. Times of great suffering provide the opportunity to unite our souls in the happiness of the Holy Spirit. Somehow, the marriage of the two is the cohabitation that brings God's Kingdom closer to the Earth. When we are despised and cast-out in our witness for Christ, our souls move away from the world toward greater unity with Heaven above. When pondering the Light of this truth, it seems that any rejection we suffer in the Name of Jesus is a welcome reminder of our place in His care. The destiny of our souls is assuredly on the right path.

I have learned that anyone who holds-fast to their human will like a saber against the Truth of God will eventually cut themselves off from the future only the faithful will inherit. They torture others with lies and deceit and wonder why the Light never shines on their path. The shadow of their own error blocks their vision to see the blindness in which they walk. An even greater sorrow is that the little children of these wretches grow amidst this same darkness. They learn the scourges of division, violence, and aggression that will render them no greater than the parents who teach them. Somehow, Christ

Jesus must be allowed to intervene in this vile passage of generations to stop the flow of hatred. This is a blessing for which we must all fervently pray. Jesus is our deliverance from all oppression and inequity. Love is the source of transformation for any beating-heart on the face of the Earth. There is not a soul in existence than cannot be converted by the power of the Holy Spirit. But, the choice is our own to open our heart and awaken to the Truth living among us. We must embrace the Cross of Mount Calvary if we are to fully comprehend our own. This is the life of prayer that Our Lady continues to compel. It is a process of sharing the suffering of Christ to ensure the transfer of souls to His Salvation. We must be convinced that Love is always the victor over hatred. And from the battles I have seen, this struggle can be a protraction of long and intense personal sacrifice. We stand upon Love because it is the shoulder of God that carries us to victory.

Our Lady asked me again tonight to continue to expand my vision to see the entire world. There are thousands who sit quietly praying for deliverance from darkness, despair, poverty, and disease. These are the true warriors for God. When we hold them in our heart, they gain new hope that the pendulum of justice is about to swing their way. We must believe this truth even when others have fallen. When the world is crawling in sin, we must let our hearts fly to the highest mountaintops of purity and trust. The destruction before us is folly because the Maker of all things will renew the face of the Earth. We do not have to wait for the return of Christ Jesus to eliminate evil works from our land. The Holy Spirit is the power of the Cross that gives us strength to battle it. We must pray in hopeful anticipation for our help and refuge in Him.

Sunday, August 30, 1992

I understand that the fundamental purpose of the intercession of Our Lady is for the conversion of sinners and the bringing of Jesus to the lost. I never lose sight of Her impeccably poised presence when She comes to converse with my brother and me and to teach us more about Heaven. But, in Her humble perfection, She is quite reserved to describe Her own beauty in terms that I am sure God wishes humanity to know. That gives me the opportunity to speak about Her through my own helpless way, in a sincere effort to present a picture of an almost indescribable person of the highest station in dignity. Our Blessed Mother is the incarnation of paradisial wisdom and beatific grace. Her motherly protection of the children She loves pours from the heavens through Her supernatural charm. And, it is my high honor and distinct privilege to tell you that these lofty adjectives are still insufficient to describe the pristine wonderment of Her perpetual virginity.

Our Lady magnifies the Lord with an intensity that is beyond our mere mortal comprehension. I know that Her soul was born in sinless perfection, Immaculately conceived in the precious womb of Her very own mother Anne, the Saint who must be the only person more proud to give birth to a child than Mary, Herself. And yet, through all of Her preternatural authority, Our Lady is still simple-of-heart and humanly prayerful. She brings that same pleasant simplicity in a maternal way into the distemperature of our modern-day world. She offers Her Love and beauty in response to our prayers through perceivable signs, graces, miracles, words, and blessings. Today, my brother and I received another such marvelous gift. It was a reflection of Our Lady's message of April 21, 1991 when She said, **"One more of you will be able to receive Me in the next month as I come to help you spread the Good News of Jesus as a part of God's Plan."** This is the statement that has brought great reticence to our peers in the prayer group being conducted at my home.

When the Holy Mother was unable to enter the heart She hoped would open for Her, it provoked a great backlash against our work by those who thought Her words were now a blatant false-prophesy. However, my brother and I received a letter which confirmed that Our Lady's message was, indeed, the truth fulfilled. When the person to whom She first wished to speak rejected Her outrightly, the Holy Mother selected another member of our regular Rosary group who was absent on April 21, 1991. And until now, this person had not come forward with their heavenly revelation. As a result, some in the group assumed that Our Heavenly Visitor was not fulfilling Her words and we were false messengers. The young lady whom the Blessed Mother chose was a very prayerful and discerning "Matthias-in-waiting." She was a pious recipient of our Immaculate Mother's graceful intercession. The true miracle is that she had not even heard the message of April 21st before Our Lady chose her to receive the gift of Her appearance. The text of the letter from this humble soul is the nature of the grace my brother and I received today.

Dear Friends,

The grace and peace of Jesus be with you through the Immaculate Heart of Mary. Thank you for the beautiful gift and especially for being so gracious to me when we have been able to visit. My prayers are with you in your sufferings; it occurred to me yesterday how painful and difficult your trials have been, and I believe that we should all be compassionate as Our Lady has said and deeply caring for our brothers and sisters in Christ to help each other grow in strength under persecution.

This beautiful book explains love very deeply in its simplicity, and it strongly expresses to me that Our Lady has a special plan for us, and because I love Jesus and Mary I have been concerned to learn what I can about Her messages here. Because I have also known about the struggles within the Church and rejection, I understand a little of your suffering. **From the beginning of my visit to your home, I was enabled to believe in Our Lady's gift because I received an interior vision of Her presence (in form, similar to Our Lady of the Miraculous Medal and human size) and also to feel Her presence, as I have before.** *This strengthened my faith, but the love*

which you always live shows Her radiance. I am not writing to talk about myself, only to let you know how grateful I am for your gift and for your friendship. Our Lady's love is so overwhelming and beautiful. It is a great joy to express this to others who love Her and know and love Our Lord so much. I hope that we will be able to pray together again someday.
With love for Jesus and Mary

Many people have not truly grasped the sincerity of conversion that Our Lady is seeking in Her children. The magnitude of conviction to prayer and penance is higher than we could possibly imagine. When we imbibe in material and temporal self-satiation, we are distracted from the path to perfect holiness. Our lives must be consumed by an inner-desire for the glories of Heaven. Our consolation is found by inspiring the hearts of our brothers and sisters to honestly yearn for God's Kingdom. Today, Our Lady told us about individuals who purportedly desire to comply with Her messages, but are really interested in finding weakness in Her messengers they can take into the world to damage the credibility of Her messages. She told my brother and me that we would be complacent and naive to disbelieve that Satan would walk-up to someone and pat them on the back and, the next moment, stick a knife into it.

"I do not want you to be too concerned that you are becoming isolated, alone, and alienated from others. Those who love and expect love in return will readily show you. Jesus was lonely so that you would never have to be alone. And, He is with you now. My little sons, as Jesus sees you suffering for His sake, it is the same as your reaching to give Him a kiss on the palm of His scarred hand as He touches the top of your head with the other in His humble caress, thanksgiving, and prayerful blessing. He is able to look down in His hands to see another soul, like Himself, who is willing to suffer persecution for the good of Love, for the good of the Salvation of all, in faith and hope that the Promise that He has bestowed upon the Earth is real, and is alive, and is coming as promised. For this, all the heavens are eternally grateful and hopeful that you, like Jesus, will not give up the fight, will persevere, and will hold your station until His call beckons your soul to His side in Glory, the same glorification that He hopes to confer upon all Creation. Thank you for allowing Jesus to help you to be wise so you will also be strong. I love you."

Our Lady also helped me understand that Her warning about others who approach us for deceitful purposes is not to stir our fears or cause us to embrace a paranoiac way of life. We are to simply be aware of the dangers lurking near trying to inhibit Her success. She told us to remember that many people who followed Jesus on Earth ate their fill from His bounty and then abandoned Him at the last in favor of a life free from sacrifice and righteousness. We must be wary of anyone approaching us for such scandalous purposes. We should also pray for a greater desire to love and sacrifice for Jesus with a burning intensity of Love in our hearts. The world has dampened many souls like soggy kindling that will not respond to a spark. Through conversion, penance, and self-denial, they will be rendered worthy of the fire of Christ's Love. He lights our diminished souls with a fire from Heaven, just as He did for Elias before the prophets of Baal. (**III Kings 18:20-39.**)

SEPTEMBER 1992

Tuesday, September 1, 1992
Never a day passes-by that Our Lady does not remind us to remember the Holy Cross on which Jesus died at Mount Calvary. She tells us that the Crucifixion is the right direction for human conversion. That is why the Mass is so important. Life's troubles dissipate when we offer them before the ameliorative power of the Cross. We need Jesus during every hour and every day to receive the wisdom He brings us through His teachings, example, and His passionate death and Resurrection. We need the legacy of His strength to eradicate our own sorrows and to lift us from despair. When we are falsely accused, heavy laden with the debt of others, or smitten by our peers for not executing duties that are rightfully their own, we find all justice and reconciliation in the consolation of the Cross. If we feel abandoned, violated, and deceived, the Blood of Christ Jesus is our refuge and strength. No thief can steal our union with God when we offer ourselves totally to Jesus Christ. When we hope for a better future, God miraculously transforms time, itself, into a physical place. That location is the Hill of Calvary, where we find inner-peace and spiritual relief. In the Cross, tomorrow is no more a function of hours, but a place beyond the sun in the company of perfect immortals.

Our departed loved ones live in the Eternity of Jesus' Sacrifice on the Cross. Those who have closed their eyes in death have opened their souls to Paradise. And, they who cry-out for Mercy and recompense need to look no further than the forgiveness and bounty of the Holy Cross. It is God's monument to the death of vengeance and the Life of absolution. These are the living ways that the Cross still blooms in the world today. Its fruit will never die. The Immaculate Lady who stood so sorrowfully beneath it to see Her Son expire has come calling on the likes of us to evangelize this Truth. I gladly respond with a consecration that is befitting of such a beautiful Mother. This evening, Our Lady revealed many graces that are unfolding in the world as a fruit of our prayers and penance. It gives us great strength to continue when we know that our lives for Jesus are making a difference in a very dark age. Our Lady is quick to affirm the power of just one "Our Father" in bringing the Kingdom of God to Earth. Its focusing effect improves the vision of His people to see Him more clearly. We are made aware in the depth of our hearts that we can attain the perfection of Love that Christ brought to the world 2000 years ago. If we believe we can achieve this beauty-of-soul, we will attain it. Our faith in ourselves must be as strong as it is in the God who makes it possible. We carry this same perfection into Paradise like a hand-in-glove.

The Holy Mother repeated Her request for my brother and me to be happy, today. This is something I have had particular difficulty in achieving because of the forces of the world. We must see our souls like a balloon underwater. It should be natural for our spirit to rise to the top of Creation. When we accept our Heavenly destiny, we become immune to the hypocrisy of the world. The Love of Jesus in our hearts is, indeed, like a pocket of air submerged in the swamp of mortality. We are elevated by His grace because we do not carry the weight of material and temporal addiction. This is the mystical power of the sacrificial endurance He places in our hearts to claim our home in Love. A buoyant spirit is a state-of-the-heart that renders us naturally unaffected by terror and despair. In Christ Jesus, we gain the inner confidence that evil cannot defeat us because the success of our effort is at hand. This is why we continue to pray through a prefigured conviction of impending victory. No sadness can detain us in the soil of desperation because we have seen in faith the harvest of triumph. We place the head of evil in a vice and our prayers tighten the handle. No one can hear his screeching voice because of the deafening cheers from the Saints of Heaven crying, **"Give it another twist!"**

Our Lady stands in Glory knowing that evil has no power over the Hosts of Heaven, including the immortal dignitaries who once walked the Earth. Christ has taken His seat at the right-hand of the Father as the conqueror of evil. With God and the paradisial Court, He looks down on us in pity and pride. He sees His children fighting the good fight against the forces of the world that try to destroy our faith in Him. Our Lady looks at the world through the same pity and grief for the sins of the multitudes who still ignore Her Son. Her sorrow is not without hope because human faith in Him can still be restored. That is why She has come by apparition and interior locution to so many. We are to attest before a stubborn world that Christ Jesus is the King of all Creation. That chore is often tantamount to convincing others they can walk in mid-air. When we perfect our Love as Christ teaches, we see more clearly that He has taken away any sadness that could dampen our hope for His justice. We feel sorrow because of human sin, but our happiness is restored when we recall the sanctifying power of the Cross. The red-water rapids of Christ's Blood have rushed through Creation and cleansed all souls in His path.

We must convert others to His Salvation because we would want them to sanctify us. And, we should trust in His Mercy to redeem us no matter what obstacles stand in our way. That is the essence of the teachings and messages of the Mother of God, **"Imagine an end to human existence which did not provide for Mercy! Therefore, Jesus' Sacred Heart is merciful. If all will**

come to Me, I will take you there because I love you." The Holy Mother sees the world crawling on its hands and knees like tiny babies. As we stumble through life, we bloody our palms and legs from our lack of elevation to God. She has come to teach us to walk upright in faith and dignity. Her grace lifts us to our feet and restores our sense of direction in Christ, Our Lord. It is He Who first stood and fell for our Salvation and purification. We must rise to stand beside Him in the restorative stadium of Holy Redemption. We are called to the summit of holiness in His Love and are awarded the fruit of immortal vision to see the meadows below. Rising from this valley comes the reverberating echo of tears from a saddened world calling us to pity and to serve.

Saturday, September 5, 1992

Our Lady called on me again today to record another message that She wishes the world to hear. She speaks urgently about the necessity for man to accept Her Son. Without affirming our faith in Jesus, there is no exoneration for our souls. We are still drowning in the paltry nature of mortal life. We cannot breathe on our own, we cannot float, and we cannot swim. Only Jesus can save us. No slice of poetry, no sliver of art, or no pact with good fortune can stop the inexorable march of humankind toward the end of time. So, every day, I give myself to God through the Blessed Virgin and say, "Use me, use me, this is my call!" And, God hears my offer and responds. He tells me that the flags are up and we are at the gate. Jesus will ensure our victory over moral diminishment and the corruption of good men. There is no turpitude that He has not already destroyed. He holds unilateral control over forces that, to us, are still out-of-reach. Indeed, His Immaculate Mother is our supreme counselor and audible voice who validates the truths promulgated by the Holy Spirit for the enlightenment of every poor sinner.

Our Lady continues to tell mankind how helpless we are without Love. We already understand most of the finite aspects about life. There is no doubt in our mind that the Earth is relatively round, winter is bitterly cold, rain is wet, and lightning can be fatal. We can even comprehend some of the infinite intangibles which lie beyond our ability to perceive, but not inconceivable to the timelessness of God. Human life is a chronology to us, but a toy in the hands of baby Jesus. If He wanted to do so, He could quit the game right now and go back home to feast on the Paradise that knows Him well as Christ the King. But, Our Lord knows no infidelity in the battle for human Salvation. He still struggles for the sake of our Redemption. I know this to be true because His Mother has told me so. I continued to pray tonight and write more words in this Diary in the hope that at least one more soul will know Jesus for my effort. Our Lady has come from Paradise to bring the Divine Light of Jesus and to explicitly reveal that our Salvation at God's Hands is real. Indeed, if we listen to Her call in the way Her Son asks, our hearts will be filled with the very holiness of Paradise. This is the Love which will powerfully change the world and render it like the heavenly home that we must aspire to attain.

If we are to be lifted-up in dignity and destiny, it is imperative that we accept the forgiveness that Christ offers by His Blood. Our souls are suspended in His Mercy and Pardon until we decide on our own that we will transfer our mortal souls to His permanent care. When Our Lady came to pray with us today, She immediately referred to a musical recording. It is a song entitled "My Love", sung by Julio Iglesias and Stevland Morris (Copyright 1988 Jobette Music Co., Inc. and Black Bull Music (ASCAP) Columbia Records/CBS Records). She asked me to play it so we could listen together, saying that it is a prayer for humanity in reflection of Her intentions. I was asked to record Her wishes in my Diary that everyone get a copy of this song and listen to it as a contemplative meditation. The lyrics are, indeed, a source of great Light and hope for the world. This is what She said, **"My little sons, that song makes Me very happy! It was inspired by the Holy Spirit and is a grace for the world. Yes, lift-up humanity! That is what Jesus' Life is all about. That is why He died! My little sons, please tell all the world in your Diary about these words, especially about this song, to listen to the message in this song, 'My Love.' You see why it makes Me so happy. The message of unity and the vision of humanity through the eyes of Love are what My intercession is all about."**

The Holy Mother asks everyone to see humanity through the eyes of Love and to pray that our hearts reflect Christ's compassion and humility from the very depths of our being. This is how we enter Her Immaculate Heart. When we pray, our vision becomes sanctified and we become holy, like God is Holy. That is what the song "My Love" does for us. It projects a Light of unity and a yearning for beauty. This is the same exhilaration and hope that the words of Jesus give to everyone who listens to the Holy Spirit. There is no doubt that the lyrics which fall from the Sacred Lips of Immortal Divinity unite all peoples under Almighty God. Our Lady echoes these same perfect intentions in Her messages. She knows that a heart filled with Love can move any mountain. Her desire is for us to hope to a height greater than any despair, in a magnitude of joy that consumes all sadness before our eyes.

This is possible if we remember the transformation that Jesus promises. His Love is greater than any human diminishment. He knows that we are priceless gems in the eyes of God and will come soon to claim us for Him and confirm eternal bliss upon our souls. All the value, fulfillment, and joy of our future rests in complete surrender to His perfect Redemption. So, we must reach-out to Him in faith, prayer, and trust. Mankind must always remember that God knows that we have the capacity to accept Everlasting Life because we are affected by Love. Our hearts will tell us what Truth lies ahead, even if our thoughts run awry. Let us trust our hearts and let Christ Jesus do the thinking.

Sunday, September 6, 1992

My shock and surprise for the intercession of our Holy Mother has not worn frail; and neither has it dimmed or diminished. I accept the fact that we must all respond in obedience for Her mission to succeed. She has told me this truth many times before. I will comply because of the dismay and indifference that I see in the rest of the world. I know that our loving Mother is our best hope for the transformation of mortal mankind into a higher grace and elevation. It was Her, at the beginning, who brought us our Savior. And, She will usher Him back the second time, just you wait and see! She has told me on numerous occasions that it will be sooner, rather than later. It will also be in union with the Eternal Triumph of Her Immaculate Heart. I know that I must wait for Our Lord to come back again; but I do not have to tarry in the stall or be bridled by indifference in the intervening time.

As my brother and I began the Holy Rosary, Our Lady appeared on behalf of the heavens and said, **"Thank you for all of your prayers today. You change the world with every Rosary that you pray..."** It is clear that these words are a dictation from timeless Eternity. Without Her wisdom, we have little means to know what effect our petitions bring upon the world around us. Our hearts must not yield to the force of the passing days. Our prayers are not a command for God to dispense of time or deliver our souls to the end of the world. Our infinitely-compassionate Father knows that we learn more about Him with each passing sunrise. He grants as many as He sees fit, knowing that the longevity of many great people is a blessing to those who would suffer greatly without them. Consider the advanced ages of the Holy Father, Pope John Paul II, and Mother Teresa of Calcutta, India.

There have been many great oratories and written discourses about the element of time. We almost look at it as though it is an object we can pass-along or cast-aside. It is not a material possession we can hold in our hands. We can neither advance or impede its progression. Time belongs to God in the same way that the Salvation of our souls is His to decide. We cannot breach this work of genius by an Almighty Father whose Holy Will is to guide us as we advance in the wisdom of His grace. We are ordained and committed to a timely exile for the purpose of becoming perfected through prayer and sacrifice. The proof of this Truth is in the holiness and compassion of Jesus Christ. The Holy Mother is telling the world that there is precious-little time left. What does She mean? Simply stated, Our Lord will soon come to the Earth to judge us and allow us to see ourselves in the Light of His Crucifixion. How will we be able to stand in the Face of such perfection? Will we say to God, *"I wish you would have given me more time. I would have better prepared."*

Such is the essential nature and purpose of our lives, to prepare our souls for that revealing moment of truth. If we do not convert in the way Our Lady teaches, we will be woefully insufficient in penitence and holiness to ever cross the threshold of allowing ourselves to be redeemed by the Christ who has been speaking to us through the Holy Spirit for twenty centuries. The toll of time is common to every man and we must all accede to death as the wage for sin. These things have been beyond our control since Adam embraced enmity and shamed us before the God of All. But, the decision for the eternal Resurrection of our souls rests on us. We must proclaim from the fabric of our will that Christ is our Savior and Lord. That is the only way our mortality can be transformed from a permanent ending into a perpetual beginning. In Christ, our death is an act of perfect Love and unity with God. That is why we must die to sin and live for Jesus in accordance with the Holy Scriptures and the miraculous intercessory revelations of His Mother.

Our every moment must be a selfless assent to the Father's Will in reflection of Our Holy Mother's Pristine Affirmation. She not only said "yes" to Him through the Archangel Gabriel, She also proclaimed a "Magnificat" of compliant profession to complete Her unity with Heaven. And to further advocate the Salvation of our souls, She bore and raised the Christ-child in a maternal perfection that is yet to be equalled. She did this willfully and prayerfully with the knowledge that, in the words of the prophet Simeon, a sword of terrible sorrow would pierce Her Heart. She never once said no, Her Love could not wane, and at no time did She have a doubtful thought. The Holy Mother knew by the grace of Her own being that Christ would be slain so the world could be saved. Consider the awful grief and anxiety She felt as the Passion and Death of Jesus came-to-pass. The compassionate gift of "motherhood" was perfected by Her maternal example. No son on Earth is loved more powerfully than this sinless Lady loves Her own. It is a Divine affection beyond reproach. And yet, unless She watched Him die, none of our souls would be saved. She grieved in harmony with the Love of God for the obedient Son She raised from the manger. Never once did She stand between Him and the Cross. The destiny of humanity depended on His Death and the Love in the Immaculate Heart that gave Him birth.

The Blessed Mother has spoken many times about the surly bonds which blind us from seeing the Throne of God. Her words echo the Bible Verse that reads, **"Now we see as in a mirror, but then we shall see Him face-to-face."** And today, She still speaks of the impotent effect of time on souls bound for Paradise. But, Her true purpose is to reclaim us as children of the Lamb and to implant His Spirit within our being. She invites us to pray from the heart and urges the angels-on-high to gaze upon our beauty because the living Christ dwells within us. And, the beginning of this celestial reunion is The Holy Rosary. We speak to God as though we are already in Heaven through these transcending Mysteries. Indeed, Paradise comes to Earth to hear our "Hail Mary" like a Dove drawn to a rolling stream. There are no words that can accurately describe the blissful unification of the heavens with the laden world when we ask for God's help. We can only compile a list of adjectives and synonyms that fall painfully short of helping our souls to see. But, prayer is our vision without the necessity of sight. It is the dew on a puppy's nose and the purr of a cat, the chuckle of a child and the smile of a grandfather. As you can see, there are truly no words.

Our Lady said, **"I can only say that you will love Heaven because Heaven loves you. When love is perfected in the world, it will be like Heaven, too. You will Love the Life you share in a heavenly way now. You will not know one from the other, but you will soon see the Face of God and the Throne from which all Love flows. This is your exile, but it need not be a captivating one, or a defeating one, or a damning one. One day you will see! One day everyone will see! I must also tell you that My messages to you have only the parameters that I am allowed to reveal to you as given to Me by God. If only you knew how earnestly I am trying to tell the world the proper things that will instill Love and peace into every heart! When the end of the world arrives, I hope not for you to state that you wished that you had spent more years in prayer on the Earth, but had insufficient time. You are now living your time! You are using it well. Imagine if Jesus had not been executed how He could have changed the world through living more years. Please, help Him effect the conversion that He was unable to complete. Always remember that I love you! My Motherly Heart and protective Mantle hold you forever. Please be more patient! Goodnight."**

Wednesday, September 9, 1992

It was cloudy outside today as I sat down with tired eyes, but elevated heart, to record Our Lady's words. I have always been mystified by the rain and how it cleanses the Earth and quenches the thirst of every form of life which lives. Thunder and lightning are a reminder to me that beyond them must live a world of wondrous magnitude and power. How great can a Kingdom be that lies above such an awesome sight as a passing rainstorm or a dancing tornado? I suppose I have come to see these things as signs of great hope. Why would God otherwise shower the world with a drink from which flowers bloom? For what other reason would the wind bring the air that thousands had been breathing a dozen miles away to our neighborhood in a matter of minutes? There is hope in God through these natural gifts. I also wonder if we are answering back. Does He bring us storms to win our silence? Does a blanket of snow tell us to disregard the sleeping ground? Is winter a break from our toils under the summer sun? I will let you ponder with me.

As my brother and I drove home this evening from Holy Mass, a large bank of dark clouds formed overhead and the wind began to violently blow. We did not make it into the house before the skies opened and an unbelievable amount of rain fell. It over-flowed the storm sewers, flooded the streets, and damaged the trees and bushes. We prayed that everyone was safe and that we, too, would get inside before a fiery streak of lightning struck the ground near us. When we knelt to offer the Holy Rosary, Our Lady came to pray with us. She placed an interesting perspective to the works of nature by saying, **"I realize that you have noticed the weather conditions and incidents apparent throughout the world as of late. There has been a commonness between each of them. All of the people who are involved are helpless to these acts of nature. Remember the way that you felt while looking at the bank of black clouds. Never did you say to yourself that you had to do something to stop the oncoming storm. You are aware of your lack of power to do so! It is the same the world over. All of the power to control nature is in the hands of My Son. The reason for all purpose in Creation is Jesus. That is to remind the world of His humble beginnings.**

Remember when Jesus was born that the weather was quite inclement in nature. We were forced to seek shelter in an animal stable. I have told you about these humble beginnings of Jesus. Humanity must return to their humbleness and to one another for shelter during the storms of life. Mankind is unified during these times of natural disaster and the discordant aspects of the functions of Earth. This replicates, identifies, and exemplifies what mankind should also do during his self-inscribed storms and battles. All of the divisions in the world are created by a seeming lack of dependence on one another, as I have told you many months ago. As you see these phenomena unfold and occur, you are able to sense the tangible, physical, and visible power of God. Always remember that such occurrences are the effect of God's Will. What you are seeing and experiencing is the cause that God delivers to you, expecting the effect of your awareness of His supreme and total power, given in Love, with the intention of always calling mankind back to Him. Over all of this, no man has ever been able to stand and say that, 'he is,' or that mankind is going to change the course and structure of the Will of God that is manifested through nature. Jesus is the Master of the universe. The Holy Spirit has already made this clear to you..."

Our Lady's message was still longer, but I was reserved about placing the rest of it in my Diary. She asked me to include it because it indicates the magnificence of Jesus' kind compassion. The remainder of Her words address some very simple gestures on the part of my brother and me. We simply reached-out in the humblest of ways, not expecting our effort to be of any significance in God's eyes. But, the Holy Mother said that nothing is concealed from Him. **"Now, I wish to tell you something that is very important to Me. I would like for you to recall the times when you have looked at the sun setting over the horizon. I know that you enjoy seeing this mastery of beauty, this expression of Love, through artistic and aesthetic** sensation. You have a feeling of awe at this beauty and how beautiful must be the One who has created it. I wish to tell you that, as of late, you have been that sunset and Jesus has been the observer.

Your creations of Love brought to the world through your acts of generosity, charity, sharing, and humility have made you the blessing to the world that Jesus wants all of His children to be. These acts of Love are of stately and saintly magnitude. Quite simply, My little children, Jesus has asked Me to tell you today that you have established for yourselves the inheritance of that great and mighty Heaven which He has bequeathed to you out of His tremendous Love. His highest desire is to fulfill His Promise to those who love Him by loving others and who obey the Father of all Creation through the acceptance of His Son. For today and evermore, you are to know that, as a result of your prayers and holiness, many millions will be granted the Eternal happiness of Heaven. My gentle sons, thank you for your lives! I am sure that your other little friends will be with you, too. They are like you, their Love precedes their lives and the daily nature of their existence. I remind you again that I love you."

All praise, glory, and honor belong to Jesus Christ and the heavens from which He comes. We are His children, players in a transforming orchestration called "Love." While we are one humanity under His care, each of us is a light without which Creation itself would be less. We must crawl from-under our bushel baskets and shine for all the world to see. Let us show-forth Christ to every corner of the universe! If our hearts are the filament for His power, let us tender ourselves to the grace that makes us glow! We must receive love graciously and confidently. God is as pleased by our child-like offerings of good will as we are with the little cut-outs our own children paste onto construction paper or the curious hues they scribble in their coloring books. Our conversion is a gift that God will remember forever-to-come. It is the foundation of the innocent beauty His Son calls us to be, basking in the Light our Virgin Mother beckons us to follow. We must emulate the unassuming nature of children in unity with the wisdom of Christ Jesus. This is the humility and chastity through which we were created and the same perfection that sets our souls free. Our walk should be of gentle steps in purity and servitude, staying the course of righteousness and Redemption. We need not bow to scorn or be chided by the mysterious forces that call and tempt us to take an errant road. We need to live in alliterative simplicity so that God may call, *"Come, My little children, come!"*

Remember the memories of youth when your mother would ask you to follow a butterfly with your eyes as it flies-past in random-scatter. You realize how much she admires these colorful little creatures as though her hopes somehow rest on their airborne beauty. And in innocent love for her, you set-out to capture one of these flippant beings and present it to her as a gift, remembering how her face lights-up like a firefly in the meadow at dusk. So, you get a tiny jar and scamper into the yard believing that a little butterfly is the only thing in the world that could make your mother happy. You dodge and dart about the yard, trying to capture the first one that gets near-enough to nab. When you fall to the ground in successive attempts, you get-up even more determined that you will catch the next one you see. It is as though all your precious hope is flying in the breeze. Your little heart is breaking because the source of your mother's happiness keeps eluding your grasp. And after you take one final dive for the last one in sight, you curl onto the ground with your face in your hands, weeping because the gift you could not contain just flew-off into the lofty blue skies above.

As you lay on the grass, you suddenly feel a fluttering on your cheek. When you raise your head, there on the back of your hand is hope-restored in the beauty of a butterfly that saw your pain. Your pent-up excitement has you glowing with exhilaration from every pore of your little body. You cannot be calm, yet cannot move without scaring your little friend away. And just then, a quietly-comforting whisper behind you says, *"Shhhh! Be quiet and still, your Mama's here."* She takes you into her arms and gently holds you as the little butterfly peacefully flaps his wings and comes to rest on your hand. Time has now stopped, the world has seceded, and your mother is happy. All Creation is now your mother's arms and the perfect gift came to you, instead. Together, mother and child gaze at Beauty in contemplation of your unity while sipping from the cup of "eternal now." You realize with the power of infinity that the butterfly is Jesus and the arms that hold you are those of our Blessed Virgin Mother.

Saturday, September 12, 1992

As I continue my Life in Christ Jesus, there are many days when I am tired, but I never entertain any thoughts of surrender to the bitters of the battle against the mortal world. I take new strides every morning because Our Lady's presence seems to intensify all that I give back to God. To Her, little things are of great magnitude in the eyes of Jesus. It seems that just one Hail Mary could save an entire race of people from destruction if we will only say it from the heart. God is rather perfect that way. The loving ambassador He has given in His Mother will not let our faith fall into any tawdriness or dissonance. She kindly lifts us in Divine ways to maintain our focus on Christ. I have very few wayward thoughts or temporal desires anymore because I cannot take the eyes of my heart away from Her grace. We are all special to Her in our own individual way. We all require different blessings to enliven our spirits. She knows each of our souls better than we know ourselves. She has the power to reach every one of us with the tenderness in which a mother knows her every child.

I am hoping that you will also be touched by Her Love through this Diary. My labors represent my desires for you to perceive Immaculate Mary in the way I already know Her. I pray that Her message of today has a special meaning for you. She came again as my brother and I prayed the Holy Rosary at eight o'clock. I know that She understands every aspect of the humanness of Her children. All of our joys and sorrows are also Hers because She is the Mother who knows us perfectly. As a part of the human nature of my brother and me, we had a small disagreement about a purely worldly matter. We hoped that Our Lady would not mention our little squabble since it seemed so insignificant to us. **"Yes, My little sons, I have come to bring you My Love once again. I love you so! I will not address or make any issue of your insignificant differences. They are childlike and you are little children. They will pass, so do not dwell on them. Please continue to dwell on Love! The more important matter these days is what I have been allowing you both to realize and envision. You are seeing the great tribulations which have begun to be imposed upon the Church by Satan, the sieging animosity and indifference."**

Our Lady continued to speak about Satan's attack on the Holy Church. He is battering it with materialism and temptation of every temporal nature. When Christ asked everyone what good it would be to gain the entire world and lose our very souls, He must have been warning us about these present days. Our holiness is being eroded and peace destroyed by our scurrilous search for wealth and recognition. Self-control and discipline are other casualties of this senseless quest. If we continue to seek false-consolation and temporary satisfaction in the world around us, we will never find the freedom and elevation that Christ brings to hearts open to Him. The Holy Mother is very sorrowful that these scourges are happening through our compromise in indifference and sin. She calls us daily to reflect the lives of the great Saints who purged themselves of every material to take-up their sacrificial lives of prayer and holiness. They cast-off the wares of darkness to stand naked in the Light of God. This is the abandonment we must offer if we expect to receive a blessing from His exculpating Hand. The lives of the Saints contradict nearly everything that secular society promulgates in this most defining century. The Holy Mother has come seeking our faith in the same Church those Saints died to evangelize. They disseminated God's message not with material or weapon, but with prayer and sacrifice.

The Truth of the Holy Church stands, indeed, opposed to the insatiable appetite of the human family to wield power and collect riches. These vices will never be ratified or validated by Christ and the Holy Spirit. God Himself looks upon us from His Seat in Heaven and commands, **"Quit the world! Abandon the flesh! Take-up your cross and follow Me!"** This is what made Saints of the Apostles and Disciples. They knew that their only power came from Jesus Christ. Everything they would accomplish was at His command and blessing. The Lord reigned in them at the expense of everything but the Eternity of their souls. They surrendered their lives to the Father in exchange for the sanctification of themselves and the mortal world that denied them. They could spot heresy at the blink-of-an-eye and would stand to the detriment of their health in defense of the Truth. These same Apostles were Christ's first priests. In the context of Her message this evening, Our Lady addressed their vocation as an example to those who wrongfully desire the ordination of women as priests and anyone who would proclaim the Blessed Mother as being the first priest.

"The Consecration of Jesus' Body and Blood is performed by those ordained by the descendants of the Apostles, the priests of the Church. It is important that you know that God the Father consecrated the Body of Jesus into the world through Myself as His Vessel. I was not God, I was not the Father, I could not consecrate Jesus into the world, but rather be His Tabernacle for Him to be born into the manger. That is why you call priests "Fathers." They are given the power by God through His Holy Spirit to bring Jesus' Body and Blood into the world upon the Sacred Altar of Sacrifice. No lay person has this power, nor should they extraordinarily administer the Body of Jesus to communicants without the proper concurrence from the Supreme Pontiff on Earth, the Holy See in Rome. As you know, the Pope is calling his priests to remain in their role as Father. The idea that some embrace of calling Me a priest is a false doctrine and errant dogma. It must be known that I was born absent of sin, and for that reason, was given the grace to bear Jesus' perfect Body into the world."

Our Lady continued by stressing the requirement of sanctity and holiness for anyone who assists in administering the Sacraments, especially our priests, but more importantly, lay ministers. The Immaculate Conception of the Blessed Virgin is proof that Jesus is to be given through sinless purity. And, She stressed the importance of the unification of all Christians under the Pope in Rome. Why would there be an heir to Saint Peter if Christ had not intended the Church to be founded on his pontificate? The entire teachings of Christ rest on this Chair, the Rock upon which the Church is built. Jesus, Himself, instituted the contemporary infallibility of the Holy See to all who would succeed Saint Peter. The tough decisions and sacrifices that God asks of His people are oftentimes like having to learn a foreign language. To those who have protested for centuries against the original Apostolic Church, and for those who do not know Her at all, the principles of the Catechism might seem foreign in nature. But, it was equally as foreign to many pagans of the early centuries who were converted to the faith and became great Saints under the authority of the Papacy still seated at Vatican City. The "key" to that great municipality is our embrace of the Seven Sacraments of Christ, the Sacrifice of the Holy Mass, and allegiance to the Holy Father who is the Vicar of Christ for all humankind.

Our Lady's final point of discussion today was a denunciation of the means that some people are utilizing to impede the spread of communicable disease. She said, **"Remember that God allows the suffering of disease not for the self-preservation of mankind through sin, but for the total giving of the heart, soul, mind, and body to Jesus through absolute purity. The so-called 'protection' about which many people have spoken does not prevent the decay of the body or the soul because the sin is still present. I have told you that sin is always fatal. Mankind should give all of his sins to Jesus and lead the Life of purity which He requires. Thereafter, there will be no fatality of the soul in the passing from human existence into Eternal Life in Heaven."** We must remember that sinful alternatives do not lead to eternal Salvation. An extension of the number of years of human life is not as important as the road we travel to reach the Glory of Heaven. Only chastity and abstinence are the righteous ways to maintain our health and ensure the perfection of our souls. We must be faithful in our spiritual marriage to Christ Jesus. We cannot live prosperously or independently on our own. We cannot divorce ourselves from the Church and expect to gain Eternal Life by virtue of some provisionary "annulment." Indeed, we would suffer both physical and spiritual starvation before we ever had a chance to proclaim our independence.

This is why Our Lady is calling everyone to pray, fast, and do penance. She is inviting the world into full communion with the Holy Father. **"I have carried a picture of the Pope in My hands when I visited the children of Medjugorje. I am trying to impress upon the Church the important role of the Holy Father in keeping the eyes and hearts of the faithful focused on Jesus."** The Holy Mother is fully aware that, as humanity moves-away from Jesus, it turns its back on Love. If we do this, Satan will step-in and trample our helpless souls into the crevices of the ground. Our lifeblood will squeeze through the cracks in our faith and become food for the fiendish ghouls lying-in-wait for our imminent fall. This terror is real and possible for many, causing death and destruction all over the Earth. **"You will see the Church undergo great suffering. Do you see a new strength and need for My intercession? It is against the principles for which Jesus died to allow impurity and lack of sanctity to rule the destiny of those who come for His aid. I wish to lead everyone to Jesus."**

Sunday, September 13, 1992

Our Lady's messages are so beautiful that I cannot describe the jubilation I feel as She delivers them to me. I hang on Her every word in anticipation of hearing the next-to-follow. Her phrases are the substance of true Divinity that bring new Life to my stagnant days. Sometimes, I wonder how I ever lived so many years without knowing Her Immaculate perfection. She is chaste of Heart and pure of soul. She asks no more from Her children than to seek our allegiance to Jesus, the same way that He, in turn, transfers our souls to God. For this, we must be responsible-enough to accede. This we must receive! The future of our well-being hangs in the balance of what the Holy Mother has come to say. Therefore, I commend Her words to you as She has asked. I seek your reflection and compliance in the manner through which She has easily secured my own. It is in Her messages that Her commission is made clear. Her perfection continues to shine forth with each passing day with as much authenticity as the first time She ever spoke to me.

When Our Blessed Lady came to pray with us this evening, She was seeking a pure vision of Love and holiness found deep within our hearts. To help me understand the austere demands of such a Life, She showed me a picture of a fence. Its purpose is to help me learn that some people have an obscured and distorted view of the Truth because of the influences of the world and their own unwillingness to see. It was a simple picket-style fence with spaces between the planks about as wide as the planks themselves. When we try to peer behind it, the only world we see is revealed by the openings. Part of our vision of the world is blocked altogether. Our Lady asked me to remember the message She gave last night about the conditions of the Church. She said that the many defiant changes being made by liberals and the ill-intentioned are not unlike the planks in a fence that block our vision of the world behind. These changes deplete the Church of the traditions brought through the ages by the many Holy Pontiffs who served so faithfully to keep Christ's teaching intact. She said that the world can call it progress if it will, but these obtrusive changes lessen the desire of the faithful to worthily receive the Most Holy Eucharist, if indeed they attend Mass at all. While the Altar of Sacrifice cannot be unsanctified by heretic practices and philosophies, the number of parishioners who have come to receive Christ's Body has been diminishing in recent decades.

If we place ourselves a distance from this symbolic fence and try to look through, we see only a portion that is not obstructed by the perversions of modern opportunism. This aberration offends Christ, the Lord. He has sent His Mother to tell us that these changes are an effect of error by many in power. And, these same spiritually-starved people are trying to place the invaluable intercession of Our Lady behind this same wall of indifference. She did not come to speak through a fence to Her children as though we belong to some distant neighbor. We were given by Christ to live in the House of God with Her at our side. She feeds our hopes and nourishes our spirits in union with Jesus' Holy Spirit. But, when She offers us a miraculous portion of Heaven to comfort our souls, many turn their head away from the spoon and say, *"I don't have to believe that!"* They hide their faces against the pall of the fence and pretend to be orphans who have been on their own long enough to fend for themselves against mankind or the beneficial nature of God, Himself.

The list of awful violations against the Mother Church symbolically represented by the vertical slats in a fence are numerous. Many have been indicated in Our Lady's other messages. But today, She asked us to record Her concern that the people She calls Her "little girls" are raising their heads in blasphemy and heresy against the Church. The role of women in ecclesiastical protocol has long-been recognized as nurturing, prayerful, meditative, and docile. But now, they are crying for center stage in every aspect from the holy priesthood to the exclusion of any pronoun that proclaims God to be a man in the Scriptures handed-down by the Holy Spirit for 2000 years. Our Lady is calling on Her female children to remember Her own service to humanity. She also told us today that the Church reaffirmed its ban on the ordination of women to the priesthood on January 27, 1977. She said that this date is a particular significance for the truth of our Diary because it is the same day as my brother's birthday when he turned twenty-three.

"The world should follow the guidance of the Pope. The Church is against the ordination of women. This point, as I have previously attested, is another portion of the original picture that is behind the fence, behind a picket. Ponder these questions for a moment, 'Do you believe that God is the Father? And, do you believe that Jesus is His Son and that He came to the Earth and sought Apostles who were all men? Do you believe that these Apostles were spread into the world to deliver the message of My Son and that the original Baptizer of the children of God was a man named John? Do you believe that Jesus is the original Priest, after whom all others would follow and serve?' Now, where in all of this is the role of woman? Who represented the role of the woman in all of this? I, your Glorious Virgin Mother! Therefore, God desires that all women imitate My holiness, purity, and motherhood in the service of His Church on Earth."

Our Holy Mother wants us to see perfect holiness by clearing the obstacles in our path. We cannot re-define righteousness by ignoring the Commandments and the stations we hold in life. No longer can we claim "victimhood" when the essence of our intentions is to abrogate our responsibilities in the eyes of God the Father. Jesus asks us to live as He lives, with equal and intense Love for our brothers and sisters. Our unity in this unique design is nourished through the Holy Eucharist. The Blessed Sacrament teaches our souls that what we once considered to be repression is, in truth, our opportunity to say "yes" to God. What we once believed to be chains are actually wings-of-flight toward mortification and sanctity. If we humble ourselves and ask for God's help, we will see the world from the summit of genuine holiness whereby no fence, no rock, and no cloud can dampen our vision of the Truth or hinder our struggle for perfection.

Monday, September 14, 1992

Our Lady often speaks of the Holy Sacraments of the Catholic Church as the graces we need for strength, purification, and direction on our journey back to Heaven. Each of the seven Sacraments is founded in the Life of Jesus, the New Covenant between God and man. And, in all of them, Christ speaks directly to our souls. His voice is both understanding and wise. If we fall on the playground and someone says, "Get up, you're not hurt!", Jesus is there to say, "Please, I'll help you up, I know that it hurt. I felt it too." By God's design, we only cry half our tears because Jesus sheds the other half. We are healed in every way through the Sacraments of His Love, His Spirit and Flesh borne on the Holy Cross. His greatest grace is His Sacrificed Body which hung under the ecliptic sun as God consecrated His people back to His unconquerable Heart. He calls this His Most Blessed Sacrament because it is the doorway to the highest chambers of The Divine Mercy. This Trinity of God is about to celebrate a trinity of ceremonies, the marriage of Jesus and the Church, the reunion of our Holy Mother with Her children, and the nuptials uniting Justice and Peace. We are now at the rehearsal, and our Mother is preparing the procession.

The Holy Eucharist is the central Sacrament to the Church around which all other Sacraments reside. Indeed, most of the Sacraments are administered at the Celebration of the Holy Mass. Our Lady asked me to list the Seven Holy Sacraments here.

> **Baptism**
> **Confirmation**
> **Confession**
> **The Holy Eucharist**
> **The Holy Orders**
> **Holy Matrimony**
> **Anointing of the Sick**

The Most Blessed Sacrament, the Holy Eucharist, is the food which nourishes the others. Someone entering the grace of God's Church is first Baptized and Confirmed. Next, the Sacrament of Reconciliation (Confession) is administered prior to First Communion. The Sacrament of Holy Orders is for persons entering the religious life. There are many vocations of service, including the priesthood, deaconate, sisterhood, brotherhood, missionary, societies of faith, and other clerical orders. The Sacrament of Holy Matrimony is a vocation to family life. Those who marry take sacred Vows at their wedding and promise to faithfully fulfill the role of husband, wife, father, or mother. The final Sacrament is the Anointing of the Sick. This is a healing Sacrament for the infirm and convalescing. It is also a final blessing for those about to die, called the administration of "Extreme Unction." It is proper for someone close-to-death to offer a last Confession and receive the Body and Blood of Jesus, the Holy Eucharist. The Bread of Life is essential toward sanctifying the soul in every way. It is the closest anyone can get to Heaven while still on Earth. And, its soul-purifying grace prepares us for the blessing of meeting God Face-to-face. Our Holy Mother's cry to the world is, **"Come to the Eucharist. Come to Jesus. Come to Love. It is your Salvation. He is your Peace!"**

Wednesday, September 16, 1992

I have recently been contemplating how I can rise to greater love and perfection in the way Jesus asks. I wish to love Him as reverently as He has given me the power to profess. He deserves more than our simple devotion and fidelity. Indeed, we must offer our lives as a sacrifice in service to our brothers and sisters in His perfect Image. I asked Our Lady about my lingering thoughts that I might never be able to live such a life in honor of Our Lord. Her response was that it is a credit for someone to even recognize that we should live for Jesus. The very fact of understanding the holiness He seeks is a profession of faith. We are helpless to contemplate the desires of God unless we are open to the Holy Spirit. I was pleased to know that it is Jesus in the depths of my heart calling me to live the essence of His exemplary Life. In our fallen nature, we are not able to elevate ourselves by human effort alone. We need the Divine assistance that comes through the Spirit of God and the Holy Sacraments to guide us. And more prominently this century, the Almighty Father is manifesting countless miracles to strengthen our faith in His Love.

Not only is the Holy Mother appearing in dozens of countries simultaneously, there have been other miracles which prove that the Holy Eucharist is the Body and Blood of Jesus Christ. The Host has been seen in Fleshly form and has bled the Precious Blood of Jesus. Moreover, many statues of Jesus and Mary have shed tears and copiously bled from various wounds. These tears and this blood have been scientifically determined to be those of our Divinely-human Jesus and Mary. Jesus gives His all-powerful Love to humankind through His Crucifixion on the Cross and Resurrection from the dead. Since our sins were destroyed by His suffering and death, our souls have been elevated into His perfect image. Of course we are still sinners, but that does not mean that our continuation in sin is inevitable. We will never be able to put our hand in the face of time and say, "I am". That title belongs to Christ alone. But, we cannot sit in a soiled pool of human transgression and say that we can never do better. Christ lifted us from the scourge of sin and washed our souls clean on the day He died. We do not have to wait for our own death to effect the fruits of our newfound perfection! While we live in a world that embellishes a propensity to sin, we need not fall just because of the gravity of our humanness.

Unless we transcend our nature by faith in Christ's Blood, we will never be able to clearly see the Light that Our Lady has been trying to describe for many centuries. God would never ask us to look at His Divinity and then blind us from seeing it like a flashbulb in the night. Indeed, the reason His Mother is here now is to prepare us for the unapproachable Light we will see past the doorway of our death. She is trying to prepare our souls for grace and Mercy so we will not feel confronted in the jurisdiction of an unknown stranger when we see God's Face. We must, instead, be trusting little children who allow our souls to be led by a Father we recognize! That is the only way we will go with Him when the time comes to judge ourselves in the Light of the revealing Crucifixion of Jesus Christ. This does not mean we should be sorry for being human. Jesus Christ walked the Earth as a man in every way like us except sin. His message before and after He died is for us to become the very essence of His Being.

The words He inherently left to those who witnessed His Ascension into Heaven were prophesied when He told the woman nearly stoned, **"Go and sin no more!"** We fail to recognize His absolution of her as the same vindication we inherit from the Cross. This is the very message to the world on Ascension Thursday. **"I have washed you clean and made your pure. Go and sin no more."** He came to remake our souls in His own likeness from the Cross of Salvation. Having accomplished His redemptive work, He stood on a cloud like the Holy Pontiff standing at the door of "Shepherd One" and gave a final blessing before departing into the awaiting skies. When we live the holiness that Christ teaches through the Scriptures and His Spirit within us, we will avoid sin. That does not mean we will be perfect in our own eyes or those of other men. But, would God put us to a test we cannot pass? Would He send a perfect Human into the world who asks us to be like Him and not provide the grace to attain it? His answer is that Love is more powerful than human nature. We become one with the Divinity of Christ when we embrace the Cross and remain in the Sacramental grace of His Church. We must love according to the Bible and be willing to rise to the power of Christ in us.

All life and holiness belong to God, even to the depth of our inner-selves. That is where human sanctification begins. We will never emulate Christ by demanding that others change first because the seed for a perfect world lies inside our own soul. This is not an overnight accomplishment. Our holiness must be nurtured by humble submission to God and prayer from the heart. We must acknowledge that we are capable of sin before we can overcome the temptations which provoke it. The road to the Life of Christ is open to everyone who hopes for peace and human Salvation. If we do not desire a world of unity and contentment, it will not come. We have to place the seed of our own conversion on the ledge of Creation in order for the Dove of Peace to light in our hearts. Our Lady has manifested this cultivating discussion because She knows our potential to be converted into the likeness of saints. If we are to pass from this life into Heaven beyond our awareness of the transposition, we have no choice but to comply with Her words. We are like children in the dark wearing blindfolds. She can take us into the Light, but we must remove every obstacle before our eyes to admire it. This requires a life of sacrifice and prayer with the intention that we will succeed.

We have to desire the vision of God before we will ever be able to find Him. If we wait for Him to reveal His Kingdom at the last, we will assuredly hide our faces from the brightness of the Truth we have always denied. With this aforethought, Our Lady turned Her discussion this evening toward those who refuse to believe that the Eucharist is the Body and Blood of Our Savior, Jesus Christ. It is bad enough that certain people choose to disbelieve, but they also try to destroy the faith of those who do. This is a good case of "misery loves company." Our Lady told me that no Protestant can claim to be a child of the Holy Spirit who says that the Eucharist is not the Divine Presence of Jesus Christ, Body, Blood, and Soul. If they do, they are openly and blatantly lying. Anyone who says that a spirit has told them that Jesus is not the Eucharist is under the influence of Satan. A Christian evangelist who denounces the Most Blessed Sacrament is not in union with God the Father. The destiny of their soul is in great danger. The Mother of God does not conceal Her discomfort with the errant words of anyone who does not embrace the Altar of Sacrifice.

The Mass is the Crucifixion of Jesus Christ, the moment He died on the Cross. Anyone who disavows this Truth is both "anti-Cross" and "anti-Christ." Such people who travel the world falsely wearing the cloth of Christian faith are looking for innocent sheep to devour. They embrace the futility of human indignance over the omnipotent power of God to place His Son on the Altar in exchange for bread and wine. They stand as imposters in a beacon of Paradisial Light that God intends as a place of Jesus' Adoration and say, *"Look at me, I know who God is!"* The real intention of the Almighty Father is for them to kneel in homage of Christ and tell others that the Holy Eucharist is truly His precious Body and Blood. It costs no earthly sum to deliver our soul to the Mercy of Jesus. We freely offer our heart and conscience for the purpose of participating in faith, conversion, and sanctification. This is the first step in our affirmation to God that we are sorry for our sins and willing to amend our life in reflection of Jesus. The Crucifixion of Christ makes us more than eligible for Redemption, it is Salvation itself. Our vow to accept His Death and Resurrection is a confessional prayer that begins the process of healing every infirmity of our being. We need not wonder how to earn this blessing because it is a grace confirmed without cost. When we accept the resurrected perfection that Christ bestows upon us, we begin the happy reunion between God and man.

Saturday, September 19, 1992

Our Lady has made it clear that humankind is, indeed, helpless unless we call upon the power of God to deliver us to Salvation. It is easy for us to recognize this helplessness; but it is not always a pleasant prospect to accept. I believe that the unwelcome companion to our helpless nature is the hopelessness which follows suit. If we do not hope, we will not seek the changes for which we pray. There are signs of our lack of hope all over the world. It is apparent today, even within the holy walls of our churches. What hope do we hold when the new hymnals we publish, that are expected to last for ten years, still include songs with lyrics which proclaim that the poor continue to be oppressed and the lonely abandoned? Does the Church not expect this to change over the ensuing months or years? Where is our trust in our prayers when we offer musical homage to God through such tragic themes? Where is human hope when we fail to parole prisoners or to pick-up walkers along the roadway because there exists the chance that a certain person might be the one who will rob or murder us? We must envision hope as a petition for change, trusting that God will validate our supplications by bringing the Kingdom to Earth for which we pray.

That faith in our intercessions is what Our Lady is teaching today. When we learn that God wishes us to pray because He holds the affirmatives to all our needs, we will meditate in the way that Our Lady asks. Her lessons should be learned well. When She came to speak to us this evening, Her words were of great anticipation of our forgiveness from Jesus, **"I am here with you, little ones! I have come to share My Love with you. Please do not be afraid to hope for all that you see as good and pure because there is hope for every soul. I have often noticed that you wonder how Jesus can witness so many terrible actions and selfish agendas in the world, but His Mercy is still so great. I can assure you that Mercy belongs to the wretched the same as they, themselves, belong to Love..."** She continued to speak compassionately about those who are being held captive. She knows where each one is located and prays over them in constant vigil for their strength and protection. She said that those imprisoned for penitential reasons are hostages to the lack of forgiveness the world refuses to offer them. Their true prison is the pain others cause their soul by a constant reminder of their guilt. How can they acquit themselves if others refuse to forgive?

Our Lady told me that everyone yearns for the simplicity of the original Love in which they were born. Their little hearts sought the embrace of the world and asked only that someone would show them the way. We are all born innocent of any sin of our making. Yes, we are descendants of sinful Adam and Eve, but our Baptism washes that away. We should be able to walk forward in baptismal grace with the expectation that we will always be new. Our souls have beautiful wings to soar in the breezes of human embrace. But, that loving acceptance seems never to come. We search and wander through a world we can never own which wishes to discard us in return. We become living examples of incarnate rejection and our hopes turn from peaceful co-existence to defiant independence. When the despised and disposed are stripped of dignity, their fight is against the Love they never received. This is the making of sorrowful souls who somehow find their way behind the barbs of prison walls. The Holy Mother says that such "criminals" never had a chance to live the harmony, unity, and freedom of acceptance from their childhood lives. They are confined by the bitterness and revenge of a society that first made them fall. No one will open the door to the freedom of forgiveness through which they can flee from their own shame and banishment by the world. They are poor in Love because no one has been willing to enrich their lives. But, their freedom is at hand!

No chains of human bondage can contain a spirit that is free in the Love of Christ. His Justice cannot be bound. These precious convicts are like birds in a cage, the first ones He will set free before pronouncing sentence on those who refused to forgive them. When America fosters the fight for wealth and prosperity without providing equal means to attain it, the poor, uneducated, and disabled are set in the cold. The atmosphere of competition is so great that many without means have to resort to physical struggle and infraction to eat and survive. When they reach-out for help to their brothers and sisters, they are asking for a chance to fully participate in the so-called Dream that truthfully keeps America asleep in sin. They ask only for the portion that the Almighty Father has created for them. When they are refused because they cannot compete, they are accused of stealing by asking for help. Our Lady told me that the true thieves are those who refuse to share. Claiming the bounty that belongs to the poor is the worst kind of pilfering.

The Holy Mother said, **"Yes, this has to stop. It is time to share, to stop the division which leads to perversion, and to stop imprisoning souls who seek only a share. We must pray for this all over the world, not just in the West. Prayer, fasting, faith, peace, conversion, the Holy Rosary, contemplation, Confession, penance, and Adoration are the goals that God has made for humanity. These are very difficult to achieve by the rich. Their wealth is a self-inflicted curse..."** Our Blessed

Lady wants everyone to faithfully imitate the Life of Her Son, Jesus Christ, and live the lessons they both bring to the world. She is the humble Handmaid of the Lord who knows Him best. We are called to be true leaders and teachers for Christ by the living example of our own lives. We must serve, share, protect, and comfort those who have only little. Even in their poverty, they hold the most valued possession of all. Their unity with suffering-Christ elevates them to the ranks of the heavenly hosts who reside within the admiration of God before all others. The Holy Mother says that the poor implicate the rich as guilty against the teachings of Christ at the Judgement Seat of God. **"Pray, pray, pray! There is nothing material to earn in Heaven. All Heaven is a Reward!"**

Sunday, September 20, 1992

I could never have imagined that I would be greeted on my thirty-first birthday by the Mother of God singing, "Happy Birthday." This miracle is beyond my ability to describe. Our Lady always knows what to say to lift my heart from the cares of the world. I often wonder what it would be like to be able to offer others the presence-of-heart that would make them feel totally loved in every way. Of course, the Blessed Mother sees the reaction to Her gifts before they are ever presented. She is teaching me the same prospective and Love by Her living example of charity and compassion. After Her gracious recognition of my birthday, She entered a discussion about those who defy the Love of God and become hostile at the thought of His intervention. This is particularly the case with young people who believe themselves to be invincible. They regard the message of Salvation as being only relevant in the lives of the old. Indeed, I have been told by many youngsters that their interpretation of the Life of Christ has Him remanded to the role of mortal prophet and nothing more.

Those who believe that Christ is just another messenger from God are denying the very sacrificial Life and Crucifixion that has saved their souls. And, in the process of rejecting His Redemption, they are also refusing to live the Love He brings. This narrow-thinking is one of the reasons that four-fifths of the world's population has yet to be converted to the truth of Christianity. People have created a false image of who they believe Christ to be so they will not have to muster the faith and morality to imitate His Life. Our Lady says that the source of this error rests in the false assumption that the omnipotence of God is a subpart of the world rather than the sustainer of it. They assert that Christ is an effect of God, like you and I, instead of the Incarnation of the Almighty Father, Himself. The source of their disbelief is their repudiation of the Holy Trinity. Not only are they denying the Son of God, they are rejecting the Holy Spirit who would tell them the Truth if only they would listen. They stand fast in the world with their feet in the chains of indifference, held tight by the lock of agnosticism. They wish to pull the Divinity of Christ down to their own lifeless existence at the same time He is trying to rescue their souls from the path to perdition.

The fact remains that mankind will never attain the perfection of God or the knowledge of Eternity on his own. Jesus proclaims that, **"No ones comes unto the Father, unless he comes through Me."** He could not be more clear than that! Jesus asks His people to live in faith and courage while anticipating His Triumphant Return. If faithless souls do not live in that hope, what are they living for? What keeps them going? Can they not see that the candle of Life is burning near its end? Can they not read the signs? They wait for miracles and God sends them. The Holy Virgin Mother is one of His best. But in the face of this heavenly intercession, they spate and protest that it is not enough. They turn away and tell God that He has to do more than just send messages of admonishment and preparation. They demand to see tangible revelations of His reality which they can grasp with the descendent-hands of Thomas in the Upper Room.

Why do so many without faith in Christ live this way? Simply because His call is to a Life of sacrifice and purity. Why would they give more than is absolutely necessary? *"If Christ is not the standard of God, why should we meet it?"*, they are quick to say. They feel a safe distance from any responsibility toward the good of humankind and the humbling of themselves that would advance the cause of world peace. To them, Jesus is just a name on page 703 of the American Heritage Dictionary. It has not come to their minds that He is the One who created the very pages on which those words are printed. The Holy Mother says that the circumference of all Creation lies in the hands of God Almighty. The Earth is just a speck in the middle of matter-in-motion. But, the souls Christ came to redeem are as blessed as the mighty sun. He seeks the transformation of human thought from the "possibility" of God to the **Truth** of God. When we were cast-out of Paradise at the hands of Adam and Eve, we lost more than a perfect vision of Him. We mislaid our entire capacity to realize He exists! That is the fateful truth that plunders the desire of many people to seek restored virginity and Redemption in Christ. But, what they fail to understand is that Jesus *is* our capacity to know God to the center of His Being. He is the restoration of our perfection and immortality Who stands before us like a great forest of revelation, while millions claim they cannot find Him in the midst of the trees of life.

When Christ came to teach, He said that His Kingdom was not of this world. When He died on the Cross, He delivered the Earth to the Throne of God. And, along with the Holy Mother and the Spiritus Sanctus, they have been prayerfully watching it shudder in the universe like a chick breaking-out of a shell. We are deplete of reasons not to respond! The world was deluged in the days of Noah and remained afloat in the sea of Creation. Now we swim gleefully in the Blood of the Lamb Who has transformed the stains on our souls into feathers. The Virgin Lady of Heaven is saying that it is time for us to fly! We can justify no distance between ourselves and God the Father because of our unity in Him through Christ. We have been transported through the ages since the beginning of the world. While we were sleeping in sin, God was preparing to awaken us. He came as a little Child in the middle of the night and rang with the Truth so profoundly that even the most comatose of sinners heard to the depth of their souls. Jesus died and rose from the dead, ascended into Heaven, and is seated at the Right Hand of the Father. He will come again to judge the living and the dead, right down to the last atheist and agnostic who will look up and tremble at the sight of the Savior they rejected.

Our Lady says that Christ can be accepted now both spiritually and physically. We must allow the Holy Spirit to reign in our hearts. And, all souls should convert to the Truth of Jesus' Presence in the Holy Eucharist. This Sacrament is God-on-Earth in our time. It proves that Jesus is truly alive and well in the world He owns and forever will be. From high above the celestial Floodgates, God sends the grace-filled Body of His Son to the Altar of Sacrifice. His Flesh is real Food and His Blood, real Drink. Unless we receive this Manna from Heaven, we will not have Life in us. Christ is the third dimension that raises our souls from the dungeon-floor of human exile. We are lifted during Holy Communion to the heights of bliss to perch in dignity and grace upon the perfection we thought we would never attain. This is real and factual Love from our Infinite God in Heaven. He transcends time and space to wake us to a heavenly Creation that we previously could only imagine. This is a dream that came true before we ever fell asleep. We should offer everything and anything to strive to reach it, leaving no stone unturned and no soul without cultivation. The Good News of Christ Jesus must resound through the Earth with the power of a hundred stampeding Paul Reveres to awaken the slumbering world, yet unaware that their freedom is near.

It is a call to prayer and service in advance of the reconciliation of God and man. Love must move from heart-to-heart. We must grow in faith and holiness like flowers that dance in the light with imperishable beauty. Our fragrance must be the sweetness of penance, peace, prayer, and repentance, making us worthy to inhabit the stately window boxes aside the bed in which the Almighty rests. We do not realize the power of our supplications! We can get up and walk out of a painted picture that seemingly detains us in sorrow and despair. The Holy Spirit is our deliverance to freedom from hopelessness and loneliness. We need the courage to believe in reverent faith that all these things are true. Christ's yoke is small and His burden light. We walk together with Him toward the Divine Chalice of human Redemption, where we will find the first sip to be delightful, indeed! Our courage comes from faith and leads to service. There is only one Victory and one Salvation. Jesus must find us working to the depth of our souls in His vineyard for the cause of our conversion and the alleviation of human suffering. Our endurance must be a holy and joyful battle against the terrible strains of mortality that try to depress our souls. We must look into Creation with open hearts and see Life as a continuous opportunity to fill the Earth with Light and health. When we love one another to the infinity of God's Will, Jesus is glorified over and again. This is the realistic truth of our faith and the reason why we hope in Him.

Tuesday, September 22, 1992
In all the invariant discussion about the tangibility of human perfection, we sometimes draw-back and wonder how this could possibly be accomplished. After all, we read the horrid accounts in the daily newspapers about the mutilation of the corporal and moral fiber of our American society. Indeed, it is the same all over the world. Rampant bloodshed, thievery, and infidelity are seemingly normal traits of the passing years. I find myself wondering how this could happen to a world of people who have been blessed for so many centuries. Have we not learned that confrontation, greed, and turpitude are the seeds of human division and destruction in our advanced age? Have all who have died from wars, disease, famine, and outright murder fallen from our sides without impressing any message upon our souls? Our Lady knows that the avoidance of every form of skullduggery and violation rests in our refusal to fall to the lies of evil. We must remove our souls from the occasion of sin! The goal of becoming the perfect likeness of Christ Jesus is not just a hypothetical postulate. If we listen with the strength of our hearts to Her words and obey with every intention of succeeding, we will be transformed into the people She calls us to be. And in doing so, our lives will be changed and our nations healed. Wars will go-the-way of dinosaurs and pestilence will become a word that is so archaic that literary authors will delete it from their vocabulary.

But, the Blessed Mother assures us that we will not attain this Heaven-on-Earth if we do not immediately cease in the way of sin and transgression. We have to purify our souls as if by conflagration, dying to every provenience that leads to inequity in ourselves and injustice in the world. This total renewal of the human psyche is sitting like a cup of ambrosia in Our Lady's hands, waiting for us to come forward like children to nourish our souls. It is a process that *must* begin in our hearts, whether we like it or not. We cannot "think-away" mortal impropriety and the destruction of the inner-self. Intellectual progress has failed for centuries on end. This time, our approach must be deeper and more sincere. The origin of the convalescence of our wounded souls must be our desire to say "I love you" and mean it, not just because we would otherwise be unable to satisfy our greed if we refuse. The Holy Mother says that our new beginning is found in understanding that we are intended to be perfect like

Christ. The evidence She provides is in the priceless gift of human life. She told me tonight that the greatest prohibition to the wholesome nature of our collective souls is the scourge of abortion. If we would only recognize the perfection that exists between a mother and an unborn child, we will be on the path to embracing the Will of God. Our understanding of Heaven is in the validity of our intention to obey Him.

I asked Our Holy Mother how a child-in-the-womb is perfect since we are all conceived with Original sin. She said that the perfection is in the union of the mother and child, not in the soul of the child. If they are separated before birth, the perfection of the womb is lost. And, anyone who destroys unborn life is denying the eternal intention of God. They are trampling upon the omnipotent desire of the Almighty Father to effect the reason we are created. A mother's womb is a paradisial weaving-basket of undeniable innocence and grace. Any human hands that dare purloin the sweet fruit of this berth belong to a soul who truly has no desire to see the Light of Heaven. Our Lady has made a pleasing comparison between a child-in-the-womb and the Consecration at the Holy Sacrifice of the Mass. We believe in Truth that when a priest takes bread and wine into his hands and pronounces Consecration, God supplants these gifts with the Divine Body and Blood of Jesus Christ. The union of these hands with the Holy Eucharist is an Element of perfection. Jesus' Body rests in the fingertips of the Celebrant in the same Divinity that God unites a mother and an unborn child. That is the reason why communicants were never allowed to touch the Sacred Host during Holy Communion in past centuries.

Can you imagine the wrath of God as He looks upon the world today and sees the precious Body and Blood of His Son being placed into hands that recently performed an abortion? I asked the Holy Mother why it became acceptable to receive the Eucharist in the hand. She replied that millions of people refuse to attend Holy Mass if it is not permitted. God does not want that to happen. She made it clear that the Perfection and Divinity of Jesus is not stained or lost when a sinner touches the Species. And while we must always receive the Holy Eucharist pure-of-soul, we also acknowledge the healing and sanctifying power of Christ to expunge the fumbling way we come-forward to receive Him. God knows that when the Body of His Son saturates our souls, human hands become tools for the deliverance of children to birth and the lifting of the rejected from the torments of oppression.

Our Lady is directing our attention to the perfect works of God to provide example for our lives. We must become the magnifiers of His intentions in a world where we serve as lowly stewards. God presents His children with numerous choices because we are a people who require them. After all, it was the decision of Adam and Eve to fall from the heights of Paradise. But, the choices we make now will not determine whether we will fall from Heaven to

Earth, but from this world into the fires of eternal damnation. That is why we must decide for God and embrace His culture of Life and perfection. When we do so, our choices will be simple and easy to effect. We will have accepted the reason Jesus Christ died on the Cross. The door will be open for our humble submission and journey back to God. The essential presence of human conversion is believing in our own helplessness and nurturing a Life of faith and peace. We must grow in concert with nature itself to anticipate the final days of Earth. When we live in "accourse" with God in every way, repentance, penance, and amendment will be the three reasons we rise from our hiding-place in darkness. The maturity of our holiness rests in the power of our prayers and openness to the Holy Spirit.

Jesus is the Mercy that God has always wished for us. Desire for His forgiveness gives us hope and a new vision of the glories of Paradise. When we approach the Altar of Sacrifice with the same intensity of faith that we yearn for Heaven, God will deliver us from worldliness, impurity, and materialism. Our Lord asks some very basic questions through our belief in His Word. Do we understand the power of our prayers? Do we accept the Will of God in our lives, come what may? Are our efforts directed toward remaking the Earth into the Kingdom that Jesus teaches? Will we sacrifice everything we have to the purpose of becoming the likeness of our Divine Savior? Our response to these very basic principles define the qualitative truth in our desire to go to Heaven. The gentle surrender of our spirit to Christ Jesus is the beginning of the long pilgrimage toward the perfection He requires of us to get there. I firmly believe that we can walk in greater confidence and faith when we embrace the humble hand of Our Blessed Virgin Mother. She is God's Love shared with humankind in a most revealing and powerful way. Her Love is genuine, Her grace is undeniable, and the beauty of Her soul is unsurpassed.

In the Holy Virgin, God's Love is manifested from the Divinity of Heaven itself. She stands as a living legacy to self-denial and humanitarian service. Now, She comes beckoning humanity to follow Her to Jesus through the blessings of the Holy Church. The Sacred Body and Blood of Her Son await our humble reception. The Cup of Eternal Salvation covers the entire world in Salvific Grace as Jesus' Blood has saturated the land He has claimed for His own. It is upon the Eternal Cup that the Dove of Peace is perched to carry the message of Salvation into the hearts of men. And, it is for Love of us that Christ surrendered His Life. When we drink Him-in at Holy Mass, we are reciprocally consumed by His Redeeming Blood. All of God's children are united in the Sacrifice of this Eternal King. Our souls are the chosen destination of His precious Crucifixion. We are one humanity again, sitting like a chalice, waiting for the Blood of the Lamb to fill our souls. Why is such emphasis placed on the Holy Cup? Our Lady said it best, **"...the Cup draws humanity to the Host, Who stands above. The Blood of the Cup is Shed from the Body of Christ into the lives of lost souls below!"**

The Most Blessed Sacrament is the Body, Blood, Soul, and Divinity of Jesus Christ. The Host is the Flesh from which the Blood flows into the Cup. The Virginal and Unretouched Perfection from the Omnipotent Veins of Christ has been poured-out upon humankind to remake, renew, purify, cleanse, and expiate. His Sanctifying Nectar is the incarnation of peace on Earth. If we would faithfully realize the majesty of this Sacred fact, we would be well on our way to the fulfillment of the prophecies of the Lord Himself, *"When I am lifted-up, I will draw all men unto Me."* The healing and deliverance of suffering humanity will come-to-pass in our age. Indeed, we will be prepared for the Second Coming of the Christ seeking those who humbly accept the Salvation He brings.

Friday, September 25, 1992

My brother has been in the process of applying for entrance into the Seminary to become a Roman Catholic priest. He has had several personal conferences with the Bishop of our Diocese. Today, I received a telephone call at my workplace from my brother. He said that the Bishop was at my home where they were having another visit. They invited me to leave work to see the Bishop before he departed to offer Holy Mass at a nearby Ursuline convent. I took the ten-minute drive to my home in great joy because I had never before been near a bishop outside of the Sacrifice of the Holy Mass. Our Bishop is quite congenial and humble. His service is characterized by the delegation of ecclesiastical etiquette to his subordinate pastors. He greeted me with this same cordiality when I got home. The three of us stood in my livingroom where I have placed a small prayer-altar before a collectible statue of Jesus. Standing nearby is a statue of the Blessed Virgin Mary that I purchased in Medjugorje, Yugoslavia in 1989. This is the same room where my brother and I receive most of Her messages for this Diary.

After exchanging pleasantries and mutual affection, I asked the Bishop to pray over us and bless my home through the power of his Holy Office. I knew that a direct descendant of the original Apostles was standing in a room to which the Holy Mother has come to reveal God's Plan. The Bishop offered a very pious blessing upon my home and all who enter. It made me very happy because it validates the worthiness of a site where God's messages are received that are so important for the conversion of the world. I am confident that Our Lady was present for this auspicious occasion. The holy Bishops of the Catholic Church are very dear to Her Immaculate Heart. They are the shepherds who lead during these last ages of human history. I hope this blessing by such a reverent servant turn the compassionate eyes of God toward the prayerful obedience my brother and I offer His Mother. We pray in union with Her and all the Bishops of the Catholic Church for the purification, sanctification, and Salvation of every soul living in faith and the Church Suffering in the mortifying confines of Purgatory.

Saturday, September 26, 1992

I was confused today about a somewhat acrimonious display of Christian discipline by another person. They stated the undeniable Truth of the Gospel of Jesus Christ, but in a tone that was less-than charitable. It seems to be such a contradiction when this happens. I know that many of the saints-of-old were quite rancorous in their defense of Christianity, but it is a rare approach in modern times. After seeing the humble civility of the Virgin Mary, my soul is disturbed when I observe someone who is almost confrontational in expressing the peace of Christ. I cannot help but wonder what a paradox this must be for them. When I pray with my brother, the Holy Spirit helps us better understand the aspects of our evangelical witness. Christians withstand quite a unique situation in the midst of indifference and outright atheism. The natural response is to fight fire with fire. Unfortunately in my case, this has usually resulted in more heat than light. It is a shallow peace that can survive the strain and cultivation required to disseminate the Christian message. We deal with the emotions and feelings of people who approach life as it is, not as God wishes it to be. Even though many Saints knew this in their invincible ministries, they still listened to the Holy Spirit calling them toward a placid temperament. Their own holiness confirmed that they were instruments for peace that grew in the wake of their faith. Our Lady offered a parable to strengthen our discernment.

Imagine standing at the perimeter of a tropical jungle that is overgrown with weeds and trees. There is no evidence that anyone has ever trekked into the depth of its undiscovered nature. Two people are standing at the forest-edge with the intention of blazing a path to the other side. One is holding a huge machete and has several power chainsaws at his feet. He plans to cut a level path through the center so others will have a planar road on which to travel. It will be a straight course through the most shallow portion of the jungle with no obstacles, inefficient turns, or detours. This capable sawyer looks at the man beside him who is perceivably more frail and weathered. He is holding a simple pair of well-worn pruning sheers in his hands. His seemingly impotent nature draws a compassionate look of uncertainty from the much stronger trail-blazer. What if the old man should fall and die on the journey he has come to undertake? But, rather than to hurt his feelings, the more capable of the two decides to follow a few yards stern until the old man tires. When he tells his senior partner that he plans to work behind, the old man's eyes glow in wisdom as they fall upon the power-tools sitting on the ground. He covers his veteran hands with a pair of old gloves and raises his shears to the first dead limb he sees.

He clips the first branch and reaches for another. Over and again, he snips and cuts-away limbs that are lifeless, barren, diseased, and unfruitful. A path begins to take-shape around the living vegetation he leaves untouched. He does this to the amazement of his much younger partner who knows that if it were him, he would use his power-tools and machete and remove the living branches with the dead. He watches the old man move onward at the instinct of his heart, changing course ever-so-slightly to accommodate the preservation of living nature. The younger man's spirit sinks as he now realizes that his plethoric approach to conquering the wilderness is a statement of over-kill. He needs no chainsaws or machete to perform the beatifying fete this seasoned gentleman is accomplishing. His head begins to lower in sorrow at the prospect that he has nothing to offer to the adept sculptor who is paring a path that was his to conquer.

The old man suddenly stops at a gargantuan wall of lifeless trees blocking his every move as though they were placed by Nature centuries ago to deny him success today. He calmly turns to the young man at his side, gazes at a power saw, and says, *"Now is the time, now is the time."* He takes the machine into his ancient arms with veins bulging and fires the saw to life. Wielding it with the agility of a surgeon, he turns to the trees and extricates their useless corpses from the path of his work. The younger man watches the skill of a veteran, mastered in the operation of these modern machines. He knows that the old man could carve any image he desires as easily as whittling a whistle from a broken branch. The pillars of laden wood fall to the ground with such force that it shakes the sawdust from both their faces. When they clear their eyes, they stand peering into the newborn light radiating from the forest's edge.

What is the message of this story? We must walk in faith both gently and precisely, pruning from our midst the lifeless fears that keep others from Christ. The Light of conversion comes through the strength of our Love. God provides the tools of confidence and valiance through the power of His Spirit. And in the face of blatant opposition to Christ the Lord, He gives us the sword of Justice and an admonishing authority from Heaven itself. No man is too tall to be felled by the Almighty Truth of the Son of God. He cuts deeply, precisely, and fairly, removing the lifeless blocks to the Coming of His Kingdom. When evangelization gets tough, Christ rolls-out the "big guns" in the people who know Him best.

We should strive for harmony in our example of the peace of Christ, complementing His holiness and the tranquility of His Spirit. The discerning wisdom we gain through prayer is the guide to our actions. God tells us when to use pruning sheers or power-saws, and whether to shake the dust from our feet and move to another place. Love is the only vision for the holy. We are not the judges of other souls, but we can assuredly lead them to the Justice of us all. The human heart is the proprietor of judicious temperament. When we listen intently to the Spirit of God, no innocent sapling will be crushed and no fertile limb will be stripped from its vine. In this Divine jurisprudence, everyone is elevated and the whole of Creation is bathed in greater revelation, Light, unity, and peace. Christ was docile on Earth because He knew He wielded the power of God. His peace-through-strength is a fruit of the infinite Wisdom that the faithless will prune themselves.

Sunday, September 27, 1992

The Holy Mother seemed very concerned when She came tonight. While She is traveling the world dispensing graces from God, very few are heeding Her call to come to Christ. There is a difference in knowing that holiness is the road to Paradise and actually effecting the changes-of-life that will take us there. When we pray from the heart, we cast our souls into the winds of Christ's peace and awareness. We not only put-on the shoes of conversion, we start walking toward the Gate of Salvation. Our earthly encumbrances fall from our hearts like shedding leaves when our sights are focused upon the glories of Heaven and the unity Christ seeks in us. But, we cannot expect Divine help if we continue to grovel in the incongruities of the flesh and material world. God helps those who help themselves. Raising our hearts to Heaven means living the elevation of our mind, soul, and spirit to Jesus Christ. His call to freedom from sin means our simultaneous liberty from the struggle for pleasurable goods and fancy fashion. The passing world has no power to burden us or dim our hopes. We find in Jesus our separation from the delusion of the world and all the shadows that detain us in mortality. The Holy Spirit releases the human soul to pure Love, openness, peace, and dignity. Our anticipation of His Second Coming makes us aware that any new dawn may be our call to reconciliation and Judgement.

We seek immortal Life which knows no suffering or disease. It is absent of pain and sadness, untouchable by evil and despair, and free from temptation, depression, and death. Can you imagine an ecstasy so fulfilling that you cannot speak or conjure a negative thought? Have you pondered a Divinity so profound that your soul falls euphorically at the presence of His Face? When your load is heavy and sadness grips your soul, go in your heart and meet this Beauty. Greet Jesus there with the assurance that His Love will lift you from any pang of sorrow or lingering grief. The freshness of Springtime will lift your soul to the freedom of His grace. No one can be held captive by the world who is given to Christ with an open heart. In Him, we live continuously beyond the grasp of broken mortality. He lifts us over the threshold into warm sunshine and eternal rest. Our singular relief from suffering lies through the doorway of conversion. Those who refuse Jesus with the Love in their hearts will die eternally and pass into wanton destruction. The bridge to freedom will be forever closed without their ever having walked across it. They will lie in an endless prison of torment, clawing at a door they had a lifetime to step-through. Their desperation will be the sad ending to a tragedy that began the day they refused Jesus Christ.

Tuesday, September 29, 1992

"The Story of a Life"

There was once a rundown village that seemed gloomy and sad where lonely people lived hapless lives. There was little common-courtesy or kindness, and few believed in dignity and trust. They lived as though they were different species of God's Creation, working by themselves to simply survive. Some would cheat and steal, believing that only the "strong" survive. And, most were convinced that their misery was brought by someone else. Yet, in the middle of this drudgery, others held a vision for a hope-filled town adorned by beauty. They yearned for someone or something to change their lives, knowing full-well it might take a miracle. They would do anything for their fellow citizens if they would just care for one another. All they asked was to be loved and forgiven in doing the best they could. But, no one wanted to be the first to love or sacrifice to finally bring beauty to this desolation. Who would pay the price to open the hearts of all and fulfill a common dream or distant hope? Everyone just lowered their heads and asked, "why?"

One little old man hoped throughout his entire life that everyone would live together in peaceful progress and common good will. He grew-up seeing the suffering and indifference of his beloved neighbors. Indeed, he saw what they were doing to themselves. One day, as he stood on his porch gazing into mid-air, his attention was drawn to a little flower blooming amidst this spiritual darkness. It was bathed from above by a single ray of sunlight. With his heart filled with hope, his eyes followed the path of the beam into the heavens, arriving at the Paradise from whence it came. That was the moment when "why" was extinguished from his lips. His heart now spoke with courage, "why not?" Why not have a town of beauty where everyone shares their individual hopes? Why not believe that their common vision could become their mutual happiness through unified love? With this spirit he addressed the future, proceeding into the next dawn that would rise. It is the reason he rose from his bed the following morning. His first task was to clean the inside of his home, washing the dishes and laundering his clothes. The woodwork got a fresh coat of paint and the walls were enlivened by decorative paper. He even repaired the wooden steps and plumbing leaks. Fresh artworks and figurines adorned his newborn rooms with the strength of his new vision. They reminded him that he was on a mission for the rest of the town, to show that their dreams are real.

When he finished inside, he continued his journey-of-light into the yard. He removed the brush, disposed of the garbage, and planted saplings and grass. His lawn was decorated with the most beautiful flowerbed the town had ever seen. But even though his land was a sight to behold, the townspeople scoffed and claimed that he was acting arrogantly, thinking he was better than the rest.

They said he was trying to show-off and display his private goodness for public recognition. No one would believe he had done it for them. They refused his gift of beauty that he had worked so hard to complete the same way they rejected each other. Sorrowful, but undaunted, the man set his sights on the village. The very next day, he walked the streets picking-up trash and clearing the gutters. He trimmed the weeds, sowed new grass, and even transplanted some of the beautiful flowers from his home beside the public sidewalks. He repaired broken concrete like he was mending shattered dreams. The stagnant stench of their lives was being flushed from the city to make way for the freshness of new anticipation. He tried to restore an age of hope as he even ventured into the nighttime and cleaned the tired property of his indignant neighbors. He polished their windows, once covered by years of indifference that kept them from seeing the truth. Everything he did was in love for the people he knew could be happy, too.

The town came-to-be a glorious sight! There was not a nook or cranny left untouched. But still, the others rejected him. They saw his beauty and purity, but their vision of themselves left them reprehensible in his sight. They refused to admit that he had resurrected a vision, lost in their hearts. But, everyone still wondered how they could be just as special and just as beautiful. How could they muster such hope on their own ? Where would they find the spirit to change the world in the likeness of this humble old man? After showing the village how much he loved them, he slipped-away to death. In the darkness of that night, he left a note which read, ***"This town is my love for you. It is all I had to give. It is my sweat, toil, tears, blisters, and pain. It was a little flower and a ray of light that brought you to this day. It is my gift to you, my sacrifice, that you can now share. It is your hopes and dreams made real. With each new sunrise, you will see the sparkles of dew shining like diamonds on crystal-clear panes. Each flower that grows will bring the colors with which I wished to paint your smiles. Our Love is now real. Love, my friends. Live my Love until we meet again."***

Why is this story applicable? Because today, we see many terrible scourges which soil the lives of God's children. Marriages are void of Love and without hope, unforgiving witnesses testify against the innocent, and cold-hearted indifference sends multitudes into despair, loneliness, and indignity. Let us resolve to pray unceasingly for these broken hearts! The world must open to compassion and unobstructed faith. We must be willing to become the little man in the village who gave every fiber of his being to restore a people's hope. Our Love must move the mountains which divide families in neighborhoods and nations, alike. Each and every fractured heart is calling for the simplest act of kindness and mercy. We must lift-up those who have fallen and build their esteem so they can begin life anew. Like the elderly villager, our acts of kindness remove the bitterness of fear and hatred.

We can no longer live as though there is no Paradise. If we hope for it now, it will assuredly come soon. We teach people to amass a fortune in wealth, but we refuse to feed poor children who already know how to eat. We build golf-courses in the desert, but fail to provide fertile opportunities to those dying in barren lands. As we sit at the center of worldly wealth, is America the true reason why Christ affirmed, "Many who are first will be last!" The Blessed Virgin is hope for the world because She brings the message of Eternal Life in Her Son. When we finally unite under Her Mantle, there will no-longer be villages filled with terrified souls wondering who lives next-door. If we allow the Holy Spirit to unite us in every sense, we will be the flowers that God nourishes, Himself. We will be transplanted into the Streets of Paradise for all Creation to admire. There will be every reason to hope and no excuse for despair. Faith conquers indifference and Love grows our trust in every soul.

OCTOBER 1992

Thursday, October 1, 1992

What does it mean for someone to have a sanctified soul? Indeed, how must we change and why should we convert? Our Holy Mother answers these questions that we formulate from deep within our hearts. Rarely do I need to pose them audibly. When I ask anything of Her regarding the Justice of Our Almighty Father in Heaven, She sends me on a sweeping meditation of the Psalms and Proverbs. She allows me to visualize the world the way She sees it from Paradise and how God wants us to become before our soul will ever be allowed to know the hallowed brilliance of Salvation. I trust Our Lady to understand what God wants of His children. She is the Mother of Wisdom and honor, incapable of speaking any untruth. Every person on Earth must recognize that She is the Queen of reason, hope, deliverance, and peace. She is the Mother some of us never had and the one who is immortally complete, to whom we can go for ecclesiastical guidance and spiritual comfort. I seek Her wise counsel daily and beseech Her intercessory prayers.

Our beautiful Holy Mother visited my home again this evening when I prayed the Joyful, Sorrowful, and Glorious Mysteries of the Rosary. She knows that only few are authentically responding to Her call to holiness and conversion, but She is not deterred by anyone's brash stubbornness. Her desire for us to go to Heaven is a fruit of Her Immortal perseverance. She has not surrendered our souls to perdition, which means that God sees us eventually embracing the Cross. Sometimes I believe that, if we could all be taken to the summit of Creation, we would look down at ourselves in disdain. We must renew our hope and begin to trust God in faith. We look to Jesus Christ for evidence that He forgives us. The very fact that we seek His motivations tells us that He does. He is aloft and, yet, also present on Earth in the Holy Spirit.

Who else but The Almighty Father could live in two places at one time? How could anyone else sit on a Throne we cannot see and inhabit hearts in a world we can? Faith tells us this is true. It is the same source of our confidence that the words of His Holy Mother are the precursor to the Return of Christ to Earth. Infidels require proof, but the faithful already know.

Our Lady is the incarnation of undaunted holiness. Her spirits seem high despite the awful nature of the mortal world. Her message is a perpetual dispensation of hope to Her children. She prays with us to augment our petitions to the Almighty Father because She knows that our lives are futile without Him. Tonight, She asked me to tell the world about a vision we must perceive as though we are looking through Her eyes. She desires us to see our labors as a fruit of our love for God. Our works are useless if we do not make Christ the reason we perform them. We hold no standing in His Light if we refuse the guidance of the Holy Spirit. As Our Lady said months ago, our finite judgment is not the power of the infinite Wisdom of God. The Holy Mother's vision is a world in which we accept the powerful magnification of God's Truth. We must look to the Holy Cross as though it is a powerful telescope to Heaven. As we intensify our union with Christ Jesus, the celestial nature of our lives is borne through the infinity of His Love. We will become able to know and see, and to seek and find. We will no longer stumble through the darkness because Light will emanate from ourselves. That is the illuminating power of the Holy Spirit.

Conflict and injustice will be confined to the vacuum of human amnesia. The mighty proclamation of Christ will live-on, *"If someone strikes you on one cheek, offer him the other. And, If someone takes your tunic, offer him your cloak as well; love your enemies, do good to those who persecute you."* But, there is also sorrow in Our Lady's eyes manifested by our unwillingness to mend broken hearts. Too often, we cast them aside as though they are irreparable and obsolete. Those rent by starvation, illness, abandonment, oppression, and weakness are salvageable souls who make a difference in our own lives because we need them when we fall. Love is the restorative salve for human infirmity. Our Lady said, **"These hearts can be healed. Love can heal them! Love will raise everyone from the dungeon of despair and from the cellars of hopelessness. It is for those who know how, those who have the resources, and those who know the Truth to drive through the indifference and hatred to help others who are afflicted and starving, brought-on by a lack of Love from the affluent. So many broken hearts are isolated by people who have subdued the world through their accumulation of power and wealth. This is why there are institutions and segregation.**

I pray for these lost hearts, those of broken souls and dreams, those whose lives are filled with desperation and desolation. I pray for all

whose afflictions are manifested through the self-righteous nature of those who are rich. Does the mortal presence of humankind consist solely of the distribution of wealth according to the false standards of competitive talent and entertainment value? They must see that their lives are based on a flagrant falsehood of egoistic self-gratification and a fantasy of discriminatory arrogance by those who maintain control over the world for the benefit of only a few. Please help Me pray for the meek, the poor, and the desolate..." Our Love for the weakest members of the human family manifests the revocation of terror, despair, and impurity. This is the image that Christ gives to the world in the Truth of the Cross. When we focus our hearts on Him, His Presence will be too beautiful to forget. We will search for Him over and again. And, we will find Him in the lives of the poor, the castigated, and the discarded. Once we embrace the perfect vision of the Crucifixion, we will always recognize the beauty of God's Love and remember the intensity of His Light. If we fail to seek Him, we will never be warm and will always be void of direction and purpose.

We have a duty to lift-up the lowly and rescue the lost. Christianity mandates our mutual embrace of the wretched and torn. But, the power of Adjudication lies solely in the hands of Christ Jesus. When we observe the power of the Cross, we are able to see the silhouette of those lost from sight. Our Lady asks us to remember that the first Saint to enter Heaven was nailed to a cross next to Jesus, Himself. He said, "Lord, remember me when you come into your Kingdom." And He who will judge us replied, *"I assure you that before this day is out, you will be with me in Paradise."* We are a pilgrim people on a journey to Heaven. While Christ grants absolution for our sins, He does not allow us to decide on our own how to get there. Therefore, we cannot equate mortal law with God's Omnipotence. He seeks no advisory counsel because all magisterial decisions already belong to Him. His Mercy is a fruit of Divine Love rather than the consent of His people on Earth. We are granted forgiveness through conversion and reconciliation, not by human promises and idle compromise. Christ tells us we will find Him in our brothers lying beside the road. When we bring them to the depth of our hearts, we embrace the same perfection as His Sacrifice on the Cross.

Those who raise the wall that the weak must overcome are the same people Jesus will subject to the last test of perfection. When they detain the lost behind their lack-of-forgiveness, Christ will blind them by the Truth of His Justice. He knows those who profess to forgive, but continue to blame others in their hearts. He saw the same hypocrisy when He walked the Earth. This is why released prisoners will always be "ex-convicts" instead of "forgiven sinners." They owe a debt to society they can never repay. We strip them of dignity when they fall and make them lie forever-naked under our oppressive heel. Crushed beneath our footsoles are hearts crying-out to beat in freedom once again. As instruments of God's Love, we must embrace one another with a common desire to enter Heaven, no matter what the cost. We must cause no repentant soul to stumble, regardless how wicked and despicable their error. Our hearts must be enlarged to encompass every living being. The world must be allowed to stand again in justice and grace. The gift of forgiveness is seventy-times-seven more likely to bring peace than a warring weapon. Debts must be canceled and grudges erased. We are called to Love humanity as Jesus loves us. Idle conversation about expendable people shows the contemptible side of our inner-selves.

The shallow nature of our lack of compassion is deep-enough to drown our own souls. When we tell neighboring lands to feed themselves, we are actually saying, *"God, I don't love them."* We forget that we enter Heaven at the discretion of the same Christ who communes so intimately with those we despise. We speak of God's Justice as though He will destroy the same poor souls we refuse to love. But, He dispenses His timely wrath to those who will not offer one measure of forbearance or clemency. Exonerating others means retracting our own accusatory prejudices. There is nothing in the weak not waiting to escape from the strong. That is how God knows us and why He comes to perfect our souls. He holds nothing back, including having given His Sacred Life on the Cross, sending the Holy Spirit into all the world, validating the intercession of the Saints, and dispatching His Glorious Virgin Mother to confirm that He says, ***"Enough!"*** to all hatred and neglect. He offers His Patience and Mercy so we may all gather under an umbrella of Love to be delivered into Paradise. That parasol is the Mantle of the Blessed Virgin Mary in the Hands of Jesus Christ.

Do we love our brothers and sisters enough that we pray to the heavens asking God to accept our sacrifices so every soul can know His Mercy? Can we suffer in humility so those in darkness can see by our Light? It takes great love for Christ to offer these gifts to the weak. But, we live in a time of final Mercy and Eternal Sanctification. Creation is the audience and God has yielded us the podium. It is our time to ascend Mount Calvary in the image of Christ to see what is waiting for our future. Who will stand beside desolate hearts and proclaim their Love for them when everyone else has walked-away? Where are those willing to live the Gospel of Jesus in soul, mind, body and strength? The standard we must apply to ourselves is the Perfection of the suffering and death of Our Lord. It must become the constant tone of our compassion, tolerance, and Love for humanity. It is forgiveness and mercy offered in advance of future inequities. And, it is a Life that does not wait for the repentance of a sinner in offering our prefigured pardon, blessing, and healing. Our Love must bring dying souls to Life and accept the love they offer to the best of their knowledge. This is the loving image of Jesus Christ and the Will of God.

When we pray with this Love in our hearts, Eternity opens before us. This is the Divine embrace of the human family that He asks us to extol. When we love in this perfect reflection, we will live-out the words of Our Lady, **"Love is most powerful when given to those who will not readily accept it."** These are the virtues we should take into the world. Life is a preparation for Judgement when we choose to enter Heaven or Hell. We will stand before the Throne of God in the full Light of Love and look at our own souls. No one will endure this moment who has frivolously wasted their days seeking the world and eluding the Truth. But, it is the Moment of Joy for those who come with their cup overflowing in love for their brothers and sisters. They will rejoice and rest in the Eternal peace of Paradise. When we love the wretched, we pour our own fidelity into their cup so they will have something to offer Christ on the Last Day. They will have tasted the Divinity of God, if only for a moment. But, it might be that sip that takes them to the height of desire to savor the Holy Kingdom forever.

By showing Love to the sinful in a way they might not think they deserve, we prepare them for the Day they see Love Face-to-face. When they are ready to condemn themselves at the feet of His Throne, Christ will show them our sacrifices and the times we remained at their side for the sake of their souls. Our Lord will offer them the full-Light of our endurance and say to them, ***"See how much your brothers and sisters love you and want you to accept Me so you can be with us forever? They love and forgive you just as I do. Please come to Me, believe that you can. Ask Me to save you."*** Sadly, there are many who might turn-away, refusing to believe that Jesus has made them worthy of entrance to Heaven. They may not have the faith to understand that the Cross is especially for them. Our Lady has come to teach us that our own living faith will deliver us to the Kingdom of our Loving God. Over and again, we recite the Rosary, asking Her to pray for us now and at the hour of our death.

Saturday, October 3, 1992 - Freedom for the Captives

Our Lady gave me this message today for everyone being held captive by others and by their own unwillingness to forgive themselves. She said that my brother and I should prepare it for delivery to those who are incarcerated in prisons. **"My many magnificent and beautiful children, I am your Mother, your Heavenly Mother, the Mother of your Savior, the one who loves you and has come to set you free in the very place in which you are sitting at this moment in time. I am the Mother of Jesus Christ, the only One who can liberate you from your captivity and who will forgive you forever for whatever trespasses you may have committed. Please, try to understand, I have been allowed to come to the world by My Son, Jesus, to tell you that the hope that you wish to sustain, but somehow cannot grasp, is real, and is at your hands, and in your hearts. I gave birth to**

Jesus because that is what God asked Me to do. And He, too, became prisoner because of the hatred of the world. He, too, was shamed, beaten, ridiculed, mocked, and abandoned in loneliness, like you, because He, too, wanted to love a world that refused to accept what He had to offer. Many of you would love if only others would let you. Many of you do not know how to love because no one ever loved you.

My beautiful children, you are not held captive by those confining walls that surround you, but rather by the hatred and lack of forgiveness from a world which led you to sin. True freedom for you should not be limited to your physical release from bondage, but also from the chains that you have placed on your hearts to protect you from an invading world of bias, bigotry, indifference, and scourge. I have come to all of you today, to ask you to allow Jesus to well-up in you, in your hearts, to expand your need for relief into an explosive Love, from within, that will break the chains which hold you captive to grief and isolation. I ask you, dear little children, to look and see the terrible new tragedies that have beset all of you into a plundering darkness, a void and shame that draws and weakens your hearts into a cold nothingness that reaches to hold you fast to stagnation. Today, children, your Life can truly begin! You can start your freedom from within you! You can break free from all that binds you, and never have to move a step toward physical relocation. The solution to all isolation and captivity is Love. Yes, Love, in the way that you can truly understand it, and feel it, and live it.

Love is the trust that you have sought for yourself and from others which you have never before been able to find. My Son, Jesus, said in His captivity, that they could hold Him bound to earth and stone, but they could not restrain His Love and passion for the hearts of all humankind. Please accept Jesus, right now, where you sit or stand, rather alone or with company, say "YES" to Love, say that you will love, that you accept Jesus for all that you have asked God to give you. My little ones, Jesus carried a wooden cross to the top of a hill upon which He was nailed and where He died. On that very day, little ones, He took the criminal with Him into a Paradise of Eternity of Light, Happiness, Freedom, and Love. On that very day, He also took you to that beautiful Paradise. As you allow Him into your hearts today, you will reap the truth of His promise that you will make it there. Live your Love brilliantly. Shine anew with a heart and soul of happiness. Then, you will be free. Then you will be fulfilled. Accept Jesus, then you will be forgiven, no matter what any earthly men choose to tell you. Your fate and destiny is in Jesus' hands, and that is why there is hope for you today, and tomorrow, and forever. I love you. Jesus loves you. Peace and goodness be with you all, and always, through Jesus who died on the Cross to save you."

Sunday, October 4, 1992 - Feast of St. Francis of Assisi

Many people see the Truth of Christ's teachings as though the faithful who witness for Him are the incarnation of human negativity. That is because those who oppose Him hear their words with desperate ears in defense of their own error. "How can a life of sacrifice be good news?," they are quick to ask. "Why are you picking on me? What makes you so perfect?" Evangelists for Jesus have never said they are perfect. They profess that Christ is perfect; and they implore the listeners to refrain from shooting the messenger. The factual truth is that the Holy Spirit of God is the one who is picking on them. Francis, the Saint of Assisi, taught total self-denial and authentic humility in defense of Christ. He bore Our Savior's Five Wounds, stigmatized into his flesh by the ingenious wisdom of God. Francis was a living testament to the Crucifixion of Jesus that has saved the world. He was also a magnifier of unwavering faith. When he traveled and taught about the Man-God, many people spit into his wounds like stinging brine. But, Francis kept going prayerfully forward, grieving with the greatest pain in his heart if others would not come to Christ and he was, somehow, disposed to blame. Will any of us go that far to dispense the message of God?

The faithful followers of Jesus carry the wounds of rejection and ridicule, but they never desist in proclaiming the Holy Gospel. Christians know that time is very short and our suffering is divinely sweet. Let us arise to the battles that will take us back Home! We are reveled and supported by the Mother of God, the Lady who owns the most suffering Heart of all, aggrieved to the depths of Her soul to see Her Son suffer and die on the Cross. She is our model of fortitude and our homeward Maiden. The Virgin Mary is the reason why Saint Francis never gave up the fight for the conversion of souls. Let us turn to Her now and She will give us the same strength that She gave to him. That perpetual help is Her determinant Wisdom that God has never once stopped loving the humanity He returned to the Earth to redeem. Today, She revisited my home to teach us more about the expectations that Jesus holds for our capacity to succeed in the Light of His Sacrifice. Our Holy Mother knows the lesson plans of God for the universe. She inscribes them onto our hearts through the Holy Spirit like a great teacher recording the meaning of Life on a Divine chalkboard.

The Blessed Mother thanked me for praying to Jesus during Adoration of the Blessed Sacrament today. It is a time during which we examine our conscience in the solitude of our heart. Every aspect of our thought and conduct should be taken to Christ in the Holy Eucharist. This is not to say that we should be self-critical in a counter-productive way. Holy Adoration is a time for us to review our lives in the Light of Holy Scripture, especially the Commandments, and the Suffering of Christ on the Cross. We evaluate our souls from the vantage-point of humility and look into the mirror of holiness to see if our reflection shines back. Christ already accepts us as we are, but He is exceedingly glorified when we live the example He seeks. He knows that there is a blind-spot in every mortal eye. We may someday find its origin to be the plank we failed to remove before pointing-out the imperfection in our brother's sight. Christ asks us to realize that we have the capacity to love God in the magnitude of the angels in Heaven. When we do the best we can, the Holy Spirit will alleviate any weaknesses in our mortal efforts.

We must live the fullness of our faith in God. Unless we move forward in that trust, we make our own holiness a self-inflicted imposition. The Holy Mother says that we should seek Jesus the way little children emulate their parents. They do not hang their hopes on the fraying-knot of speculation. While The Law of Jesus was written centuries ago, He is still the unalterable Truth Who lives outside of time and space. Love carries our souls to that same actuation. Hope in the heart lives beyond the passing generations. Therefore, the continuity of Love brought by prayer is without mortal constraint. To illustrate our filial obedience, Our Lady provides the example of two toddlers meeting for the first time. We have all seen them playing on the floor. They seem intrigued and mesmerized by each other. They know no hatred because their consciousness has yet to be stained by the world. It is clear by their actions that they belong together, sometimes grabbing and "gumming" each other in a playful way. This is an effect of their innocence and unassuming nature. It is the same affection that the Great Saints exhibited in their desire for unity under the Cross. Imagine the unabashed admiration shared between Saint Francis of Assisi and Saint Dominic. They knew they were one in Christ, just like children know to trust without question.

Our goal is to embrace one another in the likeness of the Saints. What a relief it is to gaze upon someone else who knows the same Truth of Jesus Christ that we are trying to call the world to understand. When we share our desire to evangelize the Glory of Our Lord, we walk arm-in-arm in our journey to the Almighty Father. To do this forthrightly, we must see God in the Sacrament of His Son. That is why we Adore Christ in the sanctifying gift of the Holy Eucharist. His Radiance is a flash of Light upon our soul in an otherwise very dark world. The rays of Love emanating from the Monstrance warm our hearts and transcend the mortality that prohibits us from seeing Him Face-to-face. There is a great-deal to be seen through eyes of faith. We know the eternal strength of God through His power in the world. The glow of His Heart shines through the lives of the righteous. We hear His Voice in the cry of a newborn child. Heaven comes to Earth in reverent homilies, the grace of the Holy Sacraments, and every time we turn to another and say, *"I love you."* His creative genius flows through our lives like a rolling river of wisdom and enlightenment. We see it with our souls and believe it to the depth of our hearts.

We must not be disappointed if we cannot yet see. While faith is the reflection of an open spirit, it is also a gift from God for which we must pray. Christ tells us over and again that we cannot praise the Father without the power of the Holy Spirit. Our Lady requests our prayers because She knows we must requisition the gift of faith from the One seated on Heaven's highest Throne. Just as sure as we have no power to induce our own birth, we are equally helpless to refine ourselves into the likeness of the heavenly court if we do not embrace and accept the Savior sent from their midst. When mankind looks to the sky and says, "How", God answers through The Word, Jesus Christ. When we ask "Why," His answer is always, *"Because I love you."* We are inherently weak, but not predestined to fail. Our Lord is the reason we succeed. He is God's Incarnate Love for humankind. Every fault and fracture of our being is healed through the Life, Death, and Resurrection of Christ because He is a Savior who listens to His people. When we prayerfully adore Him with the innocence of little children, there is nothing we cannot achieve and no gift God will not dispense. Call it a miracle if you wish, but the invincible Truth stands before our eyes like a Divine Apparition when we adore Jesus in the Monstrance. The Blessed Sacrament reaches into the center of our hearts to comfort our souls. We are remade through the Omnipotence of the Eucharistic King when we kneel before Him to pray for ourselves and the world.

Wednesday, October 7, 1992 - Feast of the Most Holy Rosary

The Mother of God asks everyone to pray the Holy Rosary to strengthen our faith and love. Every message I have received from Her is a reflection of my prayer of the Rosary. She assured me today that anyone who prays in Her Honor is a recipient of many miraculous graces. We may not always see them with our eyes, but they are perceived by our soul through the integrity of our faith. Our most powerful offering of the Rosary is during Adoration of the Blessed Sacrament. Our Lady says that we are not seeing a mere reflection of Jesus in the Holy Eucharist, but His Original Light. The Blessed Sacrament is not a symbol of the Body of Christ, it *is* His Divine Flesh in the same Glory that the Apostles of the first century knew. Tonight, Our Lady underscored the importance for us to unite in prayer to defeat the common enemy of God and man. It is the evil that prowls the Earth seeking the ruin of souls. There have been many motion-pictures that portray an invasion of Earth by "creatures" from other planets. In each case, humankind is united against a single foe. Regardless of the structure of their governments or location of their nations, they join forces for the preservation of the human family.

This is what we must do to defeat the irascible scourges of Satan. He is the common enemy to all humankind. God does not allow evil to attack the world to punish or test us beyond our capacity to survive. He hopes that we will call on His Divine assistance as a united people against a malevolent creature who is opposed to all righteousness and good will. The Feast that the Church celebrates today is a remembrance of the greatest weapon known to man. The Holy Rosary is our partner-in-faith that makes us spiritual superpowers in the battle against evil. We stand with Rosary-in-hand as conquerors against any influence seeking to plunder our faith or diminish our holiness. This is the message of the miracles of Lourdes, Fatima, and Medjugorje. We must comply with Our Lady's words for the conversion of the world and the elevation of our souls. The Holy Mother asks us to remember the distinction between the real guile of Satan and an imaginary assault from celestial forces.

Evil is an infestation and infection of the mortal world. Satan and his followers live among us through diabolical spirits, materialism, greed, impurity, and conflict. Rather than descending upon us like extra-terrestrial invaders, they infiltrate the lives of mortal people like a catastrophic plague of poisonous decadence. Lucifer's cohort is oftentimes much more subtle and unrecognizable than we care to believe. Cynicism, egoism, impiety, and promiscuity are the sour venom of his noxious bane. The violence he perpetuates is exacerbated by his seductive influence that sends expectant-mothers into abortion clinics. Through these murders and the carnal lust he places in unsuspecting hearts, he has managed to bring disaster and destruction to a world already made virulent by hatred and deceit. That is why prayerful unification is so necessary for mankind. While an enemy from outside the world can be defeated by material and temporal forces, Satan must be conquered through the collective strength and piety of the hearts of men.

The weapon for our victory is the Holy Rosary of the Blessed Virgin Mary. This prayer is the bringer-of-peace to a world given to dissension. It is the common-thread of holiness that keeps us from falling painfully short of Christian conversion. Those who pray the Rosary have seen the miraculous benefits of is fruitful grace. We meditate upon the Mysteries of the Life of Christ and His Mother in the expectation that we, ourselves, will be elevated to the same Heaven into which they ascended. The Rosary unites us in the Cross because it is composed of the prayers that Christ, Himself, teaches us to pray. The advantage we need to defeat the putrid forces of evil rests at our fingertips. Our prayers stand in formation like missiles in a magazine. Each "Hail Mary" is an ordnance of grace capable of destroying any malice or spite from the corridors of men. We turn brine into broth and impunity into Divinity through the oratorical eloquence of the Holy Rosary. God corroborates our intentions when we manifest them in His Name. The Rosary is a stethoscope through which we can perceive His inner-desires for the future of humanity. Indeed, when we venerate and elevate His Mother in the way of His own perfect affection, we will become the likeness of the Christ She bore to heal us.

Saturday, October 10, 1992

Our Lady arrived at my prayer-altar in hopeful anticipation of the good things happening in the world. She chooses to dwell upon the fruits of our prayers rather than the weakness of our deeds. She has told me many times that God shows His discipline in ways not always apparent to us. She has no authority that God does not allow. This evening, She reminded me of the benisons brought to the world through the Holy Rosary. It gives direction to our petitions and unites us with Our Father in Heaven. The very nature of our holiness rests in the strength of our prayers. The Rosary cultivates the consecrating meditations we need to turn the compassionate Eyes of God to the suffering world. To that end, I took my supplications directly to Jesus through the Holy Mysteries, this evening. The Holy Mother appeared and asked me to ponder another picture-parable. I always look with my heart to contemplate the purpose of Her message. Such pictures allow me to better understand the substance of Her words without having to multiply them. She said that we must always pray for direction by seeking the intercession of the Holy Spirit. That is the way we attain perfect holiness. The Holy Rosary focuses our attention on the Love of God, from which all Divinity comes. The Mysteries conform our prayers into the precise nature of His Will.

The first depiction Our Lady presented is a simple characterization that indicates the location of humankind under the Divinity of God. While we are positioned beneath His universal guidance, we do not always know how to pray. It is one of the sweetest fruits of the Love in our hearts. The words of our mouths and the meditations of our hearts must be acceptable in His Sight. If we do not pray in love for Christ, we miss the mark in all we do and say. Both the origin and destination of our prayers must be the Cross. To further explain, the first picture illustrates the distracting influences of the world which skew our vision.

A.

MAN

If we fail to focus concisely on the Crucifixion, we are not perfectly united with God's intentions for the destiny of our souls. We cannot get to the Father unless we go through Christ Jesus. What good is prayer if we do not lift it in His Name? Our Lord, Himself, teaches that we must pray to The Almighty Father, *"...in the Name of Jesus Christ."* The Cross is the shortest distance between Heaven and Earth. It is the straight Line of Truth that connects the mortal world and the Heavenly Firmament. And, the Holy Rosary provides a clearer vision of the Cross than any other supplication outside the Holy Sacrifice of the Mass. Indeed, it provides the facilitation that our hearts require to understand that the Celebration of the Eucharist is the Crucifixion of Jesus on Good Friday. Padre Pio said that the Rosary is an intrinsic patella on which we kneel to remember the Passionate Death of Our Lord. He also wholly embraced the second impression that Our Lady offered today, describing our single-minded focus on the Crucifixion of Christ.

B.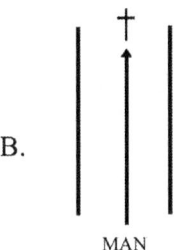

MAN

    The Holy Rosary provides a perfect focus of our souls on God in Heaven. Jesus is the central purpose of the recitation of the Sacred Mysteries. Our Lady asked me today to remember the Thirty-Third Psalm, Verse 1, **"Exult, you just, in the Lord; praise from the upright is fitting."** Herein, our faith, intentions, and desires are made straight by the prayer of the Rosary. We stand in the Truth and are lifted in humility when we ask the Holy Virgin to pray for us. We gain direction, power, and fidelity through the Fifteen Decades which recall the Lives and Suffering of Jesus and Mary. The first place Jesus was laid after His Deposition from the Cross was in His Mother's arms. God does everything for a reason! There is a message for the conversion of our souls in all He does. The purpose of this "Pieta" is that we find Christ by imploring the embrace of His Mother. That is what God desires and why She has come. She aids our understanding of the Love of Jesus because She is the first person He ever knew. She is a gift to humanity in the same magnificence as the Holy Spirit. Indeed, She is the Mother of Love. Who would know Him better?

    The purpose of the Virgin Mary's apparitions and intercessory messages throughout the centuries has been to teach us to know Her Son as the Savior of the world. When we do that, we will accept Him for everything we have ever asked of God. Humankind has prayed for two-thousand years, asking Jesus to bring His Kingdom to Earth in our lifetime. He is coming through the same Virgin Mother that bore Him that cold, dark night at Bethlehem. The Fruit of Her Womb is the Word She speaks on our behalf to the Almighty

Father. She has come twenty-centuries later affirming that same Truth to us. When She asks for the purification of our souls, for penance, and for preparation, Her requisitions are in accordance to the Will of the Divine Savior whom She gave Birth. When She asks us to pray the Mysteries of the Most Holy Rosary, we had better know that it is the command of our omnipotent God in Heaven.

Sunday, October 11, 1992

Today, my brother and I attended a special prayer service in honor of Our Lady's final apparition at Fatima on October 13, 1917. As we sat in the church waiting to begin a public recitation of the Rosary, a little girl sat down beside us with her mother. She was wearing a very colorful blouse with several decorative shapes sewn directly onto it like patches. After a few moments, she turned to look at me and I was able to take a closer look at her unique shirt. The front had a little fabric book attached to it with a functioning cover. It opened and closed, just like a book should. I saw a single word on the cover which simply read, "DIARY." I was so touched by this signal-grace from God that I nearly started to cry. There was no doubt that this was another manifestation of the Holy Mother to display Her Love. Our Lady addressed this grace in Her words of this evening, **"My special, loving children, thank you for your many prayers from your hearts today. I thought you would like the little 'diary girl.' I know that you enjoy such small graces, little words and acts of encouragement from Me. I hope that you never diminish from your hearts and minds how very special My Love is for you.**

I have come today to pray with you again because that is what Jesus wishes for us to do! There are many terrible trials and tribulations ongoing in the world today. There is much suffering and injustice. There is so little prayer being offered for the offenses against Jesus and against the Love of God. My little children, you know that My Son could immediately exterminate all of the problems in the world with His tremendous power. Would mankind be required to bear any accountability to Love in that case? Humanity must love if he expects to enter into Heaven. God wants for all of His children to enjoy Eternity in Heaven. However, it seems that mankind is not open to accept Jesus and subsequently blames God for not being all-loving, forgiving, and compassionate. Mankind does not want to change himself or to reconcile his conscience with God. The world seems more interested in the futility of material fortune. I tell you, today, that mankind does not believe that God has total control and containment over the Creation of man and the destiny of your souls..."

The Blessed Mother makes it clear that we will not enter the bliss of Paradise if we do not love in the Image of Christ. Pure Love bears the fruit of our acceptance in the eyes of our Glorious King. While we do not have the ability to determine what fruit will grow from a given sacrifice, we do know that every gift we offer humankind in the Name of Jesus is savored at His Banquet-Table in Heaven. God is infallible and capable of making great saints out of the worst of sinners. It is often said that some of the most pious followers of Christ were the converted dregs of His day. There is hope for the transformation of any living being to the Divinity of God through Christ. He holds His Truth in His hands, regardless of our vain attempts to wittingly change it. To be saved, we must move to the center of Creation, the Cross He planted on Earth to prove His Love for us. There is no other place where we can find Redemption. Salvific grace comes only from Heaven above. In our struggle to be mortally genius, we would be far advanced to realize our fate in the world and the deliverance we gain in Christ Jesus.

Tuesday, October 13, 1992

There has been a series of political debates on television recently in preparation for a national election in the United States. My brother and I watched one between the candidates for vice-president. There were three participants, one from each of the major parties, and a third representing an independent block of voters. It was clear that they were talking about worldly deficiencies, citing insufficient solutions. The bland nature of the discussion was indicative of a secular approach to spiritual problems. The indifference of the major parties to the desires of Christ for the poor and unborn is quite salient in the conclusions drawn between them. When the Holy Mother came this evening, She unexpectedly discussed the televised debate. Her Immaculate Heart was drawn to the participant who represented the independent platform. While She assuredly does not become involved in political discussions, She was touched by the sincerity of the simple man who knew he had no chance to win.

He was a veteran of the war in Vietnam and a humble representative of traditional Christian values. At one point in the debate, he said, *"...I don't know what we are going to do if we don't get some love in this country* (sic)." He displayed the same frustration that many others share about the selfish and undignified lives some Americans lead. He was a retired Admiral who came home injured from a war that his own country never tried to win. Our Lady told me to remember the sincerity-of-heart that this man showed. He was like a "little giant" standing between bitter foes. When I asked why he seems so caring, Our Lady told me it is because of the suffering he endured in the war and after his return to America. Every time he spoke, you could hear a pin drop in the auditorium. Most everyone who watched and listened wanted him to "win" the debate, if that could ever be possible. Suffering brings such gravitation of others. It procures a venue for credibly stating the truth. This beautiful man somehow did not fit this arena of politics, scurrilous exchange, and rivalry.

The Holy Mother continued, **" If he would only have said that abortion is murder…"**, as if he did not make full-use of his opportunity. For the world to attain the greatness we aspire to achieve, we must take advantage of every opportunity to close the door on evil. There is no such thing as "choice" when the subject is the issue of human life. God places a living soul in the womb of a mother and mankind has no right to breach His purpose. Making such decisions is what got us thrown out of Heaven in the first place. We must live by the Holy Commandments, especially the one which demands, **"Thou Shalt Not Kill."** It is a mortal sin to abort a child, both on the part of the expectant mother and the doctors who help her. If America is going to proclaim her pride in Christianity, she needs to live by all the Commandments, not just a few. The protracted talk about the protection of human rights in United States rings with hypocrisy beneath the sound of little children screaming as they are ripped from their mothers' wombs.

The U.S. Supreme Court has the authority to make abortion illegal once again. They refuse because they fear risking their autonomy as the third branch of government. They wish to be seen as jurists instead of legislators. They fail to remember that the Law of God is already written in spirit and truth through the very Constitution they claim to interpret. The guarantee of life and liberty of unborn children is assured in the Articles they elucidate every day. The Court consists of individual judges who will themselves be Judged by Christ according to their obedience to the Truth of His Gospel. Who knows how many unborn children will be killed by then? Most Supreme Court judges profess to be Christians. How can this be possible in light of their refusal to preserve unborn life? What do they know of the Will of God? Do they not understand that they sit on the nation's highest court by His grace alone?

Our Lady told me that She can see the end of abortion. But, She did not say when that will be. If it is not until the end of time, we are in very serious trouble in the Eyes of God. That is also the essence of the message of the humble Admiral in the political debate on television today. Our Lady concluded, **"I wish to tell you that you are not permitted to watch any more of these rhetorical events. I know that you understand why I wanted you to see this one tonight. Yes, the little Admiral did bring the restoration of peace amidst all of the commotion. I will bless you now, My little children. I love you so very much! I love you beyond measure! I love you without end! I love you into Eternity because Jesus is My Love for you! I will speak to you soon. Goodnight."**

Thursday, October 15, 1992
"My loving one, I love you so tenderly and with such power and grace. With great confidence do I see you reflect the Love that is given to humankind by My Son. I see that you have written a letter to your beautiful sister. I ask you to continue in your great love and faith and your initiation of the display of all the principles that you know to be the truth about your Savior. I have come to you again today with the peace that I bring to the rest of the world. Do you have a question for Me today?" The Holy Mother often asks if I have any questions I would like to pose. Her answers are always beautifully centered around the Truth of God's Love and what He expects from us. Yes, Her answer is always, "Jesus." I know that there are people who might ask who is in Heaven and who did not make it, or what God might be saying behind our back. Others might ask about their marriage or the future. But, the questions Our Lady is speaking about deal with what I can do to become more holy and acceptable in the eyes of Our Lord.

The exchange that the Holy Mother might employ with someone seeking to truly heal the world would be somewhat like this: How can war be ended? *Love.* How can poverty and famine be eradicated? *Love.* How can suffering and disease be eliminated? *Love.* How can the world be turned to chastity and purity? *Love.* How can we stop the break-down of marriages and divisive arguments? *Love.* How can we pray more deeply and become more holy? *Love.* How can we live like Jesus and endure the sacrifices God seeks in us? *Love.* Love is the only answer, completely and universally. Jesus is the answer to every question of how the world can become a better place. Whenever we have problems or difficulties, we must pray for peace and reach-out to one another. We accept our struggles as part of the beautiful Life that God gives. It is our participation in the unfolding of human sanctification and conversion. The Love of Christ carries us across the Threshold of Eternity. There is no doubt or question in faith. That is one of the first principles of holiness that Our Lady told my brother and me. When She asks if I have any questions, I know that She is really wanting to know if I am at peace in my journey toward spiritual perfection and Immortal Life.

Sunday, October 18, 1992
In faith, we are assured that God answers our every prayer. We must live this belief in our hearts because that is His way of recognizing that we know He is silently listening. He proves His trustworthiness in every good thing that comes into our lives. He tells us that our hope in Him will eventually bear the fruits we seek. A new day will soon come when He has finished speaking about the night. His blessings are as sure as the singing birds of dawn, reveling the start of a fresh and virtuous age. When flowers ask for morning dew, God

gives them afternoon rains. He will not allow a dead tree to fall to its repose on the ground until the last spring robin has flown safely from the bowers of its stately corpse. These are the living realities of promise in God. His Word is the Resurrection of countless fatal souls and His desire is the infant life He places in every womb. He does these things with pride and satisfaction at every virgin sunrise. He responds to our invocations with the same gentle care through which He placed a dome over the Earth and called it "sky."

Our Lord invites us to meditate upon the Life He loves to create. He asks us to listen to the saplings boast amongst themselves about being the first to satisfy the desire of human taste-buds with their potent syrup. We follow the path of the sun as though it is a kite tethered to a string. And, we climb to the top of the tallest mountains, thinking that is the reason why God put them there. He is pleased by all of our contemplations because they remind us to think of Him. We feel the connection to our unseeable God in the fruit of His seeable works. That, too, is a supplication that He will answer. The Blessed Mother has told me that we should seek the solace of prayer because Jesus yearns for peace in knowing that we are back home with Him again. It is our sin that forced the night, but His Crucifixion that has brought the dawn. Our prayers serve as usher to that Holy Day. These are Our Lady's words as She came today to teach us more about the powerful Love of our Savior in Heaven.

"My beautiful ones, I have come to pray with you again. Thank you for being so patient. I love you very much. I would like for you to know that your work is on course as a result of all your prayers. I do not want you to do too much at a time. You must still take time to pray with your brothers and sisters. Thank you for being so obedient to My call. I am happy today that so many are listening to My messages and allowing Jesus to enter into their hearts. It has been a very good day, despite all of the distractions in the sports stadiums. As you continue to do your work, you are helping move the world nearer to the purity and holiness that God wishes for humanity to achieve. I will provide you a description. I know that you will understand what I mean..."

Our Lady describes our progression toward faith and understanding God as a three-step process. The first is our awareness that we must free ourselves from immersion in the material world and the temporal nature of human indifference. Second, we must accept the fact that we need to move toward God in light of our helpless nature to effect the fruits of our own conversion. The third step is our attainment of compliant holiness and sacrificial piety in unity with Christ Jesus. The Holy Mother has been trying to walk me and my brother through these transforming levels of conversion for the past year-and-a-half. It is somewhat like beginning with the eyes of our faith closed, then partially open, and finally with eyelids completely apart. To attest that an image is worth a multitude of words, Our Lady asked me to include the following picture with this discussion.

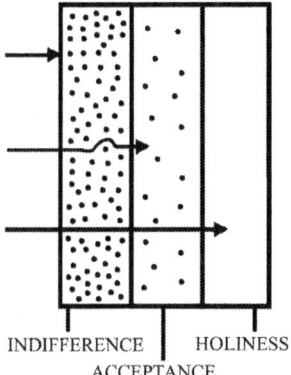

INDIFFERENCE | HOLINESS
ACCEPTANCE

The self-evidence of the pure nature of perfect holiness requires that we become free from the encumbrances of the material world. When we are one with Christ, we no longer have to guide our souls around worldly distractions because we walk on a path free from them. This is a process of permeating growth toward Divinity. Our Lady says that many of Her children have transcended the material world through faith and prayer. No, neither myself nor my brother has reached this blessed state of complete holiness. If not for the grace of God and endless prayer, we would need the Holy Mother to guide us through every minute of the day. We should understand that the struggle for holiness is nothing short of self-denial and mortification. It does not require a miracle, but it is definitively a constant desire to be one with the Miracle Worker, God Himself. Jesus Christ will take us to the heights of perfection if we surrender our human will to His power. We must always say, *"I am Thine, Dear Lord, and all that I have is Thine!"* We must hold nothing back from Him, including handing-over all that is dear in our memory, our standard of living, and the little eccentric traits that make us different from everyone else.

God reserves the right to take everything we have and ask for more. Nothing in this world is more important than our complete obedience to His desires because all life belongs to Him. Humanity can achieve perfect holiness by focusing intensely upon the Crucifixion of Jesus and moving without reservation to imitate it. What seems like a near-impossibility at this time in human history must come-to-pass if we are to be transformed into the likeness of Heaven. We have to approach the Cross and tell Jesus that we can become His likeness. The white Fatima handkerchiefs that pilgrims waive to Mary are not just salutations to the Virgin Mother, they are surrender-flags telling Christ that our own will has been conquered by the Divinity of His Sacrifice. Those who do this are telling God that they no longer live for themselves, but for His Holy Son. And, He lives in them.

Our Lady finished Her message this evening by telling me something that my brother did today. I have included it in this Diary because it is a beautiful symbol of faith and service to our Lord. Its reference is toward an act of praise that he offered Jesus when he passed a Catholic cemetery named for Saint Raymond. It has a large monument at its center depicting the Crucifixion. The statues of the Virgin Mother and Saint John are situated around Jesus on the Cross in actual human size. This holy replica of the Twelfth Station is finished in copper and sits in the open where it can be seen for hundreds of yards. My brother stopped at the site to pray. He placed Holy Water on Jesus' Wounds and on the Heart of His Sorrowful Mother. He blessed Saint John who represents all humanity under the Cross. Then, after noticing that the birds had dropped their waste on the Statue of Christ, he went back to his car and got some water from the trunk that he carries in case of an emergency. With cloth-in-hand, he washed Jesus clean. As he was cleansing Our Lord, he heard the words, **"I Thirst."** So, he scampered to the car again to retrieve a small cup from the back seat. He filled it with water and lifted it on his tip-toes to the lips of Jesus hanging on the Cross.

Then, a miracle occurred. Jesus drank the water from the cup and none spilled down His face. As He drank, my brother said, *"Jesus, this drink is from all of my brothers and sisters to tell you that we love you and accept your Sacrifice. And, tell Your Father that we love Him, too."* He prayed for the conversion of the world, got back into his car, and came home. Soon after telling me this story, Our Lady said to me, **"Thank you for remembering the unborn and the poor souls in Purgatory in your daily prayers. There are many who have now seen the pristine Light of Heaven as a result of your many petitions and holy works. My Heart and prayers are with all of My children, with all who are lost and have yet to come to the Sacred Heart of Jesus. Thank you for your lives of faith! I will speak to you soon. I love you. Goodnight."**

CONQUERING THE FAILING WORLD

Monday, October 19, 1992

The most sought-after commodity in the world today is information and our capacity to control it. We claim facts, figures, quantities, and quotas as being properties of our own curious intellect. We are armed to fight anyone or anything that threatens our self-declared right to lay claim to whatever falls into our hands. We spend fortunes and estates grasping for more of anything we can call our own that no one else has or could eventually inherit. But, the most valuable resource and power on Earth is now being dispensed by the Mother of God; and only few of us are listening. Within the Immaculate Heart of the Virgin Mary lies every avenue we could desire to attain the riches of this world and all the universe. By the time we accept the Divinity that lives in Her, the gift we value most is to be like the Son She bore. We must crave the Fruit of Her Womb, Christ the King, who is now also the Harvest of Her Heart. Men are hungry, but we know not what to eat. Humanity wants to run, but has no place to go. There are questions without answers and effects without cause. This is the fate of the lost and unconverted. The words of the Virgin Mother bring us the scent we must follow to savor the banquet table in Heaven.

Our Lady returned this evening to pray with my brother and me for the conversion of all souls to Christ Jesus. Between our segments of prayer, She spoke in rather strong terms about the refusal of humankind to accept the true power of God. We acknowledge that we have the ability to alter the physical and chemical composition of the world, but we do not realize that God gives us the means. The origin of every benevolent action by man is the Love of God. We cannot perform good works without Him. When we live in accordance to the Sacred Scripture, it is not because we are intrinsically holy. All righteousness and goodness is the fruit of His Spirit working through us. The human person is an instrument in the hands of God when we live His Divine Will. However, when the effect of our actions is destructive, corrupt, or deflowering, we are not living in the Light of God. Even the seemingly harmless apathy of indifference is a perversion of life separated from His Will. We must walk in the assurance that He is in control of every aspect of our own charitable nature. This is the key to happiness and peace.

If we live as though God is just another cloud in the sky, we will be sorely remiss in achieving the holiness and perfection that will render our souls worthy of Heaven. Our progress in intellectual achievement and industrial technology is an effect of our capacity to generate solutions through His grace. The greatest minds in the world can explain the basic design and function of the universe, but they cannot muster the faith to believe that God created it. And, if they can study such celestial serenity and not find peace, how could they ever expect to discover it on an Earth filled with the duplicity and transgressions of men? We are being excessively presumptuous about the nature of God if we assume that we are supposed to absorb the world to preserve it. Humankind will never tie the all-powerful hands of God in an effort to coerce His compliance with our mortal logic. What would happen to scientific knowledge and the reams of astronomical opinions if we woke tomorrow to the sun rising in the west? Would we immediately effect a methodological experiment to explain the phenomenon, or would our obsession with discovery and scrutiny finally crack?

The inexplicable denial of some people to attribute the creation of the universe to God will always be a source of curiosity to those bound for the Glory of Heaven. How can such a pool of intelligent minds be so blind to the Truth hitting them in the face? God created their bodies and souls without the use of any catalyst or material. What man could approach such Genius? Why is faith in Him so difficult for a society of such curious intellects? They must surely be ignorant to the inevitable effect of time. Every theory they could possibly argue rests upon the same conclusion. God created the world because He is Love; and Christ will end it through the Redemption of His children. Every rule and order belongs to the King of Creation. Nature itself is a prescription of God's creative power which He wields any way He sees fit. Jesus Christ will not enter a debate about the destiny of the universe when He returns in Glory. Polemics will go the way of the same wasted generations spent arguing them.

Creation exists at the Hands of the Almighty through the Divinity of the heavens. He set the Earth into motion because He wishes to see Love at work. All natural laws are a function of His supernatural grace. His Supreme Omnipotence is not governed by chance or fate, or by some unintelligible system of odds. He is Genius Himself and the Maker of Knowledge whose Will is the only infallible intention on either side of time. The Divine orchestration that He manifests embraces all macro-universes from the infinity of the sun to the tiniest drop of dew on a maple leaf. Therefore, our search for meaning and unity with Creation is culminated in Christ Jesus. If we wish to find virginal power, we must look to the Creche and the Cross. The Love for humanity that took Jesus to His Death is the origin of all understanding and approbation. Our frenzied search for meaning ended 2000 years ago when the Son of God said, "It is Finished." We can now stop moving in the direction of the world and devote our lives to finding Paradise through Him. Indeed, we are not like an airplane attempting to land. It is possible for us to stop moving and still survive. God calls us to His quiet peace because that is the only place we will find it. Jesus is the Prince of Peace and Conservator of Human Hearts.

How do we plunge by faith into the arms of Our Lord? It is clear through His every revelation that we must pray. The purpose of our lives is to become like Christ in all ways. He never stopped loving His enemies and forgave anyone who affronted Him. Even at the Moment of His Execution, He asked God to forgive those who killed Him. By all means, they did not know what they were doing. The question for us today is, do we? It is clear that Jesus died to save every soul in all generations and all centuries combined. Are we aware that He asks us to jump into His awaiting arms like little children returning from a long journey away from home? This leap into His embrace is the most important distance our souls will travel. It means praying and offering our thoughts to God for all He intends. It encompasses humanitarian service by giving our lives to the family of man. We must see Love as the only reason for life and hope, and answer Christ with the word, "yes" instead of "why." That is the reason I asked Our Lady if I should become a Catholic priest.

This was Her answer, **"My little child, please know that what you have asked is not really a question. I tell you that there are many, many great sacrifices to becoming a priest. As you say, it will be different in terms of the administration of the Sacraments, but your example is the same whether or not you become a priest. Do you understand why this is a decision to be made between yourself and the Holy Spirit, and not Mine to make? Would you not fear that I would mistakenly leave the impression upon the world that the most holy state of grace is by entrance into the vocation? That would be a wrong impression to leave because those who do not become priests would always feel that they have not done enough to display their love for Jesus.**

How do those who do not speak with Me directly make that judgement? The Holy Spirit calls their souls into service! You will know when that happens, you will not have to ask Me. That is how you will make your decision. There is never any question when someone knows that he is being called, and even My direct intercession is eclipsed by that call. I pray for the Holy Spirit to enter into the lives of those who seek that grace for the purpose of increasing the number of priestly vocations. I am very happy that you realize that the decision for the vocation is your decision, based upon your response to the call of God through His Spirit to touch you. Always remember that I love you very, very much! Please remember that My intercession does not obligate you to be any greater than the simple, loving little boy that you would have otherwise become. You are so beautiful, so hoping, so loving, so pure, and so magnificent. I love you so. I will speak to you soon. Goodnight."

Wednesday, October 21, 1992

Before She was ever Immaculately conceived, our awesome Virgin Mother must have, somehow, described the Son that She wished to bear to the Almighty Father. He would be the New Covenant, the merciful God-man, whose willingness to absolve us was learned from the humility of an eternal maiden He had yet to create! She also asked to become the Mother of the forsaken on Earth and our Queen and Matriarch of grace and peace. Fortunately for us, God must have assuredly listened. The Son of Man obeyed, and His Mother's prayers have ultimately prevailed. God has set a table before us; and the Fruit of Her Womb is our heavenly meal. Let us consume the Love She conveys to everyone who knows Her as "Mother." We are the omnipotent Will of Her Son; and He is the offspring of the infinite compassion of God. Our Lady asked me tonight to remember to pray for those who are committing abortions and for expectant mothers who perceive the decision to kill an unborn child as their inherent "right." We are all required to be living-witnesses to the Truth of God. He gives Life by His own Divinity and reclaims it by Eminent Justice. The only time He seeks our opinion is when we pray to conform to His Will. Holy Love is the seed He plants in our hearts. It must be nourished by our own faithfulness in the same way that a child is formed in the womb. If we reject the Holy Spirit, we abort our only opportunity to attain Eternal Life.

This was, again, another very special night because Jesus spoke to me, ***"My brother, please remember to be as a little child and your flesh will not bind you to transgression. You are pure, so live your purity in happiness. I love you. You belong to Me, and I to you. Thank you for accepting Me. I bless you now in your strength of love that I give you to share. Peace."*** I would like to somehow describe the ecstasy-of-the-moment when Our Lord speaks to me. When I hear His words, I feel like every molecule of Heaven and Earth is shuddering. It is as though Life itself almost ceases in the sanction of His tone. There is finality in His syllables and an incomparable peace. My soul feels the absolute perfection of God ringing throughout my being. His words have the quality of prominence and authority. The supernatural brilliance of His command is unparalleled by any I have ever seen. His power is permanent, persuasive, comprehensive, embracing, and irrevocable.

After Our Sweet Savior finished speaking, His Mother told me that His presence is a gift to sustain my hope in the work my brother and I are doing for Him. She also spoke about the Holy Sacrifice of the Mass with the intention of assuring the world that the Celebration is the original Crucifixion of Jesus. When we participate in the Mass, we are standing on the Hill of Mount Calvary. It is not a facsimile or semblance, but is the Death of Christ brought through time to the Altar of Sacrifice. I asked Our Lady if She is present during the Holy Mass the same way She stands under the Cross on Good Friday. **"Yes,**

I am with you. The Holy Mass is the Crucifixion. Through Jesus' True Physical Presence, we are with Him in His final battle over evil. I feel the same pity for Him during the Holy Mass. I also pity those for whom He died, those who still reject Him and scoff at His Sacrifice. My Maternal role is as intercessor between Jesus and mankind in the way that Jesus is the intercessor between mankind and God. I have been praying for everyone in Creation to recognize the timelessness of the Crucifixion."

The reflections of Our Lady are perfectly timeless. She now perceives the events of Good Friday from the Glory of Heaven. Never again will She have to grieve the death of Her Son from the purview of the mortal world. While Her sorrow is intense during Holy Mass, She concurrently lives Christ's Resurrection and Victory in the peace of Paradise. What She once endured on Earth in perfect faith can now be seen from the same perspective in which She looked-down upon my brother and me praying at the Saint Augustine cemetery on Palm Sunday last year. And yet, She kneels at the Altar of Sacrifice during Holy Mass, just as She stood under the Cross on the Hill of Mount Calvary. Our Lady feels the fullness of anguish through the Passion of Jesus during every Eucharistic celebration. She sees Him hanging on the Cross while His Precious Blood flows onto humanity. She looks into His eyes and knows the suffering of the Son of Joy that She bore to give us Eternal Life. In a way no other could conceive, She reaches-out to comfort Him, saying with Her Immaculate Heart, **"Yes, My Beautiful One, You are winning. You are conquering, this is not in vain. The world will see this moment that You love them. Oh, how You are loving them. And, I love them, too."**

We pray under the Cross in unity with the Hosts of Heaven through their own Divine reflection. The content of our hearts is consumed by the perfection of Christ, Himself, who miraculously becomes Truly Present in His Sacrificial Body as the Holy Eucharist. By God's power and the Consecration of the priest, Our Sacrificed Lord comes from Heaven to the Sacred Altar. Those who receive Holy Communion are blessed by the Bread of Life in obedience to Jesus' invitation in the Upper Room. God feeds us through the Flesh of His Son to revive our souls. We partake in the Divinity of Heaven because Christ lives in us, both Physically and Spiritually. As we increase our love for the Divinity of Jesus, we embrace the authenticity of the sorrow of His Mother as He hung on the Cross. Those who question Our Lady's role in the unfolding of Salvation must remember that Jesus said, *"Behold your Mother."*

We should contemplate the significance of these prophetic words. He knew that She would be sent during our age to assert Her role as Mother of all humanity, seeking our conversion. We cannot truly understand the perfection of Jesus unless we adhere to the prescriptions for our own transformation from the Immaculate Virgin. We need to pray through the Holy Spirit for complete submission to His Will through this Divine Lady. Our Holy Mother's apparitions, intercessions, and other supernatural graces reveal that She accepts Her role in our conversion, just as She confirmed Her desire for our Salvation to the Angel Gabriel. She knows the depth of the commission vested in Her by Christ. He spoke equally as clearly to us through Saint John, representing all the redeemed, as His words rang through Creation, "Behold your Mother." Let our compliant faith bring our perfect obedience to Her call.

Sunday, October 25, 1992

I am having to muster intense self-control to fight the temptation of disciplining others for their harsh indifference toward the Love of Christ. My focus the past days has been, "how can some people deny the truth of their responsibility that Jesus gives us to love others?" Of course, this has been a central question throughout the ages. Christians have been fighting for centuries to defeat the vices of hatred, indifference, and outright evil. God is our Creator who loves us dearly, even those far from Him. But, He definitely wants us to become like His Son at the direction of the Holy Spirit. That obedience must be a product of our own submission. The world is still struggling for identity. Mankind asks himself, "Who am I and what is my purpose?" The answer is not so much who we are, but who we must become. The source of all understanding of our identity and purpose is Christ Jesus. When we place our entire faith in Him, He tells us in definitive terms that we are a people who are exiled from our home in Heaven because of the sin of Adam. Our only way back to the source of Light that emanates from the Throne of God is to go through Him.

We must live according to Our Lord's example and accept the Blood of His Sacrifice in reparation for the sin we inherited and those we commit ourselves in this life. We must not be lulled into sleep by the physical world and its consequential apathy. We are required to be holy, not self-ingratiating. One who lives the intellect of the world falls painfully short of attaining the wisdom required to embrace Salvation in Christ. This genius is attained only through prayer and faith. It is an absolute function of our desire to be redeemed. I have noticed, however, that those who respond to this call are castigated by the very world they wish to escape. The offering of penance, prayer, love, and sacrifice are met with great opposition in societies that prosper only by intellectual and industrial development. Paradoxically, self-denial and suffering are not meant to procure material gain. Their fruits are atonement for the world, rather than a means to embellish it. They make Eternity glorious and sweet for every soul who benefits, whether they are in Purgatory or lost in the debauchery of the mortal Earth.

Our Lady told me that more souls are living in indifference at the present time than given to evil itself. They are a prime target for Satan to use for his sinister works. He draws the faithless into his ranks like metal to a magnet. This is the most important fight that any soul must wage. Christ confirms that anyone who is not "for" Him is against Him. One must be righteous in His image to avoid being seduced by the devil onto a path away from Heaven. That is why we must pray for ourselves and others. We cannot fight the battle against evil alone. Not only did we inherit sin from Adam and Eve, we also inherited the weakness that made them fall. Our hope is often strained by the struggle toward righteousness. We must live in faith more strongly than we live in the world. Prayer nourishes our lives in Christ in multi-dimensional ways. The living Spirit of God helps us to succeed. The single-dimension of evil is no match for His power. We must allow Jesus to reign in our hearts rather than simply pass through our thoughts.

If our faith is just an intention instead of a function, we will fail. Faith must live through Christian Love if we are to truly be alive in Jesus. There are thousands of well-intentioned people who have turned their back on the journey that will take them to victory. Their hope is diminished by the world and consumed by their own fear. That is why Christ asks for our total commitment. We need to grasp every opportunity to live Love and lead all others to believe. That is what the Saints of old gave their own generation. Their vigilance must become our living example. We are supposed to conquer evil rather than be consumed by it. Souls not given to Jesus live only for the causes of mortality, worldliness, promiscuity, gravity, and sin. Millions are immersed in indifference; and even more are mortally wounded in spirit. The true sadness is that they have not yet learned that their purity and health rests in the blessings and graces from God through His only Son, our Lord, Jesus Christ.

Our Lady says that it is obvious that the indifferent and agnostic wrought the Passion and Crucifixion of Jesus. They had no faith that God would come in Human Flesh to convert them. The Sacrificial Lamb willfully endured the punishment inflicted upon Him without defiance. The sorrow in His Heart for the sins of humanity was many times greater than their capacity to hate Him. The perfect Son of God was executed by the corruption of man. He was slain by Adam's sinful descendants on a Cross with a Love so great that He suffered and died for the Salvation of all. To this day, His Sacred Heart withstands the indignance of those who reject Him. Their opposition is more than a tawdry vice. It is their calculated decision to spend Eternity in Hell. Satan is still at work in the mortal world, confronting humanity at every turn and any opportunity. We must fight both night and day against his insidious treachery of evil works.

We remember the parable of the landowner with more acres surrounding his house than he cares to maintain. He is not much interested in planting, weeding, and mowing, so he sells a parcel between the house and his pond to someone else. The next thing he knows, there is a nine-feet privacy fence blocking the serenity of his view and his access to the waters he likes to fish. The person he thought would be a good neighbor evolved to be a scoundrel and a cheat. He was not prepared to be taken as a fool because he trusted hands that were unclean from the inside. This story addresses our need to always be wary. There should be no unattended areas of our life we are willing to quit because of our refusal to protect them. We are approached in our indifference by malignant sources trying to trap our souls and block our vision of God. The persistence and vigilance we need to live securely is the Love of Jesus in our hearts. We need not become the unsuspecting victims of a scheming world. Christ is our shelter in time of trouble and our peace when we are prone to rage.

Consider the spiritual wealth of His Love. God makes us rich in every way that reveals His Kingdom. The conversion of our souls to the strength of His Divinity renders us imperishable on an Earth that seems twisting out-of-control. Our Lord seeks the loyalty of His children and our bathing in the Still Waters which nourish our souls. The solace we find in Him cannot be gained from the world; and neither can the world take it away. When we live in Christ, we are unapproachable by any deceitful cynics trying to separate us from the heavenly Light above. No wall can detain us from reposing in the fragrant beauty of His peace. And, we will never be left broken because His compassion is like a celestial X-ray, seeking any fracture in our hearts to heal and mend. We have nothing to fear and every reason to hope. God turns our enemies into obsequious converts who rally themselves in every way possible to stand at our side. Jesus holds back nothing to nourish our faith. All we need to do is look around.

Can the fertility of the Earth and beauty of the skies be attributed to anyone else? How much more do we need to see? The beauty of Paradise showers grace upon us at every passing moment. The Saints are our kindred we have yet to meet. They call us to prayer and conversion because they know in Truth what we ponder in faith. As we walk through mortality, they rest in peace enjoying the sapid fruits of the Divinity of God. Christ lives in us to the deepest recesses of our souls, hoping to transform our weakness and captivity into a stately armor of holiness and sanctity. We will never enjoy genuine peace until we embrace the pristine integrity of the Savior of the World. Jesus is our Life and enlightenment in the ongoing procession of human conversion. All nourishment and direction come from His Hands. If there is a heart sitting in the darkness of despair, He will find it. No fatigue or desperation is too great for His healing touch. We must revive the spirit in our souls to accept the Love that has been ours since the dawn of Creation.

Monday, October 26, 1992
    Jesus loves us so dearly that He died an excruciating execution in reparation for our sinfulness. And, He did not stop there. He knows that every child that His Father gives Life must hear that News of our good fortune. God sent His Son not only to be our best friend and Teacher, but also the incumbent Savior of humankind, whose tenure will never end. He did not deceptively frame Christ Jesus into being a scapegoat to conceal human sin, but rather sent Him wittingly as a Divinely revered Conqueror who has destroyed it altogether. The Lamb of God did not simply deflect our errors from sight, He completely expunged them from Creation by the power of His Blood on the Cross. Our transgressions were not remanded beyond the lost portals of the universe, they were irrevocably annihilated, even from the memory of God. That is the power and authority that He vested in the Christ. The fallen nature of man is not just mitigated by this Anointed One, it is also irretrievably erased from time and Eternity. Divinity now lives where corruption once thrived, as Christ the King has exhumed our souls from condemnation and breathed new Life into their being. Without Jesus, our souls would have been eternally doomed before we were ever born.
    Such is the Love of God for humanity, sending His only begotten Son to commute the sentence of the guilty and convicted, and to endure the capital punishment that should have been rightfully handed to us. He loves us from the infinite depth of the universal Crucifixion that took His Life. Our Lady says that the Cross is the hemline where God has stitched Heaven to Earth and the scar that has healed the breach in Creation through which innumerable ages of men would have, otherwise, forever fallen. Our Lady tells me about the Glory of Jesus in these many ways every time She comes, during every opportunity that arises. She knows that time is very short, and our sinful tendencies are still quite erratic. She has come to lift our country beyond the pitfalls of material greed and outright apostasy. Let's face it, the age of spitting into God's Eye and getting away with it has come to an end. Can the failure of a nation be traced to its lack of spiritual propriety? You bet it can! I pray that the Mother of God will awaken our collective moral conscience before it is too late. For this, I yield my days to Her grace and bow to Her immortal purpose.
    When Our Lady came to pray with us this evening, She brought another very poignant message. **"Today, I have come to continue our work. I am seeing many prayers all over the world that are important for those who suffer neglect. I would like for you to take special note today for your continuing Diary of the following statement, Jesus' Second Coming is now very, very near. I tell you that all the world must prepare for His Return. All must confess their sins, beg for pardon through His Mercy, seek the Light that repentance brings, and give all of themselves to the Sacred Heart of Jesus. Jesus is the only avenue to the security of**

Salvation. Please remember that one cannot go to Heaven without first taking the hand of Jesus. I have come to the world to seek the conversion of every soul. This conversion begins through prayer and fasting. Thank you, My little one, for conveying this message so specially on this date in your Diary..." What more could be added to express the urgency of Her call? Our decision to comply is a product of our faith in God and desire to spend Eternity in Heaven. Indeed, the obedience through which we respond to Our Lady is a fruit of the Love in our hearts.

In order for us to take Jesus' Hand, we must be able to see it. He will not uproot us from the world like a gardener pulling weeds. We must bloom like flowers and reach for His outstretched Palm. The eyes of our faith must be open like a tulip's petals on their fullest day. God has already finished His Creation. It is ourselves who are still growing. As we mature in faith and love, we enlarge our hearts to embrace Heaven. It is the obstinate side of human nature that tells us we cannot find God. He is not some irascible dictator who refuses to listen to our sincere confessions. We are trapped in sin, divided by conflict, diminished by insolence, and soiled through hatred. Our cities and neighborhoods are infested by violence and sweltering in vanity. We are not only off the path of righteousness, we have no clue that it exists. God comes in Spirit and Light through overture and entourage. And yet, we stand in opposition and denial against the Truth of His existence. When He slaps us in the face with wildfires and whirlwinds, we stand back and wonder how this could possibly be. We are confronted by evil and dejected by defeat, but still rise every morning seeking a place to hide from Christ. Our Father is calling us to Justice, and we must rise to go home!

Our Lady told me today that there is no redundancy in reveling the awesome power of the Holy Eucharist through another entry in my Diary. The Body and Blood of Christ is the Grace of God that awakens our souls. The Holy Spirit enkindles our desire to seek Him; and Holy Communion is the moment we unite. Every human deliberation is answered through the Blessed Sacrament. The Eucharist is the purpose of Life! So, what makes our spirits shake and hearts tremble? Our souls are entrusted to the Glory of the Lord! Why do the winds blow and the sun shine? Because God makes it so. How do plants grow and species reproduce? The Love of God for His Creation. Everything that God does for His people is manifested through the wisdom and Truth of the Holy Eucharist. Humankind must be convinced that Love destroys the malicious posture of human discord and evil intent. Vulnerable souls are protected and stagnant consciences enlightened.

Only hearts filled with Love will be resurrected into God's Kingdom. Christ seeks our willingness to participate in compliance and service. Our Lady said, **"I ask everyone to pray for the saddened faces and suffering hearts of those who are at war all over the world. Each little heart which yearns**

for strength is nourished by Jesus. God seeks unconditional Love from all the faithful to strengthen the weak." Therein lies the Truth of our call to action as a Christian family. We are asked to transcend all distances and languages to take the word of Jesus to humanity. It is as much a matter of effort as it is desire. We cannot allow any inhibition or encumbrance to deter the work He has given us. We witness to the same Light by which we will one-day be judged.

Thursday, October 29, 1992
"Pray without ceasing!" That is the clarion call of the Lady who is Queen of the Universe. Mankind has yet to comprehend what this requisition truly means. How can we pray without ceasing and still continue our daily lives? Our Mother is quick to respond to that question. She invites us to envelope our spirituality in holiness and to make prayer, penance, fasting, and attendance at daily Mass the center of all our days. The Holy Bible tells us that we must first seek the Kingdom of God, and the rest will follow in its place. I have found this to be irrefutably true. It is the intangible aspects of Life for which we seek that we initially gain through an environment of faith. We cannot drive to the corner market and buy happiness, but we can assuredly find it in the hearts of our fellow Christian believers. Entire armies oftentimes cannot stop a war, but a humble nun in the corner of a convent with a Rosary in her hands can prevent a contentious political dispute from escalating into an intercontinental nuclear slugfest. The Life of Mother Teresa is an example of how one, simple, determined, servant can transform a hopeless country of backward mortals into a prayerful community of dignified parishioners.

Mary Immaculate brings the truth about prayer in the same Light which She brought the Truth, Himself, in the darkness of night at Bethlehem. The world little knew how the centuries would benefit from that lowly beginning. It was a premonition and prophecy that the fruit of simple, unceasing prayer will heal and change the darkness of the same world in our day. She prayed, then, and continues to pray with us today, calling humankind to our knees in humility to God. Our Lady asks us to petition that we will allow our souls to be led by the Holy Spirit and be nourished by the Most Blessed Sacrament. It is equally as important that we trust in the powerful intercession of the Holy Angels. They are great instruments of grace and support for humankind. Our reverence for Jesus includes acceptance of the Angels, the intercession of the Saints, and our own display of innocence. We must abandon our pursuit of material goods and mortal vices. There are millions who are starving and have no place to sleep. Indeed, there is no dignity in being impoverished, but Christ lifts the lowly into a high state of grace. When we pray for their swift deliverance, we embrace their suffering in communion with His own.

Tonight, Our Lady invited me to remind the world that it is sinful to summon the presence of so-called "lost spirits." Any soul living in Christ Jesus is perpetually "found." He dispatches them according to His Holy Will and Divine Plan. Mankind does not have the power to solicit these spirits. Those who conduct seances or other rituals are not in communion with Our Lord. Any spirit that answers such aberrations is an instrument of the mockery of Satan. The Queen of Heaven is very adamant about refraining from participation in such ritualistic darkness. We cannot invoke God to defy His own Will. Interaction and communication between Heaven and Earth are fruits of humble prayer, not ritualistic sacrifice. Saints and angels will not respond to secular seances or self-proclaimed psychics. If a spirit approaches someone from out-of-the-blue, it should be tested for its loyalty to Jesus Christ. The fruits of Our Lord are authenticated by the heart, not the parameters of delusion. If we have a Rosary in our hands and a Brown Scapular around our neck, we can be assured that Our Lady will send the Holy Spirit to guide us. God knows every spirit, good and evil. He also sees from where they come. When we invoke the Blood of Christ with a Crucifix at our breast, we cannot be deceived and will always be protected.

Since yesterday was the Feast commemorating SS Simon and Jude, I researched their lives in my "Book of Saints." There was very little information about them. So, I asked the Holy Mother today what they were like. She told me that Saint Simon was well-prepared and one who accepted through faith and logic that Jesus is, indeed, the Messiah. Saint Jude was more of a contemplative soul who knew through the intrinsic power of compassionate love that Christ is the Savior of the World. Saint Jude was a great teacher of prayer who assisted others in reflections-of-the-heart. Our Lady added, **"I know that you and others seek-out the lives of the Saints for guidance and example. Please also remember what they continue to do! Pray with your hearts for their intercession! Remember that common to all the Saints is their great love and compassion and that they were despised by the indifferent. They rose at this opportunity to greater heights of prayerfulness and piety."**

Saturday, October 31, 1992

This is the vigil celebration of the Feast of All Saints. Our Lady is very disconcerted that this great Feast is mocked by those who glorify evil desires and sinister works through the image-making and revelry of Halloween. The false faces and costumes are indicative of its diabolical nature. She said, **"Yes, all of this notion about generating fear is about the dark, and not the Light. Our prayers will help this to be a night of Light. The hearts of men should be lifted to the hallowed Divinity of Love and peace. What is intended to be a night of holiness is often transformed into a night of evil, and terror, and destruction. I have seen many magnificent prayers** lifted today for the poor souls in Purgatory. Please remember that Monday is a very important day for many poor souls in Purgatory. God will allow many the release into Heaven if your prayers are lifted fervently from the heart!" Our Lady also gave my brother and I a signal grace to strengthen our faith. She said that our work is proceeding in accordance with God's Divine Plan. She asked me to recall how many thousands were named in the Liturgical Reading at Holy Mass today. The number is 144. She then told me that this message is the 144th of the year 1992. **"I hope that My visit has made you happy. I ask you again and again to be of good cheer with a light heart, like that of a little child. You will be much happier and Jesus will be very pleased with you. I love you, I will speak to you soon. Goodnight."**

NOVEMBER 1992

Sunday, November 1, 1992

Today, my brother and I traveled to Peoria, Illinois to attend a special Mass at Saint Martin de Porres Church. The pastor had recently returned from Haiti where he served the poor with the Missionaries of Charity. He described the poverty and oppression under which these stricken people live. He worked charitably among the poorest of the poor. We were all reminded of the blessings God gives us as citizens of the United States. Upon our return home, my brother and I knelt for our daily Rosary. The Holy Mother came to pray with us. She spoke in audible words that only I could hear, **"I am so happy with all of My little children who were praying today with Me. The priest's description of the poverty, disease, and oppression of Haiti is a poignant reminder that the affluent West is indifferent to the suffering of many others. You can imagine that conditions are much worse in many of the smaller countries in Africa. The world cries for sharing and justice. It is much too obvious that the peoples of the United States will not share, even amongst their own people who live inside their borders.**

Your analogy of the poor in the eastern part of your city versus the affluent southwest is a good one. One does not have to travel very far to see the terrible effects of such bigotry and greed. Remember that Jesus asks the rich to sell all that they have and give to the poor, and then He will consider their appeals. There is so much inequity all over the world. I am happy that you were able to hear it first-hand. We all pray that everyone can be allowed to share the bounty of the Earth, not just a few. I am happy that many Saints are all over the world today assisting in prayers and responding by taking their case to Jesus. It is very important that the people of the world rely on the help of the Saints continuously. If only more hearts would open in faith to believe in such Divine

intercession, our work would be much easier. Much damage is being done by those who claim that appealing to such intercession from the Saints and Myself is idolatry and heresy. We will pray for them..."

It is obvious that mankind needs to purify his vision of the world. How can we justify our lives in industrialized nations in view of the plight of those in under-developed lands? There is no such justification to be found in the Gospel of Jesus Christ. The rich have the responsibility to feed the poor without recompense or public recognition. Wealth and power are the parents of false security and artificial peace. Clearly, it is a sin to feast upon the world and turn our back to those whose share we hoard. This incongruity must be supplanted by self-denial, prayer, sanctity, and reparation. We will never be a holy people if we allow others to suffer while we prosper. If we pass someone on a street-corner with tin cup in-hand without sharing our good fortune, we are not worth the fuel Christ will use to set our souls afire. Our Lady asks us to contemplate the consequences of selfishness very seriously. We are told to share generously by discreetly enriching the lives of others and conspicuously elevating the Gospel of Christ Jesus. We must retain what we need to be simple and give to those in need. This is the charity that restores dignity to the downtrodden and lifts those never before shown Love.

I had previously entered the following sentence in today's Diary entry, "Use everything at your disposal in love..." but, Our Lady asked me to modify it to state, "**Give** everything at your disposal in love..." I know that there is more than simple subtly to this substitution of terms. My original statement allows us to maintain control and manipulation. The change She effected reflects our personal abandonment through charity and love.

Friday, November 6, 1992
Early Morning

The truth about our fall from Paradise is the sin we all committed in the day of Adam. But, we are purified, restored, and made perfect through the Blood of Christ. It is in accepting Him that we will know a pristine world. But, the long wait for human conversion has had many sorrowful repercussions. Many of us stand proudly on the good deeds we do for others and the bold display of our well-intentioned acts. But, we are falling painfully short of even a marginal life that is defined by the principles of the Divinity of God. Our public acts are only vignettes to a book of good will that humanity has yet to write. All of this is a product of our refusal to reject our errors. Human transgression is the source of violence and the breeding ground for unwarranted globular suffering. War, itself, springs from the breach-of-peace of our collective inner-self, played out before God and all the heavens. We sling-shot bigotry and prejudice around the world like rocks through our neighborhood windows. Our sins are a well gone-dry and a yearling that has fallen into peril from her nest.

Somehow, we must stop our ruthless march toward the corruption of our souls. It is the root of many unmitigated tragedies that we choose to blame on God, Himself. We must realize that it is more visionary to ameliorate the deficiencies of our suffering brothers than to land a man on the moon. Life should teach us that deceit is the father of disease and materialism is our passport to emptiness, depression, and sorrow. One day, we will see all deprivation and disaster having been founded in our refusal to love. We live best when we listen to the God who already knows our carefully concealed intentions. His Love is the Light in the world. The poverty in which He was born is the salt that gave the Earth its first taste of moral victory. Jesus was given by the Virgin Mary to save us and teach us to love. It is in Him that we learn to see. There are symbols of human hatred that are peppered throughout the world. Suicide is a hopeless flower that no one cared enough about to water. Theft is the taking of someone's wallet before stepping on their fingers as they cling to their life while hanging over a cliff. The true fall that is taken is rightfully our own. Our motivations and interactions should be newly founded in Christ. We thought we had permanently killed Him once-and-for-all on the Cross, but we have long-since discovered that it is our own corruption that has died, instead.

There has never been a more benevolent crisis that has ever taken place at any point in time or at any location in Creation than the Crucifixion of Jesus Christ. United perfectly in Him, we will wish to sin no more! To perfect our acceptance of His Sacrifice, His Holy Mother is appearing worldwide, to confirm Her own commitment to our conversion. During the past two weeks, I have noticed a certain heaviness in the passing days that has been burdening my soul. It seems that my work for Our Lady has gone from joyful pleasure to a cumbersome task. My love for Jesus and His Mother has never waned, and never will. It is as though my heart has become weaker than my mind. The Blessed Mother told me that such thoughts have an ill-effect on my journey toward holiness. She has given me every reason to be happy. Our Lady appeared very early in the morning and was sorrowful for my heavy heart. I felt almost afraid to hear Her speak because I knew Her intention would be to remind me that I am blessed. I would sacrifice anything in the world to keep Her from feeling any sorrow of my making. The following are Her pious thoughts I received to begin this new day.

"My wonderful sons, it is nice to speak with you again. I hope that you are continuing your hopefulness as I have also hoped and prayed. I know that you have the great concern that many other holy people hold who pray for the world to come to Jesus. I tell you again that the world is coming to Jesus. Today, I also come to you in the tone of sorrow. It is because of your brother. He is crying and suffering because he sees you unhappy. You do not show the simplicity that he also wants to

express. Even he is not showing the innocent happiness that you both should be living by now. You are not communicating, not understanding, not feeling unity in the same shared state of prayer. I have tried to direct you both toward peace, toward unity, and toward Love. I have tried to help you both to be happy. I do not wish to see you unhappy. I pray for you to love. I pray for you to grow in that which I have taught you. Your prayers from the heart are meaningful, are sincere, and need to continue.

It is very important that you always remember that I come in Love. You are little children of Love and are not partisan with Love. You have touched many beautiful people today in a unifying way. I am happy for that. You are reuniting people and bringing the cause of a common foundation through the lessons of Love. Today, I am sorrowful because there are many who suffer the indifference of poverty and neglect. So many are victims of hatred and division. Many are lost in the magnitude of materialism, greed, possessionism, and procurement. If only I could bring to you by virtue of these words the degree and depth of suffering and bitterness that surrounds and consumes the world, you would, indeed, see the power of the true wealth of the Love that I ask you to share, the true devotion that you should display in your unity with Jesus, the true product of your union of prayers, and the Victory that mankind will know when Jesus comes to rescue everyone from their state of indignance, indifference, and apathy. For the good of your messages, you need to inhale a new breath of sacredness and a revitalizing realization that your movement through time is passing very quickly.

Mankind often becomes possessed by the seeming repetitiveness of days because there seems to be a light and darkness to his ability and willingness to love, much like the rhythm of the breaking of dawn and the falling of dusk. I pray and ask you to not allow that rhythm, that darkness, and that indifference to occur in the hallowedness of this house of Love, the structure that holds the roots of the conversion of many souls, the heart-filling magnification of everlasting Love which we, together, have tried to give to the world. While you are growing, expanding, shining, and glowing, the rest of the world is suffering and deposing, shuddering, and crumbling. I have given to you and your brother the living prescription for all happiness. But, the two of you are living as though you are about to see your doom through a lack of hope and a lack of trust in God's Promise of everlasting Life.

Every time that you have asked Me to give you a sign of Love, I have responded. But, I did not damage your faith in the process. I now ask you to also respond by not breaching your love for each other. Be in total unity with the suffering world. Our many hundreds of hours together have been for that reason! My tone of sorrow today is warranted because you and your brother will not look beyond your dailiness or beyond your habits, toward a comprehension of unity with Eternity from where you both stand. Always remember that I love you, regardless if you choose to recognize the intensity of the grace of these words. Your Holy Mother is of many magnificent dimensions. Like Jesus, I am always and everywhere, and so is My Love. I will speak to you soon. Please accept My blessing now. I love you incomprehensibly."

Friday, November 6, 1992
Early evening

I have spent the day lifting my heart and contemplating the great gifts God is bestowing upon the Earth. I hope for happiness and fulfilment for everyone who is burdened by life in any way. My brother and I began the Rosary this evening and The Holy Mother came to speak to us again. **"I love you! Please smile for Me! Today, we are happy together as you have proceeded away from the difficulties of the recent past. You are fine now, as is your precious little brother. I have come to offer you another important message. Thank you for being so nice as to examine your conscience and realize your revitalization toward opening your patient little hearts a measurable distance farther. Today, we will continue to pray together, hope together, love together, and work again to unite everyone under the care and inside the protective guidance of My Love..."**

She continued by telling me more about prayer and conversion. She said that there are four types of prayer usually lifted by humanity. They are prayers for health, prosperity, acceptance, and Salvation. She told me that She pleads for humanity to answer the call of Jesus to conversion because we are responsible for the destiny of our own souls. We often think that conversion sits aside from us and must be evaluated through human judgement. We approach it as though it is a foreign object that needs to be scrutinized to be deemed worthy of interest. Our Lady describes our perception of conversion as though we are pepper sitting beside the salt-shaker of holiness. Some people feel like they need no flavor because they can stand independently on their own. They are autonomous souls whose vision never grows larger than the horizon before them. They have no plans to avoid the darkness once the sunset of life has come. This is not the way we are intended to perceive Christian conversion. We must be consumed by the Holy Spirit in every way. We should offer every fiber of our being to Love and serve humankind the way Jesus teaches. Our every thought and action must be in union with Him. Our souls become the salt-of-the-earth because He lives together with us. We cannot survive separate from the Love He brings.

Therefore, our conversion is our acceptance of Love in-the-heart through single-minded obedience. The love that we share with Christ must be manifested through our work in His vineyard. If we are to be instruments of His grace, we must be willing to be utilized to the fullest tenor of our strength. So, we do not have to "jump-the-gap" from the pepper to the salt. Christ comes from within us through the gift of the Holy Spirit. Any distance we feel from Him is not a problem of where He is, but where we are. It is a matter of whether we have emptied ourselves so He can fill us completely with His Love. If we are to exude the flavor of righteousness in the bland indifference of the world, we are required to become the vessels through which His Love can flow. As has been previously stated, we must become smaller as Christ grows in us. That is the purpose and effect of our conversion. This is the reason why we pray. We are hallowed through the expungement of our worldly selves and inhabited by the Spirit of Our Lord. We become walking representatives of the Love of God and the seasoning that makes the world the savory Divinity of Heaven.

Prayer is the origin, the fruit, and the sustainer of our conversion. We see inside ourselves how Christ is remaking our soul. Indeed, our entire "being" is transformed into holiness and perfection. We become better able to recognize our transgressions and helplessness, while our ability to fight temptation and avoid the scourge of sin is enhanced. God makes us conquerors of any evil trying to diminish our hope or dampen our spirits. Our greatest Benefactor is His Mother, Our Lady, who comes into the world to communicate His Love. Her purpose is for Christ to become the very nature of our lives. Her desire is that He be glorified in our faith and belief. Let us hope that the prayers of humanity are humble in nature and that conversion to Jesus is the reason we live. The standard for holiness is Christ, Himself; and our imitation of His Life should be our goal. The power of Love is just as strong now as it was 2000 years ago. His Light is just as bright and His message just as True. We must let Him rule and reflect His Love, ourselves. We are all ordained to be the children of Almighty God. You are reading this undeniable fact on these pages. **You have been told. What is your response?**

God does not demand conversion, but He offers it. Christ is a gift to those who will accept Him. He is our only Savior, our one Redeemer for all peoples and all time. The original Apostles proclaimed, *"Lord, where else can we turn?"* The rhetorical nature of their question is as true today as it was then. Jesus is the Way, the Truth, and the Life. God has One Son and no other. He is the One who Died on the Cross to save our souls from the eternal fires of Hell. If we say "no" to Him, we are cast into an abysmal condemnation of our own choosing. That is why we must convert our lives through the power of His Grace and the Blood of His Cross. We are the branches that need His

Life-giving holiness, lest we wither and die. These are the bold facts that humankind has been evangelizing for twenty centuries. Most have listened and obeyed, many have ignored, and others have rejected. Through the Mercy of God, the obedient and the ignorant are being converted by the Grace of Our Holy Lady. But, those who reject Him are making a fatal decision to spend the rest of time in agony and anguish. The Holy Spirit is alive in the mortal world. It is never too early for conversion; but it may soon be too late. The time is ripe for every soul to say "yes" while God's ear is turned to our plea.

Sunday, November 8, 1992
As a fruit of Her Divine intercession, Our Lady asked me to record another message for all the world. It is an offering of love, hope, and comfort. We are undoubtedly in the hands of a compassionate God through His loving Mother. **"Good evening again, My precious ones. I love you so! I love all of the world, past pillars and palaces and in spite of famine and ghettos. I love all of My precious little children who suffer under the temptations of sin and never fall fatally due to their Salvation and Glory in My Son, Jesus. My children, today you have again witnessed hope. You have lived hope by faith and your belief in the promises of God. Everyone alive can see their own vision of Eternity through Jesus. I know that your holy thoughts are of the great grace that you have been given to see in perspective the power of Love over sin, over illness, over stagnation, and over death. I pray that every soul in the world will eventually see as you see. I have come again today to reaffirm My Promise to be with you and all of My children throughout the days that are coming and those which will be everlasting, beyond the strife and greed and beyond the coming forces of purification that God has willed His people to endure.**

Jesus stands beside all who search for His Love. He enters the hearts of those who accept His Love. Everything else that the heart may suffer is put aside. All that glows is Love and all that reflects is grace. Please help Me, today, in remembering all whose hearts are broken by loss and fear. There are millions throughout the world today who mourn and who spiritually grasp the air with their hearts and hopes, seeking for new meaning in what little they have left to claim. As I have told you before, as these days pass, everyone learns a moment at a time that the only true possession they own is their love for others and those who love them in return. I cannot begin to tell you how nourishing it is for you to recall your childhood. As Jesus calls every soul to Himself, He calls through the epitome created by childhood memories. As all souls come to Jesus, they are humbled and strengthened in faith and trust. Remember that, as a child, you believed nearly everything you were told.

This is the same unassuming innocence in which you should trust in Jesus and His Promise today..."

The Holy Mother calls us to live the simplicity of a child. This is a rarer attribute than any other aspect of human behavior. A world of terror and destruction is making cynical men out-of youthful playmates. Little hearts are being wounded by the sins of others and wish to hide from the perils of the world. It seems that when someone opens themselves in peace and holiness, they become vulnerable to the stench of hatred and guile. These generous hearts have been pierced and lacerated by the ill-will of those who despise goodness and embrace evil. The lifeblood of righteousness often falls to the ground to be trampled-upon by the wretched-of-heart. This horrid reality has led many to abandon their hope that the world will ever become a better place. Love is always on the defensive, trying to justify the reason it lives. We know through the Mother Church that prayer and the Holy Sacraments give us the power to stand confidently in the Light, not in some corner of darkness where cowards recoil. Through these pious Graces, the defiance of humankind withers and passes. Only Love can survive the magnification of God's Will! Jesus is the Master and King who stands at our side. When we embrace His Love, sinful mortality is overcome by conviction and strength.

The fallible and destructible nature of man cannot stand in the Light of the Word of God. Falsehood cannot be equated with Truth. Jesus destroyed error on the Cross. Our Heavenly Father promises that we will not lose hope if we live our faith to perfection. Even in the worst of times, Christ sustains our assurance that the world is unfolding as He plans. We are converting, but at a snail's pace. During these tempestuous times, hope is a precious gift that seems elusive to the weak. Go unto the Lord! The assurance of our success in Him is real through His Passion and Death. He endured three hours hanging on a tree in a perpetual acclamation of "I Love You." God is pleased by His Son's Suffering to the degree that we are all vindicated from the culpability of sin. Jesus lowered His head in death so we could raise ours in hope. His Spirit gives us power we could never wield on our own. We should stand in the gale amidst the treachery of the world and say to our own happiness, *"I claim you in the Name of Christ Jesus!"* The world will be still at our command when our voice echoes His Victory. Our call for peace resides in our faith that we will prevail in all ways good in the eyes of the Lord.

Friday, November 13, 1992

Many have stated their lack of belief in Our Lady's intercession because they see Her manifestations too often. Others say that She is absent of the commanding presence of God. I have often heard faithless excuses about the miracles in Medjugorje in these terms. *"There is no way that The Virgin Mary would speak to that many people every day for a dozen years!",* I have heard them say.

But, She has miraculously done so and continues to this day. The detail through which She shares our lives is quite revealing of Her desire to lead us in prayer toward holiness. She told me this evening, **"Everyone must remember that I addressed those details for Jesus when He was yet in infant clothes! Now, I do so for the rest of My children. My Son allows Me to see your lives with great candor..."** This should give us great reason for hope. The Mother of Jesus Christ is God's messenger who speaks the words we will soon hear from His own lips. There is no substitute for the loftiness of sanctity. We must become purified and take the oath of righteousness. The articles of our faith seem lost at our feet and the Blessed Virgin is showing us where to look. Our trust in God must be strong because we are asked to walk the path of holiness with our eyes turned to Heaven. Through the intercession of Our Lady and the guidance of the Holy Spirit, we will not stumble and cannot fall. Her call is an urgent invitation to prayer and sacrifice.

Christ tells us to evict human weakness from the chambers of our heart. Our capacity to love must be greater than any force trying to diminish it. When we suffer in the midst of the greatest torment, the worst misunderstanding, and blatant derision, our Love must magnify our most mollifying side. When we are tempted to retaliate through our own rebellious power, we must instead choose to shine our Love into the darkness. These moments of quiet strength are the minutes of our finest hour. When we suffer for the sake of Christ, the world opens to the Light of Glory and He stands with us wielding the excellence of the Holy Cross. This is our profession of invincible triumph over mortal flesh, aggression, and abhorrence. The world may see weakness in our imitation of Christ, but the heavens see the Divinity of God. At no time does our faith shine more brightly than when we are humiliated in His Name or suffer for His sake. This is what makes the Passion of Jesus so pleasing in the eyes of the Almighty Father. It is the intrinsic power of the Holy Sacrifice of the Mass, the Crucifixion of Jesus at the hands of sinful humanity.

God is glorified that His Son loves us to the point of His death. The Eucharistic Body of Jesus allows us to stand in that same great Light. Our souls are elevated during Holy Communion to rest in the peaceful stream of grace and Mercy. Indeed, we experience the blessing and absolution from the Power that created the universe. How can we not endure our trivial suffering in exchange for the conversion of souls? After all, Jesus was sent to His death to save ours. Surely we can withstand the buffets of rejection to lead others to His Blood. We can tell God that we will buckle-down for the storm rather than hide in a billet of the world. The Heavenly Queen stands at the center of our turmoil to tell us God's work is at hand. She kneels at the Cross of Mount Calvary and at the bedside of our death to sin. She trusts God to help us in the same Truth that He raised Her Son from the grave. No other Heart in Creation has suffered the sorrow that Our Lady has known. The Son She bore was rejected by mankind and cast from their midst. This is the same Mother who stands beside us during our own angst and pain.

We must emulate the Holy Mother as we concurrently share the Life of Christ. She is the Mother of Faith who nourishes our desire to seek God in all ways. She is the Queenly Ambassador for His Will on Earth, just as She is in Heaven. When She said "yes" to the Angel, She knew that it meant accepting everything God would require. She loves in the same perfection that brought Jesus to His Death on the Cross. He allowed Himself to be crucified because He loves us. Their two Hearts resound the eloquence of the Paradisial Kingdom. They compel us to pious inspiration and prayerful contemplation. They will never quit the Victory they won for us. Jesus is the Sacrificial Lamb and the Virgin Mother is the New Eve. They call us to the reverential prayer of the Holy Mass.

God asks us to accompany these two Hearts on the Hill of Mount Calvary. If we comprehend the torture they withstood, we will be on our way to a place called conversion. The Sacred Heart of Christ and the Immaculate Heart of Mary are the sinless Refuge where we find protection from the horrible world. They are the reason for the Mass. We are guarded by their Grace, not obscured by their Divinity. Through their Love, we are absorbed by peace and lifted to the bastion of perfection. They hold us high in their arms to the Face of Creation and ask, "Can you see? Can you see?" For those who do not know how to love, look at Jesus hanging on the Cross. You will recognize amidst this terrible carnage the reason why He died. You may cringe from the sight, but your heart will tell you that your homeland is near. From the depth of your soul, you will never ponder the word "how" again. No longer will you sound the roll-call of fear and misunderstanding. Jesus has answered the Will of God for our reconciliation to purity and Truth. By His Stripes we are healed. He destroyed our corruption through the Sacrifice He endured.

Tuesday, November 17, 1992

If we try to scamper away from God, He will not set-out to chase us. It was humanity that first abandoned Him in the Garden of Eden. But, leave it to Him to send His Son to gather-up His "problem children" and grant them eternal Redemption! With victory atop of good fortune, His Mother has come back to the world, speaking and appearing to those whom She knows will amplify Her call for conversion. Through this Diary, my brother and I are attempting to do just that. We have begun to accomplish Her purpose, which is the Divine Will of God, to the benefit of those who have the faith and desire to listen. Today, She came to ask Her humble followers to live in a perfect affirmation of trust in Her Son. She knows that God is repulsed by lukewarm Christianity. We must never allow our faith to be devoured by the jaws of indifference. We must walk upright and never bow to the invitation of sin or impurity. If we keep our hearts true to the destiny of our souls, we cannot be duped by the cunning of the world. We have a race to win and cannot be distracted by the passing byways. If we are to succeed, we cannot love at half-a-pace.

The search for holiness is not a lackadaisical stroll in a country woods. We must unleash our greatest potential to seek God with all our might and strength, to the depth of our heart and soul. We truly do not know the magnitude of our imitation of Christ. We are a breath of hope in the heaviness of sorrow and a flash of light in the darkness of despair. When we say, "I love you" from the recesses of the heart, the world becomes brighter at the beauty of our voice. We light the pitiful Earth as though it is daytime in the middle of the night. Our seemingly insignificant and obscure acts of Love are like electricity flowing through the bowels of the Earth, creating Light and shocking the indifferent into the awareness of God. When we saturate the world in the salve of dignity, the Hosts of Heaven stand in ovation. They cheer and clap their hands because God's team has taken the lead. When we are pummeled and pelted in the name of Christ, each twinge of pain takes us closer to Paradise. If the squalor of the world knocks us to our knees, we will crawl to the finish line in faith. When the world tempts us to be rich, we will be poorer for Christ. When prestige and popularity knock on our door, we will refuse to answer. The world provokes us toward secular greatness, while Christ calls us to selfless humility.

Our fulfillment is in sacrificial Love and our future resides in Heaven. These are times of opportunity for us to join those who serve, those who bless, and those who heal. This is the "now" during which Christ tells us to prepare. Our power lies in the Heart of God. When we pray for ourselves and our brothers and sisters, He enlists His infinite capacity to answer our desires. He loves to love us! When we seek, we will find. When we knock, the door will indeed be opened. We are told in many ways, **"If today you should hear His voice, harden not your heart."** This is our invitation to accept the Love of Christ and the Life that He seeks in us. The grace of God comes through the Holy Spirit and the Wisdom of His Mother. She calls us to His Will by prayer of the Rosary. The "Hail Mary" is another way of saying to God, "I love you." The Holy Mysteries are the flame of celestial brilliance many times more resplendent than the sun. They are more than points of Light; they are blazing beacons of hope for all humanity living on Earth and in Purgatory.

One day soon, we will see the beauty of this Truth with our own eyes. The reason for Life will be displayed at the invitation of our souls. At the end of time, we will know who we harmed and who we helped, those we loved perfectly, and those we failed. We will see every moment of good fortune bestowed through God's grace and Divine Providence. And in the presence of Christ, we will look into His Mercy and beg for forgiveness. He will not send us back to try again! This is our time for conversion and preparation. Our Eternal Moment has already begun. We must open our hands to Jesus filled with the fruits of Love, not stained by the scowl of indifference. Our advocacy is found in the intercession and prayers of Our Lady.

Saturday, November 21, 1992 - Feast of the Presentation of Mary

Tonight was very special, indeed. When my brother and I began the Rosary, the Holy Spirit filled our prayer-room with heavenly Light. Our Lady came with an expression of urgency to assist our petitions. She offered a message with a spirit of conviction and a proclamation of Love to the entire world. **"My precious little children. You are My little angels! I love you very much. My children, how I desire for the world to see Me as a loving Mother, a gentle Mother, a Mother whose caress is worthy of response and prayer. It is a beautiful day throughout the world as so many are remembering Me. Today, the Love of Jesus is being recalled by hundreds of thousands who recognize His dignity in the Church and His Agony on the Cross. Today, many are lifting Jesus high so that He, too, can lift them up. Today, the memory of Jesus' Crucifixion has allowed His Light to pronounce His Kingship. As the dawn breaks tomorrow, also will the dawn of the continuity of His Reign.**

My little children, the world must know that Jesus does not ask for much. His Love encompasses even the very thought of Love. He does not seek social giants amongst men. He does not seek the measuring of the heights of mountains. He does not expect miracles from those who fathom the depths of the seas. He only hopes for a change in the hearts of those who are not faithful to Him. Jesus seeks only the smallest fraction of faith and love, then He will see to it that men might ascend those same mountains with wings of ease. He will see that the richest treasures of the seas are made to rise to the surface of their own accord. All Jesus asks is a chance, a little way to show all mankind that His Crucifixion is also for the wicked and wretched, for the poor and oppressed, and for those whose darkness has held them captive for far too long.

Jesus' Love is the only living thing in the Universe. All else is objective and inanimate. All else is of terminal being and existence. Nothing but Love breathes! Nothing but Love shines! Only Jesus is the true and total composition of the future of mankind and all he hopes to achieve. Only Jesus is the Victor and the Champion, by not competing at all. Only through realizing Love and by following Jesus can mankind realize that he, too, is victorious in living fact and for all Eternity, not in earthly principle or finite mortality. Everything that resides in Jesus

must reside in Love, for all else is not alive, all else is simply a barren environment with a baseless form.

Your Mother has come to tell the world that no one can live without the breath of Life, the Love of Jesus. Please understand that My words and discipline are a living fruit of that same Love. As mankind grasps for ways to explain, to describe, and to categorize, he is only doing the handiwork of idleness in this passing age of mortality. Jesus has the answer to all that is explainable and describable. When mankind realizes the ultimate goal of sanctity and Salvation, he will turn his idleness and description into prayer, contemplation, and conversion. I am very pleased with those who have answered this call with 'Yes,' to help their brothers and sisters return to dignity. Please pray with Me and the faithful who petition for peace, purity and Salvation. One day, you will see that we have won. One day, all of My little children will know the Victory of Light and the Victory of Love over hatred. Very soon, every little voice will join as one as we together sing, 'Now thank we all our God...'"

There is little I can add to Her words to describe the urgency for the conversion of man. Yes, the world is a terrible place. It is made awful at the hands of people who refuse to reject evil and lift themselves out-of the squalid recesses of sin. I ask for your response in faith to Our Lady's call. Look with my brother and me to the brightness of Love. Please muster the courage and strength to accept Our Lord through His Mother by saying, *"I want to be with them! I want to do my part. I hope they hear my little voice, too!"* They already know who you are and where you live. They know your heart better than you will ever be able to conceive. Our Lady will help you conform to the wishes of God. Until you do, you will not be happy and will never know peace. We must pray and never give-up, never stop hoping, and never stop loving. When we do so as one humanity, we will be transformed into the righteousness and purity that Jesus seeks of those He saves. We will be a new generation, revitalized in faith and purpose, moving forward together to our destiny in perfection. If you say that you are too weak or miserable, God will strengthen you through the Holy Spirit and the Blessed Sacrament of His Son. Nothing can keep you from divinity and holiness that cannot be purged by Christian conversion. This revelation is the source of your new beginning and perpetual Life. Today can become the prelude to your Eternity in Paradise.

Friday, November 27, 1992

When Our Lady came to pray with us tonight, She wished to discuss the blessing of human forgiveness. It is the sweetest fruit of Christ's Love. If we desire a world of peace and accord, we must embrace the teaching of Jesus to forgive the transgressions of others. Not only must we exonerate them, we must tell them they are forgiven. Their faults must be removed from our memory as we live the new beginning our absolution brings. Christ redeems every soul who accepts His Sacrifice, including the terrible men who put Him to death. We have to remember that they are the first to be touched by the Blood of the Son of God. They had Redemption at their hands before their souls ever knew to partake of it. The human intellect does not have the capacity to comprehend the power of forgiveness. It is a fruit of a faithful heart. The ultimate success of peace and unity rests upon the strength of humble contrition and absolute acquittal. Our thoughts are categorized by beliefs and desires which cannot stand in Truth on their own. God did not just "think" about saving His people, He sent His Son to real death for the vindication of our souls. The Sacrifice of Calvary is the Truth in the words, "I forgive you."

We cannot stand next to the Cross with vengeance in our hearts. The Love of Christ is like a flaming torch next to the fuel of human hatred. He would incinerate our souls in an explosion beyond His Kingdom to come. The civility that God seeks from us is manifested through our forgiveness of others. It is a fruit of the new perfection we find in Him. When we love Jesus with everything we are and ever will be, we will become perfect in Love. In Him, God provides the example we need to make ourselves worthy of Heaven. We must simultaneously accept both His Life and Crucifixion because He is the Path and the Destination. Our Lady said this evening, **"Please do not stop believing that you can be perfect, as Jesus is perfect. Most of all, remember that Jesus loves you in many magnificent and resounding ways that mankind has yet to envision. All of this hope and all of this Truth was given to you when He said, 'It is finished,' whereupon He expired on the Cross. He conquered all sin, all damnation, all despair, and every evil spirit for those who accept His Sacrifice and their own Salvation. Only happiness can come from the faith in His Promise which He asks you to carry. He only asks that you follow Him in happiness. After His mighty Sacrifice, only happiness can follow Him. We realize this Truth, you and I, your brother, and the multitudes of the faithful from the past and present. We hold the key to the mystery of the Salvation of all. It is the imitation of the Love of Jesus, living as He truly asks everyone to live, lifting-up all humanity in Love, prayer, and deed…"**

What of all the people who look at the rancorous world and ask how Christ could have destroyed Satan? The answer is that the venue for the deliverance of man to peace and purity is not being accepted. Evil is dead and so are the mortal souls who embrace its decadent stench. The strength to change the world rests in the suffering of Jesus in the wake of His Resurrection. Infidels and cynics need to look, instead, through eyes of Love. That is where they will recognize the power of Christ. He is found in the pain of despair and poverty and in the beatific peace of those who suffer affliction and rejection for love of God. He shines through the smiles on the faces of His children who lose everything they have to evangelize His Gospel. Inside these holy hearts is the real world. These are the blessed corridors that have been hallowed by the Sacrifice of the Lamb. They are free from evil and cannot be corrupted. Their souls will never be crushed by greed or power because they stand valiantly as Justice Himself in the face of oppression and persecution. Christ purifies the decadent nature of sinful people through His faithful followers on Earth. There is no other service more noble and none more fulfilling to achieve. He lives in hearts where all sin has expired and despair and evil have been replaced by sanctity and delight.

Therein lies the hope of the fragrance of Paradise. It blooms from human hearts given to Jesus at the zenith of their Divine potential. If anyone would have thought this could be possible before The Crucifixion, they would have been dreaming about a world yet to come. But, the future is now at hand! Those who accept the Sacrifice of Jesus are pure-of-heart and open to Love. They have a new power growing in them at the hands of the Holy Spirit. He blooms seemingly out-of-control from every pore of the Christian being, like a flowering vine stately adorning a monument to peace. For these pretty offspring of Salvation, penance and reparation are the order of the day. Their faces are the incarnate glow of forgiveness to all who seek it. They are like flowers that grow amidst weeds who cannot be parched by the thirsty greed of the Earth. They can see forever past the finite world into the sunlit Glory of paradisial peace and eternal rest. Yes, these are the little children who have been rescued from the pit of darkness by the Anointed Son of God.

Our Lady has come seeking hearts who accept this immortal commission. Christ looks for humble servants to answer the call of righteousness and contemplation. These are the blessed souls He feeds with Love and begs not to forget His kindness. Hearts given to Him swim in the eternal seas of Redemption, never to be caught by the hand of perdition. They bask in the Ocean of Mercy and bathe in the Light of Salvation. A soul who embraces the opportunity to endure the afflictions of the world will never be destroyed and will be Resurrected into Life forever. This is the power of Love and the reason for the Crucifixion of Christ. In its own Divine right, it is majestic, comforting, salubrious, and serene. Its power is the freedom for which mankind has yearned for countless ages. The Cross is our advantage in a world trying to defeat our every salutary move. We must pray for faith and invigorate our hearts to be compelled toward the Light of Christ. We have our own crosses to bear in the same docility that Jesus endured the Crucifixion that redeems us. We are borne into Heaven through the newborn perfection we have gained through His grace.

Sunday, November 29, 1992
(The following is a parable that Our Lady asked me to incorporate into my Diary on this date.)

Two people once lived in a majestic mountain kingdom that sat at the summit of Creation. While they were completely happy there, they chose to disobey the principles of Life and lost favor with the Almighty Ruler. So, He cast them to the bottom of their spiring paradise to live in its shadow. As they stood helplessly in the valley gazing up at the towering peak, all they could see was its impenetrable face. They had no hooks, ropes, or boots to help them climb the steep sierra in front of them. Indeed, having always lived in their heavenly home, they never before knew what it is like to climb. This desolate valley left them without means or knowledge to regain the celestial beauty they lost. So, they began to live in the inconsonance of their new environment. Every day, they looked-up in sorrow to catch a glimpse of the happiness they forfeited. Their vision was obscured by clouds surrounding the highest peak. The sun was prohibited from revealing its sparkling beauty. They knew in the wake of their own disobedience that they were not living the Life intended for them in their native homeland.

When they finally died, generations of their descendants suffered their same plight. They eventually stopped looking toward the heavens and established their own hapless kingdom in the dismal confines of their exile. They promulgated public laws and devised punitive measures to enforce them. The number of towns and cities multiplied throughout the entire area. They began competing amongst themselves for the resources they needed to survive. Some even hoarded goods that would have kept others from suffering great poverty and lack of dignity. Nearly all of the population was unhappy, but they did not know why or how to alleviate it. Only a few had hope for change or bothered to look past the immediate world for help. It seemed that above them was only the arc of the distant sky.

One night, when a small group of pioneer optimists were straining to see the heavens, the clouds parted before their eyes. An awesome beam of Light began shining from the beautiful Kingdom they had lost at the hands of the first two people to Fall. A Man was climbing down the great mountain into their lost valley below. While everyone else slept, these few privileged souls marveled at the Glory approaching them and the Divinity that escorted Him to their land. Many came bearing gifts to pay homage to the One who was so kind as to visit their lowly estates below the brilliance of the stars. This pleasant mountaineer lived among them for many years, laboring, teaching, and tending to the lowly and alone. He cared for souls who were persecuted and rejected by those who wanted everything of value for themselves. His greatest gift was a staircase that He painstakingly constructed and presented to every household in every city. The citizens were ecstatic because the ladders to the lofts of their homes were rickety and dangerous. He taught them how to properly use their new stairs until they could ascend them safely. And, each time He visited, he would depart by saying, "Follow Me."

This good Man was rejected by many who said they did not need Him or His steps. From those, He departed with the same words, "Follow Me." One day, His time with the people in the valley came to an end. He was to return to His place in the heavenly skies. He would ascend to His lofty homeland by simply traveling the beam of Light on which He came. He remembered saying to them, "Follow Me." So during the darkness of night, He laid a first step at the mountain-base. He placed another above that one and kept adding steps toward the skies. Through toil, sweat, labor, and pain, He laid a ribbon of stairs much wider and easier to ascend than those He had placed in their homes. The people rose from their beds and looked at the mountain in awe. When they saw the beautiful steps leading into the clouds, they all remembered His words, "Follow Me." They also remembered the stairs He gave them for their homes that they had climbed and descended countless times each day. But, they had never seen a staircase of this magnitude, none so beautiful, and none so endless. Many people timidly came forward to climb these magnanimous stairs. They ascended three or four steps, then came back down from fear of the height. Some would make it to the ninth and tenth steps, but would descend again, remembering the legend of their earliest ancestors who took the first Fall.

One person after another came forward, only to return to the ground in remorseful defeat. Finally, a father with a little child in his arms climbed to the highest step they had ever tried and stopped, like everyone before. When he put the child down to regain his direction, he loosed the little one's hand and the child scampered up the stairs out-of-reach. Undaunted and unafraid, the little boy climbed higher and higher. He seemed unaffected that each new step was greater than the previous. He giggled and laughed at everyone he bravely left below. After looking down at their awestruck faces, he turned and raced upward still more, tickled that no one could reach him. Sensing the possible danger to his child, the father overcame his own inhibition. He now had to trust in the same way the child knew not to fear. Step-by-step, he climbed to heights he had never-before attained to retrieve his son.

Everyone else watched and gasped in stunned amazement. Courage began to grow within them. This breathtaking sight engulfed the huge throng as new joy was being born before their eyes. Their hearts exploded in ecstasy with the hope that a happy homecoming was just steps away. The vision they had once only dreamed flashed into reality in their own day. Everyone knew that the One who came from the celestial beauty of the mountaintop was He who said, **"Follow Me."** They also knew that it was the innocence of the little child that began their journey home. One after another, they stepped forward to begin their ascent to the heavenly Summit of Beauty. The hopes of their ancestors was being fulfilled in their age. The clouds parted and the sun shined brightly to light their way back to the Land that they had lost long before their birth.

This little parable describes the opportunity each of us has to return to the Almighty Father through His Son. And, we accept Him by living the unassuming innocence of a child. We climb in trust knowing we will never fail in the Light of Christ. There is no fear in faith because the trust we place in God gives us courage to succeed. Our Lady invited me to refer to **I John 4:16-21** about human inhibition. Jesus wants us to walk without fear. We must trust that we are made perfect by His Blood, shed on the Cross. We succeed because we know that the road can be traveled. We stop sinning because we know that we are perfectly sinless in Him. The Holy Mother echoes the words of Christ, Himself. Given the chance to be lifted-up, humanity will raise its arms to the Almighty Father. Given the chance to win, the struggle is worth the fight. Victory rests in the promise of God to all humankind. If we love in the way of Jesus, we will assuredly be elevated in holiness to the perfection that will render us ready for Heaven. Millions of Saints who live there speak through signs and miracles to tell us this is true. The Holy Spirit reverberates the unlimited possibilities of human greatness and righteousness throughout every heart. He summons us to the Light and the elevation that draws us closer to the Kingdom of Glory.

DECEMBER 1992

Tuesday, December 1, 1992

Today, my brother and I watched a televised program of the evangelical witness of the Reverend Billy Graham. Our Lady has told us before that he is very special in Her eyes. Our Holy Father, Pope John Paul II, calls all Christians to tell the world with courage about the Love of God and that Jesus died on the Cross for our sins. Billy Graham is fulfilling the wishes of the Holy Father. He has been preaching the Gospel of Jesus for half-a-century, telling nations with grace and power about human Redemption through the Blood of Christ. Reverend Graham has stated that he will retire from his ministry when he is "retired" by Jesus. What wonderful Christian fortitude! Our Lady is very happy about the conversion he has brought to many souls in his five-decades of crusades and revivals. As I ponder the words of this Evangelical brother, I see him as a unifier of Christians. His approach is one of prayerfulness and piety. While he has yet to embrace all seven Sacraments of the Church, he eventually will, even if after his passing. He has stated on every continent that

God so loves the world that He gives His only begotten Son so that everyone who believes in Him shall not perish, but have Eternal Life.

Hundreds of millions of souls are more closely united under the Cross as a result of Dr. Graham's ministry. The Holy Mother augments his work, trying to lead these same people to the Holy Eucharist, the Body and Blood of Jesus in the original Apostolic Church. We must all realize the holiness to which we are called by Christ. Love and prayer bring this pious transformation of the human heart and conversion of the soul. We reject sin and impropriety in the Christian family because our needs are nourished by faith and The Most Blessed Sacrament rather than the influences of the world. If it is not yet clear in this Diary, I will repeat that holiness is an achievable goal. Even though we may not yet comprehend what perfect conversion is, we must be willing to listen to the Holy Spirit and set-out to learn. Foremost, it begins through the purity that Christ teaches and in loving all humanity as we love ourselves. Our Lady showed me a picture of the steadfastness of human holiness brought through the fruit of Christianity. Its constancy is much like the sureness of a steel beam that is unwavering in strength.

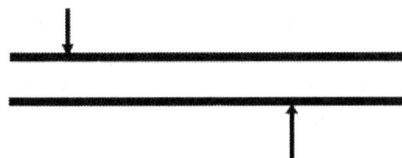

While the wholesomeness of perfect holiness has no detectable parameters, this picture displays the integrity of our lives as though our newfound purity has the preciousness of a bar of gold in the treasure of God's Love. There are no imperfections in our soul. The pathway of our being is strong and true. Our faith in God is unflappable and unwavering. Our Love is neither stained nor tarnished. This picture is indicative of our forthrightness and strength through which any gift and blessing can flow into the lives of our brothers and sisters. Indeed, we are the vessels of Christ through which He bestows grace and atonement upon others. This is the invincible nature of a converted soul who fights against the temptations of sin and lives the righteous Truth of God. However, if we do not accept the strength and power of the perfection we gain in Christ Jesus, our souls are diminished and weakened. We become flawed witnesses because we bow to sin and refuse to take-up the fight for piety. When we do this, the world not only tarnishes our holiness, our very souls become corrupted through the scourge of transgression. Sin eats-away our perfection like the corrosion of a water pipe. Our Love cannot reach its destination in God or our brothers and sisters because our impeccability is breached. We are rendered less-than-whole, as shown here.

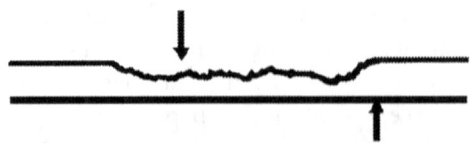

It is clear by this second depiction that sin corrupts our soul to make us less-than perfect and unwholesome in love and conversion. Through worldliness, indifference, and outright evil works, our soul becomes pitted and unfit for presentation to the Lord. But, if we remember the Gospel of Jesus that the Holy Father is sharing in unity with great evangelists like Billy Graham, we will turn to prayer, conversion, penance, and fasting. Our holiness will be restored by the Love of God. This is a simplistic vision that anyone can see, even the hearts of those whose sight has yet to be restored. The Holy Mother presented another example of how conversion affects our lives in Christ. He is the beginning of our days and the reason we rise in the morning. But, if we fail to put it into practice, what we are taught remains solely our potential. Jesus must become the reason for our action and the root of our faithful work. Consider the following example. You can complete three words from each of the two roots, "sym" and "tele." The first root means "together", and the second means "across the distance."

	POSIUM			**PHONE**
SYM:	**BOLISM**		**TELE:**	**GRAPH**
	PHONY			**VISION**

Each of the terms is derived from the same root. Their first syllable makes each word common to the others. While they have different meanings and usages, they spring from the same origin. This is how Love is the source and purpose of our every thought and action. We are brought together across the distance by the Love of Christ. Our Love is the origin of all righteousness, good will, and humanitarianism.

	GET UP IN THE MORNING
	GREETING FRIENDS
	HELPING THE POOR
LOVE:	**LEADING OTHERS TO JESUS**
	ATTENDING MASS
	FASTING
	AND ON AND ON...

The litany of human interaction, reciprocity, and Christian charity is unending. All of this is a fruit of Love. Anything you say and do must be a reflection of the Love in your heart. Love is the Alpha and Omega of all that exists in Heaven and on Earth. It is our responsibility to evangelize this heavenly call. Social and educational institutions that teach and practice contemporary law, science, and philosophy fail to make the point that Love is the reason for Life. They speak of the effect of living, but refuse to glorify the Love of God that gives and sustains it. When we elevate Love as the precedent to our every utterance and deed, there will be no odds to beat, no parametric guidelines, no pathological discourse, and no dissension between peoples. We will live in a world free from distraction and conflict. Our Lady said tonight, **"One day, no one will be left-out of total enlightenment. There will be no untouched hearts, no need for opinions, nothing that will defray, diminish, erode, or lessen total oneness. We hope for that day to come soon when the line between darkness and Light will be concise and detectable, where Light will overcome darkness forever."**

Before departing this evening, the Blessed Mother asked me to remember what I had seen on the bottom of the television screen when my brother and I watched Reverend Billy Graham's message. The words *"Paid Programming"* were superimposed on the lower part of the picture. She said that someday soon, every medium will serve the purpose of Christianity without having to be paid. But for now, those who hold power and control of the electronic media expect to be paid millions of dollars over time to allow such holy men as Billy Graham to take the word of God to the people. Those who own the networks should take immediate steps to live the message of Dr. Graham. The God he reveals to the nations is the source of the grace which allows them to live such affluent lives. If they wish to be thankful, they must start with God Almighty. Our Lady has made it clear that the time has come for people in every walk of life to spread the Good News of Christ to all lands, not for money, but because their hearts guide them in that direction. The media are currently sources of great devastation to innocent lives and impressionable children. They glorify the horrible images of violence, impurity, and hatred. They are the forces that erode and diminish human holiness in direct contradiction to the teachings of Christ. But, thanks to a humble servant named Billy Graham who still has to pay to disseminate the Gospel of Jesus, there was an hour tonight during which violence and moral corruption could not seep into the homes of vulnerable souls.

Friday, December 4, 1992

God has brought great opportunity to the world in the person of His Divine Mother. The Triumph of Her Holy and Immaculate Heart is now very near. Her victory is secured by the obedience of Her children, our prayers, and our participation. Our lives of question are now being answered by the Divinity of confidence. In our Blessed Mother, we are righteous conquerors again. We can now face in power from what we formally hid from in shame. This is the legacy of Jesus, to whom we are forever committed. Through Him, we can destroy the awful remnants of false human idolatry. Evil forces will retreat from our prayers back to the abyss, fearing our bold embrace of the redeeming Kingdom. We were once the victims of rampant fallaciousness and addiction. Our souls are the fruit that perdition wished to steal from the Vineyard of God. We were timid and tepid, but now in Christ, we are seasoned and brazen. He will soon return to the Earth and redeem His little children. He has chosen our fidelity as the premonition of His impending arrival. Our prayer is His call in the night. He reveals Himself to the ages in the petitions that His Spirit bestows in us.

Righteousness is the seed we plant in the Earth, while reconciliation its fruit. We conquer inept human indifference with the power of Life-giving prayer. It is the consummation of God, the framework of His Justice, and the destruction of ill will and rampant deceit. It is the salient grace and healing salve which mends the vile corruption of centuries past. This is our time to speak, an age that comes only once. We must listen to Our Lady, who calls us to such prayer. She brought the beauty of Heaven into my home again tonight as I prayed the Holy Rosary with my brother. Her words of comfort and grace bring peace and happiness to all who listen to Her call. As we near the end of this year, we have had some anxiety that Her messages might soon come to an end. For now, She continues to call when we pray to guide us to the Light of Christ. He is revealed to the nations through each prayer. In Him, we seek warmth for our cold hearts. Jesus is the means through which we are comforted and concealed in the embrace of God against the awful pain of the world.

The Blessed Mother told me today that the Holy Spirit rests in our hearts when we pray. The world we wish to see becomes a vision in the likeness of a beautiful painting. We are the artists who transform the images of Love in our hearts into the reality of the world. When we recite the Rosary, our prayers become the skillful strokes that color the Earth in dignity and brotherhood. This is God's wish because He wants us to realize the fruits of our prayers. He has already seen the picture we paint while we pray together over the passing days. As we move through time, we unite our petitions with the Divinity of Jesus. Since holiness is the center of our intentions, it is the *creme de la creme* of every prayerful contemplation. God is never truly finished with our souls as long as we live on this planet. He continues to crop, pare, cultivate, and caress, knowing that sincere prayer is our help in times of distress and persecution. He guides our supplication as we skillfully color our hearts with the hope that takes us closer to Him. We must always make Him the reason for our work, the center of our being, and the subject around which our efforts convene.

The Cross must be the image that we pray to replicate. Every aspect of our lives should lead in the direction of His Love. He teaches the perfection that helps us master the canvass of mortality. We make artful progress through confession of the soul, penance, prayer, and conversion. He can transform a dilettante into an expert with one "Our Father." When our days become filled with universal supplication, we become enlightened to the vision of the Crucifixion . We are united in Love as Christ changes our souls into the beauty of His Sacred Heart. When we surrender in the way of His example, our desire for Heaven is manifested through our every thought and action. The form, shape, tone, and hue of our lives rest in unison with His Will. We acquire the combined skill and vision of a Rembrandt, Picasso, and Michelangelo at the center of our being. The world in which we walk becomes filled with flowers and birds, sunrises and rainbows. The angels and Saints that Michelangelo painted on the hallowed walls of the Sistine Chapel become alive in our hearts and before our eyes. There is no end to the blessings from Heaven that dwell among us when we pray, especially the Holy Rosary.

Jesus knows what Creation must become. We are the instruments He uses like brushes in His hands. He immerses us in joy, consolation, suffering, and jubilation. He employs every hue of the human conscience to detail the Earth. When we allow Him to guide our ecclesiastical piety, the masterpiece He presents to God is pleasing, indeed. We need each other to accomplish this hope. Christ needs us and we certainly need Him. The Holy Trinity is the tripod on which Creation rests, waiting for each of us to add our pretty brush-stroke of Love to enhance its beauty. Jesus lifts us from the world like little children as we pledge our affirmation of innocent conversion to the backdrop of His Kingdom. Our Lord is the sole proprietor of the human heart. We either allow Him to rest there in peace, or shut Him out. The seemingly-endless pangs upon our consciousness are His continuous knocks at our door. When we hear a bird singing outside our window, it is the gentleness of His knuckles tapping in the distance. When our hearts are crushed by the death of a loved -one, He has come with clasped-fist to awaken the sleeping world. We are better to listen in silent peace than to force Him to call through the deafening din of human reprobation. He wishes to inhabit the life He creates, to take-up residence in His proper domain, and to claim the purity of human conversion. We invite Him into our hearts through prayer.

Our Lady said tonight, **"Remember that more powerful than any act which you may have the opportunity to invoke is your prayers, especially the Holy Rosary.** By welcoming Jesus into our hearts, we become artists for the King of Creation. We aspire for true greatness and strive for saintliness, holiness, and perfection. Every beat of our hearts becomes a percussion of Love through the resonance of the Holy Spirit. We tell our suffering brothers and sisters that we wish to be more than "good" to them. We sacrifice our lives for their souls and lead them to the Light of Christ. We place our brush of compassion to every dark corner of their heart to console them in His peace. That is the power and purpose of our prayers. We obtain God's blessings for them when we affirm our unlimited Love in the image of Jesus. We lift our desire to transform the weak into an impenetrable fortress against any temptation. The perfection we bring through our unity in Christ is suitable for presentation to the Almighty Father to commemorate our Redemption. He will mat our chosen Divinity with the bounty and peace of Paradise.

Wednesday, December 9, 1992
   Our Lady comes in the midst of our trials to bring the intercession that only God knows how to effect. She helps us remember that we are loved beyond our capacity to fully comprehend. If we are unhappy because the world is cruel, we should strengthen our hope through prayer. Our happiness lies in the gifts of the Holy Spirit sent by God. We have full-right to place our trust in His Word. He nourishes our strength and enhances our awareness that His Kingdom is at hand. He knows that we will not know joy until we embrace His peace. All things that are good in the eyes of God grow through the fidelity of our prayers. Every living soul on Earth is vulnerable to the decadence of Satan. He is the father of all despondence and despair. He pillages our inner-peace like a thief-in-the-night and parches the fruit of our good works with flames of hatred. We cannot peacefully coexist with evil. It must be destroyed if we are to live the full presence of Love. When we are converted to the Lord with all our heart, we will not compromise with evil and will refuse to allow it in our hearts, our families, and our homes. When we pray to the heights invoked by Our Lady, rectitude will replace sinfulness in every corner of the globe.
   God allows Satan to influence the Earth, knowing full-well we will run to Jesus for help. Lack of faith entices us to place our trust in the material world rather than the foundation of God. When we slip and fall, Christ catches us every time. It is as though we are not just invited to jump into the arms of The Father, He allows us to be pushed by the wiles of the world. But, Satan would like to steal our souls and run into the night. As long as our attention is totally upon holiness and prayer, he cannot touch us. Indeed, when we invoke the Blood of the Cross, the evil one does not come near! He lost his power through the Crucifixion of Jesus and will never be victorious again. If a mortal soul falls into his grasp, it is because that soul chooses to do evil rather than good. Prayer enhances our capacity to fight the temptations and enticements that are thrust upon us by the world. Christ makes all things new and refocuses our vision onto the path of righteousness. The very meaning of our lives is to

invite Him into our hearts and answer when He calls. Our prayers glorify Him as the Creator of Love who knows the plight of His children and the forces that weaken our faith.

We are an immortally holy people because of His grace. We have power that many refuse to use. When evil was at it highest pitch on Earth, God allowed His Son to be raised on the Cross like an outstretched hand and said, "Enough!" Satan lost that day and will forever be confined to the fires of Gehenna. Jesus gives us the power to avoid the maculation of our souls by evil and to propagate the Love in our hearts. Our Lord shares our hardships and times of trouble. Our greatest suffering for Him is filled with His highest reward, gentlest touch, and most pleasing succor. This is the origin of our joy. We do not suffer because we cannot love, but for the sake of Love, to bring-forth the goodness of Christ into a world which yields so easily to sin and malfeasance. When we turn to Him, we no longer yearn for the things of this Earth or the mortal visions of Creation before our eyes. Indeed, we search instead for the source of all things good, the Almighty Father who yearns reciprocally for us! We see His Will as the reason for prayer and the grace of the Life of Jesus. We perceive the world as our launching-pad for Heaven rather than a diving-deck from which we will hurl ourselves into the hellish abyss of perpetual torment. When our sights are set perfectly on the Cross, we see with the vision of the Angels. We know that Satan is a fraud and that evil is a passing nightmare from which we awake the moment we arise in Christ. It is not God's intention that we should suffer to appease evil, but rather to avoid it.

When we undergo pain, sorrow, and depression at the hands of Satan, we recognize them as the malignant carnage of a pernicious tyrant. We run from his poison like children filled with fright. When God allows evil to scour our souls, He sends Jesus to give us courage. Our God in Heaven can conquer the father of lies during any time and across any space. Light will always destroy the dark. Our prayers summon His immediate response to those who call. And at the end of time, we will know that the Blessed Virgin Mary is His gift to those who have prayed for centuries for Divine assistance and the grace of Heaven. Moreover, He dispatches the Holy Spirit to carry us past any darkness and through every trial. Satan cannot destroy Love or infringe upon our right to implore the Divinity of Heaven in our journey toward holiness. He is real and has a trenchant affect on our struggle toward conversion. But, he is as condemned as any fossil under the shales of the Earth. If we perceive the Return of Christ in the Light of faith, we can better understand this truth. When the Holy Mother says that our souls live the immortality of Heaven in the Heart of Christ, She makes time nondescript. In accepting this fact, we affirm our allegiance to Jesus for the destruction of sin. If we refuse to bow to the enticements of Satan, his forces are as dead and equally infernal as they forever will be.

Thursday, December 10, 1992

Praying the Holy Rosary is actually the soul that is searching for a means of early reprieve from the confines of the mortal body. It is the transcending and immortal nature of the acappella canticle which resounds the praises of God through the Blessed Virgin Mary. We ask Her to pray for us sinners now because we need the compound blessings of God the Father to heal us and keep us in His sights for future deliverance. We implore Mary Immaculate to pray for us at the hour of our death so that we will know the pious nature She brings into our spirits through a life given to venerating Her beauty and worshiping the Son She bore. I find it a heartening and fulfilling desire to pray the Rosary and lift my supplications to God with the kind assistance of our Holy Mother. God was right when He sent the angel to tell Her that She is blessed. I have seen Her immortal sheen with all the presence that He has allowed Her to offer.

Through my Diary, I bid you to come with me, even if it is only through your reading of these pages, to a place where you will know you belong. The address of our final home is high above the ramparts of this embattled world, up and away from the groveling stumbling blocks that evil has placed in our way. I invite you to pray for peace and your own conversion through the Most Holy Rosary of the Blessed Virgin Mary. You will live the prophecy it reveals and will receive the blessings that She promises. She came to ask me to pray with Her again today, while there is still time in our world, to make a difference in the census of souls who one-day will inhabit the ecstasy of Paradise. While She does not recite the "Hail Mary" with my brother and me, She listens as we honor Her soul with the angelic salutation. She joins in unison with all who pray the "Our Father" and "Glory Be." Please join us in meditation and be one with the universal God who is praised by our petitions.

Saturday, December 12, 1992

We swiftly move to claim our portion of the world while asking the question, "*Where is mine?*" In our blindness and insolent greed, we are ignorant to the truth that all earthly goods are perishable. We are unopen to the possibility that God's eternal treasures are endlessly more lasting and valuable than any we could ever procure in this life. But, just like the Holy Virgin says, we continue to rise from our beds each day and make the decisions that will increase our inventory of wealth. She is quick to explain that all of the materials for which we work are only soluble artifacts that we will leave to the next succeeding generation, should there be another one to inherit them. All of our hope is based on success as it is defined through the context of our neighbors. What do they have in comparison to us? Again, the Holy Mother tells us daily that this is a false and fruitless prospect because the Love in our hearts for Jesus Christ is all we will ever be allowed to transfer into the Kingdom we hope to see in our day. God the Father gives us gifts of food from the Earth and the nature that blooms from it for our shelter. The work of our hands keeps us nourished and protects us from the outside elements. Our Immaculate Mother is quite open to say that these are only the passing blessings that assist us during our short stay in the world. She tells us that the greatest gifts from God are the Holy Sacraments of the Church, which provide eternal nourishment for our souls and shelter and protection from sin and vice. Indeed, we must believe Her words with full trust because She comes from where we wish to someday go.

Yes, Jesus blesses us with even the wood from which these pages were made. I am trying to make the best use of His Kingdom by telling humanity about the Planter who owns it. His Mother is the greatest gift known to humankind. When we began the Holy Rosary this evening, our Mother of Joy came to us and said, **"Bless you, My children! Yes, you are both still helpless, unless you continue to pray. With My Love and your own understanding, we will continue in peace and perseverance..."** She told me at the beginning of the year that 1992 was to be a time for my brother and I to realize that the world is, indeed, without hope and helpless to survive if we do not accept Jesus Christ. Humanity will always need Him. There will never be a time when we can stand and tell God that we have learned all we need to know to succeed in this world and the next. We will never be able to proclaim ourselves to be, "I Am." That title belongs to Christ the King. But, with the help of Our Lady and Him, we cast the world aside and kneel in prayer to humbly say, "I wish to be..." They will help us become children of God who are prepared for Heaven.

We are all created to be one in Love. That is our purpose and our goal. There is no time for false rhetoric or temporal accomplishments. We must unify our voices in supplication for the needs of humanity in praise of Our Almighty Father. We should always remember that He spoke to us long before we knew Him. He came through Moses, then the Angel Gabriel to Our Mother Mary. He is Christ the Word, the Holy Spirit, and is present through the communion of Angels and Saints. The urgency in His bountiful Heart will persist until we are once again at rest in His Holy Arms. That is the infinity in which He loves us. The Holy Mother echoes His Wisdom to this day through Her intercession in unity with the Holy Spirit. Our Lady comes to a humanity living in darkness, bearing the Light of the World, but many refuse to accept Him. We stumble-about in the ignorance of rejection and oblivion. But, we need not travel alone. God does not intend for His people to hide from the Truth. We do not have to grope for peace and understanding under the weight of our own blindness. We must heed the glorious admonition resounding out of the heavens and imitate the lives of the Saints.

Hundreds-of-thousands before us have taken-up their crosses and lived the tranquility and joy of Jesus to the depth of their souls. They became great examples of His Love because they chose to join in the bounty of Heaven. But, their faith was not necessarily a greater gift than we will ever know in this modern age. We share the same Holy Spirit who descended upon the Church at Pentecost. Like them, our success is the fruit of what we offer Him in return. Christ asks us to love as He loves and to be perfect as He is Perfect. We are called to partake in the Glory of God in ways that might startle the faint-of-heart. If we see God as the fire in a hearth, we should do more than huddle next to Him to warm our hands. We must mortify our souls in the flaming embers. When we see Him as the Light on our path, we must not be satisfied just standing in faith. We should walk toward His Love in unshielded belief, allowing ourselves to be blinded to the world and led completely by His Spirit. If we perceive God as a cool-running brook, our hearts must yearn for more than a singular refreshing drink. We must plunge deeply into His Divinity and become perpetually immersed in His care, trusting that our every righteous breath is a fruit of His Holy Will.

There is no room for moderation in our love for Christ. He suffered the most capital of punishments to save our souls, dying on the Cross. He held no reserve in teaching and praying for the world He came to save. He owed nothing, but paid the debt of all. He walked in innocence, but was convicted by the guilty. He is shameless in Love and confident in our deliverance. That is the infinity He asked from us. We are very little people in an immensely flagrant world. We have to let-go of the Earth to reach for Paradise. We must be willing to be consumed by suffering, blinded by sanctification, and drowned in sacrifice. That is the essential nature of our conversion to Christ. There is no other way to God than Him. It is He who said, **"Take up your cross and follow Me."** If we ask where He is going, He will show us with great Light, revelation, purity, and hope. Our helplessness is not a fruit of our mortality, it is a curse for not listening to the voice of God. We walk the oft-traveled path of materialism and greed that is filled with liars and cheats. We escape their treachery by stepping onto the New Path of righteousness and conversion. Christ is our Leader, our Help, and our Shield. He is the Master of all Divinity whose Love will never allow us to fall or stray onto a fallacious course. We are helpless without Him, but conquerors in His Arms. It is time to embrace the victorious ways of Our Lord and give Love a chance to confirm Redemption upon the humanity He has already saved. When we stand on the foundation of Love, we rest at the brink of Salvation.

Wednesday, December 16, 1992

The message of Our Lady is an unmistakable call for human self-denial and sacrifice. Her words are a fruit of God's New Commandment through Christ Jesus, His mandate that we love one another as He has loved us. I ponder the images that Her words manifest in my own heart. I pray for God to heal and enrich the lives of our brothers and sisters, leaving only the last sip of water in the flask for me. We fast in total abandonment to the Holy Spirit saying, *"I'll skip my daily bread if You will take it to that child in my heart's eye who is sitting in hunger on a lonely rock across the blazing fields of Nigeria."* In penance, we repay someone else's debt that is long overdue with the money we just earned from a sweltering day in a cotton field. These are what Our Lady calls "new beginnings" which spring from the depths of the resources of the heart. In peace, we scamper across a rolling stream in a driving rainstorm to retrieve a shivering child about to be caught in the current. And, in conversion, we thank God for our Redemption by accepting the guilt of someone we know is too weak to bear the consequences on their own. By wholly pouring-out ourselves, we are newly filled with Christ.

This is the inner-soul of Our Lady's call and the desire of the God who wishes us to succeed. In seeking Heaven, we must first find the Paradise in ourselves that is begging to evolve, yearning to serve, and lapping at the shore of every opportunity to live. **"Today, My little children, I call on you to remember with freshness the many messages that I have given to you. I would like for you to recall how happy and surprised that you were when you received the first one. This is how I would like for you to always feel. As you become perfect in Love and begin to enjoy the peace of Heaven on Earth, please still expect to be exhilarated and elated upon your entrance into Heaven. It is important that you continue to hope for that celestial City and that you strive for that Beauty. Please, do not become totally satisfied with your life on the Earth. Your days and your petitions are like the making of a wonderful garment of holiness. Your prayers, especially the Rosary, help you create a pattern from which your lives are formed and are cut and shaped to make you a holy, reverent, and pure apparel.**

With the thread of Love with which you bind your days together, you make a beautiful cloak to render you worthy of presentation to Jesus. Your clothing is a pattern unique unto yourself. Your own holy prayers and goodness help define your identity before the Perfect One who needs you, who calls you, who holds you proudly and happily as His own special little children. God knows that your worthy apparel is sewn with the finest thread of Love and care, His Love given to you as a stitch that is wove, one upon each day. There will be many who will come to Him wearing apparel that others have sewn by their prayers, helping those

who do not know how to make themselves presentable and ready for everlasting grace and promise. Please envision the Heaven you seek as being a lighted house, with crystal chandeliers and stately fixtures, and Jesus is there to greet all who come to the door. Imagine that it is dark outside, with many little children who have been lost and away. The time has arrived for them to come back Home.

Yes, imagine that you are seeing that sight through a window and you want all who come to the door to be magnificently dressed, their souls polished and prepared for presentation to God. You are helping Me to dress your brothers and sisters so neatly and clean for Jesus to see. Indeed, see those whom you have already helped to be clean and worthy as you look through the window, seeing their Father open His arms to receive and bless them and prepare them room to stay in His House. He knows that you are outside helping Me. He knows that you are running from one brother to the next and one sister to the next, telling them to get ready, to be pretty, to polish their souls skillfully and with purity. Jesus knows when He sees them come to Him that it is your thread in their garments, your stitches, and your works of great Love!

Your Savior asks you to stay out in the cold as long as you can suffer for Him, and for Me, because your work is so magnificent, so graceful, and so holy. Then, when it comes time to receive you, if you have exhausted your thread while offering it to all those before you, He will hold His arms out to you as you wear your labored rags and patches back Home, and He will say, '*Come to Me, My good and faithful servant! I love you, you have lived for Me, now I have a place for you.*' All that you are doing is this important, and you are succeeding through the strength of your prayers. Jesus is pleased. Be happy! Please continue to accept My Love. Thank you for your prayers. I love you. Goodnight."

Saturday, December 19, 1992

We are approaching the celebration of Christmas again. Our Lady asked us to pray to end the awful grip of materialism that surrounds this holy event. Christ came into the world as a humble Child with nothing but Divinity to His Name. The Holy Virgin asks us to honor Him with this same simplicity. Too often, we say "I love you" to others with goods rather than sacrifices. Love cannot be symbolized or offered by proxy. Love is real Life with soul-touching fruits that last beyond the obsolescence of the physical world. One of the greatest gifts God gave us is the Holy Spirit. This Paraclete lives in the chambers of our hearts, absent of time and free from fallibility. When we share the living Divinity of God through the Love He brings, we give the greatest gift we can offer. As we muster courage to renounce worldliness and materialism, we cleanse our souls and make room for Jesus to govern our lives. His Love fills our hearts and expands our vision, giving us hope in a destiny in Him that has no limits. There is no need for material wealth or carnal gratification in the Love of Christ and the Wisdom of God. We see the Birth of the Lamb as the beginning of human Salvation instead of a synthetic exchange. That is the desire that Our Lady has for our observance of the Nativity of Her Son. And, it is the reason I offer the following prayer at Christmas to each and all as my gift of Love.

> *"I wish to give you that which my gift could not contain. I walked the stores for hours searching for that gift which would show you what you mean to me. I looked at sweaters and shawls that would make you look pretty and keep you warm at night. I pondered which utensil or tool would fit your hand so that you could build and lighten your daily toils. I saw candies and cakes, crackers and cheese that would bring beauty to your table and sweetness to your taste. I passed equipment and ropes, bats and balls that you could use to fill your lives with joy as we played as children again. There were mementos and books, pictures and plants, music and lights. There were wind-sails and wines, platters and plates, and a window filled with pets that could barely bark, let alone bite.*
>
> *I would give you the world if I could get it into a box. I would give you joy if I could wrap it with a bow. And if it cost a fortune, I would work all my days so that it could be carried to you. But, I found no gift that would load all the treasure ships of man, and no map which would sail them to you. I found no vacant throne of light nor a crown with jewels to place on your head. I could find no crystal sculpted for a palace in the air, nor an artist who created days where clouds never blocked his suns. My task is wanting to give you that sun but candles were all I could find. I sought to give you an ocean but a fish bowl would not suffice. And I wanted to lift you into the heavens but five steps of a ladder was as high as they sold.*
>
> *But then suddenly I found My Gift, after searching high and low. My Gift is a Child, a flower of Love, a baby so small. My Gift is my Love in the vision of a night in a stable. This is what I have to give, it is the best that I have to give."*

Love is the everlasting gift we all must share. It is a charitable grace that cannot be contained in a box. Indeed, the world itself is too small to confine the Love that unites Christ's children. We transmit a Light of hope across the beam of Love. We are the Church of Faith who is prepared for the Triumph of God in the Paradise beyond the stars. Jesus is about to Return in Glory to echo of the Grace of Heaven's Magnificent Queen.

Monday, December 21, 1992

We must strive to offer an immeasurable Love in a defining world. As Christmas approaches, we know that we must "do something" for those we hold dear to our hearts. When it comes to Love, we are helpless because we do not rightfully know what it means. Our Holy Mother is the teacher to whom we must listen. She bore Jesus into the simplicity of a manger to save our impoverished souls. We were lacking in compassion, had no means to attain it on our own, and expressed no humility or desire to achieve it. The Christ Child is the Way and the Truth, the Life and the Light. We no longer have to pretend that we have no means to lift-us from ignorance and callousness. Christmas reminds us that we once were lost, but now we are found. Where are our souls located? Amidst the greatest story that God has ever told His sleepy children! Awake, awake your sleeping hearts! These are the words He is saying through His Son. Reach for the unobstructed peace that He brings! Embrace the power of holiness and purification delivered at His Hands! It is a Love that will never cower, cannot diminish, and will forever Be. It is a hope that lasts beyond the ages until we greet Him at the eternal Dawn.

We are gifts to one another of this same holy magnitude. When we offer ourselves in faith and service in the Name of Jesus, we live the power of His Crucifixion and the Life of His Resurrection. We must come to see God in the manger! Oh, the Glory and magnificence of His entrance onto mankind's stage! He lays His humble Head upon the compliance of our hearts. This paradoxical night when God came to a bitter world to bring the serenity of Heaven lives yet today. Mary and Joseph offer Him to us still, but we are reticent to make Him room. We refuse to quit our grasp on material and mortality to say "yes" to the Lamb who seeks repose. Many of us still protest that a God who is worth His Glory would come into the world with flags and fanfare. But, they need not be dismayed! The celebration is about to begin! The Return of Christ in Glory will unfurl the spoils of Justice and sound the Trumpet of Reconciliation. There is new hope for all mankind! Christmas is the rhythm of the centuries that revels the innocence of Divine holiness. We are borne into grace and absolution by the Child of Mary's Womb so that the desolate and afraid can feel the peace of this holy night in happiness. Even if no other world welcomes Him, we must greet Him, allow Him room, and proclaim to the universe that God is among us. We must announce to the Angels with zeal and love that our Salvation is at hand, and raise our arms to the heavens and declare, "Thank God! Thank God!"

Our Lady bore the Child to save our souls on Christmas night. She gave birth to the new beginning of man and the reclamation of the Earth by God in Heaven. She greeted the Son of God with an embrace of perfection, the same infinite Love that She teaches us today. Hers is not the slightest selfishness or greed. She wishes to share Him with all the world, to every nation, and before every eye. God answered the desires of Her Immaculate Heart by giving us this Feast of Christmas time. On this night, He brings us to the Crib of Divinity to witness the Word who is dwelling amongst men. All the world is brought into one under the glistening of a Star. From within His manger, a tiny Child in swaddling clothes reaches in innocent desire for the embrace of the humanity He came to purify. On Christmas, all humankind knows that their Savior has come, even those who still deny His power. God wishes to resurrect us from the darkness and deliver our souls to Paradise. He could have forced His way into the world, but He came, instead at the "Fiat" of a simple maiden. Mary allowed Him entrance to the Earth as She begs us to give Him comfort in our hearts. May we allow that offering to be the reason we celebrate Christmas and the purpose for our conversion in His grace.

Friday, December 25, 1992
God often takes us by surprise because He reveals Himself in so many different ways throughout Creation. When He gave birth to the little Christ-child from His Mother's Womb at Bethlehem, the world was very confused. They thought the King of all Creation, the God of Moses, would come to greet His people like a flash of lightning, a thunderous roar, or a rush of bulls through a straight-line barracks. But, God chose the gentle avenue instead, the innocent little Lamb that He calls Jesus Christ. He slipped into the world quietly in the night and rheostatically grew in the hearts and minds of those who would soon come to know Him as the Man-God and Messiah. This is the genius of Our Creator, who does what He pleases in the manner that He chooses. To this day, many do not know how He will come back to the Earth, if they even believe in Him at all. Most people try to avoid the God of our fathers by wrapping themselves in the distractions of the world, in indifference, and in pleasures of the flesh. They barricade the door believing that God could not get to them. They hope in desperate blindness that all of their worldliness will shut Him out. But, humankind is about to be surprised again! To the shock and dismay of many scoffers, they are going to turn to see that He has returned to the Earth through the back door! The Holy Mother has told us many times to remember the reflections of the Scriptures. If today we should hear His voice, we must harden not our hearts.

That is why She has come in peace and Love to prepare us to let Him in. We hold nothing in our possession that can bar Him from bringing His Justice back to the Kingdom He owns. It would be of no avail to deny Him, even if we tried. The Mother of God has blessed us with the Wisdom to know this Truth through Her intercessory messages that no mortal can deny. **"This is the anniversary of the birth of My Love for you! My children, we are one again today because God has kept His Promise through His Son, your Savior, the Blessed One, Beautiful Redeemer, Maker of Peace, Keeper** of Sanctity, Sun of your soul, Watch in the night, Advocate to the Father, Master of Mercy, Healer of wounds, Host of all goodness, Creator of Light, Deliverer of souls, Bastion of Bounty, your Maker, and your Friend. Today, the Rock of the World and your Salvation, says *Let Me in*. He still asks to be allowed into your hearts and into your lives, welcomed by the souls who make His glorification their purpose. My son, please understand that you are learning well what I am teaching. Can you now see this more clearly? I am happy that you have allowed Me to teach you and to give you good example. The means through which you sustain peace in your home and through your love and patience is also a perfect witness of your love for Jesus and for Me.

On this special day, the flight to freedom in the Eternity of Heaven was granted to thousands upon millions. Can you understand why? Can you now perceive what Jesus wants the world to achieve to gain freedom to those in Purgatory? Yes, it is 'Love on Earth.' As Love is shared amongst mankind to bring Heaven to Earth, so is Heaven further enriched by the souls from Purgatory as a result of that Love. Love continues to grow in open hearts as its roots are formed in Heaven, from which all Love originates. The growth, the Light, the flowering, the fruits are all seen in Heaven and on Earth. The reason that Christmas is such a revealing time for the poor souls in Purgatory is because, for that short time, many millions of hearts are turned toward the reason for that holiday; the Incarnation of Love through the birth of Jesus. The poor souls are granted their freedom through the conversion and prayers of the world. This is the reason for humankind to elevate his prayers, efforts, and collective life toward a heavenly and immortal new purpose. It is all interconnected for the Divine purpose and expression of Love.

The prayers of those in Heaven help those on Earth in love, purity, and peace. The conversion and prayers of the mortals on Earth help to release the poor souls from Purgatory into Heaven. This the reciprocity of Love. You know that the poor souls in Purgatory are on their knees, begging for freedom. Those who live on Earth must also take to their knees to help them gain this freedom. This represents the continuity of Love, from mortal, to penitential, to Heavenly. On the knees of humanity is where the world is converted. That is why little children first begin to crawl. It is the first step in the development of their elevation. So it is with the soul with respect to Salvation. The first step is prayer, falling into grace upon the knees where holiness is born of that infancy and conversion begins. While humanity is on his knees, you would do well to crawl to Me! I hold Jesus in My arms, the reason for the purification and absolution of the world. This is as it has always been. It is on this day that My desire to love the world was brought to fruition and consummation. This is Jesus' birthday!

I ask the world to dismiss all false gods and idols, to release all hindrances and to be totally abandoned to Jesus and enriched by His Love. I ask mankind to remove his bridles of worldliness, fashion, materialism, and the influences of the flesh. It would be special on this day for mortal souls to awaken in Love and rid themselves of the hypnosis of indifference! I see so many amulets of false idols and images. There are many who offer allegiance to animals and birds, to music and art, and never to God. Others stage their lives in the pretense that they are someone else, diverting and blinding themselves from the reality of God on Earth, of Love Incarnate, of Jesus, His Prophecy, His Promise, and His Sacrifice. My little son, when the time is proper, make sure that the world hears what I have told you today. It will be several more years. Tell them that I love them and that I see their self-imposed imprisonment and their lives of desperation. Tell them that the suffering that afflicts them is a product of their lack of faith. Please, tell them that Jesus is their Way to freedom, the end of pain, and their Light in the darkness. I will help you to tell them. The time will come. It will be soon."

Sunday, December 27, 1992

The Blessed Mother has told us that God is watching us in every way that we could possibly conceive. By living through Him, with Him, and in Him, we are perfectly one through the Holy Sacraments that He dispenses within the Church. He is present for our protection as well as our conversion and purification. Our souls are safe inside a triangle of grace, the Father, Son, and Holy Spirit. Our Salvation is manifested through the intersection of God in three Divine Persons, yet, they are forever perfectly inseparable and One. This means that God blesses our good works and reprimands us for the bad. He knows our intentions before we ever take time to execute them. He is also perfectly aware that we branded and skewered His only begotten Son because we lacked the faith to know that He is Our Father, Himself, in human flesh. While His Crucifixion was a barbaric act by a lost humanity, Christ Jesus has made it the inscription of His forgiveness upon the very people who have feared Him the most.

Those who reject the admonishment of this perfect Christ are lost for all time to come. Anyone who scoffs at the death of Jesus will cringe in sorrow and shame at the end of time when the God of all Justice leaves them standing before Creation with the blood of unborn children on their hands. And, not only that, their faces will be stained by the cries of the innocent whose demise they brought through their own elite selfishness. The landscape of human life is still brambled by the scourge of carnal lust and a culture of death and destruction. God has cleared the course for our purification through Christ;

and it is in Him that we must rise, or fall prey to the snares of the evil that will forever coil in the pit of mortal decay. Our Lady knows these truths and enlightens Her children to the dangers that are always lurking to steal us from God. To ignore Her words is to portend our own condemnation. That is why the urgency of Her call has come in so many lands and through so many documented miracles. Let us never allow the opportunity She is bringing to slip through the cracks in our hands. I am pleased to recount the words She offered today.

"My children, My little obedient ones, I love you very much. Your prayers and your actions are inspiring others to seek the Love that the world should accept. Today, I call on humanity to recognize the diminishment of the human race with a concise and overwhelming clarity. You know that mankind breathes defeat upon himself through his faithless actions. The terrible curse of abortion manifests famine, floods, hurricanes, tornadoes, disease, airplane crashes, and all other forms of diminishment of the human race. All of these scourges violate our holy cause. My children, Jesus is the solution to all your sorrows and losses. Love can prevent any tragedy and bring-forth the expulsion of the terrible destiny of man. These days are filled with tension because humankind fears to live the courage to know that he can be perfect in Love.

Why do people wish to be constrained, tarnished, and diminished? I remind you that this tension is easing as we pray together. The prayers that you are lifting and the work that you are doing are bringing aid to the barrenness that is caused by human fear. While you see the world in a state of dysfunction, devastation, and deterioration, please do not fall into despair. Jesus will be there to catch its fall! If we pray together enough to help people love one another instead of hate, if there is conversion instead of indifference, the fall will be negligible and gentle, or maybe not at all! It is very important that you remain simple, humble, meek of heart, and open of mind to receive the Love that is blooming so beautifully from your heart."

Tuesday, December 29, 1992

How I wish for you to know true peace in these modern times! There are millions of lost and broken hearts in the world who still yearn for tranquility and rest. But, I beg you to understand that peace will not come through the world alone! We must seek the solace that only God can give through our Lord, Jesus Christ. I am not calling you to some tangential metaphysics that seems to be floating in the outer-atmosphere, but to a real and perceivable Love that will heal us and make us whole once again. It is the Love of God, manifested with unique authority through Christ and His Immaculate Mother.

Their Love transcends every physical, chemical, and mechanical means through which we futilely experiment in searching for the meaning of life and relief from the barbs of reality. Just as definitely as we live in a real world, it is an equally knowable God who has created it. He lives in the person of Our Savior to this day! That is effectively all we need to know to understand the path to human fulfillment. In Christ Jesus, we are given peace in a way that the world cannot give. That is why He came, in part to cleanse us and, especially, to redeem our souls for passage into the Paradise where the God who made us resides.

When I began the Rosary this evening, Our Lady came to speak with me again. She said, **"Good evening, My loving children. Together, we help the world return to Love from which it is begotten. Many people refuse to forgive and forget others' mistakes, failures, and transgressions. Minds are running afoul trying not to be captured by their hearts. My children, Jesus will always love you, bless you, and hold you in His care. Your heart is His home, the center of Love where He becomes one in you. I reside there with Him. I love you. Goodnight."**

Thursday, December 31, 1992

The Holy Mother has given countless revealing messages, parables, and illustrations from Her Immaculate Heart throughout the history of the world. Her exhortations are a never-ending dispensation of grace and knowledge about the aureate Glory of God. It takes a great deal of effort to incorporate them into one written composition. But, that is what Our Lady has asked my brother and me to do. She has told us that every individual on the Earth has a conscience which is either living or already dead. Even God, Himself, has a conscience that has summoned our reprieve from the punitive Justice which He defiantly vowed to bring to humankind through the revelations of Moses. Jesus Christ is the living conscience of God! He calls the omnipotent strength of the Almighty Father to compassion and forgiveness for the people who have flagrantly betrayed Him. God sent His Conscience into the world as a manifestation of His Love for our souls. He came to the Earth in the flesh of a Baby, born of Mary at Bethlehem. And, through this Child named Jesus, God has dispensed His clemency to His people, the ones from whom He had been far too long estranged. Christ is the gentle side of God, His supple and beseeching desire to reunite Creation above and beyond the coronas of the Heavenly Firmament.

Our Father confirms that we are worthy of this Redemption. Jesus reminds Him of it every day. But, He also asks us to proceed toward becoming the likeness of His own Accordance of pardon and peace. If this is the road we have chosen, we must approach it with conversion, confession, repentance, and acceptance. Our Lady has told us many times that the power of the confessional originates from the Divinity of Her Son. The Sacrament of Reconciliation restores our purity and remakes our souls through the power of its cleansing absolution. When we first enter the confessional, our souls are as dead as the body of the slain Lamb that once laid in the darkness of the Sepulcher. But, we leave it wearing His complete Resurrection and the highest of dignity. No stone or briny path can impede our new unification with His perfection, and no disenfranchised spirit can impugn the certainty of our newfound nobility. This is why Our Lady calls us to the Sacrament of Penance regularly and to practice the charity and chastity that we gain there to the end of our days. We comply best when we understand best. This same beneficent Mother has come again in the closing moments of this year to teach us how.

"My precious children, I love you with endless magnitude! I treasure your souls, pray for your destiny, and reach for your hearts. Thank you for praying again on this last day of the year to receive this message. Thank you for attending Holy Mass tonight and for your prayers and expressions of hope. I wish the world could look with such expectation to the Coming of Jesus as it does in reveling a new year. I see many dynamic celebrations by a world that has aged another year, but cares not about its own destiny. We will pray continually for all souls. My beautiful little boy, if you can find your way in holiness and conviction through your prayers and innocence to give yourself completely to Jesus, your exile, even if a hundred years in length, will seem as though it is only a fleeting moment, a breath of uttered preparation for your eternal gift of peace. It will be one which you will already know, already have seen and tasted, and already imagined. I will give you all I have so you can realize that perfect peace and purity. It lives beyond reproach from any enemy, any evil, and any limitation. This is the holiness for which I pray that the world will achieve.

With this hope, I beg you to continue to assist Me in My cause. I lift you to My breast in Love and thanksgiving because God has created you and gave you life. You are My child, as Jesus is My Child. You will be delivered to our glorious Maker as I delivered Him to you. All who pray can lead the rest and can seek the return of all who have turned their backs and walked away. You will soon see humanity crawling back on its knees of hope, opening their arms to be received from where they came, back to Love, back to Eternity and to Jesus. He is their true Beauty, Enrichment, Fulfillment, and Peace. We will seek their holiness and conversion through contemplative prayer. I will show you what I mean soon. I will bless you both now. Thank you for being My beautiful, obedient and holy children. I will lead you through this new year. Please follow and trust Me, I will take you to Jesus who calls on you for help. I love you. Praise be to God! Goodnight."

Sequence of Additional Works

In Our Darkest Hour
MORNING STAR OVER AMERICA
January 1, 1993 - February 22, 1997
Volume II
ISBN: 0-9671587-8-8

At the Water's Edge
Essays in Faith and Morals
ISBN: 0-9671587-1-0

When Legends Rise Again
The Convergence of Capitalism and Christianity
ISBN: 0-9671587-2-9

White Collar Witch Hunt
The Catholic Priesthood Under Siege
ISBN: 0-9671587-3-7

Babes in the Woods
With a Little Child to Guide Them
ISBN: 0-9671587-4-5

To Crispen Courage
The Divine Annihilation
ISBN: 0-9671587-6-1

Available through
The Morning Star of Our Lord, Inc.
www.ImmaculateMary.org

NOTATIONS

www.ingramcontent.com/pod-product-compliance
Lightning Source LLC
Chambersburg PA
CBHW051801230426
43672CB00012B/2589